1945)

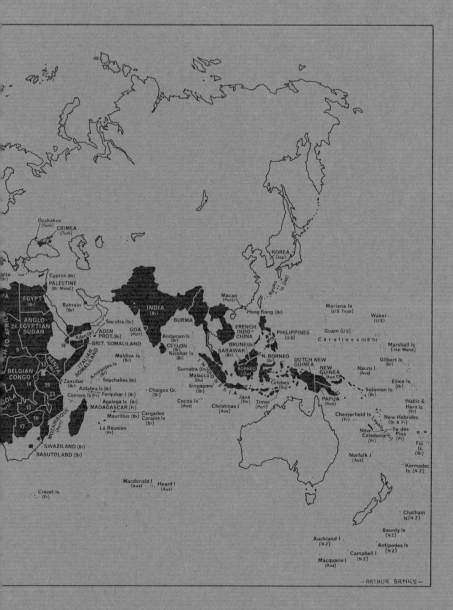

~ARTHUR BANKS~

The Colonial Revolution

Fenner Brockway

The Colonial Revolution

St. Martin's Press   New York

AFFILIATED PUBLISHERS: Macmillan Limited, London
also at Bombay, Calcutta, Madras and Melbourne

To My Friends Everywhere

Contents

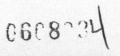

8   *Contents*

Part Two: THE EMPIRES IN PERSPECTIVE

Part Three: THE ALTERNATIVE TO EMPIRES

Introduction

This book has been written over four years during considerable public activity. I have been engaged in the struggle against colonialism for more than fifty years and have been associated with many Asian and African movements and leaders; but the more I have worked on the subject the less informed I have found myself. The original intention was to write comparatively shortly, with my personal participation prominent. I was so fascinated, however, by the study of resistance movements that my own experiences became unimportant in the drama of wider events and the typescript of history grew and grew, I hope to worthwhile proportions.

Most of the necessary research has been done by myself, but I wish particularly to thank Tom Bower, who at one time I hoped might have been associate author with me. Unfortunately his journalistic and television assignments prevented this, but he helped greatly, particularly with the sections on the evolution of theory, Ireland, Latin America and the Middle East. Let me hasten to add, lest he be compromised, that I alone am responsible for their final versions. Later, Barbara Haq gave me great help in research and correction.

Looking back, for this book reflects many unconscious years, I am indebted more than I can express to the staff of the House of Commons Library. On innumerable occasions during the quarter of a century I have been at Westminster, they have helped me with information. They have also loaned works from all over the world which I have wished to consult. Nearly every page of this book reflects their contribution to my knowledge.

One feature of this book was motivated by the *Encyclopaedia Britannica*. In an earlier edition I found a table of the members of what was then the British Commonwealth, the date of their occupation and their current status. From the editor I received permission to reproduce this table, and I then extended it considerably and adapted the idea to other empires. I have the feeling that this book may be appreciated, if for nothing else, for these tables.

The primary subject has been the revolution which overthrew empires and that is dealt with comprehensively. I have added an outline of the world order towards which I believe we must move if imperialism is to be ended.

9

To Rashida Ogilvie I am indebted for the large and not easy task of typing my manuscript, to Arthur Banks for designing the maps, to Cllr Miss Joan Hymans for providing the material for the maps and the tables, and to Mrs Jean Popper and Mrs Erna Nelki for checking corrections. And, perhaps above all, I should thank my publishers for waiting so patiently for the completion of the book.

February, 1973   FENNER BROCKWAY

Part One

The Passing of Empires

Chapter One

Turning Point in History

The Colonial Revolution is of momentous significance. By geological evidence of the presence of non-indigenous peoples, it is known that from earlier than the records of man there have been occupations of territories by invading races. These have not always been motivated by conquest or subjugation, but it is not too much to say that the history of the world until this century has been the record of successive empires.

Indeed, only since Woodrow Wilson's affirmation of self-determination at the end of the First World War has the right of peoples to govern themselves been internationally accepted, and only since the Second World War has the imposed occupation of the territories of others – the essence of colonialism – been generally adjudged wrong in practice. Empires have fallen before, but this is the first time that the conscience of man has repudiated the actual existence of empires. We are thus witnessing more than the end of an age; the whole course of human relations over the many thousand of years of history has changed.

Definitions

We pause to define. What do we mean by imperialism and colonialism and this new word neo-colonialism? Their scope is wide and complicated, and clarity at once precise and embracing is not easy. Can the early movements of peoples seeking more fertile land be described as imperialist? One would answer no; but the essence of imperialism crept in when they subjugated the original inhabitants. Can the emigration of persecuted minorities to new lands be described as colonialism? Again one would answer no; but the essence of colonialism crept in when they occupied the land at the expense of the indigenous race. The roots of imperialism and colonialism, and indeed, as we shall find, of neo-colonialism, are in the exploitation of one people by another.

Imperialism. The term imperialism is often held to mean only the

occupation of underdeveloped countries by industrialised nations.
The later Marxists identified it specifically as exploitation by monopoly capitalism. This is increasingly true in modern circumstances.
Imperialism is more and more becoming economic domination; it
operates even when nations become independent. But we reject the
Marxist limitation historically and also in immediate terms. Not
only did the exploitation of peoples begin before capitalism, but in
the present era, in the course of the ideological struggle, national
liberties may be overrun by communist countries. In this book,
whatever the stage and character of economic development, imperialism will be held to be the system of relationship between
peoples when some nations, or a class within nations, control
primarily in their own interest the collective life of other nations.
In effect, under imperialism the existence of the subjected people is
contained within a non-indigenous pattern.

During the last hundred years imperialism has taken, in greater
or lesser degree, the following forms: (*a*) territorial occupation and
political domination, (*b*) military occupation, (*c*) economic occupation, (*d*) cultural occupation. As will be seen below, territorial
occupation and political domination are not a necessary condition
of the three further occupations.

Colonialism. Colonialism, in a strict sense, is less comprehensive
than imperialism. It is the political aspect ((*a*) above), the assumption of governmental authority by a nation over another nation. In
modern terms this exercise of political power has almost invariably
been accompanied by the other features of imperialism, which has
led to frequent identity in the use of the two terms.

Neo-colonialism. Neo-colonialism is strictly a wrong term. As generally used, it means not a new form of political occupation, but
the continuing features of imperialism after political colonialism,
legalistically at least, has ended. It refers to the maintenance of
external economic, military or cultural pressures following the
recognition of the sovereignty of a nation. It is the persistence of
imperialist penetration despite the achievement of self-government.

The Motives of Colonialism

We shall find in succeeding chapters that the motives for the occupation of other peoples' territories have been diverse. The purpose
of invasion has not always been exploitation, and often it has been
accompanied by progressive development in education, health and

economic construction. But particularly from the nineteenth century onwards the main motive has been economic profitability.

The original stimulation for the invasion of new territories was probably the search for more habitable lands, warmer places in the sun, lands flowing with milk and honey. This was specially so among peoples suffering from changes of climate or land erosion: the Aryan race is believed to have moved southwards from the ice of arctic regions; the Phoenicians and Assyrians migrated from the deserts of Western Asia. In some instances the urge came from the pressure of population. Early in recorded history an uglier motive is seen in the greed for slaves and women and for personal enrichment by the ruling élite.

In the case of empires immediately before and after the beginning of the Christian era, exemplified in Greece and Rome, there was a combination of motives: the ambition of rulers, military pride, the search for wealth and, incidentally, cultural expansion. Then came the renaissance and Galileo's sweeping away of the flat earth myth, with the consequent exciting rivalry to find a route westward to India, the passion for the exploration of distant lands reaching its climax in the seventeenth century. Unknown riches and prestige for their sovereigns drew the explorers like a magnet, and there were added prizes to be won in the conflicts between the maritime powers: Spain, Britain and France. Traders followed the explorers, establishing coastal depots, which were succeeded, as in India, by invasions of the interior and the subjugation of princes and chiefs with the appropriation of their treasures.

The depths of exploitation were reached when Arab Sheikhs raided East Africa to kidnap slaves to maintain their oligarchies, and when the European colonialists, with the backing of exalted and powerful interests in Spain, Portugal, Britain, the Netherlands, France, Prussia and even Denmark, developed with incredible inhumanity the slave trade from West Africa to the cotton, tobacco, coffee and sugar plantations of the Americas (north and south) and to the Caribbean islands. When the slaves were legally freed, this was followed by the cruelties of forced labour on the rubber plantations of King Leopold's Congo and plantations in other colonies, and by the recruitment of scarcely less exploited indentured labour from Asia to the West Indies, Guiana, East and South Africa and elsewhere.

This discreditable record was accompanied by the contribution of less reprehensible motives, among them the search by persecuted minorities for lands where they could practise their beliefs, though too often they became themselves harsh persecutors of the indigenous population. There was the dedication of missionaries, not always wise, to convert those they regarded as heathen, often supplemented by commendable service of medical care and education. There was even a scientific motive, exemplified in Captain Cook's first expedition to the South Pacific in 1768 to make astronomical observations, and in Darwin's visit to the same region in 1831, which provided evidence for his historic *On the Origin of Species by Means of Natural Selection*. The new lands were sometimes used to set up penal settlements for long-term prisoners; by Britain in America and Australia, by the French in Guiana.

There can be no doubt, however, that the main motive of the great expansion of colonialism in the eighteenth, and particularly the nineteenth centuries, was economic gain. The competition by European governments for oversea possessions was partly a reflection of their rivalries within Europe, but this political pressure was increased by the demands of the industrial revolution for raw materials, markets, foodstuffs and, later, the investment of surplus capital, supplemented by the opportunities of enrichment by the exploitation of land and minerals in the virgin territories. It is significant that control in the earlier British Empire (as in other empires) was vested in profit-making corporations: the East India Company, the British South Africa Company, the East Africa Company. In more recent years there was extensive settlement by white farmers under the attractive climatic conditions of east and central Africa, accompanied by a large European labour force in the mines and in the growing industries and public services. At the same time, as European economic interests expanded in colonial territories, governments stationed troops there and set up military bases for their protection.

The greed of economic gain, the seizure of the richest land, the need for cheap labour, racial arrogance (reflecting a more developed standard of life) and a caricature of the Christian religion – these combined to make the continent of Africa, from the Zambezi to the Cape Coast, the stronghold of white supremacy: apartheid in South Africa, Portuguese assimilation in Angola and Mozambique, the assumption of sovereignty by the white minority in Rhodesia. Over this large region the Whites regarded themselves as a master race, non-Whites politically and socially outside the pale, segregated in reserves and locations, doomed by their colour to inferiority, allowed only to move from place to place by pass systems devised to regulate their function as cheap labour. The

Africans were reduced to the level of serfs, beneath civilised association, all in the name of the need to maintain what was regarded as the quality of the European pattern of society.[1]

The Motives of Neo-colonialism

Following the recognition of the independence of colonial territories, the paramount purpose of foreign influence was profitable investment. The new nations sought capital from the richer nations for their own development, but in the process they became in varying degrees economically dependent upon them. This foreign control extended beyond what operated in the preceding political colonialism, because of the increasing need for investment in expanding economies.

America, which boasted of its anti-colonialism, became the chief neo-colonialist power in this respect.[2] It already had a prominent part in ownership and investment when Africa and Asia were still politically occupied: this was enlarged. Its financial penetration and armament intervention in South American states must also be regarded as a form of neo-colonialism. There are some who would argue that Britain and Western Europe are in part dependent areas, because of the financial penetration of America and the presence of its military forces.

Economic neo-colonialism, and still more military neo-colonialism, were motivated considerably by the conflicting ideologies of the Cold War. Financial and armament aid was given according to the political sympathies of countries or to influence their political alignment. Russian aid to Egypt, China's aid to Pakistan and America's aid to strategically important countries, with its ring of military bases to contain Russia and China, are examples.

The climax of military intervention was reached in Vietnam, the consequences of which were so appalling that it may prove to be a final warning to the world. Indeed, the USA appears in part to have accepted the warning. President Nixon not only sought progressively to withdraw American troops from South Vietnam but indicated that forces stationed elsewhere in South-East Asia would be withdrawn. It remains to be seen how far the ideological conflict in this part of the world will permit these intentions to be realised, and this would only be a limitation of neo-colonialism so far as it affects the presence of personnel. American arms and economic penetration would continue.

The motives of old-time economic imperialism, and more recent Cold War concern, also linger in British military policy, despite the considerable withdrawal from Middle and Far East commitment. The base in Cyprus, a jumping-off point for the Middle East, combines both; the air-lift strips in the Indian Ocean associated with America are Cold War in intention; the artificial Federation of Malaysia was created as a defence line against Communism in Southern Asia; the speed with which troops can be transferred by air means that they can be trained at home for distant service. The conflict between Communism and Capitalism was largely responsible for foreign military and armament intervention in the less developed countries. It became the main motive of military neo-colonialism.

Nor can communist nations be absolved from blame, despite their principle of anti-imperialism. The Warsaw Pact military invasion of Czechoslovakia in 1968 was in essence neo-colonialism. Whilst that charge cannot be brought against Russia and China for the arms assistance given to North Vietnam (which was anti-colonialist in motive), their rivalry in Africa had the elements of neo-colonialism, and Russian armament aid for Egypt included the motive of extending its influence and interest.

There is a less deliberate motive in cultural neo-colonialism. France consciously endeavoured to implant its culture on the peoples of its colonial territories, and did so after they became independent, but, broadly speaking, continued cultural domination is not so much a deliberate design as a hangover from the education provided in colonial times, mostly by missionary societies, attuned to the religion, history and ideology of the occupying powers rather than to those of the indigenous people. This cultural alienation was extended by the fact that the sons of some of the wealthier indigenous élite went to universities in Europe and America, many of them on their return becoming powerful in national life and political authority. National leaders were also influenced by their indebtedness to European and American liberal philosophers who contributed so much to the concepts of freedom and equality from the eighteenth century onwards. Since independence, however, there has been a strong reaction towards the development of indigenous cultures. There has been some pressure by religious bodies, particularly through Catholicism, to maintain the image of the earlier occupying powers, and in British ex-colonies the pattern of the Westminster Parliament (though this might be challenged as within the sphere of culture) has been bequeathed with an exactness which has not been appropriate to the political climate; indeed, this is also true of Western multi-party democracy. But on the whole it is right to say that cultural neo-colonialism is more due to historical inheritance than to calculated imposition.

Civilisation?

The claim has often been made in metropolitan countries, particularly those with colonial possessions, that their empires have served as missions of civilisation. It is true, of course, that the occupation of undeveloped territories by developed nations has brought many progressive advances. Whilst invasions from the earliest times have often been accompanied by the slaughter of indigenous peoples, once established the new regimes have imposed peace upon previously conflicting tribes, saving disruption and death. However inadequately, education and medical aid have been provided; diseases like malaria have been eradicated over large areas and curative treatment of plague begun (although, on the other hand, diseases previously unknown have followed white occupation and brought decimation). Roads and railways have been built and air services established; modern industry has been introduced revolutionising the economy, and the example of technical farming given; cities with modern offices, factories, houses and sanitation have arisen; many thousands of workers, though inequitably paid compared with European artisans, have found employment and a living in mines and factories; in some colonies progressive development towards self-government has been fostered. Looking at the human race the world over, we must recognise the historical contribution which colonialism has made, though the transformation, technical and social, in Soviet Russia since the revolution and, increasingly, in China, show that foreign occupation is not a necessary condition of change. Tribute must be paid to the devoted personal service of many missionaries, doctors, teachers, technicians and civil servants in colonial territories and to the co-operation of many enlightened representatives of foreign governments in the transition to independence.

In recognising these contributions to progress, however, we must also recognise that they represent not the *motive* for colonialism, but its limited accompanying *effects*. Gain, not philanthropy, has throughout history been the reason for the occupation of other peoples' territories.[3] Economic development has been carried out essentially for the benefit of the occupying rulers, benefits which have been shared only incidentally by the indigenous peoples and often enjoyed at their expense. The purpose has been fundamentally to serve the interests of the invaders, in modern times for the exploitation of the land and resources of the territories acquired. And in the process crimes have been committed which are among the worst blots on the record of human evolution.

Notes

1. The Portuguese colonies were not so absolute in their racial discrimination. A minority of Africans could move towards assimilation.

2. The need for capital investment in the developing countries is recognised. How it can take place without imperialist control is discussed later.

3. There was some generosity in the establishment of freedom in Sierra Leone and Liberia as settlements for freed slaves.

Chapter Two

The Evolution of Anti-colonialism

From the earliest invasions there was resistance by indigenous peoples, but opposition to colonialism as a political practice did not emerge until the seventeenth century and it then took the form of denunciation of particular instances rather than against imperialism as a system. It was of particular historical significance, however, because it was expressed within nations committing aggression and reflected a moral conception.

The Pioneers

Perhaps the first anti-colonialist group were the Levellers, democratic republicans who arose among the peasantry during the English Civil War from 1645 to 1660. One of their objects was to prevent Cromwell realising his ambitions in Ireland and they attempted with limited success to spread subversion in the army.[1] In the early eighteenth century opposition to English domination of Ireland was the subject of Jonathan Swift's many satirical pamphlets, weapons of a rather lonely and unsuccessful fight, asking 'Am I a free man in England and do I become a slave in six hours when I cross the (Irish) Channel?'[2] He suggested to the Irish that they should boycott English goods, but acknowledged that they were quite unreceptive to the idea. These early manifestations of anti-colonialism were heroically pioneering, but they failed to arouse effective support.

The American Revolution

The American Revolution in 1775 stimulated the beginnings of the first anti-colonialist ideology; beyond Ireland the British empire then consisted of thirteen American states[3] and depots in the Caribbean and India. The colonies in America were regarded solely as junior partners in trade, with no self-government and without representatives at Westminster. It was extraordinary how the Establishment in Britain was insensitive to the principle of self-rule by its own people overseas. The opposition to its policy was varied. There was Dean Tucker, who supported a break with America on the conservative ground that he feared its democratic principles would be dangerous if they spread to Britain. On the other hand, there were radicals like Richard Price and Cartwright who stood wholeheartedly for the right of self-government. Both, however, urged allegiance to the Crown.

It was Adam Smith in his *Wealth of Nations* (1776) who first challenged colonialism fundamentally by his criticism of the economic consequences of an empire: he refrained, however, from advocating immediate decolonisation because he recognised the strength of national pride and the interests of the English ruling classes who would be deprived of profitable positions. His argument was that the monopoly system of trade with the colonies in fact restricted trade and necessitated heavy defence expenditure. He argued that instead Britain should adopt free trade, resulting in lower defence costs (markets no longer needing protection) and an extension of commerce through diversity.

Adam Smith mooted the possibility of a common Parliament with both British and American representation, which led to disagreement with Edmund Burke. Burke might be described as the first of the paternalists who afterwards became almost a dominant force. He discounted a constitutional partnership with the American colonies and at the same time opposed independence. He believed that the empire should continue on the basis of welfare for its peoples and proposed for India trusteeship and education. Although an exiled Irishman, he did not demand Irish independence, but only the alleviation of suffering.

The French Revolution

It was the ideals of the French Revolution, combined with the experience of the American Revolution, which stimulated the political argument against colonialism, extending it to non-Whites, epitomised in Locke's thesis of government by consent. Lincoln some years later said that it is 'self-government when the white man governs himself, but when he governs himself and also others it is no longer self-government but despotism'. In this spirit Jeremy Bentham addressed the National Convention of France in

January 1793 with a plea to 'emancipate your colonies'. James Mill had argued that colonies brought ill-will, expense and the likelihood of war for the benefit of the few who were governing. Bentham went further, arguing on the moral principle that there was no justice in ruling over another people and then calling it liberty. How, he asked the French revolutionaries, could they knock out the criminal gaoler but keep the profit of the criminal's crime? Frenchmen, he said, had no right to rule over non-Frenchmen.[4] About the same time Tom Paine, interpreting the ideas of the French Revolution in his *Rights of Man,* wrote that the American colonies would benefit from being free of the corruption of England.

Slavery

Europe experienced after 1814 a sharp reaction towards autocracy. Except in the case of the American colonies the challenge to empires failed; the British empire expanded. But it was during this period that a movement arose which successfully contested one of the foundations of the colonial system: slavery. Since the 1670s there had been an appeal to Christian conscience to support abolition, led by John Wesley, Dr Johnson, the Quakers and others.[5] But it was the Clapham Set, among them Wilberforce, who mounted the campaign which in time enlisted the support of the country. Sometimes they adopted sensational tactics to horrify public emotions. In 1811, they triumphed. Following a slave mutiny, the property owners of Britain's slave trade agreed to be bought out for £20 million.

Slavery persisted in other parts of the world and it was perhaps logical that many humanitarians in the nineteenth century advocated greater power for the British empire in the hope that its activities would help to end the slave traffic of Arabs and of other Europeans in Africa. Nor can it be denied that British intervention was a major factor in the near extinction of chattel slavery. Livingstone, inspired by missionary purpose, applied Burke's concept of trusteeship to Africa and Asia. Freetown in Sierra Leone was established by British initiative and Liberia by American influence as settlements for emancipated slaves.

What has been termed Britain's second empire followed the Seven Years War. Under Adam Smith's influence it was based on free trade, though, contradicting his theory, protected by naval bases. Commerce was unhindered by governmental tariffs, but it was also unhindered by governmental regulations. To the trade, shipping and navy of the first empire, the second added army, industry and the banks. The exploitation of colonialism was strengthened. Forced labour indistinguishable from slavery persisted in the British empire (more so in King Leopold's Congo) and indentured labourers from Asia were introduced in many British colonies.

Self-government for White Colonies

Between 1815 and 1860 co-operative relations between England and the English-speaking settlements overseas were established, but the non-white colonies were excluded from the discussions; a colony as defined by Roebuck in 1849 was a land without indigenous population looking to England as the mother country. Where, one might ask, was a land without an indigenous population?[6] Debate revolved around Lord Durham's Report of 1839, preceded by contributions by Roebuck, Molesworth and Hume. Lord Durham's suggestion was accepted that internal self-government be granted to Canada to avoid repetition of the American crisis, and later this was extended to Australia and New Zealand. The approach, however, was markedly negative, often with an overt assumption of the eventual dissolution of links. Disraeli stated bluntly that the colonies were 'millstones around our necks'. There was a widespread view that the territories overseas should be dumping grounds for surplus population, paupers and criminals, or at best markets for surplus goods. Wakefield and Molesworth put what appeared to be a minority view in the Establishment when they spoke of the colonies as democratic societies and urged systematic colonisation with a mutual exchange of food and manufactured goods.

The Liberal Attitude

The prevailing mood was reflected in the recommendation of a Parliamentary Select Committee in 1865 that Britain should leave West Africa, except Sierra Leone. The eyes of Palmerston and Russell were on the world rather than on the empire. The Free Traders, predecessors of the Liberals, formed an opposition to both colonialism and foreign intervention with a mixture of financial and altruistic motives. Cobden, the foremost critic, believed that the removal of monopoly trade by the disappearance of empires would lead, as Adam Smith had argued, to the absence of antagonisms which encouraged military forces and war. He condemned the nonchalant hypocrisy of intervening against European despotism whilst disregarding Britain's own immoral behaviour in India (especially at the time of the Mutiny), or China (during the Opium Wars). Karl Marx, who was soon to appear on the scene, dismissed Cobden's ideals, however, on the ground that he only wanted peace and *laisser faire* because they would permit cheaper exploitation of peoples.

Revival of Colonialism

In the last quarter of the nineteenth century, there was a wave of aggressive racialism and national superiority which led to a revival of colonialism. Disraeli, reversing his earlier attitude that territories abroad were a burden, actually based his election campaign in 1870 on the white colonies and the empire in India. The drive to colonialist expansion was due partly to power prestige conflicts in Europe, but still more to the opportunities sought for the foodstuffs and raw materials and the investment of surplus capital necessitated by the accumulating effects of the industrial revolution. Germany had become ascendant in Europe and France was spreading its overseas possessions. Their challenge to Britain had to be met. Rivalry between the Great Powers developed in Africa and the old competitiveness in Asia was extended. The New World could contribute the foodstuffs required, and mineral wealth was discovered which not only helped to meet demands but which provided profitable investment in their exploitation. Cobden denounced Disraeli's 'blind and tyrannical passion' for 'immoral allurement towards conquest and military prestige', but when Gladstone came to office in 1880 he betrayed the Liberal opposition to wars of expansion and 'in a fit of absence of mind' (Seeley) added Egypt and parts of South Africa to British possessions, losing many lives in Sudan and Transvaal, as well as in Afghanistan. Liberalism surrendered its stand against colonialism.[7]

Karl Marx

Challenge to the new imperialist ideology passed to the socialist movement, which came to birth in the latter half of the century. It contributed the revolutionary idea that colonialism was a reflection of a universal class struggle. Karl Marx was its exponent. He died (1883) about the time when colonialism was developing into modern imperialism and did not analyse the trend at depth, but in all his incessant, explosive attacks he emphasised the factor of capitalist exploitation. In *Das Kapital* he related the older slave trade to the newer colonialism and showed how British cities and industries 'waxed fat on slaves'. Cotton, sugar and tobacco, produced by African slaves for Britain, were purchased on the international market with produce made by 'white slaves in England'. Most of the money earned went to the privileged few, who made the 'nations of peasants' (the colonies) dependent upon the 'nations of the bourgeois'.

In continuous articles Marx concentrated on India, China and Ireland, but he also wrote about Burma, Egypt, Tunisia, Persia and other 'colonial bastions'. In a series of contributions to the *New York Daily Tribune* (1853–60) he exposed the British exploitation of India (especially its cotton industry), and the destruction of its society by interference with the balance of agriculture and industry, noting that what was an 'exporting country had become dependent upon imports'. He quoted the 1834–5 official report of the Governor-General who, commenting on the effects of British rule, said 'the misery hardly finds a parallel in the history of commerce. The bones of the cotton-weavers are bleaching the plains of India.' He cited the example of East India Company officials who in 1769–70 bought all the rice stocks in an area and by thus inducing famine were able to charge fantastic prices. Of the British ruling class in India he said: 'The aristocracy wanted to conquer it, the moneyocracy to plunder it, and the millocracy to undersell it.'[8] He criticised Bright and Hume, prominent Liberals, as only wanting administrative reforms without recognition of native rights. Marx believed that the socialist revolution would arise first in the industrialised nations, and only then would Socialism take root in the underdeveloped nations. History has shown him to be wrong on that, but history has shown him right in anticipating the end of colonialism.

Modern Imperialism

During the 1880s and 1890s the tendencies of colonisation to be a form of economic exploitation became an organised and all embracing system. It became modern imperialism. The same pressures which were operating in Britain following the industrial revolution and the development of capitalism were taking place in all Western European countries: the owning class in each began to seek overseas territories as markets for their goods, as sources of foodstuffs and raw materials, as well as for the investment of surplus capital. America was less involved at this time because it had its own vast undeveloped territory to explore and exploit; to go west towards the Pacific was the parallel to the European urge to go south to Africa or east to Asia. The competition for the continent of Africa became so critical in potential conflict that the European governments met in conference in Berlin in 1885 to share out its territories. They divided Africa without consideration of its peoples; the frontiers of European possessions were decided not by the ethnic identity of peoples but by how far traders and missionaries and troops had penetrated. An artificial pattern of colonies was established which had ill consequences even when political colonisation was ended.

The new imperialism became motivated more by financial investment than by trade. Indeed, Britain's share of trade with the empire was reduced during this period. In the decade 1883–93 profits fell from £305 million to £277 million per annum, whilst the empire grew in extent by four million square miles and one million population. But investments, supported directly by government policy, mounted. Whilst in 1877 British capital directed abroad was £600 million, by 1882 it had risen to £1,698 million (or fifteen per cent of Britain's total wealth). This financial imperialism was not limited to the British sphere. Large sums were invested in the Ottoman empire, Egypt, Liberia and Brazil. Always there was government backing. When in 1875 the Ottoman empire failed to repay its European landholders, their governments established a Board to administer the debt.

Similarly in 1879 Anglo-French control of Egypt was imposed to achieve financial authority; it rapidly became political domination, in time exclusively British. It was the financiers who backed Rhodes's occupation of Southern Africa, using either government forces or colonially-raised native armies to further their interests. The new owners in Africa, who had secured their possessions either by trickery or Ministerial Order, depended on the Government to contrive conditions (such as driving tribes from their lands) ensuring cheap labour. Thus colonialism reached a stage where government became an active partner in a gigantic business venture, with trading companies making untold profits which were never accountable.

Joseph Chamberlain

Joseph Chamberlain was the arch imperialist of the age. His visions of British domination of the world were little else than jingoistic euphoria blended with racialism. He wanted the British flag to be planted anywhere and everywhere and was quite prepared to go to war to attain British supremacy. Almost certainly he conspired with Rhodes in the Jameson Raid, although the Parliamentary Committee which investigated the alleged complicity (with the exception of a Radical and an Irish MP) found no connection. Chamberlain called imperialism 'a truly wise economic policy' and considered that it was 'the landlord's duty to develop his estate'. This estate was a quarter of the world.

The English public, including nearly all the politicians, were imbued with the writings of Dilke, Bagheot, Benjamin Kidd, Kipling, Henty and above all Darwin, extolling the white man's virtue and his 'manifest destiny' in Africa and Asia. Their adherence to social Darwinism ('the survival of the fittest') was so tenacious that the protests of humanitarian organisations met with little success, while the Liberals in Parliament were unable to suggest any real alternative. Their criticisms were directed against the activities of the chartered companies and the cost of colonial policy rather than against the conditions of the native peoples.[9]

To combat this fatalistic attitude, Mary Kingsley, E. D. Morel and John Holt of the 'Liverpool School' suggested plans for change which would encourage trade within a context of the independent development of the indigenous peoples. Theirs was a realistic attempt, in the existing circumstances, to achieve a solution by removing the worst financial iniquities of imperialism. Mary Kingsley advocated greater control of the chartered companies, thus achieving 'civilisation by trade'. Morel believed that the surest method to combine aid for development with essential economic independence was a system of indirect rule, with African landownership accompanied by free trade. But these solutions, while attacking some of the causes of exploitation, were neverthe-less combined with 'capitalistic humanitarianism'. In other words, if the natives failed to co-operate in trade or to cultivate their land they must be pressed to do so, because the rest of the world de-manded the potential products of their work. Known as the 'dual mandate', this theory was supported by the Fabians and even J. A. Hobson. The Fabians believed in a form of international trusteeship to educate the native peoples.

The Boer War

Whatever justifications the imperialists had, the sentiment they created was exposed by the revelations which arose during and after the Boer War. The war was fought for the 'Park Lane millionaires', who in 1898 wanted the gold mines of the Transvaal besides an open trade route to Rhodesia. When the Jameson Raid failed and Kruger began to arm the Boers, Chamberlain decided to negotiate through Milner about English emigrant rights in South Africa. The Boers were conciliatory, but every concession from Kruger provoked a new demand from Chamberlain, so that it became obvious that total surrender was required or war inevit-able.

The war, supported by most Englishmen throughout the world as a demonstration of empire strength and unity (the Dominions were more imperialist-minded than the British), was the climax of the new aggressive imperialism. Imperial attitudes had taken a harsher tone. There was no longer an appeal to the moral façade but rather to the power, prestige and national superiority of the English race. Characteristically, when Chamberlain went to South Africa following the war he told the Boers that it had been a mis-take for them to fight because 'the English were the fittest race in the world'. But for those in Britain who did not have a direct financial interest in this £250 million enterprise for empire expan-sion, the war meant among other things the postponement of a pension and rising payments for arms expenditure.

The Socialist Challenge

The socialist movement in Britain from its inception opposed colonialism. As early as 1885 William Morris's Socialist League issued a 'Manifesto on Sudan' which gave support to its people in what was described as a commercial war. In 1893 the ILP (Independent Labour Party) was formed and, with the SDF (Social Democratic Federation), energetically campaigned against imperialism. Keir Hardie, the ILP leader, aroused the wrath of the British in India by championing the right of its peoples and was refused permission to land in South Africa. Like Lloyd George, the Liberal leader, he had to escape from angry crowds when he denounced the Boer War. In 1896, George Lansbury proposed a resolution at a London SDF conference demanding 'the right of all nations to complete sovereignty' and denounced colonialism as an expression of capitalism. Yet the early socialist opposition to colonialism had not so far developed a theoretical analysis of the true meaning of imperialism.

Capitalism and Imperialism

It was J. A. Hobson, perhaps following the lead of Conant (who believed that the excess supply of goods and capital in relation to market demand led to the exploitation of underdeveloped areas), who translated the anti-colonialist attacks against the ruling classes into an indictment of imperialism as an integral part of the capitalist system. He exposed the new imperialism as 'the use of the machinery of government by private interests, mainly capitalists, to secure for themselves economic gains outside their country'. Instead of using their surplus production at home to improve the standard of living (which could be achieved by a more equal distribution of wealth), the financiers sought higher profits abroad, and, to secure their markets, embarked upon aggressive, militaristic imperialism. Competing empires, he prophesied, were bound to lead to conflict because protective tariff barriers limited trade on a national basis and consequently destroyed any common interest in peace.

Hobson criticised the ruling few who used the nation's money to buy weapons and armies to protect their wealth. As a result there was aggravated racialism and wars and also corruption at home, as those who ruled despotically in India continued to do so on their return. He called the system 'parasitic capitalism' with Britain living on interest returns from credit rather than by industrial development. Class rule displayed itself in the contrast between the pursuit of imperialism and the withholding of social reform; it was the outcome of finance gaining political power. Whilst the Fabians, who supported the Boer War as part of their civilising mission, maintained that European presence in Africa was necessary in order to exploit natural resources in the interests of the native peoples and the whole world, Hobson judged colonialism on the criteria of who received the actual benefit.[10]

Socialists Divided

The controversy regarding colonialism was not confined to British Socialists and was a major topic at the fifth Congress of the Socialist International in Paris (1900), where, under the leadership of Rosa Luxemburg, colonialism was condemned for imposing cruel injustices upon native peoples. There was still uncertainty, however, about the nature of colonialism. Faced with the difficulties of how to protect uneducated natives, while simultaneously aiding economic development, the 1904 Congress in Amsterdam adjourned a decision to await investigation. The result in 1907 at Stuttgart was division on whether Socialists could be colonisers. At the end, however, a resolution carried (127 to 108) expressed total opposition to colonialism and asserted the right of each nation to develop freely.[11]

Marxists disagreed on the effects of imperialism. Hilferding, an Austrian Socialist, who shared with Hobson the initiative in the deeper analysis of imperialism, believed that by its tariffs imperialism could be equated with the capitalist control of domestic markets.[12] He forecast that the high taxation needed to pay for arms in the competition engendered by imperialism would lead to dictatorships. The consequent inevitable wars would result in proletarian revolutions and would establish the rule of the working class (prophecies largely fulfilled by the First World War and the Russian revolution). Karl Kautsky, the German theoretician, in a devastating criticism of colonialism saw imperialism as 'industrial capitalism' and anticipated even 'ultra imperialism' when the imperialists would unite.[13] Rosa Luxemburg prophesied that the further expansion of imperialism would prolong the capitalist structure despite inevitable conflicts.

Lenin

It was Lenin, however, drawing on Hobson and Hilferding, who, in *Imperialism, the Highest Stage of Capitalism*, most fully developed the analysis of imperialism as wedded to capitalism; his thesis was the advance to monopoly capitalism through the domination of finance. He put the process like this: a bank of State A gives money to State B on condition that State B buys its desired products from firms nominated by the bank in State A. State A thus earns twice over and the bank exercises controlling power. The consequent concentration of capital and production amounts to monopoly.

Lenin traced European economic development from the industrial advances of 1860–70, through the period of colonial expansion in the 1880s, to the realisation of monopoly capitalism. He concluded that not only was the process of financial investment linked with the partition of the world in colonies, but that the chief characteristic of modern capitalism was the domination of monopolistic alliances by the biggest capitalists. He cited the fact that eighty per cent of the world's railways were in the hands of the five greatest Powers. When the latter achieved control of the world's raw materials, the monopoly would be complete. Meanwhile, the competition arising from the demand for raw materials and the inequalities between nations in production capacity and available capital would, he forecast, lead to world war. He described imperialism as the 'monopoly stage' of capitalism.

After the Russian Revolution, Lenin came to the conclusion that the Western imperialists could be defeated only by alliance with the Africans and Asians in their independence struggles, and Stalin, in *Marxism and the National Question*, criticised the Social Democrats for failing at their Stuttgart Congress to establish an international organisation which included Africa and Asia.

Thus the anti-colonialism of the seventeenth century evolved to the anti-imperialism of the twentieth century. From the end of the nineteenth century recognition grew that the dominant urge for the occupation of territories arose from the nature of the economic system in the Western world, and from the greed of adventurous and ambitious politicians to use the power it gave to exploit peoples in private or national interests.

Neo-Colonialism

It was left to Socialists and Communists to maintain opposition to what was termed neo-colonialism after subject nations obtained independence. They saw that imperialism in the form of external capitalism continued and that this could be overcome only by ending capitalism itself both at its centre and its circumference.

There is a further fact to add. If the definition of imperialism in the introduction to this book is accepted, the termination of capitalism is not the whole answer. The oppression of peoples by stronger neighbours took place before the coming of capitalism, and recent years (China in Tibet and Soviet Russia in Hungary and Czechoslovakia) have shown that communist countries can also be guilty of it. The exploitation of East Pakistan by West Pakistan on a colonial pattern, and the subsequent massacre of its self-reliant people, indicated that a ruling class need be only partially capitalist to commit imperialist crimes. The last traits of imperialism will not be removed from the world until new values of freedom are accepted by all and reflected in an international order to which all belong. Before we conclude we shall hope to suggest the essentials of that order.

Notes

1. See H. N. Brailsford's *The Levellers and the English Revolution.*

2. 'Drapiers Letters', 1723.

3. See tables in Part Two.

4. Bentham twenty years later somewhat modified this principle by favouring Britain's retention of her colonies as a trustee, but he added that this should be only if the colonies wanted it.

5. Adam Smith supported, saying that slavery brought no financial benefit.

6. An exceptional view was expressed in a Parliamentary paper, 'The Report of the Aborigines Committee' in 1835. It condemned colonialists who went into the lands of uncivilised peoples and demanded government protection. 'The empire,' it said, 'was for some higher purpose than commercial prosperity and military renoun.'

7. Gladstone failed to understand that the principle of Negro slavery was at stake in the American civil war. In contrast was the

refusal by Lancashire workers to accept cotton from the Southern States and their blockade of exports to America. Marx even sent Lincoln congratulations from the First International. Bourgeois opinion was expressed by the jury at the Old Bailey, who halted the prosecution of the Governor of Jamaica on a charge of illegally executing several hundred Negroes during the 1865 uprising.

8. The Chartist leader, Ernest Jones, in 'Revolt in Hindustan', *People's Paper* (1857), was also among those who severely criticised British rule in India.

9. Not without resignations in the Party, e.g. John Morley in 1889.

10. It is fair to the Fabians to record that later, through their Colonial Bureau, they contributed much to the campaign against colonialism and for racial equality. See following chapters.

11. See Braunthal's *History of the International*, Vol. 1.

12. *Finanz Kapital*, 1910.

13. *Sozialismus und Kolonialpolitic*, 1917.

Chapter Three

Across Frontiers

There have been repeated instances of common action by anti-colonialists on an international and regional scale, as well as the major resistance by the victims of imperialism recounted later. They reflected the evolution of opinion we have described.

The League Against Imperialism

The first co-ordination of the struggle against imperialism on an international scale took place with the formation of the League Against Imperialism at a conference at Brussels in 1929. It was initiated with skill by Muenzenberg, head of the publications department of the German Communist Party. He was dynamic and at the same time a genius in organisation; he was also courageous, as his defiance of Hitler in the Second World War showed – his body was thrown into the Seine by the Nazis. The object of the League was to bring unity between the peoples of the imperialist countries and the nationalist movements resisting imperialism, and, despite its communist inspiration, the conference was attended by nearly all the known leaders in Asia and Africa and by some representatives of the democratic socialist Left in Europe and America. Nehru was present from India, Kenyatta from Kenya, Romain Rolland from France, George Lansbury from Britain.

At this point a personal reference must be made. The author went to Brussels as a representative of the Independent Labour Party and was elected chairman of the League. What happened subsequently had significance in the role of Communists and Socialists in the anti-imperialist campaign. At the time the author was also the delegate of the ILP on the Executive of the Second (Social Democratic) International. The German representatives challenged his association with the League on the ground that it was a tool of the Communists; he was given the choice of resigning the chairmanship or his membership of the Second International

Executive. The ILP decided he should remain with the International.

Disillusionment with Social Democrats and Communists

This clash (one of many) between Social Democrats and Communists was significant because it marked a beginning of the disillusionment of nationalist leaders with the official Labour and Socialist movements of Western Europe. There was in 1929 a Labour Government in Britain under the premiership of Ramsay MacDonald; it had minority support in the House of Commons and this occasioned compromise. It crushed the nationalist movement in India as ruthlessly as a Tory Government would have done, imprisoning Gandhi, Nehru and six thousand members of the National Congress.[1] British Labour's betrayal and the muted voice of the International did much to lose the confidence of the resistance leaders in Asia and Africa.

Within a few years there was a similar disillusionment with the Communists. As the Second World War approached, Soviet Russia sought an alliance with France and Britain against Hitler's Germany. To gain the confidence of the French and British Governments, Moscow toned down its support of the resistance movements in their empires. This was particularly the case in Africa, where the communist representative, George Padmore, who had been prominent in determining the anti-colonial policy of the Communist International, resigned in protest.[2] It was less so in India, where the Communists were prominent as defendants in the famous Meerut trial on the charge of subversion. The changed communist line and the concentration of opposition to Nazism led to the gradual liquidation of the League Against Imperialism. Asian and African Nationalists, disappointed in turn by Social Democrats and Communists, turned increasingly to self-reliance and non-alignment.

Effect of Second World War

The Second World War, when it came, led to divided courses within the anti-imperialist movement. In South-East Asia where the Japanese overran the British, French and Netherlands' empires, many nationalist leaders formed anti-fascist movements to resist the new alien occupations, and simultaneously thousands of Africans, particularly in the British colonies, served with the allied armies to overthrow the Germans and Italians in their territories and also went overseas, mostly to South-East Asia. The Indian National Congress took the line that it would not support Britain in its 'war for democracy' until the right of India to independence was recognised. Subhas Bose, a popular leader in Bengal, even joined the Japanese forces on a promise that they would recognise India's independence.

In Western Europe support for Asian and African independence was submerged in the conflict against Nazism. In Britain the campaign for India had been conducted largely by the India League under the dedicated leadership of Krishna Menon, with the co-operation of many distinguished British figures, including Reginald Sorensen (later Lord Sorensen), its chairman, and Kingsley Martin, later the editor of the *New Statesman*. But there was considerable communist influence in the League and when Soviet Russia allied itself with the anti-Nazi forces, support for the Indian Congress was subdued. Open backing was limited to the ILP and to an *ad hoc* Indian Freedom Committee, of which the author was chairman, and whose members included Ethel Mannin, the novelist, and Reginald Reynolds.[3] Among Indians dissatisfied with the inactivity of the India League, a basement in Soho, Swaraj House, became headquarters of activity under the lively leadership of Jan Ram. Nevertheless, despite the inevitable diversion of interest from colonial freedoms, the democratic ideology released in Europe during the war had a profound effect on the movement towards liberation which accompanied the peace. Among other factors was the experience of wider horizons gained by colonial subjects through their service abroad. They had fought for democracy; they gave themselves when they returned to its achievement in their homelands.

After the war the recognition by Britain of the independence of India, Pakistan, Ceylon and Burma in 1947 restored goodwill to a considerable extent, although in Africa this was undermined by the unwillingness of Britain to move rapidly towards the acceptance of independence. In the French colonies of north Africa the Arab peoples increasingly agitated for the implementation of democracy in their territories. Growing confidence among Nationalists strengthened the feeling of self-reliance and non-alignment. This was reflected in the circumstances which led to the formation of the second international organisation against imperialism.

Congress of Peoples Against Imperialism

In 1948 the Left in the French Socialist Party and the British ILP took the initiative in convening a conference between European Socialists and representatives of nationalist movements in Africa and Asia to prepare a common economic plan for a United Socialist States of Europe and the developing nations. The intention was sincere, but the African and Asian representatives would have nothing to do with it on three grounds; first, the record of European Social Democrats did not justify confidence; second, the proposed united front would be with Socialists in Western Europe only and this would be inconsistent with non-alignment; third, the nationalist leaders were not prepared to become committed to any plan before they had independent governments. Instead of associating themselves with the Socialists, the African and Asian representatives met separately with European supporters and established the Congress of Peoples Against Imperialism. Jean Rous, a columnist on *Combatant*, courageous organ of the French resistance to the Nazis in the war, was appointed secretary, and the author, chairman. The Congress became a considerable political force. Its headquarters were in Paris and its greatest influence was by contact with the national movements in the French colonies of Morocco, Algeria and Tunisia in Africa and of Indo-China in Asia, but from London close association was also made with the resistance in the British colonies. Congress won wide allegiance among colonial peoples and its reputation is still legendary. The organisation only functioned, however, for six years. The Paris secretariat was cut off in the early fifties from northern Africa and Indo-China by the Algerian and Vietnam wars, and the London Committee was expanded into a broader British movement which is described later.

Mediterranean Council

An attempt was made to establish an organisation on an international basis in Greece, where feeling about the conflict in Cyprus was strong. The moment, however, had passed; the disruption between the peoples of the colonial territories and Europe was too great; in Africa and Asia the resistance movements were moving towards Pan-Africanism and Afro-Asian solidarity rather than to support from within the imperialist countries. The initiative in

Greece did nevertheless lead temporarily to an influential Mediter-ranean Council representing anti-imperialist forces in the Middle East, North Africa and Europe. A successful conference was held in Athens of representatives of independent Arab nations, nation-alist movements in the French colonies of north Africa, and the resistance in Cyprus and Malta, together with anti-imperialists from Greece, Yugoslavia, Italy, France and Britain.[4] Subsequent meetings of the Council were held in Cairo, Tunis and Rome. After Cyprus gained its independence, however, anti-imperialist senti-ment in Greece became less tense and the organisation melted away. It left its mark in later co-operation at official levels between Yugoslavia, the UAR (Egypt), Cyprus and Malta.

Bandung Conference

Of all international activities against colonialism and imperialism, the Bandung Conference of Asian and African nations in April 1955 was the most impressive. The sponsors were five Asian governments, those of Indonesia, Burma, Ceylon, India and Paki-stan (the co-operation of the two last was significant). They were concerned about five issues: (1) the reluctance of the West to consult on decisions affecting Asia, (2) the tension between China and the USA, (3) a desire for peaceful relations between China and the West and with themselves, (4) opposition to continued colonial-ism, particularly by France in north Africa and (5) Indonesia's claim to western New Guinea.

The attendance at the conference was extraordinarily compre-hensive. Twenty-four countries sent representatives, mostly heads of government, including Chou En-Lai, the Prime Minister of China. The only discord was between pro-Russians and the un-aligned. Should Soviet policies in Europe and Asia be condemned as well as the West's policies in Africa and Asia? A compromise was reached condemning 'colonialism in all of its manifestations' which could be interpreted as prejudices dictated. A ten-point declaration was adopted on world peace and co-operation which did not go much further than the Charter of the United Nations, and the Five Principles laid down by Nehru were not revolutionary; they repudiated force, urged international co-operation, opposed intervention within sovereign states, accepted non-alignment in the Power struggle and denounced colonialism. The conference un-doubtedly increased sympathy towards China as a result of Chou

En-Lai's moderation and it also deeply influenced Nasser's tendency in Egypt to Socialism, African identity and non-alignment.

Afro-Asian Organisations

The Bandung Conference did not realise its hopes; the sense of solidarity between Asian and African governments became less in consequence of differences in Asia between India, Pakistan and China, and in Africa because of the rift between radical Pan-Africanists and moderate governments. Indonesia and China pressed for a second conference without success; it was postponed indefinitely and never met. The Left elements within it established an Afro-Asian Solidarity Committee with headquarters in Cairo and branches in India and some African countries, but it made little impact. The successor of the Bandung Conference was rather to be found in conferences of unaligned states called by India, Yugoslavia and the UAR which promised much but which were temporarily overcome by events.[5] In 1966 there was a Tri-Continental Conference in Cuba which brought together radical movements in Asia, Africa and Latin America, the first occasion when the unity of the struggle against imperialism in the three continents was expressed. The headquarters at Havana published continuously well-produced propaganda with valuable information in different languages, but the impact was not deep beyond communist circles. Within Africa the All-Peoples' Conference became important during the fifties before national independence was gained. It received support from most of the African parties in colonial countries and a meeting at Accra in December 1958 was decisive in its influence upon the national movements of central Africa in their conflict with the British. It succeeded in establishing union between Black Africa and the Arab north, reflected in its conference in Cairo in March 1961.

Organisation of African Unity

When independence was largely gained, the formation of the Organisation of African Unity in 1963 was important. Sponsored by Haile Selassie, the Emperor of Ethiopia, it united the thirty-one independent states of Africa. It became a centre of controversy on

Pan-Africanism, but rejected the efforts of Kwame Nkrumah and others to establish a United States of Africa. It tended to reflect the Establishment views of the African states as they became stabilised, but remained militant in attitude towards racial dictatorships in South Africa and Rhodesia and gave support also to the 'freedom fighters' in the Portuguese-occupied territories. Despite outspoken denunciation of Britain for its failure to use force to overthrow the white regime in Rhodesia and its criticism of colonialism in general, the OAU became accepted internationally as the constitutional expression of independent Africa. The OAU negotiated a settlement of the frontier dispute between Morocco and Algeria and made several attempts to bring to an end the Nigerian civil war between the Federal government and Biafra, but was inhibited by the fact that many African nations had their own minorities sympathetic to secession.[6]

In April 1969, representatives of fourteen East and Central African governments met at Lusaka in Zambia and adopted an impressive manifesto on southern Africa which became recognised as authoritative throughout independent Africa. The document was moderately worded, recognising that all peoples who had made their homes in southern Africa including Whites were Africans, and opposing any racialist black government. A clause which later became a subject of controversy declared that the African governments 'would prefer to negotiate rather than destroy, to talk rather than kill', but the context made clear that such negotiations should have to be on the subject of 'human dignity and equality' within southern Africa. The manifesto was noteworthy for uniting conservative and radical nations. It is long but we reproduce it in full, in an Appendix to this Chapter because it is of historic importance as an expression, nobly written, of all that is best in African purpose.

The ex-French colonies in West and Equatorial Africa and Malagasy associated themselves in the *Union Africaine et Malagache* (OCAM). The separate nations associated themselves with the OAU, but reflected the more conservative administrations, heavily dependent on France and leaning towards the West.

In Britain

In Britain many organisations functioned in opposition to colonialism in every sphere.

Movement for Colonial Freedom

The Movement for Colonial Freedom (MCF) followed the disbanding of the Congress Against Imperialism. It was an amalgamation of most of the anti-imperialist elements in Britain. The acute
issues which had arisen in Africa had led to the spontaneous
establishment of a number of separate *ad hoc* committees. The
exiling of Seretse Khama from Bechuanaland because he had
married an English girl led to the formation of an all-party committee which included Labourites, Conservatives like Quintin
Hogg and Liberals like Jo Grimond. The plan to establish a
Central African Federation dominated by Europeans led to the
formation of an influential committee with Leslie Hale, MP, as
chairman. There were many committees dealing with other specific
issues.

In 1954 the MCF not only absorbed the specialist committees; it
greatly extended the campaign against colonialism by bringing
in wide sections of the Labour movement, peace organisations,
academics and groups of African, Asian and Caribbean students.
Its sponsors included Harold Wilson, Barbara Castle, Anthony
Wedgwood Benn and Anthony Greenwood, Ministers in the
subsequent Labour Government. Within a year, the affiliated
membership, through trades unions, constituency Labour Parties,
University student societies and peace organisations, was over one
million.

The activities of the MCF contributed greatly to the development of anti-colonialist conviction in Britain. The Parliamentary
questions which it initiated compelled the allocation of an additional day to colonial affairs. Throughout the crises which arose –
Mau Mau in Kenya, the independence struggles in Nigeria, Ghana,
Tanganyika and Uganda, the repression in Nyasaland, the tragic
Lumumba agitation for unity in the Congo, the military intervention in British Guiana, the opposition to the Central African
Federation and the violent resistance in Cyprus to British power
(as well as to national conflicts outside the British Empire in
Algeria, Tunisia, Morocco and Madagascar) – on all these issues
the MCF carried on a continuous agitation. Many of its publications were issued jointly with the Union for Democratic Control
(UDC), a relic from the World Wars. As the colonial revolution
liberated territories activity on political independence became
necessarily less, but it campaigned on the remaining colonies,
the maintenance of democratic liberties, racialism and neo-colonial-

ism. In 1970 it adopted the name 'Liberation' to express its developing purpose.[7]

Apartheid, Vietnam, Nigeria, Aid

Issues arose which had wider support than the radical MCF would be likely to attract and it co-operated in establishing separate organisations for these purposes. Most successful was the *Anti-Apartheid Movement*, which mounted a continuous campaign on the issues of Southern Africa, not only within the Republic but in South West Africa (Namibia), Angola and Mozambique and Rhodesia. It was always in the news with its marches, demonstrations, pickets outside South Africa House and Parliamentary lobbies.

Similarly it was felt that opposition to the Vietnam war would be best served by a separate body and the MCF initiated the *British Campaign for Peace in Vietnam*, which had some influence in securing decisions by the Labour Party Conference, the Trade Union Congress and the Co-operative Party Conference urging the British Government to dissociate itself from the American Government; unfortunately the Labour Government did not respond. Another effort for peace in the colonial sphere was an all-party *British Committee for Peace in Nigeria*, also MCF initiated, which included Africans from both sides. It sent James Griffiths, ex-Colonial Minister, Dr John Wallace and the author to Biafra and the Federation; they succeeded in getting a Christmas truce. Among wider organisations there was the *Defence and Aid Fund* to help persecuted victims of white domination and their families, directed by Canon John Collins, Dean of St Paul's Cathedral.

Another organisation concerned with Africa was the *Africa Bureau*, the director of which was the Rev. Michael Scott, famous for his representation at the United Nations of the Herero tribe in South West Africa. He gathered round him an important group of politicians including Lord Hemingford, a Conservative, first chairman, Sir Dingle Foot, MP, for some time Attorney-General, and Lord Campbell of Eskan. The Bureau was a political élite rather than a popular movement, but it had association with many Universities and published fact-full literature, particularly on Southern Africa. Within the Labour Party was the *Fabian Colonial Bureau*, influential among the leadership, valuable in its information pamphlets and its monthly *Third World*, continually at the service of

MPs. The *United Nations Association*, broad-based in political membership, spoke out boldly on racial issues, its Youth Section on all colonialist issues.

Racial Discrimination

One of the biggest controversies arose from South Africa's racialism in sport. An original MCF Committee did a little to start the ball rolling (or perhaps one should say to stop the ball rolling), and the Anti-Apartheid Movement was supplemented by the *South Africa Non-Racial Committee for Olympic Sports*, run from Canon Collin's office and the militant *Stop the Seventy Tour Committee*, led by Peter Hain, chairman of the Young Liberals, which so disrupted the South African rugby engagements that the South African cricket tour was called off. Race discrimination in Britain itself projected *CARD* (Campaign against Racial Discrimination), split between moderates and extremists, but after the author had introduced a Bill nine years in succession, Harold Wilson pledged a Labour Government to legislate, and discrimination was finally made illegal in public places, housing and employment. One of the best results was the formation of *Inter-Racial Community Councils* linking whites and non-whites in districts with large immigrant populations from the Commonwealth.

Special Issues

Ireland had permanent organisations in Britain, protesting against partition, the *United Ireland Association* and the *Connolly Association*, and the Ulster crisis in the early seventies threw up many more. On this issue the MCF co-operated with others in sponsoring a Bill of Rights which was introduced simultaneously in the House of Commons and the House of Lords. Innumerable organisations sprang up in the late sixties and early seventies to deal with other specific issues. This reflected a tendency for those keen on causes to act directly rather than wait for directions from large slower organisations, a trend opposite to the fifties when united fronts were popular. Among the specialist groups was the *Committee for Freedom in Mozambique, Angola and Guiné* (chairman, Lord Gifford) which staged a great welcome for Amilcar Cabral, Freedom Fighters' leader, when he came to London.[8] In addition, each student national group had its association as concerned as much with wider politics as with its own interests.

India in Britain

There was one earlier organisation in Britain which was significant in reflecting the changed character of the struggle against colonialism. As far back as 1889 the *British Committee of the Indian National Congress* was started by English sympathisers. Its first chairman was Sir William Wedderburn, who played an important part in establishing the Congress in India, and the committee was composed of moderate politicians. They mirrored the mood in India at the time, shown by the fact that Congress even considered holding its 1892 session in Britain. This mood changed progressively and did so completely at the end of the First World War. In 1920 Congress took the decision on the initiative of Gandhi to end foreign propaganda and to rely on its own strength in action. The British Committee was closed down.[9]

Within Political Parties

We should give a wrong impression of anti-colonialism in Britain if we conveyed that it was expressed only in organisations specifically devoted to this purpose. Probably the main factor was activity within the Labour Party, earlier by the ILP, afterwards by the Left in the Party associated with the *Tribune*. The Liberal Party and Church leaders were also outspoken in the assertion of the equality of peoples. Even in the Conservative Party the sentiment grew, as indicated by Harold Macmillan's speech in South Africa, recognising 'the wind of change'.

This was an attitude rather than an analysis. There was very limited understanding of the real nature of imperialism. Only the Labour left, the small but active Communist Party, the New Left including the International Socialists, radical Youth Movements, particularly at the Universities, and the MCF, emphasised the dangers of neo-colonialism and drew attention to the identification of imperialism in its modern form with the economic motives and pressures of capitalism.

In America

In America there has always been a strong anti-imperialist sentiment inherited from the War of Independence, but until the massive opposition to the Vietnam intervention there was no popular movement or determiningly influential organisation. Every colonialist venture by the US, however, had its minority dissentients.

Early Oppositions

Following the war with Mexico in 1848 there was strongly voiced opposition by leading politicians to the annexation of territory. In 1898 a *League against Imperialism* was established to oppose the annexations of Puerto Rico and the Philippines. It was headed by distinguished lawyers and writers, including William Jennings Bryan and Mark Twain, but made little impact on the public. In the early years of this century the then active Socialist Party and its idealistic presidential candidate, Gene Debs, boldly denounced imperialism, and his successor, the much-honoured Norman Thomas, later repudiated every American intervention, from Haiti through the Bay of Pigs attack to Vietnam. There was some response to the internationally organised League against Imperialism in the late 1920s, but support came mainly from Communists and a few intellectuals. They opposed the occupations by marines of Haiti, Santo Domingo and Nicaragua as well as 'dollar diplomacy' in Latin America. Strangely it was the disaffection of Chiang-Kai Shek which led to the dissolution of the American section of the League. These protest movements had, one must recognise, little political effect.

One factor which contributed to ineffectiveness was the weakness of the opposition in the colonial territories themselves – in Puerto Rico, the Virgin Islands, Guam and Samoa. In contrast with Britain, where anti-colonialist activists could co-operate with Irish, Indian and, later, African national movements, American anti-imperialists had little resistance to support. In Puerto Rico there was some armed revolt for a time, but it died out with the first concession towards self-government. In the Philippines there was the Huk guerrilla resistance, but again formal political independence destroyed much of its *raison d'être*. American colonialism at this time had to resort little to repression and consequently there was less motive for opposition.

Negro Voices

One might have expected the large Negro population in America to be concerned about the freedom struggles of other non-white peoples, but until Martin Luther King's leadership in the sixties and the emergence of the Black Power movement they were too preoccupied with their own problems to show much interest on a world scale. There were two exceptions to this. A prominent Negro who ostentatiously retained his citizenship of Ghana, Dr W. E. B. Du Bois, might almost be described as the originator of the Pan-Africanist ideas which afterwards gained a deep hold. He recruited a group of adherents in America, but it was at a conference at Manchester in England in 1946 that he gathered African leaders around him, and it was in Ghana, after independence, that he became editor of the *All-Africa Encyclopaedia*. The second exception was the crusade led by Marcus Garvey, much revered among those of African descent, for the migration of American and Caribbean Negroes to their ancestral continent. He did not have much success in this, but he did arouse interest in the fate and future of the peoples of Africa.

The Labour movement in America never became identified with anti-colonialism to the same extent as in Britain. In earlier days some trade union leaders spoke out against imperialism, but later the unions became too closely associated with the Establishment. The brothers Reuther, Victor and Walter, officers of the Automobile Workers' Union, retained an international attitude, but when the two sections of the movement coalesced in the AFL–CIO their voices tended to be submerged. Later the Auto Workers broke away, entering in 1968 an 'Alliance for Labour Action' with the Teamsters (also Leftist), and their voices were again heard on overseas issues, most strongly on Vietnam and nuclear arms.

Civil Liberties, Freedom of Peoples

Meanwhile, concerned individuals began to form organisations. There was the *Civil Liberties Unions*, mainly interested in defending democratic rights within America, but extending its interest to democracy and freedoms overseas, for example to Korea and to Okinawa, the Japanese island appropriated by the USA as a military base. There was the *League for the Rights of Man*, directed by Roger Baldwin, active for freedom over fifty years. There was the *Friends Service Committee*, for whom the author did three lecture tours on colonialism all over the United States.

There were organisations which specifically devoted themselves to the freedom of peoples. The first was known as *Towards Freedom*. It was established by William Bross Lloyd Junior in 1951 and was centred in Chicago with Dr Homer Jack, an outspoken Unitarian Minister, as president. Dr Jack paid visits to Asian and African countries and wrote objectively. *Towards Freedom* gained the cooperation of Negro leaders in Chicago and many important liberals. It was also a pioneer in opposing the Vietnam war. The group served as a kind of Fabian Society among a limited circle concerned about colonialism and the constitutional problems of the newly independent states.

Committee on Africa

The second anti-colonial organisation, the *American Committee on Africa* (ACA), had a more direct political effect. It was set up in New York in 1953 by a handful of activists in civil rights campaigns who felt that domestic interest should become international. In 1955, with faith rather than funds, a small staff was engaged in an office in New York with George Hauser, who remained the dynamic figure, as director. Support was recruited not only from the east but from the west, principally from California. A measure of the wide constituency reached was the file of twenty-five thousand on its mailing lists. The ACA developed close associations with virtually every liberation movement in Africa, assisted by the visits of George Hauser. It sponsored speaking tours in America by African leaders, including Kenneth Kaunda, Kamuza Banda, Joshua Nkomo, Tom Mboya, Oliver Tambo, Holden Roberto, Eduardo Mondlane and Kanyame Chiume. Help was given to persecuted movements through its Africa Defence and Aid Fund, which not only provided legal defence for prisoners but enabled representatives to present their case to the United Nations and paid the rent of African offices in New York. Through sympathetic Congressmen and Senators and by direct pressure, it sought to influence White House policy, not always with results; but there was spectacular success when the Government prohibited the crew of the aircraft carrier, *Franklin D. Roosevelt*, from docking at Cape Town because of the discrimination practised towards non-white sailors.

The ACA had considerable responsibility for initiating hearings on US policy towards South Africa by the Sub-Committee on Africa of the Foreign Affairs Committee of the House of Representatives. One of its specialised campaigns was to encourage individuals and organisations to withdraw their accounts from banks which loaned funds to the Government of South Africa. There was some response, particularly from Churches and students who influenced the Universities. The Methodists transferred $10 million of investment from the First National City Bank of New York and students began to agitate that their Universities should withdraw their accounts.[10] In recent years the ACA had the advantage of working within a climate, stimulated by opposition to the Vietnam war, which was opposed to American intervention against indigenous peoples.

The Vietnam War

The Vietnam war was the turning point. Opposition began among students and professors. The author was present at a conference of 'intellectuals' at Ann Arbor University in Michigan as early as 1964, followed by a teach-in attended by four thousand students. He remarked on the isolation of the movement from the general life of America. 'The students come from a cross-section of the American people,' he was told. 'Soon their parents will influence a wider circle.' How far due to the students and intellectuals it is difficult to estimate, but with astonishing rapidity opposition to the war spread throughout America. This was helped by the outspokenness of a group of Senators and Congressmen; Fulbright, McCarthy, McGovern, Javitts, Clerk, Edward Kennedy and others, by the challenging radical group within the Democratic Party, *Americans for Democratic Action,* and by the strong criticism of influential daily papers.

The mounting opposition found dramatic expression in the remarkable vote obtained by Eugene McCarthy in the Democratic primary in New Hampshire. When President Johnson said he would not contest the presidential election, reflecting a feeling of inadequacy to handle Vietnam, it became clear that American policy would have to be reviewed. Hopes were damped by compromises at the Democratic Congress and by the election of the Republican candidate, President Nixon. Nevertheless, opposition to the war strengthened as reports of American casualties came in, reflected in marches of half a million in Washington, prominent among them servicemen from Vietnam who threw away their medals. President Nixon sensed opinion. He announced that in future the Vietnamese forces at Saigon must progressively take over the fighting and that US troops would be periodically withdrawn. This had some effect in moderating opposition to the war but it revived when American forces invaded Laos and Cambodia and particularly when the entrance to Haiphong was mined and Hanoi was bombed. The success of George McGovern in the primary elections for the Democratic candidature for President indicated this.[11]

World-Wide

The opposition to the Vietnam war was world-wide. In every European country movements of protest arose, and they extended to Asia, Africa and South America. Activities were co-ordinated by a series of conferences held in Stockholm, with scarcely hidden governmental support, representing organisations in more than thirty countries. In each of them there were active campaigns. A climax was reached in Paris in February 1972 when delegations came from all over the world calling on America to withdraw all its forces and military weapons. There was never a more unpopular war.

Opposition to colonialism and imperialism on an international scale was not confined to the Vietnam war. Movements parallel to those we have described in Britain and America sprang up in many countries. It was particularly significant that the student revolts which broke out nearly everywhere in the sixties and seventies invariably included opposition to racialism and imperialism.

Notes

1. The author raised the issue on the executive of the International of which Arthur Henderson, a British Minister, was Chairman. There was considerable disappointment among its members with the actions of the Labour Government, but concern not to embarrass it. On this, as on other occasions, the distinguished Austrian leader, Otto Bauer, a sincere anti-imperialist, secured the adoption of a compromise resolution reasserting the principle of

national independence, but appreciating the difficulties of the MacDonald administration.

2. Padmore, a West Indian of African origin, became a leading constructive influence in African liberation. His book on Pan-Africanism as an alternative to Communism contributed much to African thinking. He was an adviser to Nkrumah in Ghana during the earlier period of social and economic advance. His death was a great loss to African unity and Nkrumah's subsequent course might have been different had he lived.

3. Equally known as an author and as Gandhi's messenger to the Governor-General with his 'ultimatum' on non-co-operation.

4. An unhappy feature of this conference was the refusal of the Arab representatives to sit with left-wing Socialists from Israel. This led to the withdrawal of the French delegation.

5. The unaligned nations recovered initiative at a very representative conference at Lusaka in Zambia in 1969. It was mainly concerned with opposition to white domination in southern Africa.

6. The OAU has been criticised for failing to contribute constructively to African co-operation in the economic sphere, but in February 1972 it boldly organised an All-Africa Trade Pact at Nairobi in Kenya with the object of extending intra-African trade and development.

7. The author was the chairman until 1968 and is now president. Stan Newens, ex-Labour MP, and Bob Hughes, MP, are now joint chairmen and Barbara Haq was secretary until 1973.

8. Cabral was assassinated on January 21, 1973, in Conakry. An impressive memorial service was held in the St Pancras Town Hall, London.

9. The author was one of the last joint secretaries.

10. The American example was widely followed in Britain from 1970 onwards, particularly among students, who succeeded in getting Universities to withdraw investments in banks operating in South Africa.

11. His vote in the Presidential election was disappointing. The pressure of public opinion undoubtedly influenced the Vietnam cease-fire in January 1973 and the withdrawal of American troops from the war.

The Lusaka Manifesto

Manifesto adopted by a conference of African leaders at Lusaka, Zambia, in April 1969. It was endorsed by representatives of Ethiopia, Kenya, Rwanda, Malawi, Congo (Brazzaville), Congo (Kinshasa), Somalia, Burundi, Central African Republic, Sudan, Tanzania, Chad, Uganda and Zambia.

The Future of Southern Africa

1. When the purpose and the basis of States' international policies are misunderstood, there is introduced into the world a new and unnecessary disharmony, disagreements, conflicts, of interest or different assessments of human priorities, which already provoke an excess of tension in the world, and disastrously divide mankind at a time when united action is necessary to control modern technology and put it to the service of man. It is for this reason that, discovering widespread misapprehension of our attitudes and purposes in relation to Southern Africa, we the leaders of East and Central African States meeting at Lusaka, 16th April 1969, have agreed to issue this Manifesto.

2. By this Manifesto we wish to make clear, beyond all shadow of doubt, our acceptance of the belief that all men are equal, and have equal rights to human dignity and respect, regardless of colour, race, religion or sex. We believe that all men have the right and the duty to participate, as equal members of the society, in their own government. We do not accept that any individual or group has any right to govern any other group of sane adults without their consent, and we affirm that only the people of a society, acting together as equals, can determine what is, for them, a good society and a good social, economic or political organisation.

3. On the basis of these beliefs we do not accept that any one group within a society has the right to rule any society without the continuing consent of all the citizens. We recognise that at any one time there will be, within every society, failures in the implementa-

tion of these ideals. We recognise that for the sake of order in human affairs there may be transitional arrangements while a transformation from group inequalities to individual equality is being effected. But we affirm that without an acceptance of these ideals – without a commitment to these principles of human equality and self-determination – there can be no basis for peace and justice in the world.

4. None of us would claim that within our own States we have achieved that perfect social, economic and political organisation which would ensure a reasonable standard of living for all our people and establish individual security against avoidable hardship or miscarriage of justice. On the contrary, we acknowledge that within our own States the struggle towards human dignity is only beginning. It is on the basis of our commitment to human equality and human dignity, not on the basis of achieved perfection, that we take our stand of hostility towards the colonialism and racial discrimination which is being practised in Southern Africa. It is on the basis of their commitment to these universal principles that we appeal to other members of the human race for support.

5. If the commitment to these principles existed among the States holding power in Southern Africa, any disagreements we might have about the rate of implementation, or about isolated acts of policy, would be matters affecting only our individual relationships with the States concerned. If these commitments existed, our States would not be justified in the expressed and active hostility towards the regimes of Southern Africa such as we have proclaimed and continue to propagate.

6. The truth is, however, that in Mozambique, Angola, Rhodesia, South West Africa and the Republic of South Africa, there is an open and continued denial of the principles of human equality and national self-determination. This is not a matter of failure in the implementation of accepted human principles. The effective Administrations in all those territories are not struggling towards these difficult goals. They are fighting the principles; they are deliberately organising their societies so as to try to destroy the hold of these principles in the minds of men. It is for this reason that we believe the rest of the world must be involved. For the principle of human equality, and all that flows from it, is either universal or it does not exist. The dignity of all men is destroyed when the manhood of any human being is denied.

7. Our objectives in Southern Africa stem from our commitment to this principle of human equality. We are not hostile to the

Administrations of these States because they are manned and controlled by white people. We are hostile to them because they are systems of minority control which exist as a result of and in the pursuance of doctrines of human inequality. What we are working for is the right of self-determination for the peoples of those territories. We are working for a rule in those countries which is based on the will of all the people and an acceptance of the equality of every citizen.

8. Our stand towards Southern Africa thus involves a rejection of racialism, not a reversal of the existing racial domination. We believe that all the peoples who have made their homes in the countries of Southern Africa are Africans, regardless of the colour of their skins; and we would oppose a racialist majority government which adopted a philosophy of deliberate and permanent discrimination between its citizens on grounds of racial origin. We are not talking racialism when we reject the colonialism and apartheid policies now operating in those areas: we are demanding an opportunity for all the people of these States, working together as equal individual citizens, to work out for themselves the institutions and the system of government under which they will by general consent live together and work together to build a harmonious society.

9. As an aftermath of the present policies it is likely that different groups within these societies will be self-conscious and fearful. The initial political and economic organisations may well take account of these fears, and this group self-consciousness. But how this is to be done must be a matter exclusively for the peoples of the country concerned, working together. No other nation will have a right to interfere in such affairs. All that the rest of the world has a right to demand is just what we are now asserting – that the arrangements within any State which wishes to be accepted into the community of nations must be based on an acceptance of the principles of human dignity and equality.

10. To talk of the liberation of Africa is thus to say two things: First, that the peoples in the territories still under colonial rule shall be free to determine for themselves their own institutions of self-government. Secondly, that the individuals in Southern Africa shall be freed from an environment poisoned by the propaganda of racialism, and given an opportunity to be *men* – not white men, brown men, yellow men or black men.

11. Thus the liberation of Africa for which we are struggling does not mean a reverse racialism. Nor is it an aspect of African Imperi-

alism. As far as we are concerned the present boundaries of the States of Southern Africa are the boundaries of what will be free and independent African States. There is no question of our seeking or accepting any alterations to our own boundaries at the expense of these future free African nations.

12. On the objective of liberation as thus defined we can neither surrender nor compromise. We have always preferred and we still prefer to achieve it without physical violence. We would prefer to negotiate rather than destroy, to talk rather than kill. We do not advocate violence; we advocate an end to the violence against human dignity which is now being perpetuated by the oppressors of Africa. If peaceful progress to emancipation were possible, or if changed circumstances were to make it possible in the future, we would urge our brothers in the resistance movements to use peaceful methods of struggle even at the cost of some compromise on the timing of change. But while peaceful progress is blocked by actions of those at present in power in the States of Southern Africa, we have no choice but to give to the peoples of those territories all the support of which we are capable in their struggle against their oppressors. This is why the signatory States participate in the movement for the liberation of Africa under the aegis of the Organisation of African Unity. However, the obstacle to change is not the same in all the countries of Southern Africa, and it follows therefore that the possibility of continuing the struggle through peaceful means varies from one country to another.

13. In *Mozambique*, *Angola* and in so-called *Portuguese Guinea*, the basic problem is not racialism but a pretence that Portugal exists in Africa. Portugal is situated in Europe; the fact that it is a dictatorship is a matter for the Portuguese to settle. But no decree of the Portuguese dictator, nor legislation passed by any Parliament in Portugal, can make Africa part of Europe. The only thing which could convert a part of Africa into a constituent unit in a union which also includes a European State would be the freely expressed will of the people of that part of Africa. There is no such popular will in the Portuguese colonies. On the contrary, in the absence of any opportunity to negotiate a road to freedom, the peoples of all three territories have taken up arms against the colonial power. They have done this despite the heavy odds against them, and despite the great suffering they know to be involved.

14. Portugal, as a European State, has naturally its own allies in the context of the ideological conflict between West and East. However, in our context, the effect of this is that Portugal is

enabled to use her resources to pursue the most heinous war and degradation of man in Africa. The present Manifesto must, therefore, lay bare the fact that the inhuman commitment of Portugal in Africa and her ruthless subjugation of the peoples of Mozambique, Angola and the so-called Portuguese Guinea is not only irrelevant to the ideological conflict of power-politics but it is also diametrically opposed to the politics, the philosophies and the doctrines practised by her allies in the conduct of their own affairs at home. The people of Mozambique, Angola and Portuguese Guinea are not interested in Communism or Capitalism. They are demanding an acceptance of the principles of independence on the basis of majority rule, and for many years they called for discussions on this issue. Only when their demand for talks was continually ignored did they begin to fight. Even now, if Portugal should change her policy and accept the principle of self-determination, we would urge the Liberation Movements to desist from their armed struggle and to co-operate in the mechanics of a peaceful transfer of power from Portugal to the peoples of the African territories.

15. The fact that many Portuguese citizens have immigrated to these African countries does not affect this issue. Future immigration policy will be a matter for the independent governments when these are established. In the meantime we would urge the Liberation Movements to reiterate their statements that all those Portuguese people who have made their homes in Mozambique, Angola or Portuguese Guinea and who are willing to give their future loyalty to those States will be accepted as citizens. And an independent Mozambique, Angola or Portuguese Guinea may choose to be as friendly with Portugal as Brazil is. That would be the free choice of a free people.

16. In *Rhodesia* the situation is different in so far as the metropolitan power has acknowledged the colonial status of the territory. Unfortunately, however, it has failed to take adequate measures to reassert its authority against the minority which has seized power with the declared intention of maintaining white domination. The matter cannot rest there. Rhodesia, like the rest of Africa, must be free, and its independence must be on the basis of majority rule. If the colonial power is unwilling or unable to effect such a transfer of power to the people, then the people themselves will have no alternative but to capture it as and when they can. And Africa has no alternative but to support them. The question which remains in Rhodesia is therefore whether Britain will reassert her authority in Rhodesia and then negotiate the peaceful progress to majority rule

before independence. In so far as Britain is willing to make this second commitment, Africa will co-operate in her attempts to reassert her authority. This is the method of progress which we would prefer; it would involve less suffering for all the people of Rhodesia, both black and white. But until there is some firm evidence that Britain accepts the principle of independence on the basis of majority rule and is prepared to take whatever steps are necessary to make it a reality, then Africa has no choice but to support the struggle for the people's freedom by whatever means are open.

17. Just as a settlement of the Rhodesian problem with a minimum of violence is a British responsibility, so a settlement of *South West Africa* with a minimum of violence is a United Nations responsibility. By every canon of international law, and by every precedent, South West Africa should by now have been a sovereign, independent State with a government based on majority rule. South West Africa was a German colony until 1919, just as Tanganyika, Rwanda and Burundi, Togoland and Cameroun were German colonies. It was a matter of European politics that when the Mandatory System was established after Germany had been defeated, the administration of South West Africa was given to the white minority Government of South Africa, while the other ex-German colonies in Africa were put into the hands of the British, Belgian or French Governments. After the Second World War every mandated territory except South West Africa was converted into a Trusteeship Territory and has subsequently gained independence. South Africa, on the other hand, has persistently refused to honour even the international obligation it accepted in 1919, and has increasingly applied to South West Africa the inhuman doctrines and organisation of apartheid.

18. The United Nations General Assembly has ruled against this action and in 1966 terminated the Mandate under which South Africa had a legal basis for its occupation and domination of South West Africa. The General Assembly declared that the territory is now the direct responsibility of the United Nations and set up an *ad hoc* Committee to recommend practical means by which South West Africa would be administered and the people enabled to exercise self-determination and to achieve independence.

19. Nothing could be clearer than this decision – which no permanent member of the Security Council voted against. Yet since that time no effective measures have been taken to enforce it. South West Africa remains in the clutches of the most ruthless minority

government in Africa. Its people continue to be oppressed and those who advocate even peaceful progress to independence continue to be persecuted. The world has an obligation to use its strength to enforce the decision which all the countries co-operated in making. If they do this there is hope that the change can be effected without great violence. If they fail, then sooner or later the people of South West Africa will take the law into their own hands. The people have been patient beyond belief but one day their patience will be exhausted. Africa, at least, will then be unable to deny their call for help.

20. *The Republic of South Africa* is itself an independent Sovereign state and a member of the United Nations. It is more highly developed and richer than any other nation in Africa. On every legal basis its internal affairs are a matter exclusively for the people of South Africa. Yet the purpose of law is people and we assert that the actions of the South African Government are such that the rest of the world has a responsibility to take some action in defence of humanity.

21. There is one thing about South African oppression which distinguishes it from the other oppressive regimes. The *apartheid* policy adopted by its Government, and supported to a greater or lesser extent by almost all its white citizens, is based on a rejection of man's humanity. A position of privilege or the experience of oppression in the South African society depends on the one thing which it is beyond the power of any man to change. It depends upon a man's colour, his parentage and his ancestors. If you are black you cannot escape this categorisation; nor can you escape it if you are white. If you are a black millionaire and a brilliant political scientist, you are still subject to the pass laws and still excluded from political activity. If you are white, even protests against the system and an attempt to reject segregation will lead you only to the segregation and the comparative comfort of a white jail. Beliefs, abilities and behaviour are all irrelevant to a man's status; everything depends upon race. Manhood is irrelevant. The whole system of government and society in South Africa is based on the denial of human equality. And the system is maintained by a ruthless denial of the human rights of the majority of the population and thus inevitably of all.

22. These things are known and are regularly condemned in the Councils of the United Nations and elsewhere. But it appears that to many countries international law takes precedence over humanity; therefore no action follows the words. Yet even if international

law is held to exclude active assistance to the South African opponents of apartheid, it does not demand that the comfort and support of human and commercial intercourse should be given to a government which rejects the manhood of most of humanity. South Africa should be excluded from the United Nations Agencies, and even from the United Nations itself. It should be ostracised by the world community. It should be isolated from world trade patterns and left to be self-sufficient if it can. The South African Government cannot be allowed to both reject the very concept of mankind's unity, and to benefit by the strength given through friendly international relations. And certainly Africa cannot acquiesce in the maintenance of the present policies against people of African descent.

23. The signatories of this Manifesto assert that the validity of the principles of human equality and dignity extend to the Republic of South Africa just as they extend to the colonial territories of Southern Africa. Before a basis for peaceful development can be established in this continent, these principles must be acknowledged by every nation and in every State there must be a deliberate attempt to implement them.

24. We reaffirm our commitment to these principles of human equality and human dignity, and to the doctrines of self-determination and non-racialism. We shall work for their extension within our own nations and throughout the continent of Africa.

Chapter Four

Patterns of Resistance: Hungary, Korea, Ireland

Our main purpose is to describe the course of the colonial revolution which has come to its climax since the Second World War, but it is worth pausing to note how similar in pattern, adjusted to the time, was the preceding resistance. It would be repetitive and tedious to detail the long series of conflicts. Instead, we take three struggles, one from central Europe, one from Asia, one from the United Kingdom, typical of many, indicating how more recent struggles had their precedents in both method and spirit. They are patterns of national resistance.

Hungarian Example

Two hundred and fifty years ago, when the peoples of Austria and Hungary had together freed their territories from invasion, they agreed to unite under one monarchy. The treaty laid down that they should be 'free and equal nations', but the Austrian emperors ignored Hungary's rights. Resistance began when a levy of troops was ordered. 'Our Diet (Parliament) alone has the power to levy troops,' said the Hungarians. After a dispute of five years Austria gave way and the election of a Diet was ordered. Its first session in 1833 was marked by an incident which set the people of Hungary aflame. Count Szechenyi, a rich young noble, dared to address the assembly in the Hungarian language. This was dismissed as an indiscretion of youth but on the next occasion he coolly repeated the offence; as the deputies sat spellbound he passionately told in the despised tongue the story of Hungary's woes and foretold her resurrection. His defiance created a wave of popular enthusiasm, but he declined to become a political leader, concentrating upon the revival of education and industry, and the national leadership passed to two remarkable men – Francis Deak, a Catholic land-owner, and Louis Kossuth, a Protestant barrister. Deak's spirit may be judged by his reply to the moderates in the Diet who urged caution. 'Woe – Woe to the nation which raises no protest when its rights are outraged! It contributes to its own slavery by its silence. The nation which submits to injustice and oppression without protest is doomed.'

The radicals in the Diet of 1836 demanded national education; Austria refused and arrested Kossuth, Szechenyi and others. Two years passed before the Diet was allowed to meet again. Austria agreed to release the prisoners if the nationalists would moderate their claims. 'No,' said Deak. 'Our duty to our country is greater even than sympathy for our friends. Liberty gained at such a price would be more painful to them than their sufferings.' Austria gave way; the prisoners were released. Kossuth then devoted himself to mass propaganda; his *Pesth Gazette* became a dominant influence in Hungary. The Nationalists pressed two demands: equality of taxation with the Austrians and official recognition of the Hungarian language. The latter was won, the former refused. The election of 1847 returned Kossuth to power in the Diet, and it proceeded to claim the restoration of Hungary's independence. Temporarily Austria had to concur; in 1848 a constitution establishing a sovereign government was promulgated. But only temporarily. Emperor Ferdinand revoked the constitution and ordered his grenadiers to march on Buda-Pesth. There was resistance, but when the Russians joined the Austrians defeat was inevitable, the Diet was suppressed, the Hungarian language banned, the County Councils dissolved, the country divided into military regions under Austrian officers, and the name of Hungary was erased from the map of Europe.

For a time there were no visible signs of activity by the Nationalists, but the Austrians were uneasy. They offered Deak a judgeship to conciliate him. 'When my country's constitution is acknowledged, I will consider your offer,' he replied. They asked him to go to Vienna for discussions. 'I cannot negotiate with Vienna while the constitution is illegally suspended,' he replied. Meanwhile the Nationalists devoted themselves to the furtherance of education and industry. Kossuth and others who had been exiled carried on propaganda abroad. By 1857 Hungary's self-reliant progress caused apprehension in Vienna. How was the popularity of the Austrian Emperor to be revived? Franz Josef made an impressive visit to Pesth, announcing he would inaugurate a new era. There were processions, banquets, balls, fireworks and religious celebrations; the Empress visited convent schools wearing Hungarian dress, 'Let us present the Emperor with an address,' said the moderates. 'No,' said Deak. 'While Franz Josef violates the constitution, Hungary cannot recognise him.'

The Emperor had a worse humiliation; in 1859 he was defeated in war by the French. It became necessary for him to consolidate and he invited six Hungarians to join his Privy Council. Those summoned asked Deak what they should do. 'Don't go,' said Deak. 'If the Austrian Emperor wants to consult Hungary, let him come to Pesth and consult her through her Parliament.' Three of the invited declined. The Emperor made another attempt. He appointed a Hungarian Royal Commission to re-establish the County Councils; the nobles wanted the Councils and hoped Deak would concur, but he was inexorable. 'Return your patents,' he said to the Commissioners. 'None but the King of Hungary can appoint a Royal Hungarian Commission.' The Emperor gave way; in 1861 he reluctantly decided both to re-establish the County Councils and to convoke the Hungarian Diet and Hungary was offered home rule under an imperial Parliament in Vienna. Deak rejected the compromise with derision, insisting on full independence. In the Diet election he won 270 of the 300 seats, and the deputies declined to send representatives to the imperial Parliament, telling the Emperor that if he desired to be King of Hungary he must accept the constitution and be crowned at Buda. When the Emperor retorted by dissolving the Diet, keeping the deputies out of the Chamber at bayonet point, every County Council protested. They too were dissolved. A military regime was reimposed.

Deak did not lose confidence. He admonished the people not to be betrayed into acts of violence, nor to abandon the ground of legality. 'This is the safe ground, on which, unarmed ourselves, we can hold our own against armed force,' he said. The Hungarians declined to pay taxes; their goods were distrained, but, when auctioned, no one bought; the Austrians found it cost more to distrain than the taxes were worth. Vienna attempted to defeat the passive resistance by declaring the boycott of Austrian goods illegal; result – the gaols were filled. Meanwhile, the Hungarian deputies continued to meet, not in their troop-encircled Chamber but in the halls of national institutions. A threat of war, this time with Prussia, again compelled Franz Josef to offer conciliation. Deak was asked his price for Hungary's friendship; he answered, 'The restoration of our free and national constitution.' Once more the Emperor visited Pesth to inaugurate a new era; he was delighted by the display of flags until he found they were all green, white and red, the tricolours of independent Hungary. The only hint of a new era was a promise that the Diet should be reconvened, but, war with Prussia declared, Austria had to go further in concession. On September 20, 1865, the Emperor issued a proclamation announcing the abolition of the imperial Parliament, recognising Hungary's right to manage its own affairs, and accepting the authority of the Diet. 'So far so good,' said Deak, 'but this must not be a mock Parliament.'

The former deputies, meeting under the chairmanship of Deak, resolved to accept nothing less than the restoration of the constitution. An election gave the Nationalists 200 of the 333 seats. Franz Josef opened the Parliament wearing a Hungarian costume and speaking in Hungarian. He used nationalistic rhetoric, but he repeated only the previous formula of home rule under an imperial Parliament. The Diet declined compromise; the Emperor refused to go further; the Diet informed him that until he recognised Hungarian independence he would be regarded as the enemy of the nation; the Emperor left for Vienna. But the war situation got worse and Franz Josef again sent for Deak. 'What am I to do now?' he asked. Deak's reply is enshrined in Hungarian history: 'Make peace and restore Hungary her rights.' Said the Emperor: 'If I restore the constitution will Hungary help me to carry on the war?' Deak was unbending. 'No,' he said, 'I will not make the restoration of my country's freedom a matter of barter.'

Austria suffered a humiliating defeat in the war and conciliation with Hungary became urgent. The Emperor had a hawk Prime Minister, Belcredi, and an opportunist-realist in the Ministry, Beust. Deak and Beust came to an understanding. Beust would overthrow Belcredi and restore the Hungarian constitution; Deak would prevent an uprising in Hungary so as to avoid playing into Belcredi's hands. Meanwhile, Deak maintained an unyielding attitude. The Diet again sent the Emperor an address (which Deak had drafted) demanding the constitution. The reply, under Belcredi's influence, was despotic, followed by an imperial decree imposing compulsory military service. Deak had the greatest difficulty in holding back the Hungarian people from insurrection; he did not want that because he was confident that Vienna, despite its show of sternness, was becoming convinced at last that its own security depended on peace with Hungary. He proved right. When the Diet presented its firm 'last word' to the Emperor he gave way. He dismissed Belcredi, appointed Beust as successor, cancelled the conscription law, promised immediately a responsible Hungarian Ministry and pledged himself to Deak that all his demands would be conceded. The date was February 1867.

Franz Josef had been obstinate, but was unreserved in his surrender. He asked Julius Andrassy, who had fought for independence in 1848 and for whose head the Austrians had offered several thousand crowns, to form a National Ministry, authorised an agreement with Deak, recognising the independence of Hungary, endorsing the constitution and accepting the right of the people to decide their contribution to the army. He invited the Hungarians whom he had exiled to return to share the new freedom of their country and, when the people of Pesth made him a presentation of 100,000 ducats, insisted that it should be distributed among the widows and orphans of the Hungarians who had been slain in the War of Independence. On June 8, 1867, when he visited Pesth to restore the constitution, all Hungary abandoned itself to feasting and dancing.

During the century which has followed Hungary has typified the conflicts which have tormented mankind. Its peasants and workers learned that independence did not mean emancipation; they were exploited by their own nobility. Hungary suffered with most of Europe in two World Wars and following the Second was a victim of the division of Europe. It has had its communist revolution and its second revolution suppressed by the aid of Russian forces. It is now responding to the liberalising tendencies which are growing up in much of the communist world. But in all this drama of history the struggle for independence in the last century is a glowing story remembered not only in Hungary but among many peoples who have subsequently striven for and won their national freedom.[1]

Korean Example

Our second example is from Asia – Korea, fated for more than a century to be the sport of external powers, its people resisting, dividing, and now a tragic casualty of the Cold War. The disasters from which Korea, north and south, is now suffering cannot destroy pride in the heroic and, until the disruption at the end of the Second World War, successful struggle for independence against Japan, China and Russia in turn.

Japan from early times had eyes greedy for Korea. Hidejoshi,

Japan's Napoleon, attempted conquest in 1852, but was driven back with the aid of the Chinese who exercised some powers of protectorate. In 1876 the Koreans opened several ports to Japanese trade and later did the same to American (1882) and British (1883). A clause in the treaty with the US was afterwards the subject of an appeal for help; it pledged Washington to exert good offices 'if other powers deal unjustly or oppressively with Korea'. The traders exploited the Koreans and anti-foreign feeling arose; Japanese were killed, Chinese threatened. Japan obtained an indemnity, China sent in ten thousand troops. In 1885 the two powers (if such they could yet be called) agreed to withdraw their troops, but Japan incited a rebellion in the Korean army. War followed; China and Japan quarrelled over the body of Korea. Japan won, and imposed political control and a monopoly of trade. When Korea's Empress attempted resistance, she was murdered.

Then Russia, spreading her empire over northern Asia, intervened. The Korean Emperor escaped to the Russian legation and the Japanese, not yet prepared to challenge the Tsar, acquiesced in the revival of some Korean power. In 1896 an agreement was reached between the Russians, Japanese and Koreans by which the Emperor returned to his palace, the Japanese Government undertook to restrain her citizens, and Korean control of her army and police was recognised. There was now the chance of self-government, but, as has so often happened, the Korean élite who took over were corrupt. A new leader arose.

Philip Jaisohn, who had led a students' revolt in 1884 and had been exiled in America, became a member of the Government. Disillusioned, he resigned and began an educational campaign for true nationalism and democracy. He started two papers and an institution which became historic, the Independence Club, which attained a membership of ten thousand within three months. The Club won a notable victory when the Government, fearing the democratic wave, decided to hand over the training of national troops to Russia; its members assembled in thousands before the Emperor's palace and refused to move until the Russian officers were asked to withdraw.

In 1898 Jaisohn returned to America, but his work was carried on by Syngman Rhee. Whatever criticism may be made of Syngman's subsequent presidency of divided South Korea, he showed courage and qualities of leadership at this time. He led the Independents in demanding the abolition of foreign control, caution in granting foreign concessions, the public trial of political offenders, honesty in state finance and a popular representative assembly. A nation-wide movement arose in support; the women came out of their traditional retirement to demonstrate, an infallible sign, as later instances will show, of the depth of feeling. When the Emperor dissolved the Independence Club, its members went *en bloc* to the police headquarters and asked to be arrested. Seventeen leaders were imprisoned, but such large and angry demonstrations erupted throughout the country that within five days they were released and reforms promised. The demonstrators returned to their homes, but no more was heard of the reforms.

Demonstrations were renewed, larger than ever. The police were ordered to attack the crowds with their swords; they refused, throwing down their weapons, tearing off their badges, saying the cause of the people was theirs. The troops, who were less involved, were ordered to break up the demonstrations; they did so – only to find next day that thousands had seated themselves before the palace, where they remained for fourteen days and nights. The Emperor gave way, promising to maintain national integrity and to fulfil the reforms: again deception, aided by division among the Nationalists, extremists and moderates, but still no reforms. Syngman Rhee was among those arrested in this break-up of the national movement; for seven months he lay in his cell fastened to the ground, his feet in stocks, his hands in chains. He was tortured to such a degree that, when informed that he was to be executed, he welcomed the end of his misery. By mistake the man next to Syngman was executed and in 1904, after six years' imprisonment, he was able to go to America where before returning he graduated as Master of Arts and Doctor of Philosophy.

The conflict between Russia and Japan to dominate Korea continued. The Korean Government tended to side with the Russians, and the Japanese, having sunk the Russian fleet, retorted by taking virtual control. They introduced martial law, confiscated land, commandeered the postal and telegraph services, gave Japanese names to towns, appointed Japanese foreign affairs advisers, prohibited political parties, placed a censorship on political documents and imprisoned or exiled nationalist radicals. The Emperor appealed to President Roosevelt to intervene in accordance with the treaty of 1882. The American reply was somewhat cynical. 'To be sure, by treaty it was solemnly covenanted that Korea should remain independent,' the President said in effect, 'but it is out of the question to suppose that any other nation would do for the Koreans what they are unable to do for themselves.' The

Emperor appealed in vain to the Hague Conference; still he would not sign the agreement which Japan had presented. Thereupon the Japanese deposed him and substituted his weak-willed son. In 1909 a military dictatorship was imposed and Korea was annexed and made a province of Japan. When the people resisted by demonstrations and boycott a reign of terror began. According to official figures 82,121 Koreans were fined, flogged or imprisoned without trial in 1916–17. Seventy-five thousand Koreans fled in one year to Manchuria. The Christian community was prominent in the resistance and the Japanese were particularly ruthless with it. Preachers and teachers were arrested and 123 leaders were charged with conspiracy to murder the Governor-General, a fantastic accusation.

For ten years the underground struggle went on. At last came hope when President Wilson declared, on the eve of the Peace conference which ended the First World War, that freedom should be given to small nations. Three Koreans in America were chosen to present the Nationalist case to the delegates at the Peace Conference. They were refused passports. Nevertheless, the climate of self-determination engendered at Versailles stimulated a resurgence of the resistance in Korea. When the old Emperor died, thirty-three leaders met secretly and contrived a daring plan to declare both independence and a republic. On the day of the funeral they invited the most prominent Japanese officials to dine with them; the meal concluded, they read to the astonished guests a Declaration of an Independent Republic, and then telephoned the Central Police Station, informed the incredulous superintendent of what they had done, and said they would wait the coming of the police van. The occasion had been well prepared. The van bearing the leaders passed through streets crowded with people shouting '*Mansei!*' and Korean flags – the penalty for the possession of which was death – were in everyone's hands.

The Declaration, like so many written on occasions of liberation, is an inspiring document, noble in its dignity of words, generous in spirit, calling for service to the future. It began:

'We herewith proclaim the independence of Korea and the liberty of the Korean people. We tell it to the world in witness of the equality of all nations and we pass it on to our posterity as their inherent right. We make this proclamation with five thousand years of history and twenty millions of united people behind us. We take this step to ensure that our children shall have for all time to come freedom in accord with the awakening consciousness of this new era. This is the clear leading of God, the moving principle of the present age, the just claim of the whole human race.'

The Declaration described the struggle for independence and then with some generosity referred to the Japanese occupation:

'We have no wish to speak of Japan's absence of fairness or her contempt of our civilisation or the despotic principles on which her state rests; we, who have greater cause to reprimand ourselves, need not spend precious time in finding fault with others; neither need we, who require so urgently to build for the future, spend useless hours over what is past and gone. Our urgent need today is to rebuild our house, not a discussion as to who broke it down . . . Let us not be filled with bitterness or resentment over past agonies or occasions for anger . . .'

There was recognition of Japan's influence in Eastern Asia:

'Annexation has built a trench of resentment deeper and deeper the farther the Japanese have gone along the road of tyranny. Ought not the way of enlightened courage to be to correct the evils of the past by ways that are sincere, and by true sympathy and friendly feeling make a new world in which our two peoples will be equally blessed? . . . Today Korean independence will mean not only life and happiness for us, but the departure of Japan from an evil way and her exaltation to the place of true protector of the East, so that China, too, will put all fear of Japan aside.'

The peroration:

'A new era wakes before our eyes. The old world of force is gone and the new world of righteousness and truth is here. Out of the experience and travail of the old world arises this light on life's affairs. It is the day of the restoration of all things, it is on the full tide of this day that we set forth without pause or fear . . .'

The declaration was read to great meetings in every town and village in Korea. The shops were closed, the women came from their homes, policemen in the Japanese service threw off their uniforms. The Japanese gave the order that normal life be resumed. The schools reopened; there were no scholars. Shopkeepers were ordered to open; they did so whilst soldiers stood on guard, but informed the few customers they had not the required article. The schoolchildren's strike lasted for weeks; they were told they would not receive certificates unless they returned. The boys at Seoul apparently yielded; the occasion for presenting the certificates came. The head boy, a lad of thirteen, came to the front to deliver the school speech. He was all courtesy and the Japanese officials were delighted. Then came the end. 'I have only this to add further,' he said. 'We ask one thing more of you.' He pulled a Korean flag from his coat and waving it shouted, 'Give us back our country! May Korea live for ever! *Mansei!*' The defiance had been organised; all the boys leaped to their feet, pulled flags from their coats, echoed '*Mansei! Mansei! Mansei!*' and tore up their certificates. The next day the boy and girl students of Seoul united in a great demonstration. Police beat down boys and girls alike; over four hundred were arrested. Fifteen nurses from a missionary hospital attended to the wounded; they were arrested, too.

The persecution throughout Korea was worse than it had ever been. During three months in the spring of 1919 no fewer than 166,183 persons were arrested. Authenticated cases of torture in the prisons were too terrible to describe. An American holding a responsible position said personal friends had been beaten to pulp. 'The Koreans are a marvel to us all,' he wrote. 'Even those of us who have known them for many years and have believed them to be capable of great things were surprised. Their self-restraint, their fortitude, their endurance and their heroism have seldom been surpassed.'

At the height of the terror, on April 23, 1919, the Koreans with superb heroism elected delegates from each of the thirteen provinces to draw up a constitution for an independent Republic. The constitution was democratic and liberal, allowing for equality between men and women, religious liberty and freedom of speech, writing and association. Dr Syngman Rhee, still serving the cause by propaganda in America, was elected first president. The Governor-General was summoned to Tokyo; he returned to announce that more Japanese troops would be sent, severer laws would be enforced and that self-determination was not applicable within the Japanese empire. An ordinance was published providing that anyone who attempted to bring about political changes would be liable to imprisonment for ten years; the law was made retrospective and leaders who had been arrested before its enactment were sentenced under it.

This intensified Japanese oppression broke the resistance organisation. When half a million people took part in demonstrations in favour of the Republic the Japanese shot them down, killing, according to their official records, 553, wounding 1,509 and imprisoning 19,054. Japanese officials took over all administrative posts, even the headship of villages. At this point the Korean nobles and businessmen deserted the national cause; they agreed to serve on an advisory council set up by the Japanese. Many of the nationalist leaders had to escape to China, Manchuria and Siberia. The headquarters of the movement were transferred to Shanghai, where a government in exile was set up with Syngman Rhee as head. It lobbied the League of Nations and a permanent commission was set up in Washington.[2]

These activities were carried on until the Second World War, when the Koreans gained Western sympathy because of Japan's alliance with Germany and Italy. In December 1943, China, the United Kingdom and the USA in conference at Cairo, promised independence, and at the Potsdam conference at the end of the war their promise was confirmed. Meanwhile, in 1944, a second government in exile was formed in Chunking, leaning towards Soviet Russia, with Kim Koo president and Kim Kuisic vice-president. In August 1945 Soviet troops entered north Korea and in September US troops entered the south. For purposes of military operations to implement the Japanese surrender, Korea was divided into Soviet and US areas at the 38th parallel.

Thus Korea became a victim of the Communist–West conflict. In February 1946 with Russian support, a Provisional Peoples' Committee, with Kim Il Sung (now president in North Korea) and Kim Kuisic (still a Minister) as heads, was set up in the North. Simultaneously the US military government in the South created a Representative Democratic Council, and in October a Legislative Assembly, the US appointing half the members, was established. Efforts to unify North and South failed, Russia rejecting a United Nations proposal for joint elections. In May 1948 a National Assembly was elected in the South with Syngman Rhee as president; in the North in August there was a one-list election, followed by the establishment of the Democratic Peoples' Republic. Both America and Russia ostensibly withdrew, but the damage of the division had been committed. The worsening subsequent events are well known. There were raids across the frontier from the North, a raid on June 25, 1950, in force. In the absence of Russia, the Security Council authorised United Nations military intervention. More than one million were killed in the three years' war which followed and two and a half million Koreans were rendered home-less. This appeared to be the tragic *finale* of the heroic years of struggle of the Korean people to establish a united and indepen-dent Korea, but even now the tragedy has not ended. Among many the hope of a united Korea persists.[3]

Irish Example

Irish resistance has been both courageous and tragic. Its romanti-cism lay in the deep conviction of those who died for what was called 'the blood sacrifice'; if its violence surpassed all credibility this must be ascribed to the deep hatred resulting from eight hundred years of English rule. Ireland was 'John Bull's Other Island' or even worse 'John Bull's Plantation'; its national heritage was deliberately suppressed and the people kept in a semi-barbaric state. The Irish Catholic population were subject to the most repressive penal laws and their standard of living until this century was mere existence, the majority of the people half starved as they cultivated the land for others. It is in this context that the struggle for independence must be read.

The Norman rulers of England met with some resistance when they 'inherited' Ireland from Pope Adrian IV in 1155, but they subdued the people by 1171. Resulting from the subjection of Catholics and the confiscation of their land, there was a fruitless rebellion in 1641, followed by the cruel repression by Cromwell. During the Stuart Restoration there was a brief respite, but Protestant ascendancy was secured after the defeat of James II at the Battle of the Boyne in 1690, with severer penal laws against the Catholics.

It then became the turn of the Protestants (mostly centred in Ulster, where many had migrated from Scotland) to threaten revolt against the English. On their behalf in 1750 Henry Grafton and Henry Flood demanded in the Irish Legislature (no Catholics could be members) more self-government and, faced by the organ-isation of an armed force, the Government at Westminster had to concede greater powers. The French Revolution encouraged the Protestants to go still further. They formed the United Irishmen Party, supplemented by secret working-class clubs, to establish a

Republic of Eire. Wolfe Tone even succeeded in getting Catholic support and for a time there was united resistance. England retorted by rigid control and Tone sought refuge in France. He attempted to return in 1796 with seven thousand French troops, but weather conditions in Bantry Bay prevented a landing. He made another attempt later, but was captured and committed suicide rather than be hanged. The English Government's continuing repression and its refusal of Catholic Emancipation caused rebellion to spread from Ulster to the south in 1798. The Catholics were suppressed, but they showed tremendous courage, facing mass slaughter, as at Wexford. 'Ninety-Eight' became a legend and Tone's ideas of insurrection and revolutionary violence a tradition.

Pitt decided that only union with England would stay the unrest and bribed the Irish to accept by the promise of Catholic Emancipation. The Union came about in 1800 but not Emancipation. Continuous resistance was the result, beginning with Robert Emmet's uprising in Dublin in 1803. In fact, the Union led to the more direct exploitation of Ireland. The Catholics were still denied any rights; they had no votes and suffered from ruthless extortion by agents acting on behalf of absentee landlords. This 'demoralisation, devastation and destitution' (Engels) sowed the seeds of later history. The Irish, whilst existing on potatoes, began to feed on revolution.

At first the struggle against the English was led by O'Connell, a skilful lawyer who used the court-room to propound his policy of repeal of the Union (though not the formation of a Republic). He won the Clare election in 1828 and his refusal to take his seat in Westminster until Catholic Emancipation was granted forced the issue through. He then organised huge mass meetings throughout Ireland, with the message to its sons 'agitate, agitate, agitate', but his insistence on a struggle strictly within the law became unpopular and in 1843 he backed down in the face of authority. According to Cavour, moderation blunted the nationalist movement; in his view there had to be a resort to arms. This issue divided those concerned in the future struggle. While all were united on the ending of English land ownership and the need for Irish self-determination, the methods of arriving at their goal were in dispute.

In 1846 the English aristocracy displayed to the world a greater interest in the price of corn than in the lives of Irishmen. There was a famine in some part of Ireland annually but in that year it affected the whole country, resulting in a fall of population by death and emigration of two million. Ireland was in despair; according to de Beaumont it was at 'the lowest ebb of human misery'. There was the permanent wretchedness of a nation of farmers without land who had become a nation of beggars. The despair led to continuous violence. Despite 114 commissions and sixty select committees appointed by Parliament, England did nothing and her rulers did not even visit Ireland. In the view of John Stuart Mill, even if they had done so they would not have been able to understand what they saw.

The revolutionary movement which emerged after 1846 had no connection with the Protestant north, not only because of sectarian differences but also because the growing wealth of the Protestants due to the introduction of industry (completely absent in the south) created class differences. In 1848 the Young Irelanders, militant agitators in Dublin inspired by events in France, planned a revolt which resulted only in a skirmish with the police; failure was a foregone conclusion due to lack of organisation. Although not the first, definitely the most important movement in these 'early days' was the Gaelic revival. If Ireland was to return to nationhood, its traditions had to be restored and Hyde's appeal was simple and to the point. A revival of Gaelic civilisation was popular everywhere and laid the foundations of an Irish Republic.

The new movement which developed after the 1850s adopted Wolfe Tone's policy of revolution. O'Mahony and Stephens in 1858 founded the Fenians (or the Irish Republican Brotherhood) on the basis that nothing could be achieved by constitutional means and British power had to be overthrown by force. The Brotherhood became a secret military organisation and continued well into the twentieth century, exploiting every opportunity to injure English interests. While no planned insurrections actually materialised at first, the threat presented by the IRB's mere existence forced Gladstone to initiate reforms, including the extension of votes to the Catholics.

Another important development was Isaac Butt's Home Government Association, which, after its transformation into the Home Rule movement in 1873, gained great electoral success in 1874. Its leadership fell to Parnell, the nineteenth-century champion of Irish nationalism, whose basic demand was Home Rule, and who also was President of the Land League, which called for the eviction of the absentee landlords. In the British Parliament, Parnell held the balance of power with his eighty-five seats, and his tactics brought business to a halt. But the Catholics were divided. Parnell condemned the Fenians who in 1882 had murdered two British representatives in Phoenix Park, the grounds of the Governor's residence.

Long before the end of the century the great division between north and south Ireland became apparent. The Protestants feared a loss of ascendancy and successfully fought to prevent the passing of the first Home Rule Bill. When Gladstone's second Home Rule Bill of 1893 had passed through the House of Commons only to be rejected by the Lords (the Irish in Parliament led now by Redmond), Arthur Griffith founded the Sinn Fein (Ourselves Alone) movement to present a more challenging platform. He suggested a complete break from England and Irish self-reliance, thus opposing the more moderate nationalist demands of the Parliamentarians. He urged that the Irish MPs should leave Westminster and form an Assembly in Dublin; from them a government would be formed and, relying on moral authority for obedience, it would administer the country. The nineteenth century saw little reform as a result of agitation in Parliament and Griffith said it was wrong to imagine that one could win on a battle ground chosen by and filled with one's enemies. The fight had to take place in Ireland itself. At first, however, he did not support the Fenian revolutionary violence, basing his ideas on the Magyar success in 1868 (already described) as shown in his book *The Resurrection of Hungary*.

There was also the Labour movement, not very strong but playing a crucial role. Of its leader, Connolly, it was said, 'he was not merely a nationalist rebel, he was a world-wide revolutionist'. Although there was no great desire in Ireland for a socialist state, the Belfast dock strike of 1914 showed that workers' unity could break sectarian differences.

When the third Home Rule Bill was introduced in 1912, the Liberal Government was totally dependent upon the Irish under Redmond to remain in office, and was therefore committed. Moreover the House of Lords, due to the Parliament Act 1911, no longer had the power of continuing veto. By May 1914 the Bill had passed through all the Parliamentary stages and only required the Royal Assent. However the reward was not to be forthcoming.

The Unionist Party, which had been formed in North-East Ireland to prevent Home Rule and which was associated with the English Conservatives, had in 1910 adopted Sir Edward Carson, a distinguished lawyer, as its leader. Having lost its last constitutional safeguard against Home Rule, Ulster began making plans to resist it physically (although a third of its inhabitants were Catholics). Carson addressed a demonstration of eighty thousand in Belfast who pledged him their support, and from these the Ulster Volunteers were recruited, their arms being imported without hindrance. In response, across the border, the Irish volunteers were formed, soon numbering 129,000. Only world war prevented immediate war in Ireland. The Home Rule Bill was abandoned.

From 1914 onwards the southerners no longer fought merely for land security or Home Rule; instead, their object was the ownership of all Ireland by the Irish. Even Griffith became convinced that force would be necessary to achieve independence. Although 200,000 responded, Redmond's appeal to enlist in the British forces was unpopular among the militants and he lost contact. Plans were made to take advantage of the English involvement in the war by opening a front against them in Ireland. Casement went to Germany to get arms and to enlist captured Irish soldiers in the struggle. He returned in a German submarine which was captured and he was hanged for treason.

The British Government did not believe an insurrection would take place. They failed to take account of men like Patrick Pearce and James Connolly who believed that only a blood sacrifice would create the necessary atmosphere for popular support of the liberation struggle. On Easter Monday 1916, a smaller force than planned (only two thousand) entered the Dublin Post Office, and Pearce read out a declaration from the steps to a few hundred people. The proclamation was from the 'Provisional Government of the Irish Republic to the People of Ireland'. It said that Ireland belonged to the Irish and that those inside the Post Office were prepared to give their lives for that cause. A week later the insurrection in Dublin ended. It could have been a serious moral defeat for the Irish had not the English turned it into inspiration. They executed fourteen of the leaders, making them revered martyrs and Easter 1916 a legend. The 'blood sacrifice' had succeeded.

Any settlement besides total independence for the whole of Ireland was unacceptable to Sinn Fein, who continuously gained support so that by 1917 (when Redmond died) Home Rule within the United Kingdom was no longer acceptable. The threat of conscription was sufficient to unite Sinn Fein and the Nationalists. Sinn Fein's strength increased in response to the absolute dedication of its leaders. De Valera, Griffith and others were imprisoned; Thomas Ashe organised a hunger strike in prison and died after forcible feeding. His self-sacrifice brought thousands out to follow his funeral, spreading the Easter spirit and increasing the hatred of the English. In the 1918 elections Sinn Fein gained large successes. Those returned refused to go to Westminster and instead thirty-five of those elected (thirty-four were in prison) met in Dublin at the first Irish Parliament, *Dail Eireánn* (which had been proclaimed on the steps of the Post Office in 1916). De Valera, who had escaped from prison, formed the first government.

During the next three years the Irish lived through unparalleled violence. It was a story of murder, outrage, counter-murder and counter-outrage. Michael Collins organised flying guerrilla columns in the IRA (Irish Republican Army). There was also his special 'Squad' who, dressed as civilians (as were all in the IRA), systematically killed political opponents, and especially the detectives of Dublin. On 'Bloody Sunday' army intelligence officers, replacements for the dead detectives, were killed; six were buried in Westminster Abbey, attended by Churchill and Lloyd George. The Irish intensified the rebellion. Informers were executed, prisons raided, IRA men released, soldiers stabbed in the streets, their arms seized, property was destroyed, notably tax offices, government buildings and barracks. In 1920, with sixty thousand English troops in Ireland, 176 police were killed and 251 wounded; the figures for the army were 54 and 118. To support depleted force, the Government enlisted irregulars called the Black and Tans (because of their improvised dress) and the war assumed a horrific rhythm of brutal attack and reprisal, once resulting in £3 million of damage by the English to the city of Cork. Of this the Archbishop of Canterbury said, 'You cannot justifiably punish wrong-doing by lawlessly doing the like. Nor by calling in the Devil, will you drive out devilry.'

Complete lawlessness existed by the end of 1920. English administration of south and west Ireland had ceased and was performed by Sinn Fein. Many railways didn't run. In October Terence MacSwiney, the Lord Mayor of Cork, died in Brixton prison after a hunger strike lasting seventy-four days. The whole world condemned England for the conditions created. The war against the Catholic population was also waged by Protestants in Ulster; the Unionists refused to consider any form of union with the south, a stand which the English government did little to oppose. By 1921 the violence had become intolerable for public opinion and on July 4 a truce was arranged. Under the *Government of Ireland Act* 1920, six counties of Ulster and southern Ireland were partitioned, but provision was made for their ultimate reunion. This was later amended excluding promise of unification. In Section 75 of the *Government of Ireland Act* 1920, Westminster retained 'supreme authority over all persons, matters and things', and its power to determine the legislation adopted by Stormont, the Northern Ireland Parliament.

The Treaty negotiations, following the truce, resulted in a disastrous split between those in Sinn Fein prepared to accept dominion status for the south, with acknowledgement that the treaty would be as final 'as this is the final generation' (Griffith and Cosgrove), and those like De Valera who would accept nothing less than an independent Republic, with no oath of allegiance to the Crown. To this end the dissenters even turned against their old comrades in arms who formed the first government of the Irish Free State, and embarked upon civil war, although the nation in elections had already approved of the treaty. Many of the leaders of the independence struggle died fighting each other (the Government using English-supplied guns), but at last in May 1923 De Valera accepted the need for peace and surrendered to Cosgrove, who had become leader when Griffith died of heart-attack under the great strain.

Ireland remained divided, north and south, and the violence continued; Irish against Irish. The Free State grew wealthier; but this was threatened when De Valera became President in 1932 and began a tariff war with England to achieve a Republic. He abolished the oath of allegiance, though it was 1948 before the Republic was declared. The partition continued firmly entrenched, but when in 1970 serious riots occurred between Protestant and Catholic communities in Belfast and Londonderry and a British force had to intervene, the northern government promised to remove some of the discriminations from which the Catholics suffered.

This did not satisfy the Catholic leaders and the IRA, both its sections, Official and Provisional, led fierce resistance by continuous bombing in Belfast and Londonderry and by sniping at British soldiers. When internment was introduced, the Opposition in the northern Parliament (Stormont) withdrew and declined to enter into discussions until detention without trial was ended. The violence grew; Protestants murdered Catholics and Catholics murdered Protestants in return.

At the same time, the Civil Rights Association initiated massive non-violent resistance through the refusal to pay rents and rates and organised marches, in defiance of prohibitions, in Catholic areas. The bombing and shooting became so serious that the

British Government insisted on taking responsibility for security and, when the northern Ireland Cabinet objected, Westminster suspended Stormont and imposed direct rule, appointing a minister to administer Ulster. A better atmosphere among Catholics was created by the release of many internees, but bitterness arose again when thirteen civilians were shot in Londonderry in clashes with the military following a civil rights march.[4] The IRA then took over the Catholic districts of Londonderry, refusing entry to the British military, which in turn led to attempts by Protestants to establish similar 'No Go' areas in Belfast. A situation of civil war, opposed by a small minority. The Official IRA contributed substantially to the ending of violence by announcing, on May 29, that it would cease its attacks, but the Provisional IRA declined to participate in the truce. The Prime Minister of Eire assisted a settlement by denouncing violence in the north and outlawing the IRA in the south, but at the end of 1972 conditions were still far from approaching agreement.[5]

After three hundred years of rebellion the Irish revolution has not yet achieved its aims.

Notes

1. The author is indebted among others to Arthur Griffith, the distinguished constructive voice in Ireland's Sinn Fein, for his book, *The Resurrection of Hungary*.

2. The author is indebted to F. A. Mackenzie's *Korea's Fight for Freedom* for much of this record.

3. The histories of the Hungarian and Korean resistance have been given in some detail not only because they are typical of the national struggles against imperialist occupation before the spreading colonial revolution which followed the Second World War, but because they reflect how the Cold War of the post-war years bedevilled the character of the independence when it was gained; in one case by Russian arms maintaining in the north a totalitarian state, and in the other by the West initiating civil war, among a people who had been united in their resistance to tyranny. It is a tragedy repeated in Vietnam and still a warning for the future. Surprisingly at the end of 1972 negotiations began for the reunion of North and South Korea.

4. The author was in Londonderry, intending to address a civil rights meeting, legally permitted. It was distant from the military

confrontation, but suddenly hundreds of people ran into the open square, followed by shooting from the military. The audience fell to the ground to avoid the bullets. An inquiry into the events was held by Lord Chief Justice Widgery who on balance justified the action of the troops. The author gave evidence at the tribunal.

5. Mr William Whitelaw, the British Minister, acted with a combination of firmness and reconciliation. British troops occupied the Catholic 'No Go' areas but marches and meetings were permitted. Sectarian violence nevertheless grew. Then early in 1973 the British Government issued a White Paper with proposals which were largely accepted by moderate elements among both Protestants and Catholics. They established an elected National Assembly with limited powers and promised a Bill of Rights to ensure equality for Catholics and discussion with the Southern Republic to set up a Council of Ireland. The oppressive *Special Powers Act* was to be withdrawn but some detention without trial was to continue. This prejudiced Catholic co-operation.

Chapter Five

India, Pakistan and Bangladesh

We begin our record of resistance to modern imperialism with India, of greatest significance because of its size, and because its people were the first to gain independence in the colonial revolution which followed the Second World War.

The earliest records of Indian resistance to alien occupation were during the sixteenth century when the great Mogul invasion from the north began. The resistance was ineffective and became modified under the rule of Emperor Akbar, who showed tolerance to all religions, stimulated economic progress, appointed Hindus as Ministers and generals, and gave relief to the peasants. After his death, Muslim bigotry was renewed and Hindu temples destroyed. Challenging resistance was offered by Sikhs in the north and Mahrattas in the west. When Persians invaded India, the Mahrattas, always fiercely independent, turned on the new enemy, but they were defeated. The Persians, critically poised in their homeland by the Turks, nevertheless had to withdraw.

English and French Invasions

The English and French subdued India in the seventeenth century by force of arms, bribery of princes, betrayals of allies and robbery of riches. The phrase of Clive, when charged with expropriating jewels and silver, 'I stand astonished at my own moderation', reflects the attitude of the British and French conquerors to the Indian rulers and people.[1] That stage passed, but the stance of the conqueror, of the White Sahib governing an inferior people, remained. The Europeans were a race apart, only rare souls deigning to have social contact with those they ruled, the majority using them as servants in the home, menial employees at the trading depot, soldiers in the ranks, not thinking of them as human equals. A century and more went by before the obligation of education, training and social uplift was recognised.

The Indian resistance to the English and French invasion continued over two centuries; it was defeated by a combination of division and treachery among the native rulers and by superior arms and generalship. Sporadic and localised revolts persisted. In 1756 the rebels captured Calcutta, imprisoned English officials of the East India Company and others. Then occurred the controversial episode of 'The Black Hole of Calcutta', when it was said that in one night 120 of the 143 English prisoners suffocated to death. Indian historians dispute the authenticity of this event, and there are different accounts, but the fact seems to be that the 'Black Hole' was previously an English prison in which Indians had also died. Inevitably, British opinion was deeply and widely outraged. In 1764 something happened which equally stirred Indians. Twenty-four sepoys in the British army deserted to join an Indian rebel force. They were caught, tied to guns and blown to death.[2]

The concessions made in the eighteenth century by the British were paternalistic and only favoured an élite Indian minority. A sum of £10,000 was voted 'for the revival and improvement of literature and the encouragement of the learned natives'. The education was of course to be in the English tongue. But reforms began. In Britain itself liberal ideas were beginning to influence legislation. The Reform Bill, Catholic Emancipation and the abolition of slavery were legalised. Burke, Pitt and Wilberforce led the way. They were in time mirrored to some extent in India by Governors Wellesley, Munro and Bentinck. Bentinck, who ruled from 1828 to 1835, reversed the ban on Indian admission to judicial and administrative posts, which Earl Cornwallis had imposed in the 1780s, throwing open offices irrespective of religion, descent or colour. In 1835 a further extension of education was authorised, though English orientated. Macaulay's famous Minute read: 'The great object of the British Government, ought to be the promotion of European literature and science among the people of India, and the funds for education would be best employed in English education.'

The coming of Christian missionaries with their schools extended teaching. The directors of the East India Company frowned on their arrival, fearful of proselytisation and of the effects of Western learning in upgrading the people. The schools were few; more than ninety-eight per cent of school-agers remained illiterate. Christian influence led to the abolition of suttee between 1829 and 1835. For over a hundred years widows had often thrown themselves in the flames of their cremated husbands. There was opposition by many Indians to its abolition.

First Nationalist Groups

With some Indian education, supplemented by sons of rich Indians
who went to schools in England, a politically conscious class arose.
They eagerly seized on the principles of Mill and Adam Smith. A
group began to demand education for the masses and internal
development, roads and irrigation as well as schools. In Bengal an
association was formed to send a spokesman to London; Ram
Mohan Roy defied the Hindu prohibition to cross the seas and
presented India's case to a House of Commons Select Committee.
In 1852 an Indian Association in Bombay delivered a petition
to Britain for constitutional change. It aroused controversy in
London. Cobden was one of its supporters, perhaps the first
Englishman to declare in principle for Indian self-government.
'Hindoostan must be ruled by those who live on that side of the
globe,' he said. 'Its people will prefer to be ruled badly, according
to our notions, by its own kith and kin than to submit to the
humiliation of being better governed by a succession of transient
rulers from the antipodes.' Other liberals became active. At a meeting of 'Friends of India', held in Charles Street, St James's Square,
in London, an India Reform Society was formed. Despite this reformist emergence, however, Parliament passed the Charter Act in
1853 maintaining administration by the East India Company and
British Governors-General. Nevertheless, the joint pressure from
Indian and English liberals bore some fruit. During the later years of
Lord Dalhousie's Governorship (1848–56) education was extended
– higher education in English, elementary education in the ver-
nacular – and a programme of roads, railways, postal services and
irrigation was begun.

The periodical outbreaks of resistance to British rule assumed a
serious form in the mid-nineteenth century. In 1824 there had been
an ugly event at Barrackpore, where a regiment which refused to
embark for Burma was shot to pieces by artillery. Even under
Lord Bentinck's enlightened rule the Sikhs and Punjabis revolted.
In 1855, forerunner of worse events, there was a rebellion of the
Santals, aboriginal peasants who had been driven from their lands.
The uprising spread through Bengal, resulting in the massacre of
both Europeans and Indians.

The Great Mutiny

Next year came the Great Mutiny. It was sparked off by an event seemingly incidental, but the manner in which it spread showed that opposition to British authority was rife. Lord Canning announced on July 25, 1856, that all army units would be liable for service overseas and that refusal on the ground of caste inhibition would be regarded as mutiny. The Bengal sepoys were both Hindus and Muslims; they were given greased cartridges and instructed to bite off the ends. The rumour spread that the grease was the fat of cows and pigs, the former sacred to Hindus and the latter repugnant to Muslims. Many threw the cartridges aside. They were ordered on punishment parade, stripped of their military badges and put in irons.

That was enough to light the flame. The whole regiment rebelled, slew their officers, released the prisoners and marched on Delhi, offering their services to a descendant of the deposed Mogul emperor. The area of mutiny grew alarmingly. It was backed by the Ranee of Jhansi, a Maratha princess, and the Begum of Oudh, a Muslim princess, both of whom had been denied the right to adopt heirs. Bombay and Madras remained unaffected but at Cawnpore the British garrison surrendered. They were promised safe conduct to Allahabad, but their boats were set on fire and only four survived. There was a general massacre of the English residents who remained, including women and children. When Cawnpore was recaptured, all the mutineers were executed. In Delhi the Indian population were massacred by the British. It was for a time touch and go for British rule. After the first shock, however, the British forces relieved isolated outposts, shot the rebels and destroyed the mutinous troops. By an iron hand disciplined order was restored.

Government Ousts BEI Company

Public opinion in Britain was revengeful and, at best, self-righteous. A prayer was read in the churches: 'Teach the natives of British India to prize the benefits which Thy good Providence has given them through the supremacy of this Christian land.' But Lord Canning urged generosity and was supported by Queen Victoria. When the mutiny ended administration was still in the hands of the East India Company. The directors at first protested against the moderation of the British Government, but accepted the inevitable in the grand manner. They offered the Empire to the Queen: 'Let Her Majesty appreciate the gift.' Free pardons were extended to the remaining rebels except to those convicted of the murder of British subjects, and assurances were given to the princes that there would be no encroachment on their territories or on their personal privileges. On August 2, 1858, British India passed to the Crown. Control was vested in the Secretary of State; administration continued through civil servants advised by a Council of retired officials; Lord Canning became the first Viceroy.

The mutiny shocked both Britain's officials in India and Ministers in London into a realisation that substantial reforms were necessary. Under Lord Canning universities were established in Calcutta, Madras and Bombay, rural development enlarged and justice made more equitable in the courts. Lord Mayo, who was Governor-General from 1869 to 1872, pressed reforms further. It was under him that Indians were permitted to become nominated members of Provincial Councils, and later he began to liberalise local and rural administration.

Progress in Indianisation nevertheless slowed down during the next decade; the British continued to dominate every sphere. It was not until liberal Lord Ripon became Viceroy in 1880 that any further progress of significance took place, and then it was met with almost hysterical opposition by many of the British in India. The introduction of Indian self-government in city, district and local Boards aroused consternation among the European community, and consternation turned to horror when Indian judges were allowed to try Europeans on criminal charges.[3] A former Minister in the Indian Government, Seton Kerr, said in London that the Bill outraged the cherished convictions of every Englishman in India 'that he belonged to a race whom God had destined to govern and subdue'. The agitation among the British in India took the most extravagant forms. At meetings of protest threats were made to kidnap Lord Ripon and put him on a ship to England.

National Congress Established

Meanwhile, campaigns had been launched in England in defence of the rights of Indians. Towards the end of 1866 the East India Association, broad-based with both English and Indian members, was formed as a forum of discussion and as a means of providing information to Members of Parliament and the public. It had the help of many British officials who had served in India. Lord Lyveden was the first president; Parsi Dadabhai Naoroj, afterwards to become the pioneer Indian to be elected to the House of Commons, was the secretary. Leading English politicians gave their support, notably John Bright and Henry Fawcett, who became known as 'MP for India'. Branches of the Association were also established in a few centres in India itself, again composed of both English and Indians.

Most significant was the development in the eighties of nationalist activity. Almost simultaneously the National League was formed in Bengal, the Mahajan Sabha in Madras and the Presidency Association in Bombay. Historically, however, the great occasion was the inauguration on December 27, 1885, at Bombay of the Indian National Congress, destined to be the instrument not only of the achievement of independence but of government following independence. It is strange to remember, in view of the long conflict which developed between the Congress and the British, that English officials had much to do with its establishment. Part of the intention was to direct national sentiment into constitutional channels rather than in subversion and violence, but there was real sincerity for Indian rights. Most prominent among these supporters was Allan Octavian Hume, a member of the Civil Service; others were William Wedderburn, David Yule and Henry Cotton, all genuine liberals. At the inaugural meeting there were seventy Indians drawn from many parts of the country, mostly belonging to the professional élite. The initial object of Congress was to provide opportunities for the free discussion of Indian problems, but there was also the more forward-looking aim of creating the nucleus of an Indian Parliament which in course of time would show that India was fit for responsible government. Official approval was indicated by a speech of welcome from the Governor-General, Lord Dufferin.

Following the second meeting of Congress held at Madras, however, British official opinion became nervous. Dadabhai Naoroj presided and urged the enlargement of the provincial Legislative Councils and the admission of Indians to the higher ranks of the civil service and army. These were not very revolutionary claims, but Europeans again became fearful. The attitude of the more intransigent was expressed by Lord Roberts, later head of the British army. 'It is the consciousness of the inherent superiority of the Europeans which has won us India,' he said. 'However well educated and clever a native may be, and however brave he may have proved himself, I believe that no rank which we could bestow upon him would cause him to be considered as an equal by a British officer.'[4]

Towards the end of the nineteenth century there was a wide growth of Indian self-reliance. This was due partly to a Hindu religious revival, to the influence of European liberal thought and action (Garibaldi, Mazzini and Kossuth in addition to Sheridan, Burke and Mill), to response to Japan's defeat of Russia boosting Asian prestige, and to resentfulness from unemployment among educated Indians. The Indian National Congress grew in representative authority. By its third meeting in 1888 there were 1,882 delegates. The leadership at first remained moderate: Surendranath Bannerjee and G. K. Gokhale. But soon these were superseded by Lokamanya Tilak, scholar and editor, and Arabindo Ghose, a graduate from Cambridge. Tilak, whom Gandhi afterwards described as 'the maker of modern India', aroused the people by his militant defiance of British rule for which he was sentenced to prison for eighteen months with hard labour in 1897 – the first sedition trial in India. A revolutionary spirit was emerging; students in secondary schools and colleges were swept into the movement. There were allegations of an assassination conspiracy. The Public Prosecutor and Deputy Superintendent of Police were shot in Calcutta.

Morley–Minto Concessions

The British Government again realised it must make concessions. Lord Morley was Secretary of State at Westminster, Lord Minto was Viceroy. They were authors of the Morley–Minto reforms in 1909. Indians were added to the Council of the Indian Department in London, the Legislative Council and Provincial Councils were enlarged and some elected members admitted to the latter, although the Governor could veto any candidate. In response to Muslim pressure, inspired by British officials clinging to 'divide and rule', communal representation was introduced; a small cloud on the horizon, an anticipation of later fatal division. The reforms did not go far enough, however, to meet pressing Indian opinion. The franchise remained restricted; the Legislative and Provincial Councils remained advisory. Extreme nationalism grew. Tilak was deported to Mandalay in Burma for publishing an article which was regarded as seditious, and between 1906 and 1914, on the eve of the First World War, 'terrorism' spread; Lord Hardinge, the Governor-General, was wounded in a bomb attack in Delhi. There was then a moderate reaction. At the 1910 National Congress the Viceroy was invited to give an address of welcome. A year later the partition of Bengal, which had incited Indian opposition, was revoked.

When the First World War came in 1914 Indian national opinion was split. The great majority rallied to Britain, contributing 302,000 troops and suffering 106,584 casualties (36,696 killed). But there were minorities, first in rebellious Bengal, then among Sikhs resentful about immigration discrimination in Canada, and finally from Muslims when Turkey joined Germany.[5] The Khilafat (Caliphate) Movement of Islamic Solidarity was born. As often the case, however, the experience of fighting in common released democratic impulses. At the 1915 National Congress Sir Satyendra Sinha urged Dominion status for India, though not immediately. This did not satisfy educated Indians. Tilak, released from prison, inspired the people with the idea of Swarajya and in 1916 Mrs Besant, whose broad-minded Theosophy embraced India, started the Home Rule League. In the same year there was the hope of Hindu–Muslim co-operation. A pact was signed at Lucknow by Tilak and M. A. Jinnah, the Muslim leader, retaining communal representation. It was hailed by Jinnah as 'the birth of United India'.

The National Congress reacted to the Tilak and Besant agitation. At its 1916 meeting it demanded immediate Home Rule and initiated a nation-wide campaign. Once more the British Government responded to Indian pressure. The Secretary of State, E. S. Montagu, announced a policy of gradual development to responsible government within the British empire. Once more, also, the reassurance did not satisfy. The Muslims were estranged because they wanted more representation; Indians generally were impatient. The end of the war saw rebellion in the Punjab met by emergency powers, including detention of subversive suspects and trials without juries; Indians could not be depended upon to find offenders guilty.

Gandhi Returns

Gandhi had arrived in India in 1914. His reputation preceded him because of the success of his non-violent resistance to the grievances of Indians in South Africa. He was a practising lawyer and was outraged when he first went to Natal by restrictions on Indian dress in the courts. Then an incident happened which determined his life. At Pietermaritzburg railway station, holding a first-class ticket, he was turned out of his compartment because he was coloured and bundled into a dark waiting-room. 'There was a white man in the room,' he wrote; 'I was afraid of him. What was my duty? I asked myself. Should I go back to India or should I go forward, with God my helper, and face whatever was in store for me? I decided to stay and suffer. My active non-violence began from that day.'

Gandhi's uniqueness was that he combined active resistance with non-violence. He saw repression as violence and concluded that its essence could not be overcome by retaliatory violence. It was in South Africa that he developed his philosophy and practice of *satyagraha* – 'a force which is born of truth and love or non-violence'. He formed the Natal Indian Congress in 1894 and applied his faith in 1906 when the Transvaal Government passed a law requiring every Indian to register fingerprints. Two thousand men and women courted imprisonment by marching behind him. They won; the law was rescinded. Gandhi identified himself with the most victimised of the Indian people. He abandoned law and embraced voluntary poverty. When he returned to India, Gandhi was welcomed almost with reverence. Rabindranath Tagore hailed him as 'Mahatma' ('great soul') and that became inseparably his name. Thousands rallied to his cause.

Gandhi's method was soon put to the test. He heard that peasants at Champaran in Bihar were compelled by law to plant indigo on their land for sale to European planters instead of their customary crops. With Rajendra Prasad (afterwards to become president of independent India) he went to Champaran. Ordered to leave, he refused, was summoned, pleaded guilty. The case aroused such interest that the Governor intervened and not only appointed an inquiry but made Gandhi a member. The recommendations went in favour of the peasants and the Champaran Agrarian Act legalised them.

Amritsar Massacre

Soon there came a severer test. In March 1919 the Government passed the Rowlatt Acts which empowered the authorities to arrest without warrant anyone suspected of sedition, and legalised indefinite detention without trial as well as imprisonment at secret trials without defence counsel and with no appeal. Gandhi called for a *hartel* – abstention from work, shops closed, no business, a peaceful protest. Nevertheless there was violence in Delhi, Ahmedabad and the Punjab, particularly at Amritsar. Distressed, Gandhi, although he had been arrested, suspended the *hartel*; but the British Lieutenant-Governor, Sir Michael O'Dwyer, retorted to the murder of five Europeans by instructing the military to act. They did so by an action which has been described as the blackest blot in British imperial history. In defiance of a prohibition, most of them unaware of it, twenty thousand people attended a demonstration in a large enclosed space, Jallianwalla Bagh at Amritsar. General Dyer, the commander, ordered the army to fire upon them and 379 persons were killed and 1,208 wounded.[6] Subsequently General Dyer ordered Indians, as a further humiliation, to crawl on hands and knees in a street where an Englishwoman was alleged to have been assaulted; if they failed to obey they would be shot immediately. There were violent Indian protests, severely repressed. Martial law was declared throughout Punjab, no one was allowed to leave or enter the Province; eight Indians were sentenced to death, twenty-eight were transported for life; villages were bombed and armoured trains machine-gunned the villagers. Ironically, festivals were organised by the Government to celebrate peace in Europe. The processions of British officials and troops passed through empty streets.

Nationalist feeling in India became intense. Indeed, from this moment the movement against British rule became that of the whole people. In London the response was conciliatory. It was encouraged by the climate of world opinion, following the championship of self-determination by President Woodrow Wilson towards the end of the World War. The Montagu–Chelmsford Reforms were introduced (1919). A central Legislature with elected members was established and Provincial Legislatures were introduced with elected majorities. The central Legislature was bicameral: a Council of State with 40 members elected on a severely restricted franchise (less than one-fourth of the population) and 20 nominated members; and an Assembly of 145, with 105 elected members (again on a limited franchise), 52 from general constituencies and the remainder from the Muslim and Anglo-Indian (mixed race) communities and from landed and business interests. Ordinances could be issued by the Governor-General, however, even against the decision of a majority in the Legislature, and law and order remained in his hands. In the Provinces a principle was applied which afterwards became the centre of controversy. It was known as 'dyarchy'. It divided responsibility between the Governor and the Ministers responsible to the Legislature. The former controlled 'reserved subjects' and the latter 'transferred subjects'. The reserved subjects included law and order, justice, the police and land revenue.

Nationalists Enter Legislatures

Congress rejected the reforms as inadequate and boycotted the first elections in 1920. Only one-third of the electors voted and the Legislatures were controlled by moderates. At the second elections in 1923, however, there was a change of policy. The Swarajist Party, associated with Congress and led by Motilal Nehru and C. R. Das, nominated candidates, but with the declared purpose of destroying the constitution from within. This strategy was only partially successful. Many Congressmen were elected and there were majorities in the Central Provinces and with independent support in Bengal. The Bengal Legislature voted against Ministerial salaries, with the result that its right to control 'transferred subjects' was withdrawn. The Constitution remained and some Congressmen began to co-operate with it.

Beginning of Civil Disobedience

We return to Gandhi. He identified himself with the Muslims in their Khilafat opposition to the Treaty of Sèvres imposed on Turkey in 1920, and proposed a programme of non-co-operation, including the surrender of titles and honours, the boycott of schools, colleges and Law Courts. He himself returned his Kaiser-i-Hind medal (presented for humanitarian work in the Boer War) and decorations he had received in South Africa. Gandhi was arrested, charged with sedition for writings in his weekly paper *Young India*. As usual, he pleaded guilty. 'I am here to invite and submit to the highest penalty that can be inflicted upon me,' he said from the dock, 'for what in law is a deliberate crime, but what appears to me to be the highest duty.' He was sentenced to six years imprisonment, but after two years he had to undergo an operation for appendicitis and was released.

Gandhi had opposed the decision of Congress to enter the Provincial Councils. At the time he was intensifying his campaign against British rule. In August 1920 he informed the Viceroy, Lord Chelmsford, of his intention to practise non-co-operation with a government for which he had 'neither respect nor affection'; he denounced British imperialism as a 'satanic sin'. When released from prison in 1924, disappointed by the trend in Congress, he devoted himself to campaigning in the villages. He laid stress on the making of home-made cloth, *khadi*, by the use of the spinning wheel. He advocated this partly because he believed in hand-crafts rather than factory mechanisation, partly to provide an income for peasants unemployed except at harvest time, and partly because he wished to encourage Indian economic self-sufficiency. He argued that the only essential foreign import had been material for clothes; *khadi* could replace Lancashire textiles. But he did more than propagate *khadi*. He aroused the villagers to a sense of their human status. He brought to them a new confidence, changed peasants, wrote Jawaharlal Nehru,[7] 'from a demoralised, timid and hopeless mass, bullied and crushed by every dominant interest, into people with self-respect and self-reliance, resisting tyranny and capable of united action and sacrifice for a larger cause'.

Pandit Nehru

We have mentioned Jawaharlal Nehru. He was second only to Gandhi in the leadership of the nationalist movement. His father, Motilal, was a famous political figure, moderate and acceptable in the pre-Congress period. Jawaharlal went to Cambridge and was called to the Bar in London, returning to India in 1912. He was not then a revolutionary, but it is on record that he was shocked when attending his first Congress by the respectability of the gathering, the European clothes and manners. He never accepted in principle the non-violent philosophy of Gandhi, but accepted him as leader, devotedly after the Amritsar massacre. 'We have our differences, but he always proves right,' Nehru once said. He became a confirmed Socialist, influenced by Harold Laski and the ILP in Britain, but humanist rather than Marxist, internationalist. Like Gandhi he was repeatedly imprisoned; he spent ten of his twenty-seven years of nationalist activity in gaol. One of these sentences followed an investigation which he undertook on conditions in the Princely States in 1923. He was arrested, handcuffed and marched through the streets as an exhibit. He refused to apologise and was sentenced to a term of eighteen months. His cell was verminous and rat-infested and he became a victim of typhoid for several months.

Return to Militancy

Militancy returned to Congress. Indianisation of the civil service was demanded. In August 1922 Lloyd George, the British Prime Minister, said he could see no period when India would be able to dispense with the guidance of a British element in the service. In 1923 a Commission under Viscount Lee recommended that the civil service should become half Indian after fifteen years and the Indian police force after twenty-five years. Congress indignantly rejected the recommendations as inadequate and too distant. There was a recrudescence of terrorism; the more radical element dominated the next meeting of Congress; 150 ringleaders of a protest against a severer criminal law in Bengal were arrested; there was violence in the United Provinces and Punjab; and bombs were thrown into the Legislative Assembly at Delhi. In 1929 thirty-one trade union activists with communist associations were charged at Meerut with conspiracy. The sentences were savage. One was transported for life, five for twelve years, three for ten years and the rest sent to prison for varying periods, the least of which was a term of three years.[8] The disruption did not concern relations only between India and Britain. Muslim–Hindu antagonism grew when a Congress Commission, headed by Motilal Nehru, the respected veteran, recommended a constitution for Dominion status India excluding communal representation.

The Simon Commission

The state of the country compelled a high-powered investigation from Britain. A commission came under the chairmanship of Sir John Simon and included Clement Attlee, afterwards head of Labour's Government which recognised India's right to independence. Its purpose was to review the 1919 constitution and there was great resentment because no Indians were members. Stanley Baldwin, the Prime Minister, remarked 'when God wants a hard thing done he tells it to His Englishman'. Congress decided on a boycott, the commission was received in Bombay by a *hartel* and everywhere crowds shouted, 'Simon go home.'[9] The commission spoke in conciliatory tones and on the second visit had some co-operation from Indian moderates, but within Congress demands became more uncompromising and explicit. There were some differences at this point between Gandhi and Jawaharlal Nehru. Gandhi was satisfied with the indefinite term *swaraj*; Nehru insisted on *purna swaraj*, absolute independence. The Calcutta Congress of 1928 demanded acceptance by Britain of the Motilal Nehru constitution of Dominion status, and authorised civil disobedience if not conceded in one year. Lord Irwin, the Viceroy, hastened to London and the Labour Government, elected in 1929, endorsed the aim of Dominion status and proposed a Round Table Conference to allow Indians to express their views before the Government introduced a Bill in Parliament. Some moderate Indians agreed to go to London, but Congress, meeting at Lahore, rejected representation on Gandhi's advice because no assurance on immediate Dominion status was given, declared for complete independence on a federal basis and made preparations for civil disobedience.[10]

The Salt Tax March

The campaign was begun in March 1930 by a spectacular march, led by Gandhi, from Ahmedabad to Dandi on the coast, 240 miles. Gandhi had an instinct for attaching disobedience to a grievance felt acutely by the people, especially the poorest. They bitterly resented the salt tax, and the purpose of Gandhi's march was to defy the Government's monopoly of salt by collecting it from the sea. He set out with 178 supporters, gathering large numbers *en route*. He reached Dandi on April 6, symbolically gathered salt and thousands followed his example. Gandhi and many others were arrested. The British were shocked within the same year when Indian troops of the Garhwali Rifles refused to fire on an unarmed crowd in Peshawar; one was sentenced to life imprisonment, one to fifteen years, two to ten years and thirteen to terms from two to eight years. Lord Irwin saw the danger of the growing resistance and released Gandhi in January 1931 for negotiations. In March the Irwin–Gandhi Agreement was signed; the making of salt for personal use was legalised and about 100,000 prisoners were released. The civil disobedience campaign was called off.[11]

The Simon Commission's recommendations when published disappointed India. Whilst they replaced dyarchy in the Provincial

Legislatures by responsible government (subject to the Governor's special powers), they retained communal representation. There was no mention of Dominion status and doubts were expressed as to the suitability of Parliamentary government in India. A new suggestion was that the subsequent constitutional reconstruction should include the Princely Indian States.

Gandhi at Round Table Conference

Congress reception was hostile; nevertheless the delegates agreed that Gandhi should go to a Round Table Conference (the second) as sole representative. He found that the discussions were monopolised by the issue of minority representation. He tried to reach agreement with the Muslim and other communal delegates; he argued that only self-government could solve the problem.[12] The representatives of the Untouchables and other minorities, however, insisted on communal representation. The dispute could not be resolved, and it was agreed that Ramsay MacDonald, the British Prime Minister, should make the award. He decided in favour of separate representation of the Untouchables. Gandhi repudiated the award and claimed that he represented the Untouchables and that if a referendum were held among them he would top the poll.[13] In memorable words he stated his reasons for opposing the segregation of Untouchables. 'We do not want on our register and on our census Untouchables classified as a separate class,' he said. 'Sikhs may remain such in perpetuity. So may Muslims, so may Europeans. Will Untouchables remain Untouchable in perpetuity? I would rather Hinduism died than Untouchability lived. I will not bargain away their rights for the kingdom of the whole world. If I was the only person to resist this I would resist it with my life.'

On his return to India, Gandhi found that Nehru and Ghaffer Khan, known as the Gandhi of the North-West Frontier, had been arrested. He asked to see Lord Willingdon, the Viceroy, who refused to meet him and instead arrested him, together with Vallabhbhai Patel (later the architect of the incorporation of the Princely States with the Indian union). Gandhi regarded the segregation of the Untouchables – the 'children of God' he called them – as a personal humiliation and whilst in prison began a 'fast unto death' in protest. Only when B. R. Ambedkar, the spokesman for the Untouchables, reached an agreement with him did he end the fast. The agreement was on the basis that whilst separate electorates for the Untouchables should be abandoned they would have nearly twice the number of reserved seats originally allocated. Released from prison, Gandhi established the weekly paper *Harijan*[14] and made it his principal organ. It was published in ten languages. For a time he diverted from National Congress activities to campaigning on behalf of the Untouchables. He made a tour of Indian villages and collected 800,000 rupees on their behalf, much of it in coppers from impoverished peasants and in jewellery stripped from their necks by women. Under the influence of this tour Gandhi concentrated on his advocacy of the home-made cloth, *khadi*, and the development of village industries.

Congress Endorses Socialism

Gandhi could not withdraw from the centre of the national struggle for long. He was encouraged by Nehru to draft with him a Declaration of Rights for the 1931 Karachi Congress, demanding adult suffrage, free primary education and statutory rights for the Depressed Classes (Untouchables). Gandhi tabled a social programme of five items: (1) Hindu–Muslim unity and brotherhood, (2) Abolition of Untouchability, (3) Aboliton of *purdah* and recognition of sex equality, (4) Abstinence from drinks and drugs, and (5) Revival of the peasant crafts of hand-spinning and hand-weaving as supplementary industries to alleviate chronic unemployment. Nehru went further. He got the Lahore Congress to endorse Socialism. Gandhi concurred but rejected class warfare.

The 1935 Reforms

There was a third Round Table Conference at the end of 1932, which Gandhi did not attend (he was in prison) to consider reports of committees which had gone to India. The Government of India Act, 1935, emerged. It embodied an all-India Federation and Provincial autonomy and responsibility (with safeguards for law and order). The Federation was not to come into operation unless half of the Princely States (measured by population) agreed to accede. Dyarchy was imposed on the Central Legislature, with foreign affairs and defence in British hands. It was still to be bicameral, with a Council of State and a House of Assembly.[15]

Communal representation was retained. India was divided into eleven provinces. Burma was separated from India and Aden placed under the Colonial Office in London.

These enactments were criticised by Congress on the grounds principally that India would not have control of foreign affairs and defence and that representation of the Princely States ought to be subject to democratic election and the guarantee of civil liberties. The Muslims feared Hindu dominance in the central Legislature and the princes were reluctant to surrender their sovereignty. Nevertheless elections in the Provinces took place in January and February 1937. Congress decided to participate, though without illusions. 'India is still a prison,' said Gandhi, 'but the superintendent allows the prisoners to elect the officials who run the gaol.' The Congress programme embodied prohibition (Nationalists were against alcoholism), basic education and relief for indebted peasants. Congress gained majorities in seven of the eleven Provinces, but refused to take office unless they had assurances from Governors that they would not use their special powers or set aside the advice of their Ministers. The deadlock ended in June on an understanding with the Viceroy, Lord Linlithgow, that the Provincial Governors would not normally use their reserved powers of veto and of law and order. Congress then took over cabinets which had been set up.

Disquiet persisted. Hindu–Muslim conflict was renewed. Jinnah repudiated the claim of Congress to represent Muslims as well as Hindus, and the Muslim League alleged grievances under Congress rule in Bihar and the United Provinces. Congress began agitations in the hereditary Princely States for democracy and there were disturbances in Hyderabad, Kashmir and Travancore. The Provincial governments were faced with agrarian and industrial unrest incited by Communists. On the whole, however, the Congress Ministries had a good record in measures giving relief to tenants and to peasants exploited by usurers. Some attempted prohibition.

The Labour Movement

Recognition must be given to the part played by organisations other than the National Congress. The trade union movement was at first moderate politically, ably led by N. M. Joshi. There had been some strikes after the First World War and in 1920 the All-India TUC was formed. It concentrated on labour conditions. As a result of its pressure a Factory Act was passed but it was unsatis-factory; it still permitted working hours of sixty a week, eleven hours a day (children six hours). Dissatisfied, the TUC raised the issue at the Conference of the ILO (International Labour Office) urging that the age for child labour should be lifted to twelve years. The British representatives of the Indian Government and of the employers voted against, but Joshi carried the proposal by ninety-one to three. Later the TUC threw in its lot with Congress. It declared a general strike against the Rowlatt Acts, twenty thousand workers participated in Madras and there were stoppages in Bombay, Calcutta and Ahmedabad. The TUC afterwards passed under considerable communist control and there were splits in the national organisation. The peasants formed their own association in 1936, the All-India Kisan Sabha. It was militant but never became really representative. Mention must also be made of the Congress Socialist Party led by two men dedicated to human wel-fare, Yusuf Meherelly and Jai Prakash Narayan. The party had much to do with the acceptance of Socialism by Congress, but before independence disaffiliated from it.

Second World War

Came the Second World War. Nationalist opinion was outraged when India was declared a belligerent without any consultation with the elected representatives of the people. Congress, whilst condemning Nazi aggression, refused to associate itself with the war effort unless India was declared an independent nation. The British Government replied that Dominion status was the accepted goal and that at the end of the war the 1935 Constitution would be modified in consultation with Indian communities and parties; meanwhile, there would be an advisory council representing major interests to associate Indian opinion with the prosecution of the war. Congress rejected the offer, claiming that in a war for demo-cracy India should be accorded democracy if its co-operation was desired. In November 1939 all Congress Ministers resigned, and India became a British dictatorship with complete power in the hands of the Governors.

A difference arose between Congress and Gandhi and again between Muslims and Hindus. Congress was prepared to co-operate with the British Government in the war effort on condition that a declaration should be made pledging independence for India at the end of hostilities and that, as an earnest of this intention, there should be a national government with full responsibility except for defence and foreign affairs. Gandhi dissented, unwilling to participate in the war, and the Working Committee absolved him from responsibility for the Congress decision. The conflict between Muslims and Hindus went beyond the earlier issue of communal representation. Jinnah declared that 'the Indian nation does not exist' and the Muslim League proclaimed that its aims were an autonomous state embracing the areas where Muslims were in majority. In despair Gandhi told Jinnah that he had 'dashed to the ground all hope of unity'.

Civil Disobedience, Congress Banned

When deadlock was reached with the British, Congress sought Gandhi's lead despite their different views on defence. In October 1940 he launched still another civil disobedience campaign with the immediate object of gaining freedom of speech to oppose the war. Hundreds were arrested. The war was going badly for Britain in Asia. The Japanese armies were sweeping over Singapore, Malaya and Burma, threatening India itself with invasion. A new effort had to be made by Britain to reconcile Congress. Prisoners were released and the Churchill Government sent Sir Stafford Cripps to negotiate with proposals to establish at the end of the war an Indian Union with fully independent Dominion status, the constitution to be framed by elected representatives of India and nominees from the Indian Princely States. A new proposal was that the provinces would be permitted to opt out and form separate states. The negotiations broke down on Congress insistence that a provisional national government should be set up immediately. The Muslim League also dissented on the ground that there was no specific provision for an independent Muslim state.

A point of no return was reached. Gandhi in an article in *Harijan* initiated the slogan 'Quit India'. On August 8, 1942, the Congress Working Committee adopted it, issuing an ultimatum that if Britain did not withdraw nation-wide civil disobedience would be organised. The next day Gandhi, Nehru and all the Congress leaders were arrested and Congress banned. There was a mass uprising met by massive suppression. Gandhi suffered the personal blow of the loss of his wife, Kasturba; she died in the prison camp. In January 1943 the Mahatma wrote to Lord Linlithgow denouncing the Government for its 'leonine violence' and announced that he would begin a twenty-one days' fast. He completed this and was not released until the following year.

There were political sections of the Indian people who differed from Congress. Subhas Chandra Bose, a nationalist leader in Bengal, took the extreme view that India should side with Germany and Japan in order to overthrow the British government. He fled to Berlin in 1941; obtained a promise of independence from Hitler; headed a provisional government in exile in Singapore; set up in 1943 an 'Indian national army' to fight alongside the Japanese, recruiting prisoners, deserters and Indian residents in South-East Asia; and fought against the British in Burma. He was killed in an air crash in 1945. On the other hand, the Indian Communist Party, after Soviet Russia entered the war against Germany, actively supported Britain. There were signs – subsequent to the banning of Congress, the arrest of its leaders and the repression of the consequent uprising – that considerable opinion moved towards support for the war because of anti-Nazi feeling. In 1939 the Indian army numbered 200,000. In 1945 it stood at two million, the largest voluntary force in history. One must bear in mind, however, that this was from a population of 350 millions and that poverty encouraged recruitment at relatively high wages. Concentration on political issues was also lessened by a disastrous famine in 1943–4. Over 1,500,000 people died from hunger and disease in Bengal.

Labour Government Accepts Independence

The war came to an end. Indian hopes were aroused by the election of a Labour Government in Britain. The Congress leaders were released; a General Election was promised, to be followed by a Constituent Assembly; responsible Ministries began to function in the Provinces for the first time since 1939. The British Cabinet sent a mission headed by Lord Pethick-Lawrence, the Secretary of State for India, to meet the Viceroy and the Indian leaders. The British offered an interim plan. Until an elected Constituent Assembly had decided the future of India, there should be a provisional government in which Indians would hold all portfolios; the Muslim demand for an independent state in Pakistan was rejected as incompatible with Indian defence. Congress accepted, and on September 2, 1946, Jawaharlal Nehru became Vice-President to the

Viceroy. It looked as though the long struggle for Indian independence was nearing its end. Gandhi wrote to Nehru; 'Abolish the salt tax, unite Hindus and Muslims, remove untouchability, take to *khadi*.' But there was one disturbing feature. Muslim opposition to a united independent India grew – the Muslim League resorted to 'direct action'. There were violent conflicts where Muslims and Hindu populations overlapped, with seven thousand killed. Gandhi went to East Bengal, walking barefoot in devastated villages, mingled with Hindus and Muslims, urging non-violence.

Effects of Partition

A Constituent Assembly was summoned for December 9, 1946. The Muslim League boycotted it. The British Government lost hope of negotiating a settlement and decided that the responsibility must pass to Indians themselves. It announced on February 20, 1947, that Britain would withdraw totally not later than June 1948, leaving all power and decisions in Indian hands. Lord Mountbatten was appointed Viceroy (replacing Lord Wavell who had succeeded Lord Linlithgow in 1943) and was given a free hand. He reported that the only solution was to divide the sub-continent into two separate states. The Government promptly introduced a Bill in the British Parliament embodying the Mountbatten proposal. On August 15, 1947, two independent Dominions were set up, India and Pakistan. Punjab and Bengal were divided, West Punjab and East Bengal going to Pakistan. A great expanse of Indian territory separated them.

The immediate effects of these decisions were appalling. In the divided regions millions fled, millions were massacred. It is said that more were killed than in Europe during the war. Independence had been gained, but at a price which stunned imagination. The British were to blame because they had encouraged Hindu–Muslim antagonism during their imperial rule, the Muslim leaders were to blame in their intransigence, some of the Indian leaders were to blame for not earlier seeking agreement.[16]

Death of Gandhi

This story came to a climax of national tragedy. On January 30, 1948, Gandhi was entering a prayer meeting when a Hindu, who thought he had been too conciliatory to the Muslims, fired three shots. Gandhi uttered 'He Rama' (O God!) and died. On September 12, 1948, M. A. Jinnah also died. An end to an era.

After Independence

With independence, India became the greatest political democracy in the world. Under Nehru as Prime Minister it achieved international prestige as a champion of peace and of freedom for other peoples. For two years Lal Bahadur Shastri, a learned scholar followed him. Nehru's daughter, Mrs Indira Gandhi, became premier on Shastri's death and, defying the 'old guard' in Congress, swept an election in 1971 on a policy of ending the personal subsidies to the princes and of positive socialism.

Pakistan and Bangladesh

In Pakistan dictatorial rule was imposed in 1958. Then came a violent unforeseen interruption. The first democratic election in Pakistan led to victory by the Awami League, demanding autonomy for East Pakistan. It captured 167 of the 169 seats in the East (on a low 43 per cent poll) as well as a few seats in the West and gained an absolute majority in the National Assembly. It was assumed that its leader, Sheikh Mujibur Rahman, would become Prime Minister, but the President, Yahya Khan, delayed summoning the Assembly and, when talks with Sheikh Mujib broke down, the Pakistan army occupied the East, massacring its people. Nine million refugees fled to India. Sheikh Mujib was arrested.

The world took no action to defend democracy and responded inadequately to appeals for funds to maintain the refugees. Despite her poverty, India spent many millions in maintaining them for nine months, but the burden became too great. It was clear that only the restoration of democracy in the East would provide conditions for the return of the refugees and, after Mrs Gandhi had visited the capitals of Europe and the USA in vain, Indian troops invaded East Pakistan to assist the guerrilla resistance. In fourteen days the West Pakistan forces surrendered to the Indian Commander. Following the West Pakistan occupation, the Awami League had declared for complete independence, and India's victory was celebrated by the proclamation of the new state,

Bangladesh, with a population of 75 million, the fifth largest in the world.

Soviet Russia supported India's action. The USA and China condemned it. Britain and France maintained neutrality. The defeat of West Pakistan led to the resignation of President Yahya Khan and his replacement by Z. A. Bhutto, the leader of the majority party in the West. Sheikh Mujib was released from prison and returned to Bangladesh to become its President. The new leaders of Pakistan and Bangladesh both declared they would aim to establish socialist societies, but the widespread destruction in the East and the task of rehabilitating the refugees made reconstruction difficult. A more radical party, the National Awami Party, functioning in both East and West, which had abstained in the elections in the East, advocated a revolutionary realisation of Socialism. A month after the proclamation of independent Bangladesh, its veteran leader, Maulana Abdul Hamid Khan Bhashani, revered by the peasant population, was allowed to return from India, but agreement was delayed because Bhutto, frustrated by internal division, hesitated to recognise Bangladesh. The failure to reach a settlement meant that 90,000 Pakistani prisoners of war were detained in India and thousands of Pakistani and East Bengali citizens resident in 'enemy' territory were unable to leave for their homelands.

The future in the whole sub-continent remained uncertain. Pakistan withdrew from the Commonwealth when Britain recognised Bangladesh; Bangladesh applied for admission and was accepted. The most hopeful development was the readiness of both Pakistan and India to enter discussions. There was some prospect that all three states – India, Pakistan and Bangladesh – would transform hostility into co-existence if not co-operation.[17]

Notes

1. Clive received 280,000 rupees as a member of the Calcutta Committee of the East India Company, 200,000 rupees as Commander in Chief, 1,600,000 rupees as a donation (totalling over £200,000) and an estate valued at £30,000 per annum.

2. John Mill, *History of British India*.

3. This right was exercised previously only in a few Presidency towns.

4. Quoted in *Life of Lord Kitchener* by Sir George Arthur.

5. In 1906 the Muslim League had been formed. The motive was solidarity with Islamic victims of the Italo-Turkish and Balkan wars, to whom they felt the British Government was indifferent. The separate organisation of Muslims was to become fateful for India itself.

6. General Dyer's action was approved by the British-manned Punjab Government, but censured in Britain by the Secretary of State for India, the Army Council and the Hunter Commission which conducted an inquiry. Characteristically, at that time, the House of Lords justified his conduct. A London daily newspaper raised a fund for him in appreciation.

7. *India and the World.*

8. This trial became a judicial scandal. It lasted three and a half years and all but one of the prisoners were refused bail. Meerut was selected because there were no juries there.

9. The author was invited to the Madras assembly of Congress in 1927, but was prevented from attendance by a car accident. Attlee, Gandhi, Nehru and Mrs Besant came to see him in hospital. It was clear that there was no bridge between British and Indian views.

10. Gandhi sent the Viceroy notice of this decision through a young Englishman in his ashram, Reginald Reynolds, afterwards author of *White Sahibs of India.*

11. There was much Indian criticism of Gandhi for this compromise and his subsequent attendance at the Round Table Conference. The militancy of Congress was deflated.

12. There was some justification for this view, though it was not fulfilled by events. From the earliest times the British had practised the imperial principle of 'divide and rule' by exploiting Hindu–Muslim differences.

13. The British Press made most of the fact that a few hundred Untouchables demonstrated against Gandhi on his arrival at Bombay, but a deputation representing forty Depressed Classes' Associations presented him with an address hailing him as their only representative. Later, with very few exceptions, Untouchables' organisations throughout India endorsed his attitude by large majorities.

14. The Hindu name for an Untouchable.

15. The Council was to have 156 elected representatives and 104 nominated by the rulers of Princely States, six by the Governor-General. The Assembly would have 250 representatives elected by the Provincial Legislatures and 125 nominees of the Princely States.

16. After more than twenty years the conflict between India and Pakistan over the status of Kashmir, Muslim in population but claimed by India, persisted. In 1969 there was a renewal in India of Hindu–Muslim disturbances.

17. In June/July 1972 Mrs Gandhi and President Bhutto of Pakistan met at Simla and decided to settle differences without external intervention. The issues of the return of Pakistani prisoners of war held in India and of recognition of Bangladesh by Pakistan still remained unsettled however eight months later.

Chapter Six

South-East Asia

(Burma, Sri Lanka (Ceylon),
The Maldives, Indonesia,
Malaya, Singapore, Borneo,
The Philippines, New
Guinea, Malaysia)

The struggle which led to the independence of India and Pakistan was the pioneer in the colonial revolution which followed the Second World War. It affected 350 million people, more than all those liberated from colonial dominance subsequently. But other achievements in resistance were of equal importance in deciding the patterns of the world. We start with South-East Asia.

Burma and Ceylon obtained their independence almost simultaneously with India and Pakistan. Their story is inseparable, Burma bordering the north-east of India and for a time absorbed by it, Ceylon an island on its southern tip, always involved.

Burma

It is a little startling to find that in the first century AD Indian shipping and control of the seas brought to Burma not only traders but also Hindu and Buddhist missionaries. Different races swept over Burma, the Buddhist Mons who brought the first art of writing, the Mongols from China, resisted by Queen Shin Sawba in the fifteenth century. The first European to arrive was a merchant from Venice about 1435. The Portuguese appeared in strength in 1550, seizing Chittagong, the pirate centre of the Indian seas, helping the native king in his slave raids. Early in the seventeenth century came the rivalry of the Dutch, British and French trading companies. The Dutch and the British opened competing depots on the coast and during the 1730s the French rivalled the English in building ships at Syriam and came into conflict. The British replied to the intervention of Joseph Dupleix (the dynamic French Governor of Pondicherry in India) by seizing the island of Negrais (1753). This was simultaneous with a Burmese resurgence under the aggres-

sive King Alaungpaya, who overthrew Mons dominance, founded
the port of Rangoon and persuaded the British to provide arms; he
destroyed the French at Syriam and captured military equipment
from them. Not satisfied with restoring Burmese unity, he invaded
Thailand. Then in 1759 he turned on the British, annihilating the
settlement at Negrais on a rumour that help had been given to the
Mons. The British East Indian Company withdrew its personnel
from Burma.

Conflict with Britain grew. In 1820 the Burmese in their continuing expansion captured Assam and planned to strike at
Calcutta. War and their defeat followed, leading to the cession of
Assam to British India. There was a revolution in Burma in 1837
led by King Tharrawaddy, who denounced the peace treaty with
the British. Again war and defeat, which led to the British annexation of the wealthy province of Pegu. Progressively-minded Mindon Min then came to the Burmese throne. He introduced the
first coinage, a telegraph system, river steamers for transport,
factories with European machinery. But he also took steps to
control European traders, which led to demands from commercial
interests for intervention. Mindon Min's younger son, Thibaw,
succeeded him, and upset the British by making concessions to the
French, German and Italian merchants and, still more, by suing
the Bombay–Burma Trading Company for £73,000 for alleged
fraud. Britain acted vigorously to defend its commerce. A strong
force occupied Mandalay in 1885 and Thibaw was deported to
India. The sequence to this victory was the transference of Burma's
foreign relations to the British in India; then Burma was annexed
and became a province of India. Nationalist feeling, however,
remained strong. When Burma was excluded from the reforms in
the Government of India Act, 1919, there was a storm of protest
and the British gave way. Resistance persisted and national feeling
was so powerful that in 1937 Burma was separated from India and
its distinct status recognised by placing it separately under the
British Parliament.

After Japan overran South-East Asia in the Second World War,
Tokyo declared Burma an independent state and established a
Burmese National Army. The Burmese leaders, however, were
ideologically anti-fascist and the allied victories in Europe in 1945
led the army to revolt against the Japanese. Aung San, although he
had been Defence Minister in the administration under the Japanese, formed the Anti-Fascist Peoples' Freedom League
(AFPFL) and gained massive support. He demanded independence

for Burma, and the British Labour Government responded in 1946 by saying it would accept the verdict of the electorate. In the subsequent election the AFPFL won an overwhelming victory. Aung San succeeded in getting the support of the outlying hill peoples (except the tribal-minded Karens) and all seemed set for the inauguration of independence under him. Then, on July 19, 1947, Aung and several of his colleagues were murdered at a Cabinet meeting. Despite the confusion, the Labour Government went ahead with its plan for independence and in October 1947 a treaty establishing Burma as a sovereign nation was signed with U Nu, who had succeeded Aung San, as leader.

The independent Union of Burma was born at 4.20 a.m. on January 4, 1948. The early hour was chosen by astrologers, but events did not bear out their hopes of an easy future. There was a communist rebellion, a rising by the Karens, an incursion of Kuomintang forces defeated in China, difficulties with Communist China, and in 1962 U Nu was overthrown by the army, led by General Ne Win, anti-communist yet calling himself a revolutionary socialist. In 1972 Ne Win announced that he was establishing a civilian government and did so by the simple device of resigning from the army and requiring his fellow-generals in the cabinet to do the same. He submitted for discussion a constitition for a 'Socialist Republic of Burma', a one-party state, and an elected People's Congress. Good relations have been concluded with China and Burma appears to have established stability. Whether this lasts will depend largely on the satisfaction of the seven tribal states within the Union and the ability of the Government to come to terms with U Nu.

Sri Lanka (Ceylon)

The history of Ceylon has been largely influenced by Buddhism, which missionaries from India brought to the island in the third century BC, converting King Tissa. They were committed to poverty and celibacy and lived in caves, but they introduced the art of writing as well as architecture and sculpture, and, later, painting and poetry too. A high civilisation developed. As often, internal progress aroused foreign ambitions. King Parakramabahu in 1153 invaded Burma winning concessions, but his incursion into southern India was disastrous and the Tamils established a kingdom on the northern peninsula of Ceylon. Thus began the strife between Singhalese and Tamils which persisted to modern times.

Europeans arrived in 1505, the Portuguese on their way further east. They negotiated a treaty to trade in cinnamon, obtained permission to build a fort, and, taking advantage of divisions among the Singhalese rulers which they exploited with much duplicity, seized land. At the beginning of the seventeenth century the Portuguese annexed the whole island, but almost immediately came into conflict with the Dutch East India Company. The Dutch made a deal with the titular king of Kandy, the core of Singhalese strength, to drive out the Portuguese and by 1656 they had succeeded. They reached an understanding that they would hand over the territory to the Singhalese in return for a trading monopoly; they took the trade, they maintained control of the island. They were resisted and, though retaining the seaboard, failed to occupy Kandy. Fearing the British and the French with their trading companies, the Dutch made concessions and obtained a pledge from the king that he would have no dealing with other countries. Despite this, successive Kandyan kings intrigued with the British and French, playing off the alien companies against each other.

In 1795 the British demanded that their troops be allowed to land in Ceylon. The Dutch still controlling the coast refused, whereupon the British East India Company sent in a well-equipped expedition which captured Colombo. The technique was followed of bribing a regiment of mercenaries fighting for the Dutch (they happened to be Swiss) to transfer their allegiance, and the British forces swept over the territory. By the Treaty of Amiens in 1802 Ceylon was annexed and British Crown Colony rule established. The Singhalese stronghold of Kandy, however, remained resistant until the following year when a British expedition captured it. A treaty was signed guaranteeing Singhalese rights and protection for the Buddhist religion; but in 1818 there was once more revolt. It was severely repressed. The kingdom of Kandy ceased to exist.

For three hundred years Ceylon was the victim of the rivalry of European trading companies backed by the armies of their governments. In control, the British acted thoroughly. In the 1820s they introduced coffee plantations with Tamil labour, and later tea plantations. Colombo became an important port, particularly after the Suez Canal was built. Education spread. The first schools were opened by missionary societies, but state primary and secondary schools followed and even a University (set up in 1921, but not accorded University status until 1942). The education was in the English language and British orientated, which led to a reaction. Buddhists and Hindus established their own schools and colleges and there was the beginning of a Buddhist University.[1] With education a middle class grew; they began to penetrate the export and import trades and the civil service.

Very slowly some political rights were conceded. In 1883 three Singhalese were nominated to the Legislative Council, but it was not until 1912 that one elected member, representing 'educated Ceylonese', was permitted. During the First World War national feeling arose sufficiently to bring the Ceylon National Congress into being. With peace its agitation led to considerable reforms in 1920 and 1924, including an unofficial majority in the Legislative Council. In 1928 a Royal Commission recommended a State Council with committees sharing in the administration of the different governmental Departments, their chairmen serving as a Board of Ministers. This was less than responsible government and was only reluctantly accepted by the nationalist leaders, who had to wait until the end of the Second World War before their aims were realised. In October 1947 the right of the Ceylonese people to independence was recognised by the Labour Government in Britain. The new sovereign nation was born four months later.

Independence was made difficult by tensions between the Singhalese and Tamils. After a period of moderate government under Senanayake, the radical Bandaranaike took over. When he was assassinated his wife became the first woman to be elected Prime Minister in democratic history. Her government absorbed the schools from the religious bodies and embarked on a programme of socialisation, but alienated the Tamils by making Singhalese the official language. In 1965 she was rejected in a general election and the son of Senanayake headed the government. He made concessions to the Tamils which eased tensions, relaxed state controls of industry and succeeded in getting Western foreign aid. In 1970 Mrs Bandaranaike was again elected to power by a large majority at the head of a Left government including a minority of Trotskyists and Communists, which emphasised non-alignment in foreign affairs.

In May 1971 everyone outside Ceylon (and many inside) were startled by the explosion of a formidable insurrection, leading to guerrilla fighting, suppressed by troops with difficulty. Widespread unemployment among youth, disappointment with the failure of the Government (limited by financial strain) to implement Socialism, an unbearable increase in the cost of living, and the desperate plight of the rural population combined to incite the rising. Reactionary elements participated. Britain, America, Russia,

China and India, among others gave Mrs Bandaranaike support. The rising was crushed but at the cost of 1,200 killed. Sixteen thousand were stated to have been detained without trial, nine thousand of whom remained confined a year later. Observers voiced the criticism that members of the Government who had gained power as revolutionaries had succumbed to élitism, though considerable confidence in Mrs Bandaranaike persisted. A deep scar was left on the image of the Government.

In May 1972 the island was declared a Republic under the traditional name Sri Lanka. Five thousand detainees were released, but the Tamil Federal Party boycotted the ceremonies, demanding greater use in the administration of the Tamil language, spoken by twenty per cent of the people.

Sri Lanka, after 26 years of independence, faces formidable difficulties. It has a coalition government pledged to socialist construction, weighed down by financial stringency. It has an opposition tied to private capitalist enterprise. It has an underground revolutionary Left, young and impatient, which has the ear of many disillusioned. It has racial antagonisms. Strength, courage, wisdom and sincerity were never more necessary. In foreign affairs the Government emphasises non-alignment and now underlines national unity between Singhalese and Tamils by terming all citizens Ceylonese.

The Maldives

One must not overlook the Maldive Islands, among the smallest states in the UN with a population of only 100,000. They lie four hundred miles west of Sri Lanka, an ocean station on the way to the Seychelles and Africa. For this reason the RAF has leased a staging post on the small island of Gan until 1986, a cause of controversy in the past with the autocratic ruler, President Ibrahim Nasir, nominally responsible to the People's Majeis. In older days the Portuguese dominated the Maldives, but the islands became of little value until the air age and thus can enjoy sovereignty. Their one danger of arousing external interest beyond the RAF post is the attention of oil prospectors. The people live by selling dried fish to Sri Lanka.

The Malayan–Indonesian Archipelago: Before the Second World War

In southern Asia, towards the east, there is a complicated area sometimes called the Malayan Archipelago, sometimes the Indonesian Archipelago. It consists of the Malayan peninsula, jutting south from the mainland; Singapore at its tip; the vast string of islands, large and small, which is Indonesia, including extensive Borneo and New Guinea, even larger, to the east; and to the north, the Philippines which claim to be an archipelago in their own right. From the early sixteenth century this region became a battleground between the trading companies of Portugal, Spain, Holland, Britain and later Germany (the French concentrated on Indo-China to the north), and their governments all seized possession of territories at one time or another.[2]

Indonesia

There is a large Indian and Chinese proportion in the population. Indians settled in Indonesia even before the Christian era, when they were paramount over the East in shipping, and more emigrated through Malaya in large numbers when it was ruled by the British from Calcutta. The Chinese repeatedly swept over the area from early times and later they settled as traders. The Portuguese and Spanish were the first Europeans to arrive, agreeing in 1529 to divide the area into two spheres of trading activity.[3] Then came the Dutch with a fleet which in 1596 reached Sumatra (the large Indonesian island neighbouring Malaya). The Portuguese resisted them at first but were forced to give way in 1608. The following year the Dutch appointed a Governor-General and named the more westerly islands under their control the Netherlands Indies. The Dutch East India Company dominated Indonesia for two centuries, but for a time the British East India Company challenged. Rivalry developed to virtual war, ended by the Treaty of Westminster in 1674. The English then agreed to concentrate their economic interests in India, the Dutch in the archipelago.

There is little record of resistance by the indigenous population before the early eighteenth century, when there was a formidable insurrection on the main island of Java against the slavery which the Dutch imposed. The rebellion was crushed with severity.

Events in Europe affected Indonesia. Napoleon subordinated Holland, and Netherlands India became for a time part of the French empire. Britain, at war with Napoleon, captured Java and by the Treaty of Vienna, 1816, agreed to return the Netherlands Indies to its allies the Dutch. This was met with desperate resistance by the Indonesians. Several native states revolted and the Dutch maintained power only by strong-armed repression over a long period. In 1873 there was open war in Sumatra and it took the Netherlands thirty years to subdue the Atjeh rebellion. Only by superior military force was Dutch dominance achieved.

Malaya and Singapore

Meanwhile the conflict between British and Dutch traders was transferred to the mainland. Who should exploit the trade with China? Singapore was the key, and by clever but admittedly dishonest intrigue Sir Thomas Stamford Raffles, representing the East India Company, pocketed it. Seeking a site for a factory he was given permission by the local chief to purchase land, but this chief was subordinate to a regional chief who was under Dutch surveillance and therefore unlikely to confirm the concession. Sir Thomas then installed a brother as superior chief, who obligingly validated the purchase. This was sheer bravado, but Raffles got away with it. In London the Court of Directors of the BEIC ruled that he had contravened instructions, but did nothing more. Directors, shareholders and Sir Thomas Stamford Raffles all benefited.

In 1824 an Anglo–Dutch treaty left Malaya and Singapore in the British sphere; the same year, the island of Penang to the west of Malaya and Malacca on the mainland were taken over as the British Straits Settlements, at first the property of the East India Company but after the Indian Mutiny under the India Office in London. Objection to distant rule developed among resident British and Chinese merchants, and in 1867 the Settlements became a Crown Colony with non-official settler representation in the administration. Very soon the traders sought London support; there were attacks on their property by tribes in the rest of Malaya. This and the fear of German intervention led the British Government to appoint official Residents in the different states in 1873, to which formal consent was obtained from subservient rulers. There was still resentment by the Malayan people, however, and successive rebellions had to be crushed. Many of the states then agreed to admit non-Malay residents – British, Chinese and Indians – to their Councils, and British influence became paramount. In 1909 Britain and France came to an agreement by which the French in Siam – afterwards Thailand – ceded four additional states. By 1914 all states south of Siam came under the protection of Britain.

British companies leapt in to exploit tin and rubber, which led to an economic transformation. The companies made extravagant profits, but at the same time mounting revenue enabled roads and railways to be built and education to be extended. In Asia Malaya became second only to Japan in material advance. The miners, plantation workers and peasants remained discontented.

British Colonies in Borneo

By now possession of the whole island region to the south of Malaya was passing into European hands. The Dutch occupied not only Sumatra and Java but also the greater part of the expansive island of Borneo to the east. Britain got a hold of its northern coast which had been ruled by the sultan of Brunei. Brunei became a protectorate in 1888, but the sultan was left as autocratic ruler of his population. Later he was to become vastly rich by the discovery of oil, but meantime he lost his territories – now Sabah and Sarawak – to east and west.

The means by which Sarawak became British are unique. Malays and Dyaks (aboriginal peasants) revolted against the sultan of Brunei in 1841 and an Englishman, James Brooke (afterwards Sir James) offered assistance in restoring order. He was rewarded by installation as rajah and for twenty three years he was the virtual possessor of Sarawak. In 1864 his domain was recognised by Britain as an independent state, and after his death two descendants ruled. At the end of the First World War Charles Brooke donated Sarawak to the British Crown.

The eastern region – first known as North Borneo and afterwards Sabah – was for many centuries closely associated with the not-too-distant Philippines, whose government, indeed, later claimed it. The Portuguese and Spanish appeared in the sixteenth century, but it was not until Alexander Dalrymple, a Scottish voyager, touched the coast in 1759 that European contacts became continuous. The first recorded resistance by the people was in 1882, when the sultan of Brunei granted land to the British North Borneo Company (a successor to the East India Company). The revolt grew and by 1889 had become formidable under the leadership of Mat Salleh, an influential Muslim. His fortress at Ranau was only captured after a prolonged siege and even after that raids on the British settlements were frequent. The North Borneo Company administered the territory until the end of the Second World War.

The Philippines

The Spanish landed an expedition in the first half of the sixteenth century and before 1700 most of the archipelago was in their possession, although there was Muslim opposition, with continuous raids on the Spanish settlements. Sir Francis Drake, Britain's explosive voyager, had reached the Philippines in 1577, and Thomas Cavendish ten years later attempted to capture the Spanish shipyard at Iloilo, but failed. There was a running struggle, with sea conflicts by traders of several nationalities, to get a foothold on the islands, in the course of which the Spanish, Dutch, British, Portuguese and even the Japanese and Chinese were engaged. By the 1670s the Dutch occupied much of the territory and a century later the British captured Manila. By the package deal of the Treaty of Paris in 1763, however, the islands were returned to the Spanish, who met with persistently renewed resistance from the people.

Revolt continued over a hundred years, not only in the Philippines but also in Spain itself (where many Filipinos had become students) and even in places of exile like Hong Kong. In 1872 two hundred native soldiers rebelled at the Cavite Arsenal, killing their officers and demonstrating for independence. The mutineers' leaders were executed, others sentenced to life imprisonment. Nationalist feeling was particularly strong against Catholic Friars who had been given large estates at the expense of the peasants. In Barcelona, Lopez Jaena, after campaigning in the Philippines against both the domination of the Friars and the Spanish administrative and economic monopoly, established a paper, *La Solidaridad* to advocate reforms in religion and government. In 1891 Rizal, a colleague of Jaena, started an exiled nationalist organisation in Hong Kong, *Liga Filipina*, opening a branch in Manila the following year. He was arrested and after a farcical trial in Barcelona executed in December 1896. The name of Apolinario Mabini, courageous nationalist, is also remembered. A camouflaged organisation, the Supreme Worshipful Association of the Sons of the People, was set up in the Philippines with, it was claimed, over 100,000 members, evidence of the skill and extent of the revolt.

After these warning events, a full-scale insurrection broke out in August 1896, under the leadership of Emilio Aguinaldo. The Spanish reinforced their army to 28,000, supported by limited native mercenaries. Fierce repression seemed to crush the insurrection in the autumn, but it broke out again in the New Year when news was received of the execution of Rizal. Aguinaldo left for Hong Kong in December 1897, but returned to renew the struggle when the USA declared war on Spain in February 1898. The Filipinos announced their independence in June and Aguinaldo was made president of the Republic. At the end of hostilities in December, however, the Philippines were formally ceded to the USA; on Washington declining to recognise the Republic, Aguinaldo declared war. The USA poured in reinforcements, but for more than three years the resistance continued. Aguinaldo was captured in March 1901; even then guerrilla warfare went on until the final surrender in April 1902.

The Americans attempted conciliation. Howard Taft was the Governor and he bought the estates of the Catholic Friars for $7,250,000 and made the land available to Filippinos. In October the first Legislature, admittedly very unrepresentative, was opened; official languages were extended from Spanish and English to include Tagalog. But still the Filipinos were dissatisfied and fighting was renewed in the interior. President Harding sent a mission of inquiry, which reported that a grant of independence would be premature. Thereupon Filipino demands increased. The political climate improved, however, when Henry Stimson as Governor-General introduced reforms which won some confidence from the people, and progressive Frank Murphy, appointed his successor by Franklin D. Roosevelt in 1933, recommended independence. Incredibly to the Filipinos, a Bill for self-government was passed through both Congress Houses in Washington in March 1934, and a representative convention was authorised to meet in the Philippines to prepare the constitution. Manuel Quezon was elected the first president, but before Washington's belated recognition was accorded the World War and the Japanese invasion came. There was a courageous resistance by radical Nationalists but it was overwhelmed by Japan's military power.

New Guinea

This is a large island territory in the Indonesian archipelago – in fact, the largest on the globe except Australia. The Dutch annexed the west half, West Irian, on behalf of their traders in 1848; Queensland (Australia), only a hundred miles away, annexed the south-east in 1884; and Germany, also for its traders, annexed the north-east in 1885.[4] To underwrite the Queensland claim, Britain declared its area a protectorate in 1885; three years later it became a British colony. Germany's defeat in the First World War led to its territory on the island being mandated to Australia and at the same time Britain ceded its colony to the Dominion. Thus New Guinea was shared by Australia and Holland.

There was little opposition to the original occupations; the invaders contented themselves with establishing a few trading stations on the coast, leaving life in the interior untouched. The Dutch, for example, permitted the sultan of Tidore to maintain his nominal suzerainty. The populations were thinly scattered. Alien possession was at first easy.

The Malayan–Indonesian Archipelago: After the Second World War

The Second World War was the watershed of change. Everywhere, the British, French, Dutch and American forces evacuated their territories before the Japanese, who promised the peoples independence. They were rarely believed and co-operation was limited, often refused. When the war ended the national movements demanded self-government and independence. Nowhere did it come at once.

Indonesia

The Netherlands occupation had been unhappy. The original rule by the Dutch East India Company led through incompetence and corruption to bankruptcy. When the Dutch Government assumed authority they succeeded in extending trade, but the continued poverty of the mass of the people was worsened by the destruction of the social pattern to which they were accustomed. Pressure from within Indonesia and by liberals in Holland brought an 'ethical policy', aimed at revitalising the villages and providing credits for peasants, water for eroded land, and medical services and primary education. But the programme did not keep pace with the growth of population and discontent grew, finding expression in the birth of a nationalist movement led by the few intellectuals. The Dutch responded by setting up a People's Council in 1918; it was un-representative and only advisory and was rejected by the National-ists. There were years of repression; the people's leaders were imprisoned; in 1926 there was a rebellion led by Communists. Still severer repression followed and persisted up to the Second World War.

Under the Japanese occupation the nationalist movement was divided. Two of the leaders, Sukarno, popular hero, and Moham-med Hatta, democratic Socialist, accepted administrative posts in order to protect the people, pressing the Japanese all the time for independence. In contrast a large number of Nationalists went underground, practising non-co-operation. Before the Japanese surrendered they called the national leaders together and invited them to take over. On August 17, 1945, independence was pro-claimed.

The Dutch did not accept this. For four years they attempted by the most ruthless military means to subdue the Indonesians. Thrust back on land, they blockaded the key islands by their navy. In a radio message to the author Sukarno stated his terms of peace – independence but compensation to the Dutch – and these were conveyed to the Netherlands' delegation at the 1946 San Francisco inaugural conference of the United Nations.[5] This approach, whilst initiating discussion, did not have immediate results, but sub-sequently a United Nations Commission was appointed and under world pressure, particularly from America, Holland agreed to the establishment of an independent United States of Indonesia in nominal union with herself. On December 16, 1949, Sukarno was elected president and The Hague transferred rights to a provisional government of which Hatta became Prime Minister. The Dutch negotiators had insisted on a federal constitution, but a diversified administration could not be constructed in circumstances of early post-war chaos and the projected United States of Indonesia became the centralised Republic of Indonesia.

A more serious difference arose with the Dutch. It will be remembered that the western part of New Guinea – West Irian – had been allocated to the Netherlands (by the Berlin Conference of 1885). The agreement for the independence of Indonesia made no reference to this territory. The Indonesians demanded it; the Dutch refused. Indonesia thereupon ended its nominal union with the Netherlands and expelled remaining Dutch citizens, confiscating their property. Controversial exchange continued for eight years; Indonesia broke off diplomatic relations and threatened military action; in the end, Holland agreed to the transfer of the territory on condition that there should be a referendum within seven years. There was some revolt among the inhabitants, not from love of the Dutch but calling for independence. When 1969 came the Indonesians announced that meetings of representatives of the people had endorsed their authority. Perhaps because Sukarno, a neutralist leaning towards the Communists, had by this time been succeeded by Suharto, pro-West, the claim was not challenged.

Sukarno was a controversial President. Indonesia had only artificial unity. There were separatist revolts from the various islands; there were so many political parties that Parliamentary democracy did not work; there was deepening poverty because there was no economic planning; the Communist Party grew on the discontent. Sukarno dissolved the Parliament and established a novel system of government which he called Guided Democracy. He nominated a Council from the strongest parties and when he agreed with their advice it became law. Hatta, who had sought to give constructive leadership but had been frustrated by the President's indifference to economic reform, resigned in protest against this repudiation of democracy. Sukarno then turned increasingly towards the Communists, protecting them from the opposition of the army.

In 1965 Colonel Untung, commander of the President's personal guard, attempted a *coup*, which was held to be a conspiracy planned by the Communists to gain control. Many believed that Sukarno was sympathetic to them; whether this was true or not, he could not appease the wrath of the army. Hundreds of Communists, mostly Chinese, were slaughtered. In February 1966 Sukarno in a last despairing gesture of authority dismissed the Defence Minister responsible for this purge, but he could not withstand the racialist passion against the Chinese. His day of power was over. In March the army under General Suharto carried out its own *coup* and Sukarno was thrust into humiliating background. On February 22, 1967, he handed over his power to Suharto, who had already begun a massive round-up of the Chinese, partly because he identified them with the Communists, partly from racial antagonism.

Thousands, perhaps hundreds of thousands were massacred; those who escaped death were deported. Suharto proceeded to identify Indonesia with the West. The fear that Indonesia would become a partner with communist China was removed.

Sukarno had begun office as a popular idol. He had been the embodiment of Indonesia's successful national struggle and proved himself an indomitable leader. He was a powerful orator and swayed vast audiences by extolling Indonesia's greatness. He failed disastrously, however, in the economic sphere and the people sank to ever deeper distress in their poverty. He lived himself in ostentatious and sensual luxury and gradually disillusionment grew. For a time he diverted the peoples' minds from their own grievances by arousing their patriotism in anger against the Federation of Malaysia (its story has still to be told). He whipped up national hysteria for confrontation, but this palled, he was overthrown and General Suharto was able to make peace with popular consent. Sukarno lived in enforced retreat and died in 1970.

Malaya

The Japanese occupation lasted from 1942 to 1945. There was a brave movement of resistance motivated by anti-Fascism as well as anti-alien domination, largely led by Communists. At the end of the war, however, the four principal feudal heads of states accepted renewed British sovereignty and the political union of the territory; Harold Macmillan was sent from London on a mission to work out details. He told the rulers that their agreement must be kept secret, not revealed to the people. Somehow this was leaked to *The Times* and there was strong protest in the House of Commons; there was also violent protest in Malaya and a mass movement of non-co-operation with the British began. The Government at Westminster yielded and appointed a commission of Asian and British officials to recommend a constitution. Instead of union, federation was introduced, with a Prime Minister and Executive Council in each state and an overall Federal Prime Minister and Executive Council; there was a British High Commission and British influence remained strong. A hopeful development towards racial co-operation between the Malayan, Chinese and Indian communities then took place. An alliance was formed between the Malayan party, UMNO (the Chinese Association) and the Indian Congress. It was led by Tunku Abdul Rahman, son of a sultan, a conciliatory figure. In 1955 the alliance won a sweeping victory in the elections for the Federal legislature. The demand for full independence grew.

The militants who had resisted the Japanese did more than demand. They were not prepared to accept the return of the British presence, and they regarded the sultans and politicians who had co-operated with them as representatives of a feudalism which they also wished to overthrow. Under the leadership of Communists a force of four thousand in 1948 began war in the jungle. It was a remorseless war. They not only ambushed British troops in the swampy woodland, but attacked isolated police stations, destroyed trees in rubber plantations, burned houses of European staff and worker's dwellings at the mines and killed managers; in 1951 the British High Commissioner, Sir Henry Gurney, was assassinated. The guerrillas had hidden camps in the jungle and obtained food from the villagers, sometimes with goodwill, sometimes by intimidation. The rebellion became serious. London had to engage forces heavily and in Malaya two years' conscripted service was imposed. It was necessary to establish large camps for peasant refugees and for the population in areas cleared by the troops.

The rebellion was repulsed by political as much as by military means. In August 1957 the nine Malay states with the settlements of Penang and Malacca, were accorded independence by the British Government as a federation. The constitution was a compromise between democracy and feudalism. The Legislature was elected; the Head of the Federal State was chosen by the subordinate state rulers every five years. Britain guaranteed defence, set up bases and continued to provide troops to subdue the guerrillas. This co-operation was undoubtedly influenced by the fact that the Alliance Party, which became the government, was favourable to British interests, protected the rubber and tin companies, and proved itself a reliable ally against Communism in South-East Asia. Tunku Abdul Rahman became head of the Federation. For a time it appeared that Malaya had stability, although there was a militant socialist opposition in the Legislature. In the general election of 1969 the alliance of Malays, Chinese and Indians came under severe strain. The Opposition parties, largely manned by Chinese, did surprisingly well and serious clashes occurred between Malays and Chinese. The Government suspended the meeting of the Legislature and imprisoned Opposition leaders. At the same time guerrilla activity in the jungle was renewed. Stability was not assured.

Singapore

Singapore is divided only by a causeway from the mainland of Malaya, but the British deliberately excluded it from the independent Malayan Federation because of a desire to maintain control of its strategically important naval base and also because of its predominantly Chinese population, perhaps potentially communist-inclined, certainly upsetting the racial balance in Malaya. Its port served as the exit for Malaya's tin and rubber as well as accommodating from 1921 the naval base, which by the beginning of the Second World War had became one of the largest harbours in the world, strengthened by the opening of the Suez Canal. Its loss to the Japanese from February 1942 to September 1945 was a major defeat.

The mood of the population under the Japanese was one of disillusion with the British, but the return of naval and air forces at the end of the war confined protest. The development of political institutions in Singapore took place parallel with those in Malaya; a Legislature with an elected majority was initiated in 1955 with governmental responsibility in all spheres except foreign affairs and defence. Four years later the membership of the Legislature became entirely elected.

Singapore contributed one of the ablest political leaders in Asia. Lee Kuan Yew was head of the People's Action Party (PAP) which after the war carried on a strong agitation against colonial rule. In 1959, when returned as the majority leader in the Legislature, he refused to form a government until eight nationalist leaders of the Left had been released from prison. He was Chinese by origin but strongly, and later remorselessly, withstood communist influence. His administration was efficient, constructive and aimed at reconciling the races. He developed a large industrial estate to make Singapore less dependent upon the naval docks and Malayan trade, and in his extensive housing schemes allocated neighbouring flats to Chinese and Malays so that the races should mix.

Among the Chinese populations, however, particularly at the high schools and colleges, a movement of solidarity with communist China grew in strength and it took root in some of the trades unions. The Left in PAP broke away to form the *Barisan Socialis Party*, which denied that it was communist, but to which the Communists gave underground support. Lee Kuan Yew repressed this opposition with severity, alleging that its members felt loyalty to China rather than to Singapore. He arrested and imprisoned leaders and militant members, subjecting some to solitary confinement, and there was some disillusionment, his critics pointing to the contrast with colonial times when he had challenged the detention of political opponents. Nevertheless Lee Kuan Yew's popularity remained, partly because of his social legislation, partly because of his personality which combined leadership with the common touch, helped by the fact that he himself was Chinese. When the elections came he was returned with an overwhelming majority and the influence of the *Barisan Socialis Party* dwindled.

Singapore became independent in 1963 in association with the Federation of Malaysia (still to be described). The referendum which endorsed the decision to join Malaysia was strongly criticised for its confused presentation and there was serious doubt how far it reflected opinion. In August 1965, as we shall tell, Singapore surprisingly withdrew from the Federation and became independent in its own right.

British Colonies in Borneo

The three British colonies on the north coast of the island of Borneo – Sarawak, Brunei and North Borneo (Sabah) – were also overrun by the Japanese during the war. There was an attitude of resentful co-operation by the peoples; the occupying forces' military strength prevented effective resistance.

Sarawak

When on the retreat of the Japanese Charles Brooke handed Sarawak to the Crown, the demand arose among the people for self-government. This was mostly among the large Chinese population, some of whom, their eyes on communist China, supported the Indonesian attacks on the frontier when Malaysia was established. At the general election on the issue of Malaysia the Opposition was defeated, but there was considerable evidence of unfair influence; the British official presence was on the side of the government party. Sarawak became independent as part of Malaysia, but the Opposition was so militant that the elections due in 1969 had to be postponed. There is still considerable doubt about the future of Sarawak.

Brunei

Brunei is a different story. Its Sultan remained supreme at the end of the war, wealthy from oil royalties building a fantastically ostentatious mosque, benevolent in his disbursements to the population, which attained the highest standard of life in southern Asia. It was not until September 1959 that some democratic advances were introduced; an Executive Council and Legislative Council were then set up. The members of the Executive were entirely official or nominated; ten of the twenty-one Legislative Council were elected. At the first election in 1962 a majority of the seats was won by the radical *Partai Ray'ayat* which stood for complete democracy, agrarian reform and independence. Conflict arose between the Sultan and the elected members, and when a secret conspiracy was alleged by a group associated with the *Partai Ray'ayat* it was banned and leaders and militant members imprisoned, charged with sympathising with Indonesia. To the discomfort of the British and Malayan leaders, Brunei's Executive Council rejected membership of the Malaysian Federation. This was largely because of unwillingness to share the rich revenue from the royalties of the Shell oilfields at Seria, which produced over five million tons a year.

Brunei became a protected state of Britain, which remained for a time in control not only of defence but nominally of many internal affairs, the Sultan having agreed in 1959 to accept the advice of the High Commissioner in all matters except Malay traditional customs and the Muslim religion. In 1971, however, Britain surrendered the right to advise the Sultan and limited its participation in defence to consultation. Legally, therefore, Brunei became virtually independent, though a small number of British officers were seconded to serve the government and some British nationals worked for the Sultan under contract. This British presence was denounced by the Brunei People's Independence Front, which succeeded the banned *Partai Ray'ayat*. The Sultan is accepted as Head of the State by the Muslim majority among the Malayan population (54 per cent) and many of the indigenous (17 per cent), but 26 per cent are Chinese and owe little allegiance to the dominant religion. A good living level contributes to acceptance of the regime, but democratic pressures grow.

Sabah

In the third British colony, North Borneo, Australian forces were responsible for driving the Japanese out at the end of the Second World War and for a year there was a military administration. Then the territory became a Crown Colony under Britain with a Legislature. Theoretically there were elected members, but an illiterate peasant population absorbed in its problems of existence and long distances with few transport facilities gave the advantage to rich candidates who had little in common with the people. During the Indonesian confrontation there were attacks on the borders, but these aroused only slight support from the people despite some racial identity. Pressure for national independence was concentrated in the few towns and when the Federation of Malaysia, providing for an end of colonial rule, was proposed the leaders of all the political parties gave support, the territory being renamed Sabah. There was the alternative of acceptance of the claim of the Philippines to sovereignty, but there was little indication of any popular memory of the earlier association. The truth probably is that the great majority of the people were ignorant of the issues involved.

Sabah's government proved to be dictatorial. The emergence of Opposition parties was obstructed and leaders detained without charge or trial under an old colonialist ordinance. In 1969 the Parliamentary elections were suspended and fourteen Opposition leaders detained. They were not released until March 1972 and then only on probation, most of them required to give a written undertaking not to take part in political or trade union activity. Two trade union leaders, arrested before the resumed elections in 1970, were kept in detention.

Only one Opposition group, the United Sabah National Party, was registered and at the State elections in October 1971, all its ten candidates were disqualified on the alleged grounds that they had presented their nomination forms incorrectly. The result was that the élite-supported United Sabah Action Party of the Chief Minister, Tun Mustapha, won all thirty-two State Assembly seats. Sabah remained superficially peaceful. Unlike other parts of Malaysia, there was no suggestion of communist activity, but underneath, in the towns at least, a democratic upsurge was arising.

The Philippines

The Philippines perhaps suffered more than any Asian country except China during the war. Manila was among the world's most devastated capitals and one million lives were lost on the islands. The USA agreed to the establishment of an independent Republic in July 1946, but American influence persisted and the old feudal order remained. In 1947 a Mutual Assistance Pact was signed authorising the lease to the US of naval and air bases for ninety-nine years (later after criticism reduced to twenty-five); in 1951 a Mutual Defence Treaty was signed; and in 1954 the Government joined SEATO (South-East Asia Treaty Organisation), the western alliance against communist aggression and subversion. The Philippines continued in the American sphere.

During the war internal resistance to the Japanese had been led by the Huk movement, anti-fascist in ideology, much influenced by Communists; it carried on courageous guerrilla activity. At the end of the war the Huks, as they were called, were not prepared to accept continued American presence and they turned against the landowners' domination of the peasants. When they found that the new independent government co-operated with the Americans and accepted feudal power, they called for its forceful overthrow, identifying themselves openly with the Communist Party in 1949. They received considerable support from villagers with food supplies and information about the approach of government forces, but they could not stand up to superior numbers and weapons and by 1955 were substantially crushed. Ten years later they reappeared, but still with little prospect of the mass support necessary for success.

The Government did something to meet the grievances of the people by planning land settlements and, despite unemployment during economic stagnation in the 1950s, felt secure by American aid and the American military presence. In international affairs the Government sometimes took an independent line. In the United Nations their delegation supported the Afro-Asian group on a number of colonial and racial issues, and later we shall describe how they took the bold initiative for a Malayan–Indonesian Confederation. A little out of character was the claim which the Philippines made for sovereignty over Sabah. It was based on the long-distant authority of the sultan of Sula, from whom the territory was leased rather than handed over to Britain; but in practice British rule had become absolute.

Malaysia

We turn to Malaysia, to which frequent reference has been made. First, its background. On July 27, 1962 President Diosdedo Macapagal, Prime Minister of the Philippines, made a declaration which was described as historic, proposing a comprehensive plan for the union of Malaya, Indonesia and the Philippines in an all-embracing Confederation. Malaya and Indonesia responded by co-operating in a conference of Foreign Ministers at Manila in June 1963. They met and reached agreement. The following passage appeared in the joint communiqué issued at the end of the Conference:

'This Ministerial Conference was a manifestation of the determination of the nations in this region to achieve closer co-operation in their endeavour to chart a common future. The three Ministers examined the Philippine proposal embodying President Macapagal's idea for the establishment of a Confederation of nations of Malay origin and agreed on the acceptance of the idea as a means of bringing together their countries into the closest association.'

This was promising for peace and co-operation throughout southern Asia, but just prior to the conference a proposal for the more limited Federation of Malaysia had been endorsed in London by the British and Malayan Governments. It covered the states of Malaya, Singapore, Sarawak, Brunei and North Borneo. The Foreign Ministers were aware of this project when they met at Manila and did not rule out the inclusion of Malaysia in their proposed Confederation; but at the subsequent conference of Heads of State (President Macapagal, President Sukarno and Prime Minister Tunku Rahman), held also at Manila, July to August, there were doubts and suspicions. President Macapagal was concerned about the inclusion of Sabah within Malaysia; President Sukarno was concerned about Borneo as a whole, the greater part of which was an Indonesian possession. This led to the proposal that the Secretary General of the United Nations should send working teams to decide whether the peoples of the British colonies in Borneo favoured Malaysia.

The United Nations mission, when it visited the Malaysian countries, reported that with the exception of Brunei majorities accepted the Federation. They based their views on election returns and the referendum in Singapore; but, as already stated, doubts had been expressed about the authenticity of the election in Sarawak and of the validity of the Singapore referendum. Both Indonesia and the Philippines rejected the findings. Thus began the animosity which led to Indonesia's confrontation with Malaysia and destroyed the earlier hope of a Confederation of the whole region.

The author was a member of a Labour Party delegation of three which, at this time, inquired into the validity of Malaysia. His colleagues were Arthur Bottomley, afterwards Minister for Overseas Development, and Reginald Sorensen, MP, afterwards Lord Sorensen and a junior member of the Government. They favoured Malaysia; the author presented a minority report. His doubts were based mainly on the division of public opinion; he concluded that a considerable majority in Malaya favoured the Federation, a slight majority did so in Singapore, in Sarawak opinion was fifty-fifty, in Brunei an overwhelming majority was against and in Sabah there was ignorance of the issues, although the politically aware were in favour. There was a majority for Malaysia, but not in his view sufficient favourable opinion to justify such a fundamental change in constitutional status or to give promise of a stable political unit.

In practice, Brunei, hugging its oil revenue to itself, rejected Malaysia, and Singapore after two years withdrew, largely because the governmental parties in Malaya and Singapore campaigned against each other, leading to protests by the affronted Governments, to bitterness between the propertied class and the radicals in Malaya, and, most serious of all, to racial feeling between Chinese and Malays in Singapore. The permanence of Sarawak's membership of Malaysia is still in doubt. President Sukarno's policy of confrontation with Malaysia, not only a boycott of trade but virtual war on the borders of Sarawak and Sabah with large forces from Britain involved, ended only when Sukarno was replaced by Suharto. Malaysia killed the plan for an all-in Confederation, including Indonesia and the Philippines, as was intended when established.

In the background of this controversy was the Cold War, in this instance arising from fear of communist China with Indonesia under Sukarno as a possible ally. The British Government was determined to thrust a spear of Western defence through the body of southern Asia. Already it had established a Unified Military Command in the proposed Malaysian countries, and it desired political unity to consolidate it. When Malaya, Indonesia and the Philippines projected Confederation, the plan for Malaysia was rushed through to challenge the influence of Indonesia which, because of its overwhelming population, would have had the greatest say if the confederation plan had been realised. The future will tell whether Malaysia will live and whether, with an Indonesia unassociated with Communism, the idea of the wider Confederation may be revived.

South-East Asia became a subject of controversy in Britain in the late sixties and seventies when the Labour Government decided to withdraw its forces east of Suez. The Conservatives, following their election victory in 1970, modified this. In practice the distinction was not militarily great because of the mobility of troops by air transport, but their symbolical presence was regarded as politically influential by Malaysia and Singapore. Simultaneously Australia, New Zealand, Malaysia and Singapore supplemented SEATO by negotiations for a defence agreement with the support of Britain.

The situation in the region remains highly dangerous because of the expanding upheavals following the Vietnam war. A gleam of hope broke in 1971 when, following the succession of Tun Abdul Razak as Head of State on the retirement of the Tunku, Malaysia proposed at the Singapore Commonwealth Conference that South-East Asia should be neutralised. Malaysia also gave signs of independence in foreign affairs, challenging Britain's decision to send arms to South Africa. In February 1972 Tun Abdul Razak declared that Malaysia was unaligned and would seek agreement with China. This superseded the British purpose in creating Malaysia.

New Guinea (Papua)

When the western part of New Guinea passed from the Dutch to Indonesia, Australia was taking preliminary steps to develop self-government in the rest of the territory. While administration remained in Australian hands, an elected Legislature with restricted rights was established. In the first election twenty of the hundred members were Australian, but in the election of March 1972, only nine Whites were returned. The conservative United Party was the largest group with forty members, but four Leftist parties formed a coalition with Independents, pledged to gain self-government. The strongest element in the coalition was the Panga Party committed to 'self-government now', but to conciliate the more moderate groups its attainment was put at four years. Achievement may be expedited by a likely victory in Australia for the Labour Party which has declared for an advance to New Guinea's independence.[6]

Notes

1. It was given University status in 1959.

2. The populations up to 1971 were: Malaya 8,980,000; Singapore 2,110,000; Indonesia (including Borneo) 124,890,000; New Guinea: Australian Trusteeship 1,750,000, West Irian 736,731, Australian Papua 670,000; Non-Indonesian Borneo: Sarawak 1,010,000, Sabah 690,000, Brunei 140,000 and the Philippines 37,920,000.

3. It is of interest, in view of Spain's subsequent occupation, that even at this early date the Philippine islands were in the Spanish sphere.

4. The Berlin Conference of European Powers in 1885 confirmed this division.

5. The circumstances were unusual. A wireless officer on a Dutch ship picked up the message and brought it to the author at his London home. One of the Netherlands delegates to the UN conference, Peter Schmidt, was a friend, and the author gave him the terms as he passed through London. Thus negotiations began. Sukarno subsequently confirmed the authenticity of the message.

6. A Labour victory returned a government which declared for New Guinea's independence during 1973.

Chapter Seven

Indo-China

(Vietnam, Cambodia, Laos)

Indo-China is a part of South-East Asia, but the importance of the Vietnam war to the world (and its impact on Cambodia and Laos) requires distinct consideration.

Vietnam

From early times China invaded Vietnam. It occupied the territory almost continuously from 111 BC to AD 938, calling it Annam ('the pacified South'). The occupation was often disputed, sometimes by popular risings, sometimes by local kings. From the eleventh century onwards the Vietnamese gradually drove out the Chinese, notably under Emperor Le Thanh-Ton (1466–97), who for a time united north and south. Divided again in the early seventeenth century, the two kingdoms became known by Europeans as Tonkin and Cochin China. Portuguese and Spanish traders began to arrive during this period, followed by Dutch and English merchants and, importantly, by French missionaries. The French Catholics won thousands of converts. Father Alexandre de Rhodes romanised the Vietnam language and the script became popular because it broke from the Chinese, still resented by the people.

French Gain Power

As was the case in Japan, however, the Christian religion became divisive. Indeed, one can say that it contributed to the fatal conflict which led to the occupation of Vietnam. Emperor Gia-Long proscribed the Church because it appeared to challenge his authority. Persecution grew, over 100,000 Christians are said to have been killed, and a joint French and Spanish expedition set out in revenge. After a fierce war, the south was ceded to France in 1867, but in the north hostility against French merchants persisted. One more invasion, and by the Treaty of Saigon (1874) France gained protector status over the whole territory. By this time Vietnamese enmity to the French had become so strong that they turned to their old enemies, the Chinese, who sent in troops and by 1883 France and China were at war. The French won and by the Treaty of Tientsin (1885) Vietnam was recognised as part of their empire. It was divided into three parts – Cochin China, Annam and Tonkin. Cochin China was administered as a colony, with a Governor, a Colonial Council and a representative of the French residents in the Chamber of Deputies in Paris. Annam and Tonkin had a joint Governor, but separate Councils of Ministers, presided over by a French official; they each sent a delegate to the Superior Colonial Council in France. Separately we tell of how Laos and Cambodia came under the French. The aim of the government was to coalesce them with Vietnam in a united Indo-China. One Governor-General was appointed for all three territories in 1887, and for over forty years co-ordinated economic, financial and transport construction was advanced.

At the beginning of the twentieth century nationalism in its modern form emerged and France had difficulty in containing it, particularly after President Wilson's stand for self-determination towards the end of the First World War. In Cochin China national feeling was expressed through political pressures; in Annam it gathered round the Emperor and the chief families; it took a revolutionary form in Tonkin (close to China) where there was a rising as early as 1900.

Ho Chi Minh

It is likely that as a youth Ho Chi Minh, to become Vietnam's national hero-head, was caught up in this. Let us divert a moment to him. He was the son of a minor mandarin, took to sea, washed dishes in the kitchen of the Carlton Hotel in London, touched up photographs in Paris. There he joined the Socialist Party, which accepted him as Indo-Chinese delegate at its annual congress at Tours in 1920. He made an impassioned speech on 'the abhorrent crimes committed against my native land', but that was his last speech in the party. He voted for affiliation to the communist Third International and, defeated, was one of the breakaway group which formed the French Communist Party; he said he did so because he felt that Lenin was the hope of the victims of imperialism. After two years in the Soviet Union, taking instructions in the art of revolution, he went to Canton as assistant to Mikhail Borodin, adviser to the republican government of South China. It was at Canton that he took his first action for Vietnam. He formed the Revolutionary Youth League to recruit young Vietnamese Nationalists to train under Soviet instructors at a military academy. In 1930 he formed the Vietnam Communist Party; some say this was in Hong Kong, some say in Singapore; certainly it was not in Vietnam, where he would have been imprisoned. The original members were probably drawn from the youth who attended the military academy and from refugees, many of whom secretly infiltrated back to Vietnam. The next year he extended the party to cover all Indo-China, adding converts from Laos and Cambodia.

Despite his avoidance of Vietnam, Ho Chi Minh did not escape arrest. He was seized in Hong Kong, sentenced and appealed in vain to the Privy Council in the United Kingdom. Released from prison in 1932, he seems to have worked with Chinese Communists under Mao Tse-tung, with whom it was said he did not get on. Then, under war conditions in 1940, he moved towards Vietnam, first with exiles near the Tonkin border and the following year to a region in the north, liberated from the French, where for the first time for thirty years he was on his own soil. He formed there a coalition of Nationalists and Communists, the Vietnam League for Independence, known as Viet Minh (an abbreviation of the full Vietnamese names), destined to become the powerful instrument of struggle for the next thirty years. Imprisoned again when he crossed the frontier into China, he was released after a year under strange circumstances. Agreeing to throw his guerrillas against the Japanese forces occupying Vietnam and receiving funds and arms from his old enemies, the French and their American allies, he returned to Tonkin to lead the Viet Minh into action. When defeat became imminent, the Japanese followed their usual course of declaring Vietnam an independent state, appointing Emperor Bao Dai president. The Viet Minh was not deluded, continuing their struggle with growing strength. The war over in Europe and deserted by his Japanese allies, Emperor Dai abdicated on August 24, 1945. Ho Chi Minh took over.

Republic Proclaimed

The victorious powers met at Potsdam to decide the future of the world. They allocated the responsibility for north and south

Vietnam respectively to the Chinese National Army and the British Asia Command. Before their forces could arrive, however, the Viet Minh proclaimed the 'Democratic Republic of Vietnam', which began to function as a provisional government. The Chinese and British refrained from engaging the Viet Minh, but in Saigon the British rearmed the French. Guerrilla fighting was renewed throughout the south and, weakened by their war-time discords in Europe, the French had to compromise. An accord was signed with the Democratic Republic recognising it as a free state with its own legislative body, army and finance. The Vietnamese at first conceded that they should be part of the Indo-Chinese Federation within the French Union, but differences arose on the status of Cochin China in the south, the Viet Minh insisting that it should be a part of the Republic. While negotiations were continuing, the French set up a separate state and the talks ended. The French shelled Haiphong, the North's port; in December 1946, Viet Minh attacked French forces throughout Vietnam. The Indo-China war had begun.

French Defeated

The French, reflecting post-war opinion in Europe, did not want a colonial war. They went far to make concessions; the North and Cochin China would be permitted to become a single autonomous state of Vietnam within the French Union. Bao Dai, ready to compromise with the French as he had with the Japanese, agreed to form a provisional government, which was recognised by the USA and the United Kingdom in 1950 and subsequently by thirty-two other governments. But the Viet Minh was not now prepared for any association with France. The communist revolution in China provided arms (balanced by American arms for France) and it became more challenging, extending its activities to Laos and Cambodia. France, responding to anti-war feeling at home made more concessions, placing the administration, except for the security of its own forces, entirely in the hands of the Bao Dai government, which sought to gain popular support by announcing social reforms and universal elementary education; but still the guerrilla campaign of the Viet Minh could not be contained. Then came the final blow. A strong Viet Minh force besieged the French fortress of Dien Bien Phu and after fifty-three days captured it. The French were defeated beyond recovery.

Geneva Conference

Meanwhile the Geneva Conference (1954) on restoring peace in Indo-China was in session. It was authoritative and representative, including Anthony Eden from Britain and Molotov from the Soviet Union as joint chairmen, Bedell-Smith from the USA, Mendès-France from France and, despite non-membership of the United Nations, Chou En-lai from the Peoples' Republic of China. Delegates were also present from the Democratic Republic of Vietnam (Viet Minh), the State of Vietnam (Saigon), Cambodia and Laos. As remarkable as the membership was the political climate in which the conference met. For the first time since the surge of the Cold War there was a resurgence of a will to peace. Politicians and Press spoke and wrote of the 'new spirit of Geneva'. The conclusions of the Conference justified these expectations. Agreement was signed for the cessation of hostilities between France and the Democratic Republic of Vietnam and the governments of Cambodia and Laos, and a Declaration was accepted noting these agreements by Britain, the Soviet Union, France and China. The representative of the Saigon Government was not required to sign the document for the cessation of hostilities because the war was between France and Viet Minh, but he was involved by the French signature as Saigon was part of the French Union. Bedell-Smith for the USA made the dissentient statement that his government was not prepared to join in the Declaration, but added that America would 'refrain from the threat or the use of force' to disturb the agreements reached and would 'view any renewal of aggression in violation of the agreements . . . with grave concern and as seriously threatening international peace and security'. The US also reiterated its government's 'traditional position that people are entitled to determine their own future', said it would not 'join any arrangement which would hinder this', and renewed a decision made in Washington on June 29, 1954, that, in case of nations divided against their will, it sought to 'achieve unity through free elections' supervised by the United Nations.

We print the Declaration of the Geneva Conference as an appendix to this chapter. Important points to note are that it recognised:

> The independence, unity and territorial integrity of Vietnam (and of Cambodia and Laos).

The obligation of the governments represented at Geneva 'to refrain from any interference' in the internal affairs of Vietnam (and of Cambodia and Laos).

The provisional character of the military demarcation line between north and south Vietnam, which 'should not in any way be interpreted as constituting a political or territorial boundary'.

The provision for a general election in north and south Vietnam in July 1956, under the supervision of the International Supervisory Commission (the Agreement between France and the Democratic Republic stated that the purpose of this election was 'to bring about the unification of Vietnam').

The prohibition of 'the introduction into Vietnam of foreign troops and military personnel as well as of all kinds of arms and ammunitions' and of any 'military base under the control of a foreign state' in north and south Vietnam.

The obligation that neither north nor south Vietnam shall 'constitute part of any military alliance'.

The appointment of an International Supervisory and Control Commission, composed of representatives of India (chairman) Canada and Poland.[1] (Its terms of reference were stated in the agreement between France and the Democratic Republic as 'for the control and supervision over the application of the provisions of the agreement'.)

US Backs Saigon's Defiance

In 1955 Bao Dai was deposed by Ngo Dinh Diem as head of the Saigon Government and it soon became clear that there was no intention to apply the Geneva decision for an election in 1956 to unify Vietnam. Diem declined in 1955 to enter into the consultation for the preparation of the election which the Geneva Agreement required. His refusal was endorsed later by a US State Department Memorandum on the ground that 'the conditions in North Vietnam during the period were such as to make impossible any free and meaningful expression of popular will'. This justification ignored the fact that the International Control Commission was empowered to insist upon an election 'by secret ballot' and in conditions of 'respect for fundamental freedoms' and that it had invited consultation in order to safeguard these conditions. The

Commission continued to insist in subsequent years that the election provisions of the Geneva Agreement had not become obsolete and remarked as late as 1961 that 'no consultations had been held by the parties with a view to holding free nation-wide elections leading to the reunification of the country'.

The dominant aim of the Americans was to prevent a communist take-over of South Vietnam. In his *Mandate for Change* President Eisenhower wrote that all the experts with whom he had talked in this period believed Ho Chi Minh and the Viet Minh would have got at least eighty per cent of the votes if there had been an election in 1956. The USA welcomed Saigon's defiance of the Geneva decision. Not satisfied with giving moral support Washington assisted first by providing advisers, then instructors, then war materials. The State Department argued that until 1961 the US kept within the Geneva limitation of military personnel to seven hundred, but the International Control Commission repeatedly criticised American intervention and the non-co-operation of the Saigon and American authorities.[2] In its seventh Report, April 1957, the Commission complained that the South Vietnam Government did not ask for approval of the importation of war materials.

Meanwhile, Diem had established a ruthless dictatorship, suppressing non-communist opponents as well as Communists, abolishing village councils and reimposing feudal landownership with the extortion of exorbitant rents which had been repudiated at the end of the Second World War. This had a decisive effect on events. A peasants' revolt broke out which initiated civil war, the precursor of the wider war in which America became principally involved. In December 1960 peasant resisters and liberal opponents of the regime joined with Communists to form the National Liberation Front. The North Vietnam Government endorsed the NLF and some Viet Minh troops began to move south. Its military arm became known in America as the 'Vietcong' (Vietnam Communists) though in fact the NLF continued to include non-communist elements.

US Military Intervention

The USA then openly increased its military personnel and equipment beyond the limit of the Geneva Agreement. It was supported by a request from the Saigon Government, but the International Control Commission rejected both the request and the military aid as contrary to the Agreement and stated that they amounted to a military alliance, also prohibited by Geneva. America did not officially start military actions until February 1965; these were claimed to be in reprisal for a NLF attack on Saigon installations at Pleiku, during which seven Americans were killed, but before this US instructors had taken part in the bombing and burning of villages in South Vietnam and in defoliation operations.[3] After Pleiku, American attacks on North Vietnam began and from this point the USA was engaged in an undeclared war with the Democratic Republic. Before the end of 1966 over 380,000 US troops were in Vietnam, and later Australia, New Zealand and South Korea decided to send contingents. It had become a war of international intervention.

Diem had not lasted. The Americans themselves had to repudiate him and his repressive rule and he was overthrown by a military *coup* in Saigon and assassinated. Three months later the new government was destroyed by another *coup*, and a series of bewildering clique administrations, mostly military, followed, throwing doubt upon the authenticity of any government. In August 1964 General Nguyen Khan proclaimed himself President and Prime Minister, but there were demonstrations and a month later he had to form a civilian administration. That lasted three months, after which Kahn resumed absolute power, but only until February 1965, when he was ousted by Nguyen Cao Ky, Commander of the Air Force, and Nguyen Van Thieu, civilian politician. They succeeded in establishing a more stable government, although it still came into conflict with Buddhists and neutralists who desired peace. In September a 'constituent assembly' was elected (with severe political restrictions on electors and candidates) from among the considerable population who remained under Saigon authority. Thieu became Prime Minister and Ky's influence decreased. By this time the NLF had control of two-thirds of the territory of South Vietnam, though a majority of the people were under Saigon.

Congress Endorses War Actions

During the summer of 1965 there was some hope that an initiative would be taken for peace. U Thant proposed that the Geneva Conference should be reconvened to resolve the problems of Vietnam and South-East Asia; this was endorsed by the Soviet

Union and France and favourably received by Peking and Hanoi. But in August an incident occurred which had the opposite effect by decisively escalating rather than containing the war. The American Government announced that North Vietnamese torpedo boats had attacked two US destroyers in Tonkin Gulf and indignant Congress carried a resolution (unanimously in the House of Representatives, with two dissentients in the Senate) calling for retaliatory action and 'all necessary measures' to prevent aggression. The Congress had not so far authorised American 'war actions' in Vietnam. This resolution was accepted as the 'functional equivalent' of a declaration of war.

Ironically, in view of his subsequent attitude, it was Senator Fulbright, as chairman of the Foreign Relations Committee, who steered the resolution through Congress for President Johnson. He came deeply to regret this. In May 1966 he stated that suggestions had reached him that 'the whole affair was very questionable' and he summoned hearings of the Foreign Relations Committee. These indicated that the Government had drafted the resolution for Congress before the Tonkin Gulf incident, that unknown to Congress the US vessels were engaged on an 'intelligence mission', that they were within the twelve-mile limit accepted by North Vietnam (not by the US) as territorial waters, and that there was considerable doubt whether the alleged second and more serious attack on the American warships which gave rise to the Congress resolution had actually occurred. Senator Fulbright then said, 'I think it was very unfair to ask us to vote upon a resolution when the state of evidence was as uncertain as I think it is now. We have taken what is called the fundamental equivalent of a declaration of war upon evidence of this kind . . . Even the Commander (of the US warship) . . . recommended that nothing be done until the evidence was further evaluated.' Nine of the nineteen members of the Foreign Relations Committee took the view that the Administration had over-reacted after the Tonkin Gulf naval incidents, that it had withheld very important facts and that it had been less than candid in presenting others. The US retort had been sixty-four bombing attacks on North Vietnam.

NLF Peace Initiative and Paris Talks

In August 1967 came the first signs of a breakthrough towards possible negotiations. The National Liberation Front, with the endorsement of the North, announced a programme which included free elections by universal suffrage in South Vietnam, a democratic National Assembly, a broad government of national union, freedom of speech, publication, assembly and religious belief, the gradual reunification of North and South by peaceful agreement, and neutrality in foreign affairs. The reasonableness of this programme, despite a preamble strongly denouncing American aggression, led to speculation about discussions. In March 1970 the US announced a limitation of the bombing of North Vietnam, and three days later Hanoi stated its willingness to meet American representatives 'to determine . . . the unconditional cessation of US bombing raids and all acts of war against the Democratic Republic of Vietnam so that talks can begin'. This offer was one-sided, but it did bring the breakthrough.

Early in 1968, the Democratic Republic and the NLF agreed to enter uncommitted discussion with representatives of the USA and of the Saigon Government in Paris. They met on May 13, but it was not until January 18, 1969, eight months later, after President Johnson had completely stopped the bombing of the North and a conflict about the NLF and Saigon representation had been settled, that the four-party discussion began. At meeting after meeting there was frustration, the Americans insisting that the withdrawal of their troops must be reciprocated by North Vietnamese withdrawals from the South, a proposal rejected on the grounds that America was the aggressor and that the Geneva Agreement had recognised the territorial unity of all Vietnam and required the the withdrawal of foreign troops. The atmosphere was made worse by the intensification of the US bombing in the South. In despair of resolving the problem, President Johnson announced that he would not stand for re-election. When President Nixon became Head of State he was expected to be less conciliatory, but a wave of protest was rising in America and he pledged himself to bring the war to an end.

Proposals by Both Sides

The Paris talks proceeded with seeming futility, but on May 8, 1969, the NLF again aroused hope among moderate people by elaborating its 1967 programme in Ten-Point Proposals. They included the suggestion that between the restoration of peace and the election of a Constituent Assembly a provisional coalition government should be formed by negotiations between 'political forces representing various social strata standing for peace, independence and neutrality'. The objectives of the provisional government would include not only the implementation under international supervision of the unconditional withdrawal of US and allied troops and war material but healing the wounds of war and outlawing acts of reprisal. Negotiations would be authorised for the return of prisoners. America was required to accept responsibility for the destruction it had inflicted.

A week later, May 15, 1969, President Nixon replied with Eight Points for a settlement. He proposed that over a twelve months' period the major portions of US and allied forces should be withdrawn and that the remaining forces should move to complete their withdrawal 'as the remaining North Vietnamese forces were withdrawn'. The proposals for international supervision and elections were accepted and the release of prisoners on both sides was required 'as soon as possible'. Both sides would be committed to the Geneva accords. President Nixon made no reference to the suggestion that a provisional coalition government should be set up.

It will be seen that the fundamental difference between the two sides was whether North Vietnamese troops should be withdrawn from South Vietnam simultaneously with American and allied troops or whether the latter should be withdrawn unconditionally. Despite this, the two approaches would seem to have provided a basis for positive discussion at the Paris talks; the difficulty was that the USA was confined in negotiations by its identity with Saigon, which rejected any suggestion of a coalition government with NLF representatives, although it did agree to an American suggestion that a commission including NLF representatives should be made responsible for preparing an election (rejected by the NLF because it regarded the Saigon Government as US puppets). Hope was renewed when Hanoi proposed direct negotiations with the US, but this was sabotaged by Saigon.

US Partial Withdrawal

President Nixon endeavoured to meet the opposition at home by announcing that US troops would be progressively withdrawn and responsibility handed over to the increasing Saigon forces.[4] From 1969 to 1971 half of the American ground force was withdrawn but its air force was left intact and American arms poured in and instructors remained. The troop withdrawals muted to some extent the popular opposition to the war so that even its extension into Cambodia in 1970 and into Laos in 1971 did not arouse the demonstrations of the previous year. The President assured the public that these actions were necessary to destroy 'Vietcong' supplies and pierce the Ho Chi Minh trail through which North Vietnamese troops moved to the South, thus facilitating the homecoming of American men; but informed opinion became increasingly uneasy. The incursion into Cambodia was accompanied by civil war there and the invasion of Laos met sterner opposition than expected. The earlier prospects of peace disappeared, and a settlement was made more difficult because, in effect, the conflict between Communism and American-supported regimes became extended to the whole of Indo-China. The reaction in China was fierce and any Russian contribution to moderation was nullified.

Death of Ho Chi Minh

In September 1969, Ho Chi Minh had died. There was some hope in official circles in America and Britain that this might lead to a more conciliatory attitude. The determination of the North Vietnamese was underestimated. Nothing except the withdrawal of the troops of America and its allies would satisfy. Two changes polarised the conflict. In Saigon Thieu strengthened the more die-hard representatives in his government and in South Vietnam the NLF established a Revolutionary People's Government and promoted its delegates at Paris as its representatives. They spelled out in detail the peace proposals which the NLF had made and indicated their readiness to join a coalition so long as it excluded Thieu and Ky.

An event occurred in March 1971 which was significant for the future of the war. When the American and Saigon military leaders decided to invade Laos, they planned that the newly-developed South Vietnamese army should provide the ground forces, heavily armed with modern US weapons, and that America should supply massive air support. Despite heavy bombing attacks from US planes and ceaseless transport by helicopters, the South Vietnamese fell back in confusion. This experience aroused doubts whether Vietnamisation, even with US air and arms support, would be equal to holding the North Vietnamese and NLF forces.

Secret Negotiations

On January 25 President Nixon startled America and the world by revealing that for thirty months secret negotiations had been carried on between Dr Kissinger, National Security Affairs Adviser at the White House, and two North Vietnamese representatives, Dr Le Duc Tho, from Hanoi, and Xuan Thuy, head of the delegation at the Paris talks. Washington had offered a peace plan which included (1) withdrawal of all US and allied forces from South Vietnam six months after agreement (November 1, 1971, for agreement, May 1, 1972, for withdrawal), (2) an exchange of all prisoners, (3) a cease-fire throughout Indo-China, (4) the resignation of President Thieu and Vice-President Ky one month before presidential elections conducted under international supervision by a body representing all political forces in South Vietnam, including the 'Vietcong'. Reparation for war damages was refused, but aid in reconstruction of the whole of Indo-China, to the extent of 'several billions of dollars', was offered. America promised neutrality in the proposed election and a limitation of the aid to Saigon if North Vietnam limited the aid received from 'its friends' (presumably Russia and China). For the first time the US had not made its withdrawal dependent upon North Vietnamese withdrawal from the South.

During the negotiations the North Vietnamese presented alternative proposals in a nine-point plan. According to Dr Kissinger, they called for the immediate resignation of President Thieu and Vice-President Ky, the unconditional withdrawal of military forces (that is irrespective of other agreements) on a fixed date, the ending of all military and economic assistance to Saigon and the removal of all military equipment, including that in the hands of the South Vietnamese army. In Paris the North Vietnamese delegations complained bitterly that the Americans had unilaterally reported negotiations which both sides had agreed to keep secret. They rejected the Americans plan in broad terms, but did not appear to close the door to further negotiations.

One of the major weaknesses of the American plan lay in the fact that, even after the resignation of Thieu and Ky, the basic administration at Saigon would remain. *The Times* (27.2.72) remarked that the Americans would 'keep in power the existing government, requiring only that the President and Vice President should resign one month beforehand and that the caretaker head of the government should be the present head of the Senate'. It pointed out that 'this would leave the South Vietnamese army and administration, right down to village level, still in effect answerable to President Thieu' and 'thus the independent body supervising the elections on which Communists and others would be represented would have little direct power'.

A vicious accompaniment to the publication of America's peace terms was the launching of an unprecedented bombing attack on North Vietnam by the US from Thailand and from aircraft carriers in the Gulf of Tonkin. Nevertheless, the differences between the two sides seemed to many to be negotiable. The North Vietnamese earlier proposed that a provisional government should be established prior to the elections representing all strata of society. True they would have excluded Thieu and Ky, but President Thieu had repeatedly rejected any coalition and, since he had agreed to resign before an election to permit a coalition commission to run it, no principle was involved in the suggestion that he should retire to allow a provisional coalition to prepare conditions for the election.

In May 1972 the hope of peace seemed to be shattered by a vast escalation of the war. The North Vietnamese and NLF forces began assaults in South Vietnam which seriously threatened the ability of Saigon to continue the war. They attacked simultaneously on three fronts – north, centre and south – and swept the South Vietnamese before them, confirming the earlier Laos doubts about the morale of the troops to whom America had handed over ground fighting. Hue, the second town in South Vietnam, and An Loc, only sixty miles from Saigon, were surrounded and large parts destroyed. For several days it appeared that overwhelming defeat was imminent, with troops and refugees fleeing chaotically. However, two events held back the North Vietnam–NLF final assaults. Saigon sent in its last regular troops, who were more experienced and dependable than recent conscripts, and America continuously poured down bombs from jets taking off from aircraft carriers on the coast, as well as from Thailand. The American bombing had far more effect than previously because guerrilla fighting had been replaced by mass formations.

Washington reacted to this crisis on a larger scale than ever before. US naval vessels mined the approaches to the port of Haiphong where war materials from Russia and other countries were unloaded. At the same time bombing attacks on an unprecedented level were concentrated on the rail supply routes from China and on transport communications in North Vietnam which could be used to convey arms or men to the South. Bombing of military targets was extended to industries which could serve war purposes. The bombing was ceaseless and inevitably countless civilians and hospitals and schools were struck. This enlargement of the war could have little effect on the immediate battles in South Vietnam nor was it likely to weaken the resolve of the North Vietnamese or to prevent considerable arms reaching them; but the effect in destruction and death was only less than nuclear annihilation.

President Nixon did not only order this massive military escalation. At the same time he offered terms of peace which went beyond earlier proposals. He pledged America to withdraw its troops within four months of an agreement for an internationally supervised cease-fire and the return of American prisoners of war. For a second time the condition of withdrawal of North Vietnamese troops from the South was not included. These terms were not accepted; the resignation of President Thieu and General Ky was still demanded. But the North Vietnamese and NLF delegations in Paris called for a resumption of the peace talks (America had again withdrawn) and emphasised that they had no intention of insisting on a settlement which would humiliate Washington.

These events cannot be separated from President Nixon's summit talks in Moscow which immediately followed them. It was surprising that the talks took place at all. In Vietnam America was at war with Russia's ally and American soldiers were being killed by Russian arms. That the visit proceeded after the American mining of Haiphong to prevent the arrival of Russian ships indicated how deeply both sides desired to improve relations. The conflict in Vietnam could not be excluded from these talks, even though the discussions began pragmatically with exchanges on technology, space co-operation and missile restriction. The Moscow meeting, following President Nixon's visit to Peking, must have had a deep, and perhaps decisive, effect on the progress of peace in Vietnam. It gave grounds for hope that, despite the worsening of hostilities, serious negotiations were beginning.[5]

World Reaction

In Britain, the Labour Government had supported Washington and Saigon, privately urging moderation but only once venturing to express regret publicly when Hanoi and Haiphong were bombed, but this support was in defiance of its own party and progressive opinion. The Labour Party annual delegate conference, the Trade Union Congress and the Co-operative Party representing all sections of the Labour Movement, as well as the Liberal Party, were united in asking that Britain should dissociate itself from America. In Opposition, after defeat by the Tories, the Labour Party was more forthright. Its Executive called on the US to fix a target date for the withdrawal of its troops and in Parliament the Party voted against the Government when it declined to dissociate itself from the mine-laying at Haiphong and the massive bombing of Hanoi and the North in May 1972. In Australia and New Zealand the Labour Oppositions were strong in denouncing the dispatch of troops to Vietnam; in Australia the party had sensational victories in an election contested largely on this issue, only narrowly failing to get the majority necessary to form a government.[6] Throughout the world, as we have recorded in Chapter 3, opinion against the war was impressive. Combined agitation was planned through an international committee at Stockholm.

American Reaction

In America itself there were few people who did not think that a great mistake had been made. This was implicitly acknowledged when President Johnson announced that America accepted the Geneva Agreement; if it had done so at Geneva itself and co-operated in applying it the war would never have occurred. Modern history has not seen the people of a country at war so massively opposed to its prosecution as Americans demonstrated; perhaps the nearest parallel was the opposition of the people of Russia to the First World War towards its end. Washington reported in 1970 that over 53,000 soldiers had deserted, to which must be added thousands of draft resisters, a total of nearly ten per cent of the forces engaged. The dilemma which confronted President Nixon was to get out of the war without losing face. It was much to expect that America should publicly acknowledge that she had been wrong, although General de Gaulle in effect did so for France when he recognised the independence of Algeria after a seven years' war to prevent it.

Historic

The Vietnam war will remain historic for two reasons. First, it proved that a small nation comparatively undeveloped and with limited and borrowed war equipment could hold at bay the most powerful industrial and military nation on earth using the most modern devices of destruction short of nuclear weapons. This must have a profound effect in the future on the attitudes and actions of both emerging peoples and the greater Powers. Secondly, it convinced America that it could no longer act by the use of its troops as a policeman of the world. The influence of this in limiting military imperialism may be profound.

Cambodia

Cambodia and Laos, western neighbours of Vietnam, were included with Vietnam in the colonialist state of Indo-China which the French consolidated onwards from 1887. It was 1914 before the overall *Conseil de Gouvernement* was established and 1928 before budgetary issues were co-ordinated under a Grand Council. Even then there were separate representative institutions. A popular sense of belonging to Indo-China as a nation was never created.

France Claims Suzerainty

The first Europeans to attempt to seize control of Cambodia were, as usual in South-East Asia, the Portuguese and Spanish, trading invaders who arrived at the end of the sixteenth century. In the nineteenth century Siam (now Thailand) and France were rivals for control. France claimed suzerainty after occupying nearby southern Vietnam in 1862 and the following year forced the king of Cambodia to accept protectorate status. In 1867 Siam concurred, but was allowed to retain two western provinces (reunited with Cambodia after the First World War). There were revolts by the people in 1866 and 1887, typically at this period in protest against the limitation of the prerogatives of their traditional kings, regarded as symbols of nationhood.

When Japan occupied Cambodia in the Second World War a modern nationalist movement of resistance, *Khmer Issarek* (Free Cambodia) arose, supported by the de Gaullist French as a fifth column; there was also some resistance to the occupation by small groups of Communists. At the end of the war this division remained in the nationalist movement. *Khmer Issarek*, whilst opposing the return of French authority, attached its nationalism to monarchical rights, whilst the Communists stood for the end of feudalism in a republic. The French clung to power, but, encouraging allegiance to royalty in order to by-pass any communist challenge, agreed to a new constitution in May 1947 extending self-government based on constitutional monarchy. Two years later, the French agreed to independence within the French Union.

Geneva Establishes Independence

The more radical Nationalists regarded this as paper independence. The Viet Minh in North Vietnam, accepting Indo-China as a base for extending their activities, linked with them in a guerrilla war for internal revolution as well as absolute independence. Serious civil conflict was avoided only by the Geneva Conference of 1954 which established the independence of Cambodia;[7] both the French and Viet Minh undertook to withdraw. Immediately a paradoxical situation arose which suggested that the monarchy was not as far from the people as the Communists alleged. King Norodom Sihanouk announced his conversion to Socialism, formed the Socialist People's Communist Party, and won every seat in a general election held in September 1955. His first decision was to secede entirely from France and to identify himself with the Afro-Asian policy of neutralism. In 1960 he renounced kingship, becoming Head of State in a republic, and proved that his Socialism was not merely deceptive diplomacy by introducing a five-year development plan of radical agrarian reform and of socialisation of community services. Both West and East Powers, eager for influence, gave him economic aid.

The Vietnam war, however, continually threatened Cambodia's progress. Thailand and South Vietnam (Saigon) charged Cambodia with Communism and there were frontier incidents, particularly with American forces when North Vietnam used a corridor to dispatch arms and troops to the NLF. Sihanouk tried to reconvene the Geneva Conference to secure Cambodia's neutrality and territorial integrity, but failed. Following this, relations with America deteriorated. Sihanouk charged the US Central Intelligence Agency with inciting a reactionary rebellion, complained of the bombing of Cambodian territory and in 1963 renounced all aid from Washington; in 1965 diplomatic relations were broken off. At the same time contacts with France under de Gaulle's conciliatory policy towards the East and with China improved.

Sihanouk Deposed

Crisis came in 1970. Whilst Sihanouk was paying a visit to the Soviet Union, the Cambodian National Assembly deposed him and appointed General Lon Nol as his successor. The general had the support of army officers and of the urban population of Phnom-Penh, the capital, and there was little doubt of American support spread through the CIA. Sihanouk proceeded from Moscow to China, where he was hailed as Cambodia's legitimate head, and proceeded to form a national Government-in-Exile. Civil war broke out in Cambodia itself, with much of the countryside backing their desposed leader, and the Vietnamese resistance giving their support. Following this, American and Saigon forces invaded Cambodia to destroy North Vietnam and NLF bases. The Americans withdrew, claiming that their mission had been accomplished, but throughout Cambodia the war extended with varying fortunes. Cambodia became a Vietnam.

General Lon Nol ruled with assumed power. He stripped the National Assembly of legislative rights in October 1971, and instructed its members to draft a new constitution. They called for a return of legislative authority to their Assembly and an elected Parliament. In March 1972 Lon Nol asserted absolute power, dismissing his Cabinet and announcing that he would introduce strong presidential government responsible for restoring law and order. He said that his first object was 'to chase the enemy out of the country', but in fact forces supporting Sihanouk were making formidable progress backed heavily by communist troops from Vietnam. The fate of Cambodia was in the balance.[8]

Laos

A Dutch merchant was the first-known European to arrive in Laos in 1641, but until the nineteenth century its independence was assaulted more by Siam (Thailand) and Vietnam than by European traders or governments.

French Protectorate

By the end of the century France, dominant in Vietnam, drove back the Siamese and in 1899 the territory except for some western provinces became a French Protectorate. At the end of the Japanese war-time occupation, there was division as to whether France should return. The king favoured France, but the brother Princes, Souvanna Phouma and Souphanouvong, formed the *Lao Issara* (Free Laotian Party) to demand independence. France responded by granting limited self-government within the French Union and instituting a royalist regime. This split *Lao Issara*, Souvanna prepared to work within the constitution, Souphanouvong breaking away to form the pro-communist *Pathet Lao* (Lao Nation), with a guerrilla army backed by Viet Minh and its groups in Cambodia. Once more the French made concessions, establishing virtual self-government, and Souvanna Phouma won the subsequent elections. The Americans gave him considerable support, despite his neutralism, with the object of defeating the Communists.

Civil War Between Three Armies

At the 1954 Geneva Conference there was temporary partition as in Vietnam. The *Pathet Lao* agreed to withdraw to northern provinces (Phong Saly and Sam Neua) until party differences could be tested in a general election. But antagonisms persisted. The Government and *Pathet Lao* could not agree about the elections and the *de facto* partition of the country became accepted. In 1956, however, when Souvanna Phouma took Laos out of the French Union, the *Pathet Lao* not only agreed to reunite its provinces and to integrate its forces with the Laotian army but its leaders also consented to become Ministers in a coalition administration. Again this national reunion was short-lived, the *Pathet Lao* reasserting its claims to the northern provinces. Then came the decisive event. There was an election in 1960 which was recognised by all objective observers as fraudulent. Royalist candidates with American aid swept the board, followed by the arrest of Souphanouvong and his associates, imprisonment avoided by their escape into North Vietnam. From this moment there was almost continual civil war with three armies involved, royalist, neutralist and communist. A revived Geneva conference in 1961 proposed a Swiss federal pattern for Laos with neutrality, but the war went on.

Saigon–American Invasion

In June 1962 there was still another effort for peace. A pact was
signed for a three-party coalition government with Souvanna
Phouma in the middle position as prime minister. This was confirmed by a reconvened Geneva Conference in July, which recognised the neutrality of Laos, and in November there was actually
an agreement on paper to integrate the three military forces. But
once more it did not happen. Guerrilla warfare recurred and in 1964
the *Pathet Lao* took possession of the crucial Plain of Jars. There
was a further attempt to reach agreement in the early autumn of
1964 in Paris, but again failure with an attempted royalist *coup* in
Vientiane. Uncertainty persisted, with the added complication of
US bombing of North Vietnamese supply routes and the incursion
of American troops in the autumn of 1969 to repel the *Pathet Lao*.

In 1971 American and Saigon intervention occurred on a large
and open scale with the object of destroying the 'Ho Chi Minh'
trail. A large South Vietnamese force with American tanks and
artillery invaded Laos, backed by massive American air support.
It met with an unexpected and strong counterattack. The Souvanna
Government condemned the invasion as a violation of the neutrality
of Laos, at the same time condemning communist penetration.

The truth was that neither side paid a jot of regard for the
sovereignty of Laos. Throughout the war American bombers flew
over the territory from Thailand to attack the Communists in
Vietnam and the Communists used its territory to feed the south
with arms and men. Laos in 1971 became inseparable from the
Vietnam war. Its destiny is inseparable from its conclusion.[9]

Notes

1. The official title was 'the International Commission for
Supervision and Control in Vietnam', but it became known as 'the
International Control Commission' (ICC).

2. Reports for 1955, 1956 and 1957. The Memorandum of the
State Department did not quote these criticisms, but stated that the
'considerable military equipment and supplies' provided to Saigon
had been reported to the ICC and were replacements.

3. *New York Times*, March 29, 1962, and March 28, 1965.

4. Critics in America were not impressed. Even Averill Harriman, who had been the chief US delegate at Paris, remarked: 'I think it is absolutely wrong to Vietnamese the war. We should attempt to Vietnamese the making of peace.'

5. The world was startled on the eve of the American Presidential election (November 1, 1972) by the Hanoi publication of the terms of a cease-fire agreement with Washington. Nixon did not disown the agreement, and his promises of an end to the war and the return of the American prisoners undoubtedly contributed to his overwhelming victory. Officially the Government said that some differences remained; these were soon seen to be objections by Saigon. Whilst talks proceeded, there was an amazing escalation of the war. North Vietnam and the NLF made an all-out attack on the approaches to Saigon, aiming to gain control of territory before a cease-fire. America retorted by the heaviest bombing of North Vietnam, by the re-mining of its ports, and by donating to the Saigon Government large supplies of military equipment, including bombing planes. Nevertheless, negotiations went on and at midnight, January 27, 1973, the cease-fire officially came into operation.

We must refer readers to other publications for the detailed terms of the agreement, but many asked how it was that accord could be reached in 1973 when the positions between the two sides were little further apart than in 1968 and, indeed, 1967. Fundamentally, the biggest concession by America was its signature to the declaration (as in the Geneva Agreement of 1954) respecting the unity and territorial integrity of Vietnam. What, many asked, had the war been about? There are doubts, at the time of writing, how far peace will be attainable in Cambodia and Laos, and still more doubts how far both sides will maintain the terms of agreement in Vietnam. Thieu has enormous American arms, his air force is now said to be the fourth largest in the world and charges that North Vietnam continued hostilities in strategic places may lead to renewed American intervention.

There are two statistical addenda to add to this unfinished story of the greatest human crime since World War Two. First, whilst in that war 80,000 tons of German bombs fell on Britain, the USA between 1965 and 1973 (omitting the holocaust of November–December) dropped more than 7,000,000 tons of bombs on Vietnam (*The Times*, 20.12.73), Second, the number of American servicemen who died in action in Indo-china from January 1, 1961 to January 27, 1973, was 45,941. The number wounded was 300,365;

the missing or prisoners were 1,811 (US Command). The Vietnamese casualties must have been far greater.

6. In January 1973 the Labour Parties in both Australia and New Zealand won General Elections and revised the Vietnam policy of their previous Governments.

7. Agreements were signed by the French at Geneva applying to Cambodia the same terms as contained in the Vietnam agreement, omitting only the transitional arrangements for the military withdrawal at the 17th Parallel.

8. The Vietnam ceasefire was not respected in Cambodia and Laos. In Cambodia communist forces surrounded Phnom-penh, American jets bombed them, and South Vietnamese troops invaded. Politically important was an agreement by the Communists to support Sihanouk. In Laos fighting was also continued, though on a smaller scale.

9. See Note 8 above.

Declaration of Geneva Conference

(Endorsed on July 21, 1954, by representatives of France, the United Kingdom, the Soviet Union and the People's Republic of China.)

1. The Conference takes note of the agreements ending hostilities in Cambodia, Laos and Vietnam and organising international control and the supervision of the execution of the provisions of these agreements.

2. The Conference expresses satisfaction at the ending of hostilities in Cambodia, Laos and Vietnam; the Conference expresses its conviction that the execution of the provisions set out in the present declaration and in the agreements on the cessation of hostilities will permit Cambodia, Laos and Vietnam henceforth to play their part, in full independence and sovereignty, in the peaceful community of nations.

3. The Conference takes note of the declarations made by the Governments of Cambodia and of Laos of their intention to adopt measures permitting all citizens to take their place in the national community, in particular by participating in the next general elections, which, in conformity with the constitution of each of these countries, shall take place in the course of the year 1955, by secret ballot and in conditions of respect for fundamental freedoms.

4. The Conference takes note of the clauses in the agreement on the cessation of hostilities in Vietnam prohibiting the introduction into Vietnam of foreign troops and military personnel as well as of all kinds of arms and munitions. The Conference also takes note of the declarations made by the governments of Cambodia and Laos of their resolution not to request foreign aid, whether in war material, in personnel or in instructors except for the purpose of the effective defence of their territory and, in the case of Laos, to the extent defined by the agreements on the cessation of hostilities in Laos.

5. The Conference takes note of the clauses in the agreement on the cessation of hostilities in Vietnam to the effect that no military

base under the control of a foreign state may be established in the regrouping zones of the two parties, the latter having the obligation to see that zones allotted to them shall not constitute part of any military alliance and shall not be utilised for the resumption of hostilities or in the service of an aggressive policy. The Conference also takes note of the declarations of the governments of Cambodia and Laos to the effect that they will not join in any agreement with other states if this agreement includes the obligation to participate in a military alliance not in conformity with the principles of the Charter of the United Nations or, in the case of Laos, with the principles of the agreement on the cessation of hostilities in Laos, or, so long as their security is not threatened, the obligation to establish bases on Cambodian or Laotian territory for the military forces of foreign powers.

6. The Conference recognises that the essential purpose of the agreement relating to Vietnam is to settle military questions with a view to ending hostilities and that the military demarcation line is provisional and should not in any way be interpreted as constituting a political or territorial boundary. The Conference expresses its conviction that the execution of the provisions set out in the present declaration and in the agreement on the cessation of hostilities creates the necessary basis for the achievement in the near future of a political settlement in Vietnam.

7. The Conference declares that, so far as Vietnam is concerned, the settlement of political problems, effected on the basis of respect for the principles of independence, unity and territorial integrity, shall permit Vietnamese people to enjoy the fundamental freedoms, guaranteed by democratic institutions established as a result of free general elections by secret ballot. In order to ensure that sufficient progress in the restoration of peace has been made, and that all the necessary conditions obtain for free expression of the national will, general elections shall be held in July 1956, under the supervision of an international commission composed of representatives of the Member States of the International Supervisory Commission, referred to in the agreement on the cessation of hostilities. Consultations will be held on this subject between the competent representative authorities of the two zones from 20th July 1955 onwards.

8. The provisions of the agreements on the cessation of hostilities intended to ensure the protection of individuals and of property must be most strictly applied and must, in particular, allow everyone in Vietnam to decide freely in which zone he wishes to live.

9. The competent representative authorities of the Northern and Southern zones of Vietnam, as well as the authorities of Laos and Cambodia, must not permit any individual or collective reprisals against persons who have collaborated in any way with one of the parties during the war, or against members of such persons' families.

10. The Conference takes note of the declaration of the government of the French Republic to the effect that it is ready to withdraw its troops from the territory of Cambodia, Laos and Vietnam, at the request of the governments concerned and within periods which shall be fixed by agreement between the parties except in the cases where, by agreement between the two parties, a certain number of French troops shall remain at specified points and for a specified time.

11. The Conference takes note of the declaration of the French government to the effect that for the settlement of all the problems connected with the re-establishment and consolidation of peace in Cambodia, Laos and Vietnam, the French government will proceed from the principle of respect for the independence and sovereignty, unity and territorial integrity of Cambodia, Laos and Vietnam.

12. In their relations with Cambodia, Laos and Vietnam, each member of the Geneva Conference, undertakes to respect the sovereignty, the independence, the unity and the territorial integrity of the above-mentioned states, and to refrain from any interference in their internal affairs.

13. The members of the Conference agree to consult one another on any question which may be referred to them by the International Supervisory Commission in order to study such measures as may prove necessary to ensure that the agreements on the cessation of hostilities in Cambodia, Laos and Vietnam are respected.

Chapter Eight

Western Asia:
The Middle East
(The Arab Nations and
Israel)

Western Asia, or the Middle East (as Britain rather arrogantly called it, regarding itself as the centre of the world) has throughout history, by reason of its geographical position, been the object of raids, prolonged occupations, rivalries, disputes and actual conflicts by European and Asian powers. In the past the Arabs have been the subjects of Rome, Constantinople, Paris and even marauding Mongolian tribes.

European Domination

Influenced by the French Revolution, Mehemet Ali led the first successful nationalist revolt against Turkish rule in the early nineteenth century, but its prospective success was soon severely curtailed. Thereafter the English and French slowly dominated the area to extend and defend their commercial, strategic and political interests, including the route to the East. In 1901, the British Government bought its first interests in Persian (Iranian) oil and in 1914 secured a controlling interest. It had signed a treaty with Russia in 1907 which recognised its involvement, but the Soviet revolution necessitated a new alliance if this oil power was to be safeguarded, and the Government reacted by proposing a treaty based on £2 million of military aid and assistance to rebuild the Iranian army. However, when Britain, weary of war, refused to intervene against a Russian invasion in 1920, the Persians withdrew from negotiations and in 1932 they ended London's oil monopoly. Thereafter Britain co-operated with Germany, France, Holland and the USA in oil exploitation while retaining significant political influence. The Turkish alliance with Germany during the First World War gave Britain and France, following victory, the opportunity to divide the area of the Middle East into respective spheres of influence and so assume peaceful occupation. This was arranged

through the Sykes–Picot correspondence, which reflected a strong
commitment to increased colonial and imperial possession.

Palestine Promised To Jews

In a similar vein, if also for other reasons, the British Government
in a letter from A. J. Balfour, Foreign Secretary, to Lord Roths-
child, leader of the Jewish community in England, agreed in 1917
to the principle of a national home for Jews in Palestine.[1] Although
the British Cabinet was partly motivated by genuine sympathy for
the desperate Jewish position in Europe, their prime purpose was
strategic and political. This promise ensured that the Jews would
be allies during the war and that henceforth there would be a
European population, a vanguard of sorts, which could be relied
upon in an alien area. But this declaration repudiated the pledge
given by Sir Henry MacMahon, the British High Commissioner
in Egypt, to Hussein, Sharif of Mecca, 'to recognise the independence of the Arabs' (a promise given to encourage the Arabs'
revolt against the Turks in 1916). Contradictory promises were
given because the situation demanded assurances to anyone who
could facilitate (or, if not satisfied, could prevent) the consolidation
of the British position following the war.

Peace Conference Mandates

At the Peace Conference in 1919 France was granted mandates to
Syria and Lebanon, while Palestine, Jordan and Iraq were granted
to Britain. In the Palestine mandate agreement between Britain
and the League of Nations the Balfour Declaration was explicitly
incorporated, while the Arab population, which amounted to
ninety per cent of the inhabitants in the area, were referred to as
'other sections of the population'. In Syria and Lebanon, where
France had traded since the Crusades and which she consequently
considered to be within her sphere of influence, the open recognition of this in 1919 by the League of Nations mandate was
resented by the peoples. Emir Feisal, the Syrian ruler, having failed
to dislodge the French by negotiation, was in turn driven out by
their army (the British later made him king of Iraq). In 1925 violent
revolt broke out as nationalist groups campaigned for independence; the following year Léon Blum's Popular Front in France

was prepared to concede Syrian demands, but its brief existence prevented any fulfilment of this approach. At the fall of France in 1940 in the Second World War, the position in its mandatory territories was tenuous, but de Gaulle decided to 'administer' them from London, promising independence once France was victorious. Arab sympathy for the Axis powers and a revolt in Iraq, however, stimulated an English invasion in June, 1941, to forestall an enemy advance, and by 1945 France, despite de Gaulle's promises, proved reluctant to grant independence and repressed Syrian and Lebanese nationalist demonstrations. France and Britain only withdrew the following year when subjected to pressure in the United Nations.

As stated above, Britain was alloted mandates at the Peace Conference in 1919 over Iraq, Jordan and Palestine. Because of military opposition and riots, Britain in fact refrained from establishing administration in Iraq and substituted in 1922 a treaty of alliance with its own nominee, Emir Feisal, as king. It was agreed that Iraq should have full independence as soon as possible and this was accorded in 1931 (to the disgust of British officials on the spot), followed by a preferential agreement, with a British base and military mission. Transjordan, east of the river, had formed part of Syria from November 1918 to July 1920, but came under British administration after Feisal had been deposed by the French. The British put Emir Abdullah on the throne (with a monthly subsidy of £5,000) to perpetuate their strength and forestall any other power's influence. Abdullah ruled aided by British advisers, and in 1928 conceded the Anglo-Transjordanian agreement giving Britain supreme authority. By 1940 British subsidies exceeded £2 million per annum, developing roads and a relatively strong army. During the Second World War Britain agreed to Transjordan's independence as the state of Jordan, concluding in 1946 a treaty similar to that with Iraq. The military aspects were modified in 1948 when new agreements with Iraq and Egypt were concluded. In 1949 the subsidy from London to the Arab Legion amounted to £3·5 million, but the British position was severely weakened by Abdullah's assassination in June 1951.

The Fatal Division

Britain's Mandate in Palestine was controversial from the outset and out of it arose the confrontation in the Middle East. Jews had occupied Palestine from 1800 BC until about AD 135, but it was only in 1897 in Basle that the territory was claimed in political terms as the 'Promised Land' (Zionism). In the intervening 1,700 years the one connection religious Jews had with Palestine was in their prayers.[2] It was therefore a great *coup* for the representatives of Zionism to accomplish the first part of their mission within twenty years; the assurance of a National Home in Palestine. From then until 1947 many Europeans sympathised with the Jewish desire to be free of persecution, and there could have been no more appropriate nomination of a place of refuge than their ancient Biblical home with which many were emotionally deeply identified.

Naturally, however, only the European point of view was considered and few paid attention to the near total Arab opposition towards the envisaged occupation. In fact, few in Britain were aware either of Arab nationalism or of the dedication of the Zionists to colonise Palestine. They might have read in the King–Crane Report of 1919 that ninety per cent of the Palestinian population opposed further Jewish immigration, but it had been suppressed at the Peace Conference and consequently was ignored. Confusion added to the difficulties. It was not clear whether Balfour had intimated Palestine as a Jewish *national* home or a home in Palestine for the Jews. Consequently, throughout the Mandate, the British representatives in the Middle East disastrously attempted to pursue undefined compromise with contradictory policies, becoming the common enemy of both Arab and Jew, thereby creating an irreconcilable situation.

Arab Resistance

Although very few Jews emigrated to Palestine during the 1920s, the violent Arab opposition to them indicated the problem of integration. Britain's attempts to find solutions were a succession of Royal Commissions whose recommendations were consistently rejected. The new immigrants came as colonisers to establish an exclusive society, many living on land purchased from absentee landlords by the Zionist Commission; the occupants of the land were evicted and as a rule only Jewish labour could be employed. Zionism at first found comparatively little support among Jews in Europe except in terms of financial aid and it was only the advent of the Nazis in 1933 which gave the stimulus to emigration. As it increased, so did the conflict between Jews and Arabs, resulting in a bloody Arab revolt in 1936 which lasted until 1939. Thereafter the communities openly engaged in a war of attrition, with the frustrated British suffocated in between.

In 1939, with another war approaching, the British renewed their quest for allies in the Middle East. The Jews were certain allies against the Germans, so the Arabs were to be bought off with a White Paper. A previous suggestion by the Peel Commission for the partition of Palestine had been rejected by Jews and Arabs. For the former there was insufficient provision of land, while for the latter the principle of European colonisation was abhorrent; the White Paper's proposal to limit Jewish immigration and its declaration that Palestine should not become a Jewish state were not sufficient to satisfy the Arabs. Neither side wished to underplay their claims; thus whilst the Jewish Agency criticised the White Paper for 'putting the Jewish population at the mercy of the majority' described as 'a surrender to Arab terrorism', the Arabs renewed their plea for total cessation of Jewish immigration.[3] Violent reaction became unavoidable and was postponed only until the defeat of the Axis powers. By this time the problem had become intensified, primarily because of the persecution of the Jews by Hitler, while secondary causes were the weakening of British power after six years of war and the strengthening of Arab nationalism. It is possible that violence might have been averted at this point if the Jews had dissociated themselves from Britain and the West and had shown willingness to become Middle East citizens.

Nazi Atrocities and Immigration

Before 1939 both North America and Britain had admitted comparatively few persecuted Jews to their territories; only South America was sufficiently receptive. Similarly during and following the war, despite the wishes of survivors to emigrate to the USA and Britain, the latter again pleaded incapacity to admit large numbers of Jews on account of existent overcrowding.[4] But in 1945 the European world, and especially the USA, reeled with horror at the terrifying evidence of Nazi atrocities and were prepared to sponsor any alternative refuge. The US reacted to the intense pressure of the Jewish lobby and President Truman committed himself to follow his predecessor's Zionist policy.[5] On August 31, 1945, he appealed to British Prime Minister Attlee immediately to admit 100,000 Jewish refugees into Palestine. The British reply suggested an Anglo-American Committee of Inquiry, which after deliberation submitted a report (duly considered by another committee) recommending permission for the 100,000 to enter with others to follow later. Despite American pressure, however, Britain was not prepared to admit such a large number for fear of further antagonising the Arabs, whose sympathy it believed to be vital if its oil and Suez Canal interests were to be protected. Instead, illegal Jewish immigrants packed on tramp steamers were turned back on approaching Palestine waters. There was one instance of a boat carrying illegal Jewish immigrants, stopped and diverted to Hamburg, Germany. Many of its occupants died.

Britain Surrenders Mandate

Contradictory promises made a solution impossible. Already in 1922 Winston Churchill had assured the Arabs that Palestine would not become a Zionist state, yet in 1944 he promised Dr Chaim Weizman, the Zionist leader, that Britain would grant Jews sovereignty in a divided Palestine. The new Labour Government of 1945 was determined to be rid of Palestine at any price since 'world interest' prevented Britain imposing its own solution; the Foreign Secretary, Ernest Bevin, was convinced of a Zionist conspiracy because of the intensity of the pressure. Consequently, in December 1947, London announced to a disbelieving world that the mandate would be handed back to the United Nations within one year and that thereafter Britain would accept no responsibility, nor would it impose any policy upon Palestine by force of arms. The Government were unable, however, to control the two desperate and aggrieved communities, with the result that all three sides – Jews, Arabs, British – were antagonised and resorted to extremes for political and strategic gain.

Partition and War

The UN appointed a Special Committee on Palestine, which produced a divided report, united however in recommending partition into Jewish and Arab states with Jerusalem internationalised. The Jews accepted; the Arabs rejected the proposals outright.[6] On November 29, 1947, the majority report laying down partition frontiers was approved by two-thirds of the General Assembly. Open war broke out immediately between Arabs and

Jews and the Powers took different sides. Russia proceeded to recognise Israel in order to embarrass Britain (for the same reason she had earlier agreed to the supply of Czech guns to Israel),[7] America granted Israel a $100 million loan, while Britain remained passive attempting to save its Arab connections. In May, 1948 Israeli sovereignty was proclaimed and Arab armies from Egypt, Jordan, Syria, Lebanon, Iraq, Saudi Arabia and the Yemen declared their intention to eradicate the new state. Their motives were not purely pan-Arabic; Lebanon and Syria wanted to recapture the Palestinian market, Jordan wanted to incorporate Palestine, Egypt wanted to prevent Jordan's plans. Their actual resources were incapable however of matching their zeal, and the Arabs and particularly Egypt had to admit defeat. Israel signed separate agreements with each neighbour, stipulating cease-fire lines and a promise not to resort to force to solve the Palestinian problem. It was a military and not a political agreement, because the Arabs refused to recognise Israel.

The Refugee Problem

Besides the territorial changes, the immediate result of Israel's statehood was the creation of an Arab refugee problem, resulting ironically from a project which it was hoped would solve the Jewish refugee problem. About half a million Palestinians lost most of their possessions and land. The Jews saw that the return of the refugees would create a security problem, causing an ubiquitous fifth column, but in 1949 at Lausanne they offered as a concession to accept 100,000. The Arabs insisted on a total return; finally the Israelis readmitted seven per cent of the refugees. The Americans then took the initiative in launching a United Nations Refugee Agency (UNRA) to care for the dispossessed Arabs and to resettle them in any land except Palestine. The refugees have remained in squalid camps ever since. From 1949 Israeli policy has been that a solution of the problem can be discussed only within the terms of a general political settlement, and the majority of the original Palestinians prefer to live in the sordid camps (as political pawns), hoping to return or get compensation, rather than accept an offer to be resettled outside their homeland. The Palestinians henceforth became the subjects and possibly the vanguard of the fermenting nationalism.

Arab Nationalism: Élite and Popular

Arab nationalism of course existed before the Palestine issue. One can find its roots in the late eighteenth century and it began to assume its powerful dimensions in Damascus and Beirut at the beginning of this century. The Mandatory Powers' occupation was unable to prevent Egypt forcing a limitation of Britain's military presence successively in 1932 and 1936. This resulted from at-the-roots nationalism, different from the nationalism of the rulers, who as late as 1937–8, when meeting at a pan-Arab conference, manifested pro-Western sympathies against popular anti-Western expression. Despite this, the rulers were not prepared any more than the people to tolerate a large non-Arab population in the Near East. In Palestine anti-British disturbances which had begun in 1923 culminated in massive strikes in 1936. They were directed against both the British and the Zionists.

After 1949, popular Arab nationalism was no longer solely directed against the European settlers and the Western Powers' occupation; it also turned against those rulers who for personal power and profit co-operated with the British and French. Nationalism became a force for social change which neither the Europeans nor the weaker among their Arab protegés could withstand. The humiliating defeat by the Jews in 1948 led to the overthrow of the Jordanian, Syrian and Egyptian rulers between 1949 and 1952. In 1952 the forces of nationalism and anti-colonialism were united politically and ideologically under the leadership of Nasser, who insisted that the common enemy were the imperialist powers which had facilitated and imposed the new state of Israel and had occupied the Arab countries. He declared that his intention in removing the corrupt ruling class in Egypt was to establish the political and economic sovereignty of the Arab masses. Meanwhile Cold War tensions increased in the Middle East.

Great Powers in Conflict

The position of the Powers must be briefly described. Whereas the Soviet Union did not fully identify its Middle Eastern interests until the mid-1950s, its armies drawn up along the borders of Turkey and its subversion in Iran and Iraq were sufficient to cause great fear in the West, especially in Britain, which continued to regard the security of the area as essential to her prosperity for oil reasons. British influence, however, was moving to collapse by 1951 and America and Russia were being drawn into the vacuum and future confrontation. At this time the West was essentially satisfied with the territorial settlement which had been imposed on the Middle East, and to forestall any alteration in the *status quo* they embarked from 1950 to 1956 on a succession of policies to prevent Russian penetration and to support Arab conservative governments in order to contain the popular nationalism which was arising, implying social change. The West's first gambit was the Tripartite Declaration in 1951, signed by the US, Britain and France, which announced that the signatories would permit no armed aggression across the armistice lines, that appropriate action would be taken against any aggressor, that they would maintain an arms' balance by limiting supplies and that they were the guardians of Israel and as such would ensure the maintenance of the *status quo*.

The second phase of Western policy was the formulation of defence alliances, primarily directed against Russia. Britain had already negotiated a series of pacts – a circle of military stations – in Egypt, Jordan, Iraq and the Persian Gulf Sheikhdoms, besides those in Cyprus, Libya and Aden – with the eventual object of establishing a northern and southern tier of defence. In 1951 the Allied Middle East Command was set up (US, Britain, France and Turkey), but it gained no Arab support once Egypt (although still under King Farouk) refused to be drawn into the Western plan. The West suspected Arab nationalism, and felt its doubts confirmed by the Iranian nationalisation of its oil; but it was impotent to influence the new forces. Offered no alternative, eighty thousand British troops had to withdraw from the Suez Canal from 1954, with the consolation only that they should return if the Canal's security was endangered. Egypt was offered participation in the prospective Baghdad Pact,[8] but Nasser refused and initiated a ceaseless campaign against those Arab states which considered joining, isolating Iraq at the 1955 Cairo Summit of Arab governments.

The Jordan Waters

Difficulties also arose within Israel about future water supplies. Despite the ingenuity of Eric Johnson (and his realistic report to the UN in 1955) and the initial nominal agreement of the Arab states concerned, the plan to divert and utilise the Jordan waters was subsequently rejected by the Arabs on the political grounds of the non-recognition of Israel and of abstention from any act which could aid Israel to provide for more immigrants or could impair Arab rights.[9] In addition, the Arabs continued to strengthen their organisation for a world boycott of Israel, extending it to all aspects of Israel's economy. There was a ban not only on Israeli shipping in the Suez Canal but also on cargo destined for Israel on any ship; similar restrictions applied to shipping and cargoes through the Gulf of Aqaba. World airlines could not include Arab states and Israel on the same routes, and any company found to have traded with Israel was boycotted. These measures considerably hindered Israeli economic development.

Guerrilla War

Ever since the 1949 cease-fire Israel had been hopeful of a settlement, but the rejection of her offered concessions and the failure to make realistic contact with the Egyptians led to a hardening of her position. Prime Minister, Ben-Gurion, probably the most anti-Arab in Israeli leadership, decided to launch a double reprisal policy to combat the increasing incursions into Israel by small guerrilla bands. In October 1953 the Israeli army attacked the Jordanian village of Qibya and fifty civilians were killed. This initiated a policy which was subsequently repeatedly followed with increasing casualties. During 1955 Israel suffered an increasing number of fedayeen raids from Gaza and the East Bank of the Jordan, besides disturbances on the borders with Syria. In the northern demilitarised zone, the former Syrian owners insisted on their rights to farm their land, but Israel denied their title. The result was sporadic fighting. By 1956 nearly all the armistice and security machinery established in 1949 had collapsed.

Consequences of Israel's Invasion

In 1955 Israel invaded Gaza and compelled Nasser to realise Egypt's military weakness. He sought American assistance. The US, however, still wishing to prevent any change in the Middle East's *status quo*, referred to the Tripartite Declaration for a limitation of arms' supplies (although it had not prevented France selling weapons to Israel), but at the same time contradictorily indicated that weapons would be supplied if Egypt joined an anti-Soviet alliance. Nasser was not impressed; he cautiously approached Moscow and during 1955 large consignments of Russian arms arrived. America's initial reaction was an offer to finance the Aswan High Dam project in order to forestall Russian influence. Thereafter followed a succession of events culminating in a physical attempt by Britain and France to overthrow Egypt's 1952 revolution.

The West had completely misunderstood the intentions, implications and character of the 1952 Free Officers' *coup* in Egypt. The group of young officers resented the corruption of the Egyptian government and of public life and were humiliated by Egypt's international subservience (especially Britain's influential presence) and Israel's existence. Their *coup* had minimal ideological foundations other than nationalism, and their methods were at first essentially pragmatic. The significance of the revolution lay in the advent of Nasser's assumption of leadership of the Pan-Arabic movement and his ability to expound its theory to the Arab peoples and symbolise its potential strength to the world. The division among the Arabs is discussed below; of importance here is the fact that for Nasser the pan-Arabist defence against intervention by foreign powers, both military and economic, became imperative. Economic dependence was seen to be humiliating; the Egyptian economy, for example, was subject to Turkey and Britain, and other Arab states suffered from similar domination.

Following Nasser's refusal to enter into alliances with the West against Russia and his acceptance of Russian arms, the British Prime Minister, Anthony Eden, became alarmed. Successive events convinced him that Britain's vital interests, especially oil supplies, were at the mercy of a tyrant who would have to be removed. The failure of the Baghdad Pact to draw in Arab governments, Glubb's dismissal from the Jordanian High Command, and Nasser's refusal to lessen his vehemence convinced the US also that Egyptian 'neutralism' could be interpreted only as pro-Russian. The Americans therefore withdrew the promised funds for the Aswan Dam, followed by the withdrawal of the finance which Britain had also offered. This was a great blow to Nasser; Egypt's future prosperity depended on the availability of cheap electric power and increased irrigation. He refused to submit and took the offensive by nationalising the Suez Canal. He did this both in retaliation and to gain needed revenue from the Canal and as a demonstration of Egypt's power and independence.

France–Britain–Israel Attack

This was the ultimate for Eden. Nasser attempted to compromise with him and Mollet, Prime Minister of France, but both now seemed intent on war regardless of Egypt's attitude. Eden wanted to reassert British prestige, hoping that Jordan, Lebanon and Iraq would return to London influence, while Mollet wanted to prevent Nasser from further supporting the FLN rebellion in Algeria. Both were so determined to depose Nasser that they not only ignored the public and private warnings of Eisenhower and Dulles, but purposely deceived them as to their true intentions. It was a mere handful of selected British and French Ministers and officials who sabotaged the UN's peacekeeping efforts and scorned Egyptian offers.[10]

The plan was for Israel to attack Egypt through Sinai; Britain and France would then order both sides to withdraw their forces from the Suez Canal on the pretext of saving it from damage.[11] An Anglo-French force would thereupon land under the Anglo-Egyptian Treaty of 1954 and take up positions along the Canal; Nasser would soon thereafter be deposed. Prior to the attack, Britain would activate its Middle Eastern allies to deceive the world as to the real nature of the events.[12] According to its plan, Israel, on October 29, 1956, attacked Egypt and an Anglo-French ultimatum to Nasser to stop fighting was issued. Nasser refused and the Egyptian air force was destroyed by British bombers.[13] It took some days for the British and French force to arrive at the Canal and world condemnation reflected in a United Nations resolution was so strong that it withdrew the day following. Britain faced international humiliation. There was a run on the pound sterling and an economic crisis; oil had to be rationed, the Suez Canal having been blocked by Nasser;[14] the US refused Britain any aid until withdrawal. Britain's standing in the world fell to its lowest point in modern times.

Fear of Russian Influence

The automatic result of the failure of the Anglo-French Suez conspiracy was an increase of Nasser's stature throughout the world (especially at the non-aligned conference at Bandung in 1955) as the champion of the Arab peoples and their struggle for unity against imperialism. Russia's position in the Middle East was also strengthened. Soon after 1948 the Soviet Union had turned against Israel because of the latter's close relations with the USA. It had supplied the Arabs with weapons in 1955, had financed the Aswan Dam, and had established a politically strategic position in Syria, an influential counter to the West.[15] In the Suez crisis Russia alone among the Powers unconditionally supported Egypt. The disastrous Anglo-French venture had thus aggravated the West's predicament.

Both Dulles and Eisenhower feared increased Russian penetration into what they considered a 'vital area' and decided to act. In January 1957, the *Eisenhower Doctrine* was published; it was an elaboration of the principles of the Baghdad Pact, reaffirming alignment against Russia with increased financial allurements. The response reflected the political division in the Middle East. Libya, Lebanon, South Arabia, Yemen, Iraq and Israel adhered to the doctrine, Jordan remained neutral, while Egypt and Syria rejected it outright. The leaders of the adherent Arab states feared 'Nasserism', which challenged not only colonialism but also the Arab rulers who relied upon Western support to retain office. In the following year, 1958, the forebodings of Nasser were once again vindicated when, following Kassem's successful revolt in Iraq (where Muri as Said, long-time executor and personifier of British policy, was overthrown), British paratroops and American marines were sent to Jordan and Lebanon to prevent their regimes being similarly deposed.

Egypt–Syria Unite: and then Part

While Syria was the birthplace of modern Arab Nationalism and Socialism in the Middle East, Egypt became the mainspring, providing a sufficient state structure to absorb and administer the new ideas, although in a diluted form. Syria, probably the key to the Middle East revolution, remained paralysed by the conflicting factions in its military and civilian political groups, which divided the basis for a developed social revolution. While one group sought salvation at gunpoint[16] by proclaiming in 1958 union with Egypt in the United Arab Republic (UAR), another group sought relief in the dissolution of the union three years later. Solidarity between Egypt and Syria could have been a pivot of Arab unity, but Syria's relegation by Nasser to a position of junior partner and the removal of the Syrian B'aathists (who had promoted the union) led to its collapse. The essential cause of the union's failure was the absence of mass acceptance of an ideology which could overcome sectarian interests. Nasser's immediate reaction was to summon an Arab summit conference and there he joined with conservative Saudi Arabia and Jordan to isolate Syria. Shortly afterwards Iraq (ruled by General Kassem whom Nasser disliked) threatened the invasion of Kuwait, whose Sultan immediately activated its defence treaty with Britain. English soldiers arrived, but Arab pressure soon compelled them to withdraw, replaced by Saudi Arabian, Jordanian and Egyptian contingents. The idea of a wide Arab Union still persisted. Proposals in 1963 by both Syria and Iraq to reactivate it were, however, rejected by Nasser on the ground that its basis would be reactionary.

The Six-day War

After 1956 Israel felt increasingly secure. The incursions diminished, Britain and France became further committed to defend her sovereignty, and the Eisenhower Doctrine in effect assured Israel that America's Sixth Fleet was an ultimate source of defence. With this international support, Israel's policy towards the Arabs was to exploit and perpetuate their divisions, launching massive reprisal raids whenever it was felt politic and necessary. Then came the calamitous Six-day War of June 1967. According to most accounts it had its immediate cause in reports (initially from Soviet intelligence) that Israel was about to launch a major raid against Syria. It was probable that Israel had contingency plans, but the Soviet Ambassador's refusal of the Israeli invitation to ascertain the facts by visiting the area tended to confirm doubt of the specific allegation. The Egyptian Government responded to the alleged threat by ordering the withdrawal of the United Nations peace-keeping force on its frontier; it had the legal right to do this, and it must be borne in mind that Israel had declined to allow the UN to position the force on its territory at all. But the fact that this was accompanied by the prohibition of Israeli shipping in the Aqaba Gulf, its only outlet to the Indian Ocean, and the mobilisation of Egyptian troops in Sinai indicated that Nasser took the information of a projected Israeli assault on an Arab territory seriously and intended to meet it challengingly; it is possible also that for internal reasons he was led to demonstrate a 'more anti-Israel than thou' attitude. Whatever the explanation the effect was disastrous for the Arab peoples.

The Israelis mounted a full-scale attack, smashing the fighting planes which the Russians had provided, occupying Jordan west of the river, sweeping down to the entrance of the Aqaba Gulf, and running over Gaza to the banks of the Suez Canal. Within a week Israel completely shattered the Syrian, Jordanian, and Egyptian air forces. Jerusalem and the West Bank of Jordan were occupied, while in the north the Syrians retreated from the Golan Heights.

UN Resolution

On the motion of the British representative, Lord Caradon, the Security Council of the United Nations adopted a forthright but balanced resolution. It called on the Israelis to withdraw their forces from the occupied Arab territory, maintained the right of all the nations including Israel to exist, required an attitude of non-belligerency by all, asserted the right of the free navigation of ships in international waterways, including the Suez Canal and the Aqaba Gulf, and required a just settlement of the refugee problem. Egypt accepted the resolution; Israel's response was more equivocal.[17] A mediator, Dr Jarring, was appointed to seek peace on the lines laid down, but, despite constant journeys between Cairo and Jerusalem, he failed over months to find a basis of agreement. Big Power discussions took place between the USA, Russia, Britain and France in an effort to find a solution, yet five years passed with the Israeli troops still on Arab territory, with intermittent fighting over the Suez Canal and, in retaliation for guerrilla incursions, Israeli raids into Jordan, Syria and Lebanon. The Israelis incorporated Arab Jerusalem with their part of the city and announced their intention of remaining there. They proceeded with settlement projects in other occupied regions. They made it clear that they would not accept any solution imposed by the big Powers.

On the Arab side the unity of the governments broke down. National survival became more important than Pan-Arabism. This was reflected in an abortive Summit Conference at Rabat in Algeria in December 1969, which in effect split the moderate and radical administrations. A sequel was the drawing together of Egypt, Libya, a consequence of a revolution in 1969, and Sudan which had also moved to the Left. Another sequel was the strengthening and increasing importance of the guerrilla organisation representing the determination of Arabs ejected from occupied territories by the Jewish administration to fight back since the Arab governments had consistently failed to match their deeds to their words. This development was an expression of a resurgence of Palestinian nationalism. They had been exiled from Israel and their territories were now occupied in west Jordan and Gaza. By a turn of history, they were now refugees expelled by those who had sought their own homeland. From this point on a settlement of the Palestinian problem became essential for a lasting solution in the Middle East.

Palestinian Guerrillas Defeated

During 1970 Israel became increasingly the victim of repeated Palestinian raids from across the Jordanian and Lebanese borders. Bombs exploded in Jerusalem and, of international concern, Israeli civilian aircraft around the world were hijacked and even blown up by desperate gangs of Palestinians. While European governments were held to ransom to secure the release of captive Palestinian guerrillas, the Jordanian Government was faced with a concerted attack on its sovereignty by the same guerrilla forces. The confrontation broke into warfare, resulting in a Palestinian defeat and the strengthening of King Hussein's position. The guerrillas failed because of numerical inferiority and internal division; they had attempted too much for their limited resources, and it was noteworthy that no Arab power was prepared to go to their aid. Nasser, despite all his previous criticism of the Hashimite kingdom, remained neutral. His last act before his death was to bring the two sides together in Cairo.[18]

Having defeated the Palestinian guerrillas, King Hussein of Jordan astonished all involved in the Middle East by proposing in March 1972 a Palestinian Federation joining Jordan with the Israeli-occupied territory on the West Bank and occupied Gaza isolated on the Mediterranean coast, with an Arab presence in Jerusalem. At first it was believed that there must have been discussions with Israel and goodwill, but Mrs Golda Meir, who had become Prime Minister, dismissed the proposal with what *The Times* described as a snub.

Arab countries were equally censorious. Egypt and her partners, Syria and Libya, broke off relations with Jordan, and Iraq and Algeria denounced the plan in severe terms. Almost simultaneously, Israel initiated elections for municipal councils on the West Bank in which Arabs participated more fully than expected. The Palestinian guerrillas who were meeting in Cairo derived new hope from the extensive rejection of King Hussein, but the total effect was to emphasise disunity among Arabs and the difficulty of co-operation between them either for peace or war.

Nasser's Death and After

Nasser's death threw the Arab world into temporary turmoil. Indeed, the whole world held its breath and wondered whether the region could survive the disappearance of its master hero. During their convalescence from this shock, the Arab nations became increasingly introverted. The cease-fire between Israel and Egypt across Suez, arranged only a few weeks previously under UN auspices, was hastily confirmed by the new Egyptian regime. It became apparent that whereas Nasser might have found difficulty in concluding any peace agreement with the Israelis because of past statements, the new Administration, faced with serious internal political and economic difficulties, was more prepared to search for a solution.

It was generally recognised that any peace settlement must be based on the UN Resolution 242. Although it specified the recognition of Israel and guaranteed its right to use the Suez canal and the Gulf of Aqaba, the Israeli Government made reservations, insisting on 'secure and recognised boundaries' and refused at first to specify them until the two sides met at a conference table. The Jarring mission withdrew in September 1970 on account of a Egyptian breach of the cease-fire, but returned temporarily after Christmas.

Great Power Intervention

The hope for a solution seemed to remain with the four Great Powers, but Israelis and Arabs differed about their acceptance. Whereas Israel insisted that the solution could be found only by the nations in the area, Egypt was equally insistent that any settlement should be backed by a Big Power peace-keeping force. Under American pressure a proposal was considered for the withdrawal of Israeli troops from the East Bank of the Suez Canal. Difficulties arose because the Israelis rejected any idea that Egyptian troops should cross the Canal. Washington and Moscow appeared to be urging steps towards a settlement whilst continuing to supply arms to each side. Under the promise of American Phantom bombers Israel agreed to 'indirect talks' with Egypt[19] and Jarring returned to renew negotiations. A hopeful factor was contributed by the visit of a mission from the Organisation of African Unity, received cordially both in Jerusalem and Cairo.[20] Sadat, the Egyptian President, mingled threats of war with more peaceful sentiments. Lord Caradon who had been responsible for the 1967 UN Resolution, proposed a Geneva Conference of all the governments concerned. In May 1972 there was also hope that President Nixon's visit to Moscow would lead to some accord on the Middle East. Everything pointed to the early approach of the decisive moment between peace and war.[21]

Social Change Across Frontiers

Meanwhile, the issue of social change had thrust forward. Among the Arab peoples there was a growing determination to end the feudalist regimes which permitted wealth, particularly from oil, to make a few families incrediby rich whilst the population as a whole remained in poverty,[22] and not less to free themselves from domination by the Great Powers. The Middle East was to a large extent a neo-colonialist territory subject to the strategic and economic interests of the strong industrial nations. The great oil interests of the West dominated the whole region, supplemented by the intervention of Russia and China and the financial and technical penetration by Japan in the newly rich emirates of the Gulf.

The political independence won by Arab nations was accompanied by the beginnings of a social revolution with the double object of ending both internal social inequality and external neo-colonialism. It took root in South Yemen following the departure of the British and had potential possibilities in Egypt, Syria and Iraq.[23] Far ahead one could even visualise a socialist confederation of the states of the Middle East, including Israel.[24] A Union of Socialist States is still a dream. A long way off, but who knows?

South Yemen (Aden and Protectorates)

Aden and the hinterland of earlier British Protectorates lie at the south-west corner of Arabia, the port of Aden strategically placed

near the junction of the Red Sea and the Indian Ocean, facing
Africa. They are bordered by Saudi Arabia to the north, Yemen to
the west and Muscat and Oman to the east. The total area is 62,000
square miles, but the population only an estimated one million, of
whom about 100,000 live in Aden. Before the closing of the Suez
Canal the number there was probably 250,000.

Although Aden is a forbidding extinct volcanic crater, greenless
and infertile, it became important as a port of call when trade began
with India, the Far East and Australasia. The Turks, Portuguese
and British in turn battled for possession. Centuries before, the
Roman armies had approached but were discouraged by the harsh
terrain, succeeded by Egyptians who were similarly defeated more
by the grim earth than by human opposition. Even the Turkish
and Portuguese invasions were fragmentary and temporary. The
Turks sacked Aden and withdrew. The Portuguese left the ruins
of forts and factories in neighbouring Muscat and Oman, not
regarding a continued occupation worth the cost of repressing
resisting Arabs.

The British arrived with purpose early in the nineteenth century,
establishing a colony of Aden with some twenty inland Sultanates
in 1839. British intervention was triggered off by a characteristic
incident. An Indian ship under a British flag was wrecked off the
coast and the crew held to ransom by the local sultan. As soon as
news reached Bombay a twenty-eight-gun warship and a ten-gun
cruiser with seven hundred troops were dispatched to the scene and
the British East Africa Company took advantage of the occasion
to take over Aden as a coaling station for its newly acquired steam-
ships. Thus the colony was born. Protectorates were progressively
extended over innumerable inland small states, the British promising 'in the Name of God, the Merciful Compassionate' to defend
their feudal rulers.

The opening of the Suez Canal in 1869 made Aden important
and busy. Its dock was crowded with ships for refuelling. Labourers
poured in, Arabs from Yemen, Africans from Somaliland. The
British ruled with despotic seclusion, a rich caste remote from the
poverty about them. They brought earth from India to plant a
bowling green at the Officers' Club, the only touch of colour. Prosperous business concerns were set up, not only by British traders
but by Indian, Greek and French merchants. They towered over
festering slums.

In the 1950s there were signs of some political agitation among
Arabs, but it was strike action by emerging trade unions in 1956

which first dented British self-assurance. Lord Lloyd arrived from London to assure the European residents that Britain would retain the colony. An Arab movement in the Sultanate of Lahej, the South Arabia League, then for the first time raised the demand for independence; the British retorted by exiling its leader, Muhammed Ali al Jifri, who significantly found refuge in Cairo. The British–French–Israeli attack on Egypt in October and its UN reversal made Nasser the hero of the Arabs in Aden no less than in the rest of the Middle East. Meanwhile the Imam of Yemen was influencing his eighty thousand immigrants in Aden and neighbouring Protectorates to agitate for union and independence. The only consolation for Britain was that most of the inland Sultans begged for continued protection, fearful of the radical Nationalists in Aden, and accepted a London proposal for association in a Federation and union with a British controlled Aden.

In Aden itself trade union strength and militancy increased. In 1959 there were eighty-nine strikes and the port was paralysed for five weeks. Of political importance was the establishment by the TUC of the People's Socialist Party (PSP), which campaigned for a South Arabia republic, including the Yemen, made more possible after the revolution in 1962 which initiated a republic and gained the support of Egyptian troops. The PSP leader, Abdullah al-Asnag, was educated and able; he had been an inspector in the government health service for many years. The tension in Aden broke to violence. Political strikes mounted, PSP members were imprisoned, the Assistant High Commissioner was killed by a bomb. Al-Asnag then established the Front for the Liberation of Southern Yemen (FLOSY), which became influential but afterwards lost support because it ignored the pressure for union with the Protectorates. This was followed by the formation of the National Front for the Liberation of Occupied South Yemen (NLF) which secured the support of Egypt and, reflecting the growing revolutionary mood, began guerrilla action.

This caused the British to reconsider their main reason for remaining in Aden: the retention of a British military base. Obviously a base would be untenable amidst Arab rebellion and, in conjunction with the USA, Britain began looking for an alternative in the Indian Ocean. Then came a renewed Labour Government in Britain in the autumn of 1964. After talks between all parties in Aden, it announced that independence would be accorded to a united South Arabia by 1968. In fact, the last British troops were withdrawn on November 30, 1967 although a base was retained on an offshore island, and independence then inaugurated. Aden suffered from continued economic depression whilst the Suez Canal was blocked, relieved only by the maintenance of an oil refinery which served traffic in the Arabian Sea.[25]

The Persian Gulf

The decision of Britain's Labour Government to withdraw troops from the Persian Gulf, although modified by the Conservative Government in 1971, led to tensions by the ruling emirates and to rival claims by the neighbouring states. Iraq had its eyes on Kuwait, Iran on Bahrein and Qatar, and Saudi Arabia sought to stabilise the authority of the sheikhs by consolidating a federation. Britain was concerned to retain its oil supplies and supported the idea of a federation to facilitate this, but Bahrein and Qatar supplemented Kuwait as independent states and the Union of Arab Emirates was limited to seven.

Conflict with Iran persisted. The sheikh of Sharjah conceded the island of Abu Musa, but the sheikh of Ras al-Khaimah declined to yield the Greater and Lesser Tumbs. Iran then occupied these islands much to the indignation of the Arab world.

In Muscat and Oman, long the scene of a rebellion which the British co-operated in repressing (by seconding officers to lead the Sheikh's troops and providing arms), the ex-sheikh's son on coming to the throne announced democratic changes, but guerrilla forces continued to resist with support from South Yemen. The stability of the Gulf remained uncertain, in short term because of the unsatisfied ambitions of neighbouring states and the rivalry of the sheikhdom rulers, in long term because of underlying conflict between the peoples and the privileged emirs.

The Kurds

Scattered over five countries in Western Asia are members of a race which has kept its language and character despite the fact that it has never had a unifying national home. These are the Kurds, most of whom live in Turkey, Iran and Iraq, some in Syria and the Soviet Union.[26] Until the end of the First World War, most of them were within the Ottoman empire, but agitated for recognition as a nation. From 1897 their journal, *Kurdistan,* was driven from Cairo *via* Geneva to Folkestone in England by financial as much as by political pressures. Hope rose towards the end of the war when Woodrow Wilson declared in his 'Programme of the World's Peace' (Part 12) that the non-Turkish nationalities of the Ottoman empire should be assured 'of an absolute unmolested opportunity of autonomous development' and the Treaty of Sèvres (1920) actually set up the state of Kurdistan.[27] Tragically for the Nationalists the treaty was never applied. Turkish military strength revived, reflected in the new Treaty of Lausanne (1923) which left out Kurdistan.

Following this there were rebellions in Iran and Iraq as well as in Turkey. Sometimes the Nationalists proclaimed the establishment of Kurdish states, but they did not last. In 1925 the League of Nations insisted that the Kurds in Iraq should administer their own area with Kurdish as the official language in the courts and the schools, and in 1932 the League required Iraq to accept this as a condition of membership. But still it was only half-heartedly applied.

The Kurdish agitation for national recognition continued right into the sixties, with declarations of solidarity over the frontiers of Turkey, Iran and Iraq. The Iraqi Government particularly had to meet formidable rebellions by military repression. Concessions had to be made. Considerable autonomy was provided, but, whilst among the younger generation the nationalist flame persisted, the Kurds remained forcibly divided and stateless.

Notes

1. The relevant passage reads: 'H.M. Government view with favour the establishment in Palestine of a national home for the Jewish People and will use their best endeavours to facilitate the achievement of this object, it being clearly understood that nothing shall be done which may prejudice the civil and religious rights of existing non-Jewish communities in Palestine or the rights and political status enjoyed by Jews in any other country.'

2. Palestine itself has never been a separate political entity and has been conquered thirteen times.

3. One-third of the population of Palestine was by this time Jewish.

4. See *Why Six Million Died: A Chronicle of American Apathy* by Arthur Moore.

5. On January 27, 1944, the US Congress passed a motion: 'Be it resolved that the US shall use its good offices and take appropriate measures to the end that the doors of Palestine shall be opened for free entry of Jews into that country and that there shall be free opportunity for colonization, so that the Jewish people may ultimately reconstitute Palestine as a free and democratic Jewish Commonwealth.'

6. Israel later accepted the internationalisation of Jerusalem as a condition of entrance into the United Nations, but failed to implement its promise.

7. Purchased with US money.

8. The object of the Pact was to perpetuate Anglo-Iraqi rule and to forestall Russia. Only Iran, Pakistan and Turkey joined, all being heavily dependent upon the US and not being connected with the nationalist movement (nor having anything to fear from it). It was intended to succeed the defunct Anglo-Iraqi Defence Treaty.

9. Israel thereupon unilaterally diverted the Jordan waters and attacked Syrian canals intended to channel off water before it reached Israel.

10. Britain's Foreign Minister, Selwyn Lloyd, and Egypt's Foreign Minister actually agreed on a solution which could have been satisfactory to all, but it was stalled by the French Foreign Minister, Pineau, and by Eden until war made it irrelevant. See *No End of a Lesson* by Anthony Nutting, Minister of State for Foreign Affairs, 1954–6.

11. Britain only knew of Israeli participation after it had been firmly fixed with France, see *No End of a Lesson*.

12. Iraq co-operated with Britain, not knowing the full plan, because it wanted to regain its historical influence in Syria. Iraqi soldiers were to advance through Jordan and overthrow the anti-Western regime in Syria.

13. This was to protect Israeli cities and was a pre-condition for Israeli participation in the French plan. Half of Port Said was destroyed in the bombing and many civilians died.

14. Nasser also nationalised British and French property and business interests and forced most British and French nationals to leave Egypt.

15. During 1957, three US diplomats were expelled from Syria on charges of plotting to overthrow the anti-US government. Turkey on American instructions concentrated troops on Syria's border, claiming that she was in danger of attack.

16. Patrick Seale, *Struggle for Syria.* The Syrian Ministers were cajoled on to a Cairo-bound plane at gunpoint with the alternative of going to prison.

17. UN Resolution 242 of November 22, 1967 states:

'The Security Council expressing its continuing concern with the grave situation in the Middle East, emphasising the inadmissibility of the acquisition of territory by war and the need to work for a just and lasting peace in which every State in the area can live in security, emphasising further that all Member States in their acceptance of the Charter of the United Nations have undertaken a commitment to act in accordance with Article 2 of the Charter,

1. Affirms that the fulfilment of Charter principles requires the establishment of a just and lasting peace in the Middle East which should include the application of both the following principles:

(i) withdrawal of Israeli armed forces from territories occupied in the recent conflict;

(ii) termination of all claims or states of belligerency, and respect for and acknowledgement of the sovereignty, territorial integrity and political independence of every state in the area and their right to live in peace within secure and recognised boundaries free from threats or acts of force;

2. Further affirms the necessity (*a*) for guaranteeing freedom of navigation in the area; (*b*) for achieving a just settlement of the refugee problem; and (*c*) for guaranteeing the territorial inviolability and political independence of every State in the area, through measures including the establishment of demilitarised zones;

3. Requests the Secretary-General to designate a Special Representative to proceed to the Middle East to establish and maintain contacts with the States concerned in order to promote agreement and assist efforts to achieve a peaceful and accepted settlement in accordance with the provisions and principles in this resolution;

4. Requests the Secretary-General to report to the Security Council on the progress of the efforts of the Special Representative as soon as possible.'

It was not until 1970 that Mrs Meir, the Israeli Prime Minister made a statement accepting the resolution, but it subsequently became evident that Israel had many reservations.

18. This was without effect. King Hussein subsequently routed the remaining guerrilla forces.

19. Israel had previously insisted that talks should take place

only directly across a table. The cease-fire ending the conflict which followed the proclamation of the State of Israel had been arranged at Rhodes by the opposing sides meeting in separate rooms with a mediator passing between them. Israel now indicated its readiness to resort to this method.

20. Israel informed the OAU delegation that her objective was not based on annexations, which appeared to approximate to the UN requirement of withdrawal from occupied territories. This interpretation was qualified later by Israel's explanation that security rather than annexation was her objection. This would still permit certain occupations on her frontiers and at the mouth of the Aqaba Canal. There was also no sign that Israel would withdraw from Arab Jerusalem.

21. An event occurred in February 1972, which again worsened the climate. Israeli forces entered the Lebanon in some strength to destroy guerrilla bases following raids into Israel. The UN Security Council on February 28 unanimously adopted a motion sponsored by Britain, France, Italy and Belgium demanding that Israel should withdraw. The American representative said he could not condone Israel's action. The Soviet representative said the Security Council should adopt sanctions against Israel, member-states should break off diplomatic and economic relations, and serious consideration should be given to the exclusion of Israel from the UN. World opinion was alienated from the Palestinian guerrillas when Israeli competitors in the Olympic Games at Munich in 1972 were murdered. Israel retaliated by destructive raids on Arab territories. Peace seemed doomed.

America sought a preliminary agreement by the withdrawal of the Israeli forces from the Suez Canal. In February 1973 hopes of negotiations were revived by an article in *The Times* (3.2.73) by King Hussein, reiterating Arab recognition of Israel and its necessity for secure frontiers. This was endorsed by the Egyptian Ambassador in London. Israel, however, insisted on an 'all or nothing' agreement. Exchanges of visits by both sides followed in London and Washington. The shooting down of a Libyan civilian aeroplane in February 1973 by Israeli Phantoms prejudiced seriously the moves towards peace. In April the UN Security Council by 11 votes to nil adopted a Resolution, sponsored by the United Kingdom and France, condemning Israel's 'repeated military attacks' against Lebanon and 'all acts of violence which endanger or take innocent human lives'. The USA abstained because Arab guerrilla attacks were not specifically mentioned and Russia and

China abstained because sterner measures against Israel were not included. Guinea also abstained.

22. This was not true of Kuwait and Abu Dhabi, where the ruling families paternalistically distributed a part of their wealth on social development as well as in immense industrial construction.

23. In February 1972 *Izvestia* listed as 'progressive' Arab nations Egypt, Syria, Algeria and Yemen (Aden). It omitted Libya, despite its socialist character, no doubt because of its opposition to Soviet influences. Later the Soviet Union would undoubtedly have added Iraq, which in May 1972 included two Communists to its Cabinet.

24. Despite Western finance, Israel's internal structure was democratic and largely socialist though in later years capitalist escalation occurred.

25. See *Farewell to Arabia* by David Holden for a graphic account of these events. In February 1973 there was general surprise when it was announced that negotiations had begun between North Yemen, which was pro-West, and South Yemen for the union of their states.

26. Estimates of population in 1969: Turkey, 3,200,000; Iran, 1,800,000; Iraq, 1,550,000; Syria, 320,000; Soviet Union, 80,000.

27. The Kurds in Iran, not within the destroyed Turkish Empire, were not included.

Chapter Nine

Egypt (United
Arab Republic)
and Sudan

Egypt

Egypt is inseparable from the Middle East, but the struggle of its people for independence against British and French domination demands separate treatment.

Expansions and Occupations

It has a magical place in history. We know of its mural inscriptions and sculpture, its tombs and pyramids, its pharaohs and philosophies, from the First Dynasty in 3100 BC onwards. Its situation on the Mediterranean at the meeting point of Africa, Asia and Europe involved it in every wave of the civilisations which swept about it. It went through alternating periods of expansion and occupation. It conquered Syria and Palestine in the seventeenth century BC and Libya and the Sudan in the fifteenth century BC. It was in turn occupied by Libya (945 BC), Persia (525 and 343 BC), Greece (332 BC), Rome (from the last century BC to the end of the Empire), the Muslims (the seventh century AD to the twelfth century), and the Turks (from the sixteenth century AD to the eighteenth). In between imperial adventure and subjection, whilst the few enjoyed luxury and the arts, the many strove for existence as peasants on the delta and banks of the Nile or suffered the worse existence of slaves.

European Intervention

It was not until Napoleon's aggression of the late eighteenth century that Western Europe intervened in force. His troops landed in 1798 and set up a military government with indirect rule. It was on the whole an enlightened occupation, but short-lived; the

British defeat of Napoleon led to the withdrawal of the French in 1801. After a period of anarchy, Egypt recovered unity and power to revert to its earliest expansionist ambitions, establishing an empire from the Euphrates to the Blue Nile, claiming the coast of Somalia after the opening of the Suez Canal in 1869. The cost of its military adventures, however, led to bankruptcy. Its debts were to British and French bondholders, and their governments stepped in to take financial control of the administration. The Finance Minister was British, the Minister of Public Works in control of expenditure was French.

Nationalist Resistance

The response was the beginning of the modern nationalist movement, initiated in 1872 by a Pan-Islam propagandist from Afghan, Jamal al-Din, who stirred large crowds in Cairo by appeals for Muslim unity against alien domination. He was joined by an influential Egyptian sheikh, Mohammed 'Abduh, and, despite differences about methods – Jamal al-Din advocated violence, Mohammed 'Abduh persuasion – they formed the Free National Party. They received such support from within the army and civil service that, alarmed, the British exiled them. From Paris they continued to publish their paper, denouncing the government in Cairo as a puppet of the British and French, particularly the British. The revolt which they had started grew within Egypt. There were army mutinies in 1871 and 1881 and a popular rising in 1882. The British and French conceded a moderate national government, but this did not satisfy and resistance to foreign influence became so threatening that London and Paris sent a joint fleet to Alexandria. Still rebellion mounted, met by a British expeditionary force which marched into the interior. By superior arms the resistance was crushed. The British totally occupied the country.

British Occupation

The administration under Evelyn Baring (Lord Cromer) was at first reformist. Legislatures were established with half elected membership, irrigation planned, forced labour except in emergencies abolished and taxation of the peasants lifted. But Britain and France renewed the claim that the debts due to their bondholders should be the first charge on the revenue and for a time it appeared that Egyptian co-operation would be withdrawn. The breach was bridged by the London Convention of 1885 which provided a supporting loan at reduced rates of interest. An external event, however, broke the British–Egyptian coalition. In 1885 General Gordon was defeated and killed in the Sudan by the Mahdist revolt and British prestige suffered severely. When the Egyptian forces in the Sudan were ordered to withdraw by the British, the Egyptian Ministers asserted historical claims to possession and resigned rather than co-operate.

Rivalry for Sudan

There was continuous rivalry between the British and French in northern Africa, and much intriguing to gain Egyptian support. When in 1892 Abbas Hilmi became Khediv, under French pressure he dismissed the Prime Minister, Mustaf Pasha, who was pro-British, and appointed Husain Fakhri, a Francophile, in his place; but the British had the greater power and Mustaf was soon back. The nationalist movement had been subdued, but in 1894 it revived under Mustafa Kamil, a French-educated lawyer who established a broad-based party, which included the Christian community of Copts. Meanwhile, the struggle for Sudan began again, the British and French competing. Lord Kitchener compelled the retreat of the French at Fashoda, and by a treaty in January 1899 Sudan was made a British–Egyptian condominium; control was vested in a governor-general appointed formally by the Khediv but only on the recommendation of the British. Tension between the British and French continued until April 1904, when they agreed that Britain should have paramountcy in Egypt and the French in Morocco. London pressed its unchallenged power. In January 1905 the Khediv recognised its protectorate status over Egypt; in return Britain restored nominal financial independence, but still insisted on British guidance.

Lord Cromer's rule had become increasingly authoritarian and criticism developed in the Egyptian civil service. The discontent burst into flame by rural affrays in June 1906. For the first time the nationalist movement embraced the peasants as well as the middle class. Sir Eldon Gorst, who succeeded Lord Cromer in 1907, was less authoritarian and extended the powers of provincial councils. The nationalist movement rejected his advances, but had a set-back in 1908 when the assassination of the Christian Prime Minister (he had aroused opposition by concessions to French and British interests in the Suez Canal) led to a break with the Copt community which persisted to later times.

On becoming Pro-Consul Lord Kitchener continued the Gorst reforms, establishing in July 1913 a single-chamber Legislative Council with sixty-six members elected by the provincial councils and seventeen nominated to represent minorities.

Nationalism Becomes a Force

When the next year World War broke out, there was anxiety about Egypt's attitude, but, fearing Turkey, the nationalist leaders supported Britain and France. Their claim to independence was strengthened towards the end of the war by President Woodrow Wilson's declaration for self-determination and they found a dynamic leader in Zaghlul Pasha Saad, who had been elected vice-president of the Legislative Council. He demanded to go to the Paris Peace Talks; Britain's refusal made the nationalist cause a decisive force. All the Egyptian Ministers resigned, moderates joined the movement (known now as the Wafd), the whole people were aroused. Britain reacted by arresting Zaghlul and his three leading lieutenants, deporting them to Malta. Egypt exploded. There were angry demonstrations in Cairo, railway lines were cut, telegraph lines torn down, six British citizens murdered. Ruthless repression followed, so ruthless that there were international protests. The British realised they had gone too far and in April 1919 Zaghlul and his associates were released. Zaghlul proceeded to Paris, but he was denied a hearing at the Peace Conference.

The British, sensitive to international opinion, sent a mission to Egypt under Lord Milner. It was boycotted, but it recommended independence with some recognition of obligations to Britain. Zaghlul was invited to London and the Milner–Zaghlul agreement was signed. But the Government hesitated to apply it; first it delayed; then behind Zaghlul's back it negotiated a compromise with Egypt's compliant sultan. Feeling in Egypt was so strong, however, that when Britain declined to limit their military forces to the Suez Canal Zone, even the sultan's representatives broke off talks and there was nation-wide rebellion. Once more Zaghlul, with five supporters, was deported; again ruthless repression. Nevertheless, Britain thought it best to make concessions. The Government announced its desire to recognise Egypt as an independent state, with reservations regarding imperial communications, the protection of foreign interests, and British rights in Sudan.

The British–Egyptian Condominium in Sudan had not worked easily. The British military dominated and the Egyptians resented this. It was Sudan which for a second time caused a rift. The sultan proclaimed himself 'King Fuad of Egypt and Sudan' and when the British declined to recognise his Sudanese title, disorder and repression under martial law were renewed. Calm restored, there was a repetition of democratic advance. In April 1923 a new constitution established a two-chamber Legislature: a Senate, with three-fifths of its members elected, and a Chamber of Deputies elected. Martial law was ended.

Nationalists Fight on Two Fronts

The nationalist movement now began to fight on two fronts. It opposed the British presence in Egypt and Sudan; it also opposed the royal family's subservience to the British. Zaghlul returned from exile and swept the elections in 1924, becoming Prime Minister. There were hopes of reaching agreement with the first Labour Government in Britain, but Ramsay MacDonald declined to compromise on Sudan. Simultaneously, Zaghlul attacked Palace power in Egypt. He brought the public services, previously an adjunct of royalty, under government control, and when King Fuad obstructed offered to resign, knowing he would have popular support. Then the Sudan controversy erupted again; the British Governor-General was assassinated in Cairo. Zaghlul's government agreed to pay compensation of £500,000 but refused to withdraw Egyptian forces from Sudan. There was a less justifiable refusal: Cairo objected to a British plan to irrigate the Gezira, a triangle of land between the White and Blue Niles, on the ground that Egyptians alone had the right to use the Nile waters.[1] The British retort to Zaghlul's intransigence was to occupy the customs at Alexandria. Zaghlul thereupon resigned.

The partnership between King Fuad and the British Foreign Office became closer. The Palace formed a new Union Party (*Ittihad*) to counter Zaghlul, and, when he won the next election dissolved Parliament and restricted the franchise. Despite this, Zaghlul won again, 150 members to 65, but he declined to form a government whilst royal power persisted. King Fuad thereupon went to London and was received with much pomp. To undermine Zaghlul's fuller demands Britain promised to support Egypt's claim to membership of the League of Nations, thus legalistically recognising her claim to sovereignty. But there was no undertaking that British troops would be withdrawn from Egyptian soil and there was no reference to Sudan.

Conflict Between Parliament and Palace

During these negotiations Zaghlul died. He had proved himself one of the most indomitable of national leaders against foreign occupation. Mustafa-al Nahas was elected Zaghlul's successor as head of the Wafd. He opposed the London agreement because of its limitations; his popular backing was so great that even in the Cabinet of moderates a majority supported him against the pressure of the Palace, and there was nothing for King Fuad to do except appoint him Prime Minister. The feud between Parliament and Palace grew. Taking advantage of some personal allegations against Nahas, King Fuad dismissed him and because of dissension in the Wafd was able to rule for three years by royal decree. Meanwhile a Labour Government had again been returned in Britain and it offered a treaty conceding in principle the confinement of British troops to the Suez Canal Zone and recognising the sovereignty of Egypt by the exchange of ambassadors.

A period of confusion followed. Before the treaty was ratified, elections in Egypt resulted in Nahas again becoming Prime Minister and the Wafd renewed with the British the issue of Sudan. The response was more conciliatory, but before any conclusions were reached King Fuad for a second time dismissed Nahas, dissolved Parliament, instituted press censorship and initiated a new constitution increasing his own powers. In consequence, the Wafd boycotted the elections and for a year there was again authoritarian rule. It could not last. In 1936 the old constitution was restored and Nahas was once more returned to power. He signed a treaty in London the same year, recognising Egyptian sovereignty and providing for the progressive withdrawal of the British forces to the Canal Zone. In 1937 Egypt was elected to the League of Nations at the instance of Britain. In that year also at a conference at Montreux the legal privileges of foreign nationals were abolished and Egypt obtained full rights of taxation of all residents.

During the next decade there was more co-operation between

Britain and the Egyptian Government because of their mutual concern about Turkish influence in the Middle East, and some opposition to the Wafd appeared on the new ground that it was too subservient to Britain. The rivalry between the Palace and Nahas was there all the time. King Fuad had died in 1936, succeeded by his seventeen-year-old son, Farouk, who was as assertive as his father. When in 1937 Farouk claimed the right to appoint the chief official of the royal cabinet, Nahas objected and, taking advantage of the decreasing popularity of the Wafd, the king dismissed him. Division in the Wafd prevented effective opposition. An influential group, known as the Saadists, broke away.

Co-operations in Second World War

The Second World War found Egypt and Britain co-operating, largely because of the former's fear of Italy, already established in neighbouring Libya and Abyssinia.[2] Egypt refrained from declaring war (Britain did not press it because Cairo was useful as an open city), but its territory was invaded and only the British victory at El Alamein prevented occupation. The Wafdists were actually the most ready to act with Britain and when King Farouk declined to call upon Nahas to form a government London insisted he should. Towards the end of the war the question of Egypt's representation at the Peace Conference arose again. When at the Yalta meeting between Roosevelt, Winston Churchill and Stalin the decision was taken to restrict representation to participants, Egypt gained the right by declaring war on Germany and Japan (February 1945). Despite the war, the feud between the Wafdists and the Palace supporters had persisted. The elections in 1942, whilst Nahas was Prime Minister, were boycotted by the anti-Wafdists; the elections in 1945 (when Nahas was out-manoeuvred by a reconstituted alliance between Britain and the Palace) were boycotted by the Wafd. During that year the new Prime Minister, Ahmed Maher Pasha, was assassinated, succeeded by Nokrashi Pasha.

In opposition the Wafd pressed more strongly than ever its demands for the complete evacuation of British troops and 'the unity of the Nile Valley' including Sudan, and it had the support of the Muslim Brotherhood, an extremist organisation standing for Islamic union. Anti-British feeling rose, disorders occurred, and Nokrashi resigned. Ismail Sidky who followed him pressed Egypt's claims, including a revision of the ten-year-old treaty with Britain, and Clement Attlee, heading the third Labour Government, offered the withdrawal of British troops on a time-table jointly accepted, as well as a treaty of mutual assistance. As evidence of sincerity, Britain proceeded to withdraw its forces to the Suez Canal and to evacuate Alexandria as a British base.[3] But on Sudan there were no concessions, and Egypt took the issue without avail to the Security Council of the United Nations and protested vigorously when the British-controlled administration at Khartoum unilaterally announced a measure of self-government.

Birth of Pan-Arabism

Meanwhile, a new and decisive factor had arisen in Egyptian politics: Pan-Arabism. Britain had something to do with this in both a positive and a negative way. Positively, it encouraged union between the Arab nations of the Middle East as they became liberated by the war from Ottoman rule. Negatively, there was the Arab reaction to Britain's promise to the Jews to recognise Palestine as a national home. In September 1944 Nahas had presided at a conference at Alexandria of leaders from Arab states which was the beginning of the Arab League. We have described the developments in the Middle East which revolved so largely round the establishment of the Jewish state of Israel. Here we are concerned with the struggle within Egypt for national independence, but the two issues were often inseparable. When Britain ended its mandate over Palestine in May 1948, Egyptian and other Arab forces intervened on behalf of the Arab population, and, driven back, violence broke out in Cairo. The Muslim Brotherhood had become increasingly militant and was held to be responsible for the assassination of the Chief of Police. Dissolved by Nokrashi, the Brotherhood assassinated him. King Farouk then appointed the head of his royal cabinet, Ibrahim Abd-al Hadi Pasha, Prime Minister, arousing much opposition; but tension was reduced by an agreement on Palestine, negotiated by Ralph Bunche, United Nations mediator, in February 1948, and also by a decision of the British and French to increase the scale of Egypt's profits from the Suez Canal and to invite seven Egyptians to join the Board of the Company.

Nahas once more became Prime Minister after a Wafd election victory in January 1950. He abolished the press censorship, ended martial law and initiated reforms, including social insurance and free primary and secondary education. He revived the issue of Sudan, proposing the end of the condominium and the proclamation of Farouk as king. Britain, backed by France and the USA, put the alternative that the Sudanese people should be given the opportunity to decide between union with Egypt and independence. Relations between Egypt and Britain deteriorated. There were clashes in the Suez Zone and British troops occupied the police barracks at Ismailia. Fierce riots followed in Cairo. Foreign-occupied offices and houses were destroyed, thousands were made homeless and British residents were murdered. Under British pressure, Nahas was dismissed by the king, two Prime Ministers succeeded him temporarily, there was political chaos.

The Colonels' Revolution

Egypt was now in a bad way. Any element of democracy had gone; it had been defeated in Palestine, the British armed forces at Suez had been increased, Sudan was lost. The poverty of the peasants was growing because British purchase of cotton had fallen and America was entering the international cotton market. Distress was aggravated by the fact that the population was growing at a greater speed than anywhere in Africa. The nationalist movement had been dismembered by differences within the Wafd and by the estrangement of the peasants who had lost their interest as politicians quarrelled. Egypt had no unifying purpose and no leader to guide or inspire. The king was distant in his wealth, was surrounded by a corrupt court and was subservient to the British. Even the Wafd was distant; its leaders were often rich landlords who exploited the peasants, or middle-class professionals who had no identity with the villagers or industrial workers. Too many of them had fallen to the temptation of corruption.

It was in this situation that a group of young army officers, dedicated to Egypt and its good name, seized power. They were led by Lieut-Colonel Gamal Abd-al-Nasser, who had been disillusioned by the corruption of high officials when fighting in Palestine. He had found that they had profited from arms orders and had taken money for useless weapons. He was equally shocked by the corruption of the Palace hangers-on and of the politicians, and ashamed that the king and court should be the playthings of Britain, protected by a foreign power which was making independence a mockery. Preparing carefully with junior officers who shared his views and were popular with the ranks of the army, he seized control of Cairo and the country on the night of July 22–23, 1952, without resistance or bloodshed. He set up a government under General Mohammed Neguib, a hero of the Palestinian war. King Farouk abdicated and was replaced for a short time by his infant son, Ahmed Fuad II, with a trusted council of regency.

The young officers were greeted with enthusiasm by vast crowds in Cairo. They proceeded systematically with the revolution. All political parties were abolished and all distinguishing titles relinquished; no one was to be called 'pasha' or 'bey'. On February 10, 1953, Neguib assumed 'supreme powers', Egypt was declared a republic, and the royal estates were made public parks. It soon appeared, however, that all was not harmony within the leadership. On February 25, 1954, Neguib was accused by the Council of Officers of personal dictatorship and, bowing to the criticism, resigned. There was immediate reaction of support from the people, so massive that he was restored to the Presidency two days later with Nasser as Prime Minister. The conciliation did not last long. Neguib was charged with jealousy of Nasser, obstructing him, and of serving as a tool of the Communists and the Muslim Brotherhood. This time the Council of Officers took steps to avoid public demonstrations and Neguib was quietly placed under house arrest. The Communists and the Muslim Brotherhood were outlawed.

The Council of Officers won confidence by their reforms. They cleaned up the corruption which had besmirched the Palace and the politicians, slashed the exploitation of the great landlords, and brought improvement in the standard of life of the villagers and the town workers. They succeeded in negotiating an agreement with the International Bank of Reconstruction and Development for a loan of $200,000,000 for the erection of high dams at Aswan to provide irrigated land for the peasants. But the total evacuation of British troops from Egyptian territory remained the first issue for leaders and people.

British Withdrawal from Suez

In July 1954, the British Government at last agreed to withdrawal from the Suez Canal Zone, the one area still occupied. It was to be a phased withdrawal over twenty months and the troops would be permitted to return in circumstances of danger to the Middle East. Nasser was condemned by past adherents of the Muslim Brotherhood for accepting these conditions, and an attempt was made to assassinate him in October 1954,[4] but Egyptians generally were satisfied that a date had been fixed when the last British soldier would leave. In June 1956 Nasser was elected President of Egypt, it was said by 5,496,965 votes to 2,857, and a new constitution with a National Assembly of 350 was introduced.

The better relations with Britain were broken by two events. The first was the signing of the Baghdad Pact, establishing a defensive military alliance between the United Kingdom, Turkey, Iraq, Iran and Pakistan. The second was the worsening of relations with Israel, which led to alienation from the West. Links with communist countries grew, although in Egypt the Communist Party was suppressed and activists associated with it imprisoned. China had become the largest purchaser of Egyptian cotton. Arms were bought from Czechoslovakia, after Cairo had rejected conditions attached to an offer from the USA which would have required a military alliance and the presence of an American military mission in Egypt. Nasser was moving steadily towards a neutralist and socialist position in world affairs. He established close relations with India and Yugoslavia and attended the Asian–African conference at Bandung in April 1955 which cemented solidarity between the peoples of the two continents against imperialism. This conference had a deep effect on Nasser's thinking. He had read Harold Laski and Aneurin Bevan, but it was from this occasion that his public acceptance of Socialism and his identification with the peoples of the rest of Africa in their struggle against colonialism arose. His Pan-Arabism was extended to Pan-Africanism.

The Canal Nationalised

Nasser proceeded to hold a balance between West and East. In July 1956 he announced his readiness to accept financial aid from Britain and the USA for the Aswan Dam, and aid was promised; but within a few weeks the American promise was withdrawn. The stated reason was economic doubt, but everywhere it was interpreted as concern about Egypt's acceptance of Russian arms and as the response to pressure in the US by supporters of Israel; Britain subserviently followed America's withdrawal. This was a turning point. Nasser retorted by announcing Egypt's nationalisation of the Suez Canal and the use of its revenues to help finance the dam project. Immediately there was consternation and crisis. Egypt declined to attend a conference of maritime powers in London and their representative, the Australian Prime Minister, Robert Menzies, failed to get concessions in Cairo.

Failure of British–French–Israeli Attack

Meanwhile, Britain and France, joint majority owners of the canal, mobilised their armies. There were official denials that Israel, Britain and France planned together the subsequent attack on Egypt, but later, as we have already told, contrary facts became known. A fortnight before the Israeli invasion of Sinai, staff agreements were signed in Paris on October 10, and on October 16 the British Prime Minister went to Paris and decisions were taken for the joint Franco–Israeli–British operation.[5] The consequences on Britain and France, less so on Israel, were humiliating and disastrous. Britain had for the first time used its power of veto in the Security Council to reject a resolution sponsored by the USA calling on all nations to refrain from the use of force, but, after the Israeli attack had taken place, it could not resist a resolution in the General Assembly, also moved by America, calling on Israel to withdraw its troops and other states to refrain from military action. Only Australia and New Zealand supported the United Kingdom, France and Israel. When London and Paris defied this resolution the Assembly passed without dissent a Canadian motion for an emergency international force to replace the troops of Israel, Britain and France. The three aggressors had to give way; their forces were withdrawn, the UN took over, the Israeli troops were required to retire to their original frontiers, and the United Nations accepted responsibility for clearing the Canal. World judgment was clear, and in Britain all progressive opinion rallied behind the Labour Opposition in denouncing the Government.

Egypt's Psychological Revolution

The failure of the British–French aggression at Suez was really the moment of Egyptian independence. British dominance was finally overthrown, its influence destroyed, economically, socially and culturally. It had to end its military occupation of the Canal Zone, and the Anglo-Egyptian treaty was terminated. There was a psychological revolution. The Egyptian people attained a self-respect which meant that for the first time foreigners were no longer regarded as privileged persons. Nasser rallied the people to his aim of socialist reconstruction. He nationalised foreign-owned industries and developed co-operative organisation among the peasants, including the provision of fertile land expanding from the Aswan Dam. He established a party with grass roots, the Arab Socialist Union, which monopolised the National Assembly. He participated actively in the nationalist struggles in Africa and was the host to the African Peoples' Conference and to a conference representing independent governments associated with the Organisation of African Unity. Cairo became the headquarters of the Afro-Asian Solidarity campaign, and Nasser took a leading part in extending co-operation between the unaligned nations, particularly India and Yugoslavia. Egypt is a one-party state, as are many African countries, and the regime has been criticised as more akin to the National Socialism of Hitler than to Democratic Socialism. How far Egypt will move towards democracy will depend on the degree to which the issues of the Middle East permit it peace and security.

Pan-Arabism or Pan-Revolution?

The record of Egypt's struggle for political independence should end here, but its future is still uncertain. Nasser at first reflected the mood of confidence by adopting a new role among Arab nations. He was no longer content to seek an alliance of Arab governments irrespective of their character; he acted for the Arab revolution. He challenged the administration of Iraq until the monarchy was overthrown and the Baghdad Pact repudiated; he sent troops in large numbers into Yemen to assist the Republicans against the Royalists; he came into bitter conflict with Saudi Arabia which supported the Royalists. But the common Arab threat from Israel overcame these conflicts. In 1967 Egypt believed the Jewish state was menacing Syria. It called on the United Nations peace-keeping force to withdraw from its frontiers[6] and prohibited Israeli ships from the Gulf of Aqaba. As told above, Israel replied by a large-scale invasion and in six days crushed the Egyptian forces, despite heavy arms received from the Soviet Union. Nasser was defeated, but Egypt became again the focus of Arab unity. In Africa, Morocco, Algeria and Sudan rallied to her and, after its *coup* in 1969, Libya also. Only Tunisia, ready to compromise with Israel, remained distant. In Asia, even Saudi Arabia and rich Kuwait came to the help of Cairo to compensate for its losses by the Israeli closure of the Suez Canal. The USA for a time gave aid from its surplus grain stocks (though its military aid was to Israel), but Egypt relied increasingly on the Soviet Union, which despite the suppression of Communists in Cairo, mounted rearmament, particularly jet bombers and missile defences.

Nasser died on September 28, 1970, succeeded by Anwar Sadat, who gave bold leadership in three directions. He took initiatives for peace, supporting American proposals and offering to reopen the Suez Canal; he negotiated federations with Syria and Libya; he dismissed members of his government, on a charge of conspiring against him, who were markedly pro-Russian. The Soviet Union renewed friendship, continuing to supply arms, but Cairo emphasised its non-alignment. Sadat held a precarious balance between peace and war, delivering militant speeches at one moment, keeping the door open for negotiations at another. He had to meet war-excited demonstrations from students and others, but welcomed negotiations by Dr Jarring, the United Nations mediator who made repeated visits between Cairo and Jerusalem in vain, and at times his efforts had to be suspended altogether.

The end is not yet, and no one can say whether war or peace will erupt. The end will not be until Arabs and Jews learn to live together as heirs of the centuries of the Middle East.[7]

Sudan

Sudan and the movements of its people for independence have been entwined with the history of Egypt. From 3000 BC to AD 1880 Northern Sudan was under the influence of Egyptian culture, and parts of Sudan were occupied by Egypt from the second to the first centuries BC. The Sudanese retorted by conquering Egypt from 730 to 160 BC. There is then a gap in historical records, but we know that by AD 500 Sudan was divided into three distinct kingdoms. A Catholic missionary from Alexandria, Father

Julianus, converted the northern kingdom on the edge of Egypt to Christianity, but the Arab conquest in the seventh century gave it to Islam. The Muslim–Arab domination of Egypt was followed by the Turkish occupation, which defeated an attempt to set up an independent Sudanese state in the south under Sultan Fung. The Turks ruled co-operatively, but were opposed by successive revolts, which they finally crushed by severe repression in 1822, establishing a fort at Khartoum as the seat of government. Then came the period of Turkish–Egyptian imperialism, extending to Ethiopia and the Somali coast. The Turks waged this aggression largely by Sudanese forces, raiding the villages of the south and kidnapping black Africans as conscripts. The British Government, jealous of a new power in Africa, intervened against Cairo's expansionism, and had its own generals and troops in Sudan. They were soon to become involved.

Mahdi's Nationalist Triumph

June 29, 1881, was the date of the birth of the modern nationalist movement for Sudanese independence. Mohammed ibn al-Sayyid 'Abdullah proclaimed himself the expected Mahdi (Messiah), divinely appointed to restore Islamic might. The revolt he initiated had two aims, one progressive, one reactionary. It demanded liberation from Turkish–Egyptian domination, but it also claimed the right of Arabs to practise their trade in slaves. The Mahdi massacred an Egyptian force sent to arrest him, retired to the Nubi mountains, annihilated two columns which moved against him and, during the next three years, won a series of dramatic victories over the Egyptians. His claim to be the looked-for Messiah captured the popular imagination. In 1884 the Mahdi closed on Khartoum and in January 1885 faced the British and General Gordon. At Omdurman, across the Nile, he won a spectacular victory, and General Gordon, idolised in Britain for his Christian character, was killed. The Mahdi himself died in June six months after his triumph, but the nationalist struggle persisted under Khalifa 'Abdullah, compelling the Egyptian garrisons to withdraw from Sudan.

British–Egyptian Condominium

London, however, acted vigorously to the reverse at Omdurman, and a new coalition between Britain and Egypt was established. In 1899 they agreed to joint control of Sudan under a condominium which, whilst giving Egypt some authority in internal affairs, placed supreme civil and military powers with a governor-general appointed on the recommendation of the British Government. Lord Kitchener was chosen and he crippled Mahdist power at a second battle at Omdurman in September 1898, confirmed by an overwhelming defeat of Khalifa in December 1899 by forces under Sir Reginald Wingate, who had succeeded Kitchener. Sudan progressed under the Condominium. Egypt subsidised its budget deficit, and there was educational development and the construction of roads and railways. During the First World War Sudan was untouched by military events, though it contributed to the Arab revolt against the Ottoman empire in the Middle East. It prospered by the growth of a new type of cotton by the irrigation of the Gezira between the Blue and White Niles under an ambitious plan administered by Arthur Gaitskell. Meanwhile, there were controversies with Italy, Belgium and France over the frontiers of their neighbouring occupied territories, all settled by agreement but reflecting the colonialist rivalry for Africa.

Nationalist Revival in Second World War

In May 1922 the challenge of the nationalist movement was repeated. A junior officer of a Sudanese battalion of the Egyptian army, 'Ali 'Abd al-Latif, issued a manifesto, 'The Claims of the Sudanese Nation', and organised the White Flag League to press them. He was imprisoned in June 1924, but this alerted a demonstration by the cadets at the Khartoum military school and mutiny in the 'Atbarah railway battalion. In November came the assassination of the British Governor-General in Cairo and the withdrawal of the Egyptian armies from the Sudan by British demand; the Sudanese units were embodied in a Defence Force with British and Sudanese officers; the Condominium was becoming more than ever British. The Second World War saw the Sudanese Defence Force extensively involved, taking part in the expulsion of the Italians from Ethiopia and Eritrea and in the north African campaign. These experiences stimulated Sudanese self-confidence, and in war-time, as always, national consciousness grew. On the eve of the war intellectuals in Khartoum had formed a Graduates' General Council under the leadership of Ismail al-Azhari, and by 1944 the national upsurgence was so great that the British thought it well to establish a Sudanese Advisory Council and to extend Sudanese representation in local government and educational authorities.

Independence Gained

The national movement was, however, divided by two opposing religious sects, the Khatmiyah, led by al-Sayyid Sir 'Ali el-Mirghani, who advocated union with Egypt, and the Ansar, led by the son of the Mahdi, al-Sayyid Sir Abdur Rahman, who claimed Sudanese independence. At the end of the war they were reflected in two parties, the National Unionists favouring Egypt, and *Umma* insisting on independence. In 1947 Britain and Egypt, supposedly partnering the administration of Sudan, came into conflict. As already told, the Egyptians proclaimed King Fuad as monarch of Sudan and abrogated the treaty of 1936 which established the Condominium. It was not more than a paper proclamation, having no effect in Sudan where by now Britain alone retained any power. In June 1948 the Governor-General established a Sudanese Executive Council and announced plans for an elected Legislative Assembly. *Umma* won the election and its secretary, 'Abdullah Khalil, became Chief Minister. The Officers' *coup d'état* in Egypt in July 1952, changed the attitude of Cairo; perhaps the fact that General Neguib was half Sudanese by birth influenced his declaration in favour of self-determination. In the following February Britain and Egypt agreed that Sudan should be self-governing within three years, and it looked at first as though a decision would be taken in favour of union with Egypt. The pro-Cairo National Unionists won the succeeding election, Ismail al-Azhari, leader of the Graduates' Movement becoming Prime Minister. Relations with Egypt did not proceed happily, however, and on January 1, 1956, Sudan declared itself independent. A coalition government was formed and 'Abdullah Khalil of *Umma* again became head of state.

Revolt of the South

We should end here the story of the struggle for independence except for events within Sudan which involve the principle of self-determination. Southern Sudan was not included within the British –Egyptian Condominium and was administered by the British separately with the ultimate idea that it should be joined to Uganda. Only at the last moment before the declaration of independence of Sudan was the South united to the North. The majority of the people of Sudan are Muslims linked with the Arabs of north Africa, but in the south, across swamps and living in jungle territory, are tribes belonging to Black Africa. We have told how at the time of the Egyptian conquest their men were forcibly conscripted in the army; the magnet of a service livelihood led many in succeeding years to enter the forces, but they resented the Muslim domination. In 1955 they mutinied in the Equatorial Battalion, the news of which sparked off disturbances over a large part of the south, ruthlessly suppressed. Christian missions from Britain and America had settled in the villages, opening schools, converting many. In Khartoum the missionaries were regarded as foreign agents subverting the people from loyalty to the Muslim north, and in 1962–3 the schools were nationalised, the Arabic language made compulsory, the missionaries expelled.

Armed revolt broke out in 1963, put down by bloody repression, thousands of refugees fleeing to neighbouring Uganda. Prime Minister Khalifa offered in 1964 to take some southerners into the Cabinet, but by this time the popular demand was for full self-government and the talks ended in disagreement. Rebellion burst out again; again the repression was harsh, but it failed to regain control of much of the country. In 1967 a more moderate government in Khartoum succeeded in getting the southern political parties to agree to participate in elections, but they could not be held in many districts still held by the rebels. Then there was a political revolution in Khartoum, following the adoption by a majority in the National Constitutional Committee of a motion to make Sudan a democratic socialist republic, and the Left government entered into discussions with the South in a more conciliatory attitude. This was followed by a second *coup* and *counter-coup* in quick succession leading to the exclusion of the Communists from the Government, the public execution of the former Minister of State for Southern Affairs, Joseph Garang, who had laid the ground for the later agreement between North and

South, and of the trade union leader, Shafir-el-Sheikh, shocked world opinion. Whilst moderate southerners accepted autonomy, extremer forces battled on for independence.[8]

Agreement is Reached

Then in February 1972 a dramatic change took place. After seventeen years of war, with a generation existing from childhood in the continuous presence of death, not only from fighting but also from disease, agreement was reached at Addis Ababa in Ethiopia between representatives of the Sudanese Government and the Southern rebel movement, the Anyanya. The southern region was to become autonomous with its own National Assembly and President and also to be proportionally represented in the national army. The agreement was the result of the combined efforts of OAU, the World Council of Churches, Christian Aid and Liberation (MCF) whose secretary, Barbara Haq, was a pioneer in bringing the two sides together. Sir Dingle Foot, Labour's former Solicitor-General, was invaluable as legal adviser and success was largely due to the conciliatory negotiations of the Vice-President of the Sudan Republic, Abel Alier, a Southerner and Minister for Southern Affairs. The task of rehabilitation was recognised to be immense, but representatives of United Nations agencies, the International Red Cross, and relief organisations, met at Khartoum and prepared plans for co-operation. This was one of the most cheering developments in Africa in recent years, though it may yet be that die-hards in the South may not concur.

Notes

1. Afterwards the Gezira Plan became one of the most successful developments in Africa.

2. To save Egypt's economy Britain bought its entire cotton crop in 1940.

3. Ismail Sidky had become ill and these negotiations took place with Nokrashi, who was again Prime Minister.

4. Six members of the dissolved Parliament were executed for conspiracy in this attempt.

5. Mr Anthony Nutting, Minister at the British Foreign Office, resigned and later revealed the truth. The most factual record

appeared in *The Suez Expedition 1956,* written by General André Beaufre, who was in charge of French forces and himself participated as French representative in the negotiations with the Israelis and Sir Anthony Eden.

6. Egypt had the legal right to do this. Israel had declined to allow the UN force in its territory.

7. Towards the end of 1972 world public opinion was startled by the expulsion of Russian military personnel from Egypt. Nevertheless, good relations with Moscow were maintained.

8. The second *coup* led to the withdrawal of Sudan from federation with Egypt, Libya and Syria and the alienation of Russia. Leading members of the previous government were hanged and the Communist Party banned.

Chapter Ten

North Africa

(Morocco, Mauritania, Algeria, Tunisia, Libya)

North Africa, the southern coast of the Mediterranean, is mostly Arabic in population, descending from the Arab invasion of the seventh century. Not entirely so; there are the assertive Berbers of Morocco and Algeria and others of indigenous stock. But from Morocco in the west with its offshoot Mauritania, across Algeria, Tunisia and Libya to Egypt, and then south to Sudan reaching to Black Africa, we have olive-skinned peoples, distinct from the rest of the continent. They feel their first identity, perhaps, with their fellow-Arabs in western Asia, but they are a part of Africa and are increasingly demonstrating their unity with it.[1]

Following the end of French and Italian occupation of North Africa, there was much talk of the union of Morocco, Algeria, Tunisia and Libya in Maghreb. Indeed in 1964 they were linked within a Maghreb Permanent Consultative Committee. Feelings of national prestige and differences in ideologies and constitutional and economic structures obstructed approaches to union. Libya federated with Egypt, and it was not until May 1972, that the three ex-French colonies moved together. President Boumedienne of Algeria visited Tunisia and King Hassan of Morocco telegraphed accord. At the moment the co-operation is in industrial development and common relations with the European Community, but the joint communiqué indicated wide political interests in concern to be involved in conferences on the Mediterranean and even European security. Maghreb unity may yet develop.

Morocco

Few territories have been the victim of colonialist power rivalry more than Morocco. France, Spain, Portugal, Britain and Germany have all been involved. Indeed, Morocco, climax of the conflict between competing imperialisms, dramatised one of the major causes of the First World War. But that was near the end of the long story of Moroccan occupation and resistance.

Occupations and Resistance

Far back in the twelfth century BC the Phoenicians established ports in Morocco and in the fifth century BC came the Carthaginians. Then from the first to the fifth centuries AD there was Roman domination with peace enforced, and later temporary Christianisation. In 682 the Muslim conquest swept across the northern coast, enslaving the Berbers. It was the aggressive Berbers of the Sahara who subsequently conquered Morocco in 1061. Yusuf ibn Tashfin, leader of the Almoravids, after much tribal conflict brought the whole of Morocco under his authority, extending it to Algiers and Tunisia, and across the straits to parts of Spain. In turn, the Almohad tribe overcame the Almoravids, and the Marinids overcame the Almohads. The population became Arab–Moorish, the ports Spanish–Moorish.

Europeans Compete

During the fifteenth century the Portuguese arrived, disrupting the territory into small tribal states. From southern Morocco came the cry for a holy war against the European invaders, who were defeated by joint Arab–Berber forces at the battle of the Three Kings in 1578. For more than two centuries Morocco was free from serious European intervention, but in 1830 France began its assault on northern Africa, starting in Algeria. Morocco went to the aid of the Algerians, but were defeated at Wadi Isly in 1844, and the sultan surrendered to the French in 1847. Portugal and France had opened the European armed gamble for Morocco. The conflict now became three-sided – Moroccan resistance to foreign occupation and the two foreign nations acting against each other.

Spain was next in the field. Troops built a fortification at Ceuta which was attacked by tribesmen, and in October 1859 the Spanish declared war. At this point Britain also intervened. Its government, concerned about the control of the Straits of Gibraltar, declared that it would not accept permanent Spanish occupation of the Moroccan coast. When peace between the Moroccans and the Spanish came in April 1860 it was a compromise. Spain received an indemnity for the attack on the Ceuta fortification, its enclave there was extended, and it was ceded fishing rights in perpetuity; but there was no wider occupation. Encouraged, Moroccans used the rivalry between the European powers to limit concessions,

Tangier was given special status and protection was guaranteed to its Moorish citizens. Britain, still thinking of Gibraltar, exerted influence on the side of Moroccan independence, expanding its trade and gaining privileges. In 1880, on British initiative, a conference of the involved European powers was held at Madrid. It confirmed protection for the rights and interests of Moroccans. Meanwhile, Sultan Mulay al-Hasan (1873–94), who had vigorously resisted European intervention, succeeded in unifying the country again, only for his successor, Abdul-Aziz, a playboy, to fritter it away in division and decadence.

European Powers hastened to take advantage of Morocco's weakness. France and Spain signed a secret agreement in 1902 allocating the Marrakech area in the south to France and all the rest of the territory to Spain (for some reason Spain failed formally to ratify the agreement). At the same time France and Italy agreed not to obstruct each other's plans in Morocco and Libya respectively, and in 1904 came the fateful Anglo-French *entente*. It gave France a free hand in Morocco, conditional on no fortification of the coast of the Straits, in return, as we have told, for a free British hand in Egypt. Later the same year France and Spain came to an agreement by which the Spanish should occupy the northern zone in Morocco. At last the colonial bandits had decided to share the spoils. Portugal appeared to be left out; it was busy colonising Angola, Mozambique and Guiné.

Germany Challenges

Germany was also an African coloniser, with occupied territories in Tanganyika, Togoland, the Camerouns and South West Africa. It resented the Anglo-French agreement to settle spheres of influence on the Mediterranean coast and in 1905 its government dispatched a warship to anchor off Tangier as an assertion of its right to participate. After much diplomatic discussion an international conference was held at Algeciras in 1906. Here it was solemnly affirmed that Morocco was independent, but nevertheless the conference nominated European agencies to intervene if thought necessary, with France dominant and Spanish participation. In addition, a 'state' bank controlled by the French was set up, Paris was given the monopoly of government finances, and French–Spanish gendarmerie were imposed on the ports. Not surprisingly there was Moroccan rebellion. France thereupon occupied the mountains on the Algerian frontier and landed troops at Casablanca, whilst Spain sent in ninety thousand troops after attacks from the militant miners of Rif. From 1910 to 1911 French and Spanish forces controlled most of Morocco.

In 1911 an event occurred which had little effect on Morocco immediately, but which profoundly affected the future of the world. The German Intelligence Service claimed to have found that the 1904 Anglo-French Agreement included secret understandings which went much further than was publicly admitted in dividing Africa into British and French spheres. Ostentatiously the German Government in July 1911 sent a gunboat to anchor in the harbour of Agadir. This incident caused excited reactions in all diplomatic circles. France compromised, ceding territory in the Congo basin to the German-occupied Camerouns in return for recognition of her authority in Morocco, but the British Government took a sterner view, relating the Agadir challenge to Prussian assertiveness in Europe. It was the gunboat in Agadir harbour which sparked off Britain's heavy naval expansion and the arms rivalry with Germany which finally exploded in war. Competition to control Africa was one of the causes of the First World War.

French Protectorate

France took full advantage of European acknowledgement of her authority in Morocco. The sultan, Abd-el-Hafidh, submitted in March 1912, signing the treaty of Fez which established a French protectorate over the whole country except for stretches of Spanish possessions on the coast. When Abd-el-Hafidh, ashamed of his surrender, abdicated, the French contrived the appointment of his brother whose first principle was co-operation with Paris. But resistance had not been crushed. There were revolts in Fez and Mauritania, and a Moroccan hero arose. Abd-el-Krim defeated the Spanish at Annal and for four years made Rif and the country around an independent state. Only in 1926 was the rising suppressed by large French and Spanish forces and even then there had to be some compromise. Legislation would be authorised in the name of the sultan, though in fact France and Spain determined it. Three years earlier Tangier had been given international status outside direct French or Spanish control.

Independence Movement

Recognition must be given to the economic and social advance under the administration of France. Roads and railways were built, ports developed, and education and medical services introduced. European residents numbered half a million and Morocco became a modern state. As always, education created a younger generation, more self-respecting and self-reliant, demanding rights. Experience of war intensified this Arabic confidence. General Franco in 1936 recruited Muslim Moroccan troops to serve in his rebellion against the Republican Government in Spain and they returned claiming self-government; liberalisation had to be conceded. The Second World War had the same effect. A vigorous Independence Party arose, *Istiqlal*, demanding the restoration of Moroccan sovereignty. The sultan, Mohammed V (Sidi Mohammed ben Yusuf), outspokenly identified himself with the aims of the party and with the Arab movements for independence in Algeria and Tunisia. He became immensely popular in the postwar years, regarded with almost idolatry in Morocco and by demonstrating students in Paris. France tried conciliation through minor reforms; *Istiqlal* became more demanding. Then France took the opposite course, arresting the *Istiqlal* leaders in December 1952, and in August 1953 deposing the sultan and exiling him in Madagascar.[2] Resistance exploded, mounting to an armed rising by the challenging Rif in 1955.

Independence Gained

France was now in difficulties with rebellion in neighbouring Algeria. The exiled sultan, Mohammed ben Yusuf, was brought to Paris from Madagascar, and the compliant sultan whom the French had appointed was deposed and replaced by a Regency Council. Still the people rallied to *Istiqlal*. A dramatic incident symbolised the invincibility of the Moroccan cause. El-Glaoui, who had led a French-sponsored clique against the Sultan Mohammed, fell on his knees before him and begged forgiveness. Paris realised that its day was over. By the Declaration of La Calle St Cloud (November 1955), France recognised the independence of Morocco, completing formal agreement in March 1956. Spain followed suit in April. Tangier lost its international status to become a part of Morocco. Sultan Mohammed returned.

Dictatorship and Concessions

Unity behind the sultanate did not continue when Mohammed died, succeeded by his son Hassan II. A moderately socialist Opposition arose, combining intellectuals and trade unionists, named the *Union Nationale des Forces Populaires* (UNFP). One of its leaders was Ben Barka, who had been the chairman of the National Assembly. Following an election, when the Socialists were defeated (it was alleged) by intimidation of the rural voters, the party was suppressed and the leaders arrested. Ben Barka escaped to Paris, where he was kidnapped and apparently murdered. The head of the Moroccan security force was among those found guilty, leading to a break in diplomatic relations between France and Morocco for several years.

The sultan ruled in semi-dictatorship. In July 1971 a *coup* was attempted by radical dissidents and the sultan only narrowly escaped assassination. He realised that moderation was necessary and of the thousand arrested and tried by a military court only one was sentenced to death and seventy-three sentenced to imprisonment. In February 1972 the sultan announced democratic changes to be submitted to a referendum. Two-thirds of the National Assembly would be elected by direct suffrage and a third by electoral colleges. His own power would be limited to that of 'arbitrator'. These concessions followed considerable unrest including a boycott of the National Assembly by the Opposition parties and strikes of soldiers and fourteen thousand students, which closed all universities and schools. The Opposition parties, supported by trade unions and students, rejected the sultan's reforms, insisting on conditions for genuinely free elections, the Arabisation of education (largely run by French teachers), land reforms and the elimination of corruption in high places. The referendum was stated to have resulted in a favourable vote of 98·75 per cent. The Opposition urged the electors to refrain from voting. The outcome of the struggle for democracy remains uncertain.[3]

Mauritania

Mauritania lies to the south of Morocco, divided by a strip of Spanish Sahara, extending along the Atlantic coast to Senegal. Its population is only one million, but its largely desert territory stretches to nearly five times Morocco's size.

The first known inhabitants were Negroes and Berbers, the latter important, as we have seen, in resisting foreign occupations of Morocco. In the eleventh century the Berbers of Mauritania, the Almoravids, not only swept across North Africa to Tunis but repulsed the empire of Ghana ruling from the Congo to the Sahara. In the fifteenth century, however, the Arabs infiltrated south and submerged the Berbers.

European Penetration

The Portuguese, as so often, were the first Europeans to arrive, founding in 1448 a fort at Aquin, an assault post for gold and slaves. Then came the English and the French, the latter the more persistent, settling at Saint Louis on the mouth of the river Senegal and occupying the interior. In 1920 Mauritania became part of French West Africa, later a colony, still later integrated with France, governed from Senegal. There was no effective resistance from the people, partly nomads, partly isolated villagers.

Independence

The Moroccans insisted that Mauritania was their territory and there were raids in 1956 and 1957. As late as 1964 King Hassan II revived this claim, but in 1957 the Mauritanian people elected an independent government under Mohtar ould Daddah and the following year voted in favour of self-governing membership of the French Community. In November 1960 their full independence was recognised by France, and the following year Mauritania became a member-state of the United Nations. There is still minority support for union with Morocco.

Algeria

Small incidents often provide the excuse for big events. In 1827 two Algerian farmers pressed French payment for wheat deliveries outstanding since the 1790s. The Dey Hussein discussed the matter with the French Consul and threatened to withdraw the concession of a fortified trading post near Annaba. The two men quarrelled and the Dey flicked the Consul with a fly-whisk. To avenge the insult, Charles II sent a naval and military expedition and Hussein was compelled to capitulate in July 1830. Thus French occupation began. The city of Algiers was taken over and a virtual protectorate established on the coast.

French Oust Turks

French possession of Algeria followed many other occupations. Its Arab population are derived from the Muslim conquest of North Africa from 647 to 711. There was resistance by the indigenous Berbers, who even to this day are a militant minority. We have told how Berber tribes overran Algeria from Morocco during the eleventh, twelfth and thirteenth centuries. The Arabs recovered power, but in the sixteenth century came the Spanish invasion, occupying towns on the coast, levying tribute, enforcing a protectorate. A very unofficial diplomatic channel was the means of ending this occupation. The Arab leaders asked Turkish pirates, who used the Algerian coast as a base, for their help and the pirates appealed to the Ottoman sultan, who responded by sending strong forces. The Spanish were expelled (1529), but the Algerians exchanged one master only for another. They became a vassal state of the Ottoman empire. Some resistance developed, but it was not until the early nineteenth century that the supremacy of the Turks was overthrown. In 1830, as already described, came the French invasion.

Aided by Moroccans, resistance to French rule was persistent. The city of Constantine was occupied by the Arabs and fell only after seven years. Abd-el-Kader called for a holy war in 1837, to which the French retorted by deciding to colonise the whole territory. They sent columns deep into the interior to seize cattle and crops and to destroy olive trees; in December 1847 Abd-el surrendered. This was the end of serious resistance for a century, though periodically the French had to renew minor campaigns of suppression. Meanwhile, France in 1848 integrated Algeria with itself, Napoleon III declaring: 'I am just as much Emperor of the Arabs as I am of the French.' In 1865 a Senate decree declared that the Algerian Muslim was a Frenchman, though without political rights he was a subject rather than a citizen. France colonised thoroughly and took advantage of an uprising in 1871 to confiscate tribal land. An Act was passed to give the settlers the right to acquire communal lands.

Nationalist Resistance

In the 1930s the nationalist movement revived. There was division regarding tactics. Ferhat Abbas, influential intellectual, advocated assimilation with the French through education and enfranchisement. Massali Haj, forthright leader of the *Mouvement pour le Triomphe des Libertés Democratiques* (MTLD), demanded independence. By 1943 Ferhat Abbas had become disillusioned. Only one in eight of the Arab children of school age was receiving education and there was widespread unemployment and hunger. In the war-time atmosphere of democracy versus Fascism, he issued a manifesto claiming an independent Arab State federated with France. General de Gaulle responded by praising Muslim loyalty in the North African campaign, by extending French citizenship to educated Algerians (1944), and by admitting fifteen Deputies to the National Assembly and seven Senators to the Council of the Republic (1946). Ironically it was at a celebration of the Allied victory over Nazism that the conflict between the Nationalists and French burst into flame; at a demonstration at Setif there was a clash between the police and Africans carrying nationalist flags. This was enough. Violent spontaneous uprisings occurred followed by ruthless repression. Eighty-eight Frenchmen were killed and the official estimate reported 1,500 Arab deaths. The French Constituent Assembly refused to discuss Ferhat Abbas's proposal, but created an Algerian Assembly, half of whose members would be elected by 58,000 voters, half by an electoral college. Reforms were promised, but the Assembly failed to enact them.

Seven Years' War

On the night of October 31–November 1, 1954, the seven years' war began. Preparations had been carefully made by activists who had seceded from the MTLD to form the *Front de Libération Nationale* (FLN). Its manifesto declared for the complete restoration of sovereignty, with all residents accepting Algerian nationality (including the French) as citizens. The rising began with attacks on police and forest guard posts, but by the summer it took a more savage form on both sides. When in August 1955, Algerians massacred French near Skikda, this was met by a large-scale execution of Arabs in the stadium. The Algerians had the fervent support, short only of armed intervention, of their fellow-Arabs in North Africa and set up their headquarters in Cairo, later, in Tunisia, which turned a blind eye to forces which re-formed across its frontier and provided as best they could for Algerian refugees.[4]

In 1956 France had a socialist Prime Minister, Guy Mollet, with a programme for peace. He proposed an imposed cease-fire, elections and negotiations; he went to Algiers, but he had a hostile reception from the settlers and the peace move fell away. The Algerian forces, greatly increased, were holding the French at bay. Meanwhile there were two interludes which were important for the future. In October 1956 a plane from Morocco *en route* for Tunis, convoying five Algerian leaders, including Ahmed ben Bella, was diverted to Algiers and the five were arrested; Ben Bella was afterwards to become Prime Minister. Secondly, oil was discovered in southern Algeria. France promptly detached two provinces from Algeria and administered them directly from Paris under a Minister for the Sahara.

De Gaulle Negotiates

The war was now fierce. France became notorious for deliberately torturing prisoners;[5] the Algerians were charged with intimidating villagers. The settlers in Algiers and the coastal towns were suspicious that Paris would negotiate peace and staged vast and angry demonstrations, with the support of the Right in France, demanding that de Gaulle assume power and fight the war to a finish. Their protest was so intimidating that it caused a political crisis and, almost overnight, General de Gaulle was acclaimed President. The settlers, however, had a shock. The man they had jerked to the Presidency repudiated a continuation of Algeria's integration with France, opted for its associated self-government, announced an impressive plan for Muslim educational and economic development, and finally offered to discuss terms of peace with the FLN.[6] At first there was no response. The war was on a major scale; there were half a million troops. But de Gaulle persisted. In September 1959 he proposed that four years after a cease-fire the Algerians should by a free vote decide between (1) integration, (2) independence in association with France and (3) independence with secession. The settlers were now thoroughly disillusioned. They exploded in an insurrection in January 1960; it collapsed, but in April 1961 four French generals led a second revolt which took three days to crush.

Independence

De Gaulle then assumed extraordinary powers and initiated secret negotiations at Évian-les-Bains between the French Minister for Algerian Affairs, Louis Joxe, and Belka-cem-Krim, the Foreign Secretary of the Algerian Provisional Government (GPRA). On March 18, 1962, a cease-fire was signed at Evian. A referendum on independence would be held and France would accept its decision; in return, France would be allowed to maintain its experimental rocket and nuclear testing sites in Sahara for five years. Ben Bella and the four other Algerian arrested leaders were released. Temporary administration was placed under a council composed of nine Algerians (six FLN) and three Europeans.

The French people endorsed the Evian agreement in a referendum by a 90·7 per cent vote, but the settlers formed a secret organisation, *Organisation de l'Armée Secrète* (OAS) to resist its application and commenced terrorist activity, killing Algerian Muslims, blowing up schools, hospitals and town halls. Its leader, General Salan, was captured in April 1962, whereupon the majority of the French fled from Algiers to France. On July 1, the referendum of the Algerian people gave a vote of 5,975,581 to 16,534 in favour of independence in co-operation with France. Two days later General de Gaulle recognised the independence of Algeria. In October Algeria was accepted as a member-state of the United Nations.

Leadership Conflict

As in Morocco, hostility broke out among the leaders, but, again like Morocco, it was more than personal; the differences were ideological. It happened earlier in Algeria. On the day independence was recognised, Ben Khedda, who had replaced Ferhat Abbas as Prime Minister of the Provisional Government, moved with his Ministers from Tunis to Algiers. He was received with enthusiasm, but the still more popular Ben Bella was absent. From Morocco he announced that he differed from Ben Khedda on neo-colonialism and declared that the revolution must be continued to realise Socialism. Reaching Oran he ordered the army to march on Algiers and it did so under Colonel Boumedienne. Ben Bella triumphed. When the elections came the Political Bureau of the FLN excluded Ben Khedda and his supporters and the National Assembly voted Ben Bella Prime Minister with Boumedienne

Defence Minister. The conflict in leadership did not end here; once more it had an ideological basis. With the army behind him, Boumedienne carried out a bloodless *coup* in January 1964, to modify the revolution.

Ben Bella's government had socialised the vineyard estates, factories and shops deserted by the French and instituted workers' control, but the economy had suffered from lack of technical management. Boumedienne limited workers' control and risked the charge of neo-colonialism by co-operating with the French, making an agreement with them for the joint exploitation of Sahara oil. In foreign affairs, however, Boumedienne followed a militantly Left line. He broke diplomatic relations with Britain over Rhodesia in December 1965, and declared war on Israel in June 1967. The most satisfactory event was a frontier settlement with Morocco initiated by the Organisation of African Unity, after a sharp conflict. Algeria intervened in the Middle East, supporting the Palestinian guerrillas.

Tunisia

Tunisian early history is similar to that of its North African neighbours: the Phoenician occupation from the twelfth century BC, the conflict between Greeks and Romans until the latter's victory in 146 BC, the Islam conquest which reached Tunis in AD 647, creating a potentially Arab population. Characteristically the Berbers offered periodical resistance, and it was the Berber tribes, the Almohads and Almoravids, who swept in from Morocco and Algeria and united the Muslim west in the twelfth century. Once more the story of Algeria was repeated. Turkish pirates extended their domination of the coast to the interior and Tunisia became part of the Ottoman North African empire.

French Preferred to Turks

It was not until the eighteenth century that the Arab–Berber population under the Hussein dynasty reasserted themselves. Hussein challenged the Turks by turning towards Europe, copying its modernisation and encouraging trade. This pro-European attitude led to hostility with the Arabs of Algeria who, as we have told, resisted both the Turkish occupation and the French invaders at the beginning of the nineteenth century. Preferring the French to the Turks, the Tunisian Bey supported their invasion, thinking it would be temporary, but by so doing created a serious breach of Arab unity. Modernisation and Europeanisation were advanced further by Bey Ahmed (1837–55) who abolished slavery, emancipated Jews, gave facilities to Christian schools and established an army under British and French officers.

Ahmed sought to play off the two European powers against each other, but he got into financial difficulties by the cost of modernisation and had to offer both high rates of interest for loans. The next Bey, Mohammed, whilst extending democratic rights and reforms, under pressure made further concessions to Britain and France: railway construction to Britain and telegraph installation and aqueduct repairs to France. By now taxation to meet the interest on loans had become oppressive and there were widespread uprisings, the people even looking towards Turkey for relief. In 1869 came total bankruptcy, leading to financial control by Britain, France and Italy (increasingly interested in northern Africa). An international commission was set up to receive all state revenue and to distribute it among the European creditors. There was considerable rivalry between the three Powers, but they were united against a return of Turkish influence.

French Protectorate

British influence was greatest for a time and there was even the possibility of a British protectorate. The defeat of France by Prussia in 1871 strengthened Italian ambitions, but when Rome threatened a naval demonstration it was held back by British–French intervention in which Turkey also co-operated. Public feeling by this time was so strong against the European Powers that the Bey reaffirmed Turkish suzerainty (1871); the treaty between them recognised the Bey's authority in internal affairs whilst reserving foreign relations to the sultan. But the British–French objective to control persisted. In 1878 London and Paris made a deal. France recognised the British occupation of Cyprus and in return Britain gave France a free hand to penetrate Tunisia. The French had a growing fear of Italy, which actually had the greater number of settlers, and seized the excuse of a tribal incursion from Tunisia into Algeria, by now under French control, to send in a force of thirty thousand men. The Bey yielded and signed the Treaty of Bardo, which, whilst guaranteeing safety for himself and his dynasty, authorised French military occupation, transferred the direction of foreign affairs to France, and imposed conditions for the repayment of Tunisia's debts. The spirit of resistance to foreign domination, however, was still vigorous among the people, and a rising in the south spread over the country. The French retaliated by a naval bombardment of Tunis and large troop reinforcements, and in 1883, came the final blow, a French protectorate was instituted. Theoretically, the Bey was left as ruler, but in fact control passed to France in all fields, legislative, administrative and judicial.

Nationalist Parties

The historical argument for a period of colonialism was borne out in Tunisia by economic progress under the French, mostly in the interest of the settlers, who poured into the country in large numbers, but from which the Arabs also benefited. Railways were extended, ports built, hospitals and schools opened, national finances restored. The newly educated Arab middle class asserted itself by forming in 1907 the Young Tunisian Party to demand independence and after the First World War, in 1920, *Destour* (Constitution), the first national-scale party, was established. When in 1922 Bey Sedi-Naceur threatened to abdicate in support of the nationalist demands, France realised that it faced a serious challenge. It reacted with the classical colonialist response – first repression and then reforms, which kept Tunisia quiet for a time and *Destour* subdued. The year 1934 was the next crucial date. The younger Nationalists set up *Neo-Destour*, with a thirty-year-old lawyer, Habib Bourguiba, as Secretary-General. Both party and president were destined to be determining in Tunisia's history.

Neo-Destour acted with political maturity despite its youth. Whilst militantly resisting the French occupation, it had sufficient sense of world affairs to co-operate with the *Front Populaire* government in Paris even before the World War against Nazism began. Nevertheless, the French arrested Bourguiba and his principal colleagues in 1939 and they remained in a fortress until the Germans occupied Vichy in 1942. The Nazis transferred Bourguiba to Rome and endeavoured to get him to endorse the Axis cause, but he courageously refused. In March 1943 they took him back to Tunisia, then under their occupation, and tried to get acceptance of a Vichy-French and fascist Italian condominium, but Bourguiba and the Bey rejected it.

On the defeat of the Germans and Italians, Bourguiba approached the new French Government with a proposal for a gradual evolution to autonomy, but there was no response and he had to escape to Cairo in 1945, leaving Salah-ben-Yusuf to lead. Moderate politicians and notables in Tunisia who had co-operated with the French then appealed for internal autonomy. Paris, reflecting settler opinion, turned this down, with the result that the moderates endorsed *Neo-Destour's* demand for independence. By 1950 the French thought better of their intransigence and promised Tunisia autonomy by negotiated stages and instructed the resident-general, Louis Perillier, to initiate discussion. The Bey appointed a Ministry of Negotiation, including the acting-leader of *Neo-Destour*, Salah-ben-Yusuf. The talks broke down, however, because France would not concede an elected Parliament and repression recurred. Bourguiba, who had returned to Tunis, and other national leaders were arrested, though ben-Yusuf got away to Cairo. Nearly three years of disturbances followed, begun by guerrilla fighting in the mountains. *Neo-Destour* had by now made itself into a comprehensive national movement, including a powerful trade union organisation, a large and active women's league, and a virile youth section. All were nominally suppressed, making public gatherings impossible, but they carried on under cover. The cause suffered a great personal loss in the assassination of Ferhat Hashad, loved Labour leader, by French extremists.

Independence

The situation was changed by the premiership of Pierre Mendès-France in Paris. He withdrew the ban on the trade union and political movements and accepted the right of Tunisia to complete autonomy. The author was present at the first trade union congress in 1954 after the proscription was removed and, with the agreement of Ben Sellah, the new Secretary (well trained by service at the Brussels headquarters of the International Confederation of Free Trade Unions), he urged in the new circumstances a policy of 'negotiation and non-violence'. Mendès-France sent for the text of this speech and shortly afterwards opened negotiations with *Neo-Destour* representatives in Paris to work out a programme for an elected Parliament and self-government. The programme fell short of absolute independence, nor was Bourguiba's release promised, and at first the *Neo-Destour* delegates declined to accept it on these grounds. However, Bourguiba himself, under house-arrest near by, urged them to do so, confident that independence would follow rapidly. On June 3, 1955, a convention was signed. Within a few weeks Bourguiba was released and a *Neo-Destour* government formed in Tunis. On March 20, 1956, France recognised the independence of Tunisia, which was admitted to the United Nations under its sponsorship. By agreement the French retained troops in Tunisia and a military base at Bizerta. The monarchy was abolished in July 1957, and Bourguiba became President.[7]

Military Presence Ended

The story of Tunisian struggle for freedom does not end here. The *Neo-Destour* administration, eager for economic independence, came into conflict with French business interests. The world was surprised by news in February 1958, that the French had bombed the village of Soqiyat Sidi Yusuf. Tunisia reacted by confining all French troops to barracks, and an Anglo-American Committee of Good Offices was appointed to prevent a deepening of the crisis. On assuming power General de Gaulle eased the situation by withdrawing all troops except from the Bizerta base. The customs union with France was abolished, Tunisia was permitted a state bank and its own currency, education was Arabised. In foreign affairs Tunisia leaned towards the West and received aid from the USA. Although temporarily a member of the Arab League, the Government angered Egypt and other Arab states by making conciliatory proposals for a settlement with Israel.

But the conflict with France regarding its military presence was not over. In 1961 Bourguiba pressed for the termination of the base at Bizerta and for a readjustment of the Sahara frontier of Algeria, still occupied by France. The French were obdurate and Tunisia isolated Bizerta by erecting barricades at the exits and attacked the French on the Algerian frontier at Fort and Thiriet. French aircraft bringing reinforcements to Bizerta from Algeria were fired on and some fighting followed. The French responded by bombing a largely civilian protest march carrying banners demanding withdrawal from the base. Official figures put the Tunisian dead at a thousand and the French at twenty, but many Tunisians estimated their casualties even higher. Tunisia took its case to the Security Council of the United Nations, a truce was arranged, and the French promised to evacuate the Bizerta base. It did so in December 1963, followed by a mass exodus by the French from Tunisia.

Meanwhile, relations with the Arabs in Algeria improved by Tunisia acting as hosts to the government in exile, providing for refugees and allowing the rebel forces to re-form on its side of the frontier. After Algeria obtained its independence in July 1962, estrangement was renewed, however, on Middle East policy, because of Bourguiba's conciliatory line towards Israel. Tunisia pursued a moderate policy of socialisation, the most striking feature of which was an elaborate co-operative scheme for agriculture planned by Ben Sellah, former Secretary of the Trade Union Congress, then made a Minister. It proved too elaborate and broke down. Ben Sellah was dismissed and imprisoned on other allegations.[8] Political independence did not revolutionise the conditions of the mass of the people. Without the oil of its neighbours, Algeria and Libya, Tunisia faced economic difficulties and some discontent grew, particularly directed to the élitist standard of living of its governing class. Changes will still come.

Libya

In original Greek the name Libya meant all of northern Africa and for a time, in the tenth century BC, a Libyan dynasty ruled Egypt, but historically Libya has been associated with the three regions, Tripolitania, Cyrenaica and Fezzan, all lying to the east of Tunisia. It is of interest that early engravings indicate, even before the Arab invasion, a population of a Mediterranean type distinct from the Negroid races beyond the Sahara. In succession, the three regions were colonised by Greeks, Romans, Muslim–Arabs and Turks (continuously resisted by the aboriginal Berbers), parallel with the occupation of most of the Mediterranean coast.

Italian Occupation

These occupations were periodically interrupted from Europe and by other North Africans. Tripoli was captured in 1146 by Sicilians, who were driven out by the Berber Almohads, Moroccan conquerors of Tunisia, in 1158. In 1355 Italians invaded from Genoa, sacking Tripoli, and in 1510 Charles V, taking possession of the city, transferred it to the Knights of St John in Malta. The Turkish occupation followed, challenged by British, Dutch, French and Portuguese naval expeditions, and later, from 1801 to 1805, even by the USA, concerned about shipping rights. Ottoman rule, which was fiercely resisted by the Tripolitanians in the nineteenth century, was finally overthrown by the Italians in 1911 when they declared war to claim security for Italian lives and property. To their surprise, the Arab people did not welcome Italian rule any more than Turkish, and it was only after a severe conflict that the territory was declared annexed in November 1911; by 1914 the Italians had occupied the whole of what is now Libya. With the First World War they had to retire to the coastal towns, but at the end of the war more liberal governments in Rome sought co-operation by establishing Parliaments, still with Italian governors, in Tripolitania and Cyrenaica.

The Libyans retorted by declaring independence and fervently resisted under the heroic leadership of Omar Mujhdar, a Senussi sheikh and head of Islamic purists. When he was executed by the Italians, the nationalist rebels offered the throne to another Senussi chief, Mohammed Idris, who showed similar courage against European occupation but never established himself. The subsequent fascist governments in Italy were more ruthless. They crushed the resistance in Tripolitania in 1923, in Fezzan in 1929, and Cyrenaica in 1932, herding the opposition in concentration camps. In 1934 they united Tripolitania and Cyrenaica as a colony, treating Fezzan purely as a military territory. The Italians built cities, constructed roads, piped water supplies, all of which permanently benefited Libya, but they did so, as ever by colonialists, mostly in the interest of their own settlers. They placed thirty thousand Italian peasants on irrigated land. In 1939 Libya was incorporated as a part of Italy.

Independence

The Second World War ended Italian colonisation. A Libyan force co-operated with the British army, and London promised Mohammed Idris that the territory should not revert to Italian domination. When the United Nations Organisation was established, the future of Libya was referred to the Security Council.

The principle of independence was accepted and, with the co-operation of the UN High Commissioner, Adriaan Pel, a Dutch representative, the Libyan Assembly drafted a constitution for a federation of the three territories under King Idris. Independence was achieved in December 1951.

Libya, however, did not gain participating democracy or economic independence. Its government was more dependent upon the royal family than Parliament, and its budget was balanced only by grants from Britain (Treaty, 1953) and the USA (Agreement, 1954). In return military and air bases were placed at the disposal of the Western Powers. Libya joined the Arab League in March 1953, contributing a moderating influence in line with the foreign policy of Whitehall and Washington. Then, in 1959, came the discovery of oil in Tripolitania and Cyrenaica, which revolutionised the economic and, eventually, the political situation; the revenue made Libya no longer dependent upon Britain and America. The first sign of democratic self-reliance was the abolition in 1963 of the federal constitution, whose division between Tripolitania and Cyrenaica, always rivals, assisted the rule of the king, and the establishment instead of a unitary state.

King Idris, once their hero, lost touch with the people. Oil riches brought corruption, nepotism and vaunting extravagance in the royal circle. When both Houses called for the abrogation of the treaties with Britain and the USA giving them military bases, the king dissolved Parliament and there seemed little doubt that the subsequent election to the Chamber of Deputies was rigged, whilst all the members of the Senate were nominated from the Palace.

The Revolution

On September 1, 1969, came the *coup*. It was secretly prepared and took all the Powers – Britain, America, France and Russia – by surprise. King Idris was in Turkey for health treatment and at first dismissed the news as unimportant, but the revolution was accepted without bloodshed by the people and great demonstrations showed popular support. The Crown Prince Hassan, the King's nephew, threw in his lot with the rebellion and abdicated.

As in Cairo in 1953, when King Farouk was overthrown, and in Baghdad in 1958 when General Kassem was brought to power, the *coup* was the work of young colonels who largely remained anonymous and called themselves the 'Free United Officers', of whom

Colonel Moammar Kaddafi became known prominently. They established a cabinet of eight, which included only two army representatives, though the real head of the government remained Colonel Kaddafi. The Prime Minister was Dr Mohammed Soliman al Maghrabi, thirty-four years of age, a graduate in philosophy at George Washington University in USA, sentenced to four years imprisonment and deprived of Libyan nationality before the *coup*. The Foreign Secretary was Salah Bousseir, who had been the young vice-chairman of the Chamber of Deputies and an exile in Egypt since 1955. The Government's programme was announced as Socialism and Arab Nationalism, 'dedicated to the struggle against colonialism and racism'. The banks, British and Italian, were immediately nationalised, radical reforms announced in land-ownership and agriculture, and women given equality in political and social life. The agreements with the oil companies were continued on the understanding that technical posts would be open to Libyans as they became trained.

Notice was given to the British and American Governments that their military presence should end. This involved 2,500 British servicemen in garrisons at Tobruk and El Adem. For the Americans it meant the evacuation of their most important military installation on the Mediterranean coast at Wheelus Air Base. Both governments agreed to evacuate during the first half of 1970. Libya proceeded to associate itself with the more radical Arab governments and formed a close alliance with Egypt and Sudan. There was a breach with Sudan following the overthrow of its government in 1971, but Libya went along with Egypt in establishing federation with Syria.[9] On the Middle East it took an ultra-left line, backing the guerrillas, denouncing Jordan. Libya disturbed Britain and the West by the help offered to Malta in 1972 during Mr Mintoff's dispute over the retention of military bases. For a time relations with its neighbour, Chad, were broken off in 1971 because of Libya's sympathy with Muslim rebels there, but diplomatic relations were re-established in April 1972.

More important to world affairs, there was temporary alienation from the Soviet Union because Colonel Kaddafi, committed to non-alignment, warned against growing Russian influence in the Middle East, instanced by Iraq, and in Africa, instanced by Sudan, but in March 1972 an agreement was signed in Moscow for Soviet technical help in the exploration and production of oil, and it was said that a promise of missiles and jet bombers was also given. Russian co-operation, however, became less due to Kaddafi's outspoken opposition to communism as conflicting with Islam. Abundant oil supplies have made Libya rich. The Government nationalised British Petroleum, a decision which led the company to threaten court action against any company which bought oil from the state corporation and Britain to approach non-communist countries with requests not to accept the oil.

The Libyan revolution experienced growing pains with less enthusiasm from the people and some criticism of Colonel Kaddafi and his colleagues for not changing the standard of life.

Notes

1. The populations and territorial extent of the territories of northern Africa are:

	Population	Sq. Miles
Morocco	15,230,000	166,000
Mauritania (Mauritius)	1,200,000	379,956
Algeria	14,770,000	952,198
Tunisia	5,140,000	63,362
Libya	2,010,000	679,358
UAR (Egypt)	34,080,000	386,198
Sudan	16,090,000	967,500

2. The author was closely associated with *Istiqlal*, but was not permitted to see the sultan when visiting Madagascar.

3. On August 16, 1972, a second carefully planned attempt to assassinate the Sultan led to the execution of many army officers.

4. The author visited the refugee camps, dark grass-mud huts, and one meal a day for the children. Morocco opened even larger refugee camps.

5. Among those tortured, Djamila Bouhired became a national hero. She refused, despite terrible physical maiming, to reveal information.

6. De Gaulle diplomatically called the FLN an 'external organisation' although at its headquarters in Tunis its leaders claimed to be the Provisional Government of the Republic of Algeria (GPRA) with Ferhat Abbas as Prime Minister.

7. President Bourguiba presented the author with the Order of the Republic of Tunisia for his part in the peace discussions.

8. Ben Sellah escaped from prison in February 1973.

9. On September 1, 1972, Libya and Egypt declared for the union of their states. The implications are not yet clear.

Chapter Eleven

East Africa
(Ethiopia, Somalia, Kenya, Uganda, Tanzania, Zanzibar, Mauritius, Seychelles)

It is the custom to accept five territories – Ethiopia, Somalia, Kenya, Uganda and Tanzania (with Zanzibar) – as constituting East Africa. Despite ethnic and historical differences, there is more than a geographical link between them and there have even been suggestions of some form of confederal association, never more than an aspiration. We are associating with them Mauritius and the Seychelle Islands, isolated in the Indian Ocean, because their contact with the rest of the world is mainly through East Africa, and if the idea of economic and political grouping ever comes to realisation it would appropriately extend to them. Like Kenya, Uganda and Tanzania they are within the Commonwealth.

Ethiopia

Ethiopia, to the south-west of Egypt, overlooking the Red Sea and the Gulf of Aden, has been particularly the victim of its geographical situation. It has suffered from the rivalry of greater Powers for trade routes to India and the East, and from the conflict between the Christian and Muslim religions for which it has been a frontier. Trade and religion have determined Ethiopia's history.[1]

There is little evidence of the earliest times. Before the fifth century BC a people of unknown origin, the Cuthitas, drove Sudanese tribes westward. The first Ethiopian state, the Kingdom of Aksum, was established in that century by immigrants from South Arabia who set up trading depots on the coast and who, in the tradition of invaders, penetrated inland with armed men. In the first century BC, the Romans, who had conquered Egypt, extended their presence to the Red Sea seeking trade outlets. With the Romans later came Christianity, Saint Frumentius, wrecked in a ship bound for India, converting the court and chiefs. Dedication to the new religion led the king of Aksum to invade Yemen to protect a Christian community there from Islam. In turn, Muslim Arabs crossed the Red Sea in large numbers, compelling the Ethiopians to move southward where they established churches and monasteries. One of their more powerful kings was Menelik I, said to be the son of Solomon and the Queen of Sheba. The conflict between Christians and Muslims persisted for centuries.

Trade Routes to East

In 1517 the Turks conquered Egypt, but their advance into Ethiopia was challenged by the Portuguese, who had taken over ports on the Red Sea coast in pursuance of their pioneering trade to the Far East. The Portuguese entered into an alliance with Ethiopia's rulers and their joint forces drove back the Turks. Ethiopia was also attacked by African tribes from Somalia and Kenya, and chiefs and people had to retreat to the limited region of Gondar, which became an isolated citadel of Christianity. It was not until the nineteenth century that power was recovered under Theodore II, a ruthless dictator, who crushed local chiefs, massacred Muslims and destroyed villages. At this point the British came on the scene, also interested in the trading advantages of the Red Sea. Their envoy, C. D. Cameron, was charged with conspiracy in alliance with Egypt to overthrow Theodore and he was imprisoned with other British subjects, including missionaries. London sent an expeditionary force under General (later Lord) Napier, which was welcomed by the population suffering from Theodore's oppression. The king committed suicide; the British exiled his son to England. A period of internal conflict between rival chiefs followed. An Egyptian invasion was repulsed in 1876, but Mahdists from Sudan occupied the western borders.

With the opening of the Suez Canal in 1869 the Red Sea and the Gulf of Aden became still more important. The British and French established themselves in Somalia. In 1885 the Italians occupied Massawa on the coast, marched into the interior, and by a deal with King Menelik declared Eritrea, bordering the Red Sea, a colony. Different interpretations of a treaty with Menelik – the Italian version claiming protectorate status over the whole of the territory – led to war in 1896. Rather surprisingly the Italians were defeated at Adowa and the independence of Ethiopia was recognised. Menelik succeeded in uniting the country and the frontiers were fixed by a series of treaties with Britain, France and Italy between 1894 and 1908.

When World War came in 1914, King Lij Yasu, who had succeeded Menelik, supported Turkey and Germany. For this he was dethroned by the chiefs and the Church, and Menelik's daughter, Zanditu, declared Empress. There were intrigues by Britain and Italy at the end of the war. In December 1925 an agreement was signed between them under which Italy would have a sphere of economic influence in the east and Ethiopia would be required to build a dam at Lake Tana to provide water for irrigation in Egypt and Sudan, both under British tutelage. The terms of this treaty caused such tension in Ethiopia that neither Britain nor Italy insisted it be applied. Indeed, Italy went publicly to the other extreme and signed a treaty of friendship with Ethiopia, promising that any future disputes should go to arbitration. Ethiopia gave Italy access to the port of Assab in Eritrea.

League of Nations Sanctions

A point of later significance was the crowning of Haile Selassie (Ras Tafari) as Emperor in 1930. Relations with Italy deteriorated. First there was a dispute regarding the road to Assab; then a more serious dispute about the possession of wells at an Italian armed post at Walwal, which led to fighting between troops from Italian Somaliland and Ethiopians. The Italians demanded heavy reparation. When Ethiopia appealed to the League of Nations for arbitration in accordance with its 1928 treaty with Italy, the League appointed an Enquiry Commission, which, in September 1935, asked both sides to shake hands on the ground that neither was to blame. The Italians nevertheless began military operations, troops advancing from Eritrea and Somaliland.

The League of Nations thereupon imposed sanctions on arms and finance with export–import restrictions, but there were divided opinions behind this decision. In December, Sir Samuel Hoare, the British Foreign Secretary, and Pierre Laval, the French Prime Minister and Foreign Secretary, secretly agreed on terms which undermined Ethiopia's claims and involved its dismemberment. The agreement was leaked, and opinion in England and France exploded in indignation; Sir Samuel Hoare was compelled to resign, replaced by Anthony Eden. The sanctions, which did not include an embargo on oil, accessible from the Middle East and valuable for Italy's troop movements, had only limited effect and in March 1936 Italy shattered the Ethiopian forces at May Chaw. Haile Selassie sped to Geneva to state his case to the League, but by now belief in effective pressure had gone and he received little support. After a futile attempt by the League to bring about a ceasefire, the decision was taken in June to end sanctions. Italy proceeded to annex Ethiopia and united it with Eritrea and Italian Somaliland in Italian East Africa. Haile Selassie took refuge in England.

The story of other colonial territories was repeated. Italy built roads and carried out efficient agricultural and industrial development, but among the people national pride lived. There was resistance to the Italian occupation in western Ethiopia, led by Ras Imru, and in the regions of Gojam and Shoa under Ras Abbaba Aragawi. There was an attempt to assassinate the Italian Viceroy in Addis Ababa, bringing severe repression. Even when greater moderation followed, resistance was maintained.

Independence Regained

The Second World War changed the picture. Haile Selassie went to Khartoum in Sudan to contact anti-Italians. In 1941 there was the British offensive in East Africa and Addis Ababa was captured. Five years after he had been driven out, Haile Selassie returned and resumed his reign. Under the Paris Peace Treaty of February 1947 Ethiopia's claim to independence was recognised. The problem of Eritrea, where there was considerable sentiment for separate independence, remained. In 1950 the General Assembly of the United Nations decided that Eritrea should be 'an autonomous unit federated with Ethiopia under the sovereignty of the Ethiopian Crown'. Much nationalist feeling persisted among the Muslim people of Eritrea.

Haile Selassie resurrected the Christian image of Ethiopia and implemented a programme of modernisation and some reforms. He modified the feudal system and established Parliamentary government. He identified Ethiopia with the United Nations, sending contingents to the UN forces in Korea and the Congo, and also with other independent African states, becoming chairman of the Organisation of African Unity when it was established in Addis Ababa in 1963. He had difficulties with the Somali Republic on the grazing rights of Arab nomads on his side of the frontier, but sought to reach agreement by negotiation.

Ethiopia was not radical enough to meet the aims of its younger generation, reflected by its students, and considerable feudal oppression persisted, but its experience since independence was more harmonious than many African countries. The problem of Eritrea has still to be solved. Its people remain militant for independence.

Somalia

Until 1960 Somaliland was divided in threefold occupation – a British protectorate, a French Community state and an Italian trusteeship. In that year the British and Italian regions became independent and joined to form the Somali Republic. In 1967 a referendum of doubtful validity resulted in the third region remaining in association with France.

Somaliland covers most of the Horn of Africa, the easterly point of the continent, jutting into the Gulf of Aden and the Indian Ocean; inland it borders southern Ethiopia. French Somalia is a restricted area of nine thousand square miles at the mouth of the Red Sea. In the centre, facing the Gulf of Aden, is the ex-British region, 68,000 square miles. Further south, the Italian region, 189,000 square miles, edges the Indian Ocean and, inland, touches north-eastern Kenya. The Somali interior is mostly a barren plateau, descending to a coastal plain, thirty to sixty miles in width. The peoples are of mixed race, indigenous Somalis and Afars, Arabs, Persians, and at the trading ports on the coast a minority of Europeans.[2]

European Penetration

The first contact with the outside world was trade in hides, guns and slaves to Arabia. Between the seventh and tenth centuries Arabs and Persians established coastal depots for their trade with India and even China. It was not until the first half of the nineteenth century, following the occupation of Aden as a coaling station by Britain in 1839, that penetration by Britain, France and Italy began seriously. Britain took over a claim by Egypt for control of much of the coast, France opened a coaling station at

Obok on the entrance of the Gulf of Aden and developed a port
at Djibouti, whilst Italy extended its colony in Eritrea southward.
By 1886 Britain established a protectorate over the main northern
tribes, ostensibly guaranteeing their independence. There was
nearly an armed clash between Britain and France when the latter
extended its occupation of Obok southward, but this was averted
in 1888 by an agreement recognising frontiers. Italy's occupation of
the southern region was the outcome of a trading agreement with
the British East Africa Company which had leased the land from
the sultan of Zanzibar. The BEAC sub-let to an Italian company
and when it closed down the Italian Government assumed power
in 1905.

Resistance by 'Mad Mullah'

Effective resistance by the people to this expanding European
possession of their land did not reach formidable strength until the
end of the nineteenth century. The Somali chief who led it was
dismissed by the British as the 'Mad Mullah'. His name was
Mohammed bin Abdullah Hassan, and he was in fact a scholar,
revered as a spiritual leader, with qualities of statesmanship as
well as military skill. In 1899, as Muslim spokesman, he had a
dispute with a Christian mission; it was not serious, but he began
to cultivate the co-operation of his fellow-chiefs, and the success of
the Mahdist rebellion in Sudan incited him to action. He called for
'Muslim solidarity against the infidel colonisers', assuming the
title of Sayyid and enrolling recruits as dervishes. A pioneer of
guerrilla tactics, he repulsed four major British campaigns between 1900 and 1904, moving his men quickly whilst the heavy
artillery and lorries of the British were held up. Orders came from
the Colonial Office, which took over control in 1905, for the forces
to retire to the coast and it looked as though the interior was lost to
Britain. Then a new military idea was born. An officer, Richard
Cornfield, founded a camel corps and, although he was killed in
battle in 1913, the camel army held Abdullah Hassan at bay until
1920, when a massive combined operation by air, sea and land
ended the rebellion. Abdullah died of influenza whilst still rallying
his forces.

Independent Republic

Somali resistance, fierce and persistent, was also given to the Italian occupation in the south, particularly after the appointment of a fascist governor in 1923. It was crushed in 1926, and the Italian conquest of Ethiopia in 1934 gave the government at Rome dominant power; colonialist occupation, British, Italian, French, became entrenched until the Second World War. In the early years of the war Britain evacuated its region of Somaliland, but its forces recaptured it, together with Italian Somalia, when Ethiopia was liberated in 1941. Except for the French region, the whole of Somaliland then passed under British military administration, which continued until 1948 when authority was restored to the Colonial Office. In recognition of the democratic character of the new regime at Rome, its previous region in Somaliland was returned to Italy as a Trust Territory of the United Nations in 1950. Under the watchful eye of the UN, Italy outdid Britain in the social and political advance of its territory and competition arose as to which should obtain independence first. Britain ended its protectorate on June 26, 1960, and six days later the United Nations ended the trusteeship of the Italian region. The two then united to form the Republic of Somalia.

On the whole the new state was stable. There were disputes with Ethiopia regarding grazing rights and with Kenya regarding claims to a border province inhabited by Somalis, but both were made the subject of negotiation after a period of hostilities. The Republic participated in the All-African Peoples' Conference and the Organisation of African Unity and indicated its desire to join an East African Federation. It came into conflict with Paris by campaigning in the United Nations for self-determination by the people of the French region. It did not escape the African habit of the overthrow of governments by *coups*. In 1969, following the assassination of the President, officers of the army and police took over the administration, but they appeared to do so with popular support and made preparations for a fuller participating democracy, socialist directed, than had previously functioned. There is some discontent about the slow extension of political democracy, alleged approximation to the Soviet system reflecting the acceptance of Russian aid.

French Region Rejects Independence

Separate reference must be made to the French region. As told, the French invaded in 1862 and in 1888 the *Côte français des Somalis* was established, its frontier with British Somaliland defined. The French made coastal port Djibouti the capital and built a railway to Addis Ababa in Ethiopia. There was no serious resistance from the nomadic people whose life in barren country changed little. The Second World War did not avoid the territory. The French administration at first sided with Vichy and it was only after Djibouti had been blockaded that the region declared for de Gaulle and the Free French (1942). In 1946 the colony was integrated with France as an 'overseas territory' and in 1958 the people voted to be a member of the French Community.

It was at this stage that a division among the people became evident. The Somalis either abstained or voted against the recommendation; the Afars, more Europeanised, voted in favour. This conflict came to a head in March 1967, when a referendum was taken on the issue of independence or increased autonomy within the Community. Prior to the voting several thousand Somalis were expelled by the French authorities, who exerted every kind of pressure for a favourable result; they obtained a sixty per cent majority. The region is now known as 'the French Territory for the Afars and Issas' (a Somali clan).

The Somalis refused to enter the government after the 1967 referendum, and their party, *Parti du Mouvement Populaire*, was banned; a more compliant party based on the Issa clan was then formed. Autonomy was still restricted. Whilst the elected Chamber of Deputies appointed the Cabinet, France retained control of external relations, defence and finance, and its High Commissioner had the power not only to veto legislation but to promulgate laws. Grants from Paris, however, met the costs of road and harbour construction and of health, housing and education services.

Somalia is still torn by the division between the Republic and Afars and Issas. As with Ethiopia and Eritrea, the final solution may be an East African Confederation.

Kenya

Kenya, which lies to the south of Somalia on the eastern coast and extends west to Uganda, was little known until the nineteenth century except for trading relations with southern Arabia.[3] The first recorded invaders were the Masai tribe, cattle breeders, who moved into central Kenya from the north in the mid-eighteenth century, resisted by Bantu peasants and the Kikuyu, land cultivators, who sought protection on mountain slopes and in forests.

British Occupation

Joseph Thomson was the first British traveller to explore the interior in 1883, followed by the British East Africa Company (BEAC) which opened up the land. Competition with German companies was settled by an agreement which defined spheres, and in 1880 the British Government gave the BEAC the right of administration. Famine, small pox and herd diseases in the 1890s compelled the withdrawal of Kikuyus and Masais from large areas and Europeans began to settle in the healthy and fertile highlands, renamed the White Highlands.[4] Conflict in neighbouring Uganda in the 1890s compelled a restriction of European occupation, and, anxious about communications and the stability of its protectorate in Buganda (the central Uganda province), the British Government required the BEAC to surrender its charter, paying £250,000 in compensation. London then proclaimed a British East African Protectorate over the whole area. At first little administrative intervention took place; the High Commissioner, Sir Alfred Hardinge, was content to direct affairs intermittently from Zanzibar where he was Consul-General. When, however, the tribes discovered they were subject to British orders, they resisted strongly and military expeditions had to be sent in 1896 and 1897 against the Masai chiefs on the coast and the Kikuyu and Kamba tribes inland; the Naidi in the west maintained their resistance until 1905, despite a series of armed columns sent against them. During this period the British were able to impose a disciplined order only at the centre.

European and Indian Settlers

Kenya at this time was valued mainly as a corridor to the fertile land on the banks of Lake Victoria. The British required that land not cultivated or regularly occupied by Africans should be leased to Europeans, but few of the latter regarded the available soil as inviting. This changed when the fertile White Highlands were transferred from Uganda within the East African Protectorate in 1902. Sir Charles Elliott, Commissioner, encouraged Europeans to settle and they began to do so in considerable numbers, many coming from South Africa. The White Highlands and later much of the Rift Valley were allotted exclusively to Europeans, causing much resentment. This was particularly aroused when land in the Kiambu district, still farmed by Africans, was transferred to the settlers.

Perhaps a still greater encouragement to European settlement, certainly to Asian immigration, was the construction of the railway from Mombasa to Kampala, the capital of Uganda, completed in 1903. The work was done by Indian indentured labourers, and British businessmen and Asian traders arrived with the development of Nairobi and other towns. The indentured labourers remained to become workers in the tailoring and other shops which Indian immigrants opened. The retail trade became virtually an Indian monopoly.

Meanwhile, a labour problem arose for the European farmers, many of whom had acquired extensive estates at low prices. To meet this Africans were restricted in 1904 to reserves and permitted outside only as employees of the Europeans; in effect such employment became compulsory for the Kikuyu, because there was not enough land in the reserve for them to cultivate. Their conditions on the farms were those of serfs. An African family was allowed a little plot of land and a few sheep and poultry, but parents and children (as soon as they were able to lift and dig) had to work for the farmer for a pittance. They were not permitted to leave the farms without permits even to visit relatives or friends in the reserves or towns.

In 1905 the administration of the East African Protectorate was placed under the Colonial Office and an Executive Council at Nairobi was made responsible. Two years later a Legislative Council was established, composed of four official representatives and two selected Europeans. The European settlers began to campaign for the right to elect members, but the outbreak of the First World War postponed political change. At the end of the war agitation leading to political development occurred. In 1919 the demand of the white settlers to elect members to the Legislature was conceded. Immediately Indians made the same demand. They were offered two representatives, but refused to co-operate because they were denied equality. For a time Europeans and

Indians were ranged in opposing camps, but the Indians compromised in 1927, accepting five members in contrast with eleven Europeans. In 1920 Kenya had become a Crown Colony and the coastal strip leased from Zanzibar taken over as a Protectorate.

Kenyatta Initiates Resistance

Of more significance for the future was the emergence of African self-reliance and organisation. It began among youthful Kikuyu labourers on the European farms, who in 1921 formed the Young Kikuyu Association, renamed four years later the Kikuyu Central Association, with Jomo Kenyatta as leader. It demanded African representation in the Legislative Council; attacked the low wages paid to farm and industrial workers, serfdom on the farms and the inadequate housing in the towns; condemned the prohibition of coffee cultivation by Africans; called for the ending of the European monopoly in the Highlands in order to relieve African land hunger; and denounced the Churches for their campaign against tribal customs, including what was known as girls' circumcision. The only immediate concession by the Government was the appointment of an unofficial European member of the Legislative Council, a missionary, to watch African interests.

About this time, a proposal was made for union between Kenya, Uganda and Tanganyika (now Tanzania) and a Commission visited East Africa in 1924–5 to investigate the possibilities. European settlers at first opposed the plan because of their fear of African domination, but in 1930, when in Europe the Reich was reasserting itself, the settlers supported union with Tanganyika as a protection against German claims to their former colonies. In Uganda and Tanganyika, however, there was opposition by the African majority populations, fearing the influence of Kenya's Europeans, and agreement was still distant when the Second World War erupted. It was 1948 before the East African High Commission was set up to administer limited common services between the three territories.

Meanwhile the Kikuyu Central Association (KCA) under the dynamic campaigning of Jomo Kenyatta, its general secretary, and supported by Senior Chief Koinange and a whole range of clan elders, had become a force. A major feature of its demands was the recovery of Kikuyu land incorporated in the settler White Highlands. When the KCA was banned, Kenyatta went to London to present the Kikuyu case and in 1932, conducted a propaganda campaign throughout Britain, largely in association with the Independent Labour Party, and travelled over much of Europe, including a visit to the Soviet Union. Kenyatta was stated to have become a Communist, but this was not so; his political association was with parties which were not allied to either the Social Democratic or the Communist International. During his visit to England he studied at the London School of Economics and published in 1938 a notable book on Kikuyu traditions, entitled *Facing Mount Kenya*. He returned to Kenya in 1946.

African Christians Break With Churches

A serious rift grew up between the European ministered churches and African Christians over the issue of girls' circumcision. The Kikuyu practice was not only to circumcise boys but to remove the sensitive surface of the female clitoris when girls reached puberty. Both operations were carried out at impressive ceremonies recognising the attainment of adulthood. The purpose of the girls' operation was to protect virginity by removing the enticement of sexual stimulation. It will be generally agreed that the practice was deplorable in restricting natural experience, sometimes leaving the victim painful consequences in full sexual intercourse and in the delivery of offspring. The churches were justified in condemning it, but they went to the extreme, not appreciating the strength of tribal customs, of excluding from the Christian community any family which conformed. The reaction of many African Christians was not only to establish their independent churches but to set up a network of schools, including a training centre for teachers, in competition with those of the missionary societies. Jomo Kenyatta and Mbyu Koinange, son of the Senior Chief, were the founders of this movement. The African Churches and schools became more than an indigenous expression of the Christian religion. They developed into a major reflection of the growing demand of the Kikuyu for equality, political representation and the return of land. Enthusiasm was extraordinary. The schools were built by the voluntary work of hundreds of men and women.

World War and 'Mau Mau'

The Second World War began in Kenya with some fear of Italy's advance from the north, but this was soon removed by British victories. The most influential effect of the war probably came from the overseas service of African soldiers. They learned of democracy and race equality, and, even when equality was not observed, of movements which were advocating it. On their side the Kenyan authorities responded to the climate of the democratic aims of the war by at last admitting an African to the Legislative Council; indeed, Kenya was the first East African country to do so. One African was selected in 1944, and in following years African membership was increased to two in 1946, four in 1948 and eight in 1951. There were still no African elected members. Local Councils were asked to forward names from which the Governor-General made his choice.

By now the Africans' nationalist movement had become powerful and demanding. The banned Kikuyu Central Association had been replaced by the Kenya African Union, still most strongly supported by the Kikuyu but extending to all the tribes. In 1951 attacks on Europeans and their farms began and rumours spread of an underground oath-taking movement which became known for some obscure reason as 'Mau Mau'. In October 1952, a state of emergency was declared and Jomo Kenyatta and six other leaders of the Kenya African Union were arrested. With Leslie Hale, MP, the author visited Kenya soon after these arrests and through the KAU, whilst endorsing the claim to self-government, we appealed to Africans not to turn to methods of violence. Very nearly we succeeded in getting the representatives of the three races in the Legislative Council – European, Indian and African – to announce an agreement for radical political and economic advance by Africans. The document was endorsed and was to be released at a press conference the following morning, but that night the farm of Michael Blundell, the European leader, was attacked by Mau Mau and the European representatives withdrew their signatures. This was a turning point. The agreement had been endorsed by the officers of the Kenya African Union and would almost certainly have prevented the growth of Mau Mau and the worst events of the next seven years.

Was Kenyatta Guilty?

After a long trial, Kenyatta and five colleagues were sentenced to seven years' imprisonment for responsibility for Mau Mau activities; one of those charged was acquitted, though immediately detained without trial. There was much controversy as to how far Kenyatta was responsible for Mau Mau. He delivered a speech to a vast meeting of Africans shortly before his arrest, warning them against resorting to violence, but the authorities alleged that he had his tongue in his cheek and that his audience was aware of this. Kenyatta certainly was not responsible for the later outrages and obscenities of Mau Mau; he was in prison and isolated. In 1950 he had planned with the author a programme of constitutional advance. It is possible he lost faith in its possibilities, but his record when released from prison in 1959 (at first under restrictive residence), particularly when he became Prime Minister and President, did not reflect a character directed to violence. He won the esteem of the Europeans and the British Government by his emphasis upon racial concord and co-operation.

Rebellions are always accompanied by cruelties. Mau Mau was guilty not only of the assassination of European civilians, men and women, but for the massacre of non-co-operating Africans. Indeed, more Africans were killed by Mau Mau than Europeans, sometimes by savage mutilation. On the government side there was also inhumanity, such as by the indefinite detention of Africans found innocent in the courts, among them ex-chief Koinange, a dedicated Christian, released only when he was dying. The most publicised atrocity was the beating to death of eleven African prisoners in Hola camp, which Barbara Castle exposed in the House of Commons.

Progress to Independence

The Emergency ended in 1960. One important social change accompanied the rebellion. It had been African custom, specially among the Kikuyu, for peasants to live separately on their holdings. Under the pressures of the rebellion, the dangers of subversion and of attack, the British rounded up the Africans in rows of huts, the beginning of consolidated villages. This initiated a revolution in the pattern of African life which persisted. A concession was made to the peasants during the Emergency; for the first time they were allowed freely to grow coffee. Even before the end of the Emergency in 1960 a political concession was also made. In March 1957 it was agreed that eight Africans should be elected to the Legislative Council on a limited qualitative franchise, based on education and income. The Emergency over, it was conceded at a conference in London in 1960 that Africans should become a majority in the Legislature.

Following this, democratisation moved rapidly. Two African political parties emerged, the Kenya African National Union (KANU), of which Kenyatta was president, directed largely by Tom Mboya, an able trade union leader educated in America, and the Kenya African Democratic Union (KADU), led by Ronald Ngala. The basic difference between them was the degree to which tribal autonomy should find a place in the constitution. KANU stood for a unitary state, KADU for federation. They formed a coalition in 1962, but at the general election of May 1963 KANU, with a democratic socialist programme, gained a majority and Kenyatta became Prime Minister under a constitution providing internal self-government with considerable provincial autonomy. In December of the same year Kenya was recognised as independent and a year later became a Republic with Kenyatta as President.

Kenya's troubles were by no means over. Reference has already been made to the conflict with Somalia over the Muslim-inhabited north-east province. This was negotiated but dissatisfaction continued. An easier solution was found for the status of the coastal strip leased from Zanzibar as a protectorate; Zanzibar surrendered her sovereignty on Kenya becoming independent. A good deal of internal discord persisted in the country. In 1965 the governmental party, KANU, absorbed the Opposition KADU, but the following year, Oginga Odinga, popular Leftist leader from the Luo tribe, who had been vice-president to Kenyatta, broke away and formed the Kenya People's Union (KPU), alleging with some truth that the government had not fulfilled the socialist programme on which it was first elected. Tribal feeling still remained. When Tom Mboya, a Luo, was assassinated in 1969 feeling arose against the Kikuyu who dominated the government. On Kenyatta visiting the Luo capital, he was met with rioting and the Government arrested Odinga and suppressed his party. In the election which followed there was only one party (although Kenyatta insisted Kenya was not a one-party state), but it resulted, through primary elections on the American model, in sweeping from the National Assembly many of the old guard and adding a new young reformist element. Nevertheless, tribal loyalties remained strong, suppression of the Opposition was severe and little was done to realise socialist hopes. In foreign affairs Kenya followed an unaligned policy, but was among the moderates in the Organisation of African Unity.

Kenya has controversial years ahead. There is danger of division when Kenyatta dies.

Uganda

Uganda lies to the west of Kenya, bordered by Sudan on the north, Tanzania on the south, Congo on the east.[5] Its recorded history begins in the mid-nineteenth century, when Arab traders sought ivory and slaves. Before that we know only that in the fifteenth century invaders from the north subjugated the Bantu people for a time. The territory was divided into tribal areas, the most assertive of which was Buganda, headed by a series of able Kabakas (Chief-Kings); one of these, Mutesa, had admitted the first European explorer, John Hanning Speke in 1862.

Missionaries, Traders, Occupation

The North was still devastated by slave kidnappers from Egypt and Sudan, and Mutesa welcomed a suggestion from H. M. Stanley that Christian missionaries should come to moderate Muslim influence. Anglicans associated with the Church Missionary Society arrived in 1877 and Roman Catholic White Fathers in 1879; both Anglicans and Catholics had a wide influence on Uganda's future. The next notable European visitor was the irrepressible German adventurer Karl Peters, who in 1889 hoodwinked the Kabaka Mwanga into appointing him protector of the state. His rule was short-lived. The following year an Anglo-German agreement declared the greater part of the country to be a British sphere of influence and London authorised the British East Africa Company to administer on the Government's behalf. This was done without consulting the tribal chiefs, but the BEAC agent, Captain F. D. Lugard (afterwards to win fame as Lord Lugard, colonial administrator) persuaded Mwanga to place Buganda under the company's protection and subsequently he got the chiefs of Ankole and Toro to do the same. When the company got into financial difficulties, Britain established the protectorates and extended them over the rest of Uganda. In 1897, Mwanga revolted against British overlordship, but was overthrown and was replaced by his infant son, which meant further overlordship; in the same year there was also a mutiny of British recruited Sudanese troops which was severely suppressed. Then came more definitive relations with Britain. Sir Harry Johnston in 1900 signed an agreement with Buganda representatives which remained in force for fifty years. The Kabaka was recognised as ruler, but he was required to be faithful to 'the protecting authority'. His Council of Chiefs, the *Lukiko*, was given statutory authority and the chiefs were granted freehold possession of land. Less binding agreements were also concluded with the regions of Toro and Ankole. Elsewhere in Uganda, where the chiefs were less strong, the British assumed they had the right to administer without agreements.

No Alienation of Land

Soon after this the future of Uganda became a subject of controversy within the British administration. Sir Hesketh Bell, the British Commissioner, announced that he wished to develop the territory as an African state. He was criticised by senior officials and by the Chief Justice, William Morris Carter, who was also chairman of the Land Commission and who urged that provision should be made for European planters. Sir Hesketh was active on behalf of the African peasants; in 1904 he encouraged cotton growing which rapidly became Uganda's most profitable product; by 1914 the state had become virtually self-supporting, no longer needing a grant-in-aid from the Treasury. In the Second World War the territory was not invaded, but its exports were threatened. The war over, the question arose again whether Uganda was to become a land for settlers or an African nation. The fundamental and historical decision was then taken to forbid the alienation of land for freehold occupation by European or other immigrants; Uganda was not to become a Kenya. Cotton, to which coffee was later added, had revolutionised the economy.

A second innovation had an equally transforming effect. Prior to the war there had been the beginning of limited internal railway communication, but it was not until the 1920s that the line from Mombasa on the Kenyan coast reached the Uganda frontier through Nairobi and it was ten years later, in 1931, before the trains ran to the capital, Kampala. The railway led to great economic development, but another important effect, similar to that in Kenya, was to bring a growing Indian population, which captured the retail trade in the expanding towns and the processing of cotton.

World War Brings Upsurge

In 1921 a Legislative Council was established. It had only six members, four officials and two unofficial Europeans. The Indians demanded equal representation (they did not get any members until 1926), but the African population was indifferent. The Legislature made little impact on the more distant tribal regions, and in Buganda, the centre of positive political interest, the people regarded the *Lukiko* as their authentic authority. When the proposal for a closer association of the East African states was made, Africans and Asians opposed, the Africans partly because of tribal parochialism, both because they feared domination by the European settlers of Kenya. Indifference to the Legislature did not deter its gradual penetration of the administration. British officials began to be more important than the chiefs; with the extension of Anglican and Catholic schools, the Education Department became influential by grants to the missionary schools and by establishing some state schools. The Second World War brought democratic pressures and unrest. In Buganda there were demands that the *Lukiko* should cease to be an assembly of chiefs. Protests became riots. At the end of the war selected Africans entered the Legislative Council for the first time.

There now emerged an effective national movement. It arose by a combination of economic and political demands. The most self-reliant Africans were the cotton growers. They established a Farmers' Co-operative organisation which objected to the government monopoly of exports and to the Indian monopoly of the processing ginneries. They argued with some justice that the Indian middlemen were exploiting the cotton producers, and that the British export agency was taking an undue share of the revenue from world sales. These economic demands led to political demands accompanied by a growth of African consciousness. In 1949 there were militant demonstrations and rioting, followed by repression and casualties. The Farmers' Co-operative movement was banned and its leader, Musazi, who had gone to London to present its case, was held to be guilty of subversion. At this point the author went to Uganda and was astonished by what he found. The banned Co-operative organisation proved to be challengingly and efficiently alive. At a dozen places stadiums had been prepared, with elaborate platforms and large leaf-covered spaces where audiences of many hundreds could sit protected from the sun. Their spirit was intoxicating, listening excitedly to rousing speeches for hours, singing and dancing all night. The Government did not dare to impose its ban. Here was revolution in the making.

Advance to Independence

An advance had to be conceded politically. By 1954 African representation in the Legislative Council increased to half the unofficial membership, 14 in 28. They were selected from the different regions. The following year a ministerial system was introduced, with five non-official members out of eleven in the Executive Council. The Kabaka of Buganda, Mutesa II, and the *Lukiko* viewed this development towards a unified Uganda with misgivings; they were concerned to maintain independent autonomy. When Mutesa refused to co-operate he was deported to England; he compromised and was allowed to return in 1955, but relations remained cool. As a result of discussions in London in 1962 the considerable step forward of internal self-government was accepted. Benedicto Kiwanuka became Prime Minister, soon succeeded by Milton Obote, leader of the Peoples' Congress Party. The problem of the relationship of Buganda to the central government persisted. It was agreed that the province should have wide autonomy within a federal constitution.

The progress from self-government to independence was rapid, thanks to co-operation by the Labour Government in Britain. On October 9, 1962, Uganda became sovereign and concord with Buganda appeared to have been reached when Mutesa II was appointed President in 1963. The accord was short. By 1966 conflict had become so acute that Obote arrested five of his Ministers who were alleged to be plotting against him and suspended the constitution. The *Lukiko* rejected a new constitution under which Obote became Executive President and the Kabaka demanded the withdrawal of the federal troops from Buganda. Obote reacted by taking possession of the Kabaka's palace; Mutesa escaped to London, where he died in 1969. The new constitution of Uganda was federal with four kingdoms: Buganda, Ankole, Bunyoro and

Toro. The National Assembly was composed of ninety-one members, of whom sixty-one were directly elected; Buganda had twenty-one representatives selected by the *Lukiko*, and there were nine members selected by the three remaining kingdoms. The kingdoms had Legislatures, mostly elected, responsible for local administration.

President Obote Overthrown

In January 1971, whilst President Obote was at the Commonwealth Conference denouncing the British intention to sell arms to South Africa, he was overthrown by a *coup* in Uganda. It began in the army with junior officers who requested General Amin, the popular head of staff, to take over. The *coup* was without bloodshed and was popular in Kampala, the capital, largely inhabited by Bagandans who had never forgiven Obote for dethroning their Kabaka. Obote's support was mainly in the countryside, but the people of the villages were incapable of effective resistance.[6] There was suspicion of external co-operation because of Obote's socialisation of the economy, and the British Government and the West hastened to recognise the new regime. Tanzania (where Obote fled), Zambia, Somalia and Sudan declined to recognise Amin, but the OAU was divided. Obote's administration had been radical not only in its socialisation but in its bold identity with the struggle against white domination in southern Africa. On the other hand, he had ruthlessly imprisoned political opponents (immediately released by Amin) and there was much corruption around him. The Army Council declared there could be no election for five years, but Amin made concessions by ending the state of emergency and holding out hopes for a return to democracy at an earlier date. Meanwhile he pursued policies which gained him increasing support among African states. Most dramatic was an agreement of co-operation with Libya signed in February 1972, which indicated an unaligned position and incidentally lost him the goodwill of Israel, which had earlier given him considerable technical aid. Amin outdid Obote in his denunciation of white domination in southern Africa, urging the formation of a united military command to aid the freedom fighters. Opposition to him in other parts of Africa decreased, but within Uganda disorder persisted widely. A question mark hangs over its future.[7]

Tanzania

The early story of Tanzania is much the same as that of the more northerly countries on the coast. Tanzania itself is bounded by six countries as well as by the Indian Ocean. To the north are Kenya and Uganda; to the west is the Congo across Lake Tanzania; and to the south Mozambique, Malawi and Zambia.[8] Trade with Arabia and as far east as India is known to have taken place in the first century AD with Arab settlements on the coast. The Portuguese largely replaced the Arabs in the fifteenth century, the latter returning in the eighteenth century as slave traders, backed by the Sultan of Muscat (at the mouth of the Persian Gulf) who gained enough power to appoint a governor over part of the coastal area. In search of slaves the Arabs made the first raids into the interior, followed by two Indian merchants whose interest was in ivory. The Muscat sultan, Sayyid Sa'id, found the trade in slaves so profitable that he transferred his capital to the neighbouring island of Zanzibar, and financed Arabs to go as far into the interior as Lake Tanzania where some of them settled. This was in a sense the first alien occupation and it was resisted by local chiefs who were forcefully ejected. The Arabs were obstructed temporarily in the 1860s by Chief Mirambo, who cut off their trade routes when they declined to pay him tribute. During this period the French also became involved in the slave trade.

Germans Follow Arabs

The British appeared on the scene with the Church Missionary Society, followed by the explorers, Sir Richard Burton and John Hanning Speke, and the famous David Livingstone and H. M. Stanley. Livingstone's purpose was to expose the horrors of the slave trade, and his work led to many missionary societies starting stations. The first European attempt at colonisation was initiated by the ubiquitous German, Karl Peters, endorsed by Bismarck. Peters landed in 1884 and succeeded in seducing chiefs to sign contracts which virtually surrendered their territories to the German East Africa Company. By the Anglo-German Agreement of 1886 the sultan of Zanzibar's possession of the coast was limited to a ten-mile strip and, in return for recognition of the British sphere in Kenya, German overlordship was conceded of the rest of the territory, which became known as Tanganyika. The Germans leased the coast from the sultan of Zanzibar, but administered it with an arrogance which incited a strong Arab rising in 1888, only suppressed by an expedition of German troops helped by the British navy.

The failure of the German East Africa Company to gain the co-operation of the people led to the termination of its rule in 1891 and the declaration of a protectorate. German administration, if still ruthless, became efficient. Railways were built and sisal, coffee and cotton growing introduced. State schools supplemented those of the missionary societies. Nevertheless, there was continued African resistance by chiefs and people, culminating in the Maji Maji rising of 1905, which spread throughout the country and was not suppressed for two years. In fact, the resistance was so formidable that the German administration had to be largely military. Revolts overcome, the German Government established a Colonial Department to apply a more liberal policy.

Mandated to Britain

The defeat of Germany in the First World War, preceded by a General Smuts-led Commonwealth victory over its forces in East Africa, led to the colony becoming a British mandated territory under the League of Nations. Two regions of the previous German East Africa were dismembered, Ruanda-Urundi going to Belgium, already occupying nearby Congo, and Kionga to Portugal, already occupying Mozambique. War conditions had destroyed the German-created economy in Tanganyika and the African people had largely gone back to subsistence existence, living on the food they grew. Slowly export production and exchange trade was re-established and from 1923 reforms were put in train; a Land Ordinance legalised African rights in tenure, and local administration was set up under African tribal authorities. In 1926 Sir David Cameron, the Governor, advised the formation of a Legislative Council with European and Asian (but not African) unofficial members; that this should have been regarded as a considerable advance shows how conservative opinion persisted. The Governor was also in favour of European settlement, but this was rejected by the Colonial Office. The depression of the thirties held up economic development and when the Second World War erupted conditions became still more severe. After the war there was an elaborate plan for a large groundnuts project, but it failed to realise hopes because of an inadequate understanding of African natural conditions and because it was directed primarily to providing Britain with products rather than to African reconstruction. The project was not entirely a failure. It left facilities for large African rural development.

As everywhere, the war released new democratic forces. The Tanganyika African National Union (TANU) was established and the growth of TANU among Africans was stimulated when the British Government agreed in 1947 to administer the territory under the Trusteeship system of the United Nations (in succession to the League of Nations Mandate). Progress was slow, however, with only small forward steps. The African unofficial membership of the Legislative Council was changed from two to four (with four Europeans and three Asians), and in 1955 to equality, with ten members from each race, still grossly disproportionate considering that Africans were seventy to one in the population; the official members remained a majority. In the House of Commons there was constant pressure by the group of MPs associated with the Movement for Colonial Freedom for majority rule and encouragement was given to the speeding of democratisation by a report from the Visiting Mission of the United Nations criticising the tardy progress.

European and Asian Support

In the first election after the equal representation decision an extraordinary thing happened. TANU stood for majority rule and secured the nomination even among the European and Asian electorates of candidates who supported this. And they won every seat, African, European and Asian! Radical change became inevitable. A constitutional commission in 1959 unanimously recommended that a majority in the Legislature should be African and that the elected members should form the basis of the government. The Labour Colonial Secretary at Westminster accepted the recommendation and in September 1960, a predominantly TANU government took office. Fifteen months later, December 9, 1961, Tanganyika became independent. The genius of TANU was Julius Nyerere, in character, ability and courage among the best leaders Africa has produced. He was the only choice for Prime Minister and in November 1962, he was elected President by an overwhelming vote. On the anniversary of independence in the same year the nation became a Republic within the Commonwealth.

Nyerere's Indigenous Socialism

The course of the new government was not easy. Tanganyika was united with Zanzibar (see below) in difficult circumstances, and became the United Republic of Tanzania in October 1964, but wide autonomy was extended to the island and dictatorial policies were pursued with which Nyerere had no sympathy. In developing the economy the President was determined not to become subject to foreign financial investment, which he regarded as an instrument of economic imperialism. Instead, he concentrated on the growth of indigenous crops, sisal, coffee, cotton, groundnuts – finding a good basis in co-operative movements already established – and on the construction of finishing factories for these products. He established sisal- and coffee-processing plants, textile mills and oil refineries. To meet the cost he accepted loans (not share capital) from governments in both ideological camps to demonstrate his neutrality: from Britain and West Germany and from the USSR, China and East Germany. The Government acquired fifty-one per cent of the shares in the diamond industry. Nyerere's aim was to establish a participating democratic socialist society based on egalitarian communities in the villages.

TANU issued a declaration of purpose which expressed the spirit of all that is best in the aims of the builders of a New Africa. Nyerere strove to be true to it, but he would admit that he has not wholly succeeded. In practical terms the importance of the Declaration lay in its repudiation of the view, already stressed, that foreign investment should take precedence for development, and its insistence on the priority of indigenous village progress, and in its requirement that the leadership should not be distinct from the people in conduct and personal standards of life. The Declaration was unique among official documents in emphasising that Socialism is not only an economic transformation but a way of life to be followed by individuals. The Arusha Declaration will stand for all time as an ideal to be attained. We print the greater part of it as an Appendix to this chapter.[9]

The Government had to face one serious internal crisis, a mutiny in the army, so serious that the British were asked to send in controlling troops.[10] Grievances were met and order restored. Tanzania also had problems arising from its identification with the struggle for independence and racial equality in other parts of the continent. It became the headquarters of the Liberation Committee of the Organisation of African Unity which assisted freedom fighters, particularly in southern Africa. This created clashes with governments. For example, Tanzania broke off diplomatic relations with Britain when the white minority government in Rhodesia declared itself sovereign and London failed to overthrow it.

Tanzania adopted a one-party state, but there was room for democratic discussion within TANU and at elections two members representing different tendencies or groups could stand for each seat, giving the electors choice. On the whole, Tanzania progressed well. It was a daring experiment in self-reliant and principled conduct.

Zanzibar

The island of Zanzibar lies off the coast of Tanzania and politically includes the neighbouring island of Pemba and the islets of Lama, Manda, Patta and Siu.[11] Its position made it in early days the leading African trading centre in the Indian Ocean; ships stopped on their way to the East and the Arabs carried on a profitable trade in slaves and ivory from the mainland. The Arabs, although a minority, would appear to have ruled the island from the later centuries BC,[12] but little is known until 1503 when the Portuguese invaded and exacted tribute. The Muslim rulers entered into an alliance with the Portuguese against Africans, joining in attacks on the mainland and deporting subversive African leaders. When Mombasa in Kenya was captured, the Portuguese transferred there, leaving Zanzibar to the Muslim sheikhs. As we have told, Sultan Sayyid Sa'id of Oman appreciated the island so much that he settled in Zanzibar, expanding his possessions across the African coast. On his death he left the kingship of his African dominions to one son, Majid, and of Oman to another. But the European presence grew.

Britain Replaces Arab Rule

It will be remembered that Britain and Germany with the support of France insisted in 1886 (when Sultan Barghash had succeeded Majid) that Arab dominion on the mainland should be limited to within ten miles of the coast, and in Zanzibar itself British authority became greater. In 1890, although the rule of the sultanate nominally remained, Britain proclaimed the island a protectorate, and in 1896 demonstrated its authority by a naval bombardment of the palace when occupied by a claimant of whom the administration disapproved. A beneficial result of British influence was the abolition of the legal status of slavery in 1897. British power grew, but it was sixteen years before Zanzibar was transferred from the control of the Foreign Office to the Colonial Office in recognition of its dependent status. In 1913, also, a Protectorate Council was established as an advisory body. Democratic progress was very slow. The Second World War was over seven years before a Legislative Council and Executive were set up, and then both were composed of only nominated members.

Arab–African Conflict

There was little change until after the Second World War. National movements began to arise, weakened by division between Africans and Arabs. The Arabs formed the Zanzibar Nationalist Party (ZNP), the Africans the Afro-Shirazi Party (ASP). There was a good deal of violence between them which gave the British Government justification for delaying political advance. In the House of Commons, however, there was pressure from Leftist MPs, and in 1960 the Labour Government enacted a constitution providing for an elected Legislature. The first election in January 1961 gave no party a majority and a second election was held in June; it was accompanied by large-scale rioting and by clashes between Arabs and Africans with heavy casualties. The result was again close, with the ZNP and the ASP each winning ten seats, but an offshoot of the ZNP, the Zanzibar and Pemba People's Party (ZPPP), returned three members, so that a working coalition could be formed. A constitutional conference was held in London in 1962 to settle the date for the introduction of internal self-government, but no agreement could be reached between the ZNP and the ASP. An independent commission was therefore appointed and its recommendations for adult suffrage and constituency boundaries were accepted by the Legislative Council. Internal self-government was introduced in June 1963, the ZNP winning the subsequent election by eighteen seats to thirteen ASP seats. In September a second conference in London made the final arrangements for independence, and in December 1963 Zanzibar became a sovereign state within the Commonwealth. The last stages of advance had been rapid.

The new government did not rule long. The conflict between Arabs and Africans persisted. It was a class conflict as well as a racial conflict: the Arabs were mainly an economic élite, the Africans, labourers and poorer peasants. In January 1964 there was a revolution. It was led by China-trained 'Field Marshal' John Okello, but it was not entirely communist and was acclaimed by great demonstrations of Africans. It was not a disciplined revolution; there was brutality and bloodshed, before which the Arab administrations folded up. The People's Republic of Zanzibar and Pemba was proclaimed and the leader of the Afro-Shirazi Party, Sheikh Abeid Amani Karume, became Prime Minister, and Abdul Rahman Mohammed, popularly known as 'Babu', Minister of Defence and Foreign Affairs. 'Babu' had been a member of ZNP, but left it to form a radical party entitled *Umma* ('The Masses'). The Cabinet was made subservient to a Revolutionary Council of thirty, which proceeded to nationalise the land with power to confiscate all immovable property without compensation, except in the case of hardship. Large numbers of Arabs and Indians took refuge on the mainland.

Union as Tanzania

The African population of Tanganyika had not hidden its support of Afro-Shirazi, and it was perhaps natural that the government in Zanzibar should seek association with Nyerere's government. No doubt the Revolutionary Council also desired the stability which this would give. In April 1964 the two states united, with Nyerere as president and Karume vice-president. The marriage was not always happy. Zanzibar retained major autonomous rights and was alone responsible for its internal administration. The tolerant nature of Nyerere was not attuned to the toughness of the Zanzibar leaders, and it was with reluctance that he handed over to them political opponents who had sought refuge on his territory. Members of the Revolutionary Council became members of the National Assembly without election and they did not permit their people to participate when Tanzania voted on a new constitution.

The union between Zanzibar and Tanganyika continued uneasily; there was a persistent contrast between the approach of Nyerere and that of the dictatorial revolutionaries. Nyerere's reputation was spoiled by occurrences within Zanzibar, such as the kidnapping of Arab girls to become the unwilling wives of Revolution's leaders, excused on the ground that this contributed to inter-racialism! In fact, Zanzibar had complete autonomy and Tanzania's president had the choice only of separation or forcible intervention, and he believed either would make things worse. In May 1972 Karume, Zanzibar's head of state, was assassinated. Some of the conspirators were arrested and executed in Zanzibar; others fled to the mainland and were arrested there. Among those arrested was 'Babu', who had been a Minister of the Tanzanian Government. There were fears that he and others would be returned to the island, but Nyerere gave the author a promise that if investigation indicated that trials were necessary they would take place on the mainland. There was some hope that following the death of Karume a more liberal regime would develop in Zanzibar, but the first reaction to the assassination was not unnaturally greater isolation of the Arabs.[13]

Mauritius

Mauritius is far away, 500 miles east of Madagascar, beyond the French Rodrigues. Only 750 square miles in area, the island carried an estimated population of 780,000 in 1967,[14] more than a thousand to a square mile, one of the highest densities in the world. Two thirds were of Indian origin, a quarter Creoles of mixed stock (African-European or African-Indian), three per cent Chinese, two per cent European, mostly French. The uniting language was a French patois.

European Occupations

The earliest records show invasions by Arab sailors and by Malays in the middle ages. The ubiquitous Portuguese followed, led by Domingo Fernandez, though, dispersed over much of Asia and Africa, they did not settle. From 1598 to 1710, the Dutch, runners up of the Portuguese, took possession, calling the main island Mauritius after their chief coloniser, Maurice of Nassau. They exploited the ebony forests and introduced cotton growing and, more importantly, sugar. The expanding French East Africa Company ousted the Dutch, claiming the islands in 1715, temporarily renaming them Îles de France, the government in Paris taking over in 1767. Governor Mahé de la Bourdonnais made Mauritius prosperous with French-owned sugar plantations which became the dominant crop, and also succeeded in creating a sense of nationality.

War with France early in the nineteenth century made the islands a British possession, the name reverting to Mauritius. The Treaty of Paris, 1814, retained the language, customs and religion of the people who remained characteristically French. The British pattern of colonialist development was followed, however. As early as 1825 an administrative council was set up, consisting of the Governor and four officials. The next year nominated unofficials were added. The people suffered a series of disasters, cholera, malaria, cyclones, fires, drought. It was not until the First World War that prosperity was renewed with a high price for sugar, followed by low prices and depression; with a one-product economy the livelihood of the people was dependent on what the industrialised nations would pay. Mauritius went into the depths in the Second World War, trade restricted by shipping difficulties. Renewed prosperity came with peace, and with it national political consciousness. In 1947 broad enfranchisement was granted, the voters increased from 12,000 to 71,723. It was not until 1957, however, that universal suffrage was introduced, and full internal self-government was delayed until 1965.

Independence

There were two main political parties, the Labour Party, Indian dominated but combining at first the Creole proletariat, and the *Parti Mauricien*, dominated by the French élite, sugar plantation owners, aristocratic cultural traditionalists. In the election which followed self-government the Labour Party, standing for independence, won thirty-nine seats, the Opposition, advocating the retained authority of Britain, twenty-three. Dr Ramgoolan, the Labour leader, who had previously been Chief Minister, became Prime Minister. Independence was recognised on March 2, 1968.

The *Parti Mauricien* was renamed the Social Democratic Party and succeeded in gaining the support of a large section of the Creole population. Party controversy was subdued by a realisation of the crisis arising from the one-product economy and overpopulation and a coalition government was formed under the continued premiership of Dr Ramgoolan. A number of light industries and tea plantations were established, but sugar remained the dominant production. Unemployment and the moderate policy of the government led to the formation of a more radical socialist party which won considerable support.

The economic future of Mauritius, as that of many Caribbean and Pacific islands, was largely dependent upon the outcome of Britain's negotiations to enter the European Common Market and their effect on sugar exports. It became clear that if the economy suffered severely, conditions would encourage the growth of the revolutionary Left, which became increasingly aggressive, leading to clashes in the streets in the first months of 1972. A visit by the Queen in May aroused some enthusiasm, but discontent and dissent persisted. A Commonwealth Sugar Conference in 1973 made proposals satisfactory to some Caribbean islands, but left Mauritius dissatisfied.

The Seychelles

The Seychelles Islands, with the Amirante Isles and the Cosmoledo group (145 square miles), about ninety islands in all, mostly uninhabited, form a British Crown Colony. They lie in the Indian Ocean east of Africa, six-hundred miles north east of the Malagasy Republic. It is said that they were uninhabited when first visited by Arabians in the twelfth century and by Portuguese in the sixteenth. The islands were explored by a Frenchman, Lazare Picault, in 1744 and annexed by France and administered from far-away Mauritius. French settlers brought African slaves who added a Negro element to the largely Polynesian population.

British Conquest from French

During the Napoleonic wars the main island, Mahé, fell to a British naval force in 1794 and the group of islands was surrendered by the Treaty of Paris in 1814. Britain, which had also acquired Mauritius, adopted the French system of distant administration, but in 1903 the islands were made a separate Crown Colony and five elected members (the franchise qualified by education and income) were permitted in a Legislative Council of twelve. It was not until 1967 that a constitution was introduced providing for an unofficial majority and election by adult suffrage. The Legislative Council became a governing council with three *ex-officio* members, four nominated (two unofficial) and eight elected. In discussion with the British Government in 1970 a majority of the elected members favoured integration with Britain. The Opposition advocated Associated Status with Britain and in February 1972 there were demonstrations in Mahé in favour of independence led by F. A. Réné and the Peoples United Party, who have since been recognised by the Organisation of African Unity as the authorative voice of Seychelles nationalism.

The estimated population in 1964 was 46,472, four-fifths of whom lived in Mahé island. The people are of mixed race, to which Asians, Africans and Europeans all contribute, speaking a Creole *patois*, mostly French.

Notes

1. Area, including Eritrea, 395,000 square miles. Population in 1971, including Eritrea, was 25,250,000.

2. Estimated population in 1967 in Republic: total, 2,750,000; Bantu and Negroid, 80,000; Arabs, Asians and Ethiopians, 40,000; Europeans (mostly Italians), 4,500. Estimated population in French Somalia: total 101,000; Afars, 45,000; Somalis, 40,000; Arabs, 9,000; Europeans, 7,000.

3. Estimated population in 1969: Africans, 10,774,192; Asians, 137,037; Europeans, 40,593; Arabs, 27,886.

4. The White Highlands were on the Uganda side of the frontier until 1902.

5. The estimated population in 1969 was: Africans, 9,456,466; Non-Africans, 92,381 (Indians and Pakistanis, 74,308; Europeans, 9,533; Arabs, 3,238; Others, 5,302). The Africans are ninety-six per cent rural.

6. In February 1972 evidence was given by two survivors that many thousands of Obote's followers had been killed.

7. During 1972–3 President Amin aroused controversy be expelling all Asians who had not obtained Uganda citizenship. His purpose was to Africanise their considerable part of the economy which was stated to be 90 per cent of commerce and 50 per cent of industrial investment. Difficulties arose with the British Govern-

ment who had to receive the expelled Asians as 'British citizens'. Other controversies arose. Milton Obote was charged with sending invading forces from Tanzania and difficulties occurred with Kenya regarding Luo citizens in Uganda. Internally, there were doubts about the fate of Kiwanuka, who had been imprisoned by Obote and appointed Chief Justice by Amin, but who with other prominent Ugandans disappeared. The Africanisation of the economy was extended to the transference of British-owned Companies to Africans and to the departure of their staffs, whilst other British residents were exiled. Amin was regarded in Britain as racialist and a dictator. His expulsion of Asians was certainly ruthless in method and cruel in its effects and he ruled autocratically, but his policy of instant Africanisation was popular among Africans.

8. Area, 362,688 square miles of which 20,650 square miles are water. Estimated population, 1965: total 11,175,000 (Africans, 10,046,000; Indians, 86,000; Arabs, 26,000; Europeans, 17,000).

9. Among African countries Zambia, under the leadership of Kenneth Kaunda, will probably at present be alone in endorsing the Arusha Declaration.

10. The British had to do this in Kenya and Uganda as well.

11. Area, 1,044 square miles. Population in 1967: Zanzibar, 190,117; Pemba, 164,243. A census in 1958 gave Africans 67 per cent, Arabs 16 per cent, Asians 6 per cent. But since then the proportion of Arabs and Asians has been greatly reduced by exodus.

12. The city of Zanzibar is still in appearance Muslim with its mosques and white houses.

13. Nyerere later laid down four conditions for returning the arrested to Zanzibar: (i) an open trial, (ii) the right of Defence representation, (iii) a Tanzanian Security Force to protect the prisoners, and (iv) the right to appeal to the Union judiciary. The Zanzibar Authorities have rejected these conditions and have indicated that maintained prisoners will be tried *in absentia*.

14. The 1962 census gave the population as 681,619. The estimated population in 1971 was 820,000.

The Arusha Declaration

TANU's Policy on Socialism and Self-Reliance

The policy of TANU is to build a socialist state. The principles of Socialism are laid down in the TANU constitution, and they are as follows:

Whereas TANU believes:

(*a*) That all human beings are equal;

(*b*) That every individual has a right to dignity and respect;

(*c*) That every citizen is an integral part of the Nation and has the right to take an equal part in government at local, regional and national level;

(*d*) That every citizen has the right to freedom of expression, of movement, of religious belief and of association within the context of the law;

(*e*) That every individual has the right to receive a just return for his labour;

(*f*) That every individual has the right to receive from society protection of his life and of property held according to law;

(*g*) That all citizens together possess all the natural resources of the country in trust for their descendants;

(*h*) That in order to ensure economic justice the State must have effective control over the principal means of production; and

(*i*) That it is the responsibility of the State to intervene actively in the economic life of the Nation so as to ensure the well-being of all citizens and so as to prevent the exploitation of one person by another or one group by another, and so as to prevent the accumulation of wealth to an extent which is inconsistent with the existence of a classless society.

Now, therefore, the principal aims and objects of TANU shall be as follows:

(*a*) To consolidate and maintain the independence of this country and the freedom of its people;

(*b*) To safeguard the inherent dignity of the individual in accordance with the Universal Declaration of Human Rights;

(*c*) To ensure that this country shall be governed by a democratic socialist government of the people;

(*d*) To co-operate with all political parties in Africa engaged in the liberation of all Africa;

(*e*) To see that the Government mobilises all the resources of this country towards the elimination of poverty, ignorance and disease;

(*f*) To see that the Government actively assists in the formation and maintenance of co-operative organisations;

(*g*) To see that wherever possible the Government itself directly participates in the economic development of this country;

(*h*) To see that the Government gives equal opportunity to all men and women irrespective of race, religion or status;

(*i*) To see that the Government eradicates all types of exploitation, intimidation, discrimination, bribery and corruption;

(*j*) To see that the Government exercises effective control over the principal means of production and pursues policies which facilitate the way to collective ownership of the resources of this country;

(*k*) To see that the Government co-operates with other states in Africa in bringing about African unity;

(*l*) To see that the Government works tirelessly towards world peace and security through the United Nations Organisation.

The Policy of Socialism

(a) *Absence of Exploitation*

A truly socialist state is one in which all people are workers and in which neither capitalism nor feudalism exists. It does not have two classes of people, a lower class composed of people who work for their living, and an upper class of people who live on the work of others. In a really socialist country no person exploits another; everyone who is physically able to work does so; every worker obtains a just return for the labour he performs; and the incomes derived from different types of work are not grossly divergent.

In a socialist country, the only people who live on the work of others, and who have the right to be dependent upon their fellows, are small children, people who are too old to support themselves, the crippled and those whom the state at any one time cannot provide with an opportunity to work for their living.

Tanzania is a nation of peasants and workers, but it is not yet a socialist society. It still contains elements of feudalism and capitalism – with their temptations. These feudalistic and capitalistic features of our society could spread and entrench themselves.

(b) *Major Means of Production to be under the Control of Peasants and Workers*

The way to build and maintain Socialism is to ensure that the major means of production are under the control and ownership of the peasants and workers themselves through their Government and their co-operatives. It is also necessary to ensure that the ruling party is a Party of Peasants and Workers.

These major means of production are: the land; forests; mineral resources; water; oil and electricity; communications; transport; banks; insurance; import and export trade; wholesale business; the steel, machine-tool, arms, motor car, cement and fertilizer factories; the textile industry; and any other big industry upon which a large section of the population depend for their living, or which provides essential components for other industries; large plantations, especially those which produce essential raw materials.

Some of these instruments of production are already under the control and ownership of the people's Government.

(c) *Democracy*

A state is not socialist simply because all, or all the major, means of production are controlled and owned by the Government. It is necessary for the Government to be elected and led by peasants and workers. If the racist Governments of Rhodesia and South Africa were to bring the major means of production in these countries under their control and direction, this would entrench exploitation. It would not bring about socialism. There cannot be true Socialism without democracy.

(d) *Socialism is a Belief*

Socialism is a way of life, and a socialist society cannot simply come into existence. A socialist society can only be built by those who believe in, and who themselves practise, the principles of Socialism. A committed member of TANU will be a Socialist, and his fellow-Socialists – that is, his fellow believers in this political and economic system – are all those in Africa or elsewhere in the world who fight for the rights of peasants and workers. The first duty of a TANU member, and especially of a TANU leader, is to accept these.

The Policy of Self-Reliance

[*The declaration says ' We are at War!', war against poverty and oppression. It argues that Socialists are wrong in thinking that MONEY is their necessary weapon in reconstructing society. When MPs ask for water, roads, schools, hospitals, houses, the answer is that there is not enough money. Tanzania hasn't the money. Should the Government, then, get the money from abroad by grants, loans and private investment?*]

How can we depend upon gifts, loans and investments from foreign countries and foreign companies without endangering our independence? The English people have a proverb which says: 'He who pays the piper calls the tune.' How can we depend upon foreign governments and companies for the major part of our development without giving to those governments and countries, a great part of our freedom to act as we please? The truth is that we cannot.

Let us therefore always remember the following. We have made a mistake to choose money, something which we do not have, to be our major instrument of development. We are mistaken when we imagine that we shall get money from foreign countries, firstly, because to say the truth we cannot get enough money for our development and, secondly, because even if we could get it such complete dependence on outside help would have endangered our independence and the other policies of our country.

Too Much Emphasis on Industries

[*The reliance on money leads to too much emphasis on industries in towns. It is a mistake to think that development begins with industries.*]

The policy of inviting a chain of capitalists to come and establish industries in our country might succeed in giving us all the industries we need, but it would also succeed in preventing the establishment of Socialism unless we believe that without first building capitalism, we cannot build Socialism.

[*The cost of urban industrial development is borne by the agricultural community. The loans which finance it are repaid in foreign currency obtained from exports, and in Tanzania these exports are almost exclusively primary products. Industrial goods are made for home consumption as substitutes for manufactures previously imported.*]

Although when we talk of exploitation we usually think of capitalists, we should not forget that there are many fish in the sea. They eat each other. The large ones eat the small ones, and the small ones eat those who are even smaller. There are two possible ways of dividing the people in our country. We can put the capitalists and feudalists on one side, and the peasants and workers on the other. But we can also divide the people into urban-dwellers on one side, and those who live in the rural areas on the other. If we are not careful we might get into the position where the real exploitation in Tanzania is that of the town-dwellers exploiting the peasants.

The People and Agriculture

The development of a country is brought about by people, not by money. Money, and the wealth it represents, is the result and not the basis of development. The four prerequisites of development are different; they are (i) People; (ii) Land; (iii) Good Policies; (iv) Good Leadership.

[*Tanzania has more than ten million people and fertile land. Its peasants can produce food and materials to meet home needs and for export to EARN money for development. Male peasants should work harder to earn still more.*]

It would be appropriate to ask our farmers, especially the men, how many hours a week and how many weeks a year they work. Many do not even work for half as many hours as the wage earner does. The truth is that in the villages the women work very hard. At times they work for twelve or fourteen hours a day. They even work on Sundays and public holidays. Women who live in the villages work harder than anybody else in Tanzania. But the men who live in villages (and some of the women in towns) are on leave for half of their life. The energies of the millions of men in the villages and thousands of women in the towns which are at present wasted in gossip, dancing and drinking, are a great treasure which could contribute more towards the development of our country than anything we could get from rich nations.

[*Hard work must be accompanied by intelligence and modern methods of agriculture. Available money and time should be spent on technical development.*]

Furthermore the people, through their own hard work and with a little help and leadership, have finished many development projects in the villages. They have built schools, dispensaries, community centres and roads; they have dug wells, water-channels, animal dips, small dams and completed various other development projects. Had they waited for money, they would not now have the use of these things.

[*This does not mean money should not be sought.*]

None of this means that from now on we will not need money or that we will not start industries or embark upon development projects which require money. Furthermore, we are not saying that we will not accept, or even that we shall not look for, money from other countries for our development. This is NOT what we are saying. We will continue to use money; and each year we will use more money for the various development projects than we used the previous year because this will be one of the signs of our development. What we are saying, however, is that from now on we shall know what is the foundation and what is the fruit of development. Between MONEY and PEOPLE it is obvious that the people and their HARD WORK, especially in AGRICULTURE, come first.

Good Policies

[*The third need is good policies. These were stated at the beginning.*]

The principles of our policy of self-reliance go hand in hand with our policy on Socialism. In order to prevent exploitation it is necessary for everybody to work and to live on his own labour . . .

TANU believes that everybody who loves his Nation has a duty to serve it by co-operating with his fellows in building the country for the benefit of all the people of Tanzania.

The Leadership

[Finally, leadership. The Party Headquarters is called upon to prepare specific plans for the training of leaders, who must be a good example to the rest of the people through their actions and in their lives.]

1. Every TANU or Government leader must be either a peasant or a worker, and should in no way be associated with the practices of capitalism or feudalism.
2. No TANU or Government leader should hold shares in any company.
3. No TANU or Government leader should hold directorships in any privately-owned enterprises.
4. No TANU or Government leader should receive two or more salaries.
5. No TANU or Government leader should own houses which he rents to others.

[In this context 'leader' means a man, or a man and his wife; a woman, or a woman and her husband.]

Chapter Twelve

Central Africa

(Malawi, Zambia,
Rhodesia (Zimbabwe))

In this chapter we shall review resistance in Malawi (Nyasaland), Zambia and Rhodesia. Central Africa is geographically more extensive, but politically these three territories, for a time linked in the Central African Federation, represent the division between north and south. Their reactions to this bridging situation are different. Malawi compromised with the white-dominated South, Zambia stood resolutely against it; the unrecognised white government of Rhodesia became identified with it.

Malawi (Nyasaland)

Malawi[1] (as Nyasaland became known after independence in 1964) lies inland, separated from the coast by Tanzania and Portuguese-occupied Mozambique, with Zambia to the west, cupped by Mozambique to the south.[2] Nyasaland gained its name from Lake Nyasa, the third largest water space in the continent, occupying three-quarters of the eastern frontier. In Malawi it is now Lake Malawi, in Tanzania and Mozambique on the further bank still Lake Nyasa.

The earlier history of Malawi was similar to that of the countries in East Africa about which we have written. Arab traders from the Tanganyika coast penetrated in the first centuries AD (perhaps even BC); Portuguese traders arrived after the discovery of the sea route to India at the close of the fifteenth century, starting settlements, reaching the interior. Both Arabs and Portuguese traded mostly in ivory and slaves, particularly in slaves, which became a decisive factor in the country's destiny. The Arabs and Portuguese quarrelled, and at the end of the seventeenth century the latter's presence crumbled, defeated by Sultan Ibu Seif, losing by 1698 nearly every port in Tanganyika. In the next century, the Portuguese ventured to return on an ambitious project. Lacerda da Almeida, who had been the Portuguese Astronomer Royal, accompanied by a priest and seven hundred slave porters, attempted in 1797 to cross

Nyasaland to discover a route to possessions on the far west coast of the continent. He had to pay heavy tribute to African chiefs. Another Portuguese, Major Montero, seeking to renew trade, was so stripped of his resources by tribute demands that he had to give up. These chiefmanship demands were among the first African self-assertions against Europeans.

British Intervene Against Slavery

The country was severely disrupted by the Arab slave raiders in the first quarter of the nineteenth century. Village after village was destroyed, the able-bodied men forcibly rounded up and kidnapped. Many of them were suffocated in vans on the way to the coastal towns; more died in the holds of ships. One region escaped. The Ngonde and Nyakyusa peoples in the north-west, who had achieved a high and stable standard of life, defended themselves from the Arab slavers until towards the end of the century and then, overpressed, appealed for protection to European ivory traders, who in turn approached the British consul in Mozambique, Sir Harry Johnston. Britain had outlawed slavery in 1807 and he felt justified in sending in troops, who drove back the Arabs in 1895. Meanwhile, opinion at home had been stirred by Livingstone (who made several visits to Malawi from 1859 onwards), and Church and State responded in two directions, the Church by sending out Christian missions (mostly Scottish), the Government by fostering trade in ivory, iron and cotton cloth as an alternative to the slave trade. Livingstone supported both.[3]

The logic of events under a combination of humanitarian, trade and imperial pressures drove towards greater British intervention. It was opposed by some chiefs and peoples who resented the growing interference of both traders and missionaries, but their protest was ineffective. Livingstone pressed for an English colony 'in the highlands of central Africa' and Glasgow businessmen formed the African Lakes Company to develop trade and transport and began a political campaign in 1887 in favour of a British sphere of influence in the Lake Nyasa area with themselves as the governing authority. Lord Salisbury rejected their petition, but authorised a defence force[4] to protect Europeans, both traders and missionaries. This decision led to hostility with Portugal, dominating near-by Mozambique, and it became part of the wider power struggle of the

1880s between Britain, Germany, Belgium and Portugal for the control of central and southern Africa.

British Protectorate

From 1889 to 1891 Lord Salisbury negotiated treaties with the Germans in Tanganyika and the Portuguese in Mozambique by which the British mission in the Lake Nyasa area would be linked with British possessions in southern Africa. Extensions of British participation quickly followed. In 1889 Sir Harry Johnston was appointed consul to the interior in addition to Mozambique, and the chiefs were required to undertake that they would not accept protection from any other Power without the Queen's consent. The Consul proceeded to declare British protection over districts in the south, but difficulties arose with Cecil Rhodes, who wanted his British South Africa Company to take over the Lakes Company and absorb the territory. A compromise was reached under which the British South Africa Company became nominally the administrator of Zambia as well as of Rhodesia, and Britain became protector of what is now Malawi.[5] In June 1891 the new status of the territory as the British East African Protectorate was proclaimed with Sir Harry Johnston as Commissioner.

The protectorate was proclaimed but it did not operate beyond the environs of Lake Nyasa for some time. Many of the chiefs were hand in glove with the slave traders and the Commissioner realised he had to end the trade to gain authority. In 1893 with Sikh reinforcements he subdued the south, defeated the main Arab slave-driver and cut off the route to the coast. But he had other difficulties. He met with opposition from the European settlers because he insisted that they should be fair when buying land from the Africans and he also experienced resistance from the missionaries who did not want to transfer the administration of the precincts of their missions. He later remarked that 'the difficulties raised up against my work by Europeans have infinitely exceeded the trouble given me by the Negroes or Arabs'.

In 1907 the East African Protectorate became the Nyasaland Protectorate. Despite Sir Harry Johnston's concern there was little progress in the standard of life of the Africans. Education and health were left to the attention of the missionaries and they could not cope with the growing demand. Economic advance was restricted by the absence of railways.[6] In these circumstances, the British Government discouraged European settlement.

Nationalist Rising

The African people had been stunned and subdued by the British take over, but the First World War had a reviving effect. The Christian missionaries had taught the gospel of peace and goodwill; the Africans now saw Europeans slaughtering each other. African self-confidence was expanded by their importance in the campaign against the German forces in East Africa. According to John G. Poke, ex-colonial servant, out of an able-bodied male population of 200,000 no fewer than 125,000 were recruited for service.[7] In 1915 came the first nationalist rising led by John Chilembwe, regarded in Malawi now as an historic hero.[8] Chilembwe's story was unusual. He became a cook-servant in the house of a missionary, Joseph Booth, fundamentalist, pacifist and egalitarian, taught himself to read and write, and accompanied Booth to America where he imbibed radical ideas. Returning to Malawi, he established a chain of independent African schools, at first favoured by the Administration because he accepted law and order. But he became outraged by the condition of African workers on European estates and he was shocked by the war. He had protested against the sacrifice of Africans in the Ashanti and Somali campaigns and he now protested against their involvement in a European conflict. He became obsessed by anger and led an attack on one of the worst estate managers, named W. J. Livingstone (a distant relative of the great Livingstone, the opposite in character). The raiders murdered Livingstone and the assistant manager; Chilembwe was shot by the police, his followers executed on the spot or sent to prison for long terms. The rising ended disastrously, but it had a profound emotional effect. Discontent was aggravated by the poverty and unemployment which followed the war. Thousands of men had to go to Rhodesia and South Africa in search of work.

Union with Rhodesia Proposed

From now on the proposal for closer union of Nyasaland and Northern and Southern Rhodesia determined events. The British Government appointed the Hilton Young Commission to investigate in 1928. It rejected amalgamation and made the alternative recommendation of links between Nyasaland and the eastern district of Northern Rhodesia (which would have united tribes artificially divided), and of the association of both with ultimately African-directed territories to the north. The Europeans in Nyasaland were mostly favourable to complete amalgamation with the Rhodesias, the planters welcoming union with the white community in the South; the Africans were against, fearing white domination. The latter welcomed a declaration by the Colonial Secretary, Lord Passfield (Sydney Webb) in 1930 that African interests should be paramount. Another commission headed by Lord Bledislow recommended in 1938 the establishment of an Inter-territorial Advisory Council including Southern Rhodesia, laying stress on the economic argument for association. World War II held up discussion. The post-war Labour Government rejected amalgamation, but set up an Advisory Council as recommended by the Bledislow commission.

The leaders of the settlers in the Rhodesias, Godfrey Huggins (later, Lord Malvern) in the South and Roy Welensky (later, Sir) in the North, vigorously advocated the union of the three territories. Huggins actually got the concurrence of the Colonial Office for a conference at Victoria Falls in 1949 to which he invited Europeans only. It declared for federation rather than amalgamation, but in the African mind there was little difference; both would be controlled by Southern Rhodesian Whites. There was much criticism of the exclusion of Africans from the conference, but the influence of Godfrey Huggins increased. In November 1950 the Colonial Secretary, James Griffiths, announced in London that he had accepted a suggestion from the Southern Rhodesian Prime Minister that officials of the three territories and of the Colonial and Commonwealth Offices should work at a plan for the association of east and central Africa; they met and produced a blue-print for federation. With Gordon-Walker, Commonwealth Minister, James Griffiths then toured the territories and became aware of the strong African opposition. He called a second conference at Victoria Falls and this time African representatives were invited. Its decisions were a compromise. The separate status of Nyasaland and Northern Rhodesia as protectorates was confirmed, but economic co-ordination with Southern Rhodesia in a Federation was endorsed. Griffiths thereupon took the unusual step of instructing the district officials in the protectorates to call meetings of Africans to explain the Federal proposals but to refrain from advocating them. The balance in presentation was difficult. Everywhere the Africans remained fiercely opposed.

Central African Federation

The Conservatives won the election in Britain in 1951, and the new Colonial Secretary, Oliver Lyttelton (later Lord Chandos) announced that the Government would establish a Federation. In August 1953 an Order in Council was adopted against Labour and Liberal opposition authorising the Government to proceed. From Nyasaland came explosive protest, a feature of which was the support given to the African people by the Christian missions, notably the Scottish. A deputation of chiefs proceeded to London to present a petition to the Queen. When news reached Nyasaland that constitutional custom did not permit its reception, the whole African population boycotted the celebration of her coronation which had been arranged in the capital, Blantyre. The chiefs saw someone in London, however, who was to be more important for Nyasaland than the monarch. It is time that we wrote about Dr Hastings Kamuzu Banda.

Dr Kamuzu Banda

Dr Banda had a medical practice in north-west London. He was born in Nyasaland in 1902 and entered Livingstone's mission about the age of thirteen to be trained as a teacher. Expelled for some examination irregularity (said to be a misunderstanding) he started south, intending to continue studies in South Africa. His money spent, he worked as a hospital orderly in Rhodesia, moving on to Johannesburg, where he worked by day as an interpreter in the mines, and by night at classes and books. American missionaries became interested by his dedication to study and sent him to Ohio for further education. In 1931 he graduated and with more help from American friends studied medicine in Tennessee. He got his degree, but he had to have British qualifications to serve in Nyasaland. With the help of the Church of Scotland, of which he became an elder, and a government grant, he studied at Edinburgh, practising afterwards on the Tyneside and in London, awaiting the time to return to Nyasaland. His home in Harlesden became a meeting place for visitors from all parts of Africa. The Nyasa chiefs, turned away from Buckingham Palace, found their way there.[9]

A memorandum which Dr Banda wrote on the officials' plan for federation had a dynamic effect in Nyasaland. It was from this moment that he became an almost mythical figure. He argued that the Federation conception was based on the principle of tutelage, that it would extend the minority white domination in Southern Rhodesia to the African protectorates, that it would spread racial segregation and discrimination, that it was the thin end of the wedge towards amalgamation, and that the Whites would follow the example of South Africa in pressing for Dominion status and using it to entrench their power. In Nyasaland the African Congress, which had been formed in 1944 at a meeting of welfare organisations, took a radical turn. At its 1953 conference it declared for non-violent resistance to Federation, including boycott, non-payment of taxes and strikes, and appointed a Council of Action to organise the campaign. When the head chief, Gomani, of the Masako Ngoni, ordered his people to disobey objectionable agricultural regulations, he was ordered by the Government to resign and on declining was forcibly deported. The Rev. Michael Scott, a visitor, who had used his influence in favour of non-violence, was deported with him. Despite the influence of the leadership, however, the resistance did not remain non-violent. In Cholo, where land grievances were particularly acute, extreme rioting occurred, answered by severe repression. In January 1954 the Council of Action called off the campaign. Agitation continued, but support for Congress dwindled.

Africans Enter Legislative Council

Congress revived as the result of a concession by the Government. In June 1955 it introduced a constitution which for the first time permitted Africans to be elected to the Legislative Council. It was still grossly overweighted, with eighteen European members representing 7,500 and five Africans representing three million. In the elections the following year Congress won all the African seats; among the new members were Kanyama Chiume and Masuako Chipembere, later to become prominent. Chiume, twenty-six, quiet and thoughtful, had gained a diploma in education at Makerere College in Uganda; Chipembere, twenty-five, demagogic, son of an Anglican archdeacon, had gained an Arts degree at Fort Hare in

South Africa. They used the Legislature as a platform against
Federation, harassing the Government by questions and speeches
of denunciation. Popular response was great; the official record of
proceedings, *Hansard*, gained the circulation of a daily paper.
Division arose as to whether Congress should nominate candidates
for the two African seats in the Federal Parliament.[10] With some
misgiving it did so and Chirwa, also a controversial figure later,
and Kumbikano were elected. There was also division about the
leadership of the African Congress, arising from dissatisfaction
with the indecisions of the president, T. D. T. Banda (unrelated to
the Doctor). Chipembere wrote to Dr Banda, who was in Ghana,
urging him to come to Nyasaland to take over and, supported
by Chiume, made the proposal to Congress which endorsed it
with enthusiasm. A speech by Roy Welensky decided the answer.

Northern Rhodesia's settler leader visited London in April 1957,
and hinted at a programme for the attainment of Federation
sovereignty as a full member of the Commonwealth by 1960 when
its constitution was due for reconsideration. In Dr Banda's view
this not only involved amalgamation but confirmed his warning
that the white-controlled government aimed to follow South
Africa's course. He wrote immediately to Congress urging a boycott of the Federation and the withdrawal of the two members
from the Federal Parliament; the implication was that his acceptance of leadership would depend on this. Congress endorsed his
recommendation and, when the two members declined to resign,
expelled them from the party. At the same time T. D. T. Banda
was suspended from the presidency for alleged maladministra-
tion and the way was open for Dr Banda to become president-
elect.

Conspiracy Plot Alleged

A mood had been created that Dr Banda was Nyasaland's political
Messiah. Chipembere's phrase was 'a kind of saviour, a prestigious
father figure, who would provide the dynamic leadership necessary
for success'. When he arrived at Blantyre's airport on July 6, 1958,
he was ecstatically received and enthusiastic meetings welcomed
him throughout the country. His speeches were at first conciliatory.
'I am not anti-European, still less anti-British,' he said appealing
for non-violence, but after attending an All-African Peoples' Conference at Accra he became more aggressive. 'We mean to be

masters,' he declared and demanded an African majority in the Legislative Council and parity with the official membership in the Executive Council. The Governor, Sir Robert Armitage, refused his demands, but became uneasy. There were minor instances of violence, and a major riot at Karonga, where the police station, prison and airfield were put out of action. In February 1959 a number of Africans were killed in clashes with the police and troops brought in from Southern Rhodesia. African agitation became more militant. Dr Banda, although maintaining non-violence, wrote, 'Very soon I hope to have the whole of Nyasaland on fire,' and Chipembere becoming more extreme declared, 'Every European is an enemy.'

In March 1959 public opinion in Nyasaland and Britain was startled by an announcement that a conspiracy had been discovered to assassinate the Governor and European officials and to set up African rule. A state of emergency was declared and Dr Banda and 120 African leaders were deported and detained in Southern Rhodesia. The simultaneous declaration of emergency in Rhodesia indicated fear of a concerted plan to dismember the Federation. There was an outbreak of violent protest in many parts of Nyasaland; buildings were burned down, bridges destroyed and roads disrupted. The reaction by authority was ruthless. To be a member of Congress was made an offence; hundreds were arrested and fifty-one were killed; homes were demolished, women maltreated, children flogged. It took a month to restore anything like order.

The story of the conspiracy plot and its sequence were extraordinary. It proved how wrong colonial administration could be, but it proved also how effective British democracy and how just British investigation could be. On the day the emergency was announced the Labour Opposition appropriately forced an emergency debate in the House of Commons. Mr Lennox Boyd, who had succeeded Oliver Lyttelton as Colonial Secretary, startled Members by announcing that information made it clear that plans had been made by Congress not only to carry out widespread violence, but 'the murder of Europeans, Asians and moderate Africans; that, in fact, a massacre was being planned'. A White Paper was published on March 18, which outlined the massacre plot in detail. It was to begin with non-violent civil disobedience on an extensive scale, which it was anticipated would lead to the arrest of Dr Banda. A committee had been named, it was alleged, which would then take over the leadership, and they would organise a violent *coup* on 'R-day' (the day when state departments were to be transferred to the Federation), including the assassination of the Governor and officials. Members of Congress, it was stated, had been assigned to carry out these killings.

Devlin Commission Rejects Plot

The news of this conspiracy caused a demand for a commission of investigation and it was duly appointed with Mr Justice Devlin as chairman. Its report created as great a sensation as the original allegation of a massacre plan. Whilst the Commission found that the Governor had reasons other than the alleged murder plot for declaring a state of emergency, they dismissed the evidence that a plot in fact had been conspired. The Commission told how the allegation had arisen from information supplied second-hand by informers who had been present at discussions which took place in the bush at what was claimed to be an 'emergency conference' of Congress on January 25. Chipembere and Chisiza, both militants, were present, but Dr Banda was not. The Commission concluded that whilst Congress leaders other than Dr Banda had been prepared to resort to violence and whilst there had been talk at the meeting of beating and killing Europeans, there had been no consideration of 'cold-blooded assassination or murder'. Then followed a definite repudiation of what the Colonial Secretary and the White Paper had alleged. 'We do not think,' declared the Commission, 'that there is anything that can be called a plot nor, except in a very loose sense of the word, a plan.' Later they repeated, 'we have rejected the evidence, such as it is, for the murder plot'. Judge Devlin and his colleagues also specifically cleared Dr Banda of the charge of planning violence. They wrote that he would not have approved a policy of murder and, if he had been present at the bush meeting, 'would have intervened decisively if he had thought that it was so much as being discussed'.

British Concessions

The report of the Devlin Commission had a shattering effect on the ruling Conservative Party. Its responsible leaders recognised that a new policy towards Africa was necessary. Following the general election in 1959, a more liberal Colonial Secretary was appointed in Iain Macleod. Independence was forecast for Kenya and Tanganyika and more than half of the 1,328 detained Nyasa Africans were released. Dr Banda was allowed to return to Nyasaland in April 1960, though Chipembere was detained for a further period. The Congress Party was still proscribed and meetings prohibited, but the moderate Orton Chirwa, who had been expelled from the party when he insisted on remaining a Federal MP, was permitted to establish a new party. It did not get off the ground, however; loyalty to Dr Banda was too widespread. The Congress leader extended his reputation by a visit to the USA and in July 1960 was invited by the British Prime Minister, Harold Macmillan, to a constitutional conference in London. Dr Banda demanded 'one man, one vote'; that he did not get, but it was agreed to admit twenty-eight elected unofficial members to the Legislative Council, of whom twenty would be returned on a lower electoral roll, mostly African. The Emergency regulations in Nyasaland had been lifted in June and Dr Banda demanded the release of the remaining detainees. With some misgiving the Government agreed. Dr Banda made a statement unequivocally condemning violence, but Masu-ako Chipembere, liberated from prison, toured the country advocating a physical rebellion, much to his leader's embarrassment. Chipembere was arrested and sentenced to three years' imprisonment and there were fears of violent African reaction. In fact, Congress and the people, who had accepted Dr Banda's advice of non-violence, made little protest.

Monckton Report Kills Federation

Before arrangements could be made for the election under the new constitution a development took place which was to prove decisive. The British Government appointed a Commission to investigate conditions in the Federation with a view to advising the governments concerned in preparation for the review of its working, scheduled to be held in 1960. There was controversy about its terms of reference and composition. Sir Roy Welensky wanted Dominion status and pressed that any consideration of secession should be excluded, whilst in the House of Commons the Labour Party insisted that the Commission should not be limited in scope. Prime Minister Macmillan skilfully did not commit himself, hoping to obtain Labour participation in the Commission but the party declined his invitation to nominate three members. The Malawi Congress Party also decided to boycott, but Chirwa and a civil servant, E. K. Gondwe, who had also been disowned by Congress, agreed to serve. Sir Walter Monckton, who had been Britain's Defence Minister, was chairman. Of the twenty-six members nineteen were Europeans.

The composition of the Commission added weight to its unexpected findings. It reported that it had found widespread opposition to Federation in Nyasaland and Northern Rhodesia and expressed the opinion that it could not survive in its existing form. It made recommendations which would have restored to the three separate territories matters of internal concern, limiting to Federal control only a broad supervision of the economy, external affairs and defence. The death-knell to the Federation came in its final conclusion that even these proposals could not work except with the willing support of the inhabitants. Unless there was this goodwill 'the new forms will do no better than the old'. Since it was clear that the African population remained unalterably opposed to Federation the report was everywhere accepted as foreshadowing its end. Sir Roy Welensky remarked that all that remained was to discover, in sorrow and despair, when and how judgment would be executed.

The Federal Review Conference was held in December. Dr Banda attended, but walked out at an early stage, refusing to continue discussions regarding an institution which was already dying. The Federation lingered on until December 31, 1963, concluding with a sustained and bitter effort by Sir Roy Welensky to retain power in Northern Rhodesia; he no longer had hope for Nyasaland. The Africans, with strong Labour and Liberal support at Westminster had won.

Independence and Conflict

The general election in Nyasaland in 1961 brought an overwhelming triumph for the Congress Party. It won every seat on the lower roll, all other candidates losing their deposits. T. D. T. Banda, the deposed president of Congress, attempted to form an Opposition party, but withdrew before election day. Dr Banda became Minister for Natural Resources, important because agriculture was the life of the people. On the last day of 1961, simultaneously with the execution of the Federation, the date for the independence of Nyasaland was fixed – July 1964. It was six years to a day since Dr Banda had arrived at Blantyre.

As Prime Minister the African leader quickly proved his accommodating realism. He appointed two Europeans to his Cabinet because he had no African colleagues with the necessary experience. Despite his dislike of colonialism, he negotiated with Portugal for the retention of Beira in Mozambique as Nyasaland's export outlet and, despite his dislike of white supremacy, he negotiated with Rhodesia and South Africa for continued trade. This co-operation with the enemies of African independence and equality brought trouble both in Nyasaland and outside. Some of the ablest of his Cabinet Ministers, young men who had been his closest colleagues throughout the nation's struggle, indicated their dissent. There were other reasons for their discontent. Dr Banda was not prepared to let them run their departments free from his personal supervision. They pressed for more rapid Africanisation of the civil service; they condemned the introduction of payment by patients for hospital treatment; they denounced the reimposition of the preventive detention regulations which the British colonialist administration had employed. In foreign affairs they asked for a policy of non-alignment and the recognition of China, as well as non-co-operation with the racist regimes of southern Africa. The first to resign, on the preventive detention issue, was a European, Colin Cameron, a brave supporter of the African cause over the years, but more significant was the united protest of Chipembere (when released from prison Dr Banda restored him to his circle), Chiume, Chirwa, all of whom have figured in this story, and of Chisiza (Minister of Home Affairs), Bwanansi (Minister of Works), and Rose Chibambo, leader of the League of Malawi Women. Discussion of differences deteriorated to bitter accusation. Dr Banda began by dismissing Chiume, Chirwa, Bwanansi and Rose Chibambo; Chisiza resigned in sympathy, as did Chipembere when he arrived back from a visit to Canada. They left the country, some to Zambia, some to Tanzania[11], except Chipembere, who gathered together a group of supporters at Mangoche Hills, and resisted security forces a number of times before defeat. He fled to Tanzania, visited America for further education and returned to Dar-es-Salaam, the headquarters of all-African activities.

Dr Banda similarly came into conflict with the movements in other parts of Africa concerned with independence and equality. He attended the Cairo conference of the Organisation of African Unity shortly after he became Prime Minister. A resolution urged stronger action against the white-dominated countries of southern Africa. Dr Banda was frank. He affirmed his belief in African independence; 'there should not be an inch of African soil under

colonial rule'. But it was impossible for Malawi to cut off all
relations with Portugal. Colonial history and geography had denied
his people a port of their own; Beira in Portuguese-occupied
Mozambique was the life-line of the nation. He could not therefore
vote for the resolutions. At this conference there was some sym-
pathy with Dr Banda,[12] but later as his association with South
Africa (a trade treaty) and Rhodesia became still closer the Malawi
Prime Minister found himself isolated among African nations.
He was regarded as a saboteur of the freedom movements in
Rhodesia, the Portuguese colonies and South Africa.

The final act of political independence for Malawi, took place on
July 6, 1966, when it became a Republic within the Commonwealth. Dr Banda was elected President.

Zambia (Northern Rhodesia)

Zambia, as Northern Rhodesia has been known since gaining independence in 1964, lies inland to the west of Malawi. Even more than
Malawi it is a meeting place between independent African nations
and states still colonialist or dominated by European minorities.
To the north are independent Zaire (Congo-Kinshasa) and Tanzania, but all other neighbours are white-controlled. To the east
is Portuguese-occupied Mozambique; to the west Portuguese-
occupied Angola; and to the south are Rhodesia and South West
Africa. Zambia is a beleaguered outpost of racial equality.[13]

Excavations take us back to the earliest known human times.[14]
We do not know who lived there then, but there is evidence much
later of a Bushmen population and of incursions from the north
ten thousand years ago and from the south two thousand years ago.
There is also evidence of trade with the East as far as India in the
first century AD, gold and copper ornaments and cloth. The first
recorded event was the attempt in 1798 of de Lacerde to cross
Africa to the west coast, to which we have already referred. The
territory was then occupied by Bantus, some engaged in trading
copper, some as peasants or cattle farmers. Later came more
Bantus seeking refuge from a dictatorial chief in Zululand.
Malawi's history was repeated in the decimation of villages by
Arab slave-drivers until the end of the eighteenth century, and in
the arrival of David Livingstone and missionaries in the middle of
the nineteenth century.

Cecil Rhodes Takes Over

There were few Europeans except missionaries until 1890 when the agents of Cecil Rhodes arrived to cheat the chiefs into surrendering their land and mineral rights. His British South Africa Company administered the territory until it was declared a British protectorate in 1924. Some resistance was made for several years to the company's control, particularly in the regions of Bemba and Barotseland. Meanwhile, under the magnet of the BSAC white miners, traders and settlers came in considerable numbers. By 1911 there were 1,500 Europeans. During the First World War one-third of the adult African males were impressed to serve against the German forces in East Africa. The consequence was wide starvation because of the fall in the production of crops; an appalling number of Africans suffered from disease and hunger, and several thousands succumbed. For some months normal life was not restored, but after the war there was a large development of the copper mines and more opportunities for employment. The BSAC became prosperous through its mineral rights.[15] The European population reached four thousand.

Despite African suffering during the war, perhaps because of the aftermath of physical weakness, there was little nationalist resistance in the immediate years that followed. There was a change in the method of administration when the British Government took over from the BSAC. The company had ruled directly through its officers, ignoring the African chiefs, except in using them for the compulsory provision of porters during the war and in imposing upon them the collection of the poll tax, which had the incidental effect of making large numbers of men leave the villages to work for the company. Under British protectorate administration the different system of indirect rule through the chiefs and tribal organisation was introduced.

African Opposition Begins

When the protectorate was established there was first an Advisory Council and then a Legislative Council dominated by civil servants, which led the settlers to demand representation. There was no thought of any African representation; indeed, it was not until 1938 that African claims were reflected at all, and it was then through a European appointed to voice their interests. The first organisation

of Africans concerned about their conditions was the Murenzo
Welfare Association set up in 1923. Its founders were warned not
to dabble in politics and they adopted a constitution emphasising
no intention to subvert the authority of the Government; they did,
however, protest to the district commissioner about the rate of the
poll tax. The Murenzo Welfare Association was soon followed by
similar bodies in many centres, some of which began to take a more
militant line. The Livingstone Association, for instance, protested
against the eviction of Africans from land adjoining the railway
and against the arrest of forty-three Africans for walking on pave-
ments (a privilege reserved for Europeans). In 1933 an attempt was
made to form a national union of the many welfare associations,
but it was not representative and the Government refused to recognise it. The movement faded, but it was of significance as the
beginning of African self-assertion.

In the months before the Second World War official steps were
taken to give some voice to Africans. Indirect rule was maintained
in the tribal areas, but in the developing townships along the railway line advisory councils were set up 'to keep the district commissioner in touch with African opinion'. The members were
nominated by the commissioners, though it is of interest that they
included a young teacher, Harry Nkumbula, who later became an
influential national leader. The urban advisory councils were followed by regional and provincial councils (one of whose members
was Kenneth Kaunda, destined to be Zambia's president) and,
finally, by a national African Representative Council. These organisations, despite the absence of executive power, enabled opinion
to be expressed regarding racial discrimination, the absence of
educational opportunities, bad housing and, to be important later,
union with Southern Rhodesia. This recognition of African participation in national politics, despite its limitations, contributed to
the disappearance of indirect rule through the chiefs.

African Congress

Dependence upon these official bodies was challenged, however, by
a resurgence of independent welfare associations. Gore-Browne,
the European spokesman of African interests in the Legislative
Council, went so far as to assert that these voluntary bodies were
more vital than the official councils because they reflected unin-
hibited opinion. In 1942 a teacher, Dauti Yamba, also to become

prominent, suggested in the Luanshya Welfare Association that an African Congress be initiated,[16] and young enthusiasts, including Kenneth Kaunda, began campaigning. In 1945 a Federation of Welfare Societies was formed and a year later, led by Simon Kapwepwe, an associate of Kaunda from schooldays, the annual conference adopted the name Northern Rhodesian African Congress.

The growth of self-reliance among Africans was strengthened by the beginning of resistance on the part of the miners to their intolerable conditions. The European miners formed a union to protect themselves from African competition, and in 1940 they gained an increase in wages by striking. Stimulated by their success the Africans also struck. There were disturbances, and the police opened fire, killing seventeen and wounding sixty-five. The African miners went back to work, but their militancy won increases, and a commission recommended that each tribal group working in the mines should appoint an 'elder' to speak for them. There was a Native Industrial Labour Advisory Board, composed entirely of Whites, but no thought of a trade union for Africans; they were 'not ripe for it', said the commission. The initiative for African organisation came from an English trade unionist, William M. Comrie, who was sent to the Copperbelt by the Colonial Office as a Labour Officer. In February 1948 the first branch of the African Mine Workers Union was formed; they were soon functioning in all the mining centres; in March 1949 they merged in a national organisation. The authorities insisted that the Unions should keep out of politics, but in fact the branches became hotbeds of nationalist agitation. The union leaders were almost always officials of the Congress.

The settlers' demand for a Central African Federation uniting Northern Rhodesia and Nyasaland with Southern Rhodesia added fuel to the fire of nationalism. In the preceding section on Nyasaland we have traced the evolution of the Federation and the story need not be repeated. African opposition in Northern Rhodesia was as strong as in Nyasaland. When the Legislative Council voted overwhelmingly for federation in 1953, Harry Nkumbula, who had become chairman of the Congress, called a conference of delegates and chiefs at Lusaka and burned copies of the Government's White Paper before them. The chiefs decided they would adopt a policy of non-co-operation if federation were imposed; the Congress delegates threatened to 'paralyse industry', and as a first step a one-day strike and 'national day of prayer' was endorsed.

The reaction of the Government and the companies was fierce; civil servants and the employees of the mining and other concerns were told they would be dismissed if they obeyed the decisions of the conference. This threat proved effective, only a minority of African workers stayed at home. The chiefs, however, maintained their opposition, sending petitions to Parliament in London and an unreceived deputation to the Queen. 'The Europeans are trying to bring us under the same domination as our brother Africans in Southern Rhodesia and South Africa,' said the petition. On the Africans the failure of the one-day strike had both a disintegrating and reviving effect. Four hundred Congress delegates met in Lusaka in a bitter mood. Federation was to come on October 23 and the new stage of resistance required more effective leadership. Of the officials only Nkumbula was reappointed. Kenneth Kaunda was elected Secretary-General.

Kenneth Kaunda

It is time to say something about Kaunda. He was born in April 1924, the youngest of eight children in the family of a Livingstonian Christian minister living at Lubwe, eight miles from Chinseli in the north. He became a schoolmaster, joined an African Welfare Association, married an educated girl of his mother's choice (to whom he became devoted), sought teaching jobs in Tanganyika and Southern Rhodesia (where he was shocked by the humiliations imposed on Africans), and on going to the Copperbelt was nominated by the teachers as their representative on the Urban and Provincial Advisory Councils. He was outraged by the indignities of the colour bar and challenged the practice of compelling Africans to buy through a hole in the wall by entering a chemist's shop; he was frogmarched into the street by two white miners. He complained to the English district officer without effect. It was experiences like this which made him a Nationalist.

From boyhood days Kenneth Kaunda had been inseparable from Simon Kapwepwe and John Sokoni. They had gone together to Tanganyika and were with him on the Copperbelt. They decided to return to their homes in the provinces and devote themselves to the organisation and education of their fellows. Kaunda and Sokoni established farmers' co-operatives and when the African Congress was started Kenneth Kaunda formed a branch at Chinseli. From then on he became a Congress missionary, cycling

forty and sixty miles to establish groups. In 1951 he attended his
first national conference of the Congress and was active in getting
Harry Nkumbula elected general secretary. At the conference the
following year he was appointed to the Supreme Action Council to
fight against Federation and shortly after was elected organising
secretary for the Northern Province, an area stretching from the
frontiers of Tanganyika to the Belgian Congo. On his bicycle he
visited its villages and by his sincere personality and persuasive
speech made Congress identical with the people. It was these
qualities and his mounting reputation which led to his appointment
as secretary-general of Congress in August 1953.[17]

Congress continued to denounce Federation after its enactment
and its members suffered with renewed severity at the hands of the
Government and the companies. Employers dismissed active members and some district commissioners sent known members to
forced labour and prison for trivial offences. There were disturbances in the Northern Province and other areas as a result of the
arbitrary arrests. Some chiefs, whose salaries were paid by the
Administration, were intimidated into withdrawing their support
from Congress. At this stage Kaunda was cautious. Congress
decided temporarily at least to participate in the elections to the
Federal Parliament and succeeded in returning the two African
members.[18] During its first years Nkumbula and Kaunda concentrated in Congress activity on safeguarding Northern Rhodesian
rights, and claiming advances towards equality, rather than on the
destruction of the Federation. Africans had succeeded in securing
the inclusion in the preamble to the Federal Constitution an
assurance that the control of land and political advancement
would remain the responsibility of the separate territories and the
Congress leaders took full advantage of this. To meet the disillusionment which had arisen from defeat on the Federal issue Kaunda
initiated a campaign for the abolition of the colour bar. Cafés were
closed to Africans, they had to wait in queues in post offices and
shops until Europeans were served, they could not enter a theatre
or cinema, they were not even welcome in white-attended churches,
they were paid one-ninth the wage of European workers.[19] Kaunda
started a boycott of shops at the beginning of 1956 and business in
Lusaka was brought to a standstill for three weeks. The Government brought a test case for conspiracy. Congress employed a QC
in defence and won the case.

Racial Discrimination

The fight against discrimination was taken into the Parliaments. As soon as the Federal Assembly met, the Congress member, Dauti Yamba, moved that 'equal treatment be accorded immediately to all races in public places and that such action be enforced by legislation'. Lord Malvern, the Prime Minister, declared that white women could not be expected to stand in queues with African mothers bearing dirty babies, and the motion was overwhelmingly defeated. In the Northern Rhodesia Legislative Council, however, John Moffat had greater success, carrying a motion condemning discrimination in all its forms, and in 1955 the Council, whilst rejecting a proposal by Sokota that it should be an offence to practise discrimination in places licensed to serve the public, agreed to appoint a committee to make recommendations. As a result, eighteen months later, a Race Relations Board was established to facilitate conciliations. It had no teeth, however, and its effect was minimal.

Two significant events took place in 1955. Kaunda and Nkumbula were gaoled for two months for possessing prohibited literature, consisting of pamphlets distributed by the Movement for Colonial Freedom in London which the author of this book had sent them. The second event was the return to Northern Rhodesia of Simon Kapwepwe on completing a four years' Congress scholarship in India. Kapwepwe became acting chairman whilst Nkumbula was in prison and his infectious dynamism appeared to be a challenge to the absent leader; when Nkumbula came out of prison, Kapwepwe was made Congress treasurer. The new political militancy was supplemented by trade union militancy. During 1956 there were two strikes by African miners, the first an eight-week shutdown by thirty-thousand on a wage claim, the second arising from a decision by the companies that Africans in 'advanced' jobs should resign from the African union and join an exclusive staff association. The dispute became so serious that the Government declared a state of emergency and arrested sixty leaders, including many Congress officials. These two happenings greatly stimulated African opposition to white domination.

UNIP Formed

Within Congress dissatisfaction with the leadership of Nkumbula, the chairman, developed. This was partly political, partly personal. At one point he favoured separating the races by partition rather than integration within one nation; at another point he favoured an arrangement with the Constitution Party, liberal but moderate, in contesting Federal elections whilst Kaunda advocated boycott. There was also resentment against what was regarded as dictatorship within the organisation. In 1958 the split came. Kapwepwe and Kaunda broke away and formed the Zambia African National Congress (ZANC), which quickly won massive support. Both Kaunda and Nkumbula were invited to the Accra All-African Peoples' Conference, but they declined to unite their organisations, agreeing only to co-operate on immediate issues such as the destruction of the Federation.

The uncompromising tone of the Accra Conference frightened the European leaders in the Federation and its three territories. The Governors and Prime Ministers met and states of emergency were declared in Southern Rhodesia, Nyasaland and Northern Rhodesia. The leaders of the Zambia African National Congress were arrested and the organisation banned, those imprisoned including Kaunda, Kapwepwe and Sipalo, the president, treasurer and secretary. ZANC had emphasised non-violence and an official inquiry failed to instance a single act of violence, but Governor Benson compared the party to 'Murder Incorporated' in America and described its leaders as 'racketeers', who had instituted a reign of terror, practised witchcraft and threatened to kill women and children. There was no justification for these charges, though some members had used extreme language. The arrest of the ZANC leaders, however, led to an outbreak of violence; shop windows were smashed, cars damaged, and two attempts made to burn down the rest-house for Legislative Council members. A riot in the Northern Province resulted in four African deaths after the district commissioner and his assistant had been wounded. Ninety Africans were gaoled.

The banning of ZANC was met by the formation of the United National Independence Party (UNIP) under the leadership of Paul Kalichini, who had been vice-president of ZANC. When released in January 1960, Kaunda, Kapwepwe and Sipalo were reappointed as the national officers of the movement. It was ZANC revived and greatly strengthened in public support by the character of the

British repression. UNIP was more significant than all the previous African organisations. It was to lead Zambia to democratic independence.

Death-knell to White Domination

By this time the Federation was tottering. It had received a severe jolt in Northern Rhodesia in 1955 after the Federal Government had unilaterally decided to build the gigantic dam to supply electrical power to both Southern and Northern Rhodesia at Kariba, with its power station on the southern side of the Zambezi river. Six months earlier Sir Godfrey Huggins, the Federal Prime Minister, had signed an agreement with Sir Gilbert Rennie, Governor of Northern Rhodesia, that a dam should be constructed on the Kifue river, and the Northern Administration had spent £500,000 on preparatory work. Without any consultation this plan was ditched. Indignation was strong among Europeans in Northern Rhodesia as well as Africans and at a meeting of 1,300 in Lusaka the demand was made that Northern Rhodesia should secede from the Federation immediately. African concern was also about the forty thousand who would have to leave the Zambezi valley. When police forced them to move to higher ground, fighting broke out and eight tribesmen were killed and thirty-four wounded.

African opposition was also intensified when it was announced that there would be a conference in 1960 to advance the Federation to independence. Africans insisted that majority rule must come before sovereignty. In 1959 the Devlin report on Nyasaland had been published saying that African opposition to the Federation was almost universal. Then came the first findings of the Monckton Commission appointed to survey the operation of the Federation, which reported as we have told that there had been failure to demonstrate racial partnership, that discrimination still existed, and that the Federation in its then form could be maintained only by force, the majority recommending racial parity in the Federal Parliament and an African majority in Northern Rhodesia. This was the death-knell to white domination.

Iain Macleod, more liberally minded, had become Colonial Secretary.[20] Towards the end of 1959 he announced a conference to implement constitutional changes in Northern Rhodesia. Roy Welensky, who still clung to the hope of a union of the two Rhodesias even if Nyasaland were discarded, threatened armed resistance if the North were given an African majority. Under heavy political pressure in London, Iain Macleod's constitutional proposals proved disappointing. He contrived a fifteen-fifteen-fifteen formula, under which equal numbers in the Assembly would be elected by Africans, Europeans, and a roll of both Africans and Europeans. It was likely that on the common roll liberals would be elected, providing an anti-Federation majority, so reluctantly UNIP agreed to participate. At this point Welensky so mounted the pressure on Macleod with the help of Rightists in the Conservative Party that the Colonial Secretary produced an amended scheme heavily weighted against Africans.[21] Kaunda denounced the Government's 'betrayal' and UNIP decided to boycott the elections. The Churches, Protestant and Catholic, joined in the denunciation as did the secretary of the Chiefs' Council. Protest turned to resistance. Although Kaunda went on a three thousand-mile tour appealing for non-violence, bridges were destroyed, telephone wires cut, government buildings set alight and roads blocked. The Government moved in police and troops and UNIP was banned in the more critical regions. The official estimate was nineteen killed, but the number was probably much higher as Africans carried their dead into the bush. Three thousand were arrested and 2,600 gaoled, some for long terms.

African Cabinet, Independence

In the autumn of 1961 Reginald Maudling was appointed Colonial Secretary and after a visit to Northern Rhodesia announced a revision of the constitution which, whilst it maintained overwhelming European privilege, gave the Africans a fifty-fifty chance of obtaining a majority. UNIP decided on the gamble. In the election of October 1962 Nkumbula's Congress (ANC) entered into a pact with the Federalists and the result was: Federalists (UFP), 17; ANC, 7, UNIP, 14. Despite its electoral agreement with the Federalists, the ANC was against Federation; the ironical consequence was that a coalition was formed with UNIP and ANC as partners. However, the coalition instead of bringing the two African parties together separated them deeply; there were quarrels between Ministers, a split in ANC and violent clashes between supporters leading to many deaths. African opposition then swept even more strongly to UNIP and the British Government realised that it must give way by creating an electorate which would provide an African majority. In the 1963 election there were a million

African voters compared with 100,000 a year earlier, and UNIP gained fifty-five of the seventy-five seats, ANC had ten, and ten were reserved for the Europeans. On January 23, 1964, Kenneth Kaunda became Prime Minister with an all-African cabinet.

The year 1963 was very noteworthy. UNIP'S victory in Northern Rhodesia saw the end of Federation. The British Government at last recognised the right of Northern Rhodesia to secede as it had previously done for Nyasaland. As both wished to end Federation there was no issue except the mechanism and conditions of dissolution. The formality was completed at an uncontroversial conference at Victoria Falls. The conditions were left to civil servants. As we shall indicate in our next section on Rhodesia, the distribution of the armed forces was crucial.

Three Problems

Kaunda made an early announcement of Independence Day. He fixed it for October 24, 1964, partly because it was United Nations Day, partly because it would be the sixth anniversary of the foundation of ZANC. But in the eight months before his goal was reached the Government had to deal with three difficult problems. The first was a conflict with a religious sect, the Lumpa, many thousand strong, which was other worldly to the point of declining to participate in elections; the local officials of UNIP used threats to force them to register as voters. Kaunda did his utmost to bring about a settlement, but clashes occurred, developing into a local civil war with two army battalions engaged, costing at least seven hundred lives. At length the fanatical leader of the sect, Alice Lenshina, surrendered and was detained, but it was a tragic event which damaged Kaunda's image. He was distressed that his belief in non-violence had failed at this test.[22]

The second problem concerned the winding up of the British South Africa Company. At first discussions took place on the assumption that compensation of £50 million would have to be paid by Zambia, but when the African leaders came to power they investigated the dubious circumstances under which the Company had gained its right to mineral royalties and concluded that the British Government was responsible for any compensation since it had handed over administration of the territory to the Company. The African Finance Minister, Arthur Wina, proved very tough in the negotiations and the final terms were that the compensation should be only £4 million, of which the British Government paid half.

The third difficult issue concerned the incorporation of Barotseland within Zambia. This large region in the south-west had enjoyed a special status from 1900 when, in a treaty defining the right of the British South Africa Company, the paramount chief was accepted as king. Its relationship with Britain and Northern Rhodesia became complicated, the British Government having promised not to change its constitutional status without the consent of the paramount chief, who in turn demanded separate representation within the Federation and then secession from Zambia. It became evident, however, that the people did not support the chief, UNIP winning all twenty-five elected seats in the Barotse National Council in the election of 1964. Subsequently an agreement was signed in Lusaka, ratified in London shortly after the Zambia independence negotiations, under which all the obligations between the British Government and Barotseland were ended, and the region became a part of the new independent state. Characteristically, Kaunda encouraged good feeling by taking his whole cabinet to the traditional ceremony when the chief moved to his winter capital.

Kaunda's Policy

The independence of Zambia was recognised on October 24, 1964, as Kaunda desired. In international affairs the Government pursued a policy of non-alignment with either Power *bloc* and identified itself with the movements for colonial liberation and racial equality in all Africa. This meant careful handling in relations with South Africa and Rhodesia because trade with both and communications through the latter were central to its economy; but Kaunda never hid his opposition to white domination and reduced association to the minimum. He was severely critical of Britain's failure to take effective action to end the assumption of independence by the European minority in Rhodesia, and he co-operated with Tanzania in contracting with the Chinese to build a railway to Dar-es-Salaam as the alternative to the southern route. It is probably true to say that Zambia, by its loyalty to UN sanctions against Rhodesia, suffered more in economic loss than Rhodesia itself. Lusaka became the headquarters of liberation movements active in Africa and Kaunda spoke proudly of his Pan-Africanism.

In home affairs the Government followed a policy of raising the standard of living of the African people and increasing their opportunities to enter skilled posts, whilst acting in the spirit of inter-racialism. An immediate difficulty was the absence of trained personnel to maintain administration. Kaunda invited skilled Europeans to Zambia and at the same time initiated an expansion of African education probably unparalleled in Africa. The prosperity of the copper industry provided revenue, but the white miners, many of them from South Africa, were a threatening element.

Towards the end of 1970 a disturbing split occurred in the Government and in the ranks of UNIP. Kaunda's colleague from pioneering days, Simon Kapwepwe, who had been Vice-President, resigned and formed a new United Progressive Party. The cause of dissension was not very clear; Kapaepwe had always been militant. There was great indignation among the President's colleagues and within the rank and file of his party and uncharacteristically Kaunda suppressed the breakaway party and detained Kapwepwe and others, perhaps to save them from violence. The split had a deeper consequence. Kaunda had opposed as impractical the creation of a one-party state, but pressure within the UNIP became overwhelming and he came to accept the necessity to ban parties because they were based on tribalism. He then made the proposal that a commission of twelve members, including not only representatives of Nkumbula's Opposition ANC (with twenty seats in Parliament) but of trade unions, business, the churches and the civil service, should draw up a new constitution after taking evidence from the public. It was evidently his desire to make the one-party serve as a broad reflection of the community, with the same right as Kenya and Tanzania had for different groups within it to nominate opposing candidates in elections. Nkumbula, leader of the ANC, however, rejected Kaunda's proposals, and danger grew of tribal conflict in the south and among adherents of Kapwepwe.

It can be generally said that under conditions of great difficulty, Kenneth Kaunda and his colleagues proved themselves to possess great constructive ability. From 1970 onwards a challenging policy of Socialism was adopted, and the Government took over majority shares in industries and banking in an effort to divert to Zambia the flow of profits passing to foreign financiers.

Rhodesia (Zimbabwe)

On the map southern Rhodesia looks like the profile of a square head with protruding nose and narrow neck. The head is hatted by Mozambique, the nose juts into Northern Rhodesia, and the neck disappears into the body of South Africa, with a touch of Botswana (Bechuanaland). It is a large head, three times the size of England, 150,820 square miles.[24]

Like its relative to the north, Southern Rhodesia provides evidence of early man from 500,000 BC. Also like Northern Rhodesia, the first known inhabitants were Bushmen driven out to desert land by Bantus between the fifth and tenth centuries and much later, in 1830, by refugees from the Zulu chief, Chaka. The first European occupation was by the inevitable Portuguese between 1500 and 1520. Fifty years later Emperor Monomotapa was baptised by a Jesuit Father. There were also occupations by the stronger tribes of different parts of the territory. The Matabeles conquered the Mashonas, peaceful peasants, and also plundered and enslaved other tribes. In the nineteenth century came hunters, traders, and gold seekers from South Africa and many Christian missionaries.

British South Africa Company

European rivalry was reflected in the challenge by Cecil Rhodes to Portugal in 1887 when Lisbon claimed all territory between Mozambique and Angola. The object was avowedly economic profit. Rhodes, diamond millionaire, Prime Minister of Cape Colony (then a British possession), believing the land to be rich in gold, established the British South Africa Company (BSAC) to exploit it. In 1887 his agent, Charles Rudd, tricked the Matabele chief, Lobengula, into surrendering the land and mineral rights of what became Southern Rhodesia in exchange for 1,000 rifles, 100,000 rounds of ammunition, a gunboat and £100 a month. Two years later the British Government recognised this unequal transaction by declaring Southern Rhodesia a protectorate and presenting the BSAC with a royal charter to administer the territory with full governmental powers. The charter included the Company's obligation to encourage immigration and colonisation and to 'secure all mineral rights in return for guarantees of protection and security of rights to the tribal chiefs'.

A year later the Company's 'Pioneer Column', composed of

white mercenaries from South Africa and Britain, each promised fifteen gold claims and three thousand acres of land, occupied Mashonaland. The Pioneer Column have since been honoured as 'Empire Builders'. The anniversary of their arrival in Salisbury, September 12, 1890, is celebrated each year as 'national day'. For thirty years the territory was ruled by the BSAC. Cecil Rhodes' dream of an El Dorado in gold was unfulfilled, but the Company then resorted to profiting from selling land to European immigrants. As their estates spread, the problem arose of obtaining African labour. The Company solved this by enforcing a hut tax which could be met only by earning wages. It then became necessary to distribute the resulting force of labourers between the farms. To realise this the South African 'pass system' was adopted. For African families bereft of their men reserves were established in less fertile areas.

Settlers' Revolt

A conflict arose between the BSAC and settlers regarding the ownership of land. The Matabele king, Lobengula, had sold it to a Herr Lippert, for £1,000. Three years later he sold it to the Company for £1 million. The settlers challenged the Company's title to the land and many Africans who had been despoiled of their farms took advantage of the litigation to reoccupy their lost homes. The issue went to the Privy Council, which decided in favour of neither the Company nor the settlers, nor the Africans, but of the Crown. Thus the Africans ceased to be the disposessed vassals of the Company or settlers and became instead the vassals of the British Government. The conflict between the Company and the settlers became political. A Legislative Council had been established with a majority of Company representatives. The settlers protested and won the concession of a majority. There was no thought of any African representation; they were not 'civilised'. There were two views, however, among the settlers. Some wanted Southern Rhodesia to be integrated with South Africa; others wanted independent self-government. The difference was decided in a referendum of the Whites. Those voting for self-government were 8,774; those for union with South Africa, 5,989.

In 1923 the British Government acknowledged the claim of the settlers to internal self-government. There were three qualifications: there must be no discrimination against the African population, the rights of the BSAC must be respected, and nothing must be done contrary to Britain's international obligations. The concern for the African population proved illusory. Although legislation was frequently discriminatory the British Government did not intervene on a single occasion. Although the BSAC had lost its rights in land (for which it was given generous compensation), it retained its mineral rights. They became immensely profitable.

Africans Begin Opposition

African political opposition to European control developed later than in most parts of the continent. A localised African Congress was started in the fifties by Joshua Nkomo (destined to become a national leader), which in 1957 was absorbed in a more representative African National Congress (ANC) initiated through a Youth League by George Nyandoro and James Chikerema, also prominent later. The Youth League had won a reputation by a successful boycott of buses which charged higher fares; a subsidy was granted enabling fares to be reduced. Nkomo was elected president of the National Congress, Chikerema vice-president and Nyandoro general secretary. European supporters were welcomed, among them Guy Clutton-Brock, head of St Faith's Mission at Rusape, who advised on the Congress constitution, policy and programme. In these early days concentration was on immediate issues – land distribution, wages, colour discrimination. Congress campaigned against the *Land Apportionment* and *Husbandry Acts*, delaying the implementation of the latter, and aroused so much support that in February 1959 the Government declared a state of emergency, arresting five hundred Congress members, including Nyandoro and Chikerema, and subsequently banning the organisation. Nyandoro and Chikerema were detained for four years, Nkomo escaped because he was abroad.[25] The Africans were not subdued. Congress was replaced by the National Democratic Party (NDP), with the same leadership as soon as it became available. There was, however, one difference between the ANC and the NDP, reflecting a maturer mood. Whilst the former directed attention to current grievances, the latter emphasised that injustices could be removed only when Africans gained political power; it campaigned for democracy on the basis of 'one man, one vote'. This development won support from the sophisticated urban workers but tended to lose backing among the rural population.

The African agitation took a more aggressive form. In July 1960 seven thousand marched through Salisbury and there was a sit-down by forty thousand and a strike. The police moved in, violence occurred, spreading to other towns, and eleven Africans were shot. Government reaction was a Law and Order Act prohibiting demonstrations and mass protests. Gestures of conciliation followed from the authorities. A moderately worded appeal was made for acceptance of the new constitution of 1961, which permitted fifteen Africans to enter the Legislative Assembly of sixty-five and established a Commission to draw attention to any racially discriminatory legislation.[26] The NDP rejected the concession as inadequate and in a referendum 300,000 Africans endorsed the rejection. The consequence was that the NDP was banned. To this, response by Africans was immediate. They formed the Zimbabwe African People's Union (ZAPU) with the same officers as president, vice-president and secretary.[27] There was one important newcomer. The Rev. Ndabaningi Sithole, later a rival to Nkomo, became chairman. In the elections of 1962 under the new constitution only twenty per cent of the African voters participated. ZAPU in one respect differed from its predecessor the NDP. Belief in peaceful constitutional emancipation declined. A Zimbabwe Liberation army was formed with support from militant youth movements.

Reactions to Federation

When in 1953 Southern Rhodesia was incorporated in the Federation with Northern Rhodesia and Nyasaland, the Whites concurred because they required revenue from the copper-rich north and labour from Nyasaland and were conscious that they remained the strongest partner both in the Legislative and in military strength.[28] The 1960 Federal Review Conference coincided with discussions on the new Southern Rhodesian Constitution, but in neither case were Southern Rhodesian Africans (who had been violently suppressed earlier that year) invited to participate.[29] Fearing the Government would declare independence, Nkomo called leaders of ZAPU to meet in Dar-es-Salaam to be ready to set up a government in exile. Nkomo had misjudged the tempo of events and he was heavily criticised for romantic leadership. This opened an unhappy period for the nationalist movement. Returning to Rhodesia, Nkomo denounced eleven members of the Executive as plotting to overthrow him and to form a new party. He suspended

Sithole and the critics from ZAPU membership. The excluded thereupon established the Zimbabwe African National Union (ZANU) with a revolutionary socialist policy. Nkomo invited the dissentients to rejoin ZAPU, but they declined. The split was disastrous. ZANU was disappointed in its expectation of majority support among Africans – Nkomo's image was too strong and Sithole and his colleagues were dismissed as 'intellectuals' – but Nkomo also underestimated the discontent with his leadership. He decided to wipe out ZANU; he failed and the only result was gang warfare between the two parties. The African trade union movement was also a victim of the division; it split and was practically destroyed. A nation-wide boycott of schools in 1964 when fees were introduced did not unite the warring sections. Uncontrolled violence broke out inviting repression.[31]

Whites Declare Independence

When the Federation with Northern Rhodesia and Nyasaland was terminated, the Southern Rhodesian Establishment retreated within itself, confident in its ability to retain white supremacy. The British Government had surrendered its right to intervene in the interests of Africans at the time of the 1961 constitution in return for a 'Declaration of Rights' and a Commission on discriminatory legislation. The white Southern Rhodesians ignored the first and abolished the second when the Commission dared to criticise. Nevertheless, there was some conflict between moderates and extremists among Europeans. For a time there was a relatively progressive Prime Minister, Garfield Todd, who attempted to extend the vote to more Africans and to establish a minimum wage, but he was forced to resign and his United Federal Party was swept from office by the racialist Rhodesian Front led by Winston Field, who asked London for sovereign independence for his all-white government. On this being refused, the Europeans demanded absolute defiance of Britain, and Field was dropped in 1964 for the more extreme Ian Smith. There were fruitless discussions between him and the British Prime Minister, Harold Wilson, and on November 11, 1965, Smith unilaterally declared Rhodesia independent. The Government at Westminster denounced this as an 'act of rebellion', suspended the Rhodesian administration (which in turn suspended the British Governor, Sir Humphrey Gibbs), and imposed economic sanctions. The Commonwealth Prime Ministers' Conference

pressed for stronger action and the United Nations Security Council voted for mandatory sanctions.

The outlawed Rhodesian regime weathered the storm, however.
The effect of sanctions was partially nullified by continued trade
through the Republic of South Africa and Portuguese occupied
Mozambique. In April 1966 the UN Security Council authorised
Britain to use force to bar ships from carrying goods to and from
Rhodesia via the Mozambique port of Beira, but trade continued
on a considerable scale by the use of falsified documents of origin.
Trade at the second Mozambique port, Laurenço Marques, was
not interfered with, largely because of disinclination to conflict with
South Africa who used the port extensively. Sanctions had a limited effect on the Rhodesian economy, particularly at first in
restriction of tobacco exports, but the Smith administration had
the European minority behind it and the African opposition was
rendered ineffective by draconian repression. Ian Smith banned
both ZAPU and ZANU and following the arrest of Nkomo and
Sithole, arrested and detained local leaders and party officials.
Violence broke out, but African organisation and action were
severely damaged. Within a month some hundreds were detained.
States of emergency were declared in the African townships
which prevented any coming together of the rank and file and
Africans were fearful of arrest for expressing criticism even in
conversations. An uglier fact was that the bitterness between ZAPU
and ZANU led some members to 'inform' on their opposites. The
morale of the nationalist movement was at its lowest.

African Dissatisfaction

The independent African governments were deeply disappointed
with British action. Harold Wilson told them at a conference at
Lagos that economic sanctions would bring about surrender
within a few weeks, but there were no signs of this happening.
Some African governments, including Tanzania and Algeria, were
so dissatisfied with British policy that they terminated diplomatic
relations. The Organisation of African Unity called on the British
Government to use force to depose the Smith regime and the Afro-
Asian group repeatedly raised this issue in the United Nations,
compelling Britain and the USA to apply the veto in the Security
Council on one occasion. Africans argued that if a non-white
administration had rebelled against Britain there would have been

no doubt about the use of troops to suppress it. The British Government replied that the difference lay in the fact that the Smith administration was heavily armed (a consequence of the agreement dissolving the Federation) and that the dispatch of forces to Rhodesia would mean civil war with the danger of racial war throughout Southern Africa. It was at first argued that the Army would refuse to fight their 'kith and kin' in Rhodesia, but later, even in moderate circles in Britain, it was widely held that if the RAF and troops had been sent in immediately after the illegal declaration of sovereignty the resistance would have been rapidly overcome, but this moment passed with the consolidation of white power.

Britain's Five Principles

All three parties in Britain – Labour, Conservative and Liberal – were committed to five principles.[32] These were:

(1) The principle and intention of unimpeded progress to majority rule, already enshrined in the 1961 Constitution, would have to be maintained and guaranteed.

(2) There would also have to be guarantees against retrogressive amendment of the Constitution.

(3) There would have to be immediate improvement in the political status of the African population.

(4) There would have to be progress towards ending racial discrimination.

(5) The British Government would need to be satisfied that any basis proposed for independence was acceptable to the people of Rhodesia as a whole.

To these the Labour Government added a sixth with general approval:

(6) It would be necessary to ensure that, regardless of race, there was no oppression of majority by minority or of minority by majority.

Republic Established

The Labour Prime Minister made two attempts to reach agreement with Ian Smith, both at talks on warships in the Mediterranean. The first discussion was in December 1966, on board HMS *Tiger*, the second in October 1968, on board HMS *Fearless*. Harold Wilson conceded much, offered independence before majority rule, requiring only that a majority would in time be reached. Ian Smith rejected these approaches, dismissing majority rule in any foreseeable future. In February 1969 he announced a referendum of the white-controlled electorate on a new constitution which would segregate the races and ensure that the government of Rhodesia remained 'in the hands of civilised Rhodesians' for all time. Despite a warning from Britain that such a constitution would destroy any possibility of a settlement, the referendum, held in June 1969, resulted in a landslide endorsement by the European voters and for the establishment of a republic, severing association with Britain and loyalty to the Queen. In March 1970 the Republic was established, leading to the withdrawal of all foreign consulates (including that of the USA), except those of South Africa and Portugal. Rhodesia became politically isolated from almost all the world, but by the economic co-operation of South Africa and Portuguese occupied Mozambique it was able to survive.

Guerrilla Warfare

African frustration by the failure of the sanctions policy led to support for guerrilla warfare against the Rhodesian administration. 'Freedom fighters' were trained in Russia, Cuba, Algeria, Ghana, North Korea and China and crossed into Rhodesia from Zambia. The Kaunda Government did not countenance guerrilla bases in Zambia, but in fact members of ZAPU, the South African National Congress and ZANU associated together in camps. The Smith Administration ridiculed the seriousness of the guerrilla incursions, but the two hundred-mile-long border with Zambia was difficult to police effectively. The Rhodesian authorities had four thousand troops available and seven thousand police, but they had to call in three hundred armed police from South Africa to help defend the frontier. They claimed they killed some hundreds of guerrillas and that their own losses were light (one to a hundred) but the threat appeared to be graver than was acknowledged. The freedom fighters supplemented their incursions across the Zambezi by sending in infiltrators with doctored passports who became underground agents in the African townships. Kenneth Kaunda strove to bring unity between ZAPU and ZANU freedom fighters, and in 1972 many of them came together in the Front for the Liberation of Zimbabwe (FROLIZI). At the time of writing guerrillas do not seem to be a real menace to the Smith regime, but in course of time they might become so. The Organisation of African Unity decided to support them and it could be that by co-ordination between the larger armed resistance in Mozambique and the more fragmentary guerrilla activity in South West Africa they might in the future become important.[33]

Settlement Rejected by Africans

In the General Election of 1970 the Conservative Party was returned to power in Britain. Although its Foreign Secretary, Sir Alec Douglas Home, had first drafted the Five Principles which defined policy towards Rhodesia, among Conservatives there was considerable objection to sanctions and even some support for Ian Smith. It was not surprising, then, that the Government reopened negotiations, using Lord Goodman, a constitutional lawyer with a reputation as a liberal in views, as a go-between. After prolonged discussion a settlement was announced, which provided for a progressive increase of African representation in the Legislature reflecting the proportion who reached certain standards of education and income. The British Government promised £50 million over ten years to aid this development. It was assumed that in course of time this process would lead to equal representation between Europeans and Africans and even eventually to majority rule, but this was not estimated by most knowledgeable commentators to be realisable until well into the next century.

In order to judge whether the proposals were acceptable 'to the people of Rhodesia as a whole' (Principle Five) a Commission was appointed with Lord Pearce as chairman to sound opinion in Rhodesia. Ian Smith expected the majority of Africans living in tribal lands to follow the advice of chiefs (paid allowances by the Administration) to accept the settlement. To the surprise of most, not only the urban Africans but the tribesmen, the greater part of the African population, demonstrated against the proposed terms. Opponents of the settlement ZAPU and ZANU formed, under the chairmanship of Bishop Muzorewa, an African National Council which insisted on no independence before majority rule; there was some rioting at a few meetings which led Europeans to say that intimidation was taking place. The settlement required that 'normal political conditions' should be maintained during the assessment of opinion by the Commission, but Ian Smith shocked world opinion by arresting and detaining without trial Garfield Todd, ex-Prime Minister, and his daughter Judith, as well as two leading Africans, Mr and Mrs Chinamano.[34]

On May 23, 1972, the Pearce Commission issued its report. Its conclusion was stated in these words: 'We are satisfied on our evidence that the Proposals are acceptable to the great majority of Europeans. We are equally satisfied, after considering all our evidence including that on intimidation, that the majority of Africans reject the Proposals. In our opinion the people of Rhodesia as a whole do not regard the Proposals as acceptable as a basis for independence.' Thus the Fifth Principle which the British insisted was necessary for implementation was unfulfilled. There could be no doubt that the Commission was right in saying the people *as a whole* rejected the settlement when their evidence showed that a majority of Africans, who number five million, opposed the terms in contrast with the views of a majority of Europeans who number only a quarter of a million.

Whilst sanctions were having a cumulative effect on the economy of Rhodesia, they did not appear to be weakening the hold of its Government on the European population. In Britain an increasing number of Conservatives urged that they should be withdrawn. On the other hand the Left at Westminster demanded that they should be extended and action taken to defeat the defiance of the UN decision by South Africa and Portugal. In response to the Pearce Commission conclusions, the British Government announced that sanctions would be maintained; the Commonwealth Secretariat urged that they should be strengthened; in America there was strong pressure to renew sanctions on Rhodesian chrome which had been admitted as necessary for defence purposes. Ian Smith indicated that the Rhodesian Administration would not implement the settlement unilaterally and would not reopen negotiations. The African National Council and Joshua Nkomo demanded a constitutional conference with African participation. This was endorsed by the Labour and Liberal Parties at Westminster.

The situation which emerged was dangerous. European pressure in Rhodesia was towards further adoption of the South African practice of segregation and apartheid. African pressure was for physical confrontation if African representatives were not invited to consultation regarding Rhodesia's future. It is difficult to see how renewed resistance and repression, how even ultimate racial war, can be avoided.[35]

Notes

1. Prior to the colonialist period Malawi was the name given to a much wider region covering Zambia and much of Mozambique.

2. Area, 45,974 square miles. Population (1966 census): 4,039,583. Proportion of Africans, 213 to 1. In 1960 Europeans numbered 9,500. After independence the number fell to 8,000.

3. Returning to Nyasaland after his first visit Livingstone wrote: 'I go back to Africa to make an open path for commerce and Christ.'

4. It is of interest that among the volunteers was Captain Lugard, later Lord Lugard.

5. In fact, until 1894, the British South Africa Company paid a British Commissioner £10,000 to administer Zambia on its behalf.

6. It was 1935 before the rail link to the coast at Beira in Mozambique was completed.

7. *Malawi; a Political and Economical History* by J. G. Pike.

8. The Malawi Government issued a commemorative stamp on the fiftieth anniversary of the rising.

9. The author knew Dr Banda in London and spent many evenings in his sitting-room with leading Africans, including the chiefs.

10. The Parliament consisted of fifty-nine members, of whom twelve were Africans. The forty-seven European members represented 300,000 settlers. The twelve Africans represented seven million.

11. Chisiza was shot dead by security forces near Blantyre when he was said to be leading an attack on Dr Banda.

12. There was nevertheless the feeling that he should have sought association with Tanzania and its coastal ports in the north.

13. Area: 290,587 square miles. Population, census 1961–3: 3,493,590 (Africans, 3,409,110; Europeans, 74,640; Asians, 7,790,2,650).

14. A human skull was found by Dr Leakey in Tanzania, thought to date from 1·8 million years ago. Pebble tools have been found in Zambia of the same date.

15. See section on Rhodesia for details of the operations of the British South Africa Company.

16. The first proposal for a Northern Rhodesian African Congress was made by Ellison Milambo and George Kaluwa in 1937, but the inaugural meeting was proscribed by the Secretary for Native Affairs.

17. In his book *Zambia*, the standard work, Richard Hall described the election: 'There were two nominations for the key position of secretary-general and because feeling was so immense among the delegates nobody would trust anyone else to count the votes. Nkumbula turned to a local journalist, Frank Barton, and asked him to act as returning officer. The voting papers were put in a hat, and it became clear who would be the winner by the time Barton was half-way through the count. He recalls "when I pointed to the character with the bright eyes and a tattered pair of shorts there was a big roar of delight".'

18. The Parliament had thirty-five members of whom only six, two from each territory, were Africans. Three Europeans also represented 'African interests'.

19. According to the Northern Rhodesia Chamber of Mines Yearbook, 1960, the average earnings of employees in the copper mines from 1953 to 1960 were:

Year	Europeans	Africans	Year	Europeans	Africans
1953	£1,782	£124	1957	£1,910	£189
1954	£1,734	£123	1958	£1,699	£200
1955	£1,943	£134	1959	£1,868	£218
1956	£2,295	£166	1960	£2,160	£258

20. Iain Macleod on more than one occasion invited the author to personal discussions, a privilege which Labour Colonial Secretaries, except Sydney Webb, rarely accorded.

21. This was Iain Macleod's saddest hour. He showed it in his features in the House of Commons.

22. Kaunda's distress was deepened by the fact that his family was involved. His mother had been sympathetic to the sect and his brother was one of its deacons.

23. In February 1973 Ian Smith closed Rhodesia's frontier with Zambia, alleging that armed guerrilla infiltrators were crossing in considerable numbers. A few days later he reopened the frontier, stating that he had received satisfactory reassurances. Kaunda denied this, maintained the closure of the frontier and proceeded with plans to extend alternative routes for trade by the Chinese-

constructed rail and road route to Dar-es-Salaam and through Angola to the Atlantic port at Lobito. It was suggested that the heavy construction costs should be met by a consortium of nations.

24. Population, 1972: 5,690,000, Africans 5,400,000, Europeans 262,000, Asians 9,600, Others 17,700.

25. Nkomo was at Accra and his followers insisted that he should go to Britain to state their case. The Africans were in confident mood. The author presided at a large demonstration in London with Nkomo as speaker and prophesied he would be Prime Minister of Rhodesia within five years. Nkomo retorted indignantly 'within one year'. Alas, both anticipations were illusory.

26. Nkomo, consulted by the British Government, accepted too readily but later withdrew. This was the beginning of some African opposition to him.

27. Zimbabwe was the ancient African name for Rhodesia.

28. Somewhat inconsistently, Nkomo stood as a candidate in the election for the first Federal Parliament. He was defeated by an African backed by Europeans.

29. A fateful decision was reached at the Victoria Falls conference which subsequently terminated Federation. The military forces were predominantly handed over to Southern Rhodesia. These included four army battalions, an armoured car squadron and seven air force squadrons, including jet fighter bombers with a capacity to carry atomic weapons.

30. Nkomo's first response to the split was to form a Peoples' Caretaker Council, which rallied some influential recruits who deplored the division, but very soon the name was dropped in favour of the popular ZAPU.

31. After successive arrests and releases, Nkomo was detained in a remote area. Sithole was arrested, then tried and imprisoned for treason.

32. The Five Principles were first laid down under a Conservative Government by Sir Alec Douglas Home before UDI was declared.

33. Guerrilla activity became more serious in 1973. In February Ian Smith imposed collective fines on African tribes which failed to report the presence of armed infiltrators, and sentences of twenty years' imprisonment on anyone who assisted them.

34. Judith Todd was released later in 1972 and became active in the African cause internationally. Garfield Todd was released but restricted to his farm. The Chinamanos remain in prison.

35. Conservative pressure for a settlement became strong in 1973.

Chapter Thirteen

French Black Africa

(West and Equatorial
Africa, Malagasy, Réunion,
Comoro Islands)

French Africa covered one-third of the continent. In addition to
traversing the Arab north in Morocco, Algeria and Tunisia, it
occupied the vast black area of the western bulge, much of the
centre, and the islands, large and small, of Madagascar, Réunion
to the east and the Comoro Islands to the west.

Occupation

The embracing Portuguese were the first Europeans to invade West
Africa. They appeared in the fifteenth century, establishing coastal
stations as flourishing centres of the slave trade. After their defeat
by Germany in 1870, the French sought prestige by extending their
interests in Africa. Before this their occupations on the west coast
had been confined to a few trading stations with small factories in
Senegal, the Ivory Coast and Gabon. They now began to press
along the coast and into the interior, subduing Senegal between
1854 and 1865, the Upper Niger between 1876 and 1890, the Middle
Congo and Gabon between 1885 and 1891 and Dahomey between
1889 and 1894. The conquest of Chad took several decades. The
French expansion in Africa was stopped by the British at Fashoda
on the White Nile in 1898. The British had contested French
claims, but it was in the same year that the two governments signed
a convention recognising each other's spheres of influence.

In 1895 French West Africa was constituted by grouping the
western territories under one Governor-General at Dakar in
Senegal.[1] The associated territories were: Senegal, Mauritania,
French Sudan (Mali), Upper Volta, Niger, Guinea, Ivory Coast
and Dahomey. In 1910 the more distant French Equatorial Africa
was initiated by grouping Oubangui-Chari (Central African Republic), Gabon, the Middle Congo and Chad, with Brazzaville in

the Congo as capital.[2] The lives of the people of the interior were at first little affected by political changes. They had suffered grievously from slave traders, worst of all from the Arab Rabah Zabeir, who in 1892–3 laid waste wide areas despite resistance by several tribes. He was not tracked down and killed until 1900 when the French, who had outlawed slavery in 1848, intervened.

Exploitation

In later years, as the French commercial presence grew, the African communities became disturbed at the roots. Concessions of land were made to companies to develop cocoa and coffee plantations in the green vegetation regions of the Ivory Coast, Guinea and Dahomey. Africans were heavily taxed and were compelled to become wage earners to meet demands; if they failed to pay the tax they were conscripted for labour either on public works, such as railway construction, or rounded up to serve for private concerns. They were forcibly transported from the semi-desert areas such as the Upper Volga to the plantations, and frequently flogged if they did not fulfil exhausting tasks. When minerals were discovered and companies formed to extract them, the labour force was often terrorised and sometimes even decimated. These conditions were exposed by André Gide in his *Voyage au Congo* (1927) and caused such an outcry in France that territorial concessions to companies were ended.

A second cause of deep discontent among Africans was the introduction of the system of *indigènes*, under which the officers of the administration could impose punishment without reference to any court of law. Resort was made to *indigènes* mostly to deal with 'troublesome' African workers rather than criminals; offenders could be deported or sentenced to life imprisonment. This practice was not modified until 1940, when punishments without trial were limited to five days' imprisonment or a fine of £100. In addition, there was a special penal code for Africans, many offences included in this code were legal when committed by Europeans. Opposition to this inequality before the law was accentuated by the fact that Europeans presided over the courts.

French Africans

The political aim of French colonialism was to integrate the indigenous populations with France rather than to prepare the way for independence. Its purpose in the first instance was democratic. In the aftermath of the French Revolution Danton got the Convention in 1794 to declare that not only should slavery be ended but 'all men without distinction of colour who live in the colonies are French citizens and enjoy all rights guaranteed by the Constitution'. In practice, not all were accepted as citizens. Napoleon repealed the decree and citizenship was accorded only to those who deserted the African way of life for the French and who joined the ruling élite in education and social status. The opportunities for education were extremely restricted. Even 150 years afterwards (1945), only five per cent of African children of school age were going to primary schools. In Guinea the figure was 1·3 per cent; in Dahomey, much above the average, 10 per cent; and best in Senegal, 12 per cent. Senegal was the first to break through to anything like equal status. It was the most developed area and Four Communes were given the right to return a representative to the Chamber of Deputies in Paris and to elect town councils and a colonial council. On the eve of the First World War their rights were threatened; they reacted by electing a black African, Blaise Diagne, to the Chamber of Deputies in 1914. Diagne promised to recruit Africans for the war and in return all natives of the Four Communes were made full French citizens irrespective of 'personal status'. Citizenship did not extend to Africans outside the privileged communes; they remained 'subjects'. The estrangement between 'citizens' and 'subjects' became as marked as between Africans and Europeans. Paris had succeeded in creating French Africans.

Nationalism

In the period we have so far described nationalist movements did not arise in strength. As early as the 1890s there had been conflicts with authority in Dahomey, where political consciousness was encouraged by proximity to Nigeria and by the traditions of the self-contained African kingdoms, Porto Novo and Abomey. King Behanzin of Abomey so asserted the claims of his people that he was deported to Martinique in 1894. But it was not until the years approaching the First World War that further serious opposition was recorded. France then had a tough Governor in Charles Noufflard and a strong protest movement was led by Louis Hunkanrin, an African teacher, and Tovalon Quenan, an African businessman. Hunkanrin was dismissed from his post, but legalised his activity for a time by conducting it in Paris under the auspices of the League for the Rights of Man. He had eventually to flee to Nigeria, where he continued his campaign in association with two teachers in Dahomey who published a clandestine paper.

Criticism of Governor Noufflard became so strong that an investigation was initiated in Paris and he was removed from office. Hunkanrin returned from Nigeria, and was adopted politically by Blaise Diagne, the pioneer African Deputy for Senegal. Hunkanrin was even appointed in charge of colonial troops in Paris, but was court-martialled whilst in Senegal and sentenced to three years imprisonment and five years banishment from Dahomey for attending subversive meetings and writing anti-colonial articles. The agitation continued. Anti-colonialist literature from Paris was distributed widely and in 1923 there was a massive strike for comprehensive demands. The strike was immediately occasioned by increases in taxation, but the objects also included an end to direct rule from France, a return to protectorate status, the removal of the Governor and the release of Hunkanrin. Repression was severe and six leaders were sentenced to ten years' imprisonment for describing it as equivalent to 'Boche atrocities in the war'.[3] For a time the radical movement declined, but a few militants co-operated with the Pan-African Association in Paris. The Nationalists in Dahomey turned to political action when territorial councils were established. Hunkanrin, untiring, was active in this campaign.

There were protest movements in most territories. In the Middle Congo André Matsona started an organisation, *Amicaliste*, to oppose the worst abuses of the administration such as *indigènat*, forced labour, and the absence of economic development. He had a magnetic personality and was regarded by his followers more as a religious than a political leader. The movement became negatively anti-European in its refusal to apply Western techniques in agriculture and malaria prevention or to co-operate in social security measures and the taking of a census.

In Gabon there was repeated political activity among the freed slaves who were settled at Libreville. There was a lively youth movement in 1920, *Jeune Gabonais*, demanding African rights. It made the French anxious, but dissension among leaders brought collapse. Ten years later there was a promising effort to end tribal rivalries led by a civil servant, Léon Mba. He had been appointed head of a canton by the French, but was dismissed because they regarded African unity as dangerous. It is of interest that here, as in Dahomey, the League for the Rights of Man was used as a respectable sponsor.

With the election of Senegal's Blaise Diagne to the Chamber of Deputies hope for advance turned to Paris. He was rewarded for his co-operation in the First World War by an appointment to the Ministry of the Colonies, but, although he had joined the Socialists, this identity with the Establishment meant a loss of confidence at home; he was defeated in the mayoral election for St Louis in 1925 by a young radical lawyer who was to make a mark, Amadou Lamine-Guèyre. A co-operative climate emerged in Paris with the formation of the Popular Front Government in 1936. Léon Blum, the Prime Minister, had been prominent when André Gide exposed the atrocities in Equatorial Africa, and socialist Marius Montet became Minister for the Colonies. In Senegal Lamine-Guèyre formed a broad-based Popular Front Committee and closer assimilation with France was established when citizenship rights were extended and trade union membership permitted. Plans to abolish forced labour and reform the *indigenat* were destroyed, however, by the fall of the Blum Government.

Second World War

The division in France between Vichy and de Gaullists during the Second World War was repeated in Africa. In the West (though not in Equatorial Africa) support was at first given by the administration to Vichy with disastrous results for Africans. Assimilation was replaced by authoritarianism, a colour bar was introduced in shops, hotels and trains, and elected councils were abolished. There was courageous resistance by Africans and some Leftist Frenchmen. Many were arrested for conspiring with Gaullists to overthrow the regime and a number of Africans were executed.

In Equatorial Africa Felix Eboue, who had been known as the 'Black Frenchman', became Governor-General and startled Paris by differing officially for the first time from the accepted purpose of making Africans 'good Frenchmen'. He repudiated the attempt 'to recruit native society in our own image, with our own habits of mind'[4] and criticised the policy of assimilation as destructive of

African culture, but at the same time argued in favour of recognising the African élite of chiefs and notables rather than the proletariat. With the arrival in 1942 of the Free French, Africans in large numbers came under their political influence.

Brazzaville Conference

So the Black Africa of France moved forward to the fateful Brazzaville Conference of 1944. De Gaulle opened the conference and regarded it as of supreme importance because, with France overrun, the empire was the remaining territory of the Free French; Brazzaville was the capital of his exiled government, and 100,000 Africans were fighting in the army, forming more than half of its personnel. Nevertheless, there was no African representative; only Felix Eboue reflected African views by reading declarations from chiefs that traditional culture must not be crushed by assimilation. The recommendations were all directed, however, to integration with France rather than towards African independence. The civilising mission of the French was emphasised and any idea of autonomy, any possibility of 'evolution outside the French imperial *bloc*' or 'the constitution of self-government' were excluded 'even in the distant future'. On the other hand there were concessions. The colonies would be more fully represented in the Constituent Assembly in Paris and within the territories administrative councils would be established as soon as possible, containing both Africans and Europeans, elected by universal suffrage. Many reforms were promised, including the abolition of *indigènes* punishments and forced labour (except for one year in lieu of military service). The occasion was regarded as a great triumph for the benevolent unity of France with its colonies. No one foresaw the movement among Africans for their own independent status.

Constituent Assemblies

Even before the end of the war the French pressed ahead with many of the reforms promised at Brazzaville. Perhaps the most significant for the future was a decree permitting trade unions to be formed. This led many French union organisers, including Communists, to descend on the African territories, with political as well as industrial effect in the towns. But seemingly endless controversy

buried constitutional advance. Three figures who became important appeared at a commission which met in Paris in 1945 to
consider representation at a Constituent Assembly: Houphouét
Boigny of the Ivory Coast, Leopold Senghor of Senegal and Sourou
Apithy of Dahomey. They protested strongly against the retention
of the 'double college' system of voting under which a small minority of French persons were placed on a separate and privileged
electoral roll. There were only thirty-three representatives from
Africa at the Constitutional Assembly of 586 and of these twenty-
four were Whites (there was one representative of mixed race).
The French representation was dominated by three parties, the
Communists (152), the MRP Conservatives (150) and the Socialists
(145), all of whom became involved later in deals with the African
parties. There were also two small groups, *Union-Démocratique et
Sociale de la Résistance* (UDSR), a non-party Resistance Group
in the war, and the *Mouvement Unifié de la Résistance* (MUR),
fellow-travellers with the Communists. An attempt was made by
Lamine-Guèyre to form the African representatives into a *bloc*
associated with the Socialists, but they split. Five of the eight,
including Senghor and Apithy, joined him in affiliating to the
Socialists; Houphouét Boigny, strange in view of his subsequent
history, joined the communist leaning MUR and one of the others
the conservative MRP (*Mouvement Républicain Populaire*).

There was some controversy in the Assembly between those who
wished the relationship between France and the African territories
to be based on federalism and those who favoured assimilation. A
compromise was reached by which each territory would have a local
assembly with limited powers and one deputy in the National
Assembly in Paris for every eighty thousand inhabitants (as
against one for every forty-two thousand in France). The 'double
college' system would be ended by placing Europeans and
Africans on the same roll, and theretically the territorial assemblies
were to be elected by universal suffrage, abolishing the distinction
between 'citizens' and 'subjects'; but it was recognised that in
practice this could not be realised immediately. The African
representatives no less than the French accepted the maintenance
of a French Union, but they also insisted on the recognition of an
'African personality'; they were not prepared to become 'good
Frenchmen'. In January 1946 a symbolical change in terminology
was made by government decision. 'Colonies' became 'Territories
Overseas' and the responsible Minister became the 'Minister of
Overseas France'.

The proposed constitution was submitted to a referendum both in France and in the overseas territories. In France it was rejected by 10½ million votes to 9½ million; in Africa there was a massive 'Yes' in localities with a non-white majority of voters, but in those with European majorities the 'Nos' carried. It is fair to say that in France the rejection of the proposed constitution was based more on opposition to the recommendation of a French–African National Assembly in Paris rather than on the approach to equality with the colonial peoples.

So a new Constituent Assembly had to be appointed. The African representatives were re-elected with huge majorities, but the representatives in France were drastically changed by new elections to the Legislature in Paris, which made the MRP the largest party destroying the combined majority of Socialists and Communists. Recognising the danger of more reactionary decisions, all the non-European representatives formed an Intergroup to defend their interests. The Government proposed a federal constitution, with certain colonies (Indo-China, Tunisia and Morocco) recognised as Associated States, but insisted on the integration of Black Africa with France, with minority representation in the Assembly at Paris. Citizenship in the overseas territories was to be distinct from French citizenship, and would be extended only to persons fulfilling exceptional legal requirements. These discriminatory proposals were unacceptable to the non-French, who were furious with the Socialists when they deserted them; they walked out as a body and wrote to the President, 'We cannot be second-class Frenchmen'. The Government made two concessions. They agreed that overseas inhabitants should be 'citizens on the same basis as French nationals' and they omitted from the constitution the provision for electoral colleges. Twenty-four deputies in the Assembly were allotted to Black Africa, two among them to Europeans.

United African Party

The African delegates at the Constituent Assembly formed themselves into the *Rassemblement Démocratique Africain* (RDA) with the object of fusing the political parties in the different territories into a single movement. It was agreed that the deputies in the Assembly in Paris should establish a Parliamentary group. Houphouét Boigny wanted the group to enter into an alliance with the

Communist Party and MUR, but the view of Apithy was endorsed that its members should be permitted to associate with the French parties of their choice. In practice, however, the RDA became closely identified with the Communists who alone gave it whole-hearted support. This led to official pressure against it in the overseas territories, and even to persecution, particularly in the Ivory Coast, where the administration employed *provocateurs* to incite violence, arrested the leaders (except Houphouét who had Parliamentary immunity), dismissed civil servants and several hundred chiefs, burned down a village whose inhabitants refused to pay taxes, and in another village shot thirteen. Houphouét Boigny exerted restraint, protesting his loyalty to the French Union, and the fact that not a single European was attacked reflected his influence. Nevertheless, the Government banned RDA meetings not only in the Ivory Coast but in all West and Equatorial Africa.

Split with Communists

The state of conflict in the territories occasioned some doubts in the RDA about its alliance with the Communists. Another doubt was caused by the withdrawal of support by Catholic Africans. This latter reason led to a split in the Parliamentary group, Apithy and six other deputies breaking away to form the *Groupe des Indé-pendants d'Outre-Mer* (IOM). Later Senghor, who had left the Socialist Party to form the Democratic Bloc of Senegal (BDS), joined and even Houphouét began to question the wisdom of continued association with the Communists. He entered into nego-tiations with the IOM and got the RDA deputies to agree, in the interests of joint action, to disaffiliate from all French parties. The talks with the IOM broke down, however, because of difficulties at constituency level, whereupon the RDA leaders opened discussions with M. Mitterand, the Minister for Overseas. They reached agreement that in return for support of the Government it would pursue a more sympathetic policy towards the RDA in Africa. The alliance with the Communists was dead.

The RDA-Government co-operation shocked the Left. It had one progressive result: for the first time African women gained the right to vote. This was limited to mothers with two children who had served the Free French in the war, but it gave Africans living outside the towns, the great majority, predominant electoral strength. Houphouét Boigny moved further to the Right. In 1952 with two other RDA deputies he joined the UDSR, Mitterand's party. The disintegration of the African Parliamentary group did not end there. With the consent of the IOM Senghor joined the Edgar Fauré Government of 1952. The following year Apithy defected from the IOM to join the Independent Republicans.

Trade Union Aggression

Militancy among Africans was now expressed through the trade unions. As in France they were divided into Communist, Catholic and Socialist organisations, but in 1952 Sékou Touré, leader of the Communist Union in Guinea, and David Soumah, leader of the Catholic Union, took the initiative in calling a joint conference to press for the enactment of the Labour Code which had been promised by governments for years. This led to a general strike throughout West Africa which stimulated the Assembly to pass the Code before the end of the year. When employers and the administration proved unwilling to apply the provisions fairly, Touré called a second conference in French Sudan and strikes were renewed. In Guinea all work stopped for two months, ending with victory. One result of this successful union aggression was to make Sékou Touré a leading figure throughout West Africa. He became dominant in the political party attached to the RDA in Guinea and was elected to its territorial assembly. Soon he was to be recognised as the nation's leader. His association with Houphouét in RDA, despite the latter's conservatism, was made easier when he promised that his union in Guinea, which had grown strong and self-reliant, would become independently African and break with the Communist CGT in France.

Federal or Territorial Power?

From now on controversy was continuous regarding the future of French Black Africa and the relationship of its territories to France. The leaders of the different parties still insisted on close association; the only suggestion that the African territories should be independent came from a youth movement in Senegal, mostly students. But there was a strong demand for equality between French and African citizens, for the abolition in practice of the double electoral system, and for greater autonomy in the territories. Some hopes were created during the Mendès-France government of 1954, and it set a new pattern in mandated Togoland by extending considerable autonomy; but the government lasted only a month. Hopes were renewed under the socialist government of Guy Mollet in 1956. The Minister for Overseas was Gaston Defferre, a sincere anti-colonialist. In his famous *Loi-Cadre* he finally abolished the double electoral system, enacted adult suffrage, and devolved administrative services and legislative power to elected African bodies. Defferre increased the authority of the separate territories as against the authority of the West and Equatorial Federations at Dakar and Brazzaville, which aroused conflict between Senghor and Houphouét. Senghor was against 'Balkanisation' and wanted the Federations to remain strong, thinking in terms that they would ultimately be the African administrations partnered with France, whilst Houphouét argued that only at territorial level would Africans feel that they were really governing themselves. Despite this difference the African deputies acted unitedly when the decrees applying *Loi-Cadre* were debated. There was disappointment because the powers given to the territorial assemblies were less than those accorded to Togoland and because many of the services previously performed at the Federal centres were transferred to Paris rather than to the territories. It is probable that Defferre was overruled on these issues within the government. The Mollet administration became more reactionary and lost African sympathy by continuing to prosecute the war in Algeria.

Rivalry persisted, however, between the African parties. Despite Houphouét's turn to the Right – perhaps because of this, it had the support of the administration – the RDA was the strongest. In the 1956 elections, nine RDA deputies were returned against seven for the Independents and four for the Socialists. The Socialists decided to separate from the French party and to form the *Mouvement Socialist Africain* (MSA) but they made little impression. The Independents attempted to recover ground by renaming themselves *Convention Africaine* (CA) hoping to attract other parties, but again this met with limited success. Within the parties, however, more radical ideas were developing. At the 1949 RDA congress at Bamako in French Sudan Houphouét had a lukewarm reception when he urged the abolition of the West and Equatorial regional administrations and the direct federation of the local territories with the Paris Government. It was held that this would involve subordination to France, particularly because of economic domination. Out of respect for him Congress accepted in its declaration the proposal for a 'federal government and federal parliament', but the delegates insisted on the inclusion of the principle that 'independence of peoples is an inalienable right which allows them to dispose of the attributes of their sovereignty according to the interests of the mass of the population' – the first reference made to independence. Sékou Touré, endorsed by all the delegations except those from the Ivory Coast and Gabon, declared for elected federal governments at Dakar and Brazzaville which should have full management of African affairs. Houphouét, who had now become a member of the Paris Government, was stunned by the militant tone of the congress. He stayed away from its proceedings for three days.

A serious effort was made to achieve the unity of the main African parties at a *Regroupement* conference in Paris in 1958. The RDA, the *Convention Africaine* and the MSA were all represented as well as a new party in Senegal formed by young intellectuals to advocate independence, the *Parti Africain de l'Indépendence* (PAI). The PAI was led by Majhemout Diop, editor of *Présence Africaine*, devoted to the assertion of African culture as distinctive from French. The RDA, CA, and MSA reached agreement on a minimum political programme incorporating complete autonomy for the territories, regional federations based on voluntary renunciation of territorial sovereignty, and an all-in Federal Republic linked to France on the basis of 'free co-operation, absolute equality and the right to independence'. The Federal Republic would have responsibility for diplomacy, defence, currency, higher education and the magistrature and – an interesting addition – it would be entitled to contract a 'Confederal Union' with other states in Africa already independent or becoming so. The conference failed, however, to bring about unity. The PAI delegates walked out because immediate independence was not demanded and the RDA declined to modify its name for a common name. At an adjourned conference agreement could not be reached and the promising hope of a united campaign was destroyed. The CA, MSA and a number of small parties then joined to form the *Parti du Regroupement African* (PRA).

Independence Demand

At the Congress of the PRA, held at Cotonou in Dahomey later in the year, Senghor found himself repudiated in the same way as Houphouét at the RDA congress at Bamako. He rejected independence as a solution and emphasised the need for association with France in a Federal Republic. The whole Congress seemed to turn against him, rising to Bakary Djibo, trade union leader from Niger, when he declared 'you can only associate when you are really independent'. The attitude of the Congress was strengthened by news from Paris that de Gaulle had announced that the African participants in a Federal Republic would not be recognised as states. The Congress declaration emphasised 'immediate independence' as the first necessity and decided on a campaign 'to mobilise the African masses' around it. The declaration called for a national Constituent Assembly to organise the new African nation, only after which would consideration be given to negotiation with France for a 'multinational confederation'. Very significantly it was added that this did not imply 'abandoning the African will to federate all former colonies into a United States of Africa'. By these pronouncements the PRA not only gave a new radical lead in French Black Africa, it allied itself with the Left in the African movements of the continent. Senghor, always conciliatory, accepted the decisions of Congress. Indeed, it is said that he drafted the declaration.

French Community

In Paris de Gaulle was formulating his proposals. Senghor and Lamine-Guèyre (they had become reconciled) were members of the Consultative Committee which considered his draft. De Gaulle was adamant in rejecting a confederation of independent states and indicated that if any territory chose independence France would cut off co-operation. Senghor and Lamine-Guèyre leaned over backwards to influence the committee, saying that whilst for Africans the recognition of their right to independence was a matter of human dignity, they would remain 'French in our civilisation'. The committee were impressed and in their recommendations substituted 'Community' for 'Federation', although they subscribed to de Gaulle's rejection of confederation. De Gaulle accepted 'Community' and agreed that Member-States should have the right to become independent, but if they did so they would cease to be members of the Community. The new constitution was referred to a referendum in France and the African countries. Before the vote President de Gaulle made a tour of the African territories. In Guinea he had a chilly reception both from Sékou Touré and the people. This probably affected his subsequent treatment of Guinea.

There was much confusion among Africans how they should vote. The proposed constitution accepted the right to independence, but woe to any people who exercised it! In effect, decisions in the different territories largely reflected economic necessity. The two party groups were divided among themselves. Whilst the RDA and the PRA as a whole voted 'Yes', Sékou Touré's RDA affiliate in Guinea voted 'No'. Touré carried his people with him by 95·2 per cent, but in Niger economic fears defeated Bakary Djibo. The 'Yes' vote was 78 per cent. In other territories also the 'Yes' vote was overwhelming.

Guinea Independent

The wrath of de Gaulle now fell on Guinea. Although Touré assured the French President of Guinea's 'sincere wish for preservation and development of fraternal friendship and collaboration', France within two months withdrew all its civil servants, who took away everything that was portable from their offices, even the telephones, and the police smashed furniture and windows in their barracks before they left; students lost their scholarships, French public investment was withdrawn and the Government discouraged private investment. Guinea had to turn elsewhere for support. Ghana and Guinea agreed on 'union' (more on paper than in actuality) and Nkrumah's government made a loan of £10 million. With East Germany a commercial and cultural agreement was signed. Paris became fearful that Guinea would move towards the communist East, and in 1959 agreed to a compromise, under which diplomatic recognition was accorded. France undertook to provide teachers, Guinea remained in the franc zone and was accepted as eligible for technical assistance. Relations remained cold, however, and when Touré established friendly associations both with the Soviet *bloc* and the USA (then de Gaulle's *bête noire*), France excluded Guinea from the franc zone and trade practically ceased. Guinea had to pay severely for its independence but the people continued to support Touré. There were some discontents, but the Government despite economic disintegration pulled through.

The dominant issue within the African 'Yes' territories was whether they would associate with the French Community as separate states or through the two Federations. In the West it appeared that Senegal, French Sudan, Upper Volta and Dahomey would federate, but under pressure from Houphouét and the Ivory Coast, Upper Volta and Dahomey withdrew. Senegal and French Sudan then joined in the Federation of Mali, named after an empire which had stretched from Cape Verde to Nigeria. Houphouét retorted by forming the *Conseil de l'Entente* (CE) composed of the Ivory Coast, Upper Volta and Dahomey. In the Equatorial region there was a proposal not only for federation but for union within a Central African State, but it collapsed and the territories agreed only on economic co-operation,[5] with separate associations within the French Community. The Federation was dissolved.

French Community Disrupted

These divisive results nevertheless led to a controversy in Paris which brought important conclusions. The Mali Federation (Senegal and French Sudan) was recognised after some delay as part of the Community but it demanded full independence within the Community. De Gaulle agreed; in so doing he changed the basis of the Community from federation to confederation. The other territories hastened to claim independence. Even those within the Council of the Entente – Ivory Coast, Upper Volta and Dahomey – did so; indeed, they went further – they held that the Community had no relevance and withdrew from it altogether. In the Equatorial region Gabon, Chad, the Central African Republic and Congo (Brazzaville) also claimed to be independent states. The one other change was in the Mali Federation. Senegal withdrew, French Sudan became Mali, and both became separate independent states. By August 1960 the French Community had in effect ceased to exist in West and Equatorial Africa.

The Separate States

There was, however, a deep division in the ideology and social patterns of the twelve newly independent states of what had been

French West and Equatorial Africa. Except for the Ivory Coast, all the territories lived through turmoil, much of it reflecting a revolt against French economic domination. In *Senegal* Senghor, pursuing a moderate socialist policy, had to face a trade union revolt in 1968 and a students' revolt the following year. In *Dahomey* there were repeated *coups*, six regimes in ten years with eleven heads of state, a record in instability for all Africa. Although the population was only two million, there was fierce antagonism between its three regions, but their leaders came to an arrangement in 1970 to share the presidency, each to be head of state for two years; the conflicts were tribal rather than ideological, but poverty gave rise to a working class opposition from trade unions.[6] In the *Middle Congo* (Brazzaville), where a parish priest, Fulbert Youlou, pro-de Gaullist, had been elected Prime Minister in 1958, a three-day revolution overthrew him in 1963, followed by massacres and another *coup*. In 1968 a socialist administration was established under Marien Ngouabi, Marxist but pragmatically moderate; there was continuous hostility with ex-Belgian Congo (Kinshasa) across the river, both sides charged each other with incursions aimed at overthrowing governments. In *Mali* there was popular enthusiasm for socialist construction, whole villages voluntarily building roads, water-channels and schools. The National Assembly was replaced by delegates appointed on a Soviet model, but dissatisfaction grew and in 1968 the army took over, leading to an economic agreement with France in 1969.

Chad uneasily resisted the socialist tendency. Its first independent government accepted a French military presence, largely because it feared internal revolution. In 1968 Paris sent reinforcements to crush a rebellion, which had been assisted by revolutionaries in Libya. When the People's Government took power in Tripoli, this help was ended as part of an agreement with France for the sale of a hundred Mirage aircraft. France withdrew some of its troops from Chad, but it maintained a military base and its military advisers were strengthened; a French commission virtually assumed economic control and Paris announced that this would continue for several years. Chad became a full example of a neo-colonial state, with revolts repeatedly requiring French suppression. The *Central African Republic* also returned to French domination. Its first democratic government was overthrown in 1965 by an army *coup* led by Colonel Bokassa, who dissolved the National Assembly and ruled by decree. Economic planning, which concentrated on agriculture, was carried out with French advisers. Another neo-colonial state.

In 1919 *Upper Volta* had been divided by Paris between the Ivory Coast, Niger and French Sudan, only becoming reunified in 1947. Following independence in 1960, there was a continuous struggle between the trade unions and the government of Maurice Yameogo, leading to a *coup* by the army in 1966 with Colonel Lamizana as President. In 1970 the army proposed a constitution which would allow civilians in the government. There were two Left parties – the Movement of National Liberation led by Ki-Zerbo and the more extreme Party of African Independence, headed by Amiron Thiomsiano. There was a Rightist party, the Group of Popular Action, led by Dr Sogue Nouhoum. Upper Volta was under French domination, but stability was not assured; either a Right or Left government might incite another *coup*. *Niger* escaped *coups*. Its constitution, adopted in 1968, provided for election to a single-chamber Legislature of sixty members by adult suffrage, but executive power was entirely in the hands of the president. The constitution allowed diversity of parties, but in fact there was only one, the Niger Progressive Party (PPN). The president Hamani Diori, was also the secretary-general of the PPN and was a near dictator. Niger was still within the French economic sphere and France influenced its education, providing teachers. National effort concentrated on the expansion of fertile land.

The *Ivory Coast*, the richest of the ex-French territories, proved the most stable under the presidency of Houphouét Boigny. With French co-operation (an agreement was signed in 1961) forests were cleared for coffee, cocoa and banana plantations. The social atmosphere and official language remained French. There was an elected National Assembly, but the president had wide powers. The Ivory Coast was the leader in an alliance with Upper Volta, Niger and, for a time, Dahomey, which included a customs union and common development, defence and foreign policies. In foreign affairs Houphouét followed Paris. The Ivory Coast might almost be described as France in Africa.

Togoland

After the First World War, the German-occupied territories of Togoland and Cameroun were divided between France and Britain as mandates under the League of Nations. They were closely associated with the developments in West and Equatorial Africa, but had to be treated separately because they were not colonies. The earliest controversy was between the German- and French-educated élites, but at the beginning of the war they united behind the Vichy regime and, as mentioned above, introduced segregation of Africans in transport, shops and hotels. At the end of the war the United Nations Charter laid down that the aim of the Trusteeship system was self-government which was in contrast with the French policy of assimilation but Paris accepted the mandate. There was considerable opposition from the Left when Togoland and Cameroun were asked in 1945 to vote representatives to the projected Constituent Assembly of French colonies. At the Assembly Cameroun was allotted three deputies in the Paris Parliament, Togoland one.[7] In Togoland, on the initiative of the Ewe tribe, divided between the French and British territories, a movement began for union and their party, the *Comité d'Unité Togolaise* (CUT), won fifteen of the twenty-four second college seats in the Representative Assembly. In Cameroun young trade unionists of communist leanings formed the *Union des Populations Camerounaises* (UPC) in 1948. It came out not only for the reunion of the French and British zones but for independence within a fixed time limit.

United Nations Influence

Under the government of Mendès-France in 1954 extensive reforms were introduced in French Togoland, perhaps to meet Britain's claim that it should be united with the Gold Coast. The double electoral college system was abolished, a Council of Government was established in which five out of nine members were elected by the Representative Assembly, and local councils were set up with executive powers. CUT, demanding independence, rejected these reforms, but they were overwhelmingly endorsed by the electorate. In 1956 there was a referendum in British Togoland on a proposal that it should be incorporated with independent Ghana (Gold Coast) and a majority voted in favour. This stimulated Defferre, socialist Minister for Overseas, to extend the sphere of self-government in French Togoland with an elected Parliament, the first in *Afrique Noire*. This did not satisfy, however, a United Nations mission which insisted in 1958 that France should concede further powers and that a general election for the Assembly be held with universal suffrage, increasing the number of voters from

190,000 to 491,000. Paris enlarged Togo self-government to all spheres except currency, defence and foreign policy and the election was fought on the issue of full independence. CUT won under the leadership of Olympio and Togoland's independence was recognised in April 1960.

In office Olympio rejected Nkrumah's approaches for union with Ghana and drew nearer to France. In 1963 he was assassinated by soldiers who objected to the disbandment of the army. The subsequent government was led by more conservative politicians who expanded co-operation with France, which provided considerable aid. In 1967 the Government was overthrown by a bloodless *coup* initiated by young officers, who appointed Colonel Kleber Dadjo as head of a Reconciliation Administration.

Cameroun

The advance of Cameroun to independence was more stormy. Like the people of other parts of French Black Africa, its inhabitants suffered severely from *indigenat*, under which it will be remembered unco-operative workers could be sent to prison for ten years without trial. The Brazzaville Conference of 1944 decided on reform, and it was in fact in the Cameroun that a new Labour Code was first applied, legalising trade unions, appointing doctors to inspect conditions, introducing the beginnings of social security and prohibiting payment in kind. During the war the area of Douala had become industrialised and it was here that the conflict between the low paid workers with their long hours and their European employers became fiercest. The workers organised under French communist stimulation in the *Union des Syndicales Confédérés du Cameroun* (*USCC*) and the employers responded by forming the *États Généraux de la Colonisation Française*, which denounced the Brazzaville reforms and campaigned for the retention of forced labour. In the election of 1945 the employers' candidate was defeated by Douala Manga Bell, who particularly opposed forced labour, which was ended by the Assembly in Paris when it met.

Revolutionary Struggle

It was in this background of class struggle that the UPC was established in 1948 by Ruben Um Nyobe, young communist secretary of the USCC trade union. The party was thoroughly organised, with workers' committees, village committees and women's and youth sections. It affiliated with the RDA, but broke away after Houphouét disowned the Communists. From the first it stood for independence and the reunion of the French and British zones. Despite its organisational strength the UPC was defeated in elections and became convinced that the results were rigged; when a joint Catholic–Muslim candidate in 1955 was declared the victor, violence broke out. Felix Moumie, an African doctor, president of the UPC, and Um Nyobe, its secretary, decided that their aims could not be realised by constitutional means. In riots twenty-six people were killed, including three Europeans and a gendarme, and the UPC was banned. Moumie fled to the British zone and headed a 'government in exile', while Nyobe led a revolutionary struggle in Cameroun itself.

An election for a new territorial Assembly was ordered at the end of 1956, but the UPC decided on boycott when an amnesty to its prisoners and the legalisation of the party were rejected. The UPC then moved into open rebellion, cutting telephone lines, destroying bridges, tearing up railway tracks and burning houses; two moderate candidates were assassinated on election day. The Government reacted vigorously sending in paratroopers, shooting hundreds of Africans on sight.

Independence and Reunification

The newly elected Assembly advanced towards statehood by establishing a Cameroun citizenship distinct from that of France and taking control of most internal affairs. Meanwhile the UPC maintained its physical rebellion, declaring that it would refrain only if there were an inclusive amnesty, a new general election and immediate independence. Guerrilla warfare spread, and Nyobe was shot in an engagement with government troops. By 1958 the Legislative Assembly declared for independence and a reunion of the French and British zones – aims with which the UPC originated – and Paris accepted the goal of independence and began transitional arrangements. The issue was transferred to the United Nations, which after controversy about whether independence should precede or follow a referendum on reunion, proclaimed Cameroun a sovereign state on January 1, 1960. A referendum in the British zone declared in the south for federation with Cameroun and in the north for union with Northern Nigeria. On October 1, 1961, the federal state of Cameroun was proclaimed. France signed an alliance, giving military aid to suppress the continued rebellion, as well as economic co-operation. Moumie denounced the new state as neo-colonialist, which it largely was, but its stability increased. Moumie was soon after assassinated in Geneva.

Malagasy (Madagascar)

Madagascar (Malagasy since independence) and nearby Réunion and Comoro Islands are not Black Africa. Their peoples have a largely Polynesian strain. Malagasy is so large – 226,657 square miles – that flying over it one seems to be crossing a continent.[8]

French–British Rivalry

The earliest recorded incursions into Madagascar were by Indonesian and African navigators. In the ninth century Arabs attempted to form settlements, but their presence was temporary. In 1500 the first European arrived, the Portuguese voyager Diego Dias, who landed on a ship bound for India; he was followed a hundred years later by Portuguese missionaries preaching the Catholic faith without much response. During the reign of Charles I the English endeavoured to form settlements, but it was the French who aimed at possession, beginning to land in 1642. They met stern resistance and in 1674 had to evacuate after a garrison had been massacred; they returned and optimistically declared sovereignty over the whole island. In fact, foreign occupants during the seventeenth and early eighteenth centuries were almost entirely pirates haunting its coastal nooks, whilst rival tribes fought for domination in the interior.

It was not until the latter half of the eighteenth century that the French seriously renewed settlement, meeting with some competition from English traders, both dealing in arms and slaves. King Radama I abolished slavery by an agreement with the British Governor of Mauritius, Sir Robert Farquhar, and in 1820 English missionaries arrived, Congregationalists sent by the London Missionary Society.[9] They met with opposition like the Catholics and when Radama I was succeeded by his wife, Ranovalona I, she declared Christianity illegal and two hundred converts were killed. The French, unsympathetic with Protestant missions, for a time gained influence with the Queen, establishing the first industries; but feeling among the people was against all Europeans and they were excluded by royal decree. This led to the French and English making a joint attack on the port of Tamatava in 1845, but they were repulsed despite superior arms. The next ruler, Radama II, desiring aid in developing industry, opened the kingdom to Europeans and gave concessions to the French *Compagnie des Indes Orientales*. His wife, who succeeded him, went further, concluding treaties with France, Britain and the USA, but in 1883 the claim of the French to establish a protectorate of the island was rejected. The French thereupon bombarded Tamatava and occupied the port with marines. In 1885 the Malagasies agreed that their foreign relations should be in the hands of France and Tamatava and the surrounding territory were ceded.

Resistance and Independence

The agreement reached between France and Britain in 1890 regarding African territories was extended to Madagascar, London recognising the French protectorate. Nevertheless, there was continuous resistance in the territory to the French occupation. The French had to send an expeditionary force which for a time was held at bay, but in 1895 the Malagasies were crushed and the following year the royal family was deposed and the island annexed as a colony. Resistance continued, but by 1898 the French had imposed control. As the First World War approached national feeling grew again and in the war a secret conspiracy was uncovered, the leaders shot. In the Second World War the French Administration declared for Vichy, leading to a British occupation to prevent a Japanese invasion. The British handed over to the Free French, who applying the policy of assimilation, granted French citizenship to the Malagasies. In 1947 there was another formidable nationalist rising; it was put down ruthlessly, but Paris recognised that it must make further concessions and elected local Assemblies were set up. National leaders were kept under house arrest, however, and there was still the atmosphere of foreign occupation.[10] In 1958 the first gesture towards national self-government was made. A congress of the elected local Assemblies proclaimed Madagascar an autonomous republic within the French

Community. The sweep towards independence then became irresistible. In June 1960 France recognised Malagasy as a sovereign Republic, though it remained a member of the French Community. Philibert Tsiranana, leader of the *Parti Social Démocratique*, became President. In the 1965 election moderate Socialists won 104 of the 107 seats in the National Assembly.

Malagasy took a prominent part in fostering united action between the African states which had won their independence from France. President Tsiranana presided at the Conference at Yaounde in Cameroun in 1961 which established the *Union Africaine et Malagache* with a charter for political co-ordination, economic co-operation and joint defence. The policy of Malagasy was moderately socialistic.

Réunion

The first European to visit the island of Réunion was also Portuguese, Pedro de Mascarenhas, in 1513. As in Madagascar, the French took possession (1643) through Jacques Pronis. In the early eighteenth century the island was colonised by the *Compagnie des Indes Orientales* which started coffee and later sugar plantations. The character of the island in 1717 could be judged by its population: there were nine hundred free inhabitants and a thousand Malagasy and African slaves. In 1964 the administration of the island was transferred from the company to the French Governor. Rivalry developed with the English who occupied the island in 1810, the French regaining control in 1815. In 1848 slavery was abolished and sixty thousand were liberated. In 1946 Réunion became an Overseas Department of France. It was given a local administrative assembly, but it did not follow other colonies in moving towards independence.[11]

The Comoro Islands

Half of the total population of France's overseas territories live in the Comoro Islands, which are strategically situated at the north of the Mozambique Channel, between Malagasy and the East African coast. The archipelago is the world's second largest producer of vanilla, and its exports of coconut fibre and essence of perfume form 70 per cent of French production. It consists of four islands: Grand Comoro (formerly known as Angazidja), with a population of 126,205; Anjouan (population 80,032); Mohéli (10,300), and Mayotte (31,930).[12] It has a combined land area of 838 sq miles, and by early 1971 the total inhabitants numbered 260,000; this overpopulation led to the emigration of many Comorans to Malagasy, Zanzibar and France.

The Comoros were invaded by the Omayyads in AD 940 and became the centre of Arab trade with India, after previously being occupied by Malayo-Polynesians *en route* to Madagascar in the fourth century AD. Subsequently there were occupations by Persian Sharazis, Portuguese and Malagasies; of Mayotte by the French, and of Anjouan by the British. In 1866 a Protectorate was proclaimed by France over Mohéli, Anjouan and Grand Comoro, thus giving the French (already established on Mayotte in 1841) control of the whole archipelago.

France first ruled indirectly through her Governor-General in Réunion, and used the Comoros as a stepping-stone in 1895 for their conquest of Madagascar, to which the Comoros were joined in 1912 and governed from Tananarive. Internal autonomy was granted to the islands in 1962, although the French not only retained full control of defence and security, foreign relations, civil law and all financial matters, but also insisted that all administrative acts and deliberations should be 'submitted to the French High Commissioner before being exercised, published or put into action'.[13]

Although in 1958 the Comoro Islands voted for continued association with France, the leader of the ruling *Union Démocratique des Comores* (UDC) conceded in 1970 that independence might be inevitable. The growing support for independence, led by the *Mouvement de Libération Nationale des Comores* (MOLINACO) since 1963 and by the *Parti Socialiste Comorien*, (PASOCO), is made more difficult by the fact that a French law of 1961 laid down that independence would only be granted if there were a majority in favour in each separate island. MOLINACO, banned under a Law of 1901 and Article 80 of the French Penal Code, is based in Dar-es-Salaam and has the support of the Organisation of African Unity; PASOCO functions openly inside the Comoros. The UDC, while supporting association with France, nevertheless has taken a stand on the issue of greater political liberties, some of which have been granted. This stand enabled PASOCO to be formed in legal opposition, and it works closely with the banned MOLINACO. At the United Nations in June 1971, Abdou Sakari

Boina, on behalf of MOLINACO, warned that unless independence were granted soon 'appropriate measures' would be taken by the people of the Comoros. It is likely that a militant conflict will develop.

Notes

1. Area: 1,800,000 square miles. Population (1951): 19,000,000, of whom 92,000 were Europeans.

2. Area: 969,112 square miles. Population (1960 estimate): 5,145,000.

3. By the time of the trial Hunkanrin had been released and he was one of the six; he alone survived the imprisonment.

4. Quoted by Edward Mortimer in his admirable *France and the Africans, 1944–60*, to which the author has been continuously indebted in writing this chapter.

5. The only concrete result of these discussions was that Oubangui-Chari was renamed the Central African Republic.

6. Through all the changes of regimes Dahomey remained in the French orbit.

7. Afterwards changed to four and two.

8. Estimated population in 1970 of Malagasy was 6,776,970.

9. The author's grandfather was one of these. Because of their opposition to Catholicism they later tended to identify themselves with Malagasy resistance. The author was surprised when visiting Madagascar in 1954 to be welcomed in the house of a trade union leader under house arrest by a hymn written by an aunt.

10. The author visited national leaders confined to their houses in 1954. He was kept under observation day and night and required to leave the country though ill with fever.

11. The area of Réunion is 969 sq. miles.

12. 1966 Census.

13. *The Comoros: Encounter with Their Reality*, by Abdou Sakari Boina.

Chapter Fourteen

British West Africa

(Gambia, Sierra Leone, Ghana, Nigeria)

There are four ex-British colonies in West Africa, ranging from the smallest territory on the continent, Gambia, to that of the largest population, Nigeria. From north to south they are Gambia, Sierra Leone, Ghana (Gold Coast), Nigeria.

Gambia

The most imaginative writer of fiction would find it difficult to create a more improbable state than Gambia. It is only thirteen miles wide, clinging to the banks of the river of the same name, piercing 250 miles into the interior of another state, Senegal. Its area is less than 4,000 square miles. Its population is a mere 300,000. Its people are ethnically the same as those across its narrow frontiers. It produces only one article for export, groundnuts. It has no railway, one town, no daily paper and an army of 150. Its river and port, Bathurst, potentially half-used, are the natural outlet for Senegal. It is a geographical caricature, drawn by distant colonialist bargainers without thought for divided peoples.

Separation from Senegal

In the eighteenth century, from 1765 to 1783, Gambia and most of Senegal were one British colony, Senegambia. In the nineteenth century Britain and France negotiated the separation of Gambia as part of a wider deal for partition of African territories. Inevitably colonialist occupation left difficulties in the way of reunion including governmental pride and the use of English and French as distinguishing languages. In 1961 an Inter-Ministerial Committee failed to reach agreement and referred the problem to the United Nations, whose committee would have liked federation but acknowledged that it was not possible because of Gambia's doubts. Instead, it fell back on an *entente* as a means towards co-ordination. The UN report led to discussions between the two countries which made some progress. It was agreed to have a common policy on foreign affairs and defence and Gambia consented to be represented abroad by Senegal. The Inter-Ministerial Committee continued to function and Gambia adopted the metric system and changed its rule of the road. Perhaps most encouraging was a decision to ask the UN Special Fund for joint development of the Gambia river. Nevertheless, the disadvantages of division remained, the southern region of Senegal cut off, the possibilities of the river and Bathurst not exercised, Gambia limited to its one crop economy and the cost of separate administration.

Gambia's history and the rise of Nationalism are similar in essentials to all West Africa. The Portuguese had arrived in 1455 to trade in slaves and gold. In 1588 they sold their trading rights to British merchants and in 1618 James I granted a Charter to their company. There was native resistance to the slave raiders and the first agent of the company was murdered. French and British traders conflicted, building ports on opposite sides of the river, settled by a treaty in 1783 giving the river to Britain but reserving an enclave, Albreda, for the French (returned to Britain in 1857). All this was done without consideration of the native population, but after the slave trade had been outlawed some consultation with chiefs began and it was by a treaty with the dominant chief that the island at the mouth of the river, which became Bathurst, was conceded. For a time Gambia was administered from Freetown in Sierra Leone, but the colonialist controls of the two territories were finally separated in 1888. The following year the boundaries with French occupied Senegal were fixed and in 1894 a British protectorate over Gambia was officially declared.

African Parties, Independence

The Second World War released African demands for self-government. Gambians contributed to the African forces serving in East Africa and Burma and they returned claiming rights, encouraged by a new educated African élite. The demands grew so continuously that repeated advances in democratisation of the constitution had to be made, in 1954, 1959 and 1961. There were various attempts to establish political parties, the two main streams reflected in the United Party and the Congress Party. The United Party represented the new African middle class in Bathurst, pressing for self-government, moderate politicians without any fundamental philosophy, looking forward to office. The Congress Party was Pan-Africanist and socialist, led by Garba-Jahumpa, who attended the Pan-African conference in Manchester, England, in 1945 and, after travelling to Algeria, Cairo, Moscow and Peking, returned to establish first a Muslim youth movement and then the Congress Party. He was for a time a Minister without Portfolio and was elected to the Bathurst Town Council with three colleagues in 1946, but, though the party continued to exist, it made little impact subsequently.

Until 1960 only the people of Bathurst and the surrounding area had votes for the Legislative Council, which was advisory to the British Governor who retained all executive power. The United Party dominated the political scene, enjoying increasing functions until 1960, when the vote was extended to the up-river protectorate. This entirely changed the situation; the Bathurst electorate was outnumbered five to one. The few educated Africans in the interior formed in 1959 a Protectorate Peoples' Party, later changed in name to the Progressive Peoples' Party (PPP), with the motive of resisting domination by Bathurst. In the election of 1960 the PPP, reflecting the majority vote in the interior, won ten of the nineteen elected seats in the Legislature. The party then became nationwide, and set a precedent in Gambia by establishing a Western-style organisation with membership cards and subscriptions. The PPP remained in continuous office, and when Gambia became independent in 1965 held twenty-four of the thirty-six seats in the national Parliament. The Prime Minister was David Jawara, a veterinary surgeon, selected as leader in 1959 for his popularity among the peasants, but the organising geniuses were the Finance Minister, Sherif Sissay, and the Minister of Local Government, Sherif Dibba, respectively Secretary-General and Assistant Secretary-General of the party. The dominant political issue in the five years before independence was the demand that there should be no reunification with Senegal until the people of Gambia had the freedom to decide.

Within the limited terms of their small state (with virtually no industrialisation and practically the whole population engaged in groundnut production, transportation and export) the administration, assisted by fifty British advisers, was efficient but resistant to change. The Government set up public decorticating stations for peanut shelling, but otherwise did little constructively. Parliament met only for twelve days in one year. The real opposition was in the trade union movement, limited almost entirely to Bathurst and Kombo, the Gambia Workers' Union. It was militant and declared general strikes in 1960 and 1961, gaining twenty-five per cent and ten per cent increases in wages. It was led by M. E. Jallow, a powerful personality, imprisoned during the second general strike when troops were brought in from Sierra Leone, a demogogic speaker captivating large crowds. He could have become a political force in Gambia except for his isolation from the peasant majority.

Gambia did not rescue itself from its economic imprisonment within its fractional territory and a one-crop production. Britain provided £800,000 a year in interest-free loans and £260,000 in the salaries of British ex-colonial officers serving the Government. At the independence celebrations, sympathetic governments and commercial concerns contributed money and mechanical aids, enabling a little modernisation. The Colonial Development Corporation attempted a poultry project, at the cost of nearly £900,000, to export twenty million eggs yearly, but the poultry died. It spent even more, £1,075,000, on a rice project, but also had to abandon that. The most valuable aid was probably through UNESCO, which under the guidance of Ted Smead trained African technicians.

Gambia was in many ways a happy example of a small easy-going self-governing community, but if it is not to be left obsolete and isolated in the modern world it must find a basis of co-ordination with its embracing neighbour Senegal.

Sierra Leone

The British colony of Sierra Leone[1] began in a uniquely benevolent way. Granville Sharp, an English opponent of slavery, took the initiative in 1787 to establish a settlement on the coast for freed slaves. He received permission from 'King Tom', the local ruler, but two years later 'King Jimmy', who succeeded, drove the settlers away.[2] The campaigners against slavery did not accept this rebuff. They sponsored the Sierra Leone Company, which obtained permission to renew the settlement. The company shipped liberated slaves from Nova Scotia, who were joined by freed families from Jamaica. In 1807 the trade in slaves was made illegal in British territory and Westminster took over the settlement and established a naval base which intercepted slave-raiders as they transported their victims across the Atlantic.

Liberated Slaves

It is recorded that fifty thousand slaves were freed in this way and they were added to the settlement, appropriately named Freetown. This philanthropic policy was continued by Sir Andrew MacCarthy when he became Governor of the colony (1814–24). He deliberately aimed to create a homogenous Christian community, inviting the Anglican and Methodist missionary societies to establish churches and schools. Of course trade, mostly in ivory, was also an incentive, but the emphasis on education meant that from Sierra Leone came some of the earliest African doctors and lawyers and the first African Bishop.

The Portuguese, it need hardly be said, arrived before the British. In the fifteenth century they gave the coast the name 'Serra Lyoa' (Lion Mountain), which became popularised as Sierra Leone. Later in the century many European ships arrived to trade with the African chiefs in slaves and incidentally in ivory, and the English traders established two depots on islands off the coast. There was no attempt, however, to take possession of the land; the traders pursued their unsavoury business under the protection of the chiefs. They suffered a severe interruption early in the eighteenth century when Muslims from the north descended in a devastating holy war.

Interior Protectorate

As we have told, the freed slaves who settled in Freetown became Christians. With the growth of the port, the African population wanted to extend the colony into the interior, but at first the British objected, not wishing further responsibilities. Imperial rivalry, however, changed their course when the French advanced their possessions, threatening to make Freetown a small enclave. In 1896 agreement was reached with France and Liberia, recognising a British sphere deep into the interior, and it was proclaimed a protectorate. London, nevertheless, was reluctant to contribute to the cost of administration and it was the hut tax which Sir Frederic Cardew, the Governor (1894–1900), imposed which led to the first serious African revolt. The northerners found a dynamic leader in Bai Burch, and the rebellion spread and was not easily suppressed. African resistance was weakened through the non-co-operation of chiefs who had profited by a share of the hut tax, following the application to the protectorate of Lord Lugard's system of indirect rule initiated in Northern Nigeria; the administration was imposed through subsidised chiefs supervised by English District Commissioners. Before the proclamation of the protectorate, educated Africans from Freetown had held many senior posts and the substitution of Commissioners from Britain caused some discontent. Educationally the protectorate was neglected until 1920 and its people remained backward.

Independence and Coups

In 1924 a Legislative Council was established with some elected Africans from the colony and with chiefs nominated from the protectorate. This did not satisfy the educated population of Freetown and there were many protests. It was not until after the Second World War, however, that the demand for democratic institutions became imperative. In 1951 Africans gained a majority in the Legislature and a government was headed by Dr Milton Margai, whose Peoples' Party was based mostly in the protectorate. During the 1950s the functions of the African administration were extended, and in April 1961 the independence of Sierra Leone was recognised with an entirely elected Parliament.

There was an Opposition party, the All Peoples' Congress, led by Siaka Stevens, railway worker and miner trade unionist, more radical in outlook and programme. After Milton Margai's death in 1964 his successor, Sir Albert Margai, attempted to set up a one-party state which led to bitter controversy. In the election of March 1967, when Siaka Stevens won,[3] the Commander of the army, Brigadier David Lansana, intervened to retain Margai in power. Then began a unique series of military *coups*. The generals were ousted by colonels, the colonels were ousted by non-commissioned officers, and the non-commissioned officers were ousted by privates. A descending army revolution from pyramid to base! General Lansana was first overthrown by his junior officers, led by Colonel

Juxon-Smith, who set up a National Reformation Council, excluding Siaka Stevens whilst appealing to a wider circle than Margai's reactionaries. A year later came the *coup* of the noncommissioned officers, so thorough that they arrested the entire officer corps of both army and police. Even so, the All Peoples' Congress and Stevens were kept from office. Finally came the *coup* of the privates, who established a national Government and called back Siaka Stevens from exile to head it.

In Freetown and among progressive sections of the people in the hinterland the fourth revolution was popular, but some fighting broke out between north and south and a state of emergency was declared. The Government then adopted draconian methods, arresting fourteen former political and military leaders, of whom ten were sentenced to death; the trial caused great uneasiness among liberals. Siaka Stevens pursued a moderately socialist policy. The principal exports from Sierra Leone were diamonds, a high proportion of which were smuggled out. Stevens introduced drastic control, took fifty-one per cent of the shares in four foreign mining companies and established a government-owned corporation. He attempted by reforms to overcome the antagonism between the Creoles in Freetown and the Mende and Temme in the interior, and on the whole his administration appeared popular though in 1971 military officers again attempted a *coup*, suppressed by the aid of troops from Guinea. Stevens inaugurated a Republic, which remained in the Commonwealth. The International Monetary Fund showed its confidence by advancing credits; but it would be rash to say that enduring stability had been secured.

Ghana (Gold Coast)

There is little knowledge of the peoples of Ghana[4] in earlier times, except, as already told, they extended a far-flung empire. Its territory was a junction of two Saharan desert routes, one western to Morocco, the other central to Tripoli (Libya) and there was a continuous migration of tribes. The Portuguese discovered the coast in 1471, exchanging cloth, utensils and arms for gold, the origin of the name Gold Coast. They erected a chain of forts to protect their trade, but this did not prevent the arrival of European slave traders – mostly English, Dutch and Danish – who in turn built forts from which their human cargo was transported to America. From the end of the seventeenth century African strength in the interior was with the Ashanti, who invaded the coast in anger against slave raiding.

British Protectorates

In the early years of the nineteenth century the English, Dutch and Danish outlawed the slave trade and, the supplies of gold declining, only a hard core of British merchants was left. Between 1830 and 1844, under the leadership of George Maclean, the British established an informal protectorate on the coast and the Colonial Office took over the forts, buying out the Danes. The Ashanti continued to sweep down on the Europeans from time to time, leading in 1874 to a British punitive expedition which destroyed their capital, Kumasi, followed by the declaration of the territory, coast and interior, as a colony. In addition to continued resistance by the Ashantis,[5] there were conflicts with French and Germans on the frontiers of their neighbouring territories, and the British settlers, who had started gold mining as well as extending their commerce, petitioned London for protection. The Government responded by despatching a strong force, which finally conquered the Ashanti, and moved further into the interior, guarding the frontiers. The colony of the Gold Coast became three territories – the primitive north, the Ashanti interior and the coast. In 1850 there was the beginning of an English-dominated Legislative Council on the coast whilst the Ashanti and the northern tribes were ruled under a Governor, indirectly through the chiefs.

Unlike other colonies, the Africans became strong economically. Within the interior they developed cocoa-growing on a large scale and by the 1920s were exporting half the world's supplies. Cocoa production helped to unify the three territories, the coast becoming busy in exports and the north supplying labour (much exploited on the Ashanti plantations). The revenue from cocoa enabled a greater advance in road building and education than in most African territories.

Revolt

The democratic climate after the Second World War led to growing African demands for self-government. The British administration had been based not only on co-operation with the chiefs in the centre and north but also on the compliance of the new African professional class, many lawyers, on the coast. The chiefs and lawyers competed with each other for nominated representation in the Legislative Council, which in fact was little more than a façade for rule by the Governor. Then in 1947 and 1948, an aftermath of the war, a wave of rioting broke out in the towns which stunned the colonialist officials.[6] In Accra the stores of the United Africa Company, which had a large retail trade, were sacked, and British and Syrian businessmen were assaulted;[7] in Kumasi strikes stopped transport and the public services; the gold mines were closed by stoppage of work. So widespread was the anti-British feeling that even many of the indirect-rule chiefs supported the nation-wide boycott of the administration which followed. The British brought in troops from South Africa, Nigerian reinforcements crossed the frontier, and three troop carriers were on call at Gibraltar; in the fighting twenty-nine Africans were shot dead and 237 wounded.

The immediate cause of the revolt was anger against the action of a British police officer in firing upon an ex-servicemen's demonstration; thirty thousand Africans had served against the Japanese in Burma and many returned from the East in militant mood, protesting against inadequate pensions and stirred by Gandhi's ultimatum to the British to 'quit India'. The colonialist administration had not appreciated that the developing economy, railways, mining and construction industries, had created a new social force in a working class who were already forming trade unions. Ex-service workers particularly were not prepared to be ruled by alien officials and their hangers on, the chiefs and the lawyers.

African Parties

There was a nationalist party, the United Gold Coast Convention (UGCC). It was under the control of lawyers and the less subservient chiefs, moderately demanding an advance towards self-government. In 1947 they invited Kwame Nkrumah, who had gained a reputation by his University career in America and advocacy there of Negro rights, to become general secretary. The author was with him in London (where he was a student at the School of Economics) on the December night he received the invitation. He was doubtful about accepting, because of the 'bourgeois' character of the UGCC. It was George Padmore who convinced him that he should go to 'revolutionise' the movement. There were 1,500 members. Nkrumah set out to create a mass following. He concentrated on the youth leaving schools without jobs, on the villagers and on the market women (curiously at first Nkrumah did not appreciate the new element of the working class). The riots of 1948 took him and the UGCC leaders by surprise, but overnight the political psychology in the country changed. When Dr Danquah, President of the UGCC, offered to take over the Government and Nkrumah called for the convening of a constituent assembly, the British panicked. They arrested Nkrumah, Danquah and four other members of the Working Committee of the UGCC, and the Governor, Sir Gerald Creasy, appointed on officially-manned commission to investigate the disturbances and the involvement of the leaders of the UGCC. It found that Nkrumah was using 'the legitimate economic grievances of the Gold Coast people to stage a revolution which would establish a Union of West African Soviet Socialist Republics'.

Nkrumah's Triumph

The effect of the commission's report was to make Nkrumah a national hero, and the object of the British became to isolate him from the moderate UGCC leadership. They appointed a Constitutional Commission inviting Danquah and his moderate colleagues to become members, but excluded Nkrumah, who reacted by breaking from the UGCC and establishing the Convention Peoples' Party (CPP) with the aim of 'self-government *now*'. Its inauguration was extraordinary; sixty thousand people attended in Accra. The conservative report of the Commission gave the CPP its political opportunity; it quite flatly rejected full self-government and, whilst recommending an elected majority in the Legislative Assembly, proposed that one-third of the members should be appointed by the chiefs and that reserve powers should be left with the British Governor-General. To be fair to the UGCC, their representatives opposed the reserve powers and the presence of *ex-officio* members in the Executive (three in eleven), but initiative had passed to the CPP, which gained mass support for its demand for immediate self-government. The TUC called a general strike; the response was half-hearted and the colonialists felt strong enough to arrest the trade union and CPP leaders. With Nkrumah in prison the Government risked a general election (1951). It miscalculated; Nkrumah was more popular in prison than free and the CPP won thirty-four of the thirty-eight elected seats. The British Governor met Nkrumah at the prison gates and invited him to become 'leader of Government Business'.

In office, with the certainty of independence not far ahead, Nkrumah pursued a policy of 'tactical action', that is to say he concentrated on measures of immediate social and economic reform within his powers without challenging British authority. In fact, he and his fellow-Ministers carried through a comprehensive programme, the expansion of education, the setting up of dispensaries and hospitals, rehousing and the planning of new estates, the piping of water to villages, the building of roads and the development of Tema harbour. A senior British civil servant said to the author at this time that he had been required to do more constructive work in two years than he had done in the previous twelve. The Governor, Sir Arden Clarke, was impressed. Confidence was established in the advance of the first British colony in Africa to independence. In 1952 Nkrumah was made Prime Minister and during the next five years there was a progressive transference to an all-African Cabinet with responsibility to an Assembly elected by adult suffrage. In elections in 1954 and 1956 the CPP gained seventy per cent of the seats.

The Opposition in the Legislative Council was at first un-co-ordinated, but in 1954 the National Liberation Movement (NLM) was established at Kumasi, bringing many elements together, including Dr Danquah and other leaders of the UGCC. The occasion for the starting of the new party was the cocoa policy of the CPP Ministers. In 1948 the Labour Government in Britain had established a Marketing Board in Ghana with a monopoly in buying, selling and exporting cocoa. The object was to give the producers a stable price which would be unaffected by the rise and fall of world prices. For this purpose a reserve fund was created by paying the cocoa growers less than the price obtained at export, which led to protests, particularly in Ashanti, by cocoa farmers and chiefs who owned cocoa land; they had ground for criticism because by 1954 the reserves had reached £197·4 million, providing the Government with valuable credit (and incidentally Britain with sterling) at the expense of the cocoa producers. The charge was also made that a priority in loans from the fund, as well as jobs in the administration, was given to CPP members. Probably there was some truth in this. The NLM denounced

corruption in high places (there was undoubtedly some), character-
ised Nkrumah as a dictator, and alleged political discrimination.
It demanded an end to centralised power by the creation of a
federation with Ghana.

Independence

The ferocity of the Opposition was so great that the granting of
independence was threatened by civil war. Early in 1956 Nkrumah
invited the author to Ghana to try to avert violence. An interview
with the NLM leaders took place at Kumasi and after hard discussion they agreed that they would not take unconstitutional
action if Nkrumah would hold a general election before independence. The Prime Minister was at first averse to this compromise, arguing that his authority to proceed to independence
had been given in the election held a little more than a year previously, but he finally accepted a formula that he would concur if
the British Government would promise independence within six
months if the CPP obtained a majority. Back in London, the
Colonial Secretary, Lennox Boyd, endorsed the formula with the
one qualification that the majority should be 'reasonable'. The
election was held and the CPP retained its seventy per cent
authority in the Assembly. The independence of the Gold Coast
(renamed Ghana after an ancient empire) was recognised in
March 1957.

Constructive Achievement

The all-African Government continued its constructive social and
economic development. The number of children at school doubled,
a modern hospital was built at Kumasi, a spectacular hotel for
visitors was built in Accra (criticised as a non-priority), state
plantations were opened to correct the cocoa monopoly in agriculture, tarmac roads were extended, a large housing estate was
built around the completed Tema harbour, and above all, the vast
Volta project, with its dam, electricity generating station, man-
made lake for fishing and rice production, and bauxite factory,
was successfully launched. This immense enterprise was criticised
because it involved American finance, but Nkrumah justified it on
the ground that industrialisation would require electrical power.

Expenditure was high, foreign investment dwindled and the Government had to impose a policy of austerity, including import controls which sent up prices as well as compulsory savings which reduced wages. It was this which caused the first serious rift in popular support.

Dictatorial Regime

In 1961 there was a general strike in Kumasi and Sekondi-Takoradi, a large dock centre, which spread to Accra. There was some evidence that the strikers were encouraged by the Opposition, and the TUC condemned them as counter-revolutionary, but there were genuine working-class grievances. The men returned to work within three weeks in bitter mood, a beginning of the loss of grass roots support for the CPP, which deepened when the Government made strikes illegal. At the same time Nkrumah acted with increasing ruthlessness towards the Opposition. On the eve of the election there had been disturbances in the Ghanaian section of Togoland partly in protest against low cocoa payments, partly by Ewe tribesmen wanting reunion with French Togoland. Nkrumah and his colleagues were sternly against the Opposition demand for tribal autonomy and acted drastically. Regional bodies were made only advisory and what were described as tribal political parties were outlawed. Two Opposition leaders were detained for an alleged conspiracy to assassinate Nkrumah, followed by the arrest of forty-three Opposition members of the Assembly.[8] The authoritarian character of the regime increased. In 1964 a one-party state was created and judges who gave unacceptable decisions were removed.

Nkrumah Overthrown

When Ghana became a Republic greater powers were given to the President, inevitably Nkrumah, and a personality cult campaign was staged to extol him as *Osegyefo* ('The Redeemer'). As time passed, Nkrumah himself became more distant and isolated, ignoring his colleagues, some of whom, including Ghedemah, his Finance Minister, deserted him. In February 1966, when he was absent in China on a courageous mission to seek peace in Vietnam, army officers seized power, establishing a National Liberation Council under General Ankrah. There was surprisingly little opposition to the *coup*, evidence that the hero-president and his party had lost touch with the people. Nkrumah went into exile in Guinea, where he was welcomed as co-president with Sékou Touré.[9] Ghana's new government, incorporating the Opposition politicians, outlawed the CPP, imprisoning its activist supporters, and proceeded to de-socialise the public enterprises which Nkrumah had set up. It received investment support from western countries. A general election returned a civilian government under Dr Busia to power.[10]

Nkrumah died in May 1972 in Bulgaria where he had gone for cancer treatment. This is not the place to estimate fully his place in Ghana and Africa. He was described with some justice as the creator of Ghana's independence and his contribution to its social, educational and constructional advance was outstanding. The imprisonments of his political opponents was a blot on his administration; he justified it on the ground that in African conditions their sabotaging of his socialist objective could not be tolerated.[11] In the wider scene of the continent he was the pioneer voice of Pan-Africanism for a United States of Africa; if his appeal to African governments to subdue national prestige had been followed many of the continent's difficulties might have been avoided. He was among the first to realise the dangers of neo-colonialism. In the still wider field of the world he supported the United Nations and sent a Ghanaian contingent to Congo, although he was disappointed by the result. As we have recorded, he was deposed when on a mission for peace. He will be remembered in African history as one of its greatest creative influences.

Nigeria

Nigeria has the largest population of any African state, numbering, according to the 1963 census, 55,670,052. It lies to the south of the western bulge of the continent, its coast running west and east. To the west is Dahomey, to the east Cameroun, to the north Niger. Its area is 356,666 square miles.

Little is known of the peoples before the Portuguese appeared in the fifteenth century. Nigeria did not exist as an entity and there was no association between the largely Muslim north and the Pagan south.

Tribal Conflicts

The north went through a cycle of conflicts between different tribes, particularly the Hausas and the Fulani, a pastoral people who moved in from further north. Hausa domination was followed in the first years of the nineteenth century by a Fulani empire, which was in turn overthrown. Hostilities persisted until the British occupation imposed peace.

In the south there was similar tribal antagonism. The three principal peoples were the Yorubas and Beni in the west and the Ibos in the east. During the earlier period the Yorubas and Beni had a higher standard of social and cultural life than the Ibos. When the Portuguese arrived the Beni were most powerful and their chiefs co-operated profitably in the slave trade. Gradually the Yorubas rose in power and their chiefs also grew rich by the barter of kidnapped slaves. When they defeated invasions from neighbouring Dahomey and from the Fulanis in the north, they handed over their prisoners to the European slave traders in Lagos in exchange for spirits, arms and ammunition.

The European influence was at this time disastrous. It debased the people by the distribution of alcohol and encouraged inter-tribal fighting by the supply of arms. The nationals of many European countries were involved, the British following the Portuguese. By the Treaty of Utrecht in 1713 Britain extracted from defeated Spain a thirty-year monopoly for the supply of slaves to her possessions in America and the West Indies. In addition English traders had a virtual monopoly in meeting the demand for slaves in the British territories of America and the West Indies. More than half the trade in slaves at this time was carried on by the British.

British Colonisation

In 1807 Britain abolished slavery in its territories, but this at first had little effect in Nigeria as other Europeans continued the trade. The British, limited to palm oil and ivory, found it necessary to curb the activity of slave raiders who were impeding their legitimate activities. Until this point there had been no need to colonise because trade was conducted through the chiefs, but London now ordered its naval squadron to intercept ships transporting slaves and this required a closer relationship with the coastal tribes. In

1841 the British sent four ships down the Niger River with the object of concluding treaties with the chiefs, but the effort was abandoned when 48 of 145 Europeans died from malaria. Thanks to the discovery of the preventive quinine, an expedition led by W. B. Baike succeeded, and in 1849 a British consul was appointed for the Bights of Biafra and Benin.

British pressure to stop the slave trade in Lagos led to its annexation as a British colony. When King Kosoka of Lagos declined to co-operate, the city was captured in 1851 by a naval force and the succeeding King Akitoye, nominated by the British, signed a treaty banning slave raiders and giving protection to English missionaries. A third king, Dosuma, in 1881 ceded possession of Lagos to the British in return for a pension, and the following year it was declared a Crown Colony. Meanwhile, both traders and missionaries were pressing into the interior and in 1885 a protectorate was declared over the whole coastal territory and much of the hinterland; the usual pattern was followed of handing over administration to a trading concern, the Royal Niger Company. Steadily expansion moved deeper, reaching the Muslim north. By 1899 the problems of administration required governmental intervention; the northern region was declared a protectorate and Whitehall took over from the Royal Niger Company, giving generous compensation. By 1908 Britain controlled the whole of Nigeria – Lagos and its environs as a colony and southern and northern Nigeria as protectorates. In 1914 the north and the south were amalgamated.

Lugard's 'Indirect Rule'

There was a great difference between north and south. The community life of the north was mostly ruled by Muslim emirs. There was practically no education, the presence of Christian missions, which had spread education elsewhere, prohibited. In the south the two main races, the Yorubas in the west and the Ibos in the east, advanced rapidly in education and made progress in modernisation by contact with the Europeans. This difference was emphasised when Brigadier-General Lugard became High Commissioner in the north in 1900. Lugard probably had a greater influence upon British colonial policy than any administrator. We have met him before in East Africa; his first visit to Nigeria, as Captain Lugard, was in 1894 with a mission to negotiate treaties with chiefs in Borgu on behalf of the Royal Niger Company. He returned as Brigadier in 1897 to raise a native military force under British officers to deter French aggression on the northern borders; it grew into the Royal West African Frontier Force. When he became head of the British administration of northern Nigeria the territory was still devastated by slave raiding and internecine war. Within six years he had by a mixture of force and persuasion expelled the slave traders and imposed peace.

Lugard had a seemingly intractable problem. The area was vast – over 200,000 square miles – his available staff limited, and the peoples were racially disintegrated, the Hausas, Fulanis, Kamuris and thirty-two smaller tribes. He became famous for initiating the system of 'indirect rule', though in fact it had been practised pragmatically to some extent in other British territories. Lugard's originality was in making it a system. He divided the region into provinces with a British Resident in each and with district officers beneath him. But their duties were only supervisory; the day to day administration was left to paramount chiefs assisted according to traditional practice by local chiefs and councillors. The taxation routine of the emirs and chiefs was retained with a proportion passing to the British, and justice was left to the native courts. Life at the roots went on as before. The British presence was distant; troops were at its disposal to prevent strife and to deter the French and German colonialists on the frontier; otherwise it was largely unseen. In the south, on the other hand, direct British administration was exerted in Lagos and in the environs of other towns, although local authority was still left largely to the chiefs in remote areas. Revenue was obtained through customs.[12]

Rebellion

There was of course African opposition to the British colonisation. The occupation of the hinterland of Lagos was resented by the Yoruba and Egba populations, the latter closing trade routes and expelling the missionaries. It was opposition to the Royal Niger Company by the Brass people on the coast which led to the British Government ending the company's administration. The Brass were prohibited from trading in their former markets except on the payment of prohibitive dues and in 1895 rebelled, raiding the company's offices at Akassa, killing many African employees and, it is alleged, eating prisoners. A naval force meted out severe punishment; but opposition continued and the company was wound up in 1900.[13]

Benin, in the interior, had been captured in 1894. It was a centre of the slave trade and human sacrifices. The king failed to carry out a treaty (1902) to abolish both and treacherously killed seven Europeans and 200 Africans. It took six weeks to restore control. In northern Nigeria the Fulanis opposed the British advance into their empire and interference with their slave trading. When the principal raiders were removed in 1901, the sultan of Sokoto resisted and the Emir of Kano joined him, threatening to attack the small British garrison at Zaria. There was severe fighting between the British-officered Royal Niger Force and the armies of Kano and Sokoto, leading to the deposition of the sultan and his replacement by a nominee of the British. As late as 1906 there was a rising by Pagan tribes against the sultan, severely suppressed. Much of the opposition to the British up to this point was in defence of inhuman practices, but behind was resentment of alien domination.

Nationalism

It was not until the 1920s that a genuine nationalist movement began to arise. This was due partly to a new educated African élite in the south, and partly to the exclusive snobbishness of the Whites. In this period, also, Africans who had gone to Britain and America for higher education or professional training were returning to Nigeria. They were humiliated by the absence of any African responsibility for legislation, the judiciary and government. Before any parties were established, pioneer voices, responding to the post-war mood in Europe, were demanding not only political democracy but the Africanisation of the economy. The British responded by inaugurating in 1922 a Legislative Council for Lagos and the south. There were thirty-two official and twenty-one unofficial members; of the latter only ten were Africans and only four elected. In Lagos an electorate severely restricted by property and income qualifications returned three members and in Calabar one. The eleven non-African unofficial members were nominated to represent banking, shipping, mining and commercial interests.

As was to be expected, this constitution angered the emerging African élite. In 1923 the National Democratic Party was founded by Herbert Macauley, a civil engineer. Despite its name, the party was a group of the Lagos middle class protesting against racial subordination rather than expressing national aspirations. In 1934 a group of young radicals started the Lagos Youth Movement, which was militant and outward-looking in aims. They expressed this by becoming two years later the Nigerian Youth Movement (NYM). Then came a decisive event. In 1937 a US-trained graduate returned to Nigeria and immediately contributed a challenging strength to the nationalist movement. Dr Nnamdi Azikiwe combined a commanding personality with a campaigning flare and a practical ability in organisation. He started to publish the *West African Pilot*, which had a major effect immediately in spreading nationalist convictions, wrote popular pamphlets and addressed enthusiastic meetings. He backed the NYM and they won three elected places in the Legislative Council in 1938. A feature of the movement at this time was the unity between the Yorubas and Ibos. Azikiwe was an Ibo, but most of the leaders were Yorubas. Feuds arose within the NYM, however, and Azikiwe left it to establish, with Herbert Macauley in 1944, a party which was to have a profound influence on the future, the National Congress of Nigeria and the Cameroun (NCNC).[14] It was a new type of organisation for Nigeria, having not individual members but federated trade unions, student groups, professional bodies and women's associations. Unity between Ibos and Yorubas was maintained.

Constitutional Advance

The Second World War had a great effect in stimulating nationalist fervour and a sense of human rights among the people. The experience of African soldiers abroad, the democratic war aims, and the principles expressed in the Atlantic Charter led Africans to demand more and hope for more. Among the workers dissatisfaction grew with their treatment by large British firms and there was a formidable general strike backed by Azikiwe and the militant NCNC. African pressure was so great that it became clear that concessions would have to be made. In 1945 the Governor, Sir Arthur Richards (now Lord Milverton), announced the preparation of a new constitution and it became law in January 1947. Theoretically it provided for an elected majority, but the elections were mainly through the native authorities and not by direct vote. For the first time the Legislative Council included representation from northern Nigeria with safeguards against any take-over from the south. In the preparation of the constitution nationalist opinion had been ignored and the method of election increased the influence of the traditional élite rather than the new educated generation. The Nationalists, led by the NCNC, aroused so much support in their campaign against the Richards Constitution that in 1948 the new Governor, Sir John Macpherson, supported by the Labour Government in London, announced that consultations would take place for its revision. Sir John was progressive and proceeded to Africanise the civil service and to democratise the native authorities. Consultations were held with the native councils and regions, including Lagos, and a constitution prepared on their recommendations. It fell far short of full democracy, but it gave Africans effective influence. Its complicated provisions reflected the unequal development and diverse character of Nigeria.

In the northern and western regions the Legislatures consisted of a House of Chiefs and a House of Assembly; in the eastern region there was only a House of Assembly.[15] The Houses of Assembly had large elected majorities, 90 to 15 in the North, 80 to 8 in the West, 80 to 9 in the East.[16] For the whole of Nigeria there was a House of Representatives, with 68 members elected jointly by the two chambers in the North, 34 elected similarly in the West, and 34 elected by the House of Assembly in the East. Thus there were 136 elected members, who were supplemented by 7 *ex-officio* members and 6 special members appointed by the Governor to represent interests not adequately reflected. The Executives in the regions were composed of 14 Ministers of whom 9 were elected by the Chambers; the National Council of Ministers was composed of 19 Ministers of whom 12 were elected by the Chambers. The regions had control of education, agriculture, health and local government, but legislation could be vetoed by the Lieutenant-Governors. The Governor could similarly veto national legislation. Lagos was absorbed in the East and ceased to be a separate legislative unit. The constitution did not provide for direct election and adult suffrage as African radicals desired, but it proved to be the watershed between British and indigenous rule. From this moment African self-government was inevitable.

Racial Parties

The nationalist movement became divided before the elections. An opponent to Dr Azikiwe appeared in another figure who was to be lastingly important. Obafemi Awolowo, a Yoruba chief, had been active in the NYM and had opposed Azikiwe when he withdrew from it to form the NCNC. On going to London, he started in 1945 a Yoruba cultural association named *Egbe Omo Oduduwa* and when he returned established a branch in Ibadan in 1947. It became a focus of Pan-Yorubaism. Meanwhile, many of the Yorubas in the NCNC had come to dislike the Ibo influence linked with Azikiwe's leadership and there was competition between the two races for posts in Lagos. A psychology of suspicion grew, opening the way for Awolowo to announce the formation of a new party, the Action Group, on the eve of the elections in 1951. Thus started an unhappy racial organisational rivalry which damned much of the future.

In the North the prospect of elections also led to the establishment of political parties. The initiative in forming the Northern People's Congress (NPC) was taken by ex-students of Katsina (later Kaduna) College through their Old Boys' Association. The Sardauna of Sokoto, Ahmadu Bello, political and spiritual head of the Fulanis, became leader with a teacher with experience of local government, Abubakar Tafawa Belewa, as his right-hand man. Both were to become dominant and tragic figures in Nigeria's future. The anti-traditionalists founded the Northern Elements Progressive Union (NEPU) which sensationally won preliminary elections in a number of towns, but in the electoral colleges the NPC captured nearly all the seats. There was one further party. In the Middle Belt opposition to the Fulani–Hausa domination led the Birom and Twi peoples to set up the United Middle Belt Congress (UMBC). The election resulted in NPC victories in the North, Action Group victories in the West (some NCNC in non-Yoruba areas) and NCNC victories in the East. Politics were polarised by race. One progressive change occurred however. In the South, both west and east, traditionalist Africans were replaced by new thinking activists.

Representation of three regions in a national Legislature did little to increase a sense of Nigerian unity. Opposition between North and South became intense when the northern representatives voted against 'self-government' in 1956. The northern leaders seriously considered secession and explored the possibility of finding a sea outlet for their products other than Lagos. Similarly there was bitterness in the West when the representatives of the North and East voted in favour of the separation of Lagos as Federal territory. The British decision to confirm this proposal had a drastic effect on the Action Group; it became militantly anti-British and pro-socialist, ousting the NCNC as the most radical party.

Federation

In 1954 the constitution became fully federal with increased power for the regions. Considerable advance was made towards Parliamentary democracy. The members of the House of Representatives from the South were directly elected, in the East and in Lagos by adult suffrage, in the West by taxpayers; the North retained its electoral colleges. In the regions the Westminster pattern was adopted. Except in the North all official and *ex-officio* members disappeared and the governments were headed by Prime Ministers with the right to choose their own teams of Ministers. At Federal level the Council of Ministers was restricted to three from each region nominated by the largest party, and the Governor-General (who presided), the Chief Secretary, the Financial Secretary and Attorney-General. It was decided in 1956 that the question of self-government should be examined, though in fact further constitutional conferences were not resumed until 1957 and 1958. In 1957 it was agreed that the East and West should have regional self-government and in 1958 this was extended to the North. The West joined the East and Lagos in accepting adult suffrage and the North adopted manhood suffrage. The head of the Federal Government became Prime Minister. The important decision was made in 1960 that if the Federal Parliament passed a resolution asking for independence the British Government would agree.

The first Federal Prime Minister was Abubakar Tafawa Belewa, the lieutenant of the Sardauna of Sokoto in the NPC. He was able and conciliatory and after the election of 1959 suggested to Azikiwe a coalition government with the NCNC. In ideology this was illogical, the NPC conservative, the NCNC radical. In programmes and principles a coalition between the NCNC and the Action Group would have been more basic, and the Action Group proposed this, but Azikiwe put the necessity for national unity to achieve independence first and rejected Awolowo's advances. The coalition between North and East undoubtedly ensured independence, but the Yorubas of the West were further alienated.

Independence

On October 1, 1960, independence came. The constitution remained federal on the lines of 1958, but with the regional and national Legislatures entirely Nigerian in membership and control, the members directly elected, though still only by male suffrage in the North. There was some demand for new regions in the Mid-West and Middle Belt, but this problem was left to decision after independence, the rights of minorities meanwhile was safeguarded by the inclusion of a Charter of Human Rights in the constitution.

In Britain and Nigeria the achievement of independence for united Nigeria was regarded as a great triumph, the largest nation in Africa. It was held aloft as a supreme example of British decolonisation in co-operation with the peoples. The author was present at the Independence Day celebrations and was moved by the popular enthusiasm. The one disappointment was the background role given to Azikiwe, regarded as the father of independence, the crowds continually shouted 'Zee-ek', 'Zee-ek'. He was held in reserve to become the first Federal Governor-General a year later and President after the installation of a Republic in 1963.

Continued Racial Conflict

We would have wished to end this chapter here, but if we are concerned with the independence of peoples the record must be continued. Nigeria was composed of many races at its establishment and hope was high that a great example would be given by inter-community co-operation within one state, but tension persisted and unhappily the problem of integration remained unresolved. Even in the midst of the civil war which broke out in 1969 to prevent the secession of the East (see below) Awolowo, although he was a member of the Federal Government, wrote that there were fifty-one Nigerian nations which differed 'as widely and deeply in their cultures as do any group of nations in any part of the world'. He described 'their political institutions, customary usages, basic religious beliefs and even food habits' as so divergent that 'neither British rule nor Christian and Islamic civilisations have brought about any permanent assimilation'. In forthright terms he dismissed common Nigerian nationality as a complete misnomer because 'there is no such thing as a Nigerian nation anyway'.[17] The years following independence gave continuous and tragic evidence of the difficulty of stabilising harmony.

Although the North was less educationally and socially advanced than the South, its large population – 30,000,000 as against 25,000,000 – gave it a majority in the Federal Parliament and Belewa remained Prime Minister. Because of Azikiwe's concern to maintain Nigerian unity – in the 1950s he had favoured postponement of independence in the South in order to bring in the North – the NCNC continued in coalition. Then came a crisis in the isolated West. The regional Prime Minister, Chief Akintola, received the co-operation of the Nigerian business class and conflicted with Awolowo's Socialism and Pan-Africanism. When the Action Group congress endorsed Awolowo's ideology, Akintola withdrew and formed a new party, the United Peoples' Party (later the Nigeria National Democratic Party, NNDP), whereupon a majority in the West Legislature petitioned the Governor to depose him. A temporary Prime Minister was appointed, there were unruly scenes in the Legislature, and the Federal Government suspended the regional constitution and appointed an administrator. A somewhat unprincipled coalition was then formed between Akintola and the NCNC, the object of which was to crush Awolowo, unprincipled because the aim of the NNDP was to further regionalism and to collaborate with Nigerian businessmen in a conservative policy, a denial of the historical role of the NCNC. Compromise went further when the Federal Prime Minister invited the NNDP to appoint two members to his Ministry. The NCNC was losing its radical image both nationally and in the West.

The coalition between the NPC and the NCNC broke on a dispute about the census returns in 1962, important because population determined representation in the Federal Legislature. The North charged the East with inflating its figures; a new census was taken when the East in turn charged the North with inflation. The mutual bitterness was so great that in the 1964 Federal elections the NCNC invited the Action Group to join a United Progressive Grand Alliance (UPGA), which was met by the NPC and the NNDP forming a Nigerian National Alliance (NNA). This confrontation at least represented a division between radical and conservative elements in Nigerian life, which was perhaps the reason why the contest became fierce. The procedures for the nomination of candidates was so unfair that the UPGA decided to boycott the elections, though there was some local dissent about this. Whilst NNA swept the North and won most of the seats in the West, the NCNC captured the Mid-West despite the boycott;[18] in the East there was no election, because the regional government, NCNC controlled, declined to co-operate. This situation left President Azikiwe in difficulty. Initially, he refrained from calling on Belewa to form a government because he was dissatisfied with the election. Finally, he asked the Prime Minister to form a broad-based administration with equal representation in the South of the NCNC and the NNDP. An election was authorised in the East, resulting predictably in NCNC victory.

Military Coups

So Nigeria descended to a tragic climax. In the succeeding election in 1965 there was open injustice in the West. Opposition candidates were denied nomination, ballot papers were distributed to government supporters prior to the election, the intimidation was vicious. Inevitably there were disturbances, with many killed by the armed forces. The standards of government also reached a new low. There was blatant racial discrimination in the distribution of posts and corruption became notorious. Then, as in other African countries, army officers acted and they did so with brutality. They kidnapped and killed Prime Minister Belewa and the Finance Minister, and assassinated the Sardauna of Sokoto, Sir Ahmadu Bello, Akintola, and members of Parliament from the North and the West. Most though not all of the officers were Ibos with loyalties to the East.

On the morrow of these events the remaining members of the cabinet met with the army commander, Major-General Aguiyi-Ironsi, an Ibo but loyal to the Government. They could not agree on a successor to Prime Minister Belewa and General Ironsi suggested that he and the army should be made responsible to maintain authority. The cabinet agreed and Ironsi secured the surrender of the rebels. He appointed four army officers to take control of the regions. Ironsi appeared to have popular support in urging the need for a strong unitary government, but when he issued a decree to this effect racialism erupted again. Both the North and the Yorubas resisted, and many Ibos in the North were killed.

At this point, Ironsi became indecisive and confusion reigned. Then in July 1966 came the second military *coup*, initiated by officers in the North, supported by Yorubas and anti-Ibos. Ironsi and his officers in Lagos were assassinated and administration outside the East passed to the insurgents. Lieutenant-Colonel Yakuba Gowon, a Christian and a minority tribesman accept-able to both North and West, was selected as supreme commander and head of the military government.

Civil War

The worst event followed. Anger against the officers who had assassinated their Federal Prime Minister and Sardauna led to a massacre of Ibos in the North, men, women and children. The Ibos said that thirty thousand were killed; the Government admitted ten thousand; a million refugees poured into the East; the psycho-logical unity of Nigeria was destroyed. Colonel Ojukwu, who had been appointed military governor of the East, became convinced that secession was necessary. He withheld from the Federal Government revenue from large oil installations and, although agreement was reached with General Gowon at a conference held in Ghana (no venue was safe in Nigeria), the Military Council at Lagos repudiated it and civil war began, Colonel Ojukwu declar-ing the East independent as 'Biafra'. The war which lasted three years was appalling in its loss of life, mostly from starvation when Port Harcourt was blockaded and captured by the Federalists. It is estimated that one and a half million died from hunger, the majority of them children. An ugly feature of the war was the fact that the arms on both sides were supplied by big Powers and by an extensive European black market.[19] The British Government not only maintained its normal supply of arms to a Common-wealth country but increased it largely and the Soviet Union provided the Federalists with fighting planes. Despite its denials, France, competitive with Nigeria in West African neo-colonialism and its eyes on oil concessions, supplied Biafra. Many approaches to the Organisation of African Unity were made for mediation, but these proved of no avail because the majority of African governments, with their own minority problems, feared any example of secession; four African countries, Gabon, the Ivory Coast, Tanzania and Zambia, sided with Biafra. Starvation ultimately defeated Ojukwu and his people. They surrendered in 1970.

Tribute is due to the spirit of conciliation which General Gowon showed to the Biafrans. Ojukwu escaped to the Ivory Coast, but others were restored to positions of authority. During the war General Gowon had constituted a new political structure for Nigeria, with twelve states instead of five. The coastal minorities in the East, whose support for Biafra was doubtful, were given statehood. A situation of relieved weariness with racial emotions exhausted followed the civil war, but it would be optimistic to hope that the problem was permanently settled. Indeed, Nigeria remains explosive. General Gowon, who exerts a high standard of tolerance and justice, rules with the advice of the Supreme Military Council and does not foresee a return to civilian democracy until 1974. Meanwhile, there is increasing disintegration. In the first place, the new small states, under military commissioners, are asserting powers which arouse hostility from the larger tribes, the Hausas and the Yorubas (the Ibos are otherwise engaged in rebuilding their eastern state). Secondly, corruption abounds, despite General Gowon's disapproval, and this is particularly evident in the arrogant luxury of the higher ranking officers in the 200,000-strong army. The middle-rank officers are acutely aware of this and a colonel's *coup*, as in Egypt, is not impossible. Among the people there is growing discontent because of massive unemployment and the steeply rising cost of living. To establish national unity, General Gowon is concentrating on strengthening the army, and though this may be dangerous to democracy his conciliatory administration, backed by an increasing revenue from oil, may maintain, against heavy odds, the stability necessary for unity and progress.[20]

The creation of Nigeria was a great gamble in its union of uncongenial races. It was a bold attempt to reconcile the independence of separate peoples by integration in a political unit. It remains to be seen whether the Nigerians themselves can find a solution to a problem which is a cause of division not only in Africa but in much of the world.

Notes

1. Sierra Leone lies at the southern end of the western bulge of the continent before it turns east. To north and east is the Republic of Guinea and to the south Liberia. The area is 27,925 square miles. The estimated population in the 1971 census was 2,590,000.

2. The names of the two rulers were given by the English.

3. The Governor-General had actually sworn in Stevens as Prime Minister.

4. Area: 92,100 square miles. Population (1970 census): 8,545,561.

5. Negotiations in 1896 to end the Ashanti rebellion broke down by an incident which then typified British–African relations. The Ashantis staged a Durbar at Kumasi to welcome the British Governor, Sir Frederic Hodgson. The Governor demanded that he should sit on the Paramount Chief's Stool, a sacred object for the exclusive use of the Ashanti's spiritual leaders. The African Queen Mother, it is said, then summoned an assembly of women and ordered them to refuse sex with their husbands until (opposite to Lysistrata's reason in Aristophenes' play) they took up arms against the English. Governor Hodgson and his wife were besieged in the British residency for three months (Cameron Duodu, *Observer* magazine, February 25, 1973).

6. In *British Policy in Changing Africa*, Sir Andrew Cohen admitted that the British 'based their attitudes and actions on the assumption that there was indefinite time ahead'.

7. Syrian and Lebanese in the Gold Coast fulfilled the same role as Indians in East Africa. They were shop-keepers and small businessmen.

8. Danquah died in prison.

9. Ghana and Guinea had theoretically become united in 1960. The union had little effect administratively.

10. A second *coup* ejected the Busia Government. The National Redemption Council was more radical and gained considerable support from those who had supported the Nkrumah regime.

11. The author had a close friendship with Nkrumah, whose character was more sympathetic and humane than generally recognised. In later years he passed from over self-confidence to isolation and even fear. On the last occasion the author met him he was restricted to the top floor of Christianborg Castle, reached by narrow passages and stairs. The author criticised his imprison-

ment of opponents without trials. The following exchange occurred:
'It is necessary to avoid the sabotage of Socialism.' 'Some may be
innocent.' 'Better that there be a few innocent victims than
Socialism be obstructed.' 'You are making the task of your
friends in England more difficult.' With a smile, 'Perhaps, Fenner,
you are to be one of the innocent sufferers, too.'

12. In 1912 Lugard was appointed Governor of the whole of
Nigeria and introduced 'indirect rule' in the south, except Lagos,
leading to revolts with many killed. In the east, where there were
no chiefs, he created them.

13. Internal dissension within the company was also a factor.

14. The part of Cameroun mandated to Britain was administered
from Lagos.

15. This was due to the absence of ruling chiefs in the East.

16. The election to the Houses of Assembly was indirect
through electoral colleges composed of members selected in the
first instance by all who paid taxes.

17. *The People's Republic*.

18. The Mid-West was established as a separate state after
independence.

19. The author, who with James Griffiths, ex-Colonial Secretary, and Dr John Wallace went to Biafra and Lagos on a peace
mission in 1968, saw arms manufactured in eight European
countries.

20. See article by Colin Legum in The *Observer*, February 20,
1972.

Chapter Fifteen

Belgian Africa

(Zaire, Rwanda, Burundi)

Zaire (Congo-Kinshasa)

The Congo historically covered most of west-central Africa, including French Equatorial Africa. There are still two Congos, north and south of the river, Congo (Brazzaville), already considered, and Congo (Kinshasa), renamed Zaire in 1972, our present subject. The area is vast, 895,348 square miles, but it is sparsely peopled, only twenty-four persons per square mile; in 1971 the population was estimated to be 22,480,000. The territory lies at the centre of Black Africa, its core. To the north is the Central African Republic as well as Brazzaville Congo; to the north-east the Negro sector of Sudan; east are Rwanda and Burundi (ex-Belgian colonies, considered here with Zaire) and Uganda and Tanzania; Zambia and Angola are on the south. There is only a narrow coast of twenty-five miles on the Atlantic at the mouth of the river Congo.

Portuguese Slave Rule

When the Portuguese touched the coast in the fifteenth century circumstances conspired to make their presence more than the coastal trading stations established further north. In 1482 an expedition had set out from their depot at Elmina in Ghana to round the tip of Africa, but the ships did not get beyond the mouth of the Congo river. Welcomed by King Mani and invited to become his allies in repressing subordinate chiefs, the Portuguese seized the opportunity to penetrate inland with the object of creating a Christian state as a bastion against the Islamic north. With the priests came craftsmen and even the provison of a constitution. King Manoel of Portugal secured the acceptance of the *Regimento* of 1512 under which European law was introduced and the Congolese army trained in the arts of warfare. In return the Congo kings agreed 'to fill Portuguese ships, whether with slaves or copper or ivory'.

At the time no contradiction was thought to exist between Christianity and slavery. The Portuguese transformed the associated island of São Tomé from a penal colony into a centre for exporting Africans to Brazil. At first the Congolese chiefs co-operated in the trade; King Dom Affonso confirmed the *Regimento* by handing over 320 token slaves. But by 1526 he was protesting that merchants 'daily seize our subjects, sons of the land' and 'grab them and cause them to be sold'. He addressed a moving appeal to the king of Portugal: 'So great, Sir, is their corruption and licentiousness that our country is being utterly depopulated.' After Dom Affonso's death, however, the Congo was subject to civil war between rival chiefs, and his successor had to accept Portugal as a protecting power while the devastation of the slave trade continued. By the beginning of the eighteenth century the territory within Portuguese reach had been stripped of human cargo and the traders left to exploit Angola to the south. In the year 1778 the number of slaves exported from Africa was put at 104,000, one-third of them from the Congo and Angola.[1]

King Leopold's Rule

Portugal was followed by King Leopold of the Belgians. In 1884 Britain had agreed that Portugal should resume power, but other European governments objected and at the great divide conference at Berlin, 1884–5, personal possession by King Leopold was confirmed. The Belgians claimed their object was to end slavery, but conditions under which the Congolese were forced to gather rubber and ivory were as cruel as the worst slavery. When they did not fulfil extravagant tasks they were mutilated and shot by their white overseers.[2] International exposure of these conditions led the Belgian Government to take over the administration in 1908, but Leopold left behind him a consortium of financial companies to exploit an eldorado of mineral wealth which had been newly discovered. The first of these was a British company, Tanganyika Concessions, which had originated from Cecil Rhodes' design to build a railway from the Cape to Cairo and whose purpose was to gain rights on the banks of Lake Tanganyika. Its chairman, Sir Robert Williams, directed its capital instead to the exploitation of the copper belt of Northern Rhodesia and Katanga in the Congo, and when the highly backed *Union Minière du Haut Katanga*, an alliance of the royal family and bankers, was formed in Belgium, he became vice-president and technical manager, with his company holding one-third of the shares. He also initiated the British-owned Benguela Railway Company to carry the minerals to the Atlantic across Angola. Katanga virtually became the property of the Belgian–British mining company.

Belgian Rule

Belgium governed Congo as a technical dictatorship, with its civil servants, managers and army officers conducting the administration in every sphere without African rights. Leopold had recruited soldiers under rigid Belgian command to enforce his barbaric regime and these became the core of the colonialist army, the *force publique*, with no African above the ranks. There were no legislative bodies. A Governor General was responsible to the Belgian Parliament or in practice still to the Belgian king, who decreed the laws on the advice of a minister and a colonial council. At first education was meagre and there was no thought of training Africans, who were regarded *en masse* as uncivilisable. But as industry developed, particularly in Katanga, skilled African labour became necessary and a small élite was educated and trained. In Katanga mineral wealth enabled a higher standard of life to be reached.

Patrice Lumumba

The beginning of self-expression by Africans was through Old Boys' Clubs at the few secondary schools. No political associations were permitted, but the students began to discuss social questions. The only openly political assertion was by tribal chiefs claiming traditional rights, but these were quickly suppressed. It was through the students' clubs that the Congo's national leader, Patrice Lumumba, emerged. In view of his later record it is worth noting his early outlook. He was proud of the fact that he had matriculated and attained 'equal status with Belgians'. He joined the postal service and founded (and became president of) the *Amicale des Postiers*, a friendly society originally consisting of native workers but under his influence extending to Belgians. He was also president of the Belgo-Congolese Union in Stanleyville, an inter-racial society, and was so respected by the authorities that he was included in a delegation to tour Belgium in 1956. His whole activity at this time was directed to developing co-operation between the African people and the Belgian community, and he wrote a book on 'the imperative and urgent need to achieve forthwith a brotherly understanding which will lead to a definite union'.[3] His proposals were an autonomous Congo Free State federated with Belgium under the command of a Belgian High Commissioner and administered jointly by Congolese and Belgians. He did, however, insist that Congo should not be built in the image of Europe: 'it should be a fusion of Western and African civilisations'. The subsequent history of the Congo would have been very different if the Belgian authorities had responded to these ideas in 1956 and 1957.

The revolution in Lumumba's ideas took place in 1958 when he was caught up in the wave of Pan-Africanism sweeping the continent. He formed the *Mouvement National Congolais* (MNC) with four objects: first, to develop among Africans a self-reliant consciousness; second, to supersede tribal loyalty by national unity; third, to prepare for national independence; and fourth, to identify Congolese Africans with national movements throughout the continent. His conversion to these ideas was deepened by attendance at the All-African Peoples' Conference at Accra in December, 1958. He returned to Leopoldville and addressed a meeting of thousands who vociferously endorsed his demand for immediate and total independence. The revolution had begun.

Tribal Groupings

There was another party demanding that the Belgians should go, the *Association des Bakongos pour l'Unification, l'Expansion et la Défence de la Kitongo* (ABAKO). As its name implies, it was tribal, or perhaps one should say racial, for the Bakongo were a people divided between French Congo, Belgian Congo and Portuguese Angola, and its original object was unification of all in a separate state. It had begun as early as 1950 as a cultural group, but developed political aims by opposing the influx into the Lower Congo of other tribes. The Bakongo were strong among the population from Leopoldville, the Belgian capital, to the coast and came into open conflict with the administration. In 1959 leading members were arrested, soldiers occupied Bakongo districts and the property of the party was seized. The dynamic leader was Joseph Kasavubu, destined to become a dominant figure after independence.

Other tribal movements emerged; the Baluba and Balunda in Katanga and Kasai and the Bangula in the Equatorial Province. All were opposed to Belgian rule but on a divisive basis. The distinctive feature of Lumumba's MNC was its opposition to tribalism and its appeal to the people to claim independence with national unity. He succeeded in winning support in his own area of Stanleyville and among the Kasai Baluba, and even in Katanga he went far in uniting the Baluba and many Balunda in the BALUBAKAT, in opposition to CONAKAT (*Confédération des Associations Tribales du Katanga*), which the rising influence of Moise Tshombe, leading the African population (which had benefited from the economic development in Katanga) had established with the aid of Union Minière.

Concessions Blocked

The widespread disquiet throughout the Congo and the repercussions of African advance in surrounding countries made the Belgians realise they must reconsider their policies. In July 1958, plans to remove all discrimination between European and African personnel in the administration were announced and a study group was set up to prepare a new constitution. In January 1959, however, a few days before its report was to be published, serious riots broke out in Leopoldville (later renamed Kinshasa), the consequence of a combination of frustrations. Thousands of workers demonstrated against unemployment and thousands of Nationalists against political subjection, angered by the contrast with Brazzaville Congo across the river where self-government had been conceded. Crowds looted, burned buildings and attacked Europeans. The revolt was crushed only by the sustained firing of the *force publique*; the official figures were 49 African dead and 241 wounded, but correspondents reported over 200 dead. The Belgians reacted by banning the ABAKO, arresting Kasavubu and other leaders, and rusticating its officials to the Bakongo region between the city and the coast. This last action proved mistaken; the officials organised the entire area and collected funds. In July 1959, the Deputy Governor-General wrote to Brussels that 'from Leopoldville to Banana' the whole country supported Kasavubu.[4]

The ABAKO demanded that the entire Lower Congo should become independent and in October began a civil disobedience campaign which created chaos in the administration in Leopoldville; taxes went unpaid and the *force publique* lost control, so much that Brussels decided to call representatives of the Congo to a Round Table Conference in January 1960.

Before the conference met, the constitutional recommendations of the Brussels study group were published. They included proposals for elected local councils and an increase of Africans nominated to the provincial and national advisory councils. Announcing these, King Baudouin startled everyone by saying that the aim of Belgium was to lead eventually to independence. This was the first time independence had been mentioned and the Leopoldville administration was shocked. They blocked the reforms and, when the Colonial Secretary suggested that the Governor-General and a large part of his staff should resign, their resistance was so strong that it was the Colonial Secretary who had to resign.

African Parties

There were now five major African political movements. We have mentioned the ABAKO, the MNC (with its allied BALUBAKAT) and CONAKAT. In addition there were the *Parti National du Progrès* (PNP), a party of African traditionalists, backed by the Belgian administration, formed in 1959 to oppose the radicalism of Lumumba (it stood for a unitary state, but for co-operation with Belgium and acceptance of the authority of chiefs) and the *Parti Solidaire Africain* (PSA) which covered the same area as the ABAKO but was more radical, and stood for a unitary state. It entered into alliance with ABAKO after the civil disobedience campaign and influenced Kasavubu to substitute federation of the Congo for the previous policy of Bakongo independence. Its leader was Antoine Gizenga, destined to be a controversial figure.

Constitution, Elections, Independence

Originally it was suggested that representation at the Round Table Conference should be determined by the local elections held in December 1959, but the results were unrepresentative as the ABAKO and PSA secured an almost complete boycott in the

Lower Congo and the MNC participated only partially, though in Stanleyville it won 55 of the 61 seats. The delegations were therefore decided on a party basis: ABAKO 11; PNP 11; MNC 3; CONAKAT 2; BALUBAKAT 1; and *Cerea* (a small party in Kiou) 1. Despite their differences the African delegations formed a united front to demand immediate independence and insisted on the attendance of Lumumba, who had been sentenced to six months' imprisonment; when the Belgians released him, he took over the leadership.

The Belgians surrendered. They agreed that independence should be inaugurated on June 30, 1960. This decided, the differences between the Congolese parties became apparent. The MNC and the PNP wanted a unitary state, ABAKO wanted federation, CONAKAT wanted confederation. Tshombe, fortified by telegrams from Union Minière officials, asked that the minerals of the copper belt should belong to Katanga; Lumumba claimed they belonged to the whole of the Congo. Compromises were reached on the basis that sub-soil wealth should be the property of the central government but that it should 'pay regard to the mine owners and the share-claim of the province'. The constitution was also a compromise between federation and a unitary state.

The pre-independence provincial elections gave ABAKO and the PSA a majority in Leopoldville, the MNC a majority in Orientale, and CONAKAT a marginal majority in Katanga. In the central elections for the Senate and Chamber the pattern was similar but reflected the national appeal of Lumumba. The MNC won 24 seats in the Senate and was by far the largest party. In the Assembly it led with 33 seats and had 8 allies. Against this the PNP had 15, the PSA 13, the ABAKO 12, *Cerea* 10, CONAKAT 8, MNC (K) 8, BALUBAKAT 7, and PUNA 7.[5]

The success of Lumumba surprised the Belgians and in the negotiations which preceded the formation of a government they manoeuvred to keep him from office. Finally it was agreed that Kasavubu should be president with Lumumba as prime minister. The government was a coalition. The MNC had eight ministers, ABAKO and the PSA three each, *Cerea* two, and the PNP, PUNA and CONAKAT one each. Of interest for the future was the appointment of Antoine Gizenga of the PSA as deputy premier and the fact that Joseph Mobutu was one of the MNC Secretaries of State. Everyone awaited the formal coming of independence on June 30.

Mutiny, Katanga Secession, Belgian Troops

The independence celebrations were by no means formal. King Baudouin made the mistake of delivering a paternalistic address reciting how much Belgium had done for the Congo. Angry, Lumumba let loose a fiery speech telling of the humiliations which the Congolese had suffered under the Belgians. He apologised later, but Belgium became deeply bitter against the new Prime Minister. This incident was trivial compared with what followed. Within a week the African ranks in the *force publique* mutinied, beginning in Leopoldville, spreading everywhere, reaching Katanga. They regarded the independence celebration as a farce because the army was still ruled by Belgian officers, and their anger at first turned against Lumumba and the Government. They ran riot, attacking Europeans, raping women; panic-stricken, Belgians began to flee *en masse* from the country. Lumumba acted promptly. He dismissed the Belgian army command, appointed Joseph Mobutu head of staff, and with Kasavubu went from barracks to barracks supervising the election of African officers by the men. The situation became calmer, but in Brussels the demand rose for the intervention of Belgian troops to protect nationals; in Kasai and Katanga Europeans were still threatened. President and premier flew to Kasai and found Belgian paratroopers there. They were indignant, but in consideration of European safety gave permission for the troops to stay for two months. They had a worse shock – news reached them that Tshombe had declared the secession of Katanga and had appealed to Belgium and Rhodesia for assistance. They immediately flew to Elizabethville, the capital, only to be refused permission to land by Munongo, Tshombe's tough second-in-command, who was backed by the presence of Belgian troops at the airport.

This was crisis enough, but the situation was made more explosive by a third Belgian intervention. Earlier Lumumba and Kasavubu had visited the Atlantic port of Matadi and had restored order. All Europeans except a handful had left; yet Belgian forces invaded the town and occupied the docks; there was fighting and twelve Africans were killed. As news of this spread the Congolese became convinced that the Belgians were attempting to reoccupy the country and the assaults on Europeans, men and women, were renewed in many places.

The Brussels Government had at first taken the line that it would send troops only at the request of Leopoldville, but with the deterioration of the situation they dispatched large forces; in all, they had ten thousand troops available in twenty-three centres; they occupied the port of Boma in addition to Matadi, the Leopold-ville airport and, when resistance was offered, the city itself in addition to a number of other towns.

For the Congolese Government clearly a grave crisis had arisen. Kasavubu and Lumumba requested assistance from the United Nations. In Leopoldville Gizenga asked the American ambassador to send three thousand troops to restore order; the premier and president did not confirm this, but they broke off diplomatic relations with Belgium and informed Khrushchev that they might have to appeal to the Soviet Union to intervene. Then, after calling on the Belgian troops to withdraw within two days, they asked the United Nations for military aid 'to protect the national territory of the Congo against the present external aggression'. In their appeal they denounced the arrival of Belgian troops as a threat to international peace and accused Belgium of preparing the secession of Katanga.[6]

United Nations Intervention

On July 14 the Security Council met and adopted a resolution, moved for the African group by Mongi Slim, the Tunisian representative, calling on Belgium to withdraw its troops and authorising the Secretary-General (Dag Hammarskjöld) to take steps in consultation with the Congolese Government to provide the necessary military assistance until, through the efforts of the Government with the technical assistance of the UN, the national security forces were able, in the opinion of the Congolese, to meet their tasks. All members voted in favour, except Britain, France and China (Taiwan) who abstained on the ground that in their view there had been no aggression. The United States shared this attitude, but voted in favour on the ground that the withdrawal of Belgian troops was dependent on their replacement by UN forces. The Soviet Union insisted that the withdrawal be unconditional. Of special significance in the wording of the resolutions was the emphasis laid on service to the Congolese Government.

The United Nations force consisted, in the first place, of contingents from five African countries, Ethiopia, Ghana, Guinea, Morocco and Tunisia, afterwards supplemented by Sweden and Ireland; the USA, the Soviet Union and Britain co-operated with air lifts. Katanga was the crucial issue. The Belgian troops in the capital, Elizabethville, disarmed the Congolese *force publique*, occupied all centres of importance with the support of the resident Europeans, and their commander, Major Weber, was made military adviser to Tshombe's government. The Katanga Assembly was reported to have unanimously approved secession, but the BALUBAKAT representatives were not present and it is doubtful if there was a quorum. Tshombe announced that UN troops would not be allowed in Katanga.

This issue, as well as the confusion in the rest of the Congo, led to a second meeting of the Security Council on July 20 to clarify the mandate given to the UN forces. The resolution, unanimously carried, again moved by Tunisia, implied condemnation of the secession of Katanga by recalling that the Congo had been admitted to the United Nations 'as a unit' and by requesting all states to refrain from action undermining its 'territorial integrity'; but it was sufficiently indefinite for the British representative to remark that Katanga was an international matter. The resolution was welcomed by Lumumba who, before making a visit to America, said in a conciliatory mood that Russian aid was no longer necessary; later, however, he accepted an offer from the Soviet ambassador in Canada to provide lorries and aeroplanes. This lost him support at Washington.

Katanga Crisis

Katanga was a difficult problem for Hammarskjöld. The second Security Council resolution authorised the presence of UN troops, and Lumumba asked they should enter immediately. Belgium, on the other hand, urged that there was no need because law and order were preserved, and Britain argued for negotiation. Hammerskjöld sent Ralph Bunche to Katanga to arrange for the entry of troops; Bunche concluded they would be resisted by force and the Secretary-General, doubtful if his mandate covered physical conflict, decided to recall the Security Council. These hesitations caused Lumumba to lose patience with the United Nations and he toured African countries gaining general support, Ghana and Guinea offering to send troops for a separate Congolese invasion of Katanga.

On August 8, the Security Council met. Hammarskjöld stated his belief that if the United Nations indicated they were not involved in the political conflict between Katanga and the central government, Tshombe would accept their troops. The resolution, once more moved by Tunisia, called on the Belgian government to withdraw its troops from Katanga immediately and declared that the entry of the UN force was necessary; but it emphasised non-intervention in any internal conflict and there was no mention of the use of force. Tshombe responded by saying he would admit UN troops on ten conditions, which included Katanga's freedom to appoint foreign technicians and the acceptance by the United Nations of Katanga's independent constitution. Hammarskjöld declined to accept conditions but went to Elizabethville for discussions. *En route* at Leopoldville he ignored Lumumba and said that once a Belgian assurance of withdrawal had been given the UN would have no right to intervene.

No report was published of the talks in Elizabethville, but Tshombe and the Belgians appeared satisfied and Moroccan and Swedish UN contingents moved into Katanga without opposition. When Hammarskjöld passed through Leopoldville on his return, Lumumba strongly protested that he had ignored the instruction of the July 14 Security Council resolution which required that he should consult with the Congo Government. When the Secretary-General replied coldly that it was for the Security Council to interpret its resolutions, Lumumba retorted heatedly and extravagantly. It was evident that the Congolese Government and the United Nations had become deeply estranged. The Security Council met again. It was so divided that no resolution was adopted. Hammarskjöld replaced Bunche as head of the Congo operation by an Indian, Rajeshwar Dayal.

Meanwhile, disintegrating events were taking place in Leopoldville. Lumumba lost support in his own government, partly because he did not consult ministers when deciding policy, partly because of the policy itself. The division was aggravated when he proceeded with a plan to attack Katanga with Congolese troops and requested and received Russian Ilyushin planes and lorries to transport them. The attempt had disastrous consequences. Lumumba set off to Stanleyville to organise the attack through Kasai; just before his plane arrived an American Globemaster with equipment for the UN touched down. The assembled Congolese thought the crew were Belgians intending to arrest Lumumba and beat them up. Lumumba restored order, but the damage had been done. When the Congolese troops set out from Kasai they looted on a large scale *en route* in Bakwanga and, resisted by the local people, used their ammunition in a general massacre, killing two hundred. The attack on Katanga was held up.

Simultaneously with these events, the All-African Conference which Lumumba hoped would provide him with support was in session at Leopoldville. Its attitude was very different from what he expected. Delegations were present from thirteen African governments and overwhelmingly they deplored the plan to attack Katanga with Congolese troops, criticised the approach to the Soviet Union as prejudicing neutrality and urged that Leopoldville should co-operate with the United Nations despite its mistakes. Lumumba realised that he would have to revise his policy, but the change came too late. Hammarskjöld was shocked by the acceptance of Russian help and the attack on the American plane at Stanleyville; reaction in the United States was more extreme, and British public opinion was horrified by the press reports of the slaughter at Bakwanga. Lumumba was at his lowest, distrusted by fellow-ministers, deserted by the African states, alienated from the UN and rejected by Washington and London.

Lumumba Deposed

On September 5 the blow fell. Kasavubu, head of state, dismissed Lumumba from the premiership and six of his supporters from their ministries, appointing Joseph Ileo, a middle of the way senator, prime minister. Lumumba retorted by radio speeches challenging Kasavubu's right of dismissal and claiming it was for Parliament to decide. He summoned his cabinet, thirteen of the twenty-three ministers attending, who charged Kasavubu with treason and dismissed him from the presidency. Fearing civil war and the arrival of Russian planes from Kasai, the UN representative, Andrew Cordier (Dayal had not yet arrived) closed the airports to all but UN transport and placed a ban on the use of the radio by both sides. On September 7 and 8 the Chamber of Deputies and the Senate met; the more extreme anti-Lumumbists stayed away and the airport ban meant that other deputies could not attend. A Chamber of 90 (out of 137) declared by 60 votes to 19 that the declarations of both Kasavubu and Lumumba were invalid, and the Senate voted decisively by 41 to 2 against Kasavubu's dismissal of Lumumba.

At this point Lumumba appeared to be on top again, despite Kasavubu's decrees that he should be arrested; but Ileo had the advantage of the use of the radio from Brazzaville across the river having been given facilities to travel in order to consolidate support. On September 11 Lumumba attempted to force his way into the Leopoldville radio station; he was repulsed by UN guards. Dayal arrived as UN representative and attempted conciliation; he re-opened the radio station and airports, but failed to bring Kasavubu and Lumumba together. Events then climaxed. On September 6 Lumumba was arrested, but soldiers released him. On September 13 a joint session of both Houses of the Legislature by by 88 to 1 with three abstentions voted full powers to Lumumba with a parliamentary council to supervise their application; there were, however, doubts about a quorum. The following day Kasavubu adjourned Parliament for a month.

Mobutu Takes Over

The initiative still appeared to be with Lumumba. Katanga had of course been delighted by his dismissal and the Lower Congo supported their leader Kasavubu, but Orientale and North Kasai as strongly backed their hero. The division was serious, and at this point Colonel Mobutu, the army head, intervened. With the support of other officers he radioed a message to the nation on September 14 that the army had neutralised the head of state, the two rival governments and Parliament until the end of the year in order to give the politicians time to consider the situation calmly; meantime, technicians would run the administration. There was suspicion, not confirmed, that American Intelligence (CIA) had encouraged Mobutu and this was strengthened when he gave the Russian embassy forty-eight hours to leave.[7] That evening Lumumba went to the army camp to contact Mobutu, convinced of his backing as an old MNC member. He was attacked by soldiers from Bakwanga, who remembered the massacre, and rescued by Ghanaians; but he left behind his brief-case found by opponents. Its alleged documents were handed to the United Nations and were said to include appeals to Soviet Russia and Communist China and a message to the Congolese provincial presidents foreshadowing a dictatorship and authorising the torture of those who resisted. This message was almost certainly a forgery, but its publication aroused a wave of hostility to Lumumba in the Congo and the world. Kasavubu and Ileo asked the United Nations to arrest him, which Dayal refused to do.

Despite efforts by African states and UN officials to bring accord, there was no evidence of the calmer consideration which Mobutu had anticipated. Under the external pressures about him, Mobutu turned towards Kasavubu.

Russia Criticises Hammarskjöld

On the borders of Katanga, Lumumba's forces operated with little reference to events in Leopoldville. The in-fighting in South Kasai persisted, leading to civilian loss of life, to many refugees and to the danger of famine, but a second force reached North Katanga and Tshombe had difficulty in repelling it. Without pay and rations the soldiers were in effect bought off by the United Nations, which promised both. They withdrew and when Mobutu took power he wound up the whole expedition. At the same time Hammarskjöld maintained his pressure on Tshombe to disavow Belgian aid, protesting in September to the Belgian Government against its officers' role in the gendarmerie and against a consignment of arms sent to Elizabethville. He balanced this by protesting to the Russians about their supply of planes and lorries to Lumumba. This was impartiality, but then, on September 9, the Security Council resumed and the Secretary-General came out openly for Kasavubu against Lumumba. This brought a strong attack from the Soviet Union representative who contrasted intervention in internal affairs in Leopoldville with non-intervention in Katanga. Russia even went to the point of vetoing a Tunisia–Ceylon resolution because it was too mild. As a consequence the issue was for the first time referred to the General Assembly.

United Nations' Lead

Here the Afro-Asian *bloc* presented a resolution which recommended definite and decisive UN action. It differed from the Soviet attitude by loyalty to Hammarskjöld, but did not hide dissatisfaction with the policy which with the support of the West he had pursued. The American and British delegations supported the resolution not because they liked it but because they wished to isolate the Soviet Union, whose representatives rejected the text because it did not censure Hammarskjöld. The resolution repeatedly referred to the 'unity and territorial integrity' of the

Congo (thus emphasising dissociation from Tshombe); requested
the Secretary-General to assist the central government (as distinct
from Mobutu) in restoring law and order throughout the territory; appealed to all Congolese to seek a speedy solution of their
internal differences (which meant no vendetta against Lumumba);
and called upon all states to refrain from the provision of arms
and military personnel except through the United Nations. The
operative paragraph was carried by eighty votes to none with
South Africa alone abstaining. The resolution as a whole was
carried by seventy votes to none, with eleven abstentions on
contradictory grounds by the Soviet *bloc*, France and South Africa.
The General Assembly decision was not mandatory, but Hammarskjöld said he would be directed by it.

In Leopoldville Mobutu appointed a College of Commissioners
composed of graduates to run the administration. Most of them
were anti-Lumumba and pro-Kasavubu and the head of state
ratified the College as the government. The provinces, on the other
hand, dissociated themselves, only one co-operating with them.
Mobutu hoped to gain the confidence of Katanga, but Tshombe
would accept only his own terms of political and economic independence, which, in view of Katanga's mineral wealth, involved
domination. The College gave up all pretence of neutralism in
foreign relations, becoming openly hostile to the communist *bloc*,
co-operating closely with the British and American embassies, and
conflicting with African states. Mobutu may not have been involved, because he left the control of affairs to the College and
returned to his function of organising the army, difficult because many of the soldiers supported Lumumba. The new rulers
failed to achieve the national reconciliation which Mobutu had
stated to be his purpose when he took over.

The UN Acts

Following the General Assembly resolution, Hammerskjöld
showed a new seriousness in opposing the presence of Belgian
military personnel in Katanga. He estimated that, although
Belgian troops had left, there were 114 Belgian officers and 117
other ranks in the gendarmerie and 58 officers in the police. He
addressed strong letters to the Belgian representative in the United
Nations and to Tshombe demanding that the UN decision be
implemented and he urged Tshombe to reconsider his attitude to

the rest of the Congo; neither Brussels nor Tshombe responded. Hammarskjöld also took steps to neutralise areas in North Katanga where the Baluba were in revolt. Tshombe agreed that his gendarmerie would not intervene, but was indignant when the UN arranged for the Baluba leader, Jason Sendwe, to visit the disturbed districts to appeal for order and discipline. The UN at the same time came into conflict with Leopoldville when, in accordance with the Assembly resolution, Rajeshwar Dayal declined to recognise the College of Commissioners, obstructed the arrest of Lumumba and objected to the presence of Belgian advisers. Mobutu reacted by announcing that he was breaking off diplomatic relations with the United Nations, but Dayal did not retreat; in a report to Hammarskjöld he implied that only by the restitution of Parliament would the confused political situation be resolved. This was interpreted as favouring a return to power by Lumumba; not only Leopoldville and Belgium protested but also America, the State Department indicating that the US would not accept a return to parliamentary government with Lumumba as premier and dissociating itself from the attack on Belgian advisers: 'We have every confidence in the good faith of Belgium in its desire to be of assistance in the Congo', said the official spokesman. Lumumba interjected some grounds for the West's interpretation of the Dayal report by sending a message to his followers from his confinement under house arrest: 'Your government, the legal government, will soon be reinstated. My holiday approaches its end'.

Lumumba Murdered

Two events, however, led Lumumba and his supporters to doubt their ability to regain early power in Leopoldville and turned their minds instead to regrouping in their stronghold at Stanleyville in Orientale Province, where Gizenga who had become a devoted Lumumbist was in charge. The first was a decision by the UN General Assembly to seat a Kasavubu delegation as representing the Congo and the second was the expulsion of the sympathetic Ghanaian embassy. A plan was accordingly contrived to enable Lumumba and his colleagues to escape. They were under double guard; an inner ring of UN troops to prevent their arrest, an outer ring of Congolese troops to prevent their departure. A day was chosen when surveillance by the Congolese was relaxed because they were celebrating the Kasavubu triumph in the UN, and Lumumba and a group of supporters got away in cars. The Leopoldville troops caught up with them, however, in Kasai and Lumumba was forcibly taken back to Leopoldville and imprisoned. The reaction in Stanleyville, reached by escapees, was violent. Most of the resident Belgians were arrested and activity began for the secession of the Orientale Province. Reaction was also strong among African states, who endeavoured without success to get the Security Council to demand the release of Lumumba and all political prisoners and the immediate reconvening of the Congo Parliament.

In most of the Congo there was a wave of support for Lumumba. MNC troops from Stanleyville invaded Kivu and North Katanga and Mobutu failed to dislodge them. In Leopoldville Kasavubu was met with cries: 'Long live Lumumba'. There were fears of a *coup* to overthrow the Government and it was decided to remove Lumumba to a less critical place. In his fear Kasavubu went to the fatal extreme of arranging with Tshombe that the ex-premier and two of his colleagues, Mpolo and Okito, should be transferred to Katanga. On January 17 they were placed on a plane, beaten up *en route*, landed at Elizabethville blindfolded and with hands tied, kicked and struck with rifle butts, driven away in a jeep accompanied by gendarmes and never seen again.[8] On February 13 Munongo, in his capacity as Katanga Minister of the Interior, announced that Lumumba, Mpolo and Okito had been killed by the inhabitants of a small village whilst trying to escape. Few believed him. The United Nations appointed a Commission of Investigation. It stated that the weight of evidence was against this official version and accepted as 'substantially true' evidence that the three men were killed on the day of their arrival in Elizabethville 'in the presence of high officials of the government of Katanga Province'. The identity of the officials was not established, but the Commission recorded that its investigation 'bristles with evidence indicative of the extensive role played by Mr Munongo'. The Commission did not implicate Tshombe.

World Reaction

The news of the death of Lumumba stunned the Congo and shocked the world. The first effect in the Congo was stupefaction, almost anaesthetisation, rather than violence.[9] In Stanleyville twenty-five thousand people quietly attended a memorial service. But the mood changed when six Lumumbist prisoners, including the first president of the Orientale provincial government, were executed in South Kasai. In revenge, fifteen political prisoners, including five of Mobutu's officers, were shot by a firing squad in Stanleyville. Throughout the world vast demonstrations of protest took place. At many of them Hammarskjöld and the United Nations were denounced for having allowed the deportation and deaths and immediate UN action was demanded. An urgent meeting of the Security Council was called and the African representatives were in militant mood. The American presidential election had returned John F. Kennedy, and liberal Adlai Stevenson was his representative on the Council, contributing a less intransigent attitude. Hammarskjöld also moved nearer to the African–Asian position. The resolution submitted by Ceylon, Liberia and the UAR was more drastic than any previous decision. It urged the UN to intervene by force if necessary to prevent civil war, called on all states to prevent the departure of military and political personnel to the Congo, urged the reconvening of parliament and the reorganisation of the Congolese army, and called upon all states to co-operate. It was passed by nine votes to none, with France and the Soviet Union (whose own more extreme resolution had been defeated) abstaining.

Confederation Proposed

Prior to the meeting of the Security Council Kasavubu had summoned a round-table conference in Leopoldville to resolve the Congo's political problems. Katanga, Orientale and Kivu refused to attend, but moderate Lumumbists did, including the BALUBA-KAT, the PSA and parties in Kasai. The decision of the conference was to replace the College of Commissioners by a government of politicians under Joseph Ileo with the co-operation of Cyrille Adoula, also a moderate. When the terms of the UN resolution became known, however, an unexpected united front emerged between Leopoldville and Elizabethville. Both denounced it as violating African independence and they signed an agreement to pool their military resources to prevent a 'communist tyranny', having both the United Nations and Stanleyville in mind.

This was followed by a summit conference at Tananarive in Madagascar to seek a political settlement. The United Nations representatives, desiring a solution, encouraged all provinces to attend, but Orientale and Kivu stayed away. At the conference, Tshombe in a confident mood advocated a confederal solution and so keen were the Leopoldville delegates to negate the Security Council resolution and to isolate Stanleyville that they agreed. A detailed pattern for the Congo was worked out. It was to be a 'confederation of states' with Kasavubu as president. Each state would be sovereign and have its own gendarmerie and police, but the overall Council would be responsible for foreign affairs. By resolution the Security Council was condemned, but willingness was expressed to co-operate with the United Nations so long as it respected the Congo's sovereignty. The agreement was generally recognised as a triumph for Katanga.

When Kasavubu, Ileo, Adoula and other delegates from the central government returned to Leopoldville they began to have second thoughts. Tshombe did two things which in their view were contrary to the Tananarive decision. He paid a visit to Brazzaville Congo and signed an agreement for financial assistance in the construction of a dam; this they held contravened the understanding that foreign affairs should be within the province of the central authority. Secondly, his gendarmerie occupied Lualaba which had resisted Katanga authority and he announced that the province no longer existed; this they held repudiated his declaration at Tananarive that no part of the Congo should be denied self-determination. There was some justification for these criticisms, but it would seem that the Leopoldville leaders fastened on them because they had a belated realisation of the significance of their surrender to Katanga. They awoke particularly to the fact that no pledge had been given that the revenue from its mineral wealth would be shared with the rest of the Congo and to a realisation that economic power would make Elizabethville supreme. They were also shaken by the severe criticism of their subservience to Tshombe voiced by their Foreign Secretary, Justin Bomboko, who had been too ill to travel to Tananarive.

In his disquiet Kasavubu turned to the alternative of making peace with the United Nations. This was easier because Hammarskjöld had withdrawn Dayal as his representative in Leopoldville and discussions began with two UN officials who were conciliatory. They were also clever. They interpreted the Security Council resolution as though it aimed at helping the central government and assured Kasavubu that in implementing it the United Nations would respect the sovereignity of the Congo. They presented him with an agreement which, instead of imposing on Leopoldville the evacuation of foreign personnel and the reorganisation of the army, assumed that the president wanted to do this, and undertook that the United Nations would render all assistance to him. Kasavubu signed. When the respresentatives of Leopoldville and Katanga met a second time at Coquilhatville this agreement destroyed the projected alliance. Tshombe declared that it must be abrogated or the Katanga delegation would walk out.

Tshombe Arrested and Released

They did walk out, with unexpected consequences. At the airport soldiers informed Tshombe and his delegation that no politicians would be allowed to leave until agreement about the future of the Congo had been reached, and they were shut in a waiting-room under guard. Ileo and Adoula visited Tshombe and pleaded with him to return to the conference but he refused. Meanwhile the character of the conference was changed by the acceptance of anti-Katanga government delegations, including the BALUBA-KAT with Jason Sendwe. Whilst Tshombe spent a second night in the waiting-room, a resolution was carried approving the agreement between Kasavubu and the United Nations and a decision taken to expel the European members of the Katanga delegation as a first application of the agreement. That was not enough. The conference went on to vote that Tshombe should be placed under house arrest and prevented from returning to Elizabethville, and before its proceedings concluded the announcement was made that he was to be imprisoned and tried for high treason. The arrest of Tshombe aroused furious protest in Belgium, France and in six ex-French colonies, particularly Brazzaville Congo, but less so in America and Britain than might have been expected. United Nations officials and most of the Afro-Asian nations regarded it as an opportunity to press for a political settlement. Leopoldville was in a responsive mood.

At the Coquilhatville conference Kasavubu announced that parliament would be recalled and on his return to Leopoldville he asked the United Nations to assist. The UN representatives concentrated on influencing both Stanleyville and Katanga to participate in the session which was fixed to take place at the University of Lovanium outside Leopoldville. Gizenga agreed for Stanleyville and, in return for his release, Tshombe also signed a declaration which promised attendance; on his return to Elizabethville, however, the Katanga Assembly (the Opposition was not present) held that the declaration was imposed under duress and rejected it. This decision caused dismay in the UN and America, which feared that in the absence of Katanga parliament might appoint a Lumumbist government with Gizenga at its head. The State Department even tried to persuade Union Minière to exert its influence, but the company declined and instead began in July to pay to Katanga revenue due to the central government. Although when parliament met the Lumumbist *bloc* had a small majority they agreed to neutral, liberal-minded Cyrille Adoula becoming prime minister, but Gizenga was named deputy premier with Sendwe of BALUBAKAT. The government was a coalition of Kasavubists and Lumumbists and its inauguration was hailed with relief in the Congo and outside. The problem of Katanga remained.

UN in Katanga

Until Tshombe was released Elizabethville's attitude had appeared to be less obstructionist, but with the leader back defiance returned. The United Nations encouraged by the situation in Leopoldville became sterner in action against the continued presence of foreign military personnel and advisers. The issue was intensified by the recruitment of mercenaries and by the importation of arms via the British-owned Benguela railway through Angola. The Belgian and British Governments made it illegal for subjects to serve as mercenaries, but Katanga continued to enrol them from South Africa and when Swedish troops disarmed Katangese gendarmes at the airport, Tshombe forbade traders to do business with the UN, and cut off water and electricity from its buildings. In Brussels a Socialist-Liberal coalition gained office which was more co-operative with the UN. Henri Spaak asked the United Nations to supply a list of the Belgian advisers against whom it complained, and M. Renard, head of security, and General Weber, Tshombe's military adviser, were withdrawn. The UN appointed Conor Cruise O'Brien, a member of the Irish delegation to the General Assembly sympathetic to the Afro-Asians, as its representative in Katanga, and when Georges Thyssen, an influential Belgian, failed to obey an order to leave he was arrested and put on a plane for Brussels. Crisis was again in the air.

Hammarskjöld decided, in view of the obstruction from Katanga, that he should take direct action against the remaining foreign personnel. On August 28 UN forces arrested the known Belgian officers of the gendarmerie, blockaded the house of Munongo and occupied the radio station and post office. O'Brien saw Tshombe, who agreed to dismiss all foreign officers if the UN guards were withdrawn from Munongo's residence and from the radio station and the post office. O'Brien agreed and Tshombe broadcast that his government had 'bowed to the decision of the United Nations'. O'Brien also consented to a proposal by the Belgian consul that he should become responsible for withdrawing the remaining officers in order to avoid the humiliation of arrests.

The stronger UN action had a divided reception outside the Congo. Sir Roy Welensky, Prime Minister of the Federation of the Rhodesias and Nyasaland, issued a violent protest which appeared to have British endorsement by the attendance of its consul when the statement was read to Tshombe, and Lord Lansdowne, the Foreign Secretary, instructed the United Kingdom representative at the United Nations to question Hammarskjöld. Henri Spaak also protested but in moderate terms. America remained silent publicly, but supported the UN privately. O'Brien had to face not only fierce criticism in the press of the West, but the opposition of the Western consuls in Elizabethville[10] and the utmost hostility was shown to the UN by Tshombe's supporters – open conflict moved to the brink. When a Belgian mercenary confessed that he had been employed by Munongo to organise attacks on UN patrols, O'Brien called for the minister's suspension and pressed Hammarskjöld for permission to arrest him. Then events moved to an absolute crisis. The Secretary-General was expected shortly in Leopoldville and Tshombe was invited to meet him; no one expected him to do so. Mahmoud Khiari, Tunisian UN officer, second-in-command in the Congo, authorised plans for detailed decisive action if Tshombe refused. According to O'Brien, he gave orders that in this event the Katanga leader's house should be blockaded, that control should be renewed over the radio station and post office, that the Congolese flag should be run up on all public buildings, that a number of ministers should be arrested on warrants already prepared and that Tshombe should then be asked to revoke Katanga's secession. This plan had not been submitted to Hammarskjold, but O'Brien considered that he had been authorised to end secession by force. Lunner, the senior UN official in the Congo, confirmed the plan when assured that there would be minimal force.

Tshombe duly refused to go to Leopoldville and on September 12 at 4 a.m. the UN forces moved into action. Khiari and O'Brien had miscalculated. There was fierce resistance at the post office and radio station and much loss of life before the UN took possession at 8 p.m. Tshombe escaped to Rhodesia and all but one of the ministers evaded arrest. O'Brien informed a Press Conference that night that the UN had acted to prevent civil war between Katanga and the central government and that Katanga's secession was ended.

Hammarskjöld's Death

Hammarskjöld was flying into Leopoldville when he heard of these events which were a complete surprise to him. On his arrival he was indignantly pressed for an explanation by the British ambassador and he authorised a statement which in effect repudiated Khiari and O'Brien. It declared that the purpose of the action was directed against the mercenaries and made no mention of the intention to arrest the ministers. At the same time he ordered O'Brien to cease saying that Katanga was under central government control and to instruct the UN troops to fire only in self-defence. The Katanga authorities took full advantage of the discomfort of the United Nations representatives. European officers intensified resistance, including bombing by a plane piloted by a Belgian mercenary, and an Irish UN company was cut off. All over the world the press condemned the UN, and Hammarskjold decided that the only thing to do was to negotiate a cease-fire with Tshombe. A meeting was arranged at Ndola in Northern Rhodesia.

We pass to the climax. Lord Lansdowne, the British Foreign Secretary, had flown to Leopoldville and discussed these plans. It was agreed he should go first to Ndola to ensure that arrangements were satisfactory, but that he should fly on to Salisbury in Rhodesia before Hammarskjöld's arrival to avoid appearance of British mediation. Hammarskjöld feared interception by a Katanga jet and flew by an indirect route. At ten o'clock the pilot radioed that he was in sight of Ndola airport, but the plane did not arrive; there was little anxiety because it was assumed rather casually that Hammarskjöld had changed his mind. When next morning there was no news of the plane's whereabouts a search was made and its wreckage was found less than ten miles from the airport. Sixteen occupants, including Hammarskjöld, were dead; the one

survivor died three days later. There was suspicion that the plane
had been shot down and both the UN and the Rhodesian Government appointed Commissions of Investigation. The Rhodesians
rejected sabotage; the UN stated that sabotage and external attack
could not be ruled out. When one remembers the circumstances
of the Lumumba assassination, doubts must remain.

A cease-fire, only temporary, was signed. Controversy persisted
about the UN attack on Katanga and O'Brien resigned to write his
book. Gizenga withdrew to Stanleyville and there was fear in the
West that he would set up a Lumumbist government which would
attract Kasai and Kivu. U Thant was appointed Hammarskjöld's
successor and the African states secured the recall of the Security
Council. At this meeting a resolution was carried on the motion of
the Afro-Asian group which would have gone far to sanction the
Khiari–O'Brien attack if it had been adopted before it occurred.
It deprecated the secessionist activities of Katanga and its armed
action against UN forces; authorised the Secretary-General to
take vigorous action, including force if necessary, for the detention
or deportation of foreign military and political personnel; requested all states to prevent the supply of war materials and declared
full support for the central government. The US representative
sought to amend the resolution to include condemnation of the
threat of Stanleyville secession, but when this was vetoed by the
Soviet Union he voted for the resolution. The British delegate was
critical and with France abstained. The resolution was adopted by
nine votes to none.

Tshombe Surrenders to UN

Hostilities broke out in Katanga on a greater scale than ever.
Mercenaries took the initiative in harassing the UN forces and
when the latter replied in self-defence open warfare developed.
America put a fleet of Globemasters at the disposal of the UN
which established domination; Tshombe surrendered; on December 21 he signed a declaration which in effect renounced Katanga's
secession.

This UN action brought strong protests from Belgium, France,
Portugal, South Africa, Rhodesia and Brazzaville Congo, but less
so from Britain and none from America. Attention turned to the
Stanleyville boycott of the central government. Gizenga had never
formally seceded, but he had established his own gendarmerie and

America pressed U Thant to act. In January when Leopoldville asked Gizenga to return within forty-eight hours he replied he would not do so until the authority of the central government was completely restored in Katanga, whereupon Adoula arrested and imprisoned him on an island at the mouth of the Congo river. The Lumumbist elements in the Leopoldville Government weakened, and it became a close ally of America, with Mobutu as head of the army asserting greater power. 'After eighteen months of struggle the Congo was left exhausted and disrupted,' wrote Catherine Hoskyns, 'but with a legal government in power and with its territory intact. For the first time since independence, what happened in the future seemed to depend more on political developments within the territory than upon the actions of outside powers.'[11]

Mobutu Assumes Presidency

Political developments soon threatened national unity. Defeated in Katanga Tshombe reasserted himself, forming a party in the Congo, the Congolese National Convention (CONACO), heavily backed by Belgian financial interests. The Left retorted by establishing an alliance of nationalist Congolese Lumumbist movements. An election gave Tshombe a disputed majority and Kasavubu insisted that a broadly-based government be set up. When Tshombe refused, the president dismissed him, and there was a political breakdown, leading to Mobutu and the army taking over again. Mobutu acted peremptorily. He dismissed Kasavubu and proclaimed himself president, ruling firmly and providing a stability which encouraged economic improvement. The new government got into conflict with Belgium by increasing the export tax on copper from seventeen to thirty per cent and insisted that Union Minière should transfer its headquarters to Kinshasa (as Leopoldville had been renamed). When this was resisted Mobutu seized the assets, but he had not the technicians to run his new company and a compromise was reached by which the Belgian *Société Générale des Minéraux* undertook the management for the Congolese. Mobutu's effective administration and assertion of Congo's independence won the confidence of African States and he was recognised by the Organisation of African Unity. In 1969 he authorised elections in November for a national assembly, followed by the election of a president in January 1970.

His supporters had established the *Mouvement Populaire de la Révolution* (MPR) which in effect absorbed the existing parties. It swept the elections and Mobutu became the president.

Death of Tshombe

Meanwhile Tshombe fled to Europe where he intrigued to regain power. In July 1966 he appeared to have instigated a mutiny by Katangese gendarmes and in his absence a military tribunal sentenced him to death. History cruelly repeated itself. With colleagues, Tshombe in July 1968 hired a plane in Spain apparently with the intention of reaching a favourable place in Africa. The plane was hijacked to Algeria and he was arrested. He died in prison.

Mobutu proceeded with Africanisation. He realised that political independence was limited and took control of the main resources and large industry. But he was brought up against the fact that the Congolese were not capable of administering the economy, let alone developing it, and that a generation would pass before they reached this stage. How to create a self-respecting psychology whilst Europeans administered? He decided to re-create pride in the country's heritage. He re-named the Congo by its historic 'Zaire'. He decreed that the people should drop any Christian names and substitute African ones (this got him into temporary trouble with the Catholic Church), and revert to African ways of life adjusted to modern conditions. The long European interventions were to be contained. Zaire would be African.[12]

Rwanda and Burundi

These two states, lying to the east of the Congo, a distant part of German East Africa and falling to Belgian forces during the First World War, were mandated by the League of Nations to administration by Brussels after the war. Their early origin is obscure, but a kingdom was established by the physically strong Tutsis, said to be mostly six feet and more in height, before the fourteenth century. The Tutsis, thought to have come from Ethiopia, subdued the Bantu Hutus, who became menial subjects of the conquering feudal lords, rich in cattle. In contrast with the Tutsis was a pygmy tribe of Twas, who sometimes relaxed from labouring by a flair as jesters and dancers; they were less than one per cent of the population. Ruanda (Rwanda after independence) was a powerful state in the fourteenth century.

The territories are small – Burundi (Urandi before independence) 10,747 square miles, Rwanda 10,166 square miles – but the populations are the densest in tropical Africa. Rwanda in 1971 had 3,830,000 people, more than 377 per square mile, Burundi 3,620,000, about 337 per square mile. Four-fifths of the population are Hutus. The economy is largely subsistence agriculture, with some cash exports in coffee and a few other articles.

Independence, Tribal Conflict

The Belgians governed from Leopoldville but differently from their direct rule in the Congo. They administered through the Tutsi chiefs, succeeding in preventing civil war between the exploited Hutus and their masters until the unrest in the Congo swept across the frontier. In 1959 there was a fierce tribal war in Rwanda, resulting in the expulsion of many Tutsis. Independence in 1960 changed the balance of power by the introduction of adult suffrage. Elections were supervised by the United Nations which proposed that the two states should federate but this was rejected by both. In Rwanda the Hutus formed the Parmelutu Party and captured the national assembly. In Burundi, despite their minority position, the Tutsis retained predominance. The Hutus in Rwanda, disatisfied by delays in reforms and after making ferocious attacks on the Tutsis, carried out a *coup* in 1961, expelling the king and establishing a republic. The Tutsis fled in large numbers to the Congo, Uganda and Burundi. From Burundi they organised raids into Rwanda, which led to severe reprisals in 1964 and large scale massacres. The Tutsis who escaped became refugees in Uganda and Tanzania.

Burundi began independence more quietly with power exercised jointly with the king, Mwambutsa IV, but by 1965 the basic conflict between Hutus and Tutsis burst into violence. Hutu officers assassinated the prime minister and attempted a *coup*; it failed, the leaders were executed, and large numbers of Hutus were massacred. The following year, however, whilst the king was absent in Europe he was deposed by his nineteen-year-old son, Ntare, who in turn was dethroned by the prime minister, Michel

Micombero. There were conflicts between rival Tutsi aristocrats; the Hutus, although eighty per cent of the population, continued in a state of serfdom. Micombero announced a republic, declared himself president, and ruled through a committee of thirteen officers. Later he introduced civilian members and succeeded in maintaining reasonable stability for a time.

In March 1972 rebellion and massacre recurred. The circumstances were confused. Apparently President Amin of Uganda obtained the consent of Micombero for the return of the young ex-king Ntare to Burundi as a private citizen. On arrival, however, he was arrested on a charge of attempting a *coup* and placed under house arrest. It was then alleged that armed supporters attempted to rescue him and that he was killed in the fighting which followed. Widespread conflict broke out and troops from Zaire arrived to assist Micombero crush the monarchists. The suppressed Hutus thereupon seized the opportunity of division among their Tutsi masters to rebel. Hundreds of Tutsis were massacred and refugees fled to Zaire, Uganda and Tanzania. At the time of writing Micombero appeared to have retained power, capturing sixty-seven of the Hutu leaders and executing twenty-three, but it remained doubtful whether the suppression of the majority as serfs could last.

Rwanda and Burundi do not provide a happy experience of independence. The preceding colonial administration did nothing to remove the injustices from which the Hutu majority suffered or to prepare the peoples for democratic practices. There would seem to be no early end to the tragic consequences.

Notes

1. *Handbook of the Congo,* issued by the Belgian Government in 1959.

2. See Report of Sir Roger Casement, British Consul in the Congo, 1904; *Red Rubber* by E. D. Morel; *The Crime of the Congo* by Sir Arthur Conan Doyle; and *The Agony of the Congo* by Ritchie Calder.

3. *Congo My Country,* with a foreword by Colin Legum.

4. See *The Congo Since Independence* by Catherine Hoskyns. Of the many books, this is the most objective, and it tells the dramatic story so vividly that it can be classed as a thriller.

5. The MNC (K) was an anti-Lumumbist split in Katanga.

PUNA (*Parti de l'Unité Nationale*) was a new local party in the Equatorial Province.

6. The Belgian Government did not recognise the independence of Katanga and was at first opposed to it, but under pressure of powerful interests gave support to Tshombe.

7. The Russian planes left simultaneously with the closure of the embassy.

8. Report of the UN Commission of Investigation into the death of Lumumba.

9. Catherine Hoskyns in *The Congo Since Independence*.

10. See *Katanga and Back* by Conor Cruise O'Brien.

11. *The Congo Since Independence*.

12. See Judith Listowel, *The Times*, May 1, 1972.

Chapter Sixteen

Liberia

Liberia was never constitutionally a colony, but it owed its inception and maintenance to Americans and has remained an American neo-colonial state.[1] In 1816 two US Government agents and two officers of the American Colonisation Society landed on the coast with the object of establishing a settlement for freed slaves. They did not succeed until 1821 when the local chiefs agreed that the society should occupy Cape Mesurado. The liberated slaves landed the following year, followed by Jehudi Ashmun, a white American who can be termed the founder of Liberia. He gave it a government and a frame of laws and initiated commerce overseas.

Independence

In 1836 Thomas Buchanan, a cousin of the president of the USA, was appointed Governor by Washington, but his successor, Jenkins Roberts, mixed Negro in race from Virginia, repudiated his office by declaring Liberia an independent Republic in 1847 when the Colonisation Society withdrew. Although European powers, not desiring an American presence in Africa, hastened to recognise sovereign Liberia, America did not do so until 1862. There was some talk of establishing an 'America in Africa'; a constitution was adopted on the American model and the idea was even mooted of creating a state composed of immigrants from America and their descendants, although there were fewer than three thousand. The idea faded, but the constitution remained.

Liberia began as a refuge for slaves, but in the interior and from unguarded stretches of the coast the trade in humans continued, leading to the British navy from neighbouring Sierra Leone intercepting illicit shipping. In fact, the kidnapping of natives persisted surreptitiously right into the 1930s with the shipment of slaves to the Spanish plantations of Fernando Po; this led to an investigation by the League of Nations and the resignation of the Liberian president and vice-president. There had earlier been disputes with France and Britain, in possession of neighbouring Ivory Coast and Sierra Leone, about borders and custom duties as well as slavery, and a frontier police force with American officers was set up.

American Aid

Meanwhile, Liberia got into such monetary difficulties that in 1909 President Theodore Roosevelt appointed a commission on financial reorganisation, and Britain, France and Germany nominated receivers with an American receiver-general to negotiate customs debts. The First World War, with supplies cut, brought a further economic crisis. After the war it was an American Corporation which rescued Liberia from bankruptcy. In 1926 the Firestone Company obtained a concession of a million acres for rubber plantations and arranged a loan for $5 million through the Finance Corporation of America. At the same time the administration of customs and internal revenue was placed in the hands of an American financial adviser, who was also given considerable powers over the budget and state expenditure. Even so, the Liberian president, Edwin Barclay, had to appeal in 1931 to the League of Nations for financial aid and unsuccessful negotiations proceeded for three years. Again the Firestone Company came to the rescue and an aid agreement was reached, accompanied by the appointment of foreign administrators and a moratorium on the $5 million loan. Edwin Barclay was an able president and recovery began, helped by the circumstances of the Second World War. Liberia's plantations were the only source for the Allies of natural rubber, and the economy and Firestones boomed. In 1942 a defence agreement was signed with the US for strategic airports and military protection of installations; roads were built, an international airport opened and a deep water harbour constructed at Monrovia. Liberia became a modern state.

African Resurgence

From as early as the 1870s a political movement among Africans had developed. It was curiously named the True Whig Party and was moderate in its aims, whilst asserting African self-respect against the white élite which had so far dominated the political scene. In 1869 the party won the elections, Edward James Royce becoming the first African president, and, despite privileged opposition, the party won every succeeding election. In 1943 William Tubman was returned president and he was head of state until 1971 when he died. Under his rule opposition from the Right decreased, but a Left arose advocating greater Africanisation. It was defeated in a disputed election.

Liberia declared war on Germany and Japan in 1944 and joined the United Nations at its inaugural conference. President Tubman gave an African image to Liberia, whilst co-operating closely with America and the West. In African affairs, nevertheless, he followed an independent line. He associated Liberia with the African Organisation of African Unity, and in co-operation with Ethiopia challenged South Africa's annexation of South West Africa at the International Court of Justice. In contrast, America's domination of the internal economy as well as its military association persisted. When in the mid-sixties world prices of rubber and iron ore (a developed production) fell steeply, the US again helped to overcome financial difficulties which affected not only the livelihood of the people but the prospects of the American companies. Economically, if not politically, Liberia had become 'America in Africa'.

Notes

1. Liberia is bordered by Sierra Leone on the north-west, Guinea on the north, the Ivory Coast on the east. Area: 43,000 square miles. Population in 1971 was estimated to be 1,570,000.

Chapter Seventeen

Portuguese Africa

(Angola, Mozambique, Guiné, Cape Verde, São Tomé)

Portuguese Africa is more than twenty times the size of Portugal. It consists of small Guiné (Bissau) on the west coast bulge of the continent, the Cape Verde and São Tomé islands (with Principe) in the Atlantic, large Angola south of the Congo, stretching far inland from the Atlantic, and on the east coast Mozambique, also large, closely involved with southern Africa. The area is vast, but much diminished from the empire of the sixteenth to nineteenth centuries which, to Portugal's disappointment, was dismembered at the Berlin Conference of 1884–5.[1] As previous chapters have recorded, Portugal was a pioneer in modern empire-making, its navigators the first Europeans since Roman, Greek and Phoenician times to reach much of Africa and Asia.

Portugal and Holland Compete

The Portuguese began their occupation of West and East Africa in the sixteenth century, Angola for slaves, Mozambique as a port of call on the route to Asia and for dreams of gold. The occupation set the pattern for colonial development: provision stations for ships and trading depots on the coast, driving inland, playing off chiefs against each other, donating land to companies for plantations and mines, encouraging settlers, enslaving the peoples. For a time Portugal was ousted from West Africa by Holland, partly reflecting the power struggle in Europe, still more because the Dutch fiercely wanted slaves for the part of Brazil they occupied in competition with Portuguese settlers. In August 1641 an armada of twenty-one ships captured Luanda, the slave port of Angola, and the island of São Tomé, the slave distribution centre. The Dutch were expelled not by Portuguese from Europe, heavily engaged in war with Spain, but by Portuguese from Brazil, who recaptured the Angolan coastal towns and São Tomé in 1648. The Brazilian plantation owners regarded Angola as their 'Black

Mother'. As early as 1575 no fewer than 2,500 slaves a year were exported to meet their requirements.[2]

Portuguese 'Provinces'

Portugal denies that it possesses any colonies; its overseas possessions are claimed to be provinces of the homeland.[3] As we have seen, this was the original conception of France; Portugal alone maintains it in Africa. Lisbon evolved an elaborate pattern based on a three-tier classification of the inhabitants; Portuguese, Portuguese Africans and Africans. The administration started on accepted lines: a Governor-General, regional officers, chiefs. Then, as a small educated élite developed among Africans, a restricted number were accepted as 'civilised'. The *Native Assistance Code* of 1921 stated the rigid qualifications: they must speak and write Portuguese, discard tribal customs, and be regularly and gainfully employed. These non-African Africans were termed *assimilados*; the vast majority outside the 'civilised' pale were *indigenas*. As late as 1960 the proportions recorded in the census were: in Angola 30,000 *assimilados* and 4,070,000 *indigenas*; in Mozambique 4,353 *assimilados* and 5,728,647 *indigenas*. This system was maintained even during the short-lived Republic of Portugal from 1910 to 1926, when the more liberal-minded were in control and some reforms attempted. Slavery had been officially abolished in 1836 (it continued nevertheless in the Angolan interior); the Republican Government made some effort to modify the abuses of forced labour, and freedom of speech and writing was for a time permitted. Under the near-fascist dictatorship of Salazar from 1932 the differential between 'civilised' and 'uncivilised' became more pronounced. The population was divided into two hide-bound sections, the *indigenas* and the *nao-indigenas*.

The great African majority of *indigenas* suffered the imposition of forced labour (camouflaged as 'obligation to work'), identity cards and exclusion from urban areas after dark and segregated places of entertainment. On the other hand, the privileged *nao-indigenas*, consisting of Portuguese, Goans (there were many) and the few African *assimilados*, were free from restrictions, although some distinction still remained between the Portuguese and Portuguese Africans. The latter had to pass a literary test; the former were automatically regarded as *nao-indigenas* although many of them were illiterate, reflecting the absence of education in Portugal itself. In 1963 all Africans were theoretically recognised as Portuguese citizens, but this did not end the distinction between the assimilated and the unassimilated. When in urban areas local councils were set up and elected representatives joined the Legislature in Lisbon, the *indigenas* were almost entirely excluded from the franchise. In the large tribal areas, where most Africans lived, the administration was completely in the hands of Portuguese officials.

Forced Labour

The political pattern reflected the economic. The assimilated and unassimilated lived in different worlds. When the slave trade was abolished, forced labour was in many respects as cruel. Slaves, like animals, had to be kept in good condition for permanent service; conscripted labourers could be exploited ruthlessly; when they became physically useless others could replace them. The Portuguese not only followed the common colonial policy of compelling Africans to work on plantations and in the towns by seizing their land and imposing unpayable taxes; they directly conscripted workers. In the seventeenth and eighteenth centuries they operated the *prazo* system under which not only the land but the lives of people over large areas were made the property of settlers and companies, officially designated *prazeiros*. The barbarity practised became so notorious that Lisbon was compelled to end the system, but in 1854 a new labour category, *leberto*, was instituted, described as a status between 'slavery and free men', under which workers could be bound to an employer for seven years. This was reduced to two years in 1875, but a new pressure for conscripting labour arose by the development of mines in the Transvaal which offered the governments of Mozambique and Angola fees for workers supplied. In 1903 the Witwatersrand Native Labour Association was given the right to recruit labour, which in practice gave them the right to round up the able-bodied in village after village. The provision of labour to South Africa became one of the mainstays of the economy.

In the years which followed there was much controversy as to whether forced labour existed in Portuguese Africa. It had been officially abolished in 1878, but a decree in 1899 laid it down that 'all natives of Portuguese overseas territories' had not only a moral but a legal obligation to work, which in effect meant that all landless Africans were liable to forced recruitment.[4] The decree was used to compel Africans without means to take jobs both in public undertakings and for private employers. As late as the 1960s, African leaders, Protestant missionaries and visiting investigators[5] charged that forced labour persisted despite re-iterated prohibition in a *Native Labour Code* of 1928 and the signature by Portugal to the *Abolition of Forced Labour Convention* of the ILO in 1959. In 1961 the ILO sent a commission to Angola and Mozambique. It reported that it had not found evidence of a direct breach of its Convention, but it cited instances of Africans who had been ordered by subordinate officials to do work against their will. A revised *Labour Code* in 1962 repeated the prohibition of forced labour, but provided that prison sentences served on natives could be replaced by sentences of hard labour on public works. Africans charged that in the villages many were arrested for technical breaches of regulations and rounded up as a labour force.

The Portuguese claimed that they were free from colour pre-judice. This was largely true in personal relations within the same social environment. When Goans, Africans and Mulattos (mixed race) became assimilated, distinction because of pigment of skin counted little; the Portuguese certainly had less sense of colour than many English and Americans. But the condition required for this equality, the acceptance of the Portuguese way of life, was in itself racial discrimination. The assumption of superiority towards the *indigenas* was always there; they were beyond the border of association. In fact, as the settler communities in Angola and Mozambique grew, they began to withdraw within themselves. White restaurants, white cinemas and white wards in hospitals appeared. However free individual Portuguese might be from colour prejudice, the circumstances of colonial occupation inevit-ably involved racial discrimination. The human challenge arose when educated Africans declined to identify themselves with the system.

Ties with South Africa

Before we turn to the African resistance in the separate territories there is a further general consideration of fundamental importance. Salazar's New State, preceded by the 1930 *Colonial Act* and reflected in the 1933 *Organic Law*, was based on the conception of the economic unity of Portugal and its overseas territories. Salazar was not at first interested in attracting foreign capital; Portugal would herself develop her Portuguese possessions. This was done with considerable success in the cotton industry. In 1925 Portugal received only 800 tons of her required 17,000 tons of raw cotton from Mozambique and Angola; by 1960 she received eighty-seven per cent. It soon became clear, however, that Portugal did not have the necessary capital to exploit fully the natural resources of the territories and Lisbon's head of state also realised that he would need allies to meet the challenge of liberation which was sweeping through Africa. From 1960 Portugal's policy changed. Legislation was introduced giving favourable incentives to investors in Mozambique and Angola. Salazar particularly realised that the future of the 'provinces' was bound closely to the fate of their neighbour South Africa, with whose government he had much in common. Thus during the sixties a vast expansion of investment from America, West Germany, Japan, France and Britain took place, and close economic ties were made with South Africa.

The climax of these financial concentrations came in the gigantic Cabora Bassa hydro-electric project in Mozambique, the largest in Africa, with the potential transmission of power over all southern and a large part of central Africa. It involved the clearance of an area half the size of England on which many Europeans would be settled. The contract was given to a South African-based consortium including the Anglo-American Corporation and West German and French combines. Banks from West Germany, France, the USA and Britain provided long-term loans and the South African Industrial Development Corporation undertook to provide approximately $70 million to the estimated cost of $360 million. In 1968 it was reported that the South African Government sent security forces to protect the area from the guerrilla forces of the Mozambique nationalist movement.

Fundamental Confrontation

This development crystalised the real confrontation in Portuguese Africa. The project itself would undoubtedly be immensely valuable for future development; but the external financial interests behind it, its association with South Africa, its imposition by the alien occupation, the stronghold it created of white power dominating the lives of thousands, and the circumstances of its construction – not least the settlement of European immigrants – were a basic challenge to the claim of the African people to decide the possession of their country. In the face of African opposition and of protests by their supporters, the Swedish ASA, part of the consortium which gained the contract, withheld participation, the Italian Government withdrew its offer of a $48 million loan, and the British Labour Government warned companies that participation might mean involvement in breaching sanctions against the illegal administration of Rhodesia.[6]

This critical event symbolised the deepest issue which faced Portugal in its overseas territories. The nationalist forces resisting Portugal were radical in ideology. They were seeking not merely to replace foreign political administrations by native administrations; they were seeking economic self-determination as well as political self-determination, a revolution in which the economy would be controlled by the people for themselves. In this they projected the fundamental question which bestrides the future of Africa. These are issues which relate to Portuguese policy in all their possessions. We turn to consider the separate territories.

Angola

Angola lies to the south of Congo, (Kinshasa) extending from the Atlantic to Zambia in the east and south to Botswana and South West Africa. It covers the vast area of 481,350 square miles and in 1970 its population was estimated to be 5,673,046 with 5,000,600 Africans, 300,000 Europeans and the rest Mulattos (mixed race).

Early Slave Traders

We have described how the Portuguese slave raiders moved into Angola. It was in 1483 that Diago Cao, explorer-navigator, anchored in the Congo river estuary and landed in the Angolan centre of the Kongo kingdom, which at that time spread across the subsequent Belgian and French Congos. Two years later he returned with the blessing of the Lisbon king and arranged for an exchange of Portuguese priests and craftsmen for a few Angolan students. This co-operation was destroyed by the slave trade which in three centuries exported more than three million captives from Angola to Brazil and the Caribbean; the coastal area was so denuded that the slave merchants had to travel three months into the interior.[7] In 1565 Paulo Dias de Novais negotiated a traffic in slaves supplied by King Mbundu, head of a large tribe in north-central Angola, and was rewarded by the proprietary lordship of the territory. He founded the city of Luanda to export his victims, but the people of Mbundu revolted against his depredations and it was in the face of growing opposition that the trade was maintained.

Resistance

The abolition of slavery was followed, as we have seen, by the institution of forced labour; resistance was so great that the Portuguese had to retreat from the territory until 1877, when Lisbon took its part in the European rush for colonial possessions at the end of the nineteenth century. Although the Berlin Conference of 1884–5 gave Portugal the whole of Angola, effective control was limited to the coast and neighbouring plateaux until the beginning of the twentieth century. When an advance was made into the interior there was violent opposition from successive tribes, but the territory was sparsely peopled and the Portuguese were able to move in.[8] Salazar's near-fascist state in the thirties boasted of its 'civilising mission in Africa', but its extending occupation was met by fierce resistance. The Mbundu had to be crushed by force, leading to a military occupation which has been described as 'the first African nation to be subjected to European rule'.[9] Queen Nzinga Mbande and many of her people moved northward and savagely attacked the Portuguese for three years; she is still regarded by Angolan Nationalists as the African Boadicea.

Further north in the Kongo kingdom, where Diago Cao had landed in 1483, but which the invaders had deserted for the southerly slave trade port of Luanda, the Portuguese returned in the seventeenth century and defeated the king in battle at Mbwila in 1665. They bled the territory of its male population and then left the native chiefs to rule the devastation bequeathed. The Portuguese intervened actively again only in 1859 to extract an oath of loyalty from a weak monarch whom they had pressured to the throne. By the 1880s they had extended their control sufficiently to impose direct rule on the kingdom and, with their eyes on the Berlin Conference, contrived again that an illiterate monarch should sign a declaration of loyal allegiance to the king of Portugal.[10] For nearly two decades Portuguese rule was not seriously challenged, the only potentially disturbing event being the arrival of Protestant missionaries, Baptists from Britain, who competed with the Catholic government-backed ascendency.

Protestant-Backed Revolt

In 1913 revolt broke. There was mounting resentment against forced labour and when the Portuguese used the king to round up workers for the cocoa plantations in São Tomé, Chief Buta, with sympathy from liberal-minded Protestants, led a resistance which spread over the whole territory, bringing the destruction of a large part of São Salvador, the kingdom's capital. The Portuguese invited the Baptist leaders, the Rev. J. S. Bowskill and Miguel Necaca, to persuade Buta to negotiate and it was believed the Governor had agreed to his demands; but without warning the police carried out large-scale arrests, including Necaca and many Protestants, with the consequence of renewed conflict. Buta destroyed what remained of São Salvador and the Portuguese destroyed pro-Buta towns (particularly Baptist schools and churches) and arrested the Rev. J. S. Bowskill on a charge of instigating the rebellion. The revolt continued until July 1915, when a general amnesty was announced; the Portuguese used it to seize Chief Buta, who died shortly afterwards in prison. The persecution of the Protestants continued. In the 1920s many Baptist evangelists were arrested for participation in another protest and their missions were forbidden to use indigenous languages in schools. Nevertheless, by their opposition to the authorities the Baptists gained popularity among Africans, increasing their membership in Kongo from 1,500 in 1930 to 15,000 (according to the official census) in 1950.

Holden Roberto's UPA

There was a conflict over the kingship in 1955 when Eduardo Pinnock, a highly educated Protestant, led a popular movement against the appointment of a Portuguese 'yes-man'. He was out-manoeuvred, but the event was of significance in the development of the nationalist struggle because Pinnock joined Barros Necaca, son of the 1914 rebel, and young Holden Roberto, Necaca's nephew in Leopoldville; Roberto was to become one of the two controversial nationalist leaders. At first their demand for independence was limited to the kingdom of Kongo and in July 1957 they established the *Uniaõ das Populações do Norto de Angola* (UPNA) to further this. The following year Roberto attended the All-African Peoples' Conference in Accra and under its influence convinced his co-leaders that they must strive for the independence of all Angola. In December the *Uniaõ das Populações de Angola* (UPA), to become historic, was born. Roberto fitted himself for his later role. He worked as a translator in the Ghanaian Bureau of African Affairs under George Padmore, sat at the feet of Franz Fanon, the philosopher of the Algerian revolution, consulted with Sékou Touré in Guinea, attended a Foreign Ministers' conference of African states at Monrovia, and flew to the General Assembly of the United Nations in New York as a disguised member of the Guinea delegation. He succeeded in getting the issue of the Portuguese colonies raised for the first time in the Assembly and, through George Hauser of the American Committee on Africa, made influential contacts in the United States. Returning home at the beginning of 1960 he attended the Second All-African Peoples' conference at Tunis, established an enduring association with President Bourguiba and met Patrice Lumumba, who invited him to mount his campaign for Angolan independence from the Congo.

Urban Resistance

This was the beginning of the UPA which arose, as we have seen, from developing resistance among African masses in the interior. Simultaneously, protests against distant rule began to grow in the cosmopolitan urban population. As in other territories with white settlers, a demand began among Europeans for a voice in the administration. They were mostly resident in Luanda, which had developed from a slave port to a modernised city; by the mid-sixties there were over sixty thousand Whites. A small group of anti-fascist Marxists campaigned quietly among educated non-Whites and Mulattos (mixed race) as well as Africans. The Mulattos numbered fifteen thousand in Luanda by 1960, the offspring of an overwhelmingly male presence of Europeans, and they were treated by the Portuguese as an élite. Nevertheless, protest against Lisbon rule emerged among them. José de Fontes Pereira became notorious for his attacks on forced labour and even advocated Angolan independence.

The opportunity for wage-earning jobs in Luanda attracted Africans and they came to number 200,000, among whom were a minority of educated *assimilados*. Their protest movement began not in Angola but in Lisbon, where in 1921 African and Mulatto students set up a *Partido Nacional Africano* (PNA) and some of them acted as hosts to the Pan-African Congress in 1923 which led to the formation of the *Liga Africana* (LA).[11] With Salazar's rise to power, however, political opposition was suppressed both in Portugal and its overseas territories and it was not until after the Second World War that organised activity re-emerged.

MPLA Established

A feature of African reaction to injustice was protest through poetry, a traditional means of expression. This happened in both Angola and Mozambique. When after the war political organisations were still prohibited, a group in Luanda, led by a young Mulatto, Viriato da Cruz, published a literary journal, *Mensagem*, with the theme 'discover your human dignity'. It was soon banned, but this had the effect of radicalising opinion and action. A number of clandestine organisations were started, including the Angolan Communist Party (PCA), and in 1956 these were federated in the broad-based *Movimento Popular de Libertaçao de Angola* (MPLA), destined to become the rival of the UPA in Angolan resistance. The MPLA was forthright, declaring for an independent state governed by a coalition of all the forces opposed to Portuguese colonialism. The political ferment which this reflected led Lisbon to install a secret police force, the *Policia Internacionale de Defesa do Estado* (PIDE) which on Easter Sunday 1959 made massive arrests. The long sentences of imprisonments imposed at secret trials aroused international attention, but the following year there were still further arrests, which so crippled the MPLA that it was forced into exile. Students in Lisbon took over the leadership, again three poets, Viriato da Cruz, who had been editor of *Mensagem*, Dr Agostinho Neto and Mario de Andrade, names to become famous.[12] Dr Neto was so popular that when he was arrested a thousand people gathered to protest in Luanda. They were fired on, twelve were killed and over two hundred were injured. The following day troops shot or arrested everyone in the two villages from which the demonstrators came.

Resistance Extends

Political agitation was concentrated in Luanda and in the north, but the central, southern and eastern interiors were not unaffected. The Portuguese slave raiders had swept into the central highlands home of the Ovimbundu and incited war between its tribes, bribing the chiefs to hand over their prisoners. When in the 1880s the slave trade ended, the Portuguese carried out a military occupation to seize land and to conscript labour for settlers, which led to a general uprising in 1902, subdued only after two years. The construction of the Benguela railway from the coast to Katanga brought European townships (e.g. Nova Angola) and Catholic and Protestant missions and schools. From their students began nominally cultural associations which initiated a secret society, mostly Catholic, *Juventude Crista de Angola* (JCA). These young Christians adopted the United Nations Declaration of Human Rights as their basis and breached isolation by contacting the UPA in the north. At the same time students from the Ovimbundu, sent by Protestant missions to Lisbon, came under the influence of the MPLA exiles there. Angola's interior was no longer isolated.

In the far south similar tendencies developed. A new town of 2,500 settlers was established at S'a da Bandeira and here a political movement arose, the *Uniaõ dos Naturais de Angola* (UNATA), suppressed but leaving an underground influence. Beyond the town, Portuguese penetration was fiercely resisted, leading to a battle with many killed at Pembe. Perhaps most influential was contact across the frontier with the South West African People's Organisation (SWAPO). The fortitude of its members in resisting South Africa's white domination moved the Angolans on the border similarly to resist the Portuguese. There was the same trend in eastern Angola, not occupied by the Portuguese until 1960. African self-reliance grew through welfare organisations started on the Northern Rhodesian model, which developed political interests. The whole of Angola was becoming alerted.

Nationalist Rivalry

The UPA and the MPLA remained the dominant political forces. They went their separate ways, Roberto declining at the Tunis All-African Peoples' Conference to merge with the MPLA delegation led by da Cruz and rejecting a plea from Ghana for unification. The MPLA, on the other hand, urged a united front. At this stage the divergence was probably due to the fact that the UPA reflected grass roots movement among Africans in the interior, evolving by experience from traditional tribalism to nationalism, whilst the MPLA was initiated by an intellectual élite in urban Luanda and the university in Lisbon, reflecting Marxist theory rather than mass struggle. The UPA set up its exiled headquarters in Leopoldville, the MPLA in Conakry in Guinea. The UPA had some trouble with Kasavubu's ABAKO party in the Congo which still stood for a Kongo kingdom, but whilst he was Prime Minister it had the support of Lumumba, who invited Roberto to use his radio to reach Angola. Whilst the UPA leader was absent at the United Nations General Assembly (which carried a resolution requiring Portugal to report annually on its colonial administration), a meeting was held in Leopoldville of local representatives of the UPA, MPLA and smaller Angolan organisations which decided to set up a united front. On his return Roberto found himself in a difficult position. Kasavubu, who had become Congo's president, sacked Lumumba from the premiership, and the UPA was denounced as 'communist' because of friendship with the deposed leader. Roberto fled to Ghana, where he was rebuffed by Nkrumah on the opposite ground that he 'was in the pay of the Americans'. In fact, one of Roberto's reasons for opposing union with the MPLA was its alleged leaning towards Communism and, returning to Leopoldville, he repudiated the united front. Cyrille Adoula, when he became Prime Minister, gave him facilities.

Armed Rebellion

The organised armed rebellion began on March 15, 1961, but it was preceded by two events which should have warned the Portuguese of the danger. It was in the centre of Angola, not the militant north, that the first major conflict occurred. In January Antonio Mariano began a campaign with strong religious undertones against forced labour on the cotton plantations. Workers burned

seeds, threw away their tools and sang hymns to Lumumba and
Mariano (popularly 'Maria') whilst they called for independence.
A general strike broke when employers, hard hit by falling prices,
withheld wages. With leaders arrested and beaten 'hell was let
loose', roads barricaded, livestock slaughtered, stores looted,
Catholic missions attacked, Europeans driven away. The Portuguese retaliated by bombing villages and pouring in troops which
crushed the rebellion at the cost of many hundred lives. Maria was
arrested, imprisoned and almost certainly executed.[13] Ten thousand
Africans became refugees in the Congo where they established a
military base for the UPA at Kasanje just across the border.

In Luanda the conflict arose from strange circumstances. It was
expected that the hijacked luxury liner *Santa Maria*, seized by
anti-Salazar democrats, would reach the city. The MPLA planned
to use the occasion for a rising (though in fact the liner did not
arrive), and in February several hundred Africans attacked gaols
to release political prisoners. They were machine-gunned, but
several police were also killed. The police revenged these deaths by
nightly assaults in the African ghettoes, hauling men from their
huts, shooting them and leaving their bodies in the streets. A
Methodist missionary said he knew personally of the deaths of
almost three hundred.[14] African reaction was to prepare for a
wider rebellion. Many MPLA militants left for the interior to
organise the Mbundu for action.

The UPA schemed the March 15 rebellion to coincide with the
meeting of the United Nations Security Council where Liberia was
to support a demand from Roberto for the withdrawal of Portuguese troops. On March 10, with plans for synchronised action in
Angola complete, the UPA leader departed for New York leaving
Joao Batista, an ex-conscript in the Portuguese army, in command.[15]
On the appointed day there was a general uprising in the north.
The UPA had given instructions that Portuguese property and not
persons were to be attacked, but hundreds of Portuguese were
killed. The first results were greater than the UPA expected. They
found themselves in control of villages and deserted towns as far
as the Mbundu border; but they were unequipped with modern
arms and the Portuguese launched a powerful counter-offensive,
bombing and machine-gunning. Thousands of Africans were
killed and 150,000 refugees crossed to the Congo. The UPA
nevertheless retained control of a considerable area and Batista
established military headquarters at Bemba, well within Angolan
territory. From here he organised a continuing guerrilla campaign.

The Portuguese claimed that Communists and Protestants were responsible for the rebellion. The Baptist missionaries were expelled and their churches and schools destroyed or closed down.

International Support

Despite the critical stage reached in the Angolan struggle, the rivalry between the UPA and the MPLA persisted. The UPA gained prestige from the March rebellion, which the MPLA met by consolidating its contacts with African movements and governments. Its greatest success was at Casablanca where an alliance was formed with the nationalist forces of Mozambique and Guiné in the *Conferencia das Organizacoes Nacionalistas das Colonias Portuguesas* (CONCP). The MPLA leader, Mario de Andrade, succeeded in gaining the confidence of Afro-Asians and European liberals, as well as of Moscow, in contrast with Roberto whose support lay among American liberals. In London by MPLA initiative a Council for Freedom in Portugal and Colonies was formed, uniting Leftist Labour members with representatives of the Portuguese opposition. It had considerable influence in getting Dr Agostinho Neto, the MPLA's honorary president, transferred from a Lisbon prison to house arrest. Andrade also wooed the goodwill of the moderate ex-French colonies, and particularly of President Senghor of Senegal. At a seminar in New Delhi called by the Indian Council for Africa an extravagant plan, subsequently endorsed by the MPLA and CONCP, was put forward for an African expeditionary force 'to help national liberation movements overthrow Portuguese rule'. In September 1961 Andrade established an association of students from Angola, Mozambique and Guinea to co-operate with CONCP. All these approaches gave the MPLA a greater international standing outside America than the UPA.

In October the MPLA moved its headquarters from Conakry to Leopoldville and later that year succeeded in getting the Congolese Minister of Interior to allow it to run the Angolan broadcasts. Andrade renewed his efforts to persuade the UPA to co-operate in a common military front without avail. A bitter conflict arose between the forces even in Angola. UPA strength was in the Bakongo region in the north, MPLA strength in the central area of Mbundu and in Luanda. The UPA charged the MPLA with poaching its bases and a commander who had defected to the

MPLA was ambushed by UPA militia and put to death with his squad. This division facilitated Portuguese recovery. By the end of the year their troops had reoccupied the major centres and the rebels were driven to the villages, forests and mountains. From these hidden bases they conducted continuous guerrilla warfare, with ambushes and raids on plantations and transport, and the Portuguese became prisoners in their towns. The Nationalists in the north suffered a severe loss in 1962 by the death in battle of their twenty-eight-year-old commander, Batista.

Government in Exile

The year 1962 saw the formation of a government in exile by the UPA in Leopoldville. It was supported by an independent faction, the *Partido Africano de Independência* (PDA), the two parties joining in a *Frente Nacional de Libertação de Angola* (FNLA), which gave the UPA a wider image. Roberto became president of the proclaimed Government, but it failed to obtain recognition from African states following denunciation from the MPLA. Nigeria, whilst offering to train medical and administrative staff, refused military and police training; Tunisia continued aid in arms and finance, and Ethiopia and Liberia gave limited help; Algeria assisted both the UPA and the MPLA by training officers and reflected a widespread view deploring disunity. The most substantial help the UPA received was from the Congolese Government which placed at its disposal a disused military camp where an extended Liberation Army was trained.

The UPA broke through its isolation in Africa in two directions. During 1962 Roberto negotiated an alliance with the South West African Nationalists, SWAPO, which gave it some standing in southern Angola, and in February, attending a conference of the Pan-African Freedom Movement for East and Central Africa at Addis Ababa, the UPA became the sole Angolan affiliate when the decision was taken to intervene in the Portuguese-occupied territories. This assumed still greater importance when in 1963 the Organisation of African Unity representing all the independent African states, also assumed this responsibility.

Bitterness between the rival movements increased, the UPA spreading the charge that the MPLA was communist-dominated. This had some effect within the MPLA itself, leading to the dismissal of da Cruz, the Marxist secretary, and to a declaration by

Andrade of neutralism in the Cold War. A prospect of reconciliation occurred when in July 1962 Dr Agostinho Neto escaped from detention in Portugal. He was universally respected and it was hoped he would be an arbiter, but the opportunity passed when at a joint conference he allied himself with the MPLA. Distinct from UPA and MPLA a further force, UNITA, based from Zambia, operated in the South and occupied considerable territory.[16]

NATO Arms

On the international scene, Britain, the West European nations and the USA were inhibited by their association with Portugal in NATO. Britain and America claimed they did not provide military assistance which could be used in Africa, but Portugal insisted on its rights to employ NATO-equipped troops, and at the United Nations in 1962 the US delegate admitted that arms from NATO countries had been sent to Angola; Washington had protested, but Lisbon had continued to use them. The election of John F. Kennedy as president temporarily brought a stiffening of attitude. On his instructions America voted for a resolution at the 1961 General Assembly calling upon the Portuguese Government to consider urgently the introduction of reforms in Angola to prepare for independence. Lisbon was affronted, but nevertheless announced some reforms, including the recognition of all inhabitants in overseas territories (not merely *assimilados*) as citizens, its preparations for local elections and the protection of Africans against inequitable land appropriation.[17] Under pressure from Britain and France, President Kennedy retreated. At the December 1962 General Assembly the US voted with five NATO allies against a resolution, carried by 81 to 7 with 13 abstentions (8 NATO), which condemned Portugal and urged governments to cease arms supplies to Lisbon. This change of attitude by the US was due not only to loyalty to NATO nations and fear of communist penetration of Angola, but to a reaction towards Portugal following the Indian occupation of Goa and, perhaps mostly, to a desire to retain US military bases in Azores leased by Portugal.[18] The effect of the Western rally to Lisbon was to arouse a wave of anti-Americanism among African, Asian, and some Latin American countries.

Conflict Unresolved

The war in Angola continued all through the sixties into the seventies and, at the time of writing, is unresolved. It was difficult to determine how much territory the Nationalists controlled and how far the Portuguese dominated the scene. Lisbon declared the war was over, but this clearly was not the case. Whilst it would appear that government forces maintained authority in the towns and in the villages on the main roads, there was evidence that in the villages of the interior, in the bush and the mountainsides the guerrilla forces held sway, dominating a considerable area particularly in the north, establishing administration, and even schools and a rudimentary health service.

The size of the guerrilla force was comparatively small, probably not more than five thousand and they were poorly equipped with weapons captured from the Portuguese in ambushes, supplemented by arms from the Congo, some guns even left behind by the UN force; despite Portuguese propaganda, it did not seem that a significant supply had come from communist countries. No figure can be given of Africans killed; the estimates vary from ten thousand to thirty thousand. It is doubtful whether the fatal casualties among the Portuguese reached a thousand.[19] Nevertheless, time seemed to be on the side of the Nationalists; trained officers were arriving from Algeria and the number of men trained in the Congo was growing. Probably in the long run political pressures will be most important, through African independent states, the United Nations, within NATO and perhaps in Portugal itself. At some point Angolan self-government, maybe through military confrontation, maybe through political insistence, will become inescapable.

Mozambique

Mozambique is smaller in area than Angola, 303,070 square miles, but has a larger population; 8,233,034 at the 1970 Census (in 1964 it was 6,592,994). The first Portuguese contact was at the beginning of the sixteenth century when Vasco da Gama rounded the Cape. The inland territory was occupied by Arab rulers whose wealth attracted the adventurous Portuguese, and they succeeded in gaining a monopoly of trade in ivory, gold and precious stones. From the beginning of the eighteenth century there was a gold rush into the further interior to the alleged King Solomon's mines at Monomotape, extending to Zambia and Southern Rhodesia. At the end of the century a temporary Arab resurgence drove the Portuguese from many of their settlements, but they regained control and consolidated their authority in the northern and central areas. Catholic missionaries arrived, co-operating closely with the administration and traders, coming into conflict with the Muslims.

Resistance Crushed

The Berlin Conference of 1884–5 assigned Mozambique to Portugal, but in 1895 there was fierce African resistance in Gaza, the last of the traditional kingdoms. After three years Emperor Gunguntiana was captured and deported to Portugal, but armed opposition was only finally crushed in 1918. During the early twentieth century the Portuguese established their administration firmly, following the appointment of Antonio Enes as Royal Commissioner in 1894 and of General Mousintio de Albuquerque, conqueror of Gaza, who succeeded him. Rule was set up under a Governor-General, provincial governors (*intendentes*), district officers (*chefes do postos*) and chiefs. Land was leased to Portuguese companies which established plantations for sugar, sisal and cotton and traded in minerals, timber, rubber, palm oil, hides and fisheries with a large conscripted labour force. In two areas, the Niassa and Moçambique (62,000 square miles), the companies were given full administrative power. In 1901 all land not privately owned was declared the property of the administration and African reserves were founded.

Superficially the Portuguese possessions were untouched by the wave of self-determination which followed the Second World War, except among a small group of Nationalists, but the Indian claim to Goa directed attention to the colonial issue, and it exploded in the Angola uprising of 1961 (already described), leading to United Nations resolutions. The result was the *New Overseas Organic Law*, which, on paper at least, set up elected Councils and representation in Lisbon; the electoral roll for the 1964 elections in Mozambique showed how unreal this citizenship was. In the population of 6,592,944 there were only 93,079 qualified voters.

Social Structure

The *prazo*, *liberto* and *assimilado* systems (described above) were applied in Mozambique. Only a trivial number of Africans became assimilated. Figures in 1950 gave the following breakdown of the racial composition of this privileged class: Whites, 67,485; Asian, 17,144; Mulattos, 29,507, and Africans, 4,555. A study published in Lisbon in 1964 divided the population into three socio-economic strata. The smallest were the Westernised group as above, only 2·5 per cent of the population. The second group were mostly Africans serving on the fringe of urban and mineral development, unassimilated but divorced from tribal life. They constituted 3·5 per cent. But the overwhelming majority, 94 per cent, were the African *indigena* peasants, existing on subsistence growth of their own food, supplemented by occasional urban wage-work and a few cash sales.[20] Thus all but six per cent of the people were outlawed and unprotected. The same division was expressed in education. There were two systems – primary education by the Catholic missions and state secondary education for the children of the *assimilados*. Very few African children attended even the primary schools. In 1963 of the 25,742 pupils only one-fifth were African. The proportion in the secondary schools, where education was compulsory for the Portuguese-identified, whether European, Asian or African, was a mere six per cent. Illiteracy among Africans was between 95 and 98 per cent as late as the sixties.

Resistance Renewed

The modern nationalist movement was distinct from the earlier resistance of chiefs defending their kingdoms. One stream came from peasants in the north who in the fifties formed a co-operative society for the sale of their produce and the purchase of seeds and fertilisers. The Portuguese placed restrictions on their activities, imposed levies on their sales, and even kept their meetings under surveillance. The African reaction was hostility and political orientation which later became significant. Among their members was Mzee Lavaro Kavandame, to become prominent in the Mozambique Liberation Front (FRELIMO). Simultaneously groups began to grow among educated Africans and Mulattos in the towns, protesting against particular injustices, gradually developing opposition to the colonial system itself. Political associations were not allowed, but, as told above, in 1920 students in Lisbon established the *Liga Africana* (LA) which sent representatives to the Pan-Africanist conference in England in 1923 and actually acted as brave hosts to a second session. There were only twenty of them, but they contributed to the later realisation that the national struggle should unite resistance in all the Portuguese overseas territories.

In Mozambique itself a number of organisations were formed, legally limited to mutual aid and cultural or athletic activities, but which increasingly became political. Ironically it was a group of Whites born in Mozambique, the *Associação dos Naturais de Moçambique*, set up to claim democratic rights against authoritarian rule, which became most influential. It linked together liberals who opposed racism and later opened its doors to Africans, Asians and Mulattos. The different ethnic groups also had their separate organisations, all beginning to press for democracy, and the African group, *Associação Africana* (AA) established a paper, *O Brado Africano* (The African Cry) which was outspoken in moving human terms, as this extract indicates:

'We want to be treated in the same way that you are. We do not aspire to the comforts you surround yourselves with – thanks to our strength. We do not aspire to your refined education . . . even less do we aspire to a life dominated by the idea of robbing your brother . . . We aspire to our 'savage state' which, however, fills your mouths and your pockets. And we demand something . . . bread and light.'[21]

The paper was suppressed in 1936. The Salazar dictatorship succeeded by clever infiltration in subverting the different racial groups, even to the point that some of them became apologists for Portugal.

Intellectuals Protest

It was not until half-way through the twentieth century that nationalist activity resurged. It arose from different sources. As in the Congo, school associations contributed largely. In 1949 African Secondary School Students formed the *Nucleo dos Estudantes Africanos Secundários de Moçambique* (NESAM), which under cover of social and educational activities conducted a

political campaign against cultural subjection and for independence. Many of its members were arrested, including Eduardo
Mondlane,[22] but it survived until the sixties and established a network of contacts, including past students who later became
important in the national movement. In 1964 NESAM was banned
and members seeking to reach Zambia were arrested by Rhodesian
and South African police; seventy-five were still detained in
Mombazia four years later. The initiative of the school students
was followed by University students who formed a union in
Mozambique which became part of the liberation movement
centred in Lisbon; other University organisations were started
which lived precariously because of police attention. Adult
intellectuals also helped to create the atmosphere of national
revival. A remarkable group of painters, poets and writers, inspired
by their faith in Africa, compelled attention. The poet Craveirinha
and author Honwana (his short stories were appreciated outside
Africa) suffered imprisonment, and the poet dos Santos became
active in the liberation movement.

Mozambique's 'Sharpeville'

There was a serious weakness in the élite nationalist movement.
It had no contact with the ninety per cent of the population who
were peasants. On June 16, 1960, however, an appalling occurrence
shocked them into support. In the north, as we have seen, there had
been initiative in the formation of a peasants' co-operative. That
failed because of government obstruction, but the activities of
Kavandame, the leader, aroused demands for 'more liberty and
more pay' in many villages. The police authorities encouraged the
villagers to attend a meeting with the Governor at Mueda, and
Kavandame rallied several thousands to it. The Governor held
discussion with representatives in his office and invited spokesmen
from the crowd. When several indicated their eagerness to speak
they were ordered to stand aside, and the police tied their hands.
This was done with some roughness leading to angry protests from
the crowd, who, when an attempt was made to drive the men away
in police trucks, surrounded the vehicles to stop them. Violent
exchanges followed, but there was little justification for the order
which the Governor then gave to troops, hidden in the background,
to fire. The demonstrators estimated that over five hundred were
killed; certainly several hundred were. The Government in Lisbon

did not deny that excessive force was used; they dismissed the Governor. But the psychological effect was deep. To Mozambique this tragedy was what Amritsar was to India and Sharpeville to South Africa. All hope of co-operation with the Portuguese disappeared, particularly in the north. Africans concluded that they must win independence by force.

The workers in the towns were also involved in violent conflicts. A series of strikes which had political undertones took place by dockers at Lourenço Marques, Beira and Nacala. The strikers were fired on, over forty were killed and several hundred deported to São Tomé. These incidents stirred the coastal towns as the Mueda massacre had incited the interior. The mood of the people was ready for action.

FRELIMO

The mobilisation of Mozambique's militant national movement took place in neighbouring countries beyond the reach of the secret police and security forces. At first there were three separate organisations – one started in Salisbury, Rhodesia, one by groups in Tanzania and Kenya, one by exiles in Malawi; each established headquarters in Dar-es-Salaam and decided to unite. On June 25, 1962, the Mozambique Liberation Front (FRELIMO) was born and its inaugural conference was held in September attended by many adherents in Mozambique who clandestinely crossed and recrossed the frontier. From the first FRELIMO was committed to an armed struggle, but its leaders realised the gravity of the decision and spent two years in comprehensive preparation. Two hundred young volunteers were accepted for military training by Algeria, which had just concluded its seven years' war against the French, and Tanzania placed a camp at the disposal of FRELIMO at Bagamayo.[23] The freedom leaders soon appreciated that an educational programme was as necessary as military training because of the shortage of technical personnel due to the absence of higher education in Mozambique. They set up a secondary school in Dar-es-Salaam and scholarships abroad were provided for older students. Within the growing army educational courses were also organised and detailed preparations were made for schools within Mozambique as areas came to be liberated. FRELIMO established permanent missions in Cairo, Algiers and Lusaka to facilitate international co-operation.

The movement did not avoid splits, largely due either to personal rivalries or impatience with the delay in action required by preparation. One of the breakaway organisations, COREMO, independently invaded the Tete region of Mozambique in 1965, but it was crushed. Six thousand refugees fled to Zambia.

Eduardo Mondlane

The leadership of FRELIMO was collective and it avoided personality cults. The part played by its president, Eduardo Mondlane, however, was outstanding. His ability was largely responsible for the thoroughness and width of organisation. Born in 1920 in the Gaza district of southern Mozambique, he went to a mission primary school and, denied secondary education, taught himself English and won a scholarship to a high school in Transvaal and to the social science section of Witwatersrand University. With an American scholarship he proceeded to Lisbon University, but he was so harassed by the police that he contrived to transfer to the USA where he gained arts and philosophy degrees at the North Western University in Illinois. After doing research work at Harvard, he joined the United Nations Trusteeship staff. Visiting Mozambique in 1961 he decided to devote himself to its national cause. The Mueda massacre convinced him that a military uprising was necessary and he left for Tanzania to organise it. He did much to bring the separate movements together and was elected president of FRELIMO. When the armed struggle began in 1964 he was its guiding genius, often entering Mozambique in connection both with the military and reconstruction activities. He was assassinated in Dar-es-Salaam on February 3, 1969, in circumstances to be described.

Invasion

FRELIMO began its war on September 25, 1964. The invading force was only 250 trained men, but the fifth column prepared within Mozambique was much larger, taking possession of many villages. Guerrilla tactics kept a large Portuguese force stretched over the four northern provinces of Niassa, Cabo Delgado, Tete and Zambezia. Reinforced Portuguese troops reconquered Zambezia and regained strategic control of most of Tete, but the larger part of the two northernmost provinces were occupied by FRELIMO and became 'liberated areas' under its administration, leaving only a few towns under besieged Portuguese control. The fighting came to a stalemate in 1965 and 1966, but meanwhile FRELIMO was strengthened greatly by recruits within Mozambique. It is claimed that by 1967 its military strength was eight thousand and in addition it established in the liberated villages a people's militia of all adults, who continued their work as peasant cultivators but trained daily. The mobilisation of women had a revolutionary effect on social life. They shed subservience, insisted on selecting women officers and became militant propagandists.

Conflicting estimates were advanced on how far FRELIMO occupied Mozambique. Most of the northernmost provinces of Niassa and Cabo Dalgado on the borders of Tanzania passed into nationalist administration, with co-operative organisation of peasant production and education and health services. Perhaps early in 1970 one-sixth of the territory of Mozambique was in FRELIMO hands, but that year the Portuguese began an offensive which they claimed was successful. Tete, cut off by the independent state of Malawi, became critical. The guerrillas maintained constant ambushing and raids, but the Portuguese concentrated troops and bombing in the province because it was the core of plans for economic expansion and colonisation. Lisbon launched the Zambezi Valley Development project with the powerful hydro-electric dam at Cabora Bassa already described. To protect it South Africa sent in forces and the Portuguese supplemented their napalm bombing by the wide spraying of defoliants to destroy cultivation in the 'liberated' areas. Northern Mozambique was becoming a Vietnam.

Mondlane Assassinated

The nationalist forces suffered a deep disaster in February 1969, when Eduardo Mondlane was assassinated in Dar-es-Salaam. He was killed as he was opening a parcel bearing a West German postmark which exploded in his hands. His friends assumed that a Portuguese foreign agency was responsible, but the Tanzanian police found that the postmark was faked and suspicion arose that someone in FRELIMO had been bribed to post it. Mondlane's death deprived the Nationalists of a pre-eminently able freedom fighter. It was a tragedy that his gifts had to be devoted to rebellion; he would have been a great constructive statesman under self-government.

FRELIMO was for a time disrupted in controversy about his successor. Temporarily leadership was in the hands of a triumvirate including Uriah Simango, afterwards a figure of controversy. Kavandame surprisingly defected to the Portuguese, apparently impressed by the grant of citizenship to all,[24] and he tried to persuade the guerrillas of his Makonde tribe to follow him; on the other wing Simango and his supporters were expelled as extremists. After a year, the commander of the forces in northern Mozambique, Samora Moises Machel, was appointed president and Marcelino Dos Santos, the veteran literary intellectual, vice-president, becoming the main spokesman in Dar-es-Salaam. FRELIMO was by now a mass movement, spontaneously dynamic, too strong and dedicated to be more than temporarily weakened by leadership difficulties. It faces a powerful Portuguese–South African alliance, but few even in Lisbon doubt that freedom approaches.

Guiné (Bissau)

Portuguese Guinea or Guiné (Bissau) cuts into the west coast of Africa between Senegal and the Republic of Guinea. The area is 13,948 square miles. The population at the 1960 census was 521,336, including about two thousand Europeans and four thousand Mulattos.

Portuguese Penetration

Portuguese exploring traders reached the coast half-way through the fifteenth century. Slaves were the prize. 'Here you can buy slaves at the rate of six or seven for a horse, even a bad horse,' wrote one navigator in 1506.[25] The traders did not invade, satisfied with setting up coastal depots, the chief of which was at Bissau, later the capital. Even when in 1886 the frontiers were settled with France, occupying the surrounding inland, there was little Portuguese presence and when the invaders attempted to claim possession from successive tribes there was resistance which persisted until 1915. Guinea did not suffer occupation as much as Angola and Mozambique because there was little European settlement and less forced labour; the greatest exploitation was the compulsory cultivation of cash crops for export by the trading monopoly, União Fabril, which meant that there was less food for existence. Under the military rule imposed in 1926, and still more after the Salazar dictatorship in 1932, no political activities were allowed.

Amilcar Cabral

The beginning of the later resistance, as in Angola, arose from the friendship of four students in Lisbon, Agostinho Neto, Mario de Andrade and Viriato da Cruz, already mentioned as Angolan leaders, and Amilcar Cabral, the inspirer and organiser of the subsequent rebellion in Guiné. In 1948 they formed a Centre for African Studies, one purpose of which was to re-Africanise themselves; they became conscious that as *assimilados* they were alienated – their only fluent language was Portuguese – and they devoted themselves to learning their native tongues and the history and conditions of their peoples. Inevitably their discussions turned to politics and they dedicated their lives to national and social emancipation. Cabral returned to Guiné and to gain experience joined the administration. His job was the preparation of an agricultural census and for two years he travelled the country, gaining an intimate knowledge of the life of the villagers. He got into trouble in 1953 for criticising Portuguese rule and left for Angola where, with Agostinho Neto, he became a foundation member of the MPLA. This incited him to start a resistance movement in his own Guiné; he returned to Bissau and in September 1956, with five friends, clandestinely formed the *Partido Africano da Independência da Guiné e Cabo Verde* (PAIGC). They began by making peaceful appeals for democratic self-rule, but in August 1959 an event occurred which changed the psychology of the struggle. When the dock workers at Bissau struck for higher wages they were shot down by the police and over forty were killed. On September 19 the leaders of PAIGC, still with only a hundred or so members, declared for the overthrow of the Portuguese regime 'by all possible means, including war'.

Peasant Education

Cabral and his associates knew that the conditions did not permit an armed rising; but they began carefully preparing. They sought

volunteers and opened a training centre in Conakry in neighbouring radical Guinea. Cabral himself prepared his recruits, men
and women, not only for guerrilla warfare but for a campaign to
win the support of the unreached peasant population. The PAIGC
leaders were not concerned merely with political independence.
They were unimpressed by what had happened in some of the
independent African states where a political élite had replaced
colonial rulers, but where the life of the people had changed
little. They aimed at a revolution in which all the people, mainly
villagers, would join in building a participating democratic society.[26]
The first necessity, therefore, was to win the allegiance of the
peasants. For three years the members of the party went to the
villages, discussing grievances with growing groups, forming
cadres of the convinced, spreading from region to region. By the
end of 1962 they believed they had sufficient adherents to start
armed action.

From Guerrillas to Army

They began mostly with limited guerrilla action by the original
PAIGC recruits in the towns and the volunteers trained at Conakry.
Within a year peasants joined actively in large numbers, not only
in full-time guerrilla service but in Peoples' Militias of working
villagers. In 1964 a disciplined force had emerged which took on
the character of a regular army capable of mobile attacks on
Portuguese garrisons. As the seventies were approached assaults
on towns, the Portuguese strongholds, took place. To repel the
growing rebellion heavy reinforcements were sent from Lisbon,
reaching thirty thousand. Bombing, including the use of napalm,
was continuous; but increasingly the Portuguese were confined to
Bissau and two scattered towns, many of which could be reached
only by air, and to distant regions. They held on to a large portion
of the east, a considerable part of the north-west and the coastal
area around Bissau, but the vast centre, amounting to nearly two-
thirds of the territory, passed into PAIGC control. In this 'liberated
Guiné' village committees organised expanding cultivation,
people's shops, schools and health services. Creator of this social
development was Amilcar Cabral. He was little known among
African leaders, but in personality and ability proved himself
exceptional. He contributed not only the ideological basis of the
Guiné uprising, but gained the allegiance of the people by their

instinctive sense of his identity with them in the wrongs they suffered.[27]

International Support

The PAIGC always insisted that the liberation of Guiné could be gained only by its own people, but help was welcomed from others. It came from two neighbours; revolutionary Guinea, and after some hesitation from the more moderate Senegal. Sékou Touré, Guinea's head of state, not only facilitated the preparatory training, but provided a corridor for arms for trainees in other countries. President Leopold Senghor in Senegal at first supported an *émigrés'* group in FLING who regarded PAIGC as extreme, but in 1967 Cabral was invited as a fraternal delegate to his party conference and agreement was reached, necessarily secret, for support.

The PAIGC was a little disappointed by the extent of material aid received from other African states. Their struggle received early endorsement from the Casablanca group and later from the Organisation of African Unity and its Liberation Committee, but, perhaps understandably, Guiné was not regarded as important as Rhodesia, South Africa or Angola and Mozambique. The greatest help came from communist countries – arms from the Soviet Union and Czechoslovakia, uniforms from Cuba, nurses from Moscow, technical advisers for co-operatives from Yugoslavia. Five hundred fighters were trained in Moscow and a small group of officers went through a course at Nanking Military Academy in China. Cabral nevertheless insisted on non-alignment and made clear that help without strings would be welcomed from elsewhere. On one point emphasis was laid: foreigners were not acceptable in PAIGC military activity. 'We want no volunteers,' said Cabral to Basil Davidson.

Guiné's Isolation

The freedom fighters in Guiné were saved from the two most formidable obstructions which their fellows in Mozambique and Angola faced: there was little foreign investment owing to the absence of known valued natural resources and there was not the close involvement with South Africa. This difference was a decisive factor in determining the course of the struggle. Portugal did not have the interested support of large financial interests in the West and was without the military aid of a near-by ally. It may well be that the PAIGC will be the first to succeed in achieving independence in the Portuguese territories.[28]

Cape Verde Islands

The islands form an archipelago, crescent in shape, 280 miles from the West African coast, a little north-west of Guiné. There are fourteen islands with a total area of 1,557 square miles.[29] From the first the PAIGC (*Partido Africano da Independência da Guiné e Cabo Verde*) included the Cape Verde Islands, administered with Guiné, in its objectives, but the task of achieving independence and social revolution was more difficult for both historical and immediate reasons.

The islands were not only distant, they were distinct in population. Lisbon began its occupation in the fifteenth century through the invasion of slave traders and settlers who employed slaves on their plantations. The Portuguese were almost exclusively males with the consequence that nearly three-quarters of the subsequent inhabitants came to be Mulattos, who sought to identify themselves with the Europeans rather than with Africans. Of immediate significance the islands, unlike Guiné, were linked with South Africa which had an air-base there. The Portuguese could therefore look for military support.

PAIGC Contacts

Nevertheless, Cabral claimed that his party had made advances, establishing groups with African and Mulatto membership. Early armed resistance was not considered, but the Portuguese appeared to be alarmed when they came to know that political action was in preparation. They disbanded the groups forcibly and arrested and deported many PAIGC supporters.

The islands would be isolated if the Portuguese withdrew from Guiné but would not necessarily become independent simultaneously. Pressure for self-government is likely to arise from the European settlers and Mulattos to supplement the more extreme demands of the Africans.

São Tomé and Principe

São Tomé and Principe lie in the Atlantic off the coast of Gabon. Their total area is 372 square miles of which São Tomé, much the larger, occupied 330. The population was stated to be 73,811 by the 1970 census, of whom 4,605 lived on Principe. About 1,200 were Europeans and 4,300 Mulattos.

Forced Labour Scandals

As we have already said, São Tomé was the most important slave distribution centre in West Africa and for a time its commercial power dominated even coastal Congo. After slavery was abolished, the island developed in two directions: it became a rich cocoa plantation territory and a penal colony. Thousands of Angolans continued to be shipped both to São Tomé and nearby Principe, no longer nominally as slaves but almost undistinguishably as forced labour, supplemented by prisoners, sometimes for illusory offences such as vagrancy, sometimes for failure to pay taxes, sometimes as political troublemakers. In 1865 British members of the English–Portuguese Commission on Slaving protested that Negroes were conveyed *en masse* to the cocoa plantations, and thirty years later a Governor of Guiné, Justice Baker, courageously exposed in detail what happened, describing how workers were purchased in the interior of Angola, brought in chains to Benguela docks, officially registered as permissible contract labour, and crowded in the holds of ships to São Tomé. The contract was for five years, but Justice Baker wrote that no one ever returned, all victims of malnutrition and brutality. International attention was drawn to this scandal by an investigation which the well known English writer, H. W. Nevinson, made for *Harper's*.[30]

William Cadbury, head of the British cocoa company, sent his agent, Joseph Burtt, to report[31] and his firm and other firms decided to boycott São Tomé produce. Further exposures followed[32] and pressure from London led in 1917 to a large repatriation of the Angolan victims. By the time of the census of 1950, in contrast with the low proportion in Angola and Mozambique, more than half the non-white population had become theoretically equal with the Europeans. Some success attended efforts to encourage free labour by grants of land, houses and education and a high proportion of assimilated Africans were enrolled.

Massacre and Reforms

Grievances nevertheless continued, and São Tomé had its massacre. In 1953 African peasant-farmers joined workers in demonstrating against the indifference of the administration to their wrongs, and over one hundred were shot dead. The Portuguese reacted to public horror by further reforms. In 1953, both in São Tomé and Principe the *regime do indigenato* was abolished, which meant that all Africans were regarded as assimilated. The Portuguese boasted that their mission of racial equality had been accomplished.

African Nationalists recognise that these islands will probably be the last citadel of Portuguese occupation in West Africa.

Notes

1. Britain (Sir Edward Grey) and Germany sought subsequently to dismember the Portuguese territories still further. See James Duffy, *Portugal in Africa*.

2. *Portugal in Africa* by James Duffy.

3. This designation was not made officially until 1951. Portugal hoped to avoid decisions by the United Nations relating to colonial administration.

4. The decree was discreetly worded: 'All natives of Portuguese overseas provinces are subjected to the obligation, moral and legal, of attempting to obtain through work the means that they lack to subsist and to better their social conditions.'

5. See *The African Awakening* by Basil Davidson.

6. Lord Shepherd, House of Lords, December 1969.

7. Douglas Wheeler, *Race Relations in the Portuguese Colonial Empire, 1413–1825*.

8. There was a suggestion before the First World War that a 'home for the Jews' should be established in Angola.

9. David Birmingham in *The Portuguese Conquest of Angola*.

10. According to John Marcum in *The Angolan Revolution*, Volume 1, the king thought he was signing an expression of gratitude for the gift of a gold-backed chair.

11. A co-ordination of nationalist movements in the various Portuguese territories.

12. See later references under Guiné (Bissau).

13. John Marcum states in *The Angolan Revolution* that when Maria's mother brought food to the prison she was told not to bother any more. 'This was the customary if indirect way of informing relatives or friends of an African prisoner's death.'

14. John Marcum in *The Angolan Revolution*.

15. It would seem that the UPA did not expect to drive out the Portuguese, but hoped the conflict would arouse sufficient support in the United Nations to bring their withdrawal.

16. Later negotiations were begun for the union of MPLA and the UPA. It was announced early in 1973 that agreement had been reached.

17. African Nationalists rejected the reforms as inadequate and in fact they had little effect.

18. The lease was due to expire in December 1962. The Portuguese hoping to continue pressure on the US, extended the lease only on an *ad hoc* basis.

19. *Portugal in Africa* by James Duffy.

20. *Promoção Social Em Mocambique* in *Junta da Investigacto do Utramar* (Lisbon, 1964).

21. Quoted by Eduardo Mondlane in *The Struggle for Mozambique*.

22. Later President of FRELIMO. See his biography on page 412.

23. Mondlane points out in *The Struggle for Mozambique* the significance of this venue. Bagamayo means 'broken heart' and it was so named because it was a dispatching point of slaves to the East. Later Bagamayo became the capital of the German occupation of East Africa. FRELIMO now reversed its history.

24. The right to vote was limited to the literate. In Mozambique 99 per cent of Africans were illiterate.

25. Duarte Pacheco Pereira, quoted by Basil Davidson in *The Liberation of Guiné*.

26. See Basil Davidson's *The Liberation of Guiné*, authoritative after personal investigation.

27. The personality of Cabral is revealed in his contribution to Basil Davidson's *The Liberation of Guiné*. His foreword is a continuous poem.

28. On January 21, 1973, Amilcar Cabral was assassinated in Conakry.

29. The combined population returned by the 1950 census was 18,331, of whom 103,251 were Mulattos, 42,092 Negroes and 2,913 Whites. In 1970 the population had grown to 272,041.

30. *A Modern Slavery* by H. W. Nevinson.

31. *Labour in Portuguese West Africa* by William Cadbury and Joseph Burtt.

32. Including *Portuguese Slavery: Britain's Dilemma* by John Harris, and *The Slavery of Today* by Rev. Charles Swan.

Chapter Eighteen

Republic of South Africa

South Africa (a Republic since 1961) ceased to be a colony when the Liberal Government at Westminster accorded it independence as a Dominion in the British Commonwealth in 1910. The motive was democratic and there were entrenched clauses safeguarding the limited rights of the non-Whites, but the politically conscious among Africans regarded the Act of Union (four colonies were joined) as a betrayal subjecting them to the European minority, and they proved right. South Africa became the most racialist state in the world, with Africans, Indians and Coloureds (mixed race) denied all political rights and socially ostracised as uncivilised under the system of apartheid. South Africa became an occupied country within its own borders.

The Republic lies at the extreme south of the continent, bounded on the north-west by South West Africa (Namibia), virtually annexed, on the north by Rhodesia and Botswana (Bechuanaland before independence, 1966) and on the north-east by Mozambique and Swaziland (independent in 1969). Small Lesotho (Basutoland before independence, 1966) lies within it. To west and east are the Atlantic and Indian oceans.

The original inhabitants appear to have been Bushmen and Hottentots, both physically non-Negro types. They were driven out by Negroes and Europeans and became almost entirely confined to South West Africa and Botswana. Most of the African population are now Bantu-speaking Negro peoples including Zulus. There is a large community of Indians, particularly in the province of Natal where they were brought in 1860 as indentured labourers. In the Cape province there is a large population of Coloureds, descendants of the early European settlers and their women servants and slaves. The Europeans are of Dutch and British stock (German in South West Africa).[1]

Dutch and British Settlements

The pioneering Portuguese navigators ignored South Africa as apparently without resources. In 1615 the English tried vainly to form a settlement with ten reprieved convicts, and in 1620 two captains who landed optimistically annexed all Africa for James I. It was a Dutch captain, Leendert Janssen, shipwrecked on the coast in 1647, who persuaded his government to establish a settlement on the Cape. Farms were started with African slave labour, supplemented from the East Indies and Madagascar, and by 1707 there were 1,779 Dutch farmers with 1,107 slaves. Before the end of the century the European immigrants had grown to 15,000 (with 17,000 slaves), forming a highly integrated community, forced together by their religious conviction that they were the chosen of God and identifying themselves with their adopted holy land by calling themselves Afrikaners. There was some resistance by Hottentots in the 1670s and later by Bushmen and Negro Bantus. It was not until towards the end of the eighteenth century that the settlers enjoyed security from Africans, and then another European invasion disrupted them.

The British arrived in the first instance indirectly. In 1795, during the Napoleonic Wars, they invaded the Cape on behalf of the Prince of Orange who had taken refuge in Britain from Holland. By the Treaty of Amiens, 1803, they handed back the territory to the Dutch, but, finding that Napoleon's officers were in control, they returned in force four years later and under the general peace settlement the colony passed to Britain. The British and the Dutch did not assimilate. The Dutch regarded the Africans as inferior beings beyond redemption, though many cared benevolently for their slaves, and they opposed reforms which the British introduced to give the Hottentots legal protection against ill-treatment. In 1815 there was a minor rebellion after a Dutchman had resisted arrest by British police; sixty Afrikaners were killed and five hanged. The conflict was heightened by an agitation for African rights led by the Rev. John Philip, a non-conformist missionary, which culminated in 1828 in a House of Commons resolution for the emancipation of the Hottentots. In 1833 the Emancipation Act abolished slavery. The Dutch were humiliated.

Dutch Trek North

The reaction of the Dutch to British liberalisation was a mass trek north (they became known as Trek Boers).[2] Twelve thousand left between 1835 and 1843, taking with them their sheep and servants. Piet Retief, their leader, said their object was 'to reserve proper relations between master and servant'. Later their apologist, Anna Steenkamp, explained that the British had placed their slaves 'on an equal footing with Christians, contrary to the law of God and the natural distinctions of race and religion, so that it was intolerable for any decent Christian to bow beneath such a yoke: wherefore we withdrew in order thus to preserve our doctrines in purity'.

The Afrikaners first settled in Natal, but when three hundred of them and two hundred servants were massacred by Africans, including Piet Retief, treacherously murdered when signing a peace treaty,[3] the British intervened ostensibly to restore order and proceeded to occupy the territory. The Trek Boers moved further north followed by the British, who took possession temporarily of the Orange River region in 1848. In 1852 the Dutch were recognised as occupying the Transvaal, and in 1858 they established a South African Republic of the territory north of the Vaal river, with a constitution which permitted 'no equality between coloured peoples and the white inhabitants, either in church or state'. In 1854 the Orange Free State, the British permitting, was also recognised as Dutch. South Africa was thus divided into three areas – Dutch Transvaal and Orange Free State, the British colonies of the Cape of Good Hope and Natal, and a large African tribal area.

African Resistance

It must not be supposed that the British were African emancipators. Their occupation of the Cape brought an armed invasion by Bantus who were ruthlessly expelled, and as the British extended their seizure of land they were resisted repeatedly. When in 1854 they had inaugurated the Orange River Colony they limited voting to Europeans and were met by African risings. In the Cape colony they were more liberal. Whilst they applied an economic qualification for voting which excluded most non-Whites, they accepted the principle 'irrespective of race or colour'. Even then, however, there was resistance, taking an extraordinary form when Africans on the borders destroyed their stock and crops under the superstition that the white man would then vanish from the country. Thousands starved. In Natal, when native locations were set up with the retention of tribal law, the British permitted Africans to repudiate tribal custom and claim citizen rights with the Europeans, but few did so. In 1879 the actual British presence in South Africa was brought into jeopardy by war with the Zulus. King Cetywayo attacked with an army of forty thousand and only with reinforcements from London was their formidable rising overcome.

The racialist administration of the Dutch in Transvaal led to continuous conflict with the African population and the state got into financial difficulties which added to its instability. The British annexed the territory in 1877, but from 1880 they met such stern resistance from the Boers, resulting in a series of military disasters culminating in Majuba, that the following year they had to sign a convention recognising Dutch self-government. The treaty nominally acknowledged British suzerainty, but by a second convention, accepted in 1884, British control was limited to foreign affairs, and even from this the Orange Free State, which had become a close ally of Transvaal, was excluded.

Rhodes, the Jameson Raid, War

The Dutch Republics were threatened, however, by a larger design. Cecil Rhodes became Prime Minister of Cape Colony in 1890 and conceived the idea of incorporating all southern Africa and a large part of Central Africa in the British Empire. He established British authority over the vast area of Bechuanaland and through his British South Africa Company, formed to exploit mineral riches,[4] took over Mashonaland and Matabeleland in Rhodesia. With Britain in possession of Cape Colony and Natal, the Boers in Transvaal and the Orange Free State were hemmed in, both north and south.

Circumstances in Transvaal which followed the discovery of gold in the Witwatersrand in 1885–6 gave Rhodes his opportunity. There was an inrush of 'Uitlanders' (foreign immigrants) and Paul Kruger, the president, reflecting the closely-knit Boer community, discriminated against them. He taxed them heavily and restricted their citizenship rights by a law which denied the vote until they had been in the country fourteen years and then only to those over forty years of age. As the mines developed and the number of

Uitlanders, largely British, grew, Joseph Chamberlain, the Colonial Secretary at Westminster, seconded by Rhodes from the Cape, supported their claims and declined to consider modifications which Kruger wished to apply to a five years' qualification. Tension mounted between British and Boers, exploding in 1895 when Dr Starr Jameson, an officer of the BSA Company, invaded Transvaal with a force of five hundred men. Both Chamberlain and Rhodes were aware of his intention, but afterwards denied any support. The raid was unsuccessful, but the psychology of war had been created. Britain sent reinforcements of ten thousand troops to South Africa and in 1899 Transvaal and the Orange Free State issued an ultimatum which started hostilities. The British Government claimed justification as champions of the Uitlanders, but there was world-wide conviction, including that of a liberal minority in Britain, that the underlying motive was the extension of the occupation of South Africa to the newly found riches of Transvaal.

Independence for Whites

The war lasted until 1902, costing more than twenty thousand British lives. Transvaal and Orange Free State were annexed by Britain. In 1905 a colonialist constitution was granted with an elected majority, but it was revoked as inadequate by the Liberal Government elected the following year[5] and in 1910 independence as a Commonwealth Dominion was accorded to a South Africa which united Cape Colony and Natal with the ex-Dutch states. The opportunity was not taken to remove the disabilities of the majority population. Clauses in the constitution guaranteed the continued citizenship of the limited number of non-white voters in Cape Colony, but throughout the rest of the territory the African, Indian and Coloured people were left disenfranchised. Their fate was left to the European minority.

Independence did much to heal the breach between the Boers and the British, cemented later by the part played in the First World War by General Botha and General Smuts in defeating the Germans in their African territories, South West Africa and Tanganyika. Nevertheless, before the first election under independence the Boers and British established separate parties; the South Africa Party led by Botha and Smuts and the Unionists led by Starr Jameson. The Boers were the majority among the electors and Botha became Premier with Smuts as his right-hand minister.[6]

They were less isolationist than traditional Afrikaners and sought the union of British and Boers, excluding General Hertzog from the Cabinet when he insisted that there were still two streams among Europeans. At the same time they intensified racial discrimination. They passed a law in 1911 excluding Africans from other than labouring jobs in the mines and in 1913 another law to limit the right of Africans to purchase land. In 1919 Botha died and Smuts succeeded him.

Hertzog Applies Apartheid

When Hertzog was dismissed from the Cabinet in 1912 he formed a new Afrikaner party, the National Party, appealing to the old prejudices. In the general election of 1924 the Labour Party, representing white workers who feared competition of Africans for jobs, entered into an unprincipled coalition with him, and the National Party won.[7] Hertzog stood for Whites against non-Whites, for Afrikaners against the British and for South African dissociation from Britain. He pursued aggressive apartheid. In 1926 he passed an Act strengthening the exclusion of Africans from jobs, in 1927 and 1930 Acts increasing the powers of the government to repress African resistance, and in 1930–1 Acts expanding the white franchise to all men and women, whilst continuing the property and educational qualifications for non-Whites in the Cape province.

Perhaps the most repressive action against the Africans was the tightening of the administration of the pass laws. Both in the Boer Republics and the British colonies before independence Africans had been required to carry passes when moving from place to place. The Hertzog Government used the pass system to reduce the number of Africans going to the cities and to force them to become the serfs of Afrikaner farmers. In 1933 there was an economic crisis and Smuts joined Hertzog in a coalition government and in the formation of the United Party. The traditionalist Afrikaners broke away under Dr Malan to form what they termed the Purified Nationalist Party.

The Hertzog–Smuts Coalition went still further in applying apartheid. What were known as the *Hertzog Bills* made the African leaders give up hope of influencing the White minority by persuasion and representations. The Bills removed African voters from the common electoral roll in the Cape province, substituting the right to elect three *white* representatives to the Lower House; throughout the Union Africans became entitled to elect four *white* Senators. The one concession was a Native Representative Council but it had advisory powers only. This Act repudiated the enfranchisement clauses in the independence constitution, and Hertzog argued that the Statute of Westminster of 1931, for which he had fought strenuously in his desire to break free from Britain, withdrew the right of London to interfere with Dominion legislation. It now became clear that no representation in the Legislature of Africans by Africans was to be permitted.

Second World War and After

The Second World War brought division in the government and among the Afrikaners. Hertzog was for benevolent neutrality; Smuts for backing Britain. Smuts won the vote in the Assembly, Hertzog resigned and Smuts took over the premiership. Hertzog voted for Malan's resolution against 'fighting Britain's war', vainly attempted to form his own Afrikaner Party, and retired from politics. Smuts gained an international reputation and became a member of Britain's War Cabinet. Malan's dissociation from Britain gained increasing support among Afrikaners. At a war-time election his party in the Legislature grew from 27 to 43. Many of his supporters openly supported Hitler.

In the post-war election of 1948 history went full circle. Hertzog had replaced Smuts; Smuts, Hertzog; now Malan replaced Smuts. Malan won 70 seats, Smuts 65 and he was defeated in his own constituency. Malan made traditional Boer ideals the basis of the policy of his government. Expediency was joined with principle in legislation to remove the Coloureds [8] from the common electoral roll in the Cape province and to cancel the provision which Smuts had made in 1947 for national representation of Indians by three Whites; Malan's majority was only five, and he realised that the Coloureds had the balance of power in the Cape, and that the Indian representatives, though white, would be likely to vote against him. He took the more decisive step of virtually incorporating the mandated territory of South West Africa into the Union by giving its white population six seats in the Assembly. They all returned National Party candidates; Malan thus increased his Parliamentary majority to eleven.

The Government proceeded to entrench white privilege in many directions. To assist the Afrikaner farmers, Africans arrested on pass charges were released from prison on condition that they indentured themselves as farm labourers; many of them were treated as serfs. Further legislation was introduced to restrict the scope of African labour. A measure in 1951 limited skilled work in construction to 'buildings for use by natives in native areas', and in 1956 under the *Industrial Conciliation Act* the Minister of Labour was given power to reserve categories of work in all industry to Whites. The Act also insisted on the segregation of Whites and non-Whites in separate trade unions, prohibited strikes by African workers, and ruled out rights of negotiation.

The Afrikaner concept of African society was the preservation of a traditional tribal division; by this means Africans could be deterred from united action in a national movement. A *Bantu Authorities Act* was passed which ruled out contact between large tribal groups; the chiefs and headmen held office at the Minister's pleasure and regulations prohibited them from participating in any 'subversive' organisations, even moderately liberal, with the result that seven chiefs were deposed. At the same time the advisory Native Representative Council, which at least gave some expression to African views on a national level, was abolished. This legislation was supplemented by the *Group Areas Act* which enforced total residential segregation in the towns. It not only established compulsory locations for Africans but kept African tribes apart. It prohibited Indians from trading in other than Indian racial areas.

Christian Missions Close Schools

A fierce controversy arose over the *Bantu Education Act*, and many of the Christian missions closed their schools rather than operate it. The Minister responsible was Dr Verwoerd, who during the war had openly sympathised with Nazism and who believed fanatically in white superiority. The purpose of the Act was to direct the education of African children to their apartheid status in society. Dr Verwoerd was particularly concerned that Bantu teachers should fulfil this intention. In the Assembly he said that they should be indoctrinated in the belief that 'they must not think that once they are educated they can leave their own people and seek equality with the European'. The Act was followed by legislation regimenting African universities. Non-white students were excluded from colleges attended by Whites and even African universities were

segregated on a tribal basis. The Minister of Education dismissed
seven white lecturers at Fort Hare College for 'seeking to destroy
apartheid'.

Apartheid became stricter and more rigid. The *Native Laws
Amendments Act* prohibited social contact between White and
Black. The *Mixed Marriages Prohibition* and *Immorality Acts*
prohibited mixed marriages and made sexual intercourse between
the races a criminal offence. The *Nursing Act* prohibited a white
nurse from working under a non-white Sister or doctor. The *Population Registration Act* classified the whole population according
to race. In justice to the National Government we must recognise
that it supplemented its segregation policies by measures of social
betterment. The townships provided for Africans had greatly
improved housing; schools and hospitals were built, welfare
schemes introduced and certain autonomy accorded to compliant
chiefs. Many Afrikaners behaved benevolently towards Africans so
long as the master–servant relationship was maintained.

Bantustans

Segregation and the severe discrimination accompanying it was
negative apartheid. There also developed a positive aspect, the
division of the white and African peoples into separate states,
Bantustans for Blacks. This was rejected by the African National
Congress (ANC), led by Chief Luthuli, not only because it
stood for a multi-racial South Africa but because the government
proposals maintained inequality and domination. When Dr Verwoerd introduced the *Promotion of Bantu Self-Government Act* he
held out high hopes: the day of discrimination had ended and
nothing would stand in the way of the African reserves becoming
independent states. But when the operation of Bantustans began
these hopes were betrayed. In the first place there was no suggestion
of redistributing the land so that viable African states could be
established; only thirteen per cent of the territory of South Africa
was in the hands of Africans, who were more than sixty-five per
cent of the population.[9] Secondly, the Act, whilst it abolished all
representation of Africans in the South African Legislature (the
three white Assembly members and the three white Senators allotted to watch African interests were withdrawn), it did not establish
African self-government in the reserves. The Minister of Bantu
Administration and Development was given supreme power and

the administering chiefs were made answerable to him. Local Councils were set up, but their members were nominated by the chiefs and required the approval of the Minister. Thirdly, Whites were invited to open factories on the borders of the Bantustan territories, to be served by African labour from them. The purpose was to restrict the number of Africans leaving the reserves for the existing urban areas, but the effect was to extend African dependence on European industry as cheap labour.

Within the newly proclaimed Bantustan states there was vigorous opposition. Previously peaceful areas like Sekhukeneland and Zeerust became disrupted and in the Pondoland area of Transkei a state of emergency was declared and it was reported that conditions of civil war existed; the facts were not known because unofficial visitors were not permitted. Disillusionment grew when Dr Eiselen, the Secretary for Native Affairs, declared, in contradiction to Dr Verwoerd, that the Bantustans would never have complete independence.[10]

Some white liberals, including the Bureau of Racial Affairs, grasped at the idea of the establishment of separate European and African states as a solution of the racial problem, but they faced the difficulty that forty per cent of the African male population were employed as labourers by the European farmers and industrialists. It was clear that effective segregation required that the Whites would have to adjust themselves to the menial work performed by Africans, an unlikely sacrifice.

British Parties

We have omitted reference to the attitude of the minority British section of the white population. John Merriman, who was prime minister of the Cape at the time of Union, hoped it would start upon Cape lines rather than Transvaal lines, but the British surrendered to the conciliatory gestures of Botha and Smuts (particularly to their wartime support) and their policy of liberalisation in race relations became increasingly compromised. Immediately after the grant of Dominion status they joined Jameson's Unionist Party, and later most allied themselves to Smuts against Hertzog. By this time, however, they had accepted the principle of apartheid and the older tolerant Cape approach passed to a Liberal Party formed in 1953 to oppose racial discrimination. The Liberals did not achieve any Parliamentary representation, and the Labour

Party (at first racist) at last reverted to principle and opposing apartheid was entirely wiped out. In 1959 thirteen members of the United Party split to form the Progressive Party, which boldly opposed racial segregation, though standing for a qualification franchise against the African demand for adult suffrage. Some British-rooted industrialists, like Harry Oppenheimer, who wished the limitations on African labour removed, supported the Progressives, who polled comparatively high votes in subsequent elections and returned an outspoken Member, Mrs Helen Suzman.

The distinction between white liberals and the non-white movements widened, however. The Whites still placed their faith in changes through Parliament. The Africans, Indians and, to a large extent, Coloureds ceased to hold this hope. There was a split from the African National Congress by those opposed to all collaboration with Whites, resulting in the formation of the Pan-Africanist Congress. Imposed segregation of the races by the Whites created, despite the influence of Chief Luthuli, the Congress leader, a dangerous psychology of racial enmity among many Africans.

Suppression of Communism Act

As apartheid extended, there was inevitably more drastic resistance by Africans, Indians and Coloureds. The Government took stern measures to meet it. In 1950 it passed the *Suppression of Communism Act* aimed not only at Communists but at anyone who encouraged 'any of the objects of Communism' or 'industrial, social or economic change' by 'unlawful acts or omissions'. The Communist Party was declared illegal and the Government proceeded to arrest, restrict and imprison many non-Communists on the ground that opposition to racial domination was one of the objects of Communism. Powers to prohibit meetings, restrict freedom of speech and writing and to banish political offenders were extended in other Acts. The *Riotous Assemblies Act* gave the Minister power to prohibit any person from entering proscribed areas if he was held to be promoting hostility between Europeans and other races. The same Act gave the Governor-General powers to prohibit publications and gatherings. A law passed in 1961 authorised the Attorney-General to detain persons for twelve days before being charged in court instead of the former forty-eight hours and placed the onus of proving innocence (instead of the Prosecution proving guilt) on any person accused of intimidation.

African National Congress

We have referred in passing to the African National Congress. It became the leading African instrument of resistance and must be looked at in some detail. The ANC was formed at a meeting of leaders, hardly representative because they were from the educated professions, held at Bloemfontein at the beginning of 1912. The inspiration came from a young barrister from Oxford and the Middle Temple, Dr Seme. The first name of the movement was the South African *Native* National Congress, significant of the earlier moderation; the first president was Dr John Langalibalele Dube, who ran an African boarding school, attended as a boy by Chief Luthuli. The occasion for the establishment of Congress was the *Act of Union*, which stimulated recognition of the need for an African voice. Congress was originally organised on the lines of the British Parliament, a House of Commons and a House of Chiefs. The first object was to develop African unity among the different tribes, and Congress concentrated upon immediate grievances, such as the *Land Tenure Act* of 1913 and the *Pass System*, rather than the fundamental issue of citizenship and enfranchisement. It was concerned with alleviation rather than transformation, representations rather than demands, and began by appealing to the Europeans. In fact, the ANC in its early days did little more than hold yearly meetings, formulating grievances presented to the Government in petitions and deputations. There were no branches, although members carried on some educational activities in their localities. When deputations to South African Ministers met with no result, a few proceeded to London with little more result.

African Trade Unionism

Nevertheless, agitation began among the masses. As early as 1913 there were extensive anti-pass demonstrations in the Orange River province and Congress cautiously moved to its second stage of agitation. In 1919 it organised an anti-pass campaign in Johannesburg when seven hundred were arrested, but at this time popular revolts developed mostly outside Congress influence, concerned

with low wages and working conditions. In 1919 a dockers' strike
in Cape Town began a movement which, under the leadership of
Clements Kadalie and his Industrial and Commercial Workers'
Union (ICU), swept the whole country, with vast demonstrations
and massive strikes, including in 1920 a stoppage by forty thousand
miners on the Reef. The alarmed authorities acted with severity. At
a Port Elizabeth demonstration twenty-one people were shot by
police and in 1921 at Bulhock the death roll was 163. By 1924 the
ICU had eighty thousand members and it was becoming a revolutionary challenge to the South African Establishment, extending its
resistance to political measures, such as the pass laws. The movement depended, however, greatly on the personality of Kadalie and
his ability to arouse emotion at vast meetings. During an absence
in Europe to make contacts with the British TUC and the ILO, a
split arose in the organisation, and on his return Kadalie failed to
show ability to restore its strength or popular appeal.[11] The opportunity passed.

Subsequently the non-white trade unions established the South
African Congress of Trade Unions (SACTU) which constantly
championed the rights of African, Indian and Coloured workers.

All African Convention

It was not until the *Hertzog Bills* of the 1930s that the African
National Congress established itself as the recognised instrument of
African expression. There had been continued unrest and disturbance in the intervening years. In 1924 a hundred Hottentots were
massacred when refusing to pay a tax on dogs. In 1928–9 Natal had
a succession of riots arising from home-brewing restrictions and
from exorbitant taxation. In 1930 violence occurred at anti-pass
demonstrations at Durban and Worcester. Congress participated
in the agitation against the pass laws and members were active in
the local struggles over other issues, but the ANC as such had not
so far made a national impact. Even on the *Hertzog Bills* the initiative came from outside. In 1935 Professor Jabavu of Cape Town
proposed a conference of African organisations to oppose the
measures, and four hundred delegates gathered at an All-African
Convention at Bloemfontein. It was remarkably representative,
including non-political bodies like pastors' fraternals and football
clubs. There was a cleavage between old and young. The more
seasoned delegates wanted to vote for Whites to represent non-

Whites in the Legislature and for members of the advisory Native Representation Council, whilst the young militants wanted to reject participation outright. The older view prevailed. The same division occurred when it was proposed by the officials that the Convention should continue as a permanent body. This was opposed by the younger delegates from the ANC who did not wish to be deterred from action by the conservative leadership or have political decisions taken by the many non-political bodies in the Convention. The ANC endorsed their attitude and this was the beginning of the activist approach which made it the major African force in the land.

The old guard in the Convention set up the non-European Unity Movement and some more cautious members of the ANC transferred to it, including the then president, the Rev. Z. Mahabane. He was followed as president by Dr Xuma who sympathised with the younger element. He revolutionised the whole organisation, devising a new constitution based on the establishment of branches, formed a Youth League to enrol a new generation of militants, prepared a challenging manifesto of 'African Claims' and initiated a united front with the Indian National Congress, which under the leadership of Dr Dadoo was in revolt against the Asiatic Land Tenure Act limiting Asians in Natal to ghettoes. These tendencies were encouraged by the psychology of the Second World War, which had a peculiar effect in South Africa. As we have told, some of the Afrikaner leaders supported Hitler, whilst General Smuts, head of the Government, became famous on the world scene for his stand against Nazism. African Nationalists were stirred by the democratic claims of the West, but their disillusionment with the regime in South Africa grew. They compared the reputation of General Smuts abroad with his repression of democracy at home.

Chief Luthuli

About this time an event occurred in Natal which was to be profoundly important for Congress. Dr Dube, the first president of the ANC and the elder statesman of African politics, had continued to act as head of the movement in Natal after his retirement from the heavy obligations of national leadership. In 1945 he had a stroke and died, leaving the Natal presidency to be contested by a trade union leader, A. W. G. Champion, and the Rev. Mtimkulu, a moderate. The election conference was breaking up in confusion when a newcomer – Chief Luthuli – restored order. Champion was returned chairman and Luthuli was appointed to the Executive. Thus began the association with Congress of a figure whose service to freedom and inter-racial democracy was awarded the Nobel Peace Prize in 1961.

Chief Luthuli was born a Zulu at Grantville, perhaps in 1898, perhaps in 1900 (births were unregistered), educated at a Methodist school and took a course for head teachership at Adams College. He was interested in African affairs but his main concern was his Christian religion, of which he remained a devout adherent all his life. He went to India and America on the invitation of missionary bodies and these visits not only widened his horizons but impelled him to think sharply about conditions in South Africa; his public activities at the college were limited, however, to the secretaryship of the African Teachers' Association. He left teaching when elected chief of his tribe at Grantville and became deeply involved in voicing their grievances, particularly their need for land. He came to admire the stand of the ANC, but did not join it until after the death of Dr Dube. Soon after his appointment to the Natal Executive he was asked to serve as its representative on the Native Representation Council, but convinced that it was futile spoke in favour of its indefinite adjournment at his first attendance. When after the defeat of Smuts in 1948 Dr Verwoerd became Minister for Native Affairs, Luthuli gave up all pretence of consulting with the European representatives and soon the Council was abolished.

The Congress at national level progressed with its new radical policy. Dr Xuma could not keep pace with it and the pressure of a group, including Nelson Mandela and Oliver Tambo (both to become famous), led to the election in his place of Dr James Moroka as president. Under Moroka the ANC adopted its historic 'Programme of Action'. The policy of seeking adjustments of the regime and making representations to the Government was replaced by the demand for full citizenship rights for all non-Whites. Demonstrations on a nation-wide scale, strike action and civil disobedience were endorsed, and united action with Indians and Coloureds was authorised – indeed, it was the Indian example of non-violent resistance to the *Ghetto Act* which stimulated the decision in favour of civil disobedience. The first action was a combined one day stay-at-home in June 1950, to protest against the *Group Areas* and *Suppression of Communism Bills* and to mourn the many who had already lost their lives in the expanding struggle.

In May 1951 there was an impressive united strike at the Cape against the Government's intention to remove Coloureds from the Common Electoral Roll. In July 1951 a Joint Planning Committee was set up to organise a Defiance Campaign by the three peoples, Africans, Indians and Coloureds.

Defiance Campaign

Luthuli's first national recognition was when, at the request of Dr Moroka, he acted as chairman at Bloemfontein of the conference which initiated the Defiance Campaign. It was agreed that the main act of defiance would be to ignore the 'Europeans Only' restriction on trains and buses and in station waiting-rooms, parks, post offices and other public places. The movement gathered momentum and in the one month of October 1952, 2,354 resisters were arrested. At the same time Congress strength increased phenomenally; its membership leapt from 7,000 to 100,000. Congress had insisted that the defiance should be non-violent and for three months it remained disciplined. Then riots took place, alleged to be incited by *agents provocateurs*, and the Government passed an Act making it illegal to defy any law by way of protest. Dr Moroka, the Congress President, and nineteen leaders in Johannesburg were arrested. This brought about an internal crisis in the ANC. Dr Moroka dissociated himself from his fellow-accused. He could no longer be leader.

Luthuli was now a national figure. He was a staff officer of the Defiance Campaign, but, more important for his image, the Government had dismissed him from his chieftainship because of his activity in Congress. Following the Johannesburg trial the ANC national conference appointed Luthuli executive president. His first reluctant act was to end the Defiance Campaign; the riots and the use of them by the authorities to discredit the movement necessitated this in his view. Nevertheless, the Defiance Campaign was a turning point. It drew masses of Africans to Congress and consolidated solidarity with the Indian Congress, Coloured groups (there was no national organisation), and many Europeans, including the newly formed Liberal Party, whose Patrick Duncan, son of a previous Governor-General, was among those arrested. This broader co-operation was expressed by the formation of the Congress of Democrats covering all races.

As president of the ANC Luthuli toured the country addressing large demonstrations. In 1953 he was banned from attending public gatherings and from entering the larger centres. He then directed his attention to organisation, important with the massive membership which Congress had reached. The *Bantu Education Act*, restricting teaching to Africans to an elementary level, raised difficulties. There was pressure within the ANC to boycott schools, but on the other hand African parents were disinclined to deny all education to their children. The decision was taken to allow regions an option, not satisfactory in practice. Congress was rescued from a set-back by an initiative decided at its annual conference at the end of 1953. A plan propounded by Professor Matthews (a student with Luthuli at Adams College) was adopted for a conference of all peoples and organisations opposed to the regime. Luthuli welcomed this and in 1954, when the ban on attending public meetings ended, addressed meetings of Indians, Coloureds and Europeans to further it; but he was arrested at Johannesburg and a stricter ban imposed, restricting him to the magisterial area of his home at Grantville. Thousands of Africans marched passed the house where he was staying in sympathy and protest.

Congress of the People: Treason Trials

A joint meeting of the many organisations involved in the projected Congress of the People was held near Grantville so that Luthuli could attend, but he could take little part in the preparations because he had an attack of blood pressure and was confined two months in Durban hospital. The Congress met on a sports ground at Kliptown near Johannesburg in June 1955. It was the most representative meeting ever held in South Africa and made a profound impression. It adopted a Freedom Charter which in its language and principles was comparable with the Charter of the United Nations (see Appendix). Its most noteworthy feature was its outline not only of the South Africa denounced, but of the South Africa desired. The Government reacted with greater severity; there were raids and arrests throughout the Union. In the autumn of 1956 Luthuli's two-year ban ended and he was able to address the ANC Conference, but this freedom did not last long. On December 5 he was arrested on a charge of High Treason. Transported to Johannesburg Fort, he found himself with innumerable others – 'professionals and labourers, priests and laymen, Muslims,

Christians, Hindus, Infidels, Africans, Indians, Coloureds'[12] from every corner of the land (Europeans were, of course, segregated even in prison). They were the great assembly of the accused in the Treason Trial.

The trial was the longest and most memorable in South Africa's history. Luthuli was among 256 arrested; after the preliminary hearings, charges of high treason were brought against ninety-one (not including Luthuli). The trial continued until March 1961, over four years. It amounted to a full-scale investigation of the policies and actions of the organisations participating in the Congress of the People and particularly of the ANC. The defendants were charged with the intention to overthrow the state by violence and to substitute a communist or other form of state. The surprising result of the trial was a judgment of 'not guilty'. Summing up Judge Rumpff said that it had not been proved that the ANC had become a communist organisation or that it had adopted a policy to overthrow the state by violence. The Government was humiliated, but in practice achieved its aim by proceeding to arrest and detain activists under other Acts.

Luthuli had a recurrence of high blood pressure whilst the preparatory examination of the treason trial dragged on and was allowed to be absent for a month. At the end of the long preliminary proceedings, he was among those discharged. His mind remained with those sent to trial and he gave evidence day after day on their behalf. Even when, as described later, he was arrested again and seriously ill in the prison hospital, he continued his evidence. His insistence upon the non-violence principle of Congress and its goodwill towards all races, not least towards Europeans, made a deep impression.

Workers and Women

During the trial an event took place which demonstrated African determination and solidarity in an extraordinary way. The bus company which transported African workers from their locations to jobs raised their fares. To pay would have driven their families further below the poverty line and at many places the workers decided to walk even twenty miles a day. It was in the Alexandra township outside Johannesburg that the boycott was most impressive. For weeks the workers tramped every day ten miles from home to mine and factory and ten miles back after exhausting labour. Not one man boarded a bus. They won. The Chamber of Commerce subsidised the bus company and the increase in fares was withdrawn. The Minister of Transport charged Congress with engineering the boycott, but this was not true. Its significance was its spontaneity.

Women as well as workers demonstrated their spirit. When the Government passed its law compelling them to carry passes similarly to men, they joined Congress in large numbers. In 1956 they held a memorable all-races gathering in Pretoria, the administrative capital, with groups attending from all over the Union, some travelling a thousand miles. The authorities hoped to apply the measure first to the more 'backward' women in the countryside, but were stunned by the vigour of their resistance. Through 1957 the women protested in every part of the country, leading in the following year to a vast demonstration in Johannesburg, when over two thousand were arrested.

Pan-Africanist Congress

The women's example did much to influence the agitation which followed for the burning of passes by both men and women. Congress and its Women's League took an active part in this campaign, but like the bus boycott it was spontaneous and wider than ANC, which in fact, was passing through a disrupting period. A split was arising in its ranks among those opposed to the growing association with Indian, Coloured and European resisters. The division became acute when the ANC Working Committee expelled two members who had impeded its activities, resulting in the formation of the separate Pan-Africanist Congress (PAC) with the slogan 'Africa for the Africans'. Broadly, the Pan-Africanists reflected in South Africa the outlook of the Black Power movement in America and Britain.

Another cause of controversy was the association of Communists with Congress. This gave some credence to the government charge that Communists controlled the organisation and it provoked opposition from some Liberals, including Patrick Duncan, as well as from Pan-Africanists. Chief Luthuli defended the co-operation. He rejected Communism as 'a mixture of a false theory of society linked on to a false "religion"', but 'we leave our differing political theories to one side until the day of liberation'. He admitted that this might be said to be naïve, but he had no reason to believe that the number of Communists was large and if there were a danger of their using Congress for their own ends, that could be the result only of apathy among non-Communists. 'I am in Congress precisely because I am a Christian,' he wrote. 'My Christian belief about human society must find expression here and now, and Congress is the spearhead of the real struggle.'[13]

Luthuli did not allow the split with the Pan-Africanists to discourage him or alter his course. He was greatly heartened by the All-African Accra Conference of 1958 and Congress made Africa Day (April 15) a big event in its calendar. He extended his meetings with Europeans, even speaking to a group of Afrikaners. He was particularly moved by the devotion of the European 'Black Sash' women, who stood in silent vigil outside Parliament. Although the proportion of Whites participating was fractional, the Government became alarmed by the increasing co-operation of the races. In May 1959 the Special Branch police were again at Luthuli's home. This time he was confined to Grantville for five years. He was permitted to go to Pretoria to continue his evidence at the Treason Trial; he did not foresee the climax of tragedy which was approaching.

Sharpeville

Both the African National Congress and the Pan-Africanist Congress were preparing campaigns against the *Pass Laws*. The ANC planned long-term preparation, ensuring that the participants should be briefed, disciplined and ready to endure. The PAC was for immediate action, believing the people would respond. Its leader, Robert Sobukwe, appealed to Africans to leave their passes at home and go to police stations and challenge arrest. Except in parts of the Transvaal and the Cape the response was not great. But the campaign brought about an event which profoundly affected the struggle in South Africa and moved the world to closer involvement.

On March 21, 1960, a crowd of Africans – estimated at five thousand by their leaders, twenty thousand by the authorities – gathered outside the police station at Johannesburg inviting arrest for not carrying passes. Sixty-seven were shot dead and 186 were wounded; twelve police were injured, none seriously. Dr Verwoerd, the Prime Minister, reporting to Parliament said that when an African was arrested, three shots were directed at the police who then opened fire on the crowd. He admitted that no order to shoot was given. Affidavits signed by a hundred of the wounded Africans denied that the demonstrators carried any arms and asserted that their leader repeatedly said, 'We have come here to talk, not to fight.' They insisted that no order to disperse was given; a few acknowledged that some children threw stones, but all denied any firing; no attempt was made to assault the police station. The evidence of the senior district surgeon at the subsequent judicial inquiry went far to endorse the Africans' claim that they had not attacked. Seventy per cent of the fifty-two post mortems he carried out showed that the victims had been shot in the back. The reports of this tragedy, and particularly a photograph of the unarmed men lying dead on the ground, brought a wave of protest throughout the world. It was from this moment that the international agitation against South Africa's apartheid burst into flame.

Congress and PAC Banned

Sharpeville moved South Africa more intimately than the world. Luthuli called for a national day of mourning for the victims and their families. The response went far beyond the allies of Congress. Many churches were open for prayer all day and students of all races participated at their universities. This was regarded by Congress as a dedication to action. When it called for the burning of passes, bonfires spread through the land. The Government responded by declaring a state of emergency and banning Congress and the PAC. Twenty thousand resisters of all races were arrested and taken into detention; Luthuli and the leaders were arrested. An incidental consequence was that the defence lawyers at the treason trial withdrew in protest. Until the end of the state of emergency two young prisoners, Nelson Mandela and Duma Nokwe, conducted the defence.

In prison Luthuli had a recurrence of blood pressure and was transferred to the hospital. He was still giving evidence at the trial, but often was too ill to do so. At his own trial five months later, on the charge of inciting the burning of passes, he was found guilty on two charges, fined £100 and sentenced to six months imprisonment, suspended for three years on account of his health. The fine was paid by the Defence and Aid Fund in London, and Luthuli returned to his confinement at Grantville. An effort was made to overcome the effects of the banning of the ANC and PAC by the formation of the *African People's Democratic Union of South*

Africa (APDUSA), which included Whites, with some temporary influence.

Nobel Peace Prize

We have referred above to the 'positive' apartheid of the Bantustan policy. Luthuli used unusually strong terms in his denunciation, realising that the idea of separate White and Black states might appeal to opinion frustrated by the racial conflict. He denounced the Government's Act as a 'huge deceit', ridiculing the allocation of land, the caricature of self-government, and the exploitation of labour. He regarded the new reserves as compulsory retreats for rejects from the towns. With passion he wrote: 'To us Bantustan means the home of disease and miserable poverty, the place where we shall be swept into heaps in order to rot, the dumping ground of "undesirable elements", delinquents and criminals created especially in towns and cities by the system. And the place where old people and sick people are sent when the cities have taken what they had to give by way of strength, youth and labour. And still, to the day of death, whether in cities or farms or reserves, we are tenants on the white man's land. That is our share of South Africa. Our home is in the white man's garbage can.'[14] He pointed to the reports which leaked out of Pondoland, sealed off by the emergency, of shootings by the army and police as proof of the falseness of the liberal image of Bantustan. 'Is it a slow-motion Sharpeville?' he asked.

It was in 1961 that Chief Luthuli was awarded the Nobel Peace Prize. He was still confined to Grantville, but the South African Government permitted him to travel to Stockholm to receive it.[15] The award was given because of the influence which he had exerted for abstention from violence and for his insistence on the co-operation of all races both in the struggle and in the society which it would establish. 'South Africa is not yet a house for all her sons and daughters,' Luthuli wrote. 'There remains before us the building of a new land, a home for men who are black, white, brown, from the ruins of the old narrow groups.' He looked forward to the integration of the continent of Africa in a world harmony. 'Somewhere ahead there beckons a civilisation, a culture, which will take its place in the parade of God's history beside other great human syntheses, Chinese, Egyptian, Jewish, European.'[16] On July 27, 1967, Luthuli died, honoured throughout the world.

Laws Completing Subjection

The decade of the sixties saw a series of Acts which eroded all citizen rights. The restrictive legislation already described was followed by a quick succession of laws which completed the subjection of the non-white population. It began with an amendment of the General Laws, commonly known as the *Sabotage Act* (1962); sabotage was defined widely, from damaging property to embarrassing the state administration. Those charged had to prove their innocence and sentences ranged from five years' imprisonment to the death penalty. The Act authorised the banning of meetings, of attendance at meetings by listed persons, the publication of anything said by listed persons, and those regarded as guilty could be placed under indefinite house arrest. Other measures during this period were: the *90-Day No Trial Act* (1963), also an amendment of the General Laws, which provided for the indefinite and *incommunicado* detention in 90-day spells of any person suspected of committing an offence; the *180-Day No Trial Act* (1965) authorising for interrogation similar detention in 180-day spells of any person 'likely' to give material evidence for the state; the *Official Secrets Amendment Act* (1965) which legalised the examination in secret by a public prosecutor of any person thought to have evidence of an offence; the *Suppression of Communism Amendment Act* (1965) prohibiting the publication of anything written or said abroad by listed persons and presuming that anyone under charge who left the country without a passport had the intention of subversive training (he was guilty unless he proved otherwise); the *Police Amendment Act* (1965) empowering any policeman to search without warrant a person, vehicle or premises within a mile of the frontier; the *Terrorism Act* (1967) providing for indefinite and *incommunicado* detention and a minimum sentence of five years or death if found guilty (the onus was placed on the accused to prove that any action was not committed with intent to endanger law and order); the *Suppression of Communism Amendments* (1967) de-barring listed lawyers; the *Coloureds Cadets Act* (1967) imposing one year training on Coloureds between eighteen and twenty-four, requiring them to carry passes; the *Prohibition of Political Interference Act* (1968) ending representation (through Whites) in the Legislature and in the Provincial Council of Coloureds in the Cape and banning multi-racial political parties, e.g. the Liberal Party; the *BOSS Act* (1969) an amendment to the General Laws, prohibiting the possession or publication of any information about security held to be prejudicial to the state and, on the certificate of a Minister, prohibiting the presentation of evidence in court; the *Bantu Laws Amendment Act* (1969) giving the Minister power to prohibit the employment of any African in a specified area, a specified type of work, or for a specified employer; the *Group Areas Amendment Act* (1969) prohibiting African servants from having overnight visitors, including husbands, without the authorisation of an employer; the *Population Registration Amendment Act* (1969) basing racial classification on heredity (even distant) rather than appearance or acceptance, and restricting the right of appeal.[17]

Together with previous legislation, these Acts made South Africa the most racist police state in the world.

Congress Endorses Physical Struggle

Before the death of Chief Luthuli his colleagues in the leadership of the ANC had begun to doubt the effectiveness of the method of passive resistance. Their organisation was banned, every form of public activity was prohibited, they could not attend meetings, they could publish nothing, they could be confined to restricted areas, they could be arrested and detained indefinitely without charge or trial, the way of political advance was closed. They had not the disciplined following which Gandhi had inspired in India for a mass movement of non-violent civil disobedience. Out of respect for Luthuli the leaders did not commit the ANC to violence, but a number formed *Umkhonto we Sizwe* (Spear of the Nation) to prepare for ultimate physical revolution. They included Nelson Mandela, deputy leader under Chief Luthuli; Walter Sisulu, Secretary-General of ANC; Govan Mbeki, ex-national Chairman of ANC and General Secretary of Transkei Voters; Denis Goldberg, white chairman of the Congress of Democrats and Ahmed Kathrada, a leader of the Indian Congress. They began to plan long-term: the first stage sabotage without violence to persons; the second, guerrilla warfare with a growing force trained abroad; and finally the overthrow of the white government and its replacement by a multi-racial, though African majority, administration.[18]

A document, *Operation Mayibuye*, outlining this proposed plan was prepared for private discussion, but it was seized by the police and eleven leaders were arrested at the farm of Denis Goldberg at Rivonia. Eight, including those mentioned above, were found guilty in June 1964, sentenced to life imprisonment, and incarcerated on Robben Island. This removal of the most influential leaders appeared to have destroyed effective direction by the ANC within South Africa, but under Oliver Tambo continued leadership was given from abroad and the military training of volunteers was stepped up. Underground work persisted in the Republic through small local groups.

More Mass Trials

In February 1969 there was a second mass trial at Pietermaritzburg under the Terrorism Act. Twelve Africans, one a woman, were sentenced to long terms of imprisonment for conspiracy to overthrow the existing order by 'subversion, terrorism, violent revolution and warfare'. One of them was sentenced to 20 years imprisonment, six to 18 years each, one to 15 years, two to 10 years each, one to 5 years and one was acquitted. Many of the prisoners had already been banned or served terms in prison. Miss Nyembe, who was sentenced to fifteen years, had been imprisoned during the Defiance Campaign of 1952, was one of the accused in the abortive Treason Trial, had been sentenced to three years' imprisonment in 1963 for ANC activities, was gaoled again on the charge of contravening a banning order, and in 1968 was banned for five years.

A feature of the trial was evidence of the collaboration of the illegal Smith regime in Rhodesia. Several of the accused as well as State witnesses, had been arrested in Rhodesia and handed over to South Africa. The trial provided evidence of severe ill-treatment in prison. The State witnesses included ANC activists who were driven by their suffering to give evidence. Among them was Desinger Francis who was seized in Rhodesia when travelling from South Africa to Zambia to escape arrest under the *Immorality Act* because he was married to a British woman. He told the court that he had been kept in solitary confinement for 421 days and tortured. Subsequently he described his treatment in Bulawayo, where he had been beaten, burned and chained, and in Pretoria prison where he had been beaten and subjected repeatedly to electric shocks. He finally agreed to be a State witness on condition of release. His allegations in court of torture received wide publicity and the magistrate ordered an investigation.

In May and June 1969, there was further and wider evidence of the continued struggle. Forty persons were arrested and detained for interrogation under the *Terrorism Act*. Two of them died in prison – Iman Haron, a highly respected Muslim leader from Cape Town, and Cabel Mayekiso, a prominent trade unionist.[19] Other prisoners included Winnie Mandela,[20] wife of the ANC leader serving a life sentence on Robben Island, trade unionists, journalists and students. In October nineteen were tried, not under the *Terrorism Act* but under the *Suppression of Communism Act*, on the charge of membership of the ANC and the promotion of its objectives by publicising African grievances, possessing subversive literature, and organising relief for political sufferers. Seven detainees were called as State witnesses and again there was evidence that they were induced to do so by ill-treatment. Two of those called – Miss Naidoo, daughter of the ex-chairman of the Transvaal Indian Congress, and Miss Nkala, who had previously been gaoled for ANC activities – refused to give evidence and were sentenced for contempt. In February 1970 there was surprise when the Attorney-General of the Transvaal withdrew the prosecution, but the reason became clear as soon as the judge acquitted the prisoners. They were immediately re-arrested under the *Terrorism Act*, including the two 'witnesses' who had refused to give evidence. In September there was another surprise. At their trial at Pretoria Judge Vilgoen acquitted the nineteen prisoners on the grounds that the indictment was substantially identical with the indictment at their previous trial under the *Suppression of Communism Act* and that there could not be a second trial for the same offence. On this occasion the prisoners were not re-arrested but the Prosecution was given the right to appeal against the judgment. The acquittal did not apply to Benjamin Ramotse who had not been previously tried; the judge did not accept his objection that he had been captured illegally by Rhodesian forces in Botswana.[21] There was considerable press criticism of the fact that the nineteen prisoners had already been detained for nearly two years, mostly in solitary confinement without any access to their families and lawyers. Disquiet was also caused by the sworn affidavits of some of them that they had been tortured.

These trials gained world-wide attention, but it was the continuous discrimination, segregation, restriction and suppression from which the non-white majority suffered most.[22] The *Pass Laws* were the basic instrument of the police state, controlling the daily life of Africans, their location, work, and movement. Between 2,500 and 3,000 persons were arrested daily for infringements. By

September 1968, 1,100,000 were forced to move to segregated locations under the *Group Areas Act*, only 2,624 of them Whites.[23] By July 1969, 1,100 persons had been banned to restricted areas. By June 1969 thirteen thousand books had been banned. By January 1970 forty-one lawyers who had defended political prisoners suffered disabilities, withdrawal of passport, de-barring, and imprisonment on charges under many repressive laws.[24] The South African Committee of the Defence and Aid Fund, set up by Canon Collins in London for the defence of prisoners and aid to their families, was banned.

Opposition in South Africa was expressed by all the churches (except the Dutch Reformed Church), the Progressive Party, the Liberal Party until it was banned, students and professors at Universities, and some British-controlled papers, but except for Helen Suzman, the one Progressive MP, both the Opposition and the government party in the Legislature supported apartheid and measures to impose it. The Afrikaner majority among the Whites, backed by many British descendants (though with some moderate opposition from industrialists who wanted restriction on African labour removed) were in absolute control.

Withdrawal from Commonwealth

Meanwhile, international denunciation of apartheid grew. Within the Commonwealth opposition was intense, and the protests at the Prime Ministers' Conference led the South African Government to withdraw and become a Republic on May 31, 1961.[25] The United Nations General Assembly and Security Council repeatedly adopted strong resolutions, recommended that Western States should stop sending arms to South Africa, and set up a Special Committee on the policies of apartheid. The Secretariat periodically issued Notes and Comments describing the repression in South Africa.[26] The Organisation of African Unity, representing all the independent African States, established a Liberation Committee to support the military training and activity of the 'freedom fighters' in southern Africa, and the Conference of Unaligned Governments, forty-two states meeting at Lusaka in September 1970, gave major attention to the issue. A fierce controversy arose when the Conservative Government in Britain, elected in 1970, declared its intention to reverse the previous Labour Government's decision not to sell arms to South Africa and the Lusaka conference decided to send a deputation to Britain and to the governments supplying arms; the continued existence of the Commonwealth was threatened. The World Council of Churches got into trouble with many of its adherents when in 1970 it voted to contribute to the educational and relief work of freedom fighter organisations. In many countries anti-apartheid organisations carried on continuous agitation. An extraordinary impact was made when the Olympic Games Committee, most international sporting and athletic federations, and the English MCC (the cricket authority) broke off relations with South African sport because of its racist basis. To South Africans sport was a religion and the Government had to compromise to the extent of permitting mixed play in international games although it retained racial segregation in clubs within South Africa.

Over South Africa hangs a great question mark as to whether international pressures and the liberal elements within its territory can bring an adjustment of its racial relations before revolt brings civil war. Many conclude pessimistically (hoping to be wrong) that the chances are on the side of physical conflict.

Notes

1. The area of the Republic is 471,445 square miles. The population in 1970 was:

	White	Bantu	Asian	Coloured
Cape province	1,102,367	1,360,172	21,617	1,751,546
Natal	442,499	1,116,021	514,810	66,836
Transvaal	1,890,182	4,267,272	80,563	150,853
Orange Free State	295,903	1,317,308	5	36,090
Bantu homelands	20,377	6,997,179	3,441	13,128
TOTAL: 21,448,169	3,751,328	15,057,952	620,436	2,018,453

Note: Asians were excluded from the Orange Free State

2. Boer is Dutch for farmer.

3. The Trek Boers revenged this at the Battle of Blood River in 1838. It has been celebrated ever since as 'the Day of the Covenant' because the Trekkers vowed that if God gave them the victory they would commemorate it in perpetuity.

4. At twenty years of age Rhodes had made a fortune from new diamond mines at Kimberley.

5. Popular opposition to the introduction of Chinese indentured

labour in the South African mines was a factor in the defeat of the Conservatives.

6. Party strength in the Legislative Assembly was South Africa Party 66, Unionists 39, Natal Independents (pro-British) 11, Labour 4.

7. National Party 63, South Africa Party 53, Labour 18.

8. It will be remembered that Hertzog had already removed the Africans.

9. The Nationalists held out the promise that the three British Protectorates – Bechuanaland (Botswana), Basutoland (Lesotho) and Swaziland – would become Bantustan states, but in fact all remained multi-racial following independence.

10. Quoted by Patrick von Rensburg in *Guilty Land* from an article by Dr Eiselen in *Optima*, published by the Anglo-American Corporation. Asked in Parliament to reconcile the contradiction, Dr Verwoerd denied there was any.

11. The author organised Kadalie's visit to Britain and deplored the loss of his power. He became the victim of an environment to which he was not disciplined.

12. Albert Luthuli, *Let My People Go*

13. Albert Luthuli, *Let My People Go*.

14. Albert Luthuli, *Let My People Go*.

15. The author met Luthuli at Heathrow airport *en route*. He was surprised by the vitality of his personality following his illness. Here was a magnetic leader.

16. *Let My People Go* by Albert Luthuli.

17. Registration under this Act was nicknamed 'Vorster's human stud book'.

18. This subsequently became the accepted policy of ANC.

19. Fourteen persons were reported to have died in detention up to April 1970. Seven were stated to be suicidal cases.

20. Winnie Mandela courageously carried on the struggle, month after month, despite repeated detentions. She was sentenced to imprisonment again in 1973.

21. Reports of the trial made no reference to the cases of Miss Naidoo and Miss Nkala who had been arrested for refusing to give evidence.

22. There were many other trials. Immediately after the passing of the *Terrorism Act* in June, 1967, thirty-seven Namibians were charged at Pretoria. Fifteen were sentenced to life imprisonment, sixteen to terms ranging from 5 to 20 years, 3 to 5 years (under the *Suppression of Communism Act*), two were acquitted and one

died in prison. In July 1969 five Namibians were sentenced at Windhoek to life imprisonment under the *Terrorism Act* and one to 18 years (see next chapter). In December 1969 Donald Mathangela, a Malawi national, was sentenced at Pietermaritzburg to 7 years' imprisonment under the *Terrorism Act* for undergoing military training. Africans were also tried for alleged violence against chiefs. In August 1969 seventeen Bakwena were arrested for acts against Chief Lerothidi II who had imposed collective fines. Two died in prison before the trial; the inquest on one disclosed police brutality. Nine were released after many months in detention; the six tried were acquitted. Between April 1968 and March 1969 forty-seven Bakubung tribesmen were detained under the *Terrorism Act*, ten of whom were charged with the attempted murder of the Chieftainess. Six pleaded guilty and were sentenced to 3 years' imprisonment each, two years of which were suspended. The judge said he had sympathy for the reasons for the attempted murder. There was evidence of electric shock torture of prisoners. Two died in detention.

23. Eric Winchester, MP in the Assembly, quoted by Jill Chisholm in *Rand Daily Mail*, December 27, 1969.

24. Details and list of lawyers, UN Notes and Documents (Unit on Apartheid), January 1970.

25. This was after a referendum of the white electorate. The majority was small, 52·05 per cent in favour in a poll of 90·73 per cent. The total vote was 1,633,772.

26. Published by UN Unit on Apartheid (Department of Political and Security Council Affairs).

The Freedom Charter

Adopted at the Congress of the People at Kliptown Johannesburg, on June 25 and 26, 1955

We, the People of South Africa, declare for all our country and the world to know:

> that South Africa belongs to all who live in it, black and white, and that no government can justly claim authority unless it is based on the will of all the people.
> that our people have been robbed of their birthright to land, liberty and peace by a form of government founded on injustice and inequality,
> that our country will never be prosperous or free until all our people live in brotherhood, enjoying equal rights and opportunities,
> that only a democratic state, based on the will of all the people, can secure to all their birthright without distinction of colour, race, sex or belief;

And therefore we, the People of South Africa, black and white together – equals, countrymen and brothers – adopt this Freedom Charter. And we pledge ourselves to strive together sparing neither strength nor courage until the democratic changes here set out have been won.

THE PEOPLE SHALL GOVERN!

Every man and woman shall have the right to vote for and to stand as a candidate for all bodies which make laws;

All people shall be entitled to take part in the administration of the country.

The rights of the people shall be the same, regardless of race, colour or sex.

All bodies of minority rule, advisory boards, councils and authorities, shall be replaced by democratic organs of self-government.

ALL NATIONAL GROUPS SHALL HAVE EQUAL RIGHTS!

There shall be equal status in the bodies of state, in the courts and in the schools for all national groups and races.

All people shall have equal right to use their own languages, and to develop their own folk culture and customs.

All national groups shall be protected by law against insults to their race and national pride.

The preaching and practice of national, race or colour discrimination and contempt shall be a punishable crime.

All apartheid laws and practices shall be set aside.

THE PEOPLE SHALL SHARE IN THE COUNTRY'S WEALTH!

The national wealth of our country, the heritage of all South Africans, shall be restored to the people.

The mineral wealth beneath the soil, the banks and monopoly industry shall be transferred to the ownership of the people as a whole.

All other industry and trade shall be controlled to assist the well-being of the people.

All people shall have equal rights to trade where they choose, to manufacture and to enter all trades, crafts and professions.

THE LAND SHALL BE SHARED AMONG THOSE WHO WORK IT!

Restriction of land ownership on a racial basis shall be ended, and all the land redivided amongst those who work it, to banish famine and land hunger.

The State shall help the peasants with implements, seed, tractors and dams to save the soil and assist the tillers.

Freedom of movement shall be guaranteed to all who work on the land.

All shall have the right to occupy land wherever they choose.

People shall not be robbed of their cattle, and forced labour and farm prisons shall be abolished.

ALL SHALL BE EQUAL BEFORE THE LAW!

No one shall be imprisoned, deported or restricted without a fair trial.

No one shall be condemned by the order of any Government official.

The courts shall be representative of all the people.

Imprisonment shall be only for serious crimes against the people, and shall aim at re-education not vengeance.

The police force and army shall be open to all on an equal basis and shall be the helpers and protectors of the people.

All laws which discriminate on grounds of race, colour or belief shall be repealed.

ALL SHALL ENJOY EQUAL HUMAN RIGHTS!

The law shall guarantee to all their right to speak, to organise, to meet together, to publish, to preach, to worship and to educate their children.

The privacy of the house from police raids shall be protected by law.

All shall be free to travel without restriction from countryside to town, from province to province and from South Africa abroad.

Pass laws, permits and all other laws restricting these freedoms shall be abolished.

THERE SHALL BE WORK AND SECURITY!

All who work shall be free to form trade unions, to elect their officers and to make wage agreements with their employers.

The State shall recognise the right and duty of all to work, and to draw full unemployment benefits.

Men and women of all races shall receive equal pay for equal work.

There shall be a forty-hour working week, a national minimum wage, paid annual leave and sick leave for all workers and maternity leave on full pay for all working mothers.

Miners, domestic workers, farm workers and civil servants shall have the same right as all others who work.

Child labour, compound labour, the tot system and contract labour shall be abolished.

THE DOORS OF LEARNING AND OF CULTURE SHALL BE OPENED!

The Government shall discover, develop and encourage national talent for the enhancement of our cultural life.

All the cultural treasures of mankind shall be open to all, by free exchange of books, ideas and contact with other lands.

The aim of education shall be to teach the youth to love their people and their culture, to honour human brotherhood, liberty and peace.

Education shall be free, compulsory, universal and equal for all children.

Higher education and technical training shall be opened to all by means of state allowances and scholarships awarded on the basis of merit.

Adult illiteracy shall be ended by a mass state education plan.

Teachers shall have all the rights of other citizens.

The colour bar in cultural life, in sport and in education shall be abolished.

THERE SHALL BE HOUSES, SECURITY AND COMFORT!

All people shall have the right to live where they choose, to be decently housed, and to bring up their families in comfort and security.

Unused housing space shall be made available to the people.

Rent and prices shall be lowered, food plentiful and no one shall go hungry.

A preventive health scheme shall be run by the State.

Free medical care and hospitalisation shall be provided for all, with special care for mothers and young children.

Slums shall be demolished and new suburbs built where all have transport, roads, lighting, playing fields, crèches and social centres.

The aged, the orphans, the disabled and the sick shall be cared for by the State.

Rest, leisure and recreation shall be the right of all. Fenced locations and ghettoes shall be abolished and laws which break up families shall be repealed.

THERE SHALL BE PEACE AND FRIENDSHIP!

South Africa shall be a fully independent state, which respects the rights and sovereignty of all nations.

South Africa shall strive to maintain world peace and the settlement of all international disputes by negotiation – not war.

Peace and friendship amongst all our people shall be secured by upholding the equal rights, opportunities and status of all.

The people of the protectorates – Basutoland, Bechuanaland and Swaziland – shall be free to decide for themselves their own future.

The rights of all the peoples of Africa to independence and self-government shall be recognised and shall be the basis of close co-operation.

Let all who love their people and their country now say, as we say here:

'THESE FREEDOMS WE WILL FIGHT FOR, SIDE BY SIDE, THROUGHOUT OUR LIVES, UNTIL WE HAVE WON OUR LIBERTY.'

Chapter Nineteen

South West Africa (Namibia)

South West Africa (to Africans, Namibia) is as large as France and the British Isles together.[1] To its north is Angola and, across a narrow strip, Zambia; to its east, Botswana; to its south, the Republic of South Africa; to its west, the Atlantic along a coastline of 800 miles.[2] The estimated population in 1970 was only 746,328, composed of 630,661 Africans, 90,658 Whites and 25,009 Coloureds. One-third of the territory, arid land, is virtually uninhabited.

German Occupation

The original tribes were Bantus and Khoisans, often in conflict for possession of grazing land. The early coastal traders were British, Dutch and Germans, and the last, reacting to Dutch and British occupation of the Cape, imposed treaties of 'protection' on the Hereros and Namas inland. By the 1880s South West Africa became a German possession, with farmer-settlers supplementing traders. The German administration was tidily efficient for themselves, neat homes and roads, but for the Africans it was inhuman and they were treated as little above animals. There was fierce resistance, leading to appalling massacres in 1904. The Herero tribe were reduced from eighty thousand to fifteen thousand and the Namas were decimated.

South African Mandate

In the First World War the territory was taken by forces from the Dominion of South Africa and at the end it became a mandatory state under the League of Nations administered by South Africa. Responsibility in the first instance was given to the United Kingdom, but London seconded it to the Dominion. The mandate principle was 'to promote to the utmost the material and moral well-being and social progress of the inhabitants of the territory', but that was not how the Afrikaners controlling South Africa administered it. They stimulated white immigration, gave the best land to the settlers, evicted the Africans to reserves, and treated them as social outcasts. They imposed heavy taxation, but most of the revenue went to white betterment. In 1967 of the £864,000 spent on education, only £52,000 was allotted to the Africans, who were twenty times as many as the Whites.[3]

African resistance persisted. There was refusal in 1922 to pay the dog tax, unpopular throughout southern Africa, leading to the bombing of Bondelswarts, and ten years later, after sporadic revolts, there was a major attack on the village of Ipumba, the home of a chief who rejected terms of land expropriation. The same year the League of Nations asked that South Africa's economic powers be transferred to it. The issue was delayed over the Second World War, but the suppression of the Africans and the eviction from their lands continued. The Herero chief, Frederick Makarero, was exiled in Botswana. He authorised the Rev. Michael Scott, an Anglican priest who had courageously identified himself with African claims, to present the case of his tribe to the Fourth Committee of the United Nations. He did so persistently and impressively. He was accompanied by J. Kozonquizi, then President of the South West African National Union (SWANU).

Hague Court Judgment

Twenty-five years of frustration followed. The United Nations became involved in the judgment on the status of South West Africa by the International Court of Justice at the Hague, which from 1949 to 1966 delivered contradictory decisions. Its first decision was that the authority of the League of Nations over mandated territories had passed to the United Nations, including the obligation of the mandatory power to report annually to the United Nations.[4] Ethiopia and Liberia, as former members of the League of Nations, instigated proceedings against South Africa at the Court on the ground that it had broken the mandate by many policies, including the application of apartheid. South Africa objected that Ethiopia and Liberia were not parties to the dispute since their national interests were not involved. The Court by majority turned down this argument, but in 1966 by a vote of seven to six reversed its decision, and the appeal of the two African governments was rejected.

United Nations Ultimatum

The majority in the United Nations did not retreat before this negative judgment. In October 1966 the General Assembly declared that South Africa had failed to perform its duties under the mandate and by its actions had disavowed it. The mandate was therefore revoked. In May 1967, the UN appointed a 'Council for Namibia' to administer the territory and in December called on South Africa 'unconditionally and without delay' to withdraw. When the Nationalist Governments of the Republic did not comply, the General Assembly then recommended that the Security Council take measures to end their administration by October 4, 1969. The Security Council appointed an *ad hoc* committee to study ways and means to implement the decisions and declared all acts undertaken by the South African Government after its termination of the mandate 'illegal and invalid'. In July 1970 the committee recommended that consular representation should be withdrawn from South West Africa and that financial and industrial companies should end dealings in the territory.

Apartheid and Bantustans

The South African Government took no notice of these pronouncements, refusing even to admit an UN mission, and proceeded with its administration on the principle of apartheid as though the United Nations did not exist. In effect, the Malan Government had virtually annexed South West Africa when it gave the settlers elected representation in the Legislature of the Republic. The Bantustan pattern was followed by restricting the tribes to reserves, evacuating them by force if they were resident in territory seized by the Whites. The South African authorities were selective in this, allocating to the Ovambos, the strongest tribe, a reserve on the Angolan border where water and fertile soil were available, but none of the other reserves were economically viable, and the people were left to scratch existence from land that was often arid or to become ill-paid labour on eighteen month contracts for the Whites. The Coloureds were segregated in locations in the towns.

When the reserves were set up some form of self-government was promised, but only in Ovamboland was anything done. What was termed a Legislative Council was constituted of chiefs and headmen with a maximum of forty per cent elected members. The Council had little power however. All legislation had to be submitted to the South African Government before implementation and the major features of discipline and development – internal security, transport, water supply and the production and distribution of power – were reserved for white control. All the inhibitions of apartheid were imposed in the towns where the African labourers were treated as untouchables in social life.

Resistance

Resistance to the White occupation of South West Africa developed from spontaneous and unco-ordinated revolts into national organisations. The South West African Peoples' Organisation (SWAPO), the strongest, arose from a trade union formed by Namibian contract labourers in Cape Town. Its leader, Sam Nujoma, gave it a political purpose in South West Africa in the late fifties. The first agitation was against the forcible eviction of Africans from their traditional land to make room for White settlers. At Windhoek in 1959 troops and police fired on a protesting demonstration, killing eleven and wounding more than fifty; indignation led to extending support for SWAPO. African political activity was illegal and underground work was carried on at severe peril. In 1968 thirty-one members of SWAPO were sentenced in Pretoria to terms of imprisonment up to twenty years under the *Terrorism Act*. In impressive language Herman ja Toivo, one of SWAPO's founders, stated the African case. 'We are Namibians and not South Africans,' he said. 'We do not now and will not in the future recognise your right to govern us, to make laws for us in which we have no say, to treat our country as if it were your property and us as if you were our masters . . . Only when our human dignity is restored to us as equals of the Whites will there be peace between us.' Ja Toivo was one of the arrested sentenced to twenty years' imprisonment. In July–August 1969, five Namibian resisters were sentenced at Windhoek, again under the *Terrorism Act*, to life imprisonment and one to eight years.

The headquarters of SWAPO had to be transferred outside the territory. It gave up hope of achieving its object by peaceful means, declaring in January 1970, at its Consultative Congress in Tanzania, that 'armed struggle is the only effective way to bring about the liberation of Namibia'. From time to time trained 'freedom fighters' infiltrated into South West Africa, and in the Caprivi strip neighbouring Zambia there were fierce clashes in 1970 and fighting extended southward. The nationalist movement did not escape the division which marred other movements. The South West African National Union (SWANU), with headquarters in Europe, whilst not disclaiming armed revolt, placed most emphasis on revolutionary mass action within the territory.[5] The voice of protest did not go unheard in Namibia. The Herero Chiefs' Council established the National Unity Democratic Organisation to act within the limits of legality allowed. It complained to the United Nations about the removal of tribes, particularly the Hereros, from their homelands, and other chiefs and headmen petitioned. The *South African Terrorism Act* did not permit any political activity other than petitions.

Africans Criticise the UN

The failure of the United Nations to implement its declaration that South West Africa should cease to be administered by the Republic was severely criticised by Africans. Britain, France and Portugal had refrained from voting for the resolution on the ground of the inability of the United Nations to apply it, which in fact proved to be the case. Considerable cynicism and frustration arose. The OAU in 1969 endorsed a manifesto initiated by East and Central African governments calling on the UN to enforce its decision and to secure self-determination and independence for Namibia. 'If they do this,' the manifesto declared, 'there is hope that the change can be effected without great violence. If they fail, then sooner or later the people of South West Africa will take the law into their own hands.' The General Assembly of the United Nations, without apparently any twinge of conscience, welcomed the manifesto and expressed the intention of the UN to co-operate with the OAU; but no effective action emerged. SWAPO at its conference in Tanzania in 1970 remarked that the UN had 'done nothing' and called on it to live up to its obligations. The impotence of the United Nations contributed to the disrespect for it as an organisation which spread in the late sixties and early seventies through a large part of the world.

Financial Interests

It should be noted that there was one passage in the UN resolution of 1970 which suggested positive action. It recommended that member states should withdraw consular representation from South West Africa and that financial and industrial corporations should end dealings in the territory. Little was done to follow up this proposal, though in May 1970, President Nixon declared that the US would 'actively discourage American investment as long as South Africa continued to rule in defiance of the United Nations'. The discovery of minerals, in the first instance diamonds, changed the whole economy of Namibia. From fishing and agriculture it became a mining territory. In the five years to 1967 the value of mineral exports doubled to R.136 million, whilst the fishing industry accounted for only about R.50 million and agriculture for about R.40 million.[6] Copper and petroleum supplemented diamonds. British, American, Canadian and French financial and industrial interests were involved as well as South African.[7] It was clear that if the UN recommendation were applied, the effect in South West Africa would be serious.

UN Action Proposed

At a hearing of the Fourth Committee of the United Nations in October 1969, Professor Gideon Gottlieb, of the International Law Department of the University of New York, urged that a Judicial Committee should be set up to apply its decisions.[8] This proposal was extended by Michael Scott in evidence he gave to the Ad Hoc Committee of the Security Council in April 1970.[9] He urged that the Judicial Committee should not only hear appeals from Namibians sentenced to terms of imprisonment, prosecute officials responsible for inhumane treatment of prisoners, and take measures in relation to international corporations engaged in mining and prospecting operations, but should activate the UN Council for Namibia as the legal *ad interim* government. The difficulty was the absence of any UN presence in South West Africa, but Michael Scott made a series of recommendations, such as eligibility to representation at the FAO, WHO, ILO, Universal Postal Union, etc, which would have given the Council international authority. The Council could be substituted for the Republic of South Africa as a party to multi-lateral treaties and conventions affecting Namibia and be authorised to establish a provisional constitution, in consultation with representatives of the indigenous population, for the territory's future. The proposal for the prohibition of investment and industrial enterprise in Namibia could be operated by giving power to the Judicial Committee to impose sanctions on individuals or undertakings contravening it. A determined United Nations could have taken such measures, but it was very unlikely that the governments of industrial countries with extensive investment and trading interests in South West Africa and South Africa itself would agree to their limitation.

The Ovambo Revolt

At the end of 1971 an event occurred which was not only immediately important but potentially of great significance. Thirteen thousand workers of the Ovambo tribe, employed in gold, diamond and copper mines outside their reserve in white men's territory (it was popularly known as 'The Police Zone'), refused to accept the contract system of labour imposed on them. In fact, the system was much like that under which miners from the reserves lived in the Republic: housed in compounds, wives and children not allowed, wages low (less than £1 a week), segregation from the Whites. The strike extended to the fish factories at Walvis Bay and virtually halted all services in the territory. The surprising fact was that the Ovambos had revolted. Their tribe was favoured by the Afrikaners, their reserve fertile and green, a show-piece of Bantustan. When Mr Vorster had proposed to the International Court a plebiscite on the issue of continued South African rule, he had in mind the 350,000 Ovambos occupying two-thirds of the territory. He assumed their allegiance.

Twelve leaders of the strike were arrested and clashes with the security forces occurred, eight Ovambos killed. The workers then returned *en masse* to their reserve, where hundreds were arrested, compelling the erection of temporary gaols; when their chiefs sided with the Government the people disowned them. The strikers won modifications of the contract system, but more significantly they turned against the system of apartheid itself. Tribute must be paid to the non-Afrikaner church leaders who supported the protesting people; the Anglican Bishop and three other churchmen were exiled. The Government proclaimed emergency regulations under which meetings of more than five people were banned and indefinite detention without trial, similar to practice in the Republic, was authorised. Despite this, opponents of the regime met in Namibia secretly and drew up plans for a new form of government.

These events were accompanied by a political development of first importance. Mr Vorster permitted the Secretary-General of the United Nations to visit South West Africa. Dr Waldheim's mandate from the Security Council was 'to initiate as soon as possible contacts with all parties concerned with a view to establishing the necessary conditions so as to enable the people of Namibia freely and with strict regard to the principles of human equality to exercise their right to self-determination and independence'. Dr Waldheim met African spokesmen and the church leaders, but some apprehension was caused as to whether he had been influenced by Mr Vorster's argument that Bantustans in South West Africa would lead to a satisfactory independence.[10]

No such compromise would be acceptable to the African people. Increasingly it becomes clear that the liberation of Namibia is a part of the wide issue of the ending of white supremacy throughout the South.

Notes

1. Total area, 318,216 square miles.

2. The narrow strip on the Zambian frontier, 200 miles long and 20 miles wide, was conceded by the British to the Germans, then in occupation, in 1890 to enable them to have access to the river Zambezi. An area of 434 square miles at Walvis Bay was annexed by the British in 1878 to protect the British interests at the port. It is administered as part of South West Africa, but is technically part of the Republic of South Africa.

3. *South West Africa (Namibia): Proposals for Action*, edited by Richard Hall.

4. South Africa submitted one report to the UN, but after the election of Nationalist governments declined to continue.

5. The Organisation of African Unity (OAU) gave recognition only to SWAPO.

6. UN Report A/7752. The Report remarked that the African population participated in the economic expansion only as unskilled or semi-skilled labour at wages substantially below those of the Whites. In 1967 the average *per capita* domestic product was R.360, whilst the average income of the Whites was R.1,602.

7. Ninety per cent of the diamond industry was controlled by the Consolidated Diamond Mines of South West Africa, associated with the Anglo-American Corporation (South Africa). The largest producer of base metals was the Tsumeb Corporation, owned by American Metal Climax and the Newmont Mining Corporation. The United Kingdom was the principal purchaser of diamonds. The three largest buyers of base minerals, principally copper, were the USA, Belgium and West Germany. Exploratory concessions were granted to subsidiaries of British, French, American and Canadian companies, as well as South African.

8. The proposal was first made to the UN Commission on Human Rights by the International Commission of Jurists.

9. *South West Africa* (*Namibia*): *Proposals for Action* (Africa Bureau).

10. Subsequently Dr Waldheim sent a deputy to Namibia and the fear of a compromised settlement accepting separate Bantustans was renewed. It appeared unlikely that Dr Woldheim or the Security Council would accept it.

Chapter Twenty

The Ex-British
Protectorates

(Lesotho, Botswana,
Swaziland)

The ex-British Protectorates in southern Africa were Basutoland (now Lesotho), Bechuanaland (now Botswana) and Swaziland. They were known as the High Commission Territories and were so called because they were ruled by a High Commissioner stationed in Pretoria, who was also the British Ambassador to South Africa. Basutoland and Swaziland were constitutionally British Colonies and Bechuanaland a Protectorate, but in practice the administration was similar.

Lesotho is an enclave within the territory of the Republic of South Africa. It is a small mountain region, with an area of 11,716 square miles, but has a population of about 969,634, the largest of the three. Botswana to the north-west of South Africa is vast, 222,000 square miles, much of it desert, scrubland and swamp, with only 543,105 people (1964 census). Swaziland, on the north-east edge of South Africa, is the smallest in area, only 6,705 square miles, but is the most highly developed, with an estimated population in 1966 of 374,571.

Reason for Neglect

All three territories are closely linked with South Africa, not only geographically but economically. Their proximity led to their involvement in the conflict between the British and Boers for South Africa. In one respect the British occupation was unusual. London did not wish to colonise; it was reluctantly led to do so in competition with the Boers, supplemented in the case of Lesotho and Botswana by requests from the people for protection. After the establishment of the Union of South Africa in 1910 it was assumed that the territories would be incorporated with the Dominion. It was only when South Africa left the Commonwealth that this prospect was entirely given up, although the opposition to apartheid, including that of the peoples themselves, had made political integration increasingly difficult. The original British disinclination to take responsibility for the territories and to spend money on them, and the later perspective of their transference to South Africa, meant that they became the 'Cinderellas' of the empire. Their development was for fifty years almost totally neglected.

Basutoland came under British control in 1884, Bechuanaland in 1885 and Swaziland in 1903. In his monumental *An African Survey* Lord Hailey wrote that 'it was not until 1927 that the imperial Government began to give any sign of a practical interest in the means necessary to improve the local economic and social services'. There was no thought of the political evolution of the territories until even later, Lord Hailey adding that by 1931 there was 'no evidence of any consideration being given by the British Government at this stage to the policy to be observed in regard to their development or their political future'. The policy of indirect rule was applied to the point of indifference to any responsibility. The chiefs were permitted to run their tribes as they liked so long as they collected the taxes to pay for a skeleton British staff, which was designedly of a lower level of quality than elsewhere in the colonial service. Britain was in the background to maintain law and order and their territorial status, but nothing was done by the Colonial Office for the education or health of the people or to lift them from poverty by economic progress. The only welfare activity was by the missionary societies.

This state of affairs continued until into the thirties when the British began to accept some responsibility for administration by the chiefs. Only after the Second World War did Britain reveal a sense of involved concern for the social and economic progress of the territories; in 1955 help at last began through the Colonial Welfare and Development Fund. Only after the Nationalist victories in South Africa in 1948 did Westminster take the first steps to advance the protectorates towards democratic self-government and eventual independence. That story we tell in separate consideration of the three territories.

Lesotho (Basutoland)

Lesotho (independence, October 1966) has particular difficulties because it is surrounded by the territory of the Republic. Its dense population was estimated in 1965 to be composed of 746,000

Africans and 2,000 Europeans (government officials, traders, missionaries), and earlier census in the same year returned 891 Asians and Coloureds. Estimated population by 1971 was 930,000.

British Asked to Protect

Until the first half of the nineteenth century a kingdom of Lesotho stretched west across what is now the Orange Free state of the Union of South Africa and south to parts of what is now Transkei. The original Bushmen inhabitants migrated or were destroyed in tribal wars, and replaced by Bantus. In the nineteenth century the Bantus had to face an invasion by Zulus, beaten back by a young chief, Moshoeshoe, a legendary figure, who then had to face invading Boers and British. He skilfully played off the rival Europeans against each other, but he lost a large part of his territory to the Boers and in 1843 sought the protection of the more liberal British in a restricted Basutoland. He welcomed missionaries and traders, but after his death in 1870 the Protectorate was annexed without consultation as part of Britain's Cape Colony.

The British ran roughshod over traditional customs and tribal loyalties, substituting the jurisdiction of nominated magistrates for that of the chiefs; they treated Basutoland as a native reserve, anticipating Bantustans but this had the advantage of prohibiting the alienation of land to Europeans. A demand by the chiefs for representation in the Cape parliament to gain some voice in decisions regarding Basutoland was refused and anger was aroused by a doubling of the head tax and an attempt to enforce the disarmament of its people. Fighting broke out, sufficiently serious to be known as 'The Gun War', and the strong resistance by the Basutos gained them the right to carry arms.

With peace in 1884 Basutoland became, at the request of the chiefs, a Crown Colony separated from the Cape. Its people and chiefs retained a good deal of the spirit of independence and declared themselves neutral in the Boer War at the turn of the century. They were deeply suspicious of the *Act of Union* in 1910 which united Boer and British in South Africa in a Dominion. They were reassured somewhat when Britain reaffirmed the protectorate status of the three territories, Bechuanaland, Swaziland and Basutoland, but were uneasy when they were placed under a High Commissioner stationed with doubtful implications at Pretoria and who was given dictatorial powers of law making.

Prospects of Union with South Africa

There was ground for suspicion. It was assumed in the Act of Union that the territories would eventually be joined to South Africa. Under Section 151 the Dominion was given the right to apply to the British Government for their amalgamation. Colonel Seely, the Colonial Secretary, presenting the Act to Parliament foreshadowed a transfer to South Africa so gradual that the 'natives will never know from anything that occurs to them that the transition has been effected'.[1] The High Commissioner governed through the chiefs who traditionally consulted assemblies of the people, *pitsos*, and who since 1903 had participated in a National Council (with eight government nominees) to consider legislation and the use of the hut tax. Following the *Act of Union* this body was given more formal status as the 'Basutoland Council', consisting of one hundred members, six officials and ninety-four nominated by the Paramount Chief; it was still limited to advice and criticism. The intention was to protect the interests of the people, but in fact under Crown Colony rule they became more alienated from the administration. This was largely due to the tendency of the British to encourage the chiefs to look 'upwards towards government for authority and support rather than, as before, to the people'.[2] Basutoland gained economically from an arrangement by which South Africa contributed a percentage of its custom receipts and from employment for its male population in the Kimberley mines.

Democratic Beginnings

The beginning of an expression of independent opinion had taken place in 1907 with the formation of the Progressive Association, a group of teachers, traders and white-collar workers. They pressed for the addition of elected members to the Basutoland Council, and criticised the nepotism and corruption of many chiefs. Events rather than popular pressure, however, determined changes during the first forty years of British colonial rule. In 1929 a fall in world prices of mohair and wool brought many families to the edge of starvation and in 1932–3 there was a devastating drought, which destroyed thousands of livestock and only government distribution of maize relieved the most extreme suffering. London in 1934 sent out a commission under Sir Alan Pim to report on the economic position of Basutoland, extended also to the two other British territories. Sir Alan estimated that grants of £151,000 over ten years were necessary to meet soil erosion,[3] but he also insisted on administrative changes. Under these the powers of the Paramount Chief to make rules for the 'peace, order and welfare' of the Basutos were increased, but the British were given the last word in his appointment and in the listing of subordinate chiefs and headmen.

A second change arose from an ugly event, the re-emergence of a primitive practice of 'ritual murder'. A claimant to the Paramountcy believed his interests would be furthered by 'medicines' which included human flesh. He was executed, but others followed his example and in 1948 there were twenty ritual murders. Study of the circumstances indicated that the motives were political and progressive elements in Basutoland, shocked by these traditionalist barbarities, demanded the institution of a modern democratic society. Pressure grew for an extension of the authority of the Basutoland Council.' Moderate chiefs and the Progressive Association joined in a declaration calling for the British to consult both the Council and the Paramount Chief, now less hidebound, before enacting decrees, adding that this should be the practice until 'the time comes for Basutoland to have its own Legislative Council'. From 1948 onwards changes were made in the constitution of the Council providing for thirty-six elected members from districts and specialised bodies including the Progressive Association; the High Commissioner agreed to consult the Council before instituting changes affecting domestic affairs; and the Paramount Chief agreed that no local rate or levy would be valid unless approved by the Council.

The third change was the establishment of advisory District Councils in 1945. They were proposed by the Basutoland Council, but when in 1950 the British administration introduced the principle of secret voting the chiefs had a shock. Their nominees were defeated. A new democratic opinion was emerging.

African Congress Formed

The Basutoland African Congress (BAC)[4] was formed in 1952. It attacked both authoritarian British rule and the Basutoland Council as a stooge of that rule. Its leader, Ntsu Mokhehle, was to be a controversial figure. Born in 1918 of middle-class parents, he was writing about African wrongs when he was nineteen. He was expelled for a time from Fort Hare College for inciting strikes; on resuming, he gained the Master of Science degree. In South Africa he became active in the National Congress Youth League and returned to Basutoland with the one object of political campaigning. He started by securing the presidency of the Teachers' Association. His colleagues were B. M. Khaketla, editor of the BAC paper, *Mohlabani* (The Warrior) and Z. L. Mothopeng, who became an Executive member of the South African Pan-Africanist Congress. All three were teachers at the Maseru High School, and were dismissed in 1955 from their posts, a victimisation which immediately won many recruits for the BAC, including students and workers as well as teachers. The party came into conflict with the strong Roman Catholic Church which regarded it as co-operating with Communists, though Mokhehle never hid his anti-Communism.

Other parties were formed in 1958. Two prominent Catholics, Chief Jonathan (later Basutoland's first Prime Minister) and G. C. Manyeli started the Basutoland National Party (BNP) supporting self-government but also hereditary chieftainship.[5] There were two breakaways from the Basutoland Congress Party (BCP) which in 1955 had succeeded in name the BAC, the *Marema-Tlou* (United Party) and the Basutoland Freedom Party (BFP) which merged as the Marema-Tlou Freedom Party. The former was led by Chief Matete and appeared to have the support of both the British administration and the Paramount Chief. The latter was surprisingly started by B. M. Khaketla, whose differences with his colleagues were personal rather than political. In 1962 the Basutoland Communist Party was established. The earlier policy of the Communists had been to join the BCP, but they were denounced by Mokhehle and decided to organise separately. The party never had much influence.

Legislative Council

In 1955 the Basutoland Council had proposed to the British that it should be given powers to make laws in all internal matters, subject to confirmation by the Paramount Chief. London had replied sympathetically, but the Council had second thoughts when it realised that this would involve a dual administration with separate laws for non-Basutos. Professor D. V. Cowan of Cape Town University was asked to prepare a draft constitution and the Council unanimously endorsed his proposals for a Legislative Council and an Executive Council in which the interests of both Basutos and non-Basutos would be represented. Constitutional Conferences were held in London and Maseru, and in September 1959 Orders-in-Council were promulgated by the British Government to make a new constitution operational in 1960. A Legislative Council was established, named the Basuto National Council. Forty of its 80 members were to be elected from 9 District Councils acting as electoral colleges, 22 were to be chiefs, 14 were to be selected by the Paramount Chief, and four to be government officers. The Council was given power to legislate on all matters except a long list of important spheres, not only external affairs, defence and internal security but currency, customs, civil service, the mails, broadcasting and related subjects, though on these reserved subjects the Council would also act as a consultative body. Powers of delay were given to the Paramount Chief. The Executive Council would consist of four senior officials and four non-officials, one of whom would be nominated by the Paramount Chief.

The first general election took place in January 1960. It resulted in an impressive victory for the BCP which demanded immediate independence, criticised the British administration, and condemned South Africa for its apartheid and its designs to take over. The BCP secured 36 per cent of the popular vote, won 73 of the 162 District Council seats, and took control of 6 of the 9 Councils. The Marema-Tlou-Freedom Party won 8 per cent of the votes and 15 District Council seats. The Independents polled nearly as many votes as the BCP, but won only 4 seats in the Legislature. The Paramount Chief nominated 9 Independents, 2 BNP members and 3 members of the Progressive Association (PA). When the National Council met B. M. Khaketla, then still in the BCP, Chief Matete of the MTFP and M. Lepolesa, a member of the Progressive Association, were elected to the Executive Council with four officials and one nominee of the Paramount Chief. When Khaketla defected from the BCP, the policy of the Executive became openly conservative and the majority in the National Council became an Opposition, led aggressively by the BCP which demanded immediate independence.

Independence

The Executive gave way to the extent of requesting the High Commissioner to invite the Paramount Chief to appoint a constitutional commission. Significant of the mood in the country and of his subsequent behaviour was the response of the Paramount Chief, Moshoeshoe II. In a speech to the National Council he stressed the inadequacy of British rule, the need for responsible government and the importance of a reform of traditional institutions. The commission sat for eighteen months. Its report was dynamite. It called for independence by 1965, universal franchise, a bicameral National Assembly, the lower house elected, the upper house of chiefs and king's nominees with delaying powers only, a cabinet on the British model and the establishment of a constitutional monarchy under Moshoeshoe.[6] The British Government hesitated, their cautious attitude challenged by declarations by Mokhehle for the BCP, Chief Matete for the MFP and Chief Jonathan for the BNP. Constitutional talks were held in London which, after official obstruction, led to an agreement that independence would be granted twelve months after an election.[7]

Although the BCP had made all the running for independence, there was a marked decline in its support before the election. This was partly due to a renewed campaign alleging communist association which affected the large Roman Catholic electorate. It was due also to the enfranchisement of women who feared that the BCP opposition to South Africa would prejudice the position of their menfolk working in the Witwatersrand mines. The election in April 1965, resulted in the BNP gaining 41·63 per cent of the votes, with 31 of the 60 seats, the BCP 39·66 per cent with 25 seats, the MTFP 16·49 per cent with 4 seats. Both Chief Jonathan, leader of the BNP, and Dr Makotoko, the MTFP leader, were defeated. Makotoko was nominated to the Senate, Jonathan won a by-election and became Prime Minister. In October 1966 Basutoland under its historic name Lesotho became independent.

Reactions of South Africa

In the background of all these events was South Africa. It will be recalled that until the Republic left the Commonwealth in 1961 the British Government had at the back of its mind that Basutoland, Bechuanaland and Swaziland would eventually be incorporated with South Africa. This explained its indifference and neglect. Dr Verwoerd's idea was that the three territories should become Bantustans, native reserves with considerable autonomy, and it was only the 1959 constitution for Basutoland which repudiated this aim by establishing a common roll for the election of the Legislative Council. Even then a sop was thrown to South Africa by the assurance (overtaken within seven years) that Basutoland could not in the foreseeable future become a completely independent state. The fact that the territory was an enclave within South Africa and economically bound to it meant that the British administration, the Republican Government, and the Basuto political parties all had continuously to keep in mind the impact of the two territories upon each other.

South Africa's white leaders did not want Basutoland to become a stronghold of Pan-Africanism within its borders, or a place of refuge from which its African exiles could plan subversion. Accordingly help was given to Chief Jonathan's BNP, which although it rejected apartheid stood for co-operation. In the election of 1965 South Africa provided the party with vehicles and, it is alleged, money,[8] and before Chief Jonathan's by-election Dr Verwoerd presented him personally (rather than the government) with 100,000 bags of grain worth over £150,000 for distribution in relief. Chief Jonathan on his side expressed a desire to initiate conversations with Dr Verwoerd and pleased him by announcing that he would not accept a single embassy of any country 'sympathetic to the aims of Communism', among which he included Nkrumah's Ghana, Tanzania and the African Arab countries. He also announced that he would not allow refugees to engage in 'subversive action against other governments'.

South Africa's Proposals

The South African Government under Dr Malan had publicly announced in 1959 that it had abandoned the idea of the incorporation of Basutoland (and the other High Commission Territories), but Dr Verwoerd proposed close association through links with the Republic and with the Bantustan states of South Africa in a consultative body dealing with 'mutual political interests'. Whilst the Basuto Council was considering its future constitution he elaborated this plan in September 1963. He suggested that there might be an exchange of borderland territories, African areas in the

Republic and white areas in Lesotho, and, remarking that there was a very small number of Whites in Basutoland, proposed that they should be regarded as citizens of the Republic, arguing that this would be consistent with the citizenship rights of Basutos working in South Africa. He warned that whilst Britain might guide Basutoland to political freedom, London was powerless to provide economic viability and claimed that if South Africa were to become their guardian the Republic could lead the Basutos 'far better and much more quickly to independence and economic prosperity than Great Britain can do'. He looked forward to a 'Commonwealth for White and Black South Africa in co-operation', within a consultative political body of 'free Black and White states'. It was clear that South Africa was still thinking of a racially segregated Basutoland, applying the principle of apartheid.

In September 1966 Prime Minister Jonathan met Dr Verwoerd (four days before his assassination), the first African leader to sit at a table with him, and planned co-operation.[9] Economic concessions were made to South Africans, including diamond rights. In 1970 the South African electoral officer in Transkei, J. Pretorius, was seconded as Chief Electoral Officer in Lesotho. The political attitude of Chief Jonathan was reflected in the proposal he made to Malawi, also a collaborator with South Africa, that there should be a grouping of southern African states, confirmed later in the support he gave in 1970 for British arms to South Africa.

Election Declared Void

The 1970 election had a dramatic result and dramatic consequences. The early returns showed that the BCP had won; the reported figures were BCP 36, BNP 23, MTFP 1. Before the result was officially announced, however, Chief Jonathan cancelled the election, alleging that there had been intimidation. He declared a state of emergency and arrested not only the BCP leaders, including Ntsu Mokhehle, but also King Moshoeshoe, on the ground that he had exerted influence on the side of the Opposition. 'I have seized power and I am not ashamed of it,' declared the Prime Minister, saying he was confident that he had the majority of the people behind him.

The BCP asserted that the *coup* had been instigated by British expatriates; the state of emergency was policed by a force under British officers seconded to Lesotho. The charge was also made that it was given legal authority by a South African-manned judiciary: the Chief Justice suspended the High Court when an action was brought for the release of the BCP leaders. The British at first withdrew their recognition of the Jonathan Government and gave notice to end financial aid, but subsequently recognition and aid were renewed when the authority of the Government appeared to have been demonstrated.

When Mokhehle was arrested he appealed to the people to remain calm, but resistance grew. The first challenge was made by an ex-Commissioner of the king, Clement Leepa, but he was defeated, imprisoned and died within a month. Government forces then raided villages widely and fierce fighting broke out in the capital, Maseru, with aircraft dropping bombs and grenades. There was criticism at Westminster that the armed police mobile unit, the main force in suppressing the revolt, was commanded by British officers; the Government replied that they were in the service of the Lesotho administration. Chief Jonathan announced that a 'master plan' for the overthrow of the Government had been discovered and decreed a *Suppression of Communism Order* which, like its prototype in South Africa, outlawed not only communist organisations but the furtherance of the 'objects of Communism'. At the same time the Government acted to destroy the power of the king. It exiled him to Holland and dismissed chiefs and headmen favourable to him.[10]

Talks Fail

In April 1970 Mokhehle, disturbed by the violence which had led to over two hundred deaths, agreed to talks with Chief Jonathan. He made concessions which were criticised by some of his followers, offering to enter an interim government with the Chief as head, on condition that within a year there should be a general election. There is doubt about what happened at these talks, the official *communiqué* stating only that the general election was discounted. The BCP insisted that a settlement was concluded, including provisions for an interim government, an election within a year, and the release of prisoners, and that the Prime Minister had gone back on this. It was not possible to learn the truth, but the fact that Mokhehle was kept under strict house arrest after the talks indicated that disagreement persisted.[11]

The future of Lesotho is inseparable from the future of South

Africa. With the livelihood of its people dependent on the Republic it has little room to manoeuvre.

Botswana (Bechuanaland)

Botswana (independence, September 1966) lies in the centre of southern Africa. To the north is Angola and fractionally Zambia; to the north-west Rhodesia; to east and south the Republic of South Africa; and to the west South West Africa. We have already recorded its large area over much arid land and its thinness of population, only about 2·5 persons per square mile.[12] The racial breakdown was: Africans, 535,275; Europeans, 3,921; Asians and others, 420.

Botswana is named after its principal people, the Tswana, a group of Bantu tribes of Sotho stock. The original inhabitants were Bushmen, of whom about eight thousand remain. They were treated by the occupying Tswana in the seventeenth century as serfs and in recent times they still remained the most deprived. The Bantu predominance was increased by refugees from the Zulu war in 1823 and from Transvaal when the Boers trekked north in 1835. Four elements determined the evolution of Bechuanaland; first, the native peoples and their chiefs, secondly the European missionaries, thirdly the imperialist aims of Cecil Rhodes and his British South Africa Company and finally the British–Boer conflict for supremacy in southern Africa.

Missionaries Champion Africans

In the early nineteenth century Bechuanaland was divided into eight tribal administrations with subordinate peoples, the Bamangwato being the most powerful, constituting one-third of the population and occupying forty-five square miles on the borders of what became Boer-occupied Transvaal. European missionaries and traders arrived, with Robert Moffat establishing a station at Kuruman in 1820. The missionaries, Congregationalists of the London Missionary Society, identified themselves with the African people. Moffat protected them from the Zulu chief Mzilikazi, leader of the Matabele (later driven north into Rhodesia by the Boers in 1837). Between 1820 and 1870 Bechuanaland was in chaos, dismembered by conflicts between the tribes, but the missionaries and traders began some construction, beating out a track from the Cape which became important as a route to the north; it was known as the 'Missionaries' Road'. The Boer trekkers from the Cape claimed it, strongly resisted by the never-failing David Livingstone. Gold was reported in the Tati area and an invasion of Europeans took place. Livingstone appealed to the Cape for British protection, but Transvaal annexed Tati and succeeded in closing the vital route to the north. Another missionary, John MacKenzie, then became the champion of the people, urging the Governor of the Cape to occupy Tati on their behalf. In response the British Government refused to recognise the Transvaal occupation, and the added magnet of the discovery of diamonds led to the British annexation of southern Bechuanaland in 1871.

An African leader of strength and distinction arose in the seventies. In 1876 Khama III became chief of the Bamangwato and he united the tribes of Bechuanaland. Under missionary influence he became converted to Christianity and had two obsessions; the prohibition of alcoholic liquors and resistance to European concessions of land. To oppose Boer settlements Khama appealed for British protection and in response London sent a small force in 1878 and three years later negotiated the Pretoria Convention of 1881 which settled the boundary with Transvaal. When the British withdrew disturbance was renewed. In 1883 dissident Boers from Transvaal set up what they termed Republics in south Bechuanaland across the controversial North (Missionaries') Road. Missionary MacKenzie became important. As a result of his representations the London Convention of 1884 was proclaimed (despite the opposition of President Kruger, head of Transvaal) abolishing the Boer Republics and restoring the North Road. MacKenzie was appointed Resident Commissioner in Bechuanaland.

British Protectorate

Aggression by the Boers did not end. They occupied Mafeking and London sent Sir Charles Warren with a strong force to 'reinstate the natives in their lands' and to hold the country until its future was decided. In March 1885 a British Protectorate was declared, but there was controversy about its administration. Sir Charles Warren wanted complete British occupation, but London decided in favour of indirect rule through the chiefs. Chief Khama insisted on the maintenance of Bechuanaland's laws, including the prohibition of liquor and the restriction of the alienation of land. It was agreed that European claims to land should be subject to the approval of the British High Commissioner and mineral conces- sions to the approval of the Secretary of State at Westminster. Tribal courts should try natives, but there would be European courts for Whites. In September 1885 southern Bechuanaland was annexed outright and its administration placed under the Governor of Cape Colony, subsequently becoming a part of the Union of South Africa.

Rhodes' Plan

Meanwhile, Cecil Rhodes came into the picture. As leader of the Opposition in the Cape he opposed missionary identification with the Africans in Bechuanaland and urged British–Boer co-operation in the exploitation of the wealth of southern Africa, including an accord with President Kruger. In 1889 he established the British South Africa Company and offered to contribute £4,000 annually to the appointment of an imperial officer in Bechuanaland. The Colonial Office in London was at first inclined to support a propo- sal that the BSAC should take over the administration, relieving the Government of the costs and responsibility, but the chiefs were bitterly opposed to the transfer and they were backed by the High Commissioner. The BSAC obtained the concession, however, of a strip of land along the North Road to build a railway to serve as a connecting link with its enterprises in Rhodesia.

Advisory Councils

Although the Boer War was on its borders and the siege of Mafe- king at its doors, Bechuanaland was politically unaffected. Neither British nor Boers wanted African troops. But the *Act of Union* in 1910 disturbed the chiefs greatly. They protested that they would never accept the incorporation in South Africa which it forecast. The recognition which the British gave to the chiefs and their rule meant that democratic advance in Bechuanaland was slow. It was not until 1920 that representation was accorded to Africans in a Native Advisory Council which met once a year to express views on the administration. Theoretically its members were selected by tribal *Kgotlas*, assemblies of the people, but in fact they were nominees of the chiefs. The following year a European Advisory Council was also set up with elected members. On both bodies official members sat and subjects for discussion were limited to the affairs of the respective races. It was not until 1950 that the White–Black segregation was ended by the establishment of a Joint Advisory Council. By then the Native Council had evolved to the African Council and it served as an electoral college for the election of representatives on the united body.

Tshekedi Khama

But that lay ahead. In the thirties doubts began to arise about the validity of rule through the chiefs. These were strengthened by the review which Sir Alan Pim made on administration in Bechuanaland following his report on Basutoland, and independently there was criticism of the efficiency of the native courts, of the absence of supervision of funds, and of the treatment of subservient tribes. Into this controversy emerged a new dynamic figure. Tshekedi Khama became chief of the Bamangwato in 1926 because of the infancy of his nephew, the heir-apparent, Seretse Khama. Tshekedi modernised the tribal administration and extended education, but he stood challengingly for traditional authority and came into constant conflict with the British. He outraged white opinion when he authorised the corporal punishment of an European for an offence for which an African would have had similar punishment; the Acting High Commissioner ordered a naval detachment from Simonstown and Tshekedi was suspended temporarily from office. More fundamental disagreement occurred when the British issued their proclamation of 1934 amending native administration; henceforth chiefs were obliged to obey the instructions of the Resident Commissioner, to promote social and economic welfare as directed, and forbidden to demand levies without approval of the Commissioner and a *Kogtla*.

As a judicial body the *Kogtla* was replaced by a tribunal. Tshekedi challenged the validity of the proclamation on the ground that it infringed internal sovereignty, but a special Court endorsed the British Government's view that it had 'unfettered and unlimited power'. The estrangement was largely overcome by the conciliatory approach of Sir Charles Arden-Clarke who was appointed Resident Commissioner. Chiefs were given fixed stipends, and after 1940 grants were made from the Colonial Development and Welfare Fund which enabled them to expand education and agricultural development, purposes near to the heart of Tshekedi. He was not silenced, however. He protested strongly when it was proposed that the mandate to administer South West Africa should be given to South Africa. The British Government refused to allow him to go to the United Nations to press his objection.

Seretse Khama

One of Tshekedi's main aims was to preserve chieftainship rights for his nephew. There was a touch of tragedy as well as drama in the extraordinary events which accorded Seretse the post and led to the exiling of Tshekedi. Having gained his BA degree at Fort Hare in South Africa, Seretse proceeded to Oxford and married a London girl, Ruth Williams. Tshekedi opposed the marriage as an affront to the Bamangwato tribe, and South Africa, where mixed marriages were illegal, was outraged. Seretse returned to Bechuanaland to press his case. The *Kogtla* at first condemned him, but at a second meeting in June 1949 endorsed him as chief and his wife as 'the white queen'. The British Government under pressure from South Africa invited Seretse to London and offered him £1,000 a year tax-free if he would renounce the chieftainship and live in England. He refused, and was then exiled from Bechuanaland and in 1952 deprived permanently of the chieftainship. Meanwhile, Tshekedi had resigned as Acting Chief and he was also exiled from his tribe. This surrender to racialism was vigorously challenged in Britain[13] and finally Seretse accepted the proposal of Tshekedi that they should both renounce the chieftainship and return to their tribe and participate actively in political life as private citizens. In September 1956 the British Government agreed. Meanwhile, Rasebolai Kgamane, third in line of succession, was appointed chief.

During his period of exile Tshekedi became prominent in advocating the political development of Bechuanaland through elected local, legislative and executive councils, pointing out that the High Commission Territories were virtually the only British dependencies which did not possess legislatures and charging the Government with fear of offending South Africa. In 1951 the British made the concession of the Joint Advisory Council (African and European) to which reference has already been made. On Tshekedi's motion Seretse became vice-chairman of the Council and together they campaigned for internal self-government. In 1958, supported by the European chairman, Russell England, they succeeded in getting the Advisory Council to declare for the establishment of an inter-racial Legislative Council and to set up a committee to frame a constitution. The British Government was now more receptive, alienated from South Africa by the extremism of its policies, and in June 1961 it responded to the growing pressure by creating a Legislature with balanced African and European representation. Tshekedi did not live to see this fruit of his labours – he died in 1959 – but Seretse was made the senior African member of the Executive Council.

Political Parties

The radicalisation of opinion in Bechuanaland had been expressed in December 1960 by the formation of the first political party, the Bechuanaland Peoples' Party (BPP). Its membership was largely drawn from the towns, supplemented by refugees from South Africa, and it came out firmly against racial representation in the legislature, concessions to White immigrants, and political privileges for chiefs. The founder and president was Kgeleman Motsete, an intellectual with London University degrees, and a pioneer of secondary education in Bechuanaland. The party was plagued by reflection of the conflict in South Africa between the African National Congress and the Pan-African Congress. The vice-president, P. G. Matante, had been an activist in the PAC, whilst the Secretary-General, Motsamai Mpho, had been a treason trial member of the ANC. Within a few months Mpho was expelled for the alleged staging of a communist *coup*. The party succeeded, however, in organising large demonstrations against the racial basis of the Legislative Council and stirred the Resident Commissioner to pre-date to 1963 a constitutional review promised for 1968. The agitation reached proportions which frightened the Administration. In Francistown tear gas had to be used against the crowd and meetings of twelve or more people were banned. The BPP gained international attention by evidence which Matante gave in New York to the United Nations Committee on Colonialism.

Seretse Khama reacted to what he regarded as extremism by establishing in 1962 the Bechuanaland Democratic Party (BDP), which drew its basic strength from his Bamangwato tribe, but which stood for multi-racialism and thus gained the support of many white settlers and most of the African members of the Legislative Council. It declared for universal suffrage and independence following a general election. A further and more serious split in the BPP strengthened Seretse's party. Motsete, the president, shocked his members by proposing that independence should be postponed for four years and, though he withdrew from this, the party broke into two, Matante claiming the leadership and Motsete heading a breakaway, somewhat ironically called the Bechuanaland Independence Party (BIP).

Responsible Government

Irrespective of party differences public pressure for independence mounted and in July 1964 the Resident Commissioner agreed to call a conference to review the constitution. The BPP, the BDP, the chiefs and European members of the Legislative Council had three representatives each. There was rapid and extraordinary unanimity; with six days of discussion agreement was reached. The racially-based constitution would be ended; the Legislative Assembly would be composed of 38, of whom 32 would be elected by common roll adult suffrage, 4 selected by the Assembly and 2 would be officials nominated by the Administration. The British Government would retain responsibility for external affairs, defence, internal security and the civil service, but decisions in these spheres would be made on the advice of the Cabinet, except in emergency circumstances. The Cabinet would consist of a Prime Minister and five other Ministers drawn from Parliament. There would be a House of Chiefs with responsibility in tribal matters, which would be consulted before legislation in this sphere was introduced.

Although the European members of the Legislative Council accepted these recommendations, the Whites in Tati asked for its separate independence 'so that our land will not be handed over to the natives'. There was also opposition to an Act introducing racial integration in the schools, but these protests failed to get the support of either the leaders or an influential section of the European community. Dr Verwoerd made a last bid by challenging the British Government to hold a plebiscite in the High Commission Territories on a choice 'between economic prosperity in union with South Africa or economic decay under Britain', but met with no response. In June 1964 the British Government accepted with slight amendments the Legislative Council's proposals for responsible self-government and in February 1965 the first general election with universal suffrage took place.[14] Seretse Khama's BPP won an overwhelming victory, taking twenty-eight of the thirty-one seats, the minority of three going to Matante and the BDP.

Independence

In September 1966 Bechuanaland as Botswana gained complete independence with Seretse Khama as head of state. It was fifteen years since he had been exiled in London. He showed considerable skill in balancing a policy of co-existence with South Africa and opposition to racism and white domination. He recognised that Botswana was economically dependent upon South Africa and did not permit his territory to be used as a base against its regime, much as he hated it, but on the other hand he associated himself with the independent African states in the Organisation of African Unity and, when tested by the seizure of power by the white minority in neighbouring Rhodesia, refused to recognise the illegal regime of Ian Smith, banned the passage of arms and oil by the only rail route and permitted the establishment of the British opposition radio station at Francistown fifteen miles from the border. When the frontier between Zambia and Southern Rhodesia was closed, Seretse extended air flights with supplies for the Zambians.

Botswana maintained a dignified independence despite the pressures which surrounded it. Hope of economic self-sufficiency was aroused in 1972 by the confirmation of large potential mineral resources and by a project of a two-hundred-mile road linked with Zambia, providing an alternative outlet to South Africa.

Swaziland

Swaziland is one of the smallest countries in Africa, squeezed tightly in the north-east corner of South Africa on the border of Portuguese Mozambique. It had the doubtful advantage of rich mineral resources and fertile land which brought an army of concession hunters into a society which was primitive and unsophisticated even by African standards. In the second half of the nineteenth century the greater proportion of the country had become owned by Whites. Total estimated population in 1971 was 42 millions.

Request to British

The Swazi people migrated from Central Africa in the fifteenth century, coming into conflict with the Zulus, and settling in what is now Swaziland at the end of the eighteenth century. It was to hold back the Zulus that King Mswazi in the 1840s first appealed to the British for protection, and Theophilus Shepstone, Agent to the Natives in Natal, gave it. The European invasion destroyed Swazi life, however, more than the Zulus. Boer farmers occupied land in 1879, the discovery of gold, followed by other minerals, led the chiefs, bribed beyond belief, to swear away the country. In Swazi law natural resources could not be alienated, but illiterate chiefs often did not know to what they were committing themselves.

The confusion and deprivation were so great that the king again appealed to Theophilus Shepstone, who appointed his son Resident Adviser. Shepstone Junior established a concessions register and introduced regular collections of rents but did not stop the process of alienation. Indeed the concessions to monopolies grew. Significant for Swaziland's political future, he set up a council of fifteen property owners with nominees of the king to administer the economically dominant white sector in the community.[15] The Council did not function long because of quarrels between the British and Boer settlers, but it was followed by the establishment of a provisional government to frame laws for the Whites. This government existed by the side of the native administration and, whilst independence of the territory was theoretically affirmed, the last word was given to the British and the Boers. Any change in the status of Swaziland required their approval.

Boers Take Over

Continued conflict between the two European groups led to the disbandment of the White Council, and London, unwilling to extend its responsibilities, agreed in 1893 to South Africa negotiating its 'rights and powers of jurisdiction, protection and administration' with the Swazi monarch and chiefs. The Queen Regent, however, rejected this transfer of authority to the Boers and sent a delegation to London asking for British protection. The contrary result was that Britain agreed to a Boer takeover in return for concessions elsewhere. There was Swazi resistance, centred on a mass refusal to pay the hut tax, but South African domination was entrenched.

At the end of the British–Boer War in 1902 the British somewhat reluctantly took charge in Swaziland. Control was placed with the Governor of Transvaal which had been annexed and its laws were applied. The Swazis protested, claiming that their independence had never been lost; but without avail. Their anxiety was increased when the 1910 *Act of Union* indicated circumstances under which Swaziland could be transferred. South Africa assumed the collection of customs (paying a valuable percentage to Swaziland), ran the postal, rail and bus services, its currency was used, and South Africans largely manned the administrative posts. Whatever its constitutional future, the economy of Swaziland was from this time chained to South Africa.

British Control Condemned

The British were, however, nominally in control. At first they were content to let the Swazis run their own affairs under the tribal system, giving virtually no help in education, health or agricultural development. In 1939 the report published by Sir Alan Pim was scathing in its criticism, stating that the administration was absorbed in the affairs of the European population, lacked initiative in devising policies in native interests and concentrated on the negative tasks of tax collection and administering justice. Sir Alan stated bluntly that the Swazis had lost faith in the British as a result of the transference of land to the Europeans. Activated by this exposure the British attempted to introduce a system of native administration similar to that practised in other colonies, but it was fiercely opposed by the chiefs and traditionalists, was held up until 1950, and then more power was left to the Paramount Chief than in most territories.

The loss of land remained the most acute grievance. The British responded to petitions by agreeing that one-third of the territory should revert to the 'natives'. This did not satisfy King Sobhuza, who claimed that by traditional Swazi law land could not be alienated at all and that at least two-thirds be restored. He sent a deputation to London and instituted proceedings to the Privy Council, but in vain. The depth of feeling was expressed in an extraordinary movement which encouraged young men to seek work in the Transvaal in order to establish a fund to repurchase land from the Europeans. By this means the territory in Swazi hands reached nearly one-half.

Four Competing Forces

As time passed four distinct forces were revealed within Swaziland. There was the British administration which, after a period of negligence on the assumption that the territory would pass to South Africa, timidly began to reflect the accepted trend of colonial policy towards self-government by slowly phased stages. There were the European settlers concerned to maintain separate administration. There were the Swazi chiefs and traditionalists who sought to maintain tribal structure. There were the Nationalists who campaigned for an inter-racial democratic state on the basis of 'one man, one vote'.

The constitutional problem lay in the separate existence of the White and Native Administrations. By Swazi tradition government was by the king (Paramount Chief) and hereditary chiefs. There was a somewhat informal inner council, the *Liqoqo*, to advise the king, and an all-embracing council, the *Libandhla*, which theoretically every adult male could attend. Laws required the approval of this mass gathering, which met once a year for about a month. Continuing administration was conducted by the Swazi National Council, which was responsible to these bodies and which had a Standing Committee. The British maintained some contact by meeting the *Libandhla* at a special one-day session and by regular attendance at the Standing Committee.

Separately the Whites functioned through a European Advisory Council set up in 1921 and made a statutory body in 1949, the members of which were elected by European adult suffrage and met twice a year under the chairmanship of the British Resident Commissioner. Although officially the Council had no legislative power, which was limited to the British administration, in practice it had considerable influence, particularly in economic matters. The European leader was Carl Todd, a director of more than thirty companies in South Africa and the largest landowner in Swaziland.

Europeans and Traditionalists Coalesce

Swaziland responded belatedly to the wave of African nationalism which swept the continent after the Second World War, but in the late fifties events in Central Africa, particularly in Nyasaland, stirred both the traditionalists and the Europeans to action. King Sobhuza denounced nationalist acceptance of Western democracy instead of traditionally clinging to African tribal customs and he petitioned London in favour of expanding the status of the *Libandhla.* The Europeans were disturbed in 1959 by the report of an Economic Survey Mission headed by Professor Chandler Monroe which insisted that Swaziland's advance depended on political changes involving the association of Swazis and Europeans in a channel through which joint advice would flow to the Government. The Whites, fearing the growth of democratic nationalism, turned towards the chiefs' tribal structure as a means to prevent it. In 1960 the European Advisory Council proposed that a joint body should be formed with the traditional Swazi National Council. King Sobhuza also proposed a coalition between traditionalists and Europeans in the form of a Legislative Council in which the Whites would have elected representatives and the Swazis nominees in equal numbers. He insisted, however, that the new body should have no jurisdiction over Swazi custom, land or mineral rights; a double administration would remain.

African Parties

Meanwhile, democratic ideas were growing among the few Swazis who had the opportunity of education and among workers in the spreading mines and industries established by the Europeans. They opposed both the domination of the chiefs and of the British administration and bitterly resented the racial superiority of the Europeans. In 1929 a Progressive Association had been formed with the goodwill of the Resident Commissioner for the discussion of social issues, but soon political views were expressed by educated Swazis. They contrived to absorb the Association in the Swazi National Council; meanwhile, under the chairmanship of John J. Nquku (South African born teacher and first African schools inspector in Swaziland), the Association did useful work in exposing child labour and inequitable taxation. After a visit to Europe and America, Nquku returned in 1960 to transform the

Association into the Swaziland Progressive Party (SPP) with the objects of democratic enfranchisement, human rights, racial integration and opposition to South African incorporation.

By the end of 1961, however, there was a split in the party over the personality of Nquku, and he was deposed as president, succeeded by Dr Ambrose Zwane with Clement Dhlamini as secretary. Zwane was the first Swazi to graduate as a doctor. Whilst studying in South Africa he became an associate of Nelson Mandela and Robert Sobukwe, and it was the Sharpeville massacre which led him to resign as Medical Officer in Swaziland to devote himself to politics. He was held in great respect, and his leadership gained the Progressive Party much authority. Dhlamini was a nephew of the king, but as a student disowned traditionalism and became a militant champion of the underprivileged, popular by his oratory, feared both by chiefs and Europeans. By 1962 there were two other political parties with somewhat confused objects. The Swaziland Democratic Party (SDP), launched by white liberals but with a Swazi head, Simon Nxumalo, condemned the SPP as Pan-Africanist, dissociated itself from apartheid, but was friendly towards South Africa. The Mbandzeni National Convention (MNC) combined adult suffrage for a legislative council with the maintenance of the tribalist structure.

Constitutional Recommendations

The Colonial Secretary in London welcomed the *rapprochement* of the traditionalists and Europeans and endorsed the idea of a joint Legislative Council. In 1960 he set up a committee to draft a constitution, consisting of representatives of the European Advisory Council, the *Libandhla*, the British administration and the Progressive Party. The traditionalists and the Europeans demanded the prohibition of political parties, whereupon the SPP withdrew, calling on the help of Professor Denis Cowan, author of the Basutoland Constitution. Professor Cowan recommended a Legislative Council elected by a common voters' roll, the elimination of racially discriminating laws, the integration of traditional chieftainship with a democratic structure of administration, the recognition of the Paramount Chief as constitutional head of state and the establishment of responsible government. Simultaneously the official Constitutional Committee recommended a Legislative Council of equal representation of Swazis and Europeans, the

Europeans to be elected, the Swazis acclaimed by the *Libandhla*. Reservations were made by the Resident Commissioner and the Administration, who came down on the side of the generally accepted British colonial policy of evolving towards democratic self-government. They recommended the compromise that eight Swazis should be nominated by the Paramount Chief, eight Europeans elected on a European roll, and eight (four Swazis and four Europeans) elected on a national roll with a qualified franchise. They rejected the idea that a separate tribalist administration should be outside the scope of the Legislative Council's authority.

Extraordinary contradictions by the British Government followed. The Conservative Colonial Secretary, Reginald Maudling issued a White Paper which insisted that the Administration should still control the Legislature by the votes of the official members and that the Resident Commissioner should have the last word. He antagonised the king and chiefs by not excluding Swazi law and custom from the authority of the Legislature and by including the control of land and minerals within its scope. He also declared that a common electoral roll, or something like it, would be required to satisfy the rights of the non-traditional Swazis; on the other hand, the separate racial representation of Swazis and Europeans was to be maintained as the main structure of the Legislature. These proposals were rejected equally by the Swazi National Council, the European Advisory Council and the Swazi nationalist parties. A united front was formed of political parties, trade unions, academic bodies, the students' union and the Anglican Church to protest against the racialism of the proposed constitution.

Constitutional Conference

To resolve these differences a constitutional conference was called in London in 1963. The representatives of the political parties formed an alliance against both 'Black privilege and White privilege' and in favour of a non-racial democratic state with universal suffrage, independent and sovereign, and the Paramount Chief as constitutional monarch. The traditionalists and Europeans insisted on their separate race legislatures and no agreement could be reached.

The British Government compromised. There was to be no responsible self-government; executive power was to be vested in the Commissioner and a Council of *ex-officio* and nominated members. The Legislative Council would be composed of eight Swazis elected by traditional methods, four Europeans elected on an European roll and four Europeans and eight persons of any race elected on the national roll. The king would have the right to bring matters to the attention of the Executive Council, but was otherwise without political authority. Minerals were left in his possession, but the control of mineral rights passed to the Legislature and the Commissioner and his Executive.

Traditionalists, Europeans and Nationalists were all disappointed. The traditionalists, angered by the decision on mineral rights, drastically changed their policy. If the Legislature was to have any say, they would prefer that it be Swazi controlled rather than shared with the Europeans. Thus they repudiated their coalition with the Whites and urged the alternative of a democratically elected common roll Legislative Council, confident they could gain a majority. The Europeans were bitter in rejecting the Government's proposals. Carl Todd concentrated his attack on the denial of sovereignty; in this way he got some nationalist support. The Nationalists rejected the British proposals outright because they retained racial representation, denied adult suffrage and withheld independence.

Strikes and Arrests

Into this political confusion burst the complication of strikes and violence. From 1962 the workers began to form trade unions, met by dismissals. Dr Zwane identified the Progressive Party with them and entered into a coalition with the unions in a new party, the Ngwane National Liberatory Congress (NNLC). Frightened by a mass strike of sugar workers, the Administration issued a decree forbidding strikes without three weeks' notice. A ban on the sale of popular foodstuffs brought women into the struggle, leading to the arrest of sixty and the use of tear gas to disperse crowds. The climax came with a strike at the Havelock Asbestos Mine, one of the largest in the world. The Government arrested twelve leaders, tear gas was used to disperse a demonstration of two thousand, a general strike was declared, police were reinforced from Basutoland and a battalion of British troops brought from Kenya. Zwane, Dhlamini and all the Executive of the NNLC were arrested and their trials lasted for over six months. Zwane was acquitted and light sentences were passed on his colleagues, but the cost of the defence drained the NNLC of nearly all its resources. The immediate political effect was to disrupt the nationalist organisation.

Royal Party Victory

As the election under the new constitution approached the king took the unprecedented step of entering the political struggle. There was evidence of collaboration between him and South Africa and in establishing his party, the *Imbokodo* (Golden Spear), he adopted a plan outlined by van Wyk de Vries, a prominent Afrikaner. The nationalist parties were refused the right to campaign in the Swazi areas by the chiefs, with the result that the *Imbokodo* gained a sweeping victory in a renewed alliance with the Europeans; together they won every seat. Of the nationalist parties the NNLC did best with 12·3 per cent of the votes, of the others only the SDP got more than one per cent. After the election all the parties went to pieces. Zwane was arrested for debt defaults and Dhlamini left the country. The traditionalists and Europeans were in unopposed command.

Independence

The coalition, however, soon broke down. Dominating the Legislature, the traditionalists in *Imbokodo* realised that they could have greater power than in their old tribal system. The Europeans fought back. Todd proposed that in any future constitution the Europeans should have reserved seats. The *Imbokodo* refused. This changed attitude played into the hands of the British Government. In 1966 a White Paper was issued combining recognition of Sobhuza as king and tribal authority over Swazi law and customs with a Parliament elected by adult suffrage. Swaziland would have extended self-government, although Britain would retain responsibility for external affairs, defence, internal security and finance. Full independence was promised by 1969. The Legislature would consist of two Chambers, an Assembly of 24 elected on a common roll and 6 nominated by the king, and a Senate of 12, 6 elected by the Assembly, 6 nominated by the king. This constitution was accepted by the *Imbokodo*, although difference persisted on the control of land and minerals. Europeans still pressed for separate racial representation in the Assembly on a fifty-fifty basis, but this was brushed aside. Their day of political privilege was over.

In the pre-independence elections in 1967 the *Imbokodo* won all twenty-four seats, though the NNLC improved its poll to twenty per cent. The other parties were nowhere. In February 1968, the conference to prepare independence was held in London; the NNLC, though backed by the working population, was not allowed representation though its representatives came to London, only to be escorted from the doors by police. The legislative structure was maintained and independence dated for the end of 1969. The British had to accept the Swazi view on mineral rights. Whilst the king would in all other respects be a constitutional monarch acting on the advice of the Cabinet, he would in his capacity as Paramount Chief control the disposal of minerals and their assets in consultation with the Swazi tribal council. He would establish a National Fund into which royalties would be paid and devoted to the general welfare of the nation.

Independence was inaugurated on September 6, 1968. The traditionalists in power were prepared to co-operate with South Africa, but the considerable white presence in Swaziland denied its classification as a Bantustan state. The Government of the Republic would have liked to adjust the boundaries so that the territory occupied mostly by the white farmers would be transferred to South Africa in exchange for territory on the frontier mostly occupied by Blacks. European interests in the industrial economy, however, made any political segregation of the races difficult. Adjustment, as in the case of the other ex-Protectorate Territories, awaited the final determination of the wider South African problem.

The first elections after independence took place in May 1972. The traditionalist Government, with Prince Makhosini as Prime Minister, won a resounding victory, winning twenty-one of the twenty-four seats. For the first time, however, there was an Opposition, Dr Zwane's National Liberatory Congress taking three seats. The opponents to traditionalism were weakened by division. Thirty-seven candidates from separate parties were nominated, twenty-nine of them losing their deposits. Swaziland still stands at the crossroads.

Notes

1. August 10, 1909. This is what the Opposition in Basutoland said was happening after independence.

2. *Report on Constitutional Reform and Chieftainship Affairs*, 1958.

3. Later, under the Commonwealth Development and Welfare Act, the grants were made.

4. In 1955 the BAC became the Basutoland Congress Party (BCP).

5. Many Catholics, including the Archbishop of Maseru and lecturers at Pius XII University College, criticised Church involvement in the party.

6. Professor Cowan was also called in to co-operate in the preparation of this constitution.

7. The High Commissioner for the Three Territories was replaced by the transference of his powers to Resident Commissioners in each.

8. The *Observer* (London) June 19, 1966, reported: 'Funds for the competing parties came in from abroad – most of it for the BNP from South African pro-Government sources and from a Catholic organisation in West Germany, and considerably less from Russia, China and Ghana for the Opposition.'

9. Already the judiciary in Lesotho was staffed by South Africans.

10. The king declined to act as a 'constitutional monarch', claiming that according to African tradition he was 'leader of the people'. Despite this departure from democracy he retained the support of the BCP, but later accepted Chief Jonathan's terms and returned to Lesotho.

11. The author was subsequently informed that Chief Jonathan's agreement with Mokhehle's terms had been opposed by the Deputy Prime Minister and the Commissioner of Police. The Commissioner was dismissed. It was still possible that a settlement could be reached.

12. Estimated population in 1971 was 670,000.

13. The author raised the issue in the Commons and formed an all-party Committee to champion Seretse's rights. The method by which he was exiled by a Labour Home Secretary shocked many Labour MPs and was denounced by Winston Churchill.

14. Donkeys and camels had to be conscripted to take voters to the polling stations over the vast expanse.

15. A court was set up to decide the validity of the concessions to Europeans; it confirmed 352 out of 364. The principle was accepted, however, that no further alienation of land should take place.

Chapter Twenty-one

Latin America

The Spanish and Portuguese *conquistadors* and priests who, from the fifteenth century onwards crossed from Europe to South America for wealth and converts, had two consequences. The first was the destruction of the ancient civilisations of the sub-continent; the second was their failure to establish any stable political system. Spain and Portugal became involved in the European wars of the early nineteenth century and South America became a mere symbolic token of the Iberian peninsula's colonial endowment. A vacuum was left which has since been largely filled in much confusion by the arms-supported economic imperialism of the USA.

Early Liberal Revolutionaries

The simultaneous absence of efficient European control and the inspiration of the French and American revolutions encouraged an emerging white élite of Iberians to raise armies throughout South America to challenge the Spanish dictatorship and its Royalist supporters. Although its leaders, Ravelo, Miranda, San Martin and Bolivar, were not agreed on any ultimate relationship with Spain and Europe, their common ambition was to be rid of colonial dominance and to achieve national and economic independence with tolerance among the religions and races, including the indigenous Indians. Their followers showed outstanding bravery and a ferocious idealism, but there was no intention to destroy the existing social structure beyond an ambition to realise the liberal ideals and institutions of the European revolutions (which had not even been fulfilled in Europe and were to prove totally unsuitable to South American conditions).

Power became concentrated in a small landowning class, the Church and the army leaders. They were distrusted by large numbers of civilians, both white and Indian, and in the context of the feudal social structure there could be no reconciliation by adherence to European democratic changes. This, combined with the absence of communications, made the emergence of strong government impossible and prevented the realisation of national unity in the different states. Allegiance was given to local leaders resorting to force against the landowners, who retained the majority of the Indian population as a semi-slave labour force, and to the town *caudillos,* who paid lip-service to constitutionalism, whilst using authority in office to increase their own wealth.[1] The landowners and the city bosses themselves disintegrated as a result of a power fragmentation which destroyed social discipline. These difficulties confronted all the new states even before their national revolutions were completed. The legacies of the wars of independence remain the crux of the South American situation today.

From 1850 to 1920 the problems of the post-revolutionary days moved even further from solution. Political power became dependent upon an alliance between the landed interests and the military élite. Often they came into conflict, but the feudal structure was not in doubt; even when the military removed the actual rulers, the latter still maintained the social *status quo.* The rural areas, isolated from urban developments, fell under oligarchic rule, which made landownership not only a political problem but the crucial economic impediment. Although there was some industrial development in Argentina, Mexico, Brazil – this was partly caused by the absence of European goods during the 1914/18 war – static feudalism prevented a repetition of the European and North American industrial revolutions. Most of South America depended upon monoculture (largely coffee growing) economies.[2]

US Economic Domination

In this way, the sub-continent, like colonialist territories, became dependent upon North America and Western Europe for manufactured goods, paying for them by agricultural produce and some minerals and by concessions for industrial and extractive (mostly oil) privileges. After 1914 South America became almost totally dependent on North America for its markets; some states exported up to eighty per cent of their raw materials to the USA. America's domination of the economy was still more reflected in the fact that eighty-five per cent of the exporting companies were US owned.[3] There were some attempts to break through this subservience by nationalisation projects, but they were defeated not only by dependence upon the USA and Europe for markets but because their technical co-operation was required. Even after 150 years of political independence Latin America still had a colonialist economy. Industrialisation had comparatively little significance, partly because of the massive population explosion demanding close-to-hand food products and, secondly, because industrial profits were absorbed either by the small upper class or the foreign owners. They were neither distributed nor reinvested.[4]

Military Intervention

Instrumental in nearly all South America's political changes was military intervention. In the earlier years the army was an instrument of greed for power by ambitious figures of the élite. During the twentieth century military intervention became a middle-class method of gaining political control. This class impetus for change began in the urban areas of the larger South American countries in the 1920s, but, whilst coalitions of élitist groups, businessmen, intellectuals and military officers, overthrew the *caudillos* they still refrained from destroying the feudal system which left 64·9 per cent of the land in the possession of five per cent of the landowners.[5] These movements during the 1940s established nationalist governments to challenge the upper classes, the new rich industrialists and North American economic imperialists, but the army soon fell foul of the social legislation which was introduced and was easily encouraged by the same upper classes to counter revolt. Similarly, in the smaller less developed countries the aristocratic *cacquismi* was overthrown, only to be replaced by ruthless dictatorships, such as those of Somoza, Stroesner and Trujillo. Thus military rather than political power, with the sole exception of Costa Rica, came to dominate South American government, partly because it was the only coherent force capable of maintaining social order. In most countries, the military still absorbed at least twenty-five per cent of the national budgets and had a decisive influence on many government appointments.

Washington's Policy

There were, however, four revolutions in the last sixty years aimed at removing the colonial heritage and foreign financial domination. These were in Mexico in 1910, Bolivia in 1952, Cuba in 1959 and

Chile in 1970. As indicated above, ever since South America threw off Iberian colonial authority, the USA increasingly treated Latin America as its protectorate, as a market, an eldorado for investments, and a political foster-child. As early as 1823 Washington imposed the Monroe Doctrine, which ruled out any intervention on the American continent by non-American Powers. This was largely as a warning to Spain and Portugal and other European nations that it would not countenance any attempt to re-establish colonialism; but the USA itself proceeded to dominate and intervene. In the 1830s Washington 'granted' to Britain the Falkland Islands and Honduras as though it were the master of southern and central America. At the same time it provoked war with Mexico, annexing half of its territory from Texas to California. From then until 1910 it treated Mexico as an economic colony, taking over industry by large investments and continually harassing its governments to obtain increased concessions. For example, in the 1870s large US armies were stationed along the border to deter the Mexican Government from taxing US citizens and companies.

In 1898, following war with Spain, the US extended its protection to Cuba; American troops remained there until 1933, first to construct facilities for American development and then to protect them. Washington constantly intervened in the Dominican Republic, Nicaragua and Haiti. When the US decided to build an inter-Oceanic canal it was Colombia's turn. After the Colombian Senate had refused permission for the canal to be constructed, the US in 1903 organised a revolt in Panama (then a province of Colombia) and immediately recognised Panamanian nationhood and gave it protectorate status. A canal treaty was signed, Panama receiving $10 million for exclusive US rights in perpetuity. It was only in 1921 that Colombia recognised Panamanian independence. The US rewarded her with $25 million.

Time did not change the US attitude. Year by year its financial hold strengthened remorselessly. Since 1945, although South American economies have remained static, the profits of US companies have steadily increased, with an annual return on investments averaging about twenty per cent. In 1971 the profits of US companies in Venezuela had reached $500 million, of which $440 million were transferred to shareholders in the US rather than reinvested. The Venezuelan steel industry was US owned and so were seventy-five per cent of its total oil reserves, the remainder belonging to British–Dutch companies. Attempts by Venezuela to compete failed because of the lack of technical experience and marketing facilities. In fact, forty-seven per cent of Venezuela's budget was foreign-owned and sixty-eight per cent of its foreign exchange was earned by foreign companies.

Attempts in recent years by Venezuela to assume greater control over its oil resources by nationalising foreign companies have not been very successful. The lack of technical skill and marketing outlets has reimposed dependence on foreign companies.

In Chile, until 1970, three US companies owned ninety per cent of the copper mines representing seventy per cent of the national product. The copper is worth over one billion dollars. John Gerassi in his *The Great Fear in Latin America*[6] estimated that if Chile had nationalised the mines in the 1960s it could not only have paid fair compensation from the profits earned, which he put at $82\frac{1}{2}$ billion, but would now be benefiting from the profits. Gerassi also showed how foreign companies were able to avoid taxation by off-setting profits on claims of depletion of resources, depreciation of machinery, and 'loans' to other companies. Thus because the mines were foreign-owned Chile lost not only the profits but also tax revenue on the profits.

Further implications of foreign ownership were apparent from US methods of underpaying products received from South America and selling them at a much higher price in the US. In 1881 the US gained possession of zinc mines in Peru as a reward for support in a war against Chile. In 1924 the holding company paid its subsidiary in Peru 11·597 cents for a measurement of zinc, selling it to manufacturers in US for 17·556 cents, a margin much greater than transport and other costs. As the years passed the margin grew. In 1957, although the price paid in Peru had fallen to 11·399 cents, the zinc was sold by the same company in the US for 31·270 cents. This was a device to avoid taxation on profits in Peru. Peruvian revenue lost dramatically.

Alliance Against Castroism

The US attitude to South America was epitomised by the fact that its grants in aid to the region barely amounted from 1945 to two per cent of the total it distributed in profits, and even this was negatived by the US imposing high tariffs and failing to maintain stable commodity prices. Furthermore, investment usually meant no more than depositing dollars in US banks and allowing the countries concerned to receive the interest payments. These factors led to the ineffectiveness of both Eisenhower's Aid programme and its successor, Kennedy's Alliance for Progress in 1961. Kennedy hoped that industrialisation and social reform would halt the spread of Cuba's Castroism, but much of the promised money did not materialise, especially as many South American countries, with an emerging gesture of independence, refused to comply with US insistence on political influence in return for the dollars. To check this mood Kennedy hastily convened the following year a conference at Punta del Este and sought to isolate Cuba by a reinforced anti-communist Declaration. The Declaration was not unanimously endorsed. Indeed, the six countries which abstained represented seventy-five per cent of South America's area and population.

US policy was then concentrated to ensure 'internal security' against Communism. Plans to combat 'active internal subversion' were alternatively described as 'counter insurgency' or 'military civic action'. It was stated in the 1964 Democratic Party's election manifesto that, in place of the 'inter-American defence force' which had never materialised, the US, in the three previous years, trained 100,000 North and South American officers in counter-insurgency skills to fight guerrilla warfare.

US policy was to support directly the militarists in South America whom it credited as sure safeguards against subversion. The most ruthless dictators in the sub-continent retained power with American supplied weapons in return for which they signed Mutual Assistance Pacts. An earlier pact signed by the Honduras Government in 1954 included Article 8, which read:

'In conformity with the principle of mutual aid ... the Government of Honduras agrees to facilitate the production and transfer to the government of the USA for such period of time, in such quantities and upon such terms and conditions as may be agreed upon, of raw and semi-processed materials required by the USA as a result of deficiencies or potential deficiencies in its own resources.'

The later Mutual Assistance Pacts were not as explicit.

Arms for Both Sides

An extraordinary feature of US practice in southern America was that arms were supplied to both sides when states were in conflict and when there was internal conflict. This may have been an expression of the classic imperialist policy of 'divide and rule' or merely the salesmanship of armament firms (official US missions were in the background). One of the most disturbing reports of modern times was that presented by the Committee to investigate the munitions industry appointed by the American Congress in 1934. It contained evidence that US arms firms had stirred up conflict between states and parties and, with co-operation of some British colleagues, had profited by selling military equipment to the opposing contestants.[7] This was, however, before 'communist subversion' obsessed Washington.[8] In recent years elected civilian governments which reflected opinion resentful of American dominance rarely completed their constitutional terms of office. For example, President Frondizi of Argentina lost office in 1962 as a result of a Pentagon-backed military *coup* because of his opposition to US Cuban policy at Punta del Este. Similarly, Brizola of Brazil was removed by a US-backed military *coup* in 1964 for not co-operating with America, and in 1969 a successor was sought for President Frei of Chile.

Guatemala Socialist Deposed

Guatemala provided one of the most blatant of US interventions. In 1944 the Washington-supported Umbico dictatorship was overthrown and, after years of inter-factional intrigue, a liberal Socialist, Arbenz, came to power. His first object was land reform, the success of which depended upon breaking the semi-monopolistic landownership of the US United Fruit Company (which also controlled Guatemala's harbour, railways and electricity). Following nationalisation, the US State Department 'discovered' a communist plot, hastily armed the countries around Guatemala, and equipped a 'Guatemalan army' in neighbouring Honduras. To defend the country, Arbenz in 1954 bought Russian arms. The US declared this was a threat to inter-American security, moved in the exile Guatemalan army, and Arbenz was deposed. Eisenhower deepened the cynicism of central and southern American liberals by saying that the US had played no part in the affair.

Four Revolutions

We referred earlier to revolutions in Mexico, Bolivia, Cuba and Chile. In Mexico the revolt was partially successful, in Bolivia, unsuccessful, in Cuba successful, in Chile in doubt. It was as far back as 1911 that a popular uprising in Mexico overthrew the Diaz dictatorship to establish a nationalist (i.e. anti-US) government. The 1917 constitution epitomised Socialism and was far more advanced than anything in Europe (and more democratic than the subsequent constitution in Soviet Russia), but the revolution failed to realise its aims because of inter-factional fighting and the absence of an accepted ideology strong enough to counter historical pressures and US suzerainty. The revolution had little impact on South America, partly because of distance, partly because political conditions were not ripe. Nevertheless, it cannot be written off. Many benefits remained in Mexico.

The revolution in Bolivia in 1952 against a South American landowning élite was also initially successful. Paz Estenssoro, a Trotskyist, was elected president on a platform including the nationalisation of the mines and land. But primitive social conditions and an unprepared administration in isolated geographic circumstances could not overcome continuing deterioration of the economic situation and a counter-revolution occurred in 1964. The country became totally reliant upon US aid in return for which it exported its tin.

A short-lived attempt to return to the spirit of 1952 arose in October 1970 following the military overthrow of General Ovando. The new president, General Torres, proclaimed his adherence to 'revolutionary nationalism' and his allegiance to the peasant and working classes. Backed by left-wing army officers and 'popular forces' Torres attacked the US Steel Corporation. But having failed to disarm the left and right extremes and falling foul of local political manoeuvres, Torres compromised his original approach. Few were surprised when in August 1971 Bolivia went through its 187th *coup* since independence, led by a right-wing military faction, momentarily plunging the country into civil war. As in other South American countries, the Bolivian army failed to fulfil the promise of serving as the vehicle of fundamental change.

Although economically the later objects of the Cuban revolution of 1959 were not fully realised, it must be described as successful in its fundamental aims, and its political significance in South America, indeed wider than that, was great. Following the American 'liberation' from Spain in 1898 Cuba was ruled by harsh dictatorships supported by US interests. Prior to 1959 US companies owned more than fifty per cent of the sugar production and eighty per cent of the mines and cattle ranches.[9] When Batista was overthrown, however, his disappearance was not at first mourned at Washington.[10] The revolution in the first instance was a middle-class intellectual revolt against corruption. Castro saw that this could be achieved only by nationalisation of the sources of individual wealth and by universal education. It was of interest that only later was he driven by the logic of the revolution to adopt Marxism–Leninism.

From the outset Castro rejected US offers of finance and as the true significance of the revolution became clearer Washington showed its determination to crush it. The abortive Bay of Pigs invasion of 1961 and the ineffective economic blockade in 1962 followed. The Americans consistently supported the anti-Castro elements not only by finance but by facilitating hostile action from offshore islands. In his difficulties Castro turned to Soviet Russia. The Cuba crisis brought the world to the edge of nuclear war when President Kennedy insisted on the withdrawal of Soviet missiles; Krushchev gave in, but Cuba became heavily reliant upon Russia and eastern Europe for economic support. At the beginning of 1961 only two per cent of Cuban trade was with Russia; by the end of 1962 it amounted to eighty per cent. That the revolution achieved remarkable social results could not be doubted. It achieved, for example, near ninety per cent literacy within two years. It became a considerable influence in South America, particularly among the youth, towards challenging dollar diplomacy.

Failure in South America

But Castro's success failed to instigate similar revolutions in South America to destroy the powers of capitalism, landownership and the USA. Immediate revolution was opposed by Moscow and the communist parties. Castro's method, as expounded by Debray in *Revolution in the Revolution*, was to organise rural and urban guerrilla forces and to arouse the political support of the masses. This was the pattern of his own campaign in the Sierra Maestra. The mistake was made by Che Guevara, a Minister of the Cuban Government, who failed to realise that the conditions of the mainland were so different from those in Cuba, with its homogeneity and compact island area, that campaigning could have little in common with his experience. The guerrilla groups were defeated in Peru in 1965 and in Bolivia in 1967. Guevara became the hero of Cuba and of revolutionary youth throughout the world, but he did not have the backing of the rural population necessary for success.

Nevertheless, a potential revolutionary situation developed in South America. Urban guerrilla groups sprang up in many countries. Contrary to Che's ideas, these bands of middle-class students and professionals operated mainly in the towns, often robbing banks and kidnapping (sometimes with fatal consequences) foreign diplomats, civil servants and police officials. Their daring and startling success in capturing headlines has so far failed, however, to influence appreciably South America's basic political structure. Yet, spurred on by a series of developments – the killing of the Alliance for Progress in 1969 by President Nixon, the pressure of the population explosion, the resulting urbanisation of peasants in shanty towns, the mass unemployment, the malnutrition and staggering inflation – some hesitant governments have been forced to adopt policies which increasingly contradict US interests and confront US economic dominance. Challenges arose in Chile, Peru, Bolivia and Ecuador. There was also an incipient revolutionary situation in Uruguay.

Chile's Democratic Revolution

In Chile, President Frei's Christian Democratic government hesitated too long with proposals to nationalise the US-owned copper mines and for the first time in the world's history, in September 1970, a government committed to socialist revolution was voted into power, albeit with only a 1·4 per cent majority, within the framework of the democratic electoral machine. Winning the elections on promises of redistribution of land and wealth, the nationalisation of two hundred industries and the eviction of foreign financial interests, Salvador Allende's victory sent the Chilean middle classes into frenzied fear for their future financial security. Simultaneously, the poor, the students and the trade unions believed they had at last achieved a 'People's State'. Thousands of landless peasants squatted on estates and workers asserted new rights in their factories and mines. The shock of the election also sent shivers northwards to the USA. The US copper mines were completely nationalised, but the corresponding drop in world copper prices and the fall-off of foreign investment in Chile meant that after his first year in office Allende faced tremendous economic difficulties.[11]

Steadfastly, almost self-destructively, Allende has insisted on 'protecting and adhering to Chilean democracy' while working towards a socialist state. This allowed his opponents, for example, to block efforts to nationalise all the banks or to increase state control of the economy generally. Allende feared that any step out of line would invite military intervention 'in protection of the constitution'. The 'Chilean Road to Socialism' is undoubtedly unique, but its final success in challenging US economic and Chilean middle-class power remains uncertain.[12]

Military Power Decisive

Once Chile went 'red', and both Peru and Bolivia had swung left-wards, there was talk of a 'red *bloc*' along the Andes. Peru, under a leftish military government, expropriated the US-owned International Petroleum Company in 1968 and later forced US fishermen to quit Peruvian waters, claiming that these were two hundred miles wide. The US retaliated by cutting off economic aid. But, inevitably, to ensure survival the country has remained US orientated. In all three Andean countries, despite the nationalisation of US interests, some successful attempts at land reform and gradual softening of links with the US, the power of the right-wing, and that is generally the army, continues steadfast. Latin America has joined the world-wide fight against imperialism, but it is based on sporadic and radical evolution rather than on comprehensive revolution.

Fundamental changes can be realised only by direct challenges to the military throughout the whole continent. Behind the armies stands the US, which, despite its new 'low profile', still maintains a vital interest in the region. Military rule has supplanted civilian government and, irrespective of any social consciousness, South American armies retain their role as 'guardians of the nation'.

Notes

1. South America had about two hundred constitutions in 150 years.

2. Coffee accounts for more than one third of the exports of fourteen South American countries and for more than three-quarters of the exports of five countries.

3. US investment in Latin America in 1968 was $12,989 million, earning $1,586 million annually. Latin American subsidiaries of US firms exported thirty-five per cent of Latin America's exports.

4. In Uruguay, Brazil and Argentina about a thousand people owned between fifty and seventy per cent of the national production. In the rest of Latin America (except in Bolivia, Cuba and the Dominican Republic) between twenty and a hundred people in each state owned about ninety per cent of the production.

5. United Nations ECLA.

6. Published by Collier-Macmillan.

7. See *Death Pays a Dividend*, Brockway and Mullally.

8. Communist Party membership in South America is 0·1 per cent of the population.

9. There was evidence that three million acres of US-owned land was allowed to remain fallow to improve world sugar prices.

10. Batista is estimated by Lieuwen in *Arms and Politics in Latin America*, to have stolen $250 million.

11. The American chemical company *Kennecott* attempted to establish an international boycott of Chilean nationalised copper.

12. It is noteworthy that much of Africa seems to be following a similar pattern.

Chapter Twenty-two

The Caribbean

(The Islands, Guyana, British Honduras)

The Caribbean Sea is dotted with innumerable islands. Guyana borders them from South America's mainland, British Honduras from Central America.

The Islands

The Caribbean Islands form a curved archipelago between Florida in the USA and Venezuela in South America. They are probably the survivors of land dividing the Atlantic from the Caribbean Sea. The total area is 91,600 square miles with an estimated population in the mid-sixties of 20 million, of whom sixty per cent were Negro, Indian or of mixed descent and forty per cent white. Forty of the islands are inhabited. They are divided into two mains groups: the Greater and Lesser Antilles, with a separate atoll of the Bahamas close to the Florida coast. Their association is disrupted by language and an inheritance of rival colonialist occupations. Among the larger islands for example, the official tongue in Cuba and the Dominican Republic is Spanish, while in Puerto Rico both Spanish and English are recognised. In Haiti the language is French; in Jamaica and Trinidad, English. Cuba, the Dominican Republic, Haiti, Jamaica and Trinidad (with Tobago) are independent states, and Puerto Rico is a self-governing Commonwealth associated with the USA. Britain, the USA, France, the Netherlands and Venezuela are responsible for the remaining islands, devolving to them varying degrees of self-government. The area and estimated populations of the inhabited islands (to the latest, rather distant, figures) are as shown in the table on the opposite page.[1]

Slavery and Revolution

In the fifteenth century Europeans sailed west to find India and found the Americas. Columbus, when he landed in the Bahamas in October 1492 thinking he was in Asia, called the inhabitants In-

INDEPENDENT STATES	Sq. Miles	Population
Cuba	44,218	7,106,700 (1962)
Dominican Republic	18,703	3,013,525
Haiti	10,714	4,660,000 (1965)
Jamaica (with Morant and Pedro cays)	4,413	1,613,800
Trinidad and Tobago	1,980	827,957
Barbados	166	231,785
FRENCH TERRITORIES		
Guadeloupe (with Marie-Galante, Les Saintes, Petite Terre, La Désirade, St. Barthélemy, and north St. Martin)	687	283,223
Martinique	431	292,062
NETHERLANDS TERRITORIES		
Curaçao	173	125,181
Aruba	69	58,743
Bonaire	95	5,812
Leeward Islands		
St. Martin (south)	17	6,881
St. Eustatius	12	4,722
Saba	5	956

VENEZUELAN TERRITORIES	Sq. Miles	Population
Nueva Esparta (Margarita, Coche and Cubagua)	444	89,492
Federal Dependencies	46	861
BRITISH TERRITORIES		
Bahamas	4,405	130,955
Cayman Islands	100	7,622
Leeward Islands		
Antigua (with Barbuda and Redonda)	170	54,354
St. Kitts, Nevis, Anguilla	138	56,658
Montserrat	32	12,108
Virgin Islands	59	7,338
Turks and Caicos Islands	166	5,668
Windward Islands		
Dominica	290	59,916
Grenada (with Carriacou and South Grenadines)	133	88,677
St. Lucia	238	86,108
St. Vincent (with North Grenadines)	150	79,948
ASSOCIATED WITH USA		
Puerto Rico (self-governing 'Commonwealth')	3,435	2,349,544
Virgin Islands of USA	133	32,099
St. Thomas	33	16,201
St. John	20	925
St. Croix	80	14,973
Navassa Island	2	—

dians and that designation has persisted to this day throughout the Americas. He was financed by Queen Isabella of Castile to embark on a mission to Christianise the people but there was also the magnet of riches. In a decade of journeys he touched most of the islands of the Caribbean archipelago and established the Spanish empire. The women wore gold rings in their noses, but the eagerly sought gold was exhausted. Nevertheless, he brought riches to the royal family and to the traders who followed. He took sugar cane to Hispaniola (now the Dominican Republic and Haiti) which determined the history of the islands. He also took slaves, Caribbeans whom he had shipped to Spain and brought back to servitude.

The Caribbeans resisted fiercely. By 1495 there was an unequal war, resulting in defeat and decimation for the native peoples: in Hispaniola two-thirds were killed on the coast or starved in the mountains, the first recorded rebellion against European imperialism in any part of the world. Its leader, Chief Hatuey, was burnt alive. The story is still told that as he died a Franciscan friar pleaded with him to make peace with God and be assured of heaven. 'Are there Spaniards there?' asked the chief. 'Good Spaniards, yes.' 'I do not want to go to that heaven.' There was a Spanish priest, Bartolomé de las Casas, who is revered with Hatuey. He courageously defended the Caribbeans both in Hispaniola and in Spain.[2]

The depopulation of Caribbeans meant there was a shortage of labour for the plantations. Convicts and a limited number of white slaves, including women, were sent from Spain and foreigners were encouraged; but all failed to fill the gap. The Whites were unwilling to do menial work, so in 1501 Madrid authorised Negro slaves and las Casas estimated that during the first half of the century 100,000 were sold to the Spanish dominions. There were Spanish critics, notably Bartholomé de Albornoz, who denied that the law of Christ authorised the liberty of the soul at the price of the slavery of the body. His book was banned by the Holy See, but nevertheless was translated into many languages.

Rival Empires

By the first quarter of the sixteenth century the Spanish empires, besides spreading on the American mainland, had occupied the Greater Antilles. Its colonies were a royal monopoly, closed to all but Spanish trade and Catholic nationals. Opposition to this restriction developed among the white planters, who demanded trade with all Spanish ports (restricted to Seville), free trade in slaves and local government. White-elected municipal councils were conceded in Cuba, but the settler revolt faded before a Negro–Indian revolt; the planters preferred Spain to a indigenous rebellion.

Two years after the forcible coming of Negro slaves began a revolution which continued for thirty-six years. The Governor of Hispaniola had temporarily to suspend the importation of slaves because Negroes and Indians made common cause. There were riots in Puerto Rico in 1527, and in 1538 Negroes in Cuba joined French pirates in sacking Havana and rioting in Santiago. Crushed in the towns, the Negroes fled to the mountains, where they were hunted down by an armed force and dogs. Severe punishments were imposed: fifty lashes for more than four days absence, one hundred for more than eight days, two hundred for more than four months, hanging for more than six months. In Hispaniola seven thousand Negro refugees lived African-style in the mountains by subsistence cultivation. Led by Diego de Campo they defeated Spanish troops and burned sugar mills.[3]

Other European nations were not prepared to let Spain have a monopoly of Caribbean riches and possessions. In 1493 a Papal Bull in effect divided the unoccupied world between Portugal and Spain, recognising Spanish supremacy in the Caribbean islands and in North and Central America. Britain, France and Holland repudiated this 'law of God', King Francis I of France remarking he would like to see the relevant clause in Adam's will! Their assault began by piracy on the high seas. Francis Drake, concerned to challenge Catholicism but also aware that the Caribbean was 'the treasure house of the world', won the approval of Queen Elizabeth, and his successes in the West Indies were crowned by his defeat of the Armada which destroyed the power of Spain. Sir John Hawkins, who has been described as the first imperialist planner,[4] consolidated Drake's naval victories. He broke Spain's trade monopoly and Portugal's slave-trade monopoly. He began the establishment of the network of British colonies in the Caribbean.

At the start Britain did not have everything its own way. The Caribbeans repelled the invasion of the islands of St Lucia in 1605 and of Grenada in 1609. St Kitts was captured in 1623, Barbados in 1625, and Nevis, Antigua and Montserrat followed in quick succession.[5] Thirty years later, in 1655, Jamaica fell to Cromwell's

'Western Design' expedition. France was equally aggressive. It shared St Kitts with Britain, took possession of Martinique, Guadaloupe, Bartholomew, St Croix and Tobago, and partitioned St Martin with Holland. It overcame resistance in St Lucia and Grenada, exterminating the whole Caribbean population in the latter island; the precipice from which the last survivors threw themselves to death is still known as Leapers' Hill. Holland concentrated on the mainland, naming what is now New York, New Amsterdam.[6] Germany entered the scramble, succeeding only in occupying the islet of St Peter in the Virgin Islands; even Scandinavia joined in, with Denmark taking St Thomas and St John. Sweden, ambitious after the triumphs of Gustavus Adolphus in the wars of religion, failed to gain an island until the next century, when they secured a footing in France's St Bartholomew. This phase of imperialist rivalry ended in 1697 when the Treaty of Ryswick transferred Hispaniola, renamed St Domingue, from Spain to France.

The Caribbean islands were deeply affected by four events in the eighteenth century. The first was the war between Britain and France; the second, the American Revolution; the third, the final revolt against slavery; and the fourth, the French Revolution.

Franco-British War

For most of the century Britain and France were at war and to the British, French rather than Spanish possessions became a prize. In 1763, when there was a temporary peace, Britain annexed Grenada, Tobago, Dominica and St Vincent[7] and a year later repulsed a French claim to the Bahamas. In 1783, with another truce, victorious Britain, thinking of the balance of power in Europe and the American mainland more than of the Caribbean islands, allowed France to retain two-thirds of St Domingue, Martinique, and Guadeloupe, and to add Tobago and St Lucia to her empire. Britain had won the war, but in the West Indies France won the peace.

Effect of American Revolution

The American Revolution was supported by the Caribbean settlers, who were themselves continually in conflict with their home governments. In 1766 the Jamaican Assembly of white representatives defied Westminster by asserting that Parliament had no right to legislate for the colonies. Bermuda, Barbados and the Bahamas openly expressed sympathy with the American rebellion. Dr Williams, historian of the Caribbean and Premier of Trinidad and Tobago, writes that 'but for the British navy it would have been impossible to prevent the British West Indies from joining the Revolution'.[8] In the French and Spanish Colonies, both the governments and the settlers were pro-American. When London prohibited the British colonies from continuing trade with America the results were serious for the British plantation owners and traders and for their slaves. Planters became bankrupt, their foodless slaves died. Even after the independence of America the ban was maintained, despite the protest of the colonial Governors. The destruction of the trade of the British colonies, whilst the French colonies carried on, meant that the British were left behind. French-occupied St Domingue had a fantastic economic upsurge.

Negro Revolt

The white revolt was preceded and followed by a renewed Negro revolt against slavery. In 1639, at St Kitts, the slaves established a fort in the mountains and defended it against five hundred troops with many deaths. In 1649 eighteen Negroes were executed in Barbados for conspiring to kill Europeans; in 1656 there was an insurrection for fifteen days, and the leaders were hung, drawn and quartered. In 1679 the slaves revolted in St Domingue, again establishing a mountain fortress, stormed by buccaneers. In 1690 it was Jamaica's turn; three hundred Negroes on a plantation revolted, and a hundred were killed. In 1692 there was revolt again in Barbados, with many executed. In 1729 and 1731 slaves took over the copper mines of Santiago in Cuba. Negro rebellion became almost continuous in the eighteenth century. Dr Williams lists these slave risings: St John (1733); Jamaica (1734); Antigua (1736); Guadeloupe (1737); Jamaica (1746); Martinique (1752); Jamaica (1760); Nevis (1761); Jamaica (1765 and 1769); Jamaica and Montserrat (1776).[9]

The frequency of revolts in Jamaica will be noted. In fact the Negroes had rebelled there from the beginning of the British conquest, accompanied by a mass escape to the interior. From the end of the seventeenth century to 1739 there was incessant conflict.

The Maroons, as the escapees were called, led by Cudjoe, drove back the local militia and British troops, and in the end the Government had to make concessions. The Maroons were declared free and were given fifteen hundred acres with the right to grow any crop except sugar, but they betrayed the slaves from the plantations; they gave a pledge to return them and to co-operate in handing over future fugitives. Meanwhile in Europe voices were raised in denunciation of slavery. Richard Baxter, the Quaker, John Wesley, Godwyn, Thomas Browne, Adam Smith, James Battie and Tom Paine in Britain and Rousseau and Voltaire in France made a moral and intellectual challenge.

Effect of French Revolution

The French Revolution lit the fire of both the settlers' revolt and the slaves' rebellion. The National Assembly in Paris was engulfed in controversy by both. When it decided to enfranchise the Whites and only those Mulattos (mixed race) born of non-slave parents, the Mulattos rejected this compromise and made common cause with the slaves. There was civil war, in which the non-Whites were victorious, leading the Assembly to concede that all non-slave Negroes and Mulattos should have political rights. This in turn brought revolt from the Whites. The planters of French St Domingue, St Lucia, Tobago, Guadeloupe and Martinique decided to end their association with France and the St Domingue settlers approached William Pitt with the proposal that they should transfer allegiance to Britain. Welcoming the prospect that prosperous French St Domingue and the French islands would compensate for the loss of the American colonies, Britain accepted the offer of the planters and renewed its war with France, promising the settlers that political rights would not be extended to the Mulattos and Negroes and that slavery would be maintained. Only Britain's Opium War with China was as morally wrong.

The slaves brought a new element into the struggle. They fought both the planters and the British. At the same time the Revolution in Paris moved leftward and in 1794 it was decreed that there would be a total abolition of slavery in the French Dominions. From this moment the Slave Revolution and the French Revolution were hand in hand. Slaves in French St Domingue were led by a remarkable man, Toussaint Louverture (himself a slave coachman) who routed invading British troops. General Maitland with-

drew and signed an agreement with Toussaint, but when Bonaparte
assumed power he rejected the island's new constitution abolishing
slavery and colour distinction, and sent a strong expedition which
restored the old regime. Toussaint himself was captured and
died in a prison in the French Alps; but the Negroes refused
defeat. Under the leadership of Dessalines and Christophe they
destroyed the French as they had destroyed the British. On
January 1, 1804, the independence of the western area of the
islands was declared under the Caribbean name of Haiti, with
Christophe as president. Slavery was again abolished, but President Boyer, third in succession, introduced serfdom for the benefit
of a new owning class of Mulattos and Negroes. Labourers were
tied to the farms and prohibited from forming workers' associations. In 1821 the Spanish portion of the island, still known as
St Domingue, also declared its independence; it was annexed by
Haiti, but regained its separate sovereignty in 1844 under the new
title Dominican Republic.

The defeat of Bonaparte led to the confirmation of the British
occupation of Trinidad, which had been surrendered by Spain in
1797, and to the restoration to Britain of Tobago and St Lucia.
The French Caribbean empire was reduced to Martinique, Gaude-
loupe and Cayenne (on the South American mainland). In 1877 it
had the slight compensation that St Bartholomew became French
when the Swedish withdrew. Spain also had her troubles. In 1868
Cespedes led a formidable independence rebellion in Cuba, campaigning to end slavery as well as political subjection, insisting that
'a free Cuba is incompatible with a slave Cuba'. Simultaneously
there was a struggle for autonomy in Puerto Rico which won
concessions.

Abolition of Slavery

Opposition to slavery had become influential in Europe. For
twenty years Wilberforce led the struggle in Britain, supported by
Thomas Clarkson, the writer, the orator Henry Brougham and
James Stephen, a civil servant. Victor Schoelcher led the campaign
in France. From the beginning of the nineteenth century slavery
was gradually outlawed. Denmark began it in 1803. The process
was slow. In Britain, Pitt, whilst stopping the slave trade from
Africa, permitted it to continue between the islands of the West
Indies. In 1807 the British Parliament accepted the principle of

abolition, but did not apply it to the colonies until 1833 and then by stages over another five years. France took from 1817 to 1848 to abolish slavery in its colonies; Holland from 1818 to 1863; Sweden from 1824 to 1846, and Spain from 1820 to 1873 in Puerto Rico and to 1880 in Cuba. The planters were compensated for their loss of slaves.

The abolition of slavery in the Caribbean brought thousands of Negroes crowding into insanitary shanty towns; it also brought a labour shortage on the plantations, some of which passed to freed Mulattos and Negroes when Europeans evacuated with their compensation money. The slaves were replaced by indentured Asians. Many returned to India at the end of their five-year contracts (they were paid 8p a day) and to restrain others governments granted plots of land. Thus a permanent Asian population was added to the West Indies, involving some racial tension. The number was large. Between 1838 and 1917, 145,000 Indians went to Trinidad; 21,500 to Jamaica; 39,000 to Guadeloupe; 1,150 to St Lucia; 1,820 to St Vincent, and 2,570 to Grenada. In addition to Indians, there were many Madeirans, Chinese and some Japanese.

The British abolition of the slave trade aroused resistance among many European planters. In 1815 the Jamaican House of Assembly protested and again declared that they should not be bound by laws imposed without their consent. Jamaica's freed slaves challenged British rule on other grounds, demanding land, and in 1865 they rebelled, supported by George William Gordon in the Assembly. The Governor declared martial law, called on the Maroons for help, secured reinforcements, captured and hanged Gordon. A reign of terror followed; it was acknowledged by a Royal Commission that the punishments were excessive, the death penalty (354 sentenced by court martial) too frequent, flogging barbarous and the burning of houses wanton. The rebellion led to constitutional reaction. In Jamaica, where there had been an income-based franchise, following the abolition of slavery there was actually a majority of non-Whites in the Assembly.

In 1865 Jamaica was made a Crown Colony on the same basis as in Trinidad where white control had been retained. A purely advisory Council of six official and six unofficial members, chaired by the Governor with a casting vote, was established. About this time ideas of federation first emerged. Barbados violently resisted federation with smaller neighbouring islands and proposed confederation with Canada, but Ottawa would not accept the burden. Denmark succeeded in associating St Croix, St Thomas and St

John, with six representatives from each in a Colonial Assembly, supplemented by four nominated members. The Spanish colonies were still governed with absolute autocracy.

American Intervention

The nineteenth century saw the United States of America asserting its authority in the Caribbean. Jefferson dreamed of a federation of all the islands and even approached Bonaparte for the transference of Cuba to the Union. In 1823 President Monroe made his historic pronouncement initiating the Monroe Doctrine; it is often forgotten that this was directed to the Caribbean. The President warned that any extension by the European Powers of their colonial systems would be regarded as dangerous to peace. Theodore Roosevelt, before becoming President, urged in 1898 that American foreign policy should be shaped to drive every European power from the continent, beginning with Spain and including England.[10] The US passed from opposition to European expansion to planning its own expansion. It offered to purchase Cuba in 1854, but Spain declined to sell. In 1895 a fierce rebellion for independence gave US the opportunity. A battleship which it sent to Havana to restore order was blown up with the loss of 260 lives. The Spanish Government refused reparations, President McKinlay declared war, and in 1898 Spain surrendered both Cuba and Puerto Rico. Under pressure the Cuban Assembly accepted what came to be known as the Platt Amendment, which gave the US rights to intervene and to lease naval stations. In 1907 the US gained authority to control customs and debts in the Dominican Republic, and in 1915 occupied the Republic; the military government imposed was not withdrawn until 1924. In 1915 the US got Haiti to sign a treaty giving it supervision of debts and customs and from 1916 to 1924 occupied the territory. In 1917 the US purchased the Virgin Islands from Denmark.

Rise of Nationalism

Modern nationalist movements arose on the eve of the Second World War and were stimulated during the war by the Atlantic Charter and the Four Freedoms. In Jamaica Norman Manley's People's National Party, in Trinidad the West Indian Nationalist

Party, in Barbados the Progressive League, in Puerto Rico the Popular Democratic Party, and in Cuba the Independent Party of Colour, became a force. At the same time trade unions emerged everywhere. In 1938 a Labour Congress of the West Indies and Guyana demanded federation of the British area, a Legislature elected by adult suffrage, nationalisation of the sugar industry and public utilities, landholding restriction to fifty acres, co-operative marketing, social welfare and free compulsory education.

American Sphere

The objectives of the nationalist movements reflected the different external dominations. In Haiti, Cuba and the Dominican Republic, anti-colonialism was directed against America. In 1918 there had been a peasant revolt in Haiti against American imposition of forced labour in road-making; it was suppressed at the cost of more than a thousand Haitian lives. The American forces did not withdraw until 1934. In Cuba, as told later, America supported dictators Machado and Batista. In the Dominican Republic there was a ruthless dictatorship from 1929 to 1961 under Trujillo. He faked election results, handpicked the Legislature, took possession of the larger part of the economy, and in 1937 massacred over fifteen thousand Haitians when rebellion broke out. The Americans appreciated him because he paid off foreign debts, rewarding him by ending US control of customs. He was unashamedly an opportunist and, when America turned against him at the end of his career, negotiated with countries behind the Iron Curtain. He was assassinated in May 1961. Many years of confusion followed, with the US intervening with large forces in 1965 to defeat a left-wing threat to obtain governmental control. Since then the Dominican Republic has passed increasingly within American influence. Independent Haiti came into serious conflict with the American-supported Dominican Republic, whose President Duvalier was dictatorial but nevertheless won the confidence of Nelson Rockefeller, who recommended economic aid. Living conditions were still very low; and there is much speculation about what will happen when the aged president dies.[11]

For three hundred years Puerto Rico had been an appendage to Spain. Its struggle for autonomy gained further concessions in 1897 when, in addition to delegates in the Spanish *Cortes*, it was accorded a legislature with an elected Lower Chamber and powers of self-government, except law and order. The Legislature lasted only a month; in April 1898 the Spanish–American war began, and in June the US occupied the island. Washington began by appointing a Senate of nominated members and an elected Lower House, but the US Congress could annul any law. In 1917 Puerto Ricans were granted citizenship in America, but this did not satisfy the Nationalists. In 1937 there was an uprising led by Albizu Campes, which led to a massacre setting the whole population aflame. America had to make concessions, particularly after the Popular Democratic Party, led by Muñoz Marin, swept the 1940 elections with the slogan 'Land, Bread, Liberty'. In 1950 Puerto Rico was given Commonwealth status and its people poured into the US. By 1970 over a third of the population – one and a half million – had emigrated, but they became among the poorest sections of the community, most living in ghettoes like the Negroes. In New York they were one-third of the city's welfare recipients. January 1971 saw the first Puerto Rican elected to Congress, Herman Badillo, who became the voice of his people.

French, Dutch and British Spheres

The lessened group of French colonies became assimilated as departments of France. There was some nationalist resentment and uprisings in Guadeloupe in the sixties. Holland found a compromise which satisfied nationalist aspirations more fully. The Netherlands Antilles (as well as Surinam on the southern mainland) not only had internal self-government but were represented on a commission which considered defence and foreign affairs.

In the British colonies the modern revolt against the regimes began in protests against poverty. Conditions were appalling. Wages were below subsistence level and there was heavy unemployment. Anger with destitution was aggravated by the high dividends distributed by the companies which had taken over the sugar plantations and established industries. An effort was made to alleviate conditions by some land distribution, but this did not begin to be adequate. Dr Williams lists the uprisings which occurred between 1935 and 1938:[12] a sugar strike in St Kitts, 1935; a revolt against an increase of customs duties in St Vincent, 1935; an oil strike which became a general strike in Trinidad, 1937; a sympathetic strike in Barbados, 1937; a sugar strike in St Lucia, 1937; sugar troubles in Jamaica, 1937; a dockers' strike in Jamaica,

1937. The Governors called for warships and marines, but unrest grew, expressing itself in militant trade union expansion.

Cipriani of Trinidad and Rawle of Dominica initiated a West Indian conference in 1932 to consider federation and the establishment of elected Legislatures. In the same year the British Government sent a commission which declared against both federation and adult suffrage. But the democratic wave which the Second World War released impelled constitutional changes. Adult suffrage was introduced and elected Ministers made responsible for internal government.

In 1958 a serious attempt was made to establish a federation of the British colonies. A constitution was prepared, but hope was destroyed by a general election in Jamaica which returned Bustamente's party to power. It had been proposed that the Federation should become an independent Dominion; instead separate independence was accorded to the larger islands. Jamaica and Trinidad (with Tobago) became sovereign within the Commonwealth in 1962 and Barbados in 1966. The Bahamas also moved towards independence, with a non-White government replacing control by the white 'Bay Street Boys' after the election in 1967, but Prime Minister Pindling was confined by the dependence of the Bahamas on tourism from nearby US. At some stage there will be a confrontation between the wealthy white community who run an American-style society and the poorer non-Whites. Dissatisfaction threatened to take a more militant Black Panther form, which emerged in many other Caribbean islands also.[13]

Grouped smaller islands became Associated States of Britain with full internal self-government and the right to opt for independence. There was opposition from some of the islands to the grouping; Anguilla seceded from St Kitts-Nevis, and a small British security force took over whilst a commission of Caribbean representatives advised. They reported in favour of continued association with greater autonomy for Anguilla, but the Anguillans rejected the recommendations. It was clear that a final solution had not been found.

Limits of Independence

The West Indian islands should ideally form a federation or confederation, but they were disintegrated by colonialism. Even with self-government they are bound to their previous occupying powers – Jamaica, Trinidad, Barbados and smaller islands to Britain, Puerto Rico and Dominican Republic to America, the French islands to France, the Netherlands Antilles to Holland. There is incidentally but importantly the difference of languages; but most relevant is the direction of trade and political association. Economic co-operation is still predominantly with the ex-colonialist powers rather than between the islands themselves. Some of the territories have formed a Free Trade area and proposals have been considered for a Caribbean Development Bank, but neo-colonialist integration remained stronger than Caribbean integration. Puerto Rico is now virtually a part of the USA and the French territories are in effect France overseas.

The proximity and economic power of America are certain to increase its influence. After the Second World War the USA established naval bases in Trinidad, Jamaica, Antigua, St Lucia and the Bahamas, as also in British Guiana, and in addition still has its base in Cuba. The climate and beauty of the islands make them a favourite resort for American visitors; indeed tourism has become a major industry, involving a contrast between foreign luxury and indigenous poverty. American investment in new industries, hotels and casinos, not only in islands associated with itself but in the British sphere, is giving it economic domination. If these tendencies persist, the Caribbean, except for the more assertive states, will become an American Mediterranean.

Except for Cuba the Caribbean islands are neo-colonialist territories. Recognition should be given to advances in economic development, education, health treatment and sanitation under colonialist occupation, but the lives of the peoples are dependent upon industries, plantations and tourism dominated externally. The state of Trinidad and Tobago is making a constructive effort to attain genuine independence and has succeeded in ridding itself of an American military base. During the latter half of 1970 a significant endeavour was made by the small British Virgin Islands to buy out foreign developers.[14] There were disputes regarding compensation and a British Minister visited the islands in 1971 to make an assessment. The example of the Virgin Islands is likely to be followed by other islands, but the peoples may not always be so amenable to providing compensation. The political revolution has gone far in the Caribbean, but economic freedom has still to be won. Unlike some other colonies, because of their limitation in size and resources, their full emancipation depends upon fundamental changes within the dominating powers.

Guyana (British Guiana)

Guiana, which lies on the north coast of the South American mainland, was first sighted by Columbus in 1498, but the earliest settlers were probably the French in 1503. However, the 'Indians' soon drove them out, but from 1580 onwards Dutch settlers arrived and the Dutch West India Company set up offices in 1682. Soon agents arrived with the first slaves.

Effects of the End of Slavery

During the seventeenth century the territory repeatedly changed hands reflecting European wars. While the British held Guiana from 1791 the Act abolishing the slave trade was carried at Westminster, and three years after British Guiana was formally established, in 1831, the slaves working on the sugar plantations were emancipated. There was fierce opposition from the owners who lost over half their labour force. Many of the ex-slaves pooled their resources and formed co-operatives, but the world sugar surplus acted against them, forcing down prices. They were especially hard hit when imperial preference on sugar was withdrawn in 1846, throwing many out of work. The problems of the unemployed were intensified when British traders brought Indian and Chinese indentured labourers to work on the plantations.

Guiana's economic situation remained bad and social conditions outraged those who made social surveys after the Second World War. One visiting UN Representative from FAO told the Guianese Legislative Assembly that she was 'shocked to the bones' by the terrible signs of malnutrition she had seen.[15] The country was only able to struggle through its economic troubles after the discovery of bauxite, manganese, diamonds and gold, all of which were exported at low prices after extraction by Anglo-Saxon companies.

Jagan's Victory Rejected

Political power in Guiana remained, however, with the 'sugar kings'. The plantation owners dominated the Legislature and prevented any effective rise of alternative power groups. But as with so many other outposts of the empire, the war brought the first development of national consciousness. The new forces were mobilised when Cheddi Jagan, who had returned to his homeland after spending seven years as a student in the USA, began with others, including Forbes Burnham, the organisation of trade unions, called strikes and established a political party. The People's Progressive Party campaigned for the rights of the coloured workers in the colony's first democratic elections in 1953. When the PPP won, the British Government suspended this 'experiment in democracy', convinced that Jagan was a dangerous Communist. The constitution (which in any case gave Jagan very little power) was set aside and 133 days after the elections British troops arrived. The British Government issued a White Paper charging the PPP with a conspiracy to set fire to business property and the residences of prominent companies. It was alleged that there was a threat to establish a people's police and to transform the Civil Service into an instrument of the Party. The White Paper was regarded by Labour MPs as unconvincing and the Labour Party voted against the Government. Both Jagan and Burnham forthrightly denied the allegations.

The struggle between Jagan and London continued for the next eleven years. Independence for the colony under him was ruled out at Westminster, especially once Kennedy came to power in the USA. The American President feared the advent of a Cuba on the American mainland, and pressure was brought on successive British governments not only to retain control but to get rid of Jagan. The final *coup* to remove him was in fact delivered by those whom he thought were his friends – the Labour Government in 1964. There was fierce opposition by a group of Labour MPs in the House of Commons.

Successively in the elections of 1953, 1957 and 1961 Jagan's party was returned as the largest in the Legislature, despite the fact that Forbes Burnham broke away and formed a new social democratic party. Unfortunately the Jagan–Burnham split found expression in racial opposition, the Negro population in the towns supporting Burnham, the Indian workers on the sugar plantations backing Jagan. The 1961 election was accepted as a preliminary to independence and Jagan as head of the government was to negotiate with London, but negotiations were postponed when rioting occurred following austerity taxation. The humiliating position arose that Jagan had to appeal for British troops when government buildings were destroyed. The financial crisis arose from a boycott of investment and aid by capitalist countries, particularly the USA, and from British objection to aid from communist countries. Cuba attempted to send supplies, but its ships were unable to unload.

Independence Under Burnham

The British Government met this situation by amending the electoral law to proportional representation. In 1964 the PPP was again returned as the largest party, but Burnham formed a coalition government with a reactionary European-led group. Independence was granted in May 1966, under the name Guyana, and Burnham was re-elected as Prime Minister in 1969 in a contest marred by proved illegal practices. Throughout the Jagan–Burnham struggle there was evidence of intervention by the CIA, but Burnham after independence did not receive the aid from the USA which he had expected. He adopted a policy of nonalignment and identified his government with the Third World and the OAU in Africa. In domestic affairs he favoured co-operative self-help schemes rather than dependence upon foreign investment. Washington is probably still worried that Guyana may become a socialist society in South America.

British Honduras

British Honduras on the central American mainland remains a colony, largely because the population desire protection from assimilation by neighbouring Guatemala which borders it west and south (to the north-west is Mexico, to the east the Caribbean Sea). The population in 1960 was 90,121, one-third living in the port capital, Belize. The coastal people are mostly descendants of African slaves, the inland people American Indians.

The uninviting coast was deserted after the fall of the historic Maya civilisation in the ninth century and was not significantly occupied until 1638, when some British settled as cutters of logwood (used to make dyes). They competed with surrounding Spaniards who attempted to drive them out, but the settlers and their slaves defeated decisively a naval attack from Madrid in 1798. The American Indian population arrived as refugees from Mexico in 1847.

Britain Preferred to Guatemala

British Honduras was declared a British colony in 1862, at first administered under the Governor of Jamaica; in 1884 it was recognised as a separate colony. The larger inland country, Guatemala, has repeatedly claimed Belize, but the people dissented and Guatemala declined a British proposal to submit the issue to the International Court of Justice. American mediation in 1965 also came to nothing but it was stated in responsible quarters in London that negotiations were still proceeding between the USA, Guatemala and Britain. Under the constitution of 1960 British Honduras is classed as a Crown Colony under a Governor aided by an Executive Council and a Legislative Assembly elected by adult suffrage.

The future of the territory will probably depend on the possibility of political co-operation in Central America. The alternative suggestion has been made of federation with British Caribbean islands.

Notes

1. We are indebted to the *Encyclopaedia Britannica* (1970) for this comprehensive classification. Unless otherwise stated, the population figures are those of the 1960 or 1961 censuses.

2. Las Casas subsequently endorsed Negro slavery to replace Caribbean, but regretted this before he died.

3. De Campo gave way after being captured and offered to lead an attack on the refugees.

4. Dr Eric Williams, in his monumental work, *From Columbus to Castro: the History of the Caribbean, 1492–1969*, describes Hawkins's initiative as 'the Birthday of the British Empire'. The author is continually indebted to Dr Williams, as any writer about the Caribbean must be.

5. On July 2, 1627, Charles I of England granted to James Earl of Carlisle, the following islands: St Christopher, Grenada, St Vincent, St Lucia, Barbados, Mittalanea, Dominica, Margalante, Deseada, Todosortes, Guadeloupe, Antigua, Montserrat, Rodendo, Barbuda, Nevis, Statia, St Bartholomew, St Martin, Anguilla, Sebrara, Enegada and others, 'reserving a yearly rent of £100 and a white horse when the King, his heirs and successors shall go into those parts'.

6. Holland exchanged New Amsterdam with Britain for Surinam in Guiana.

7. Dominica and St Vincent had been left under Caribbean administration because France and Britain could not agree about their status.

8. Dr Eric Williams, *From Columbus to Castro*.

9. *From Columbus to Castro*.

10. In a letter quoted by Dr Eric Williams in *From Columbus to Castro*.

11. President Duvalier died in 1972 and was succeeded by his son who, to a limited degree, modified dictatorial rule.

12. *From Columbus to Castro*.

13. The Bahamas were promised independence during 1973.

14. Three years earlier a British corporation had been given a 199-year lease on four-fifths of the island and exemptions from taxation were promised for all companies within the area.

15. Cheddi Jagan, *The West on Trial*.

Chapter Twenty-three

The Mediterranean

(Cyprus, Malta, Gibraltar)

We bring together Cyprus, Malta and Gibraltar because they are of the Mediterranean Sea; two as islands, the third commanding its entrance. Their stories are different, each reflecting strategic locations.

Cyprus

Cyprus is the continuing victim of its geographical position, poised between Turkey (only forty miles away) and the Arab and Israeli western boundaries with the Mediterranean, Egypt to the south and Greece to the north. All through history it has been the pawn of empires and has been occupied more than any territory of which we have knowledge. Its area is only 3,572 square miles, its population, according to the 1960 census, only 577,615 (80 per cent Greek, 17 per cent Turkish), yet it remains in the seventies crucial in the power struggle.

Six Empires

Archaeological research has established a high state of civilisation even in the sixth millennium BC with evidence that the island was the emporium of the East from 1600 BC. Its subsequent occupations reflected empires: Greek, Phoenician, Egyptian, Persian, Roman, Byzantine, Arab, Italian, Turkish, British, until in the twentieth century it asserted its independence. About 1400 BC Cyprus was colonised by Greece, followed by Phoenician penetration from 800 BC. A hundred years of proud independence followed, with great commercial and cultural advance. Then in 560 BC the Egyptians took over, followed by the Persians who permitted considerable self-government under Cypriot chiefs styling themselves kings. Cypriot national consciousness developed and there was revolt, in the confusion of which Egypt returned, but everything was swept away by the Roman empire, which spread to Cyprus in 56 BC. In the first years of the Christian era St Paul and St Mark are said to have won many converts among the Jewish settlement in Cyprus, which became a refuge for persecuted Christians from Rome; this did not save the Jews from acts of massacre which led to their expulsion from Cyprus in AD 115.

The Roman empire fell, but for seven hundred years, with rare intervals, Cyprus remained subject to eastern emperors. Its condition was generally peaceful until it became involved in the conflict between Islam and Byzantine power in the seventh century. The Muslims attacked Cyprus, the Byzantine fleet victoriously defended, and for two hundred years the island remained part of the Byzantine empire. Then came the Crusades, with King Richard I of England presenting the island to the king of Jerusalem in consolation for his eviction, followed by an Italian take-over. Through the influence of trade Cyprus became, in the fifteenth century, involved in the Venetian wars, taking the offensive, capturing towns on the Arab mainland, including Alexandria, and suffering the revenge of Egyptian occupation in 1426, its kings paying tribute to Cairo. The Venetians returned temporarily, to be expelled in 1570 by the Ottoman empire which initiated three hundred years of rule by the Turks. Their occupation began progressively, serfdom abolished, and the Christians given autonomy, but it deteriorated to dictatorship and there were risings in 1764, 1804 and 1821.

Cyprus Ceded to Britain: Revolt

Britain entered the scene, involved in the power struggle. In 1878 Turkey ceded Cyprus to London in return for a promise to assist in her war against Russia, but Cypriot revolt was still strong, the Greek majority demanding *enosis*, union with Greece. Cyprus was formally annexed by Britain in 1914 when Turkey sided with Germany. London still used the island as a bargain counter, offering it to Greece in 1915 if she would co-operate in the war. When Athens refused, Cyprus was declared a Crown Colony. A Legislative Council with an official majority was set up.

In the 1930s widespread disturbances showed that the Cypriot people were tired of being treated as pawns in imperial interests. The Greeks massively claimed *enosis*. A state of emergency was declared, the Legislative Council abolished, and all legislative and executive power vested in the British Governor. The Second World War delayed constitutional development. There was considerable voluntary enlistment by Cypriots, but when the war was over they demonstrated for *enosis* again. Archbishop Makarios emerged as a leader, uniting the Church and political resistance. The Cypriot demand was supported within Greece. Turkey became resentful, and the British, Greek and Turkish Foreign Ministers met in London in September 1955, but failed to agree. Guerrilla warfare extended in Cyprus with further severe repression.

Makarios Deported

There followed what was virtually war between the British and Greeks in Cyprus. The Cypriot rebels were led by Colonel Grivas, a former officer in Greece, who established EOKA (*Ethniki Organosis Kypriakou Agonos* – National Organisation of Cypriot Struggle), which held at bay the British forces despite reinforcements. The conflict ignored the rules of war; any British soldier could be stabbed in the back in the streets. Inevitably there was severe reaction. In 1956 negotiations took place with Archbishop Makarios; the British rejected full self-determination but offered extended self-government. When the talks broke down, Makarios and the Bishop of Kyrenia were deported to Seychelles. Colonel Grivas could not be found and the fullest deployment of the British forces failed to suppress EOKA.

The British Government asked Lord Radcliffe to devise a new liberal constitution and in December 1956 he made recommendations endorsing the principle of self-determination. The Government accepted them and EOKA offered to suspend activities if Makarios were released. A few days later he was freed, but he was excluded for a time from Cyprus. Negotiations were slow, and the Turkish minority, favouring partition, became militant. Guerrilla warfare was renewed, becoming more divisive by conflicts between the Greek and Turkish populations.

Greek–Turkish Agreement

In the Autumn of 1958 Makarios proposed independence rather than union with Greece and the Greek and Turkish Governments negotiated at Zürich early in 1959. They reached agreement in principle, and the British Government accepted their terms. They proposed that the Republic of Cyprus should not enter into political or economic union with either Greece or Turkey, there should be a Greek Cypriot president and a Turkish Cypriot vice-president, an elected House of Representatives of fifty members composed seventy per cent of Greeks and thirty per cent of Turks, the Executive should be composed of seven Greeks and three Turks, the British would retain sovereignty over military bases at Dhekhelia and Akrotiri (ninety-nine square miles).

Renewed Conflict After Independence

Makarios accepted the proposals and there was a general election in July 1960 which resulted in the return of thirty supporters of the Archbishop and five Communists by the Greek voters and fifteen supporters of Dr Kutchuk by the Turks. A republic was declared in August 1960, and Cyprus admitted to the United Nations and the Commonwealth. The British Government agreed to make a grant of £12 million over five years; it retained its military bases. For a time the bi-national constitution appeared to work, but the conflict between Greeks and Turks erupted again and by 1963 co-operation in the Legislature and Executive ceased and Makarios and the Greeks ruled alone. Civil war broke out with British troops endeavouring to keep the Greek and Turkish communities apart.

UN Peace-Keeping Force

In March 1964 the United Nations Security Council agreed to send a peace-keeping force which had considerable success, though it could not prevent an outbreak in August when Turkish Government aircraft bombed Greek villages to repel an expected offensive. In November 1967 there was another outbreak and renewed efforts were made to bring about a settlement through the United Nations and the USA. They brought the Greek and Turkish Governments together, but again failure. So the uneasy situation continued and discussion over more than two years between representatives of the two communities in Cyprus did not succeed in bringing agreement. The Turks asked for complete local autonomy in areas where they were the dominant population, the Greeks rejecting this as virtual partition. In fact, *de facto* partition existed, the Turks forbidding Greeks to enter their enclaves.

One effect of this division was to isolate the Turks from the economic revival which occurred in the late sixties and seventies. It would be too much to say that Cyprus regained her early status as the emporium of the East, but as the months passed civilian life began to function with near normality and trade developed strongly, aided by the expenditure of the British and United Nations military personnel. There was nevertheless some nationalist opposition to the British base, which had mounted when it was used in the attack on the Suez Canal.

In 1971 General Grivas, leader of EOKA and hero of the resistance to the British, returned to Cyprus. He made it clear that he still favoured union with Greece and was opposed to the Makarios regime of independence. He remained in hiding, but his presence on the island aroused tension and division within the Greek community. Then at the beginning of 1972 crisis escalated. Makarios visited Moscow and accepted arms from Czechoslovakia valued at £5 million; at the same time he emphasised his determination to win full independence for Cyprus and indicated his long-term object of excluding the British military base. The Greek Government, still a member of NATO (despite its suppression of democracy) and an ally of the West, insisted that the Czech arms should be handed to the United Nations force and called on Makarios to form a government of national unity including General Grivas. The illegal Opposition within Greece denounced this pressure as a 'naked threat of intervention', whilst Turkey watched uneasily, pulled in two directions: it was still identified with its community in Cyrpus, but it relied on American and NATO support. Turkey joined Britain and Greece (making together the three guarantor states of Cypriot security) in urging the transference of the Czech arms to the UN force and Makarios agreed. Then a new crisis arose. The Holy Synod of the Orthodox Church presented a demand to the Archbishop to resign his presidency of Cyprus because it was incompatible with his headship of the Church. The fact that he had held the two offices for twelve and a half years without objection ever being raised indicated political pressure in the background. Simultaneously the Greek Government did not hide its view that it would be desirable for Makarios to resign in order that a government which included Grivas, still an advocate of union with Greece, might be established.

These threats to Makarios aroused large demonstrations

acclaiming him, but rumours arose that his departure was desired to facilitate the partition of Cyprus into separate Greek and Turkish spheres associated with the two mainland governments. The fate of Cyprus hangs in the balance. If partition is seriously proposed, physical resistance will almost certainly recur.

Malta

The Maltese islands; Malta (95 square miles), Gozo (26 square miles) and Comino, uninhabited rocks (one square mile), lie in the middle of the Mediterranean, 140 miles from the European main-land, 180 miles from Africa. Nearest land is Sicily sixty miles away. The population was estimated to be 320,000 in 1968, unique in density, with 3,074 per square mile in Malta and 1,060 in Gozo. Malta was not as victimised by rising and falling empires as Cyprus, but nevertheless became the prize of rival powers.

Successive Occupations

Racial characteristics continuing until today suggest that Phoen-icians were the original inhabitants, but there are megalithic monuments which date beyond them to lost and prehistoric man. In the sixth century BC, Carthaginians arrived from North Africa, ruling harshly and extracting heavy toll in taxation. In 218 BC the Maltese appealed to the Romans for protection, retaining local self-government to themselves. In the first years AD St Paul was shipwrecked on the island and is said to have converted the popu-lation to Christianity. When the Roman empire disintegrated their successors, the Byzantines, took over and then the Arab empire in its turn, massacring the Greek garrison and selling the men as slaves. In 1091 Count Roger, 'the Norman dictator' of Sicily, arrived and was hailed as a liberator. The Church became dominant, the remaining Arabs were treated as vassals and were expelled in 1245. Malta passed under a succession of feudal lords, but the Normans introduced representative communal self-govern-ment, the *universita*, probably the most democratic in all Europe in the Middle Ages. Subject to an annual tribute of a falcon, Emperor Charles V granted Malta and Gozo (also Tripoli in North Africa) to the Knights of St John of Jerusalem when they were driven from Rhodes by the Turks, placing the islands under the suzerainty of Spain. The Turks attacked Malta but were driven off in 1565, and there followed a period of indefinite rule until June 1798 when Napoleon took possession.

National Resistance

In September of 1798 came the first recorded nationalist rebellion, led by Canon Francesco Caruana, a name still honoured. The Maltese formed a provisional government appealing to Nelson for protection, and a British fleet took possession of the islands. The Maltese Assembly appointed Admiral Ball head of the government and for two years, despite thousands killed and dead from hunger, withstood a siege of two years. The Treaty of Amiens (1802) restored the islands to the Knights of St John, but the Maltese refused to accept it because the influence of the French would have been renewed. The Assembly drew up a Declaration of Rights and appealed to Britain for protection on condition that its constitution would be observed and the Catholic religion maintained. London agreed, involving a recurrence of war with the French. In 1814 by the Treaty of Paris British suzerainty was acknowledged. At first only an Advisory Council of nominated members was permitted, but vigorous Maltese protest led in 1849 to the acceptance of eight elected members in a Legislative Council of eighteen.

In the 1880s a conflict arose over the official language, with the Maltese opposing a limitation to Italian. A lawyer, Fortunato Mizzi, formed the Nationalist Party which was backed in its first stages by Gerald (later Lord) Strickland, the prominent British settler. This agitation led in 1887 to the acceptance of an elected majority in the Legislature, fourteen out of twenty members. Strickland became Chief Secretary and then fiercely opposed the Nationalist Party. The constitution was repealed in 1903 and government by an official majority established.

The Two Wars

There was a political truce during the First World War, with the Maltese sending labour battalions to Gallipoli and Salonika, but the war over, they agitated militantly for political and economic reforms, finally with rioting in the capital, Valletta, in June 1919. A National Assembly was reconstituted with a Senate and House of representatives elected by proportional representation. A compromise was reached on the language issue. Whilst English was the official speech in the administration, Italian was used in the courts. The new constitution had a rough passage. A conflict arose between the Church and Government. The constitution was suspended in 1930, restored in 1932, and revoked in 1936. In 1939 a Legislature was reconstituted, but on the basis of 1849 with a nominated majority.

The Second World War again suspended internal political strife. Malta, a crucial naval base, was fiercely attacked, and bombed day and night. The people showed remarkable endurance and courage and were given the unique distinction of the bestowal of the George Cross to the whole population. Political agitation burst to activity with peace. A Labour Party, led by dynamic Dom Mintoff, supported by the General Workers' Union, whose stronghold was the docks, challenged the Nationalist Party. A new constitution was introduced with a Legislative Council of forty members elected by proportional representation, with women enfranchised for the first time. In the 1947 election the Labour Party won twenty-four seats and formed a government, but two years later it split and the dissidents, calling themselves the Workers' Party, formed a coalition with the Nationalists and ruled until 1954. A reunited Labour Party won the election which followed in 1955.

Constitutional Controversy

Malta was precarious economically. The livelihood of the people depended largely on the naval docks, supplemented by service to the British garrison.[1] The British indicated that they would be running down the dockyard and the economic viability of Malta was in doubt. Dom Mintoff saw the solution in integration with Britain and a round-table conference in London recommended this unusual course with Malta electing Members to the House of Commons. In Malta opinion was divided. Borg Olivier, leader of the Nationalist Party, declared for complete Dominion status; Miss Mabel Strickland, who had formed a conservative Progressive Constitutional Party, urged a restricted form of Dominion status. The negotiations broke down when Westminster declined to provide the financial aid which Mintoff said was necessary for the social services under integration, and the Labour Party leader then outbid his political rivals by demanding complete independence, leaving Malta free to enter into economic arrangements with other countries. He resigned and led a massive agitation for independence, with the result that the constitution was once more suspended and complete legislative and executive power transferred to the Governor. Vast numbers of people demonstrated in protest.

Independence

A constitutional commission was sent to Malta in 1960 and recommended full internal self-government with concurrent powers in defence and foreign affairs, but Britain having the last word. A new constitution was introduced on these lines in 1961, followed by a general election in which there was fierce antagonism between the Catholic Archbishop and the Labour Party. Mintoff and the majority of his party were Catholics, but the Archbishop held that Socialism was anti-Christian and announced that to support Labour would be a mortal sin; there was a fringe split, the dissidents forming the Christian Workers' Party.[2] The Nationalists were returned with 25 seats, Labour won 16, the Christian Workers 4, and Miss Strickland was the sole representative of her party. Constitutional exchanges continued. Borg Olivier, the Prime Minister, sensing the mood of the people, was intransigent; he refused a British offer of increased financial aid and insisted on independence. There was a London conference in 1963 and an inconclusive referendum in Malta before agreement was reached in September 1966. Maltese independence was recognised, British forces would remain for ten years, emigration would be assisted to ease overpopulation and Britain would grant £50 million over fifty years. In the general election following independence the Nationalist Party was again returned. The smaller parties were eliminated, the Labour Party becoming the only Opposition.

There were serious economic problems following independence. The naval docks were taken over by a private company whose administration aroused controversy. There was heavy unemployment, but Malta began to flourish as a tourist resort. The new state became a member of both the Commonwealth and the United Nations.

Following an election in which the Labour Party gained a majority of one, Dom Mintoff, the Prime Minister, entered into negotiations with the British Government regarding its military base and with NATO regarding its Mediterranean headquarters.

Mintoff was in a dilemma. He wanted Malta to be unaligned and free from all bases. On the other hand, he could not face, until economic development took place, the unemployment which the loss of the British base would cause. He demanded, therefore, an increase of the annual payments for the base, and for NATO facilities, to the sum of £18 million for five years and a guarantee of work for the six thousand employees for that period. Negotiations continued for six months. The British Defence Minister, Lord Carrington, and the NATO Secretary, Dr Luns, had never met a diplomat of the type of Mr Mintoff before. There were no courteous niceties; he was blunt and explosive. In reply to his demand for £18 million they came to offer £14 million, of which the British contribution would be £5,250,000, the balance made up by NATO countries. As against Mintoff's claim that the military presence should end in five years, NATO and the British insisted on seven years; against his request for the employment of 6,000 the British said 3,800.

The NATO and British concern was not so much for the strategic advantages of a military presence – they declared its defence value was minimal – as to keep out an alternative Russian presence in the Mediterranean. Mintoff, whilst not desiring to be aligned with the East any more than the West, strengthened fears by negotiating financial aid from Libya and receiving the Russian Ambassador from London to discuss the opening of an embassy in Malta. Finally, Mintoff accepted £14 million from NATO and Britain for seven years with, in addition, one million pounds a year in economic aid. There were also prospects of £2½ million from Italy and a substantial contribution from the USA, concerned to block the Soviet Union. This came near to the £18 million he had first asked for, and, beyond this, he had retained his unalignment while reaching economic agreements with communist countries, including Russia and China.

Mintoff's diplomatic methods appeared to have come off. He proposed to utilise the seven years of British and NATO presence to make Malta economically self-supporting, enabling his people to become basically independent, beholden to neither of the power *blocs*.[3]

Gibraltar

The Rock of Gibraltar towers over the Straits, which link the Atlantic with the Mediterranean. It rises to a height of 1,398 feet and from early times was regarded as one of the Pillars of Hercules, partnering Mount Acho on the opposite African coast; the Pillars were regarded as the limit of seafaring in the Mediterranean, the oceanic end of the world. Gibraltar is attached to Spain by an isthmus. It is possessed by Britain almost exclusively for military purposes, the limestone rock caved with guns, an airstrip, a dock. The total area is only 2¼ square miles. The population in 1961 was 24,075, geared to the military establishment.

British Annexation

The Moors were in occupation of Gibraltar in the ninth century in order to protect the sea route to Europe from Africa. They were twice raided by Normans in the forties and fifties, but held on until 1309 when Castilans from across the border of Spain ejected them. Again from 1333 to 1462 the Moors were masters, once more ejected. Isabella I formally annexed the Rock in 1501 and it remained Spanish for more than two and a half centuries. Even when the British and Dutch captured Gibraltar in 1704 during the War of Succession, the announced aim was not to take it from Spain but to secure it for Charles of Austria, whom they held to be the rightful king. The British, however, unknown to the Dutch, entered into secret negotiations with France for possession and presented both Spain and Holland with the *fait accompli*. The Dutch withdrew, and Spain accepted the annexation in the Treaty of Utrecht, 1713. Most of the Spanish population left.

Possession of Gibraltar remained a source of friction with Spain. There was renewed war from 1718 to 1720, when the Spanish were defeated; in 1726 they made an all-out assault on the Rock and were repulsed; in 1779 the Spaniards, in what was known as 'the Great Siege', began an attack which lasted four years, and were again repulsed. Britain was prepared, however, to use Gibraltar as a bargaining counter. More than once in the eighteenth century it offered to transfer the Rock to Spain for political concessions. Spain refused to make them.

Spain Rejects Compromise

In 1830 London declared Gibraltar a Crown Colony. Spanish sense of grievance persisted, but the issue did not become politically controversial until the 1960s when the United Nations Special Committee on Ending Colonialism[4] called for a return of the Rock to Spain. In reply Britain relied on the principle of self-determination, fortified by a referendum of the inhabitants which gave an almost unanimous vote for remaining British. The Government offered to refer the legal issue to the International Court of Justice, but Spain refused, as it did when Britain proposed that there should be self-government through municipal authorities rather than by a Legislative Council (which might be held to imply national status), and through facilities shared with Spain at the dockyard and airport.

From 1964 Spain imposed frontier restrictions, beginning with the prohibition of vehicular traffic and merchandise but extended to persons. This meant that the large Spanish labour force which crossed the frontier daily was no longer available, causing considerable dislocation in Gibraltar. The people responded in the first instance by doing the work themselves, supplemented later by recruiting Moorish workers across the Straits from Africa.

Gibraltar reflected the difficult issue of self-determination *versus* the right of a nation to integrated territory. Earlier in Britain writers like H. N. Brailsford had advocated the internationalisation of Gibraltar and of all military posts controlling international waterways, but this solution was not suggested during the controversy in the seventies. That time is not yet.

Notes

1. Malta was also the Mediterranean headquarters of NATO.

2. The conflict between Church and Labour was resolved in 1971, strengthening the prospect of the re-election of a Labour government.

3. Mintoff later raised again the amount of the contribution by Britain which declined to make an increase, but NATO nations added to their contributions and agreement was reached.

4. The UN Special Committee on the Granting of independence to Colonial Territories, also known as the Committee of Twenty-four.

Part Two

The Empires in Perspective

Tables of
Occupation and
Status

As originally planned Part Two would have been an exhaustive survey of the rise and fall of empires from the beginning of known time. This would have placed the story of the Colonial Revolution we have told in historical perspective, but it would have extended these pages to an impossibly long encyclopaedia. With regret chapters were put aside; the subject was fascinating, leading one thousands of years BC to modern times, from the Arctic and the wastes of Northern Asia to the tropics of Africa.

Instead of this comprehensive survey we have included in our treatment of the different territories references to their past, which have served to demonstrate how throughout history peoples have occupied the lands of other peoples. Fortunately in earlier centuries there was plenty of room on the Earth for people to move (even in this day of population explosion wide areas of undeveloped land exist); empires arose only when concentrated states emerged under rulers eager to extend their authority and riches, mobilising armies to conquer and subject.

We have seen how the form of colonialism changed. Trade was the motive of the Europeans who preceded the first modern empires, adventurous navigators starting depots on the coasts of Africa, Asia and the Americas, spreading in neighbouring settlements. Trade extended inland and rivalries developed, financiers forming the first overseas companies to exploit the new sources of riches. In time governments gave these companies the authority to administer large territories, backing them by treaties and troops. When the companies proved incapable of handling the complex problems of ruling and often suppressing tribes, governments themselves took over and modern political imperialism established itself. There were exceptions to this evolution of empires, but it was the general rule.

Now the wheel has turned full circle. Governments have withdrawn, the financiers have resumed power. In fact, the Colonial Revolution has been only half a revolution. Whilst the colonial peoples have gained their political independence, great multi-national companies are attempting to take major control of their economies, which means control of the lives of the people. Increasingly these giant corporations are becoming more powerful than governments. Their domination is resisted by the more radical new nations, sometimes by the method of majority shares, sometimes by socialisation. The reader will find that this emerges in Part Three as the central issue for the future.

We have retained the Tables of Occupation and Status which we had intended to follow our history of empire. They condense the essential facts of modern empires. Indeed, they tell the story more completely than thousands of words could do. Except in the cases of Spain, Italy and France (who did not respond in time), they have been checked by the libraries of Embassies, High Commissions or Legislatures.

There are a few points arising from the Tables which should be mentioned. Ironically the Table relating to the Portuguese empire is one of the shortest, although they were the pioneers of the evolution of modern empires through the trading depots they stationed down the west coast of Africa, round the Cape, along the east coast and, never satisfied, until they reached the Far East as well as westwards to Latin America. Many of these explorations are not included because they were not followed by governmental occupations.

The British Table is the longest, reflecting the possession at zenith of one quarter of the Earth's surface. Note should be taken, as indeed in other Tables, of the many scattered islands, because when we come to deal with their problems it has not been possible to consider each separately.

The Russian Table is also long, but it refers to the empire under the old Czarist regime.

The list of Australian and New Zealand possessions are short. They can be expected to disappear very soon with the advent of Labour Governments.

The American list will appear long in view of the US tradition against political colonialism. It includes, in fact, many uninhabited islands arising from the fantastic decision of Congress in 1856 that all such islands with guano deposits were forthwith to be regarded as American possessions.

We also give as an Appendix the Commonwealth Declarations of Principles adopted at the Singapore Conference in 1971, reflecting the transition from the British-occupied Empire to an association of independent states.

THE PORTUGUESE EMPIRE

Territory	Date of Occupation	Method of Occupation	Status in 1972
MADEIRA	1418–19	Discovery and settlement	Metropolitan Portugal following settlement
AZORES	1448	Discovery and settlement	Metropolitan Portugal following settlement
CAPE VERDE ISLANDS	1460	Discovery and settlement. 1587 Governor	Overseas Territory, June 11, 1951
PORTUGUESE GUINEA	1471	Discovery and settlement, 1522 Provincial Governor, 1879 colony	Overseas Territory, June 11, 1951, known as Guiné (Bissau). Granted status of State on June 23, 1972
ANGOLA	1484	Settlement. Settled from 1491 Sao Paulo (1574)	Overseas Territory, June 11, 1951
BRAZIL	1500	Governor, 1548	Independent, September 7, 1822
MOZAMBIQUE	1498	Discovery. Colonised from 1505	Overseas Territory, June 11, 1951. Granted status of state on June 23, 1972
GOA	1510	Settlement	Occupied by India, December 18, 1961
MACAO	1557	Settlement	Overseas Territory, June 11, 1951
TIMOR	1586	Settlement	Overseas Territory, June 11, 1951

THE SPANISH EMPIRE

Territory	Date of Occupation	Method of Occupation	Status in 1972
CANARY ISLANDS	1344	Assigned by Pope to Crown of Castile	Provinces of Spain
HAITI	1492	Discovery and conquest. Ceded to France 1697	Independent, January 1, 1804. Republic since 1859
DOMINICAN REPUBLIC (San Domingo, Española)	1496	Discovery and conquest. Ceded to France 1795	Independent, 1821, finally February 27, 1844
NAPLES (Kingdom of)	1503	Defeat of French claimant	Part of Italy, February, 1861
ORAN	1505–10	Conquest from Turkey	Independent as part of Algeria, July, 1962
PUERTO RICO	1506	Discovery and conquest	United States Commonwealth from December 10, 1898
JAMAICA	1508	Discovery and conquest. Ceded to England 1670	Independent within Commonwealth, August 6, 1962
FLORIDA	1513	Discovery and conquest. Lost to Britain 1763, regained 1783, sold to USA 1819–21	State of USA
DARIEN (La Palma)	1513–14	Discovery and acquisition	Independent as part of Panama, November, 1903
PANAMA	1514–19	Discovery and conquest	Republic of Panama, November 3, 1903
ARGENTINA (Rio de la Plata)	1515	Discovery and conquest	Independent, 1816
URAGUAY (Banta Oriental)	1516	Conquered from Portugal	Independent, September 27, 1828
MEXICO (New Spain)	1519–21	Discovery and conquest. (Aud.[1] 1527)	United States of Mexico, February 24, 1821
NICARAGUA	1521	Discovery and conquest	Republic of Nicaragua, 1838
GUATEMALA	1524	Discovery and conquest (Aud.[1] 1542)	Republic of Guatemala, July 1, 1823 (Confederation of Central America), 1839 Guatemala

EL SALVADOR	1524	Discovery and conquest	Republic of El Salvador, 1841
HONDURAS	1524–6	Discovery and conquest	Republic of Honduras, 1838
NEW GRENADA (Colombia)	1525	Discovery and conquest (Aud.[1] 1549)	Republic of Colombia, December, 1819
VENEZUELA	1527	Discovery and conquest	Republic of Venezuela, July 7, 1811
NEW GALICIA	1529–31	Discovery and conquest (Aud.[1] 1548)	State of USA
PERU	1531–3	Discovery and conquest (Aud.[1] 1542)	Republic of Peru, July 28, 1821
QUITO	1532	Discovery and conquest	Republic of Ecuador, May 13, 1830
BOLIVIA (Upper Peru)	1534–5	Discovery and conquest	Republic of Bolivia, August 6, 1825
TUNIS	1535	Conquest – lost to Turkey, 1574 French Protectorate, 1881	Republic of Tunisia, March, 1956
PARAGUAY	1536–56	Discovery and conquest	Independent, May 1811
CHILE	1541	Discovery and conquest	Republic of Chile, February 2, 1818
PHILIPPINES	1565–71	Conqueror (Aud.[1] 1583). Ceded to USA, 1898	Republic of Philippines, April 23, 1946
TEXAS	1720–2	Discovery. Independent as part of United States of Mexico, 1826. Seceded. Annexed by USA, 1845	State of USA, December, 1845
LOUISIANA	1753	Ceded by France, 1762. Lost to Britain, 1783, ceded to France, 1800, and sold to USA, 1803	State of USA, April, 1812
FERNANDO PO	1778	Ceded to Spain by Portugal	Republic of Equatorial Guinea, October, 1968
SPANISH GUINEA (Rio de Oro)	1844–77	Exploration and conquest	Republic of Equatorial Guinea, October, 12, 1968
IFNI } Spanish Africa	1860	Occupied for purpose of founding a Fishery	Returned to Morocco, June 1969
RIO DE ORO }	1884	Exploration and Protectorate	Province of Spain, January 1958
SPANISH SAHARA	1923	Agreement with France and Britain modified 1928	Province of Spain, January 1958

[1] Aud. – *audiencia*, establishment of official colonial government.

THE NETHERLANDS EMPIRE

Territory	Date of Occupation	Method of Occupation	Status in 1972
NETHERLANDS ANTILLES			
Curaçao	1527	Discovery and conquest	Autonomous Overseas Territory, December 29, 1954
DUTCH NEW GUINEA	1634	Discovery and conquest	Ceded to Indonesia, 1963, as West Irian
NEW NETHERLANDS	1595	Ceded to Britain, Treaty of Breda, 1667	Part of County of Lincolnshire, England
CAPE COLONY	1624–5	Lost to United Kingdom, 1795–1803; finally 1814. Part of Dominion of South Africa, 1910	Part of Republic of South Africa, May 31, 1961
	1652		
DUTCH EAST INDIES	1610–41	Conquest and settlement	Independent as Indonesia, December 1949
Java	1610		
Sumatra	from 1615		
Batavia	1619		
MALACCA	1641		Independent as Indonesia
SURINAM	1667	Settlement of Dutch East Indies Co. Ceded by Britain as Surinam, Treaty of Breda, 1667. Reoccupied by Britain 1799–1802, 1804–1816	Autonomous Overseas Territory, December 29, 1954

THE BELGIAN EMPIRE

Territory	Date of Occupation	Method of Occupation	Status in 1972
BELGIAN CONGO	1884–5	Conferred by Berlin Conference upon Leopold II, who in 1908 amended it to the Belgian people as a colony	Independent, June 30, 1960, as Congo-Kinshasa. Changed name to Zaire, 1971
RUANDA-URUNDI	1919	Transferred by League of Nations Mandate from German control to Belgian Trusteeship	Independent, July 1962, as two states, Rwanda and Burundi

THE ITALIAN EMPIRE

Territory	Date of Occupation	Method of Occupation	Status in 1972
ASSAB	1882	Conquest. Settlement as part of colony of Eritrea, 1890	Transferred as part of Eritrea to Ethiopia, December 2, 1952
ERITREA	1889	Conquest. Settlement as colony, 1890. Occupied by British forces, 1941	Transferred to Ethiopia, December 2, 1952
ITALIAN SOMALILAND	1889	Conquest. Colonised 1905	Independent, July 1, 1960 (joined British Somalia as Republic of Somalia)
LIBYA	1911	Occupied. Italians expelled 1942/3. Occupied by military forces	Independent, December 24, 1954 Federated with UAR and Syria, 1971
ABBYSSINIA	1936	Conquest. Liberated by British forces, 1941	Independent as Ethiopia, 1941

THE GERMAN EMPIRE

Territory	Date of Occupation	Method of Occupation	Status in 1972
SOUTH WEST AFRICA	1884	Surrendered to South Africa 1915. League of Nations Mandate, granted to Britain, December 17, 1920, administered by South Africa. Mandate withdrawn by UN, 1972	Partly incorporated by South Africa, through the *South West Africa Affairs Act* of 1969. About two fifths of the territory to be transferred into 'Bantustans'
NEW GUINEA (Kaiser Wilhelm Land)	1884	Surrendered to Australia 1914	League of Nations Mandate to Australia, April 1921
CAMEROUN		Occupied by United Kingdom and France 1916. Mandated to them 1922	Independent, January 1960
EAST AFRICA (Tanganyika)	1885	Protectorate in support of German East Africa Company. Lost to United Kingdom 1918. Mandated to UK 1919	Independent, December 9, 1961
ANGRA PEQUENA	1884	Annexation April 24	
MARSHALL ISLANDS	1885	Occupation. Mandated Japan, 1919–46	United States Trusteeship, 1946
NAURU	1888	Annexed. Surrendered to Australian forces, 1914	Independent, January 31, 1968
RUANDA-URUNDI (part of East Africa)	1890	Lost to Belgium by League of Nations Mandate, 1919	Independent as Rwanda and Burundi, July 1962
TOGOLAND	1894	Protectorate, mandated to Great Britain and France, 1922	Independent, April 27, 1960
KIA CHOU	1898	Mandated to Japan 1920–45	Returned to China after Second World War
SAMOA	1899/1900	Occupation. Mandated to New Zealand 1920–1961	Independent as Western Samoa, January 1962

THE FRENCH EMPIRE

Territory	Date of Occupation	Method of Occupation	Status in 1972
WEST INDIES			
MARTINIQUE	1635	Settlement (1635–48). Occupied by Britain 1762–3, 1794–1802, 1809–15	Overseas Department, March 19, 1946
GUADELOUPE	1635	Settlement	Overseas Department, March 19, 1946
LESSER ANTILLES –	1635	Settlement	Overseas Department, March 19, 1946
Marie Galante			
Les Saintes			
Desirade			
St Barthelemy			
St Martin (Part Dutch)			
LA RÉUNION (Bourbon)	1642	Settlement	Overseas Department, March 19, 1946
ST PIERRE AND MIQUELON	1814	Acquired by Treaty of Paris from America 1814	Overseas Department, December 16, 1958
GUYANE FRANCAISE	1854	Settlement	Overseas Department, March 19, 1946
PACIFIC			
POLYNESIE FRANCAISE		Settlement	Overseas Department, November, 1946
Windward Islands			
Leeward Islands			
Taumorn Group			
Austral Islands (Tubai)			
Marquesas Islands			
NOUVELLE CALEDONIE		Settlement	Overseas Department, November, 1946
Île des Pins			
Loyalty Islands			
Huon Islands			
Belep Archipelago			
Chesterfield Islands			

THE FRENCH EMPIRE (*continued*)

Territory	Date of Occupation	Method of Occupation	Status in 1972
COMORO ARCHIPELAGO	Mayotte colony since 1843		Overseas Department, December 11, 1958
SOUTHERN AND ANTARCTIC TERRITORIES CROZETISLAND	6.8.1955	Discovery	Overseas Department, December 11, 1958
WALLIS and HORN ISLAND	1842	French rule established	Overseas Territory, December 27, 1959
EQUATORIAL AFRICA			
GABON	1860	Portuguese gradually ousted	Independent, August 17, 1960
MIDDLE CONGO	1891	Lost to Germany 1911, Regained 1916	Independent as Republic of Congo (Brazza-ville), August 15, 1960
UBANGI SHARI	1900	Conquest	Independent as Central African Republic, August 13, 1960
CHAD	1913	Conquest	Independent, August 11, 1960
FRENCH WEST AFRICA			
IVORY COAST	1882 (1904 FWA)	Kings Aigini and Attokpora sought protection of Louis-Philippe, 1843	Independent, August 7, 1960
DAHOMEY	1843 (1904 FWA)	Occupation of Porto Novo (1863)	Independent, August 1, 1960
GUINEA	1887 (1904 FWA)	Military and commercial penetration, complete by 1890	Independent, October 2, 1968
UPPER VOLTA	1893	Conquest 1919–32, created out of Upper Senegal and Niger	Independent, August 5, 1960
FRENCH SUDAN	1895	Conquest	Independent as Mali, September 22, 1960

MAURITANIA	1903	French Protectorate and Colony (1920)	Independent as Islamic Republic of Mauritania, November, 28 1960
NIGER	1906 (1904 FWA)	Colonisation 1883–4. French sphere determined 1906	Independent, August 3, 1960
CAMEROUN	1916	Occupied and annexed from Germany	Independent, January 1, 1960
TOGO	1914	Annexed from Germany – League of Nations Mandate, 1922 and UN Trusteeship, 1946	Independent, April 27, 1960
NORTH AFRICA			
MOROCCO	1912	French Protectorate following conquest	Independent, March 2, 1956
TUNISIA	1887	French Protectorate following conquest (Treaty of Bardo)	
ALGERIA	1830	Conquest from Spain	Independent, July 3, 1962
AFRICA (Miscellaneous)			
SENEGAL	1677	Conquest from Dutch (ceded to Britain 1758–78, 1783–90)	Independent, August 20, 1960
TERRITORY OF AFARS AND ISSAS (French Somaliland)	1862–84	Conquest and settlement	Overseas Department, March 19, 1967 (Referendum)
NORTH AMERICA			
QUEBEC	1535–6	Settlement. Ceded to Britain 1763	Part of Dominion of Canada, 1867
MISSISSIPPI	1682	Claimed and settled in name of King of France. 1763, East to Britain, West to Spain	State of USA
LOUISIANA	1699	Ceded to Britain, 1763	State of USA
INDIAN OCEAN			
ÎLE DE FRANCE (Mauritius)	1713	Lost to United Kingdom, 1814	Independent, March 12, 1968
MADAGASCAR	1886	Protectorate 1885, Full colony 1896	Independent as Malagasy, July 26, 1959, within Community

THE BRITISH EMPIRE

Territory	Date of Occupation	Method of Occupation	Status in 1972
	17th century		
BARBADOS	1605–27	Settlement	Independent – November 30, 1966
BERMUDA	1609	Settlement	Colony
THE GAMBIA	c. 1618	Settlement. Acquired by Treaties in 1816 and 1827	Independent as Gambia – February 18, 1965
ST CHRISTOPHER (St Kitts)	1623	Settlement. Did not become wholly British until 1713	Part of Associated State of St Kitts, Nevis, Anguilla with United Kingdom – February 27, 1967
NEVIS	1628	Settlement	Part of Associated State of St Kitts, Nevis, Anguilla with United Kingdom – February 27, 1967
THE GRENADINES	1628	Settlement. Divided later between St Vincent and Grenada	*See* St Vincent and Grenada
MONTSERRAT	1632	Settlement	Colony
ANTIGUA	1632	Settlement	Associated State with United Kingdom – February 27, 1967
BRITISH HONDURAS	1638	Settlement. Granted colony status 1862	Colony
ST LUCIA	1638	Settlement. Finally passed to Great Britain in 1803	Associated State with United Kingdom – March 1, 1967
ANGUILLA	1650	Settlement	Part of Associated State of St Kitts, Nevis, Anguilla with United Kingdom – February 27, 1967
GOLD COAST	c. 1650	Settlement. Danish forts bought 1850, Dutch forts 1871. Ashanti added 1901 by military occupation. Northern territories added 1896 as a protectorate	Independent as Ghana – March 6, 1957
ST HELENA	1651	Settled by East India Company. Government vested in British Crown 1833.	Colony
JAMAICA	1655	Conquest	Independent – August 6, 1962
BAHAMAS	1666	Settlement	Colony. Exchanges for early independence begun 1972
VIRGIN ISLANDS (part of)	1666–72	Settlement and conquest	Colony as British Virgin Islands
CAYMAN ISLANDS	1670	Ceded by Spain as dependency of Jamaica. Separated, 1962	Colony

Territory	Date	Method	Status
TURKS AND CAICOS ISLANDS	1678	Settlement	Colony
	18th century		
GIBRALTAR	1704	Capitulation. Ceded to Britain under Treaty of Utrecht 1713	Colony
DOMINICA	1761	Conquest	Associated State with United Kingdom – March 1, 1967
ST VINCENT	1762	Capitulation	Colony (prospective Associated State)
GRENADA	1762	Capitulation	Associated State with United Kingdom – March 3, 1967
TOBAGO	1763	Cession. Afterwards in French possession. Reconquered 1803	Independent (with Trinidad) as Trinidad and Tobago – August 31, 1962
FALKLAND ISLANDS	1765	Settlement. Reoccupied 1832	Colony of Falkland Islands and Dependencies
PITCAIRN ISLANDS	1780	Settlement	Colony
SIERRA LEONE	1787	Settlement and Protectorate	Independent within the Commonwealth – April 27, 1961
CEYLON	1796	Capitulation	Independent within the Commonwealth – February 4, 1948. Changed name to Sri Lanka in 1972
TRINIDAD	1797	Capitulation	Independent within the Commonwealth – August 31, 1962
MALTA	1800	Capitulation	Independent within the Commonwealth – September 21, 1964
	19th century		
BRITISH GUIANA	1803	Capitulation. Independent state, as Guyana, 1966	Republic within the Commonwealth – 1970
SEYCHELLES	1806	Capitulation	Colony
MAURITIUS	1810	Capitulation	Independent within the Commonwealth – March 12, 1968
ASCENSION ISLAND	1815	Military occupation	Dependency of colony of St Helena
TRISTAN DA CUNHA	1815	Military occupation	Dependency of colony of St Helena
SINGAPORE	1824	Ceded by treaty with Dutch. Independent within Malaysia – 1963	Independent within the Commonwealth after secession from Malaysia – August 9, 1965
ADEN	1839	Conquest – with additions by purchase, 1868–88	Independent as Peoples' Republic of Southern Yemen – November 30, 1967
ADEN PROTECTORATE	1839–1954	Protective treaties	Independent as part of Peoples' Republic of Southern Yemen – November 30, 1967

THE BRITISH EMPIRE (continued)

Territory	Date of Occupation	Method of Occupation	Status in 1972
NEW ZEALAND *	1840	Settlement and treaty. Self-government, 1852	Independent within the Commonwealth – 1907
HONG KONG	1841	Treaties. Kowloon added 1860; additional area leased 1898	Colony
LAGOS	1861	Cession. South Nigeria amalgamated with Lagos under style of Colony and Protectorate of Southern Nigeria – 1906	Capital of independent state of Nigeria within the Commonwealth – October 1, 1960
BASUTOLAND	1865	Protectorate. Annexation in 1868	Independent as Lesotho within the Commonwealth – October 4, 1966
FIJI	1874	Cession	Independent within the Commonwealth – October 10, 1970
W. PACIFIC ISLANDS (including Ellice, Gilbert, Southern Solomon and other groups)	1877	High Commission created by Order in Council, giving jurisdiction over islands not subject to other colonial governments nor under jurisdiction of other 'civilised powers'. Protectorates declared over all by 1900	British Solomon Islands: Protectorate Gilbert and Ellice Islands: Colony New Hebrides: Anglo-French Condominium
CYPRUS	1878	Ceded by Turkey. Annexed 1914	Independent within the Commonwealth – August 16, 1960 following Zurich Conference of UK, Greece and Turkey
NIGERIA	1884–6	Treaty, conquest and settlement under royal charter. Chartered company's territory transferred to Crown and divided into North and South Nigeria, 1900	Independent within the Commonwealth – October 1, 1960, including part of British Cameroun
BRITISH SOMALILAND	1884–6	Occupation and cession. Protectorate declared 1887	Incorporated in independent Somali Republic – July 1, 1960
BURMA	1826–86	Mandalay occupied followed by annexation of Burma to India. Separated 1937	Independent state outside the Commonwealth – January 4, 1948
BECHUANALAND	1885–91	Protectorate declared. Southern portion annexed to Cape Colony, 1895	Independent as Botswana within the Commonwealth – September 30, 1966
BRUNEI	1888	Placed under British protection	Protected State

BRITISH EAST AFRICA (Kenya)	1888	Treaty, conquest and settlement under royal charter. Transferred to Crown, 1895. Annexed in 1920	Independent as Kenya within the Commonwealth – December 12, 1963
NORTHERN RHODESIA	1888–93	Treaty, conquest and settlement. Royal Charter granted to British South Africa Company, 1890. Requested protection from Crown, 1924. Part of Federation of Rhodesia and Nyasaland, 1953–61. Granted internal dependence 1961	Independent as Zambia within the Commonwealth – October 24, 1964
SOUTHERN RHODESIA	1888–93	Treaty, conquest and settlement. Royal Charter granted to British South Africa Company, 1890. Became self-governing colony, 1923. Part of Federation of Rhodesia and Nyasaland, 1953–61. Made unilateral declaration of independence (UDI), November 11, 1965, and administration outlawed. Unilaterally assumed title of 'Republic of Rhodesia', 1970. Not recognised by the United Nations	Self-governing colony
ZANZIBAR	1890	Protectorate declared	Independent with Constitutional Monarchy, December 10, 1963. Union with Tanganyika to form Tanzania, April 27, 1964
SWAZILAND	1890–94	Cession. Under South African protection and administration, 1894–1902. Then under British administration and protection	Independent within the Commonwealth – September 6, 1968
UGANDA	1890–96	Treaty and protectorate	Independent within the Commonwealth – October 9, 1962
NYASALAND	1891	Protectorate declared	Independent as Malawi within the Commonwealth – July 6, 1964
WEI-HAI-WEI	1898	Lease from China	Restored to China, 1930
FANNING ISLAND	1898	Annexed for purposes of projected Pacific cable	One of Line Islands, Polynesia
CHOISEUL AND ISABEL ISLANDS	1899	Cession	In Protectorate of British Solomon Islands
20th century			
TONGA	1900	Protectorate declared with Niue. Separated	Independent – June 7, 1970
NIUE	1900	Protectorate declared with Tonga. Separated	Island territory of New Zealand
TANGANYIKA	1920	German colony mandated after First World War	Independent, December 10, 1963. Union with Zanzibar as Tanzania, April 27, 1964

THE BRITISH EMPIRE (continued)

Territory	Date of Occupation	Method of Occupation	Status in 1972
BRITISH CAMEROUNS	1916	Occupation. German colony in west mandated in part to United Kingdom after First World War	Part joined independent Nigeria and part independent Cameroun 1961
TOGOLAND	1922	German colony mandated in part to United Kingdom after First World War	Part joined independent Togoland and part independent Ghana 1957
PALESTINE	1915	Military occupation during First World War. League of Nations Mandate granted July, 1922	Division as independent Israel and part incorporated with Jordan, 1948
CANADA *			Independent federal state within the Commonwealth, 1867
Newfoundland	1583	Possession taken by Sir H. Gilbert for the Crown	United with Canada, March 31, 1949
Nova Scotia	1628	Settlement. Ceded to France, 1632; recovered 1713. Confederated to New Brunswick and Ontario to form Dominion of Canada, 1867	Province of Canada
North-West Territories	1669	Settlement under Royal Charter of Hudson's Bay Co. Purchased from Imperial Government, 1869, and federated with Dominion of Canada, 1870. Alberta and Saskatchewan separated, 1905	Province of Canada
New Brunswick	1713	Cession. Confederated with Nova Scotia and Ontario to form Dominion of Canada, 1867	Province of Canada
Prince Edward Island	1758	Conquest. Confederated with Dominion of Canada, 1873	Province of Canada
Ontario	1759–90	Conquest. Confederated with Nova Scotia and New Brunswick to form Dominion of Canada, 1867	Province of Canada
Saskatchewan	1766	Settlement as part of North-West Territories within which became part of Dominion of Canada, 1870. Separated from North-West Territories, 1905	Province of Canada
Alberta	c. 1788	Settlement as part of North-West Territories within which became part of Dominion of Canada, 1870. Separated from North-West Territories, 1905	Province of Canada

Manitoba	1811	Settlement by Red River or Selkirk Colony. Created Province of Dominion of Canada, 1870	Province of Canada
British Columbia and Vancouver Island	1821	Settlement under Hudson's Bay Co. Confederated with Dominion of Canada, 1871	As British Columbia, Province of Canada
All remaining British possessions in North America, other than Newfoundland (see above)			Incorporated in Dominion of Canada, 1880
AUSTRALIA*, COMMONWEALTH OF			Independent federal state within the Commonwealth, 1901, comprising the following former colonial territories
New South Wales	1788	Settlement. Provincial status granted with constitutional powers 1850	Federated state within Australia
Tasmania	1803	Settlement. Provincial status granted with constitutional powers 1850	Federated state within Australia
Queensland	1824	Settled as part of New South Wales. Separated, 1859 as province with constitutional powers	Federated state within Australia
West Australia	1826	Settlement. Provincial status granted with constitutional powers 1850	Federated state within Australia
Victoria	1834	Settled as part of New South Wales. Separated, 1851, as province with constitutional powers	Federated state within Australia
South Australia	1836	Settlement. Provincial status granted with constitutional powers 1850	Federated state within Australia
Papua	1884	Occupied by Queensland. Protectorate declared by Britain, 1885. Ceded to Dominion of Australia 1906	Dependency of Australia. Exchanges for early independence begun 1972
Christmas Island	1898	Annexed for purposes of projected Pacific cable	Dependency of Australia
New Guinea	1920	German colony mandated to New South Wales after First World War. Mandate transferred to Australia 1901	Dependency of Australia. Exchanges for early independence begun 1972
INDIA AND PAKISTAN			Independent federal states within the Commonwealth – August 15, 1947
Bombay	1608–85	Treaty and cession. Trade first established, 1608. Ceded to British Crown by Portugal, 1661. Transferred to East India Company, 1668	Divided between states of Gujerat and Mysore within India

THE BRITISH EMPIRE (*continued*)

Territory	Date of Occupation	Method of Occupation	Status in 1972
Bengal	1633–1765	Treaty and subsequent conquests. First trade settlement established by treaty as Pipli in Orissa, 1633. Raised to presidency on separation from Madras, 1681. Virtual sovereignty announced by East India Co. as result of conquests by Clive, 1765	Divided between India and Pakistan as states of East and West Bengal 1947. East Bengal independent as Bangladesh 1971
Madras	1639–1748	Treaty and subsequent conquests. Fort St George, the foundation of Madras, the first territorial possession of the East India Co. in India, was acquired by treaty with its Indian ruler. Madras was raised to a presidency in 1683, ceded to France, 1746 and recovered in 1748	State within India
United Provinces of Agra and Oudh	1764–1856	Conquests and treaty through successive stages of which the principal dates were 1801, 1803, 1814 and 1815. In 1832 the nominal sovereignty of Delhi, then retained by the Great Mogul, was resigned into the hands of the East India Co. Oudh, of which the conquest may be said to have begun with the battle of Baxar in 1764, was finally annexed in 1856	State of Uttar Pradesh within India
Central Provinces	1802–17	Conquest and treaty	State of Madya Pradesh within India
Ajmere and Merwara	1818	Conquest and cession	Part of Rajasthan state within India
Eastern Bengal and Assam	1825–26	Conquest and cession	Divided between India and Pakistan
Coorg	1834	Conquest and annexation	Within India
Punjab	1849	Conquest and annexation. Created distinct province, 1859	Divided into separate states within India and Pakistan
British Baluchistan	1854–76	Conquest and treaty	Within Pakistan
Andaman Islands	1858	Annexation	Part of India
North-Western Frontier Province	1901	Subdivision	Within Pakistan

SOUTH AFRICA * Cape of Good Hope	1803	Capitulation. First British occupation, 1795–1803. Present limits not attained until 1895	Province of South Africa
Natal	1824	Settlement. Submission by Natal Boers, 1843	Province of South Africa
Zululand	1887	Annexation. Incorporated into Natal, 1897	Part of Natal, province of South Africa
Orange Free State	1900	Annexation. Formerly British, 1848–54	Province of South Africa
Transvaal	1900	Annexation. Formerly British, 1877–81	Province of South Africa
South West Africa	1920	League of Nations Mandate from Germany to Britain. Mandate handed over to South Africa, 1920. Mandate upheld by International Court of Justice, 1971, and withdrawn from South Africa, 1972	Annexed by South Africa as Bantustan. Known by United Nations as Namibia
MALAYSIA			Independent federal state within the Common-wealth, 1963
Straits Settlements (including Penang and Malacca)	1786–1824	Settlement and cession. Vested in Crown by East India Company, 1858. Transferred from India to colonial possession in 1867. Federated with Malay States as British Protectorate. Became independent state of Malaya, 1957. Federation extended, 1963	Part of federal state of Malaysia
Labuan	1846	Cession. Incorporated in Straits Settlements, 1906	Part of Sabah State within federation of Malaysia
Federated Malay States	1874–95	Treaty. Federated with Straits Settlements as British Protectorate. Became independent state of Malaya, 1957. Federation extended, 1963	Part of independent federal state of Malaysia
British North Borneo	1881	Treaty and settlement under royal charter. Protect-orate assumed, 1888	As Sabah, part of federal state of Malaysia
Sarawak	1888	Protectorate declared. Ceded to Britain by Rajah Sir Charles Vyner Brooke, 1946	Part of federal state of Malaysia

* Dates customarily assigned to independence:
Canada   July 1, 1867
Australia   January 1, 1901
New Zealand September 26, 1907
South Africa September 20, 1909

THE RUSSIAN EMPIRE

Territory	Date of Occupation	Method of Occupation	From Whom	Status in 1972
A. Metropolitan Russia (RFSFR)				
Novgorod	1478	Conquest		Part of Metropolitan Russia
White Russia	1563	Parts, by conquest	Lithuania	Part of Metropolitan Russia
Little Russia	1503	Parts, by conquest	Lithuania	Part of Metropolitan Russia
Pskov	1510			Part of Metropolitan Russia
Smolensk	1514	Conquest. Finally incorporated, June 20, 1667		Part of Metropolitan Russia
Ryazan	1517			Part of Metropolitan Russia
Kazan	1552–6	Conquest	Tatars	Part of Metropolitan Russia
Astrakhan	1552–6	Conquest	Tatars	Part of Metropolitan Russia
Siberia	1581–3	Exploration began followed by settlement and conquest	Tatars	Part of Metropolitan Russia, 1614
Amur Region	17th c.	Occupation. Withdrawal of China by Treaty of Nerchinsk, 1689	China	Part of Metropolitan Russia, 1858–60
Ussuri region	1858	Ceded by the Treaty of Peking, 1860: foundation of Vladivostock	China	Part of Metropolitan Russia
Manchuria	1896–1903	Penetration of Manchuria by Treaty with China. Lease of Port Arthur 1898. Complete occupation in 1903 following the Boxer Rising	China	Part of China. Regained after surrender of Japan, September, 1945
Finno-Karelia	1721	Ceded after war (Treaty of Nystadt, August 30, 1721. Final conquest 1809. Claimed independence March 1917. Recognised by USSR: October 14, 1920	Sweden	Independent as part of Finland, October 14, 1920 except Karelia Isthmus ceded March 12, 1940
Sakhalin Is.	1875	Southern Islands acquired in exchange for Kurile Is. Northern acquired when Japan retired, January 21, 1925	Japan	Part of Metropolitan Russia January 21, 1925

B. *Ukrainian SSR* (established December 1919, finally formed July 6, 1923)

Crimea	1774–83	Kinburn, Yeni Kale and Kerten ceded after war (Treaty of Kutchuk Kainardji, July 21, 1774). Final annexation: 1783 with Kiev	Turk	Absorbed into Ukraine SSR February 26, 1954
Oczkakov	1792	Ceded after war (Treaty of Jassy, January 9, 1792) to the boundary of the Dniester River	Turk	Absorbed into Ukraine SSR February 26, 1954
Ukraine	June 20, 1667	E. Ukraine with Kiev ceded after war by Treaty of Andrusovo. Remainder acquired by 2nd partition of Poland (January 1, 1793) and 3rd partition of October 24, 1795. Independent government April 8, 1919 SSR: December 30, 1919	Turk Poland	SSR of Soviet Union December 30, 1919
Azov	July 28, 1696	Ceded after war. Lost to the Turk: July 21, 1711 (Treaty of Pruth). Reacquired September 18, 1739 (Treaty of Belgrade)	Turk	Ukraine SSR of Soviet Union December 30, 1919

C. *Azerbaidzhan SSR*

Azerbaidzhan	1815	Annexed by Russia by Treaty of Gulistan	Persia	Declared independence May 28, 1918 SSR April 28, 1920. Constituent republic of USSR 1936

D. *Georgian SSR*

Georgia	1813	Annexation. Daghestan and Shemakha ceded after Napoleonic Wars	Persia	Declared independence April 22, 1918. Georgian SSR: February 25, 1921

E. *Armenian SSR*

Armenia	1828	Part of Armenia and Erevan ceded by the Treaty of Turkmanchai. S. parts ceded to Turkey 1921	Persia	Declared independence: April 22, 1918. Armenian SSR April 2, 1921. Constituent republic of USSR: 1936

F. *Moldavian SSR* (first organised October 12, 1924. Reorganised August 2, 1940)

Bessarabia	1812	Annexed by Russia, 1856 (Treaty of Paris). Southern parts handed to Rumania, but transferred back to Russia by the Treaties of San Stefano and Berlin (1872). Seized again by Rumania (1918) and reacquired by Russia (June 1940)	Turk	Moldavian SSR, August 2, 1940

THE RUSSIAN EMPIRE (*continued*)

Territory	Date of Occupation	Method of Occupation	From Whom	Status in 1972
N. Bukovina	1940	Ceded by Roumania in 1940 and 1947	Rumania	Moldavian SSR
Ruthenia	1945	Ceded by Czechoslovakia (June 29, 1945)	Czechoslovakia	Moldavian SSR
G. *Estonian SSR*				
Estonia	1721	Ceded after war (Treaty of Nystadt August 30, 1721). Autonomous April 12, 1917. Recognised by USSR: February 2, 1920. Came into Soviet orbit: September 29–October 5, 1939. 'Asked' to be admitted to USSR July 21, 1940 (Ultimatum of June 16, 1940)	Sweden	SSR of Soviet Union. Confirmed by decree, August 6, 1940
H. *Latvia SSR*				
Latvia	1721	Ceded after war (Treaty of Nystadt, August 30, 1721). Recognised as independent by USSR: July 11, 1920. 'Asked' to be admitted to USSR July 21, 1940 (Ultimatum of June 16, 1940)	Sweden	SSR of Soviet Union. Confirmed by decree August 5, 1940
I. *Lithuanian SSR*				
Lithuania	1793–5	Lost from Poland to Russia by 2nd and 3rd Partitions of Poland January 23, 1793 and October 24, 1795. Part of Russian Federation: March 21, 1917. Independence recognised by Soviet Union: July 12, 1920. 'Asked' to be admitted to the Soviet Union: July 21, 1940 (Ultimatum of June 16, 1940)	Poland	SSR of Soviet Union. Confirmed by decree August 13, 1940

J. *Kazakh SSR* (constituted August 26, 1920)				
Kazakh Territory	1801–55	Most of Kazakh annexed. Firm control over Nomads by 1822	Kazakh Khanates	Kazakh SSR December 5, 1936
K. *Turkmen SSR* (formed October 27, 1924)				
Teke Turkmen Settlement	1881–5	Conquest. Merv fell 1884. Compromise with Turkmen. Great Britain June 18, 1886	Turkmen	Turkmenistan SSR, May 1925
L. *Uzbek SSR* (formed December 5, 1924)				
Uzbek	1847–76	Conquest. The major Khanates succumbed after bitter struggle in the years 1865–76 (Kokand 1868, Bokhara 1868, Chiva 1873)	Uzbek	Uzbekistan SSR, May 1925
M. *Tadzkihistan SSR*				
Tadzhiks	1895	Annexation	Tadzhiks and Afghans	Tadzhiks SSR, December 25, 1929
N. *Kirghizia SSR* (formed 1924)				
Kirghiz Steppes	1825–56	Conquest	Kirghiz	Kirghistan SSR, December, 1936
O. *Alaska*				
Alaska	1741–84	Exploration and settlement Forts constructed 1805–12		Sold to USA 1867. 49th State of Union, January 3, 1959
P. *California*				
N. California	18th c.	Exploration and settlement Forts constructed 1805–12	Aborigenes	Abandoned 1844 – state of USA since September 9, 1850
Q. *Poland*				
Poland	1772, 1793, 1795	Acquired in three partitions of Poland, 1722, 1793, 1795. Independent 1918 Treaty of Brest Litovsk and Treaty of Versailles	Poland	Polish Socialist Republic, 1944

NEW ZEALAND POSSESSIONS

Territory	Date of Occupation	Method of Occupation	Status in 1972
COOK ISLANDS	June 11, 1501	Annexed as part of New Zealand	Self-governing in free association with New Zealand, August 4, 1965. New Zealand responsible for external and defence policies in consultation with Cook Islands Government
WESTERN SAMOA	August 29, 1914	Military occupation from Germany. A League of Nations Mandate from 1920	Independent January 1, 1962. Member of Commonwealth August 27, 1970
TOKELAU ISLANDS	February 11, 1926	British protectorate administered by New Zealand	Administered as part of New Zealand from January 1, 1949
NIUE ISLAND	November 6, 1901	Annexed to New Zealand by Proclamation	Mainly self-governing. Constitutional changes under negotiation between the Niue Legislative Assembly and New Zealand Government
NAURU	1919	League of Nations Mandate to New Zealand, Australia and Britain jointly	Independent, January 31, 1968 Associate member of Commonwealth
KERMADEC ISLANDS	1886	Annexed	A New Zealand dependency with no indigenous population. Maintained as meteorological station
ROSS DEPENDENCY	July 30, 1923	Annexed	Administered territory. Permanent scientific bases maintained

AUSTRALIAN POSSESSIONS

Territory	Date of Occupation	Method of Occupation	Status in 1972
NORFOLK ISLAND	1788	Acquisition as a Penal Station until 1813 Settlement under New South Wales 1856	Territory of Australia under Minister for External Territories (1913)
PAPUA	1884	Annexation. Administration under Queensland. Transferred to Australian Commonwealth, 1906	Territory of Australia. Negotiations for independence in 1973
NEW GUINEA	1919	Mandate by League of Nations of former Germany territory, 1920	Under United Nations Trust Territory Negotiations for independence in 1973
ANTARCTIC TERRITORY	1933	Annexed and placed under Australian authority by Imperial Order in Council, 1936	Territory of Australia
HEARD and McDONALD ISLANDS	1947	Official transfer from United Kingdom 1947	Territory of Australia
COCOS (KEELING) ISLANDS	1955	Transfer from United Kingdom 1955	Territory of Australia
CHRISTMAS ISLAND	1958	Transfer from United Kingdom	Territory of Australia

THE US EMPIRE

The original thirteen states on the east coast, which gained their independence from Britain in 1783–4, expanded west; in 1803 the USA acquired Louisiana by purchase ($23m) from France; in 1819, Florida and adjacent territories were acquired by purchase ($5m) from Spain; in 1845, the Independent Republic of Texas was annexed; 1846, Oregon Territory was acquired by treaty with Britain, ending joint occupation; in 1848, there was the cession of Mexican territory for payment of $15m, following war and in 1853–4 the Gadsden purchase was negotiated with Mexico for $10m. In 1856 the *Guano Island Act* gave USA authority to take possession of any uninhabited island with guano deposits.

Territory	Date of Occupation	Method of Occupation	Status in 1972
St Pierre and Miquelon	1963	Ceded to France 1814	Overseas Department of France, December 16, 1958
Johnston and Sand Islands (Pacific)	1858	Under *Guano Island Act*	Possession
Palmyra Island (Pacific)	1862	Annexed by Hawaii, but not included in state	Possession
Swan Islands (Caribbean)	1863	Under *Guano Island Act*	Possession (disputed by Honduras)
Navassa (Caribbean)	1865	Under *Guano Island Act*	Possession
Alaska	1867	Purchase from Russia ($7·2m)	State of USA
Midway Island (Pacific)	1867	Annexed	Possession
Republic of Hawaii (Pacific)	1898	Annexed	State of USA, 1959
Wake Island (Pacific)	1899	Annexed	Possession
Guam (Pacific)	1898–9	Conquest from Spain	Unincorporated Territory
Philippines (Pacific)	1898–9	Conquest from Spain. Payment of $20m	Independent, July 4, 1946
Puerto Rico (Caribbean)	1898–9	Conquest from Spain	Commonwealth status, July 25, 1952
American Samoa (Pacific)	1898–1900	Treaty with Britain and Germany	Unorganised unincorporated Territory
Panama Canal Zone	1903–4	Leased from Panama for $10m and annual payments rising from $250,000 to $1·93m	On September 11, 1972 the Panama Parliament declared sovereignty and declined US annual payments. Status undecided

Territory	Date	Status
GUANTANAMO (Cuba)	1903	Leased for coaling and naval station. Uneasy relations with Cuba
CORN ISLANDS (Caribbean)	1914–16	Leased from Nicaragua for $10m. Right to construct ship canal through Lake Nicaragua. Turned back to Nicaragua April 25, 1971
VIRGIN ISLANDS (part of) (Caribbean)	1916	Purchased from Denmark for $25m. Incorporated territory (see also *British Empire*)
QUITA SUEÑO BANK, S.W. CAY, RONCADOR CAY, SERRANA BANK (Caribbean)	1919	Under *Guano Island Act*. On September 8, 1972 the United States abandoned claim to sovereignty and recognised the territory as part of Colombia
KINGMAN REEF (Pacific)	1922	Annexation. Incorporated in American Samoa, 1925
HOWLAND, BAKER, JARVIS ISLANDS (Pacific)	1934	Confirmed under *Guano Island Act*. Possession
CANTON AND ENDERBURY ISLANDS (Pacific)	1939	Treaty. Controlled jointly by Britain and USA (valid to 1989), 1939
TRUST TERRITORY OF THE PACIFIC ISLANDS (about 2,000 islands and atolls, including Caroline, Marshall and Mariana groups, excluding Guam	1947	United Nations decision. US jurisdiction under UN Trusteeship System, 1947
RYUKYU ISLANDS, including Okinawa (Pacific)	1952	Treaty with Japan, which retained residual sovereignty. Northern islands reverted to Japan, 1954. Okinawa returned, 1972, except for military base which remains without nuclear arms
VOLCANO ISLANDS (Pacific)	1952	Treaty with Japan. Returned to Japan, June 26, 1968
CORDOVA ISLAND (Rio Grande)	1968	Northern half ceded by Mexico in return for Chamizol, readjusting Texas border. Incorporated with Texas

Appendix

Commonwealth
Declaration of
Principles

(*Adopted at Singapore Conference of Heads of State, January 22, 1971.*)

The Commonwealth of nations is a voluntary association of independent sovereign states, each responsible for its own policies, consulting and co-operating in the common interests of their peoples and in the promotion of international understanding and world peace.

Members of the Commonwealth come from territories in the six continents and five oceans, include peoples of different races, languages and religions, and display every stage of economic development from poor development nations to wealthy industrialised nations. They encompass a rich variety of cultures, traditions and institutions.

Membership of the Commonwealth is compatible with the freedom of member Governments to be non-aligned or to belong to any other grouping, association or alliance. Within the diversity all members of the Commonwealth hold certain principles in common. It is by pursuing these principles that the Commonwealth can continue to influence international society for the benefit of mankind.

We believe that international peace and order are essential to the security and prosperity of mankind; we therefore support the United Nations and seek to strengthen its influence for peace in the world, and its efforts to remove the causes of tension between nations.

We believe in the liberty of the individual, in equal rights for all citizens regardless of race, colour, creed or political belief, and in their inalienable right to participate by means of free and democratic political processes in framing the society in which they live. We therefore strive to promote in each of our countries those representative institutions and guarantees for personal freedom under the law that are our common heritage.

We recognise racial prejudice as a dangerous sickness threatening the healthy development of the human race and racial discrimination as an unmitigated evil of society. Each of us will vigorously combat this evil within our own nation.

No country will afford to regimes which practise racial discrimination assistance which in its own judgment directly contributes to the pursuit or consolidation of this evil policy. We oppose all forms of colonial domination and racial oppression and are committed to the principles of human dignity and equality.

We will therefore use all our efforts to foster human equality and dignity everywhere, and to further the principles of self-determination and non-racialism.

We believe that the wide disparities in wealth now existing between different sections of mankind are too great to be tolerated; they also create world tensions. Our aim is their progressive removal; we therefore seek to use our efforts to overcome poverty, ignorance and disease, in raising standards of life and achieving a more equitable international society.

To this end our aim is to achieve the freest possible flow of international trade on terms fair and equitable to all, taking into account the special requirements of the developing countries, and to encourage the flow of adequate resources, including governmental and private resources to the developing countries, bearing in mind the importance of doing this in a true spirit of partnership and of establishing for this purpose in the developing countries conditions which are conducive to sustained investment and growth.

We believe that international co-operation is essential to remove the causes of war, promote tolerance, combat injustice and secure development among the peoples of the world. We are convinced that the Commonwealth is one of the most fruitful associations for these purposes.

In pursuing these principles the members of the Commonwealth believe that they can provide a constructive example of the multinational approach which is vital to peace and progress in the modern world. The association is based on consultation, discussion and co-operation.

In rejecting coercion as an instrument of policy, we recognise that the security of each member-state from external aggression is a matter of concern to all members. The Commonwealth provides many channels for continuing exchanges of knowledge and views on professional, cultural, economic, legal and political issues among member-states.

These relationships we intend to foster and extend for we believe that our multi-national association can expand human understanding and understanding among nations, assist in the elimination of discrimination based on differences of race, colour or creed, maintain and strengthen personal liberty, contribute to the enrichment of life for all and provide a powerful influence for peace among nations.

Part Three

The Alternative to Empires

Chapter Twenty-four

The New
Nations

It is too early to judge the consequences of the colonial revolution which followed the end of the Second World War. A quarter of a century is short compared with the centuries during which imperialism ruled the world and with the depth of the transformation which took place and is still taking place. That must be the subject of another book which another must write. All that can be written now is to indicate the significance of what has happened, successes and failures, the opportunities and dangers ahead, and the direction which governments and peoples should consider taking if human co-operation, liberty and justice are to be extended. The consequences have affected not only the newly independent nations, but the imperial powers themselves and world relations.

Psychological Revolution

Independence brought a new sense of self-respect and personal and national dignity to peoples. Even when material conditions remained stern this was true. The author went to Indian villages where hard work still brought little above subsistence yet the peasant had shed the attitude of subservience. Where there had been resentment, as among the educated in the towns, the sense of self-rule brought the attitude of man-to-man equality between Indians and Europeans. In the freed nations this new pride was most marked among those with political interest, but it went far down to the people. There was a spiritual rebirth.

Whilst this mood lasted there were large voluntary movements, particularly in Africa, of education and construction in which large numbers joined – adult classes in reading and writing, women's instruction in hygiene and child-care, the building of schools, dispensaries and community halls, the making of feeder roads from isolated places, the digging of trenches for irrigation, the laying of pipes for tapped water. The author saw whole villages marching out on such projects after working hours, men with pickaxes and spades, women with baskets, small boys with sticks.

In those early days of independence there was the psychology not only of a revolution achieved but of a continuing revolution. Hopes were high of social change, of betterment of life. Big things were actually done: the legal abolition of Untouchability in India (though tradition persisted), works of irrigation and industrialisation, the Aswan Dam in Egypt, land distribution in Kenya, the Tema Harbour and Volta electrification in Ghana, rural co-operative villages in Tanzania, the spread of education everywhere. The task was great, change disappointingly slow. Perhaps an even greater demonstration of a new image was given on the international scene: Nehru's lead for peace, the beginning among the new nations of a Third World,[1] the stand for racial equality. Making use of the United Nations the colonial revolution began to change the attitudes of all governments and peoples.

The end of colonialist concentration by west European powers synchronised after the Second World War with an inverted attention to social problems at home. The author heard a Cabinet Minister say at an Indian celebration of independence anniversary in 1970 that colonial liberation had also contributed to liberation from destitution in Britain through the Welfare State.[2] Certainly the political psychology of the imperialist Powers changed. They began to adjust themselves to the situation of no longer having responsibility for policing other peoples and commenced to think of their own problems in a non-empire world.

Disillusionment

Disillusionment grew in the independent nations as the early hopes of a transformed society were lost in seemingly intractable difficulties. Mass poverty continued, appalling housing and primitive sanitation in towns remained, unemployment increased. A gulf grew sometimes between the peoples and the European–American educated élite who became the political Establishment; new indigenous rulers tended to become bureaucrats and sometimes dictators. Corruption poisoned the regimes, ministers becoming rich and living in mansions which rivalled those of the previous European masters. In vast India militant oppositions erupted in the provinces of Kerala, Madras and Calcutta; in Malaya and the Philippines communist guerrillas challenged what they regarded as fictitious independence; in Indonesia pro-Chinese Communists pressed President Sukarno to war against British-designed Malaysia; power by dominant political cliques was strengthened, one-party states were decreed, sometimes reflecting national unity, sometimes exploiting it, opposition leaders were imprisoned; nineteen governments in Africa were overthrown by army *coups*, sometimes radical, sometimes reactionary and supported in the background by American and Western agencies.[3] The continued revolution tended to become, instead, the old stabilised society, with the difference that white rulers had been replaced by brown and black. Capitalist enterprises overseas regained confidence, foreign investment increased, encouraged by development opportunities and cheap labour. Russia and China more than watched, intervening with aid to socialist-inclined states, training and arming freedom fighters.

It is difficult to give an overall picture of this explosive, chaotic period. There were the achievements described earlier. In Asia there was the emergence of communist China, of modern competitive Japan, the disruption of the Vietnam war, and of the Arab–Israeli conflict at its junction with Africa. In Africa there was the contrast between the independence accorded by France to Tunisia and Morocco and the seven years' war in Algeria; the cruel drama in the Congo for which both European industrial interests and tribal intensities shared blame; the confrontation with southern Africa – the Republic, South West Africa, Rhodesia – and within the Portuguese colonies; the largest number of refugees in the world until the six-day Israeli war – partly the victims of colonialist conflict (Angola, Mozambique), partly of tribal conflict (Rwanda, Burundi and southern Sudan). These were not the conditions in which new nations could be born healthily.

The Colonial Inheritance

Most of this violent confusion was the inheritance left by the empires, both political and economic. In Asia, insoluble political problems were bequeathed: the partition of India and Pakistan, partly a consequence of Britain's 'divide and rule' policy; the imposed incorporation in Indonesia of many diverse peoples; the disintegration of Indo-China and Vietnam; the power of communist China and communist penetration of the southern mainland and the archipelagoes. At the Berlin Conference of 1884–5, the Western European powers had divided Africa not on the basis of identity of peoples but according to their own penetrations, trade routes, troops and missionaries. The result was an arbitrary and artificial pattern of the continent, dividing tribes, communities, families. Often the division was by a river which in those days, when there were no connecting roads or railways, was the highway of villages.

The independent governments inherited these unnatural states. The first reaction among the dedicated was Pan-Africanism, a unity above race, tribe and language, expressed politically in a desire for a United States of Africa; but this idealistic aim did not capture minds enough to overcome separatist interests. As independent governments were formed, the sense of national authority and power submerged other loyalties; the new rulers were not prepared for their frontiers to be attenuated by racial and tribal demands: internal strife, across-frontier revolts and flights of refugees found a climax in the Nigerian–Biafran war of 1968–70. Africa needed a new 'Berlin Conference' of African states to re-draw the maps of the continent. The conditions and the will were not there.[4]

In the British colonies, particularly, tribal loyalties had been encouraged rather than national unity. There was much to be said for the Lugard practice of indirect rule. It operated through the chiefs and traditional administration; it meant less intervention, and it had in perspective the ultimate aim of self-government as distinct from the French, Belgian and Portuguese principle of absorption by direct rule. But it often employed the method of divide and rule and had the effect of maintaining tribal solidarity. Thus when independence came there was limited national consciousness. The evolutionary process of tribes becoming nations and nations becoming a confederation had barely begun.

Too Soon?

The chaos over a large part of Africa led many to ask whether political independence had not been extended too hurriedly. Great responsibility rested with the colonialist Powers who did not allow the peoples sufficient opportunities of development and training. Europeans had been in Africa for three hundred years and three-quarters of a century had passed since the Berlin Conference had consolidated European rule, yet the peoples were left mostly illiterate and in subsistence poverty. Disease was widespread with a fractional service of doctors; there was minimal higher education to prepare potential administrators. Tribute has previously been paid to the educational and medical services of the missionary societies, and in the latter half of the twentieth century medical science contributed supremely to the conquest of malaria and leprosy. The economic advance achieved has also been recognised: the construction of roads, the introduction of hitherto unknown goods in shops, and the establishment of industries. To this must be added the devoted service of many civil servants and the enlightened co-operation of some governors. But the overall picture remained as here described. Mining and trade yielded high dividends to the European owners, Europeans took possession of good land whilst many suffered from land hunger, the mass of the people were left little touched by progress and only a small political élite were belatedly directed to any responsibility.[5] The blame for much that exists in Africa under independence lay in the failure of the preceding occupying powers to provide the conditions for success.

Positive responsibility for indifference to democracy and personal liberty, for individual aggrandisement, and for violence and resort to military power also rested with the example of colonialist administrations. We need not labour the point; it has been made clear almost without exception in the record given of country after country. Democracy was withheld, organisations suppressed, liberties of speech and writing denied, individuals imprisoned without charge or trial; dishonest aggrandisement was practised in the seizure of riches and land; violence continued from the first conquests to Amritsar and Sharpeville and military rule imposed in repeated states of emergency, often without justification as in the case of Nyasaland. The dominant record inherent in the system of imperialism is there for everyone to read.

One appreciates that the responsibility of colonialist administrations for the unpreparedness of peoples for self-government does not meet the argument that it came too soon.[6] Historic failure does not necessarily justify immediate change, and this was particularly relevant in the fifties when colonialist governments were beginning to realise that their occupations must end. But that realisation came too late and was defeated by the escalation of final injustices (Algeria, Kenya, Nyasaland, the Central African Federation, Vietnam). There is also the moral and philosophical view, which is behind much of the thinking in this book, that no people has the right to rule another people, with its logical consequence that even bad self-government is better than good imposed government. A politically free people may begin in chaos, it will suffer self-inflicted wounds, but from these it will learn and grow and fulfil itself.

There is finally a practical argument against the view that independence was granted too soon: the alternative would have been far worse. This truth was expressed by Iain Macleod, Conservative Colonial Secretary in Britain (1959–61), when he argued against die-hards in his party that the withholding of independence would lead to a racial war throughout Africa. Kenya had had its Mau Mau, Algeria its seven years' war; most of Africa would have become a Vietnam. The distresses in Africa must be seen historically. When Europe evolved into nation states during the eighteenth and nineteenth centuries there was more violence, more cruelty and more persecution than there has yet been in Africa in its similar stage of development.

One-Party States

The almost universal habit of the new African nations in establishing one-party states was condemned in the West as a repudiation of democracy. The fact that it was so widely accepted indicated that the practice reflected popular opinion; both conservative and socialist governments adopted it. The feeling behind it was the national unity gained in the struggle for independence. Why disrupt this in the national reconstruction required after independence?

There was later another reason for prescribing parties. Often there was danger that the parties would reflect tribes and so undermine the people's sense of belonging to one nation. Tribalism was seen as a threat to the realisation of sovereign nationhood.

In practice democracy was often real within the parties. In elections in Kenya and Tanzania, for example, many candidates stood representing different tendencies in the one party, and those who had served in Parliament as supporters of the administration were defeated. The undemocratic feature of this system was when opponents were persecuted as in Ghana with Danquah and others, in Kenya with Odinga, in Uganda with Kiwanuka, in Zambia with Kapwepwe and in Algeria with Ben Bella, to mention only leaders whose fate many others shared. But it should be remembered that in the politically free West tolerance grew only with the growth of democracy over the centuries. It was perhaps too much to expect all Africa to be tolerant when democracy was a new experience.[7]

The Commonwealth

The British ex-colonies, with the exception of Burma and later Somalia, joined the Commonwealth (no longer called the British Commonwealth). There were thirty-one nations in all. Will the Commonwealth last? On the surface it is an illogical association. Some of its members are monarchical, some republican, some capitalist, some socialist, some pro-Western, some unaligned. Nevertheless it has significance because of its extent and its inter-racial character. The Declaration of Principles adopted at the Singapore Conference in January 1971 endorsed the freedom of peoples, personal liberties, dedication to peace, co-operation to end world poverty, and upheld racial equality; a forward-looking statement.[8] The conference nearly split on Britain's disastrous intention to supply arms to South Africa, but the African and Asian nations, sensitive for their own independence, could not object to London's claim to act independently. That did not remove the right of dissenters to withdraw from the Commonwealth as Pakistan did in 1971 and others may do so if Britain compromises fundamentally on human rights in southern Africa.

If the Declaration of Principles is accepted in practice,[9] the Commonwealth can contribute in an important way to racial co-operation, human liberties and peace. But this will depend upon a further adjustment. How far will its conservative and radical member-states, its capitalist and socialist states, be able to integrate permanently in one political group.[10]

In the sixties and seventies a test for the Commonwealth arose in the application made by Britain to join the European Economic Community. Economic co-operation with Commonwealth countries came second to economic co-operation with Europe. Among British Conservatives, pride in the old empire was never extended in the same way to the Commonwealth, and indifference grew as the nations in Africa and Asia asserted their independence in non-alignment. The consequence of the West European consortium on the economies of the developing countries has still to be fully experienced. A number of African countries have sought association with the Common Market; but what will be the effect on those developing countries which accept association with the East as well as the West? One consequence of Britain's projected membership of the European Economic Community is evident. Identity with Europe will mean decreased identity with the Commonwealth.

Notes

1. We may use this term again. By the 'First World' we mean the USA and the industrialised nations of the West and Japan. By the 'Second World', the Soviet Union and the communist nations. By the 'Third World', the rest of Asia, Africa (except the South), much of central and southern America, the Caribbean and other islands.

2. Wedgwood Benn, Connaught Rooms, January 22, 1970.

3. These were: *UAR* (July 1952), *Sudan* (November 1958), *Congo-Kinshasa* (1960 and November 1965), *Togo* (January 1963), *Congo-Brazzaville* (August 1963 and September 1968), *Dahomey* (December 1963 and December 1967), *Gabon* (February 1964), *Algeria* (June 1965), *Burundi* (October 1965 and November 1966), *Central African Republic* (January 1966), *Upper Volta* (January 1966), *Nigeria* (January and July 1966), *Sudan* (May 1967), *Ghana* (February 1966), *Sierra Leone* (March 1967 and April 1968), *Mali* (November 1968), *Libya* (September 1969), *Somalia* (October 1969), *Uganda* (January 1971), and *Ghana* again (1972). See *The Barrel of a Gun: Political Power in Africa and the Coup d'État* by Ruth First.

4. Asia also had its frontier problems.

5. One often meets the argument that African workers flocked to the mines and industries to obtain the wages paid. That is true, but wages were low and the fact that so many sought such employment was a condemnation of their general standard of life. In addition, many of them were evicted from the land with the deliberate object of creating a pool of cheap industrial labour.

6. The most extreme case was perhaps Congo-Kinshasa (Zaire). A transition period might have saved much.

7. Especially in view of the instability of the newly-created states.

8. See Appendix on page 566.

9. For example, Australia and Britain will require to adjust their discriminatory immigration policies and some African and Asian nations their denial of civil liberties.

10. President de Gaulle likewise established a French Community of African ex-colonies, but constitutionally it is scarcely operative. Nevertheless, because they have persisted in the French pattern, the association between most of them and France is closer culturally, economically and military than between most Commonwealth nations and Britain.

Chapter Twenty-five

Unresolved

(Remaining Colonies,
Portuguese Africa,
Southern Africa)

The Colonial Revolution is still unfinished. Many peoples remain under external or internal racial domination, and when political freedom and racial equality have been won, the exploitations of imperialism persist. We are seeking an alternative to empires, and our theme has been that empires represent not only political occupation but cultural, military and, supremely, economic occupation. Let us first consider the alternative to the residues of political occupation – colonies and territories of racial domination.

The Remaining Colonies

We begin with the problems of continuing political colonialism, difficult in themselves but a fraction of the greater problem of eradicating imperialism. The remaining colonies are (1) the left-overs of empires, and (2) the Portuguese provinces in Africa.

The Mainland Enclaves

At the time of writing, the left-overs include a few territories on mainlands and large and small islands. The first, with the exception of Gibraltar, will inevitably proceed to independence, either separately or federated with neighbours. The Spanish enclaves in Africa will become absorbed, French Somaliland will either become fully independent or join greater Somalia. Similar alternatives will face French Guiana and Dutch Surinam, in South America and British Honduras in Central America. Portugal claims Macao, an enclave on the mainland of China; this is strongly challenged by Communist China.[1] In Asia, British-protected Brunei (perhaps not until its oil runs out) will in time become independent, reconciled to federation with neighbouring Sarawak and Sabah, or even Indonesian Borneo. Australia's New Guinea will pass from self-government to independence in 1973. In Europe Britain's Gibraltar represents a different problem; self-determination by its small population or integration with its geographical identity, Spain? Its value to Britain is only naval power, but the will of the people must be considered. The best solution would be to internationalise all the commanding heights of the world's communicating waterways, including Gibraltar.

The Scattered British Islands

The scattered islands present special difficulties. Of the old British empire only three island colonies of considerable population remain: Bermuda and the Bahamas in the West Indies and Hong Kong on the offshore of China.[2]

The Bahamas and Bermuda will go forward to independence as other British ex-colonies in the West Indies have done; indeed, the Bahamas very soon. They exist economically as a sunshine playground for rich tourists from the United States, mostly served by white-owned hotels, shops and night clubs. The black population are the proletariat in the towns and the peasants and fishermen in an archipelago of islands; what the reaction of Americans and Europeans will be when a black majority government takes over in complete independence one cannot foretell. Bermuda is the most eastern of the West Indian islands, one of the earliest to have a Parliament but lagging in independence because of European penetration, faced by a black opposition. The sensible solution would be for all the West Indian islands to be confederated, but this will be delayed by ideological and language differences and economic and political post-colonial associations. It will be a long evolution if ever reached.

Non-self-governing Hong Kong is at present useful both to Communist China and to Britain, serving as a naval and trade base for the latter and a means of trade and communication with the outside world for the former. The lease of the neighbouring mainland from China expires before the end of this century and what happens then (or earlier), will depend on the future mutual relations of China and the rest of the world. It will prove politically, if not militarily, impossible for Britain to retain permanent possession; a temporary solution might be to place the island under United Nations trusteeship.

Turning to the small islands, alternatives to complete independence must be considered, because they are not wholly viable units. Of those in the British empire, Tonga was exceptionally accorded independence, partly, perhaps, because of the popularity of the extrovert Queen Salote at the coronation of Elizabeth II.[3] But this can be no lasting solution. It is having difficulties in adjusting itself to the modern industrial world, suffering from unemployment, its people emigrating, almost forgotten in the role of a poor relation. Tonga was duly admitted to the United Nations, but how long will the large powers consent to equality in sovereignty, including equal voting rights, by those who represent a few thousand? Against the background of our competitive and armed world there is always the potential need of protection from exploitation and war. Tonga, like other small islands, requires wider integration.

It is not possible to consider each of the islands separately; readers are referred to the Tables of Occupation and Status on page 539. Many are directly ruled as colonial possessions by the occupying governments; some are fully integrated with the metropolitan territories; others enjoy internal self-government as Associated States with the right to opt for independence. Looking to the future, the basic right of self-determination must be accepted, but independence could include the alternatives of confederation either with neighbouring islands or with peoples on the nearest mainlands. Preferable geographical confederation would sometimes be prejudiced by language differences inherited from colonial times, but translation techniques could go some way to overcome these. Indeed, there is already in the Pacific a grouping of all the islands, whatever their colonial background, together with the mainlands the South Pacific Commission. There has also been from distant 1947 a Forum of all Commonwealth islands, linking Fiji, Nauru, Tonga, West Samoa and the Cook Islands. The functions of these two groupings are much less than administrative co-ordination, but they could provide the nucleus of the type of confederation proposed. Curiously, they are criticised as inadequate for contradictory reasons. The Commission is thought limited because it excludes political questions from consideration. The Forum is often dismissed on the ground that it devotes too much attention to politics.[4]

Others: The Canaries

There are still scattered islands associated with other old empires. Among them the Canary Islands, which deserve special mention. The Canary archipelago, composed of seven large islands (Lanzarote, Fuerteventure, Gran Canaria, Tenerife, Gomera, Palma and Hierro) and six smaller islands, has a population of 860,000 and an area of 2,807 sq miles and lies off Spanish Sahara and Ifni (a small enclave that has now been returned to Morocco). The native population, known as Guanches, are of Cro-Magnon and Khoisan origin and have never acquiesced in foreign occupation, whether Portuguese, French or Spanish. The islands were granted by Pope Clement VI in 1344 to Spain to create a Christian Kingdom of the Canaries, and although Spain proclaimed its dominion in 1496, the claim was contested by the French, Moroccans, Algerians and British, and Spain did not take undisputed possession until the seventeenth century. The *Mouvement pour l'Autodétermination et l'Indépendence de l'Archipel Canarien* (MPAIAC), based in Algiers, was recognised by the Organisation of African Unity in 1968.

United Nations Responsibility?

Often one is led to ask whether the technological advance of some of these islands represents progress. Phosphate is discovered; the inhabitants of the land on which it is found are evicted, to return as labourers amidst excavations and machinery which have destroyed the beauty of their palm groves and coral-waved sands. The simple nature of their primitive life has gone, too. Perhaps this is inevitable, but who has not desired at times to escape to such a retreat? Relevant is the problem of the Seychelles, lost in the Indian Ocean. One third of the ninety islands are uninhabited, many of them unique in their floral and bird life. General Gordon, when making a military survey in 1881, nominated a valley in Preslin Island as the original Garden of Eden. The Seychelles may be saved from phosphates or oil, but the islands are now being developed as a tourist resort with a modern airfield to deliver visitors from America and Europe. We must hope that the natural beauty will not be desecrated, but it looks very much as if the Caribbean pattern of occupation by rich aliens will be repeated.

We have forgotten our political purpose for the moment. Only fifty thousand people live in the Seychelles, but they have a Legislature much concerned about the future. The majority Progressive Party expressed a desire in 1970 for integration with Britain; the more radical People's United Party advocated Associated Status, which is more likely to be realised. Later, the Party, with the support of the Organisation of African Unity, claimed absolute independence; Associated Status would provide that option. Long-term thinking begins to turn towards confederation with Mauritius and East Africa. Another attractive solution might be United Nations protection as a world nature reserve.

This brings us to the proposal that United Nations protection should be extended to all the islands unequal to viable sovereignty. It would be appropriate, for example, for Associated States, candidates for membership, to be available for the guardianship of the UN. The precedent has been given of the Trusteeship territories, but it would be preferable not to repeat the practice of mandated authority through separate governments, which maintains the image of empire.

A Department of the UN itself should be made responsible. In this way the islands would be saved from becoming the pawns of the Great Powers either economically or militarily and there would be united incentive for constructive development. The terms of reference should be to encourage education and economic progress free from exploitation and without, one hopes, the destruction of natural beauty. The fulfilment of these aims would necessitate a deliberate expansion of the UN's authority and functions. That we discuss later.

The Forgotten Originals

Perhaps the most pathetic victims of external occupations are the original races of the Americas and Australia, lost in the expanding white invasions. The Indians of Canada, the USA and South America, and the Aborigines of Australia have been largely left outside the pale of the modern society which has replaced their own. But they are now beginning to assert themselves, claiming rights in their reserves in North America, participating as recognised citizens in some South American states. It is indicative of our age that the high achievement in tennis of a young Aboriginal girl, Miss Yvonne Goolagong, has made the world more aware of her forgotten race; her rise to fame was accompanied by a new political militancy by her people, who squatted before the Parliament buildings at Canberra in February 1972, demanding their right to land. This was rejected by the Government, but endorsed by the Labour Opposition, and Labour are likely to win the next election. Even the most forgotten are coming into their own.[5]

The Portuguese Colonies

The Portuguese possessions in Africa, Angola, Mozambique, Guinea and its Atlantic islands, are a challenge not only to its peoples but to the West. Portugal is a member of NATO which claims to be defending the 'Free World'. Although it was at first denied that arms supplied by NATO nations were being used in the Portuguese colonies, they were found there and, as already recorded, an American delegate at the United Nations confirmed their use. In any case, there can be no doubt that NATO members' arms have enabled Portugal to release for its colonialist repression weapons which would otherwise have been reserved for domestic defence. The NATO nations have turned their backs on colonialism: how can they justify their support of Portuguese colonialism? Is it unreasonable to suggest that they should logically withdraw their arms contribution to Portugal and terminate its membership of the alliance if Lisbon persists in its occupation of African territories?[6] It is doubtful whether Portugal could continue to bear the heavy cost of its military engagements in Africa without the support of the West.

And what of the United Nations? Resolutions are carried against colonialism, but there is little action. This is a test of sincerity and of depth of conviction. If we really believed that the enforced rule of peoples by another people was a crime against human rights, intolerable in the historical period we have reached, we would seek to do something effective to end it. The United Nations represent 130 governments of the world. It is impossible to believe that they could not exert a decisive influence on the one government which continues to practice and justify political colonialism. If the dominant white states felt this issue as deeply as the non-white majority, they would act.

We discuss later the ineffective powers of the United Nations, but even within present limitations it has the authority, if it had the will, to make the Portuguese Government alter its course. It could in the first instance summon Portugal to discussions together with representatives of the African peoples. It could call on Portugal to withdraw its troops from Angola, Mozambique and Guiné within a stated period. It could offer to co-operate in facilitating the transference of administration to accepted leaders of the peoples pending the setting up of democratic constitutions. It could say to Portugal that unless this were accepted its government would not be recognised in the community of nations and that all association with it would be withheld: diplomatic association, arms association, trade association, communications association, transport association, every form of association. Portugal and its African territories would thus be entirely isolated. Almost certainly, that warning would only have to be given for Lisbon to give way. Its economic position is critical, its population the poorest in Europe, over-burdened by military expenditure. Within Portugal there is a growing liberal opposition, including disquiet among its young conscripted NCOs and officers, many of whom have come from its uneasy universities.[7] In the African territories there are strong armed resistance forces compelling the presence of 150,000 Portuguese troops. The Government is deeply concerned to keep its association with the rest of Europe, America and Britain. An ultimatum from the United Nations could scarcely be rejected.

One may object that the imposition of sanctions has not been successful, illustrated by the failure of the League of Nations action against Italy over Abyssinia and the ineffectiveness of the trade embargo against the illegal white regime in Rhodesia. The first point to make is the inadequacy of the sanctions imposed; elements in the failure in Rhodesia, for example, were the half-hearted action to curb the extensive black market, the absence of containment of trade from South Africa and through Mozambique, and the continuation of communications. Similarly, whilst the United Nations endorsed a British blockade of the port of Beira in Mozambique, there was no restriction on the imports to Rhodesia through the port of Laurenço Marques, which was a principal channel for South African supplies.

Sanctions would have a considerable effect on Portugal's crucial occupation plan for the construction of its vast hydro-electric project at Cabora Bassa in Mozambique with its large-scale eviction of Africans and settlement of Europeans. Sweden and Italy have already withdrawn constructional and financial co-operation; if other countries did so the effect might be determining. We have already acknowledged a dilemma: the hydro-electric project, whilst at present consolidating Portuguese power, could be of immense economic value to a wide area of central and southern Africa; it is eminently desirable in itself. When democracy is established, we have to see that international co-operation is given generously to its realisation.

There is an incidental problem of importance here. In the three Portuguese possessions, strong African forces have occupied large areas of the territory. They have the support of the Organisation of African Unity, and logically the United Nations cannot condemn Portuguese colonialism, as it has, without giving support to those who resist it; nor can aid to the 'freedom fighters' consistently be frowned upon as it is by the British and other governments.[8] This became a controversial issue in 1970 when the World Council of Churches decided to make contributions to the medical and educational activities, which are great, of the African insurgent organisations. The decision was criticised on the ground that it was an endorsement of violence, which was answered by the reminder that the Church has historically supported wars when it has held them justifiable. Pacifists among Christians have the right to dissociate themselves, but the World Council commendably has shown recognition that racial freedom and equality are fundamentally righteous.[9]

Southern Africa

The most urgent and perilous political problem is that of southern Africa. In Rhodesia and the Republic of South Africa, including South West Africa (Namibia), the practice of white supremacy and racial separation is imposed by minority governments upon the non-white disenfranchised majority.[10] Legalistically this may not be regarded as colonialism since South Africa is an independent country, though Rhodesia is constitutionally British and South West Africa a trusteeship territory of the United Nations. In practical terms, however, these distinctions are irrelevant. Colonialism is fundamentally the occupation and political control of a people by another people, and that is exactly what applies. Europeans have seized these territories and govern without acknowledging the right of the majority indigenous population to have voice in determining their own destiny.

Association or Isolation?

There are two views as to how this position can be remedied. The first is by the influence of association to encourage reconsideration and hope of the gradual elimination of apartheid. The second is by pressure, isolation and resistance.

One is appalled by the thought of racial war in southern Africa. It would mean vicious barbarity, European families assassinated, Africans massacred. One must seek every means of a solution without this disaster; there are some faint signs of encouragement. There was the evidence of declining support for the Nationalist Government by the defeat of its candidate at a by-election at Brakpan in the Transvaal in February 1972. There was a 10 per cent swing to the Opposition United Party which, if maintained, could bring about the defeat of Mr Vorster at the general election in 1973. The United Party also stands for apartheid, if apartheid without tears, but the result of the election was significant of a trend in public opinion away from severe segregation.

There is opposition to apartheid by the Churches (except the Dutch Reformed Church), and by many academics and particularly the students. Potentially the most powerful opposition is from industrialists, led by the mining king, Harry Oppenheimer, who because of labour shortage demand that non-white workers shall be allowed to enter skilled jobs.[11] Perhaps even more significant in its effect is the issue of multi-racial sport. The Government's permission to non-whites to take part on international occasions was a considerable departure from apartheid.[12] It should be noted however, that it was the consequence of isolation.

It would be optimistic to expect that the opposition to racial segregation will become sufficiently strong to eradicate apartheid by consent. In a flight of imagination one can see, paradoxically, a possible bridge through a measure intended to be the final and irrevocable separation of Whites and non-Whites. Bantustan is rejected by inter-racialists as the climax of apartheid, but if there is any sincerity in Mr Vorster's declaration that these African reserves will eventually evolve to independent states one can begin to visualise through them a possible challenge to apartheid. Under genuine independence the African administrations would have authority to end racial segregation within their borders. This would be generous on their part so long as apartheid is maintained in the Republic, but there are strong elements in the present Bantustans, Transkei and Zululand, opposed to discrimination against Whites.

What has happened in Zululand is important. Chief Gatsha Buthelesi has won the right to become Head of State despite the claims of the reactionary royal family. He is unsparingly opposed to apartheid and has courageously denounced it in South Africa. He says he will apply segregation in the Zulu state so long as the Whites apply it in the Republic, but he would prefer not to do so. Perhaps he may come to see that a more effective method would be to break with apartheid in his own territory. Whether he does so or not, it is evident that the Bantustans can in fact become bastions of opposition within South Africa. Together with the stand in the Republic of industrialists, church leaders and universities there is the slight hope that in time apartheid could be undermined. This is only a very marginal hope in view of the large Afrikaner majority among the Whites, but nevertheless a hope devoutly to be wished.

Test of Rhodesia and South West Africa

The conflict between the methods of association and isolation first arose sharply in neighbouring Rhodesia when the white minority government declared the independence of the country in defiance of Britain, who demanded assurances of an advance to majority rule. London imposed economic sanctions and got the United Nations to make them mandatory by its member-states, but the white administration lived on. When in February 1972 Lord Pearce headed an all-British commission to Rhodesia to judge whether the terms of a settlement reached between the British Government and the Ian Smith Administration were acceptable to the people, and the African majority rejected them, the path to a solution by association seemed closed. The Blacks insisted on majority rule. The Whites would not accept democratic equality even in the distant future.

South West Africa was the next test. Administration under a League of Nations mandate protected the interests of the indigenous population; the Republic of South Africa, as already recorded, applied apartheid, with the result that the United Nations declared the mandate withdrawn and asserted its own control. South Africa rejected this defiantly. There was no room for co-operation there. Influence by association was out.[13]

The United Nations has repeatedly expressed disapproval of apartheid in South Africa. So far from responding the Republic extended its segregation of non-Whites. The Coloureds (mixed race) were disenfranchised like Africans and Indians; Africans and Indians were evicted to separate locations; the pass laws were applied to women; the rules governing detention without trial were extended; African education was restricted in standards; and segregation constitutionally instituted in Bantustan reserves. The non-white political organisations were suppressed and their leadership was either in prison or exile. There seemed to be no road for a change by constitutional means from within, nor indeed were there signs of an opportunity for effective revolt.

The conflict of view between dissociation and association came to breaking point when Britain's Conservative Government proposed in 1970 to defy a United Nations resolution by providing South Africa with arms. Insisting they were against apartheid, the Conservatives argued that co-operation in meeting the threat of a Russian fleet in the Indian Ocean and the development of mutual trade would give the opportunity of influencing South Africa. The Organisation of African Unity strongly repudiated British policy, although a breach appeared in its ranks when the Ivory Coast, Malawi, Malagasy and Ghana proposed talks with South Africa. This went further in the case of Malawi, where there was definite association, but with no effect on apartheid. Which was it to be – association or pressure?

Action Proposed

When one thinks in terms of a settlement by slow evolution, the thought of South Africa as it is – the continuing oppression of the African, Coloured and Indian majority, the intolerable humiliations which they suffer under what is a police state, the imprisonment for years of leaders of fine character and ideals, the apparent hopelessness of changing the minds of the majority of white Afrikaners, the fact that the regime is practising and promoting violence and thus inviting violence in return – these considerations compel one to look to other methods.

As in the case of the Portuguese territories, it is difficult to believe that a united world cannot stop the crime committed by some four million Whites on nearly twenty four million non-Whites in South Africa, South West Africa and Rhodesia. Resolutions of the United Nations are of little value unless they are followed by action. What action?

One would wish to see the United Nations making a serious declaration that the international community can no longer tolerate white dictatorships and the practice of apartheid in southern Africa. It could summon representatives of the Administrations and of the non-white populations to UN headquarters, calling for measures by which democratic majority rule and racial equality could be established. If the Republic of South Africa and the illegal government of Rhodesia declined to attend or failed to accept proposals, the UN should say that neither could be regarded as belonging to the world community. The logic of this decision, as in the case of Portugal, would be that they would be boycotted by the rest of the world – not only no arms but no trade, no investment, no buying of gold, no communication by post or rail or sea or air. Absolute isolation.

Alternatives to Violence

Realistically one recognises that with the present composition of the United Nations and the power of veto on the Security Council by America and Britain there is little chance of such a decision. Rejection could be defended on the ground that action of this character would lead to racial war, but there is no doubt that economic interest would be the dominating factor in the decision. British and American financial involvement in southern Africa is great. One must acknowledge, however, that a situation might occur involving physical conflict; if white South Africa and white Rhodesia did not give way, non-Whites would revolt, the infiltration of freedom fighters would increase. It is a tragic fact that there appears to be no way out apart from violence, but comprehensive UN action would have the effect of shortening the struggle and making it decisive. The alternative would be worse. Nothing is more certain than that failure to act will in time make a massive physical conflict inevitable, with the white Governments highly armed but isolated, and the non-Whites strong in numbers, supplied with arms by sympathetic governments, certainly by Russia and China, and backed, as the struggle went on, by most of the rest of Africa pouring in guerrillas. The choice is between early international intervention or inaction during which the forces for all-out racial war will mount.

The proposed United Nations action would in effect be war minus arms, though some military intervention would be necessary. A naval blockade of the ports would be required and relief would have to be flown to the three independent states, Lesotho, Botswana and Swaziland. The Lesotho Government might identify itself with the Republic, though that would be difficult to justify to its people and there would be strong resistance, whilst Botswana would probably side with the United Nations, with Swaziland divided. The UN would also have to decide how far assistance should be given to the resistance within the Republic. One must bear in mind that South Africa and Rhodesia, including Mozambique and Angola, would be economically viable, except for the loss of oil, over a considerable period. They have food and industry, though the loss of power would be serious for transport as well as overall production. The real pressure on the Administrations would be the effect of isolation on their long-term economies and the revolt of the massive non-white population and the effect of division among industrialists.

Involvement with South West Africa

South West Africa (Namibia) would be a major factor in such a conflict. In 1971 its status was for a third time considered by the International Court of Justice. South Africa objected to the judges and offered a plebiscite, confident that salaried and subservient chiefs would influence voting, an assumption doubtful after the Rhodesian experience. Indeed, in 1972 there was evidence of resistance within Namibia. There was the massive strike by workers from Ovamboland against their contract system of labour and the Government was compelled to modify it. The resistance began on an industrial issue, but it had political repercussions in the Ovamboland reserve, which had previously been the least aggrieved.

In South West Africa again, financial and industrial interests will probably deter the West European governments from supporting any drastic action. They are becoming involved in exploiting the rich mineral wealth of the country, diamonds, uranium, lead, zinc, tin. Although the UN Security Council recommended member states to discourage economic relations with South West Africa and the United States agreed to fall in with this proposal, the United Kingdom Atomic Energy Authority entered into an agreement with the South African Atomic Energy Board and the British-owned Rio Tinto Zinc Corporation in a huge uranium project in the territory. Economic advantage can be counted on to override political principles.

To sum up, United Nations action could undoubtedly be decisive in ending the fundamental human wrong of racial oppression. We must accept the probability, however, that the United Nations will not act. Power is with the industrial countries which are identified with the economy of South Africa and, notwithstanding all their disavowals of apartheid, it is this that will be the determining factor. We confess we have little hope for the near future as we look at southern Africa.

Notes

1. In February 1973 there was a massive strike by trade unions in Surinam. This led to the Netherlands Government proposing Associated Status for the territory.

2. The Bahamas were promised independence to begin in July 1973.

3. Nauru has also attained independence. It was made prosperous by the discovery of phosphates.

4. At the first meeting in New Zealand the Forum condemned the French nuclear tests in the Pacific. At its second meeting at Canberra in February 1972 a majority condemned Australia's discriminatory immigration laws. The Forum could profitably give its mind to the construction of a common plan to deal with the serious unemployment from which all the islands, except Nauru, suffer.

5. At the beginning of 1973 a Labour Government was elected in Australia and decided to grant tenure of land to the Aborigines, and to introduce many other reforms.

6. This assumes that NATO will continue to exist. It is to be hoped that the proposals for an all-European Conference on Security and Co-operation may lead to the eventual disbanding of both the Warsaw Pact and NATO.

7. The Portuguese Minister of Defence and Army, General Horacio José de sa Viana Robeto, acknowledged this in Lisbon, December 30, 1970 (*The Times*, December 31, 1970).

8. In June 1971 the Israeli Government announced a gift of £1,200 to the freedom fighters through the OAU.

9. The PAIGC has now decided to form an independent Government in Guinea and to ask for the support of the Afro-Asian Group for United Nations recognition.

10. In Rhodesia there is very limited African representation in the Legislature.

11. In February 1971 the South African Minister of Labour permitted Coloured workers to take some skilled jobs in the building trade in Johannesburg and Pretoria.

12. An illogical but much supported penetration of apartheid occured early in 1971. A group of Afrikaner men were charged with breaching the Immorality Act by sexual relations with African women, but the case did not get to the courts on the ground that conveniently the women would not give evidence. There was a demand even in Afrikaner circles that the *Immorality Act* should be amended, but the Government did not respond. It could not face the contradiction that whilst African women were not permitted to sit on benches reserved for Europeans in public places they should be permitted to share beds with them in private.

13. Towards the end of 1972 discussions took place between Mr Alfred Escher, nominated by the United Nations Secretary-General and Mr Vorster, the Prime Minister of the Republic, regarding the future of Namibia. The suggestion was made that independence should be recognised through Bantustan states, but this was not accepted.

Chapter Twenty-six

Neo-colonialism
(Cultural, Military and Economic Domination)

We can see our way forward to the end of political colonialism; we cannot see our way optimistically to the end of apartheid, though if human progress means anything it must come. We now face the even bigger task of ending neo-colonialism. One can now say that world opinion has finally repudiated the right of one people to rule another people. *Imperialism nevertheless continues: cultural, military and economic domination.* Political independence has not ended the fundamental exploitation.

Let us consider in turn what is required to end the three forms of colonialism.

Cultural Domination

The dominance of European culture in occupied territories was due principally to educational monopoly and to the early religious fundamentalism of the Christian missions which ran the schools. The psychological resistance of the peoples was greatest in Asia and North Africa where the hold of the Buddhist, Hindu and Muslim religions was strong. The racial self-respect which grew as the nationalist movements emerged, especially after independence, led to a return to an indigenous culture. Gandhi in India, aided by the scholarship of Tilak and the literary distinction of Tagore, cultivated pride in Indian philosophic and spiritual traditions. In Senegal, Leopold Senghor expounded a theory that the instinctive mental approach of Africans to an understanding of life was distinct in that it identified itself with objects of study, whilst Europeans measured them from the outside. How far this was generally true is open to doubt, but in his country a widely influential movement for the encouragement of African culture developed around *Présence Africaine*, edited by Majhemout Diop. The most evident expressions of a distinctive culture were in music, songs and dancing, the sitar of India, the drums of Africa, the rhythm and movement different from those of Europe, though in recent times African versions influenced much of what became popular among Western youth.

A marked feature of the resurgence of African culture was in the use of poetry to express the emotions and aspirations of the struggle for racial equality and human dignity. It was no accident that so many of their leaders, Senghor in Senegal, already mentioned, and Graveirisha and Marcelino dos Santos of FRELIMO in Mozambique, were poets.

The greatest contribution towards a new culture came slowly from the schools as they were brought under Asian and African control, with history taught increasingly to reflect indigenous development rather than imperial occupation, and with the philosophy and beliefs of traditional religions. Europeans also contributed to the revival. The research which revealed the old civilisations and arts of Asia and Africa, bringing pride to their peoples, was often the work of European historians and archeologists. UNESCO helped notably in spreading information through its publications.

Military Domination

The military aspect of neo-colonialism changed in character in the late sixties and seventies. As nations became independent the control of the armed forces passed to the new governments, though expatriate officers often remained to train indigenous troops. British forces were retained in Hong Kong, Malaysia and Singapore to contain communist penetration and in the Persian Gulf to maintain oil supplies; in West and Equatorial Africa there was a continued French military presence. Some British ex-colonies began independence with defence agreements, but these were ended as they decided to become non-aligned. The Cold War military bases scattered about the world by the USA and, to a lesser extent, Britain, became of decreasing importance through the development of long-range missiles and the speed of air transport. Both withdrew from North Africa, the USA from Morocco and Britain and the USA from Libya after the 1969 revolution. Supplementing NATO in Europe, Western Asia had its CENTO Alliance and South-East Asia its SEATO, both of decreasing importance; in the latter region a military alliance was formed with Australia and New Zealand, but contradictorily the independent nations met and declared for neutralism, whilst the two Dominions are progressively withdrawing.

The Vietnam war appeared to be a turning point for America. Disillusioned President Nixon announced that personnel would not in future be involved in South-East Asia, although arms would continue to be sent. This increasingly became the pattern elsewhere, but arms supplies remained important. Russia sent weapons to Egypt; the US to Israel; Britain, America, China and Russia to the competing Asian countries (Pakistan, India, Malayasia, Indonesia, Thailand, as well as Indo-China). Russia and China also supplied arms to a number of African countries and to freedom movements; France sent arms to many Asian and African countries.[1] In South America the USA was progressively repulsed politically, but its military power, close off-stage, remained relevant as the conflict between the old and new orders became sharper. Overall, America and Russia had the power to dominate the world militarily, even if opposition by the newly arising nations and international opinion made its imposition partial. It was increasingly realised that the dual might of the two Great Powers was ever in the background, ready to destroy if crisis came. This was military imperialism, world wide in scope, with the lives of all mankind menaced.[2]

Economic Domination

We turn to economic imperialism. There has been controversy ever since the books of Adam Smith and later J. A. Hobson as to how far colonialism benefited the occupying countries and how far it meant the exploitation or progress of the subject peoples. Certain conclusions seem to have been proved. It was not all advantage and not all disadvantage. The early raids on distant lands by merchant adventurers enriched the successful and contributed to military power. The occupation of India by Britain made the participants rich and the East India Company at first profitable. The slave trade and the slave-served plantations brought wealth to the perpetrators.

Generally the tribute gathered from colonialist possessions aided the development of the industrial revolution. In the nineteenth century overseas investment reduced substantially the cost of raw materials and foodstuffs. From the 1920s onwards large corporations gained control of natural resources, including minerals and oil, as well as of retail markets. Thus began the external ownership of the economies of the emerging nations, whilst investments, specially by America, led to a widening domination.[3] There is no doubt that this economic imperialism resulted in exploitation of the peoples and the appropriation of wealth by the investing class.

On the other hand, it is doubtful whether the populations of the imperialist powers, as distinct from the financiers and industrialists, benefited on balance. In cheap food, yes; in employment through raw materials for industry, yes. But as Michael Barratt Brown wrote in his authoritative *After Imperialism*,[4] with few exceptions 'Britons have suffered rather than gained from colonial impoverishment'. This was dramatically the case in the late twenties and early thirties when the loss of markets led to the great world depression; the destitute one-half of the world meant poverty for the other half. It became clear that the peoples of both developing and developed countries were dependent upon a common high standard of life.

The basis of the economic subjection of the colonial peoples was the function imposed on them by the occupying powers. It is not suggested that the poverty of the Third World was due to imperialism in the first instance. It existed before modern imperialism; the contrast between rich and poor countries from the nineteenth century onwards reflected the location of the industrial revolution. But imperialism perpetuated the poverty. The occupying powers only extended to their overseas possessions the new facilities for wealth production (mostly mining) when profitable to themselves; the colonies were treated essentially as preserves to provide food and raw materials. This was not because of any callous intent; it was the inevitable development of the capitalist system which grew up with the industrial revolution.

The consequence was an unbalanced economy in the colonial territories, which were at the mercy of the industrialised nations because they had no complementary manufacturing industries. As late as 1965, for example, the developing countries provided all the world's natural rubber, 73 per cent of the jute, 70 per cent of the cocoa, 59 per cent of the bauxite, 42 per cent of the oil and gas, 42 per cent of the cotton and 28 per cent of the minerals; yet a mere 7 per cent of the manufacture of the products took place in these countries.[5] It was only after the colonial peoples gained their independence that a serious effort was made to establish balanced economies by the introduction of industries. In many, as we shall see later, this meant an increased indebtedness to foreign investors and continued economic subjection.

This is not the full picture. The Europeans who infiltrated Asia and Africa introduced the beginnings of modern development, in the first instance to serve themselves, later adopted by the indigenous élite. Bush and marshland became towns, railways were built, sanitation introduced, mines dug, land technically cultivated. This (with education, medical service and Christianity) was termed 'taking civilisation to primitive peoples' even though the masses benefited little, existing in little-changed poverty and privation, exploited for profit. Nevertheless it was historic progress; the advance of the industrial revolution in Europe was taken, if only partially and belatedly, to the rest of the world.

Poverty and Aid

It is not necessary to describe the poverty of the Third World. We all know of it even if we do little about it. The Food and Agricultural Organisation recorded in the seventies that almost eighty per cent of the population in the developing countries suffered malnutrition, some of it from wrong foods, much of it from the want of food. The richer countries benevolently declared in 1960 that they would devote one per cent of the value of their annual production to the relief of hunger. This was not very generous, but they failed even to reach the figure; they were below it in 1970. And they incorporated in their calculation every possible asset and made the grants with all available advantages to themselves.

The assets included contributions to the salaries of their staffs and export credits. The advantages included undertakings that purchases arising from the grants would be made in the donor countries. The most extraordinary perversion was to make the one per cent cover not only governmental grants and loans but private investments requiring the payment of interest, often exorbitant. This had the ironical result that the revenue from accumulated investments received annually was up to three times the amount provided annually. The total drain from the Third World in the late sixties was one and a half times the total value of aid. 'So it is not the imperialist countries which aid the Third World, but the Third World which aids imperialism,' remarked Pierre Jalée.[6]

One does not underestimate the value of much of the aid, particularly in the technical field. This was specially the case in the constructive help given through the international agencies of the

United Nations – the Food and Agricultural Organisation, the World Health Organisation, the Economic and Social Council, the Relief Works Agency for Palestinian refugees (UNRWA), though political circumstances largely restricted the last to maintaining camps rather than resettlement. Tribute must also be paid to OXFAM, War on Want and similar voluntary efforts. There was hope when the Special United Nations Fund for Economic Development (SUNFED) was established, but it became ineffective when its operation was made conditional upon disarmament by the great powers. The World Bank and the International Monetary Fund were intended to channel US overseas lending through international hands, but both were conditioned by commercial and political considerations. The full multilateral aid amounted to less than ten per cent of the total and was woefully inadequate.

The fact that over sixty per cent of aid was through national grants and loans meant that political motives rather than human need determined their destination. They were given with a view to influencing not only advantageous trade but ideological acceptance and alignment in the Cold War. This was in the background even when no 'political strings' were attached; however self-reliant the recipient country might be, it was inevitably influenced. Aid became a competitive game, specially by the USA, the Soviet Union and China. America and Britain withdrew their financial promises to Egypt's Aswan Dam project, whereupon Russia stepped in; the West declined to finance the Zambia–Tanzania railway, whereupon China did so. The repercussions of the Aswan Dam transference were enormous – the Suez war, the escalated Middle East confrontation. The repercussions of China's participation in eastern and central Africa may in the long run be as great. When to economic aid the effect of aid for military purposes is added we begin to see the place of economic imperialism in shaping the pattern of the world.

Another profoundly important factor was the influence of overseas investment on the racialist domination of southern Africa. The maintenance of apartheid in the Republic was made possible by the stability of the economic structure, and that structure was maintained by investment from America, Britain and West European sources. Moreover, when South Africa developed its strong armament industry it was in partnership with large British monopolies. Controversy arose over the provision of arms to South Africa by Britain, France and other European countries, but there was a great deal in the argument that investment in South Africa was a greater pillar of apartheid. This was fundamentally economic imperialism, more objectionable in some ways than in independent African states because the African majority had no political participation.[7]

Reaction of Nations

The retention of neo-colonialism following independence was resented by politically aware Africans and Asians. Many of the leaders of the nationalist movements were convinced Socialists and understood the deeper meaning of imperialism. When the occupying administrations withdrew, however, the new indigenous governments took different attitudes. Some did not quarrel with the economic system they inherited and co-operated with financiers and corporations by encouraging the private ownership of industries and plantations. Malaya in Asia, and the Ivory Coast and Liberia in Africa were examples. There was a second group whose leaders were socialist gradualists, pragmatic, introducing limited changes, but welcoming foreign investment to facilitate industrialisation and not thinking in early terms of a fundamental transformation of society. India under Nehru, Singapore under Lee Kwan Yew, Kenya under Kenyatta, Tunisia under Bourguiba and Senegal under Senghor were examples. There was a third group which made a basic change to Socialism their objective. This was not always an immediate sequence to independence. Indeed, one can think only of North Vietnam, avowedly communist, in Asia and Guinea, Algeria, Tanzania and, for a time, Mali and Ghana in Africa which set out with this aim.[8] But pressures from within added to the number.

In Asia, India under Mrs Indira Gandhi responded to a considerable degree, whilst in Africa Egypt (the UAR), Libya, Zambia, Uganda,[9] Congo (Brazzaville), Sierra Leone and Sudan[10] all began in the seventies actively to reconstruct their economies on a socialist basis. They varied in degree. Many still encouraged foreign investment but attached conditions which limited the period of indebtedness, and they proceeded to take the keys of the economy into public ownership, acquiring majority share-holdings in industry generally. Julius Nyerere in Tanzania took another line. He didn't base development on foreign investment but concentrated on building Socialism from the grass roots through egalitarian co-operatives in the villages, an experiment yet to be judged. Important for the future was the fact that the nationalist movements in the Republic, Namibia, Angola and Mozambique were all socialist in aim.

The same dynamic pressure found expression in Latin America, not only in Castro's communist revolution in Cuba but in Mexico, Peru, Bolivia and Chile; perhaps the most significant development on the American continent in the early seventies was the loss of the influence of the USA as shown in the virtual collapse of the Organisation of American States with its Treaty of Mutual Assistance against Communism. The test of all these pressures was resistance to neo-colonialism, particularly in its economic aspects.

The Extent of Communist Influence

How far was this development communist? In one sense the term was irrelevant. Communism had ceased to be monolithic. There was the conflict between the Soviet Union and China, and even ideologically between communist parties, as the reaction to the Russian invasion of Czechoslovakia showed. Many parties and some communist governments dissociated themselves from this action because they believed in national self-determination; instinctively the nationalist and socialist movements which had won through in their struggles for independence in Asia and Africa shared that view. Moreover, even the more challengingly socialist administrations among the new nations accepted the democratic approach to Socialism. In Latin America the election by the constitutional franchise of Allende to the presidency of Chile was a turning point. Even in Vietnam the Provisional Revolutionary Government of the South accepted a free election as the method of determining permanent rule. In Africa reactionary elements were responsible for governmental *coups* as frequently as revolutionary elements, and these take-overs often reflected an absence of demo-cratic communication rather than a denial of democracy.

Significantly when communist countries, as well as the West, sought to influence developments in the Third World they were met by a stubborn assertion of non-alignment, not least by the socialist administrations.[11] Historians of the future will probably be surprised that Asian and African nations did not identify them-selves more with the Communist *bloc* in view of Western policy, but the truth was that they were obsessed by the independence they had won and determined not to become involved in the struggle between the great powers. Of importance also were the origins of the Socialism of most of the Asian and African leaders. Nasser became a Socialist not by reading Marx but pragmatically, and as a Muslim he rejected the materialistic philosophy of Marxism. Nehru, Nyerere and Kaunda were Socialists on ethical and humanitarian grounds. It was evident to those who observed closely that the Socialism which would emerge in Asia and Africa, whilst basically accepting public ownership of the economy, would be distinctive, reflecting their own philosophies and conditions.

Notes

1. From this stage military imperialism was reflected not so much by the presence of troops as by the influence which the aid in arms exerted in the confrontation of the opposing *blocs*. The Labour Government in Britain decided in 1969 to withdraw British troops east of Suez, but the Conservative Government in 1970 renewed a symbolic presence.

2. In the new climate of the world, and also in their own interests, the USA and the USSR began to set limits to their military power. This was particularly reflected in the summit meeting in Moscow in May 1972 between President Nixon and Mr Brezhnev.

3. The fact is often overlooked, however, that in both the nineteenth and twentieth centuries overseas investments were greater in expanding Europe than in Asia or Africa.

4. His father was Principal of Ruskin College.

5. *The Third World in World Economy* by Pierre Jalée, translated by Mary Klopper.

6. *The Third World in World Economy*.

7. To a large degree this criticism also applied to investment in Rhodesia. In 1973, arising from an article by Adam Rafael in the *Guardian*, attention was drawn to the starvation wages paid by British firms in South Africa. This led to a considerable lifting of standards of life. The *Guardian* exposure followed large and militant strikes by African and Indian workers, particularly in Natal.

8. In its domestic economic policy Israel, with its wide public ownership, its unique powers in Histadruth (the trade union

organisation) and its egalitarian Kibbutzim might be included, but it depended on foreign financial aid, and its occupation of Arab land and expulsion of Arab people made Zionism regarded widely as colonialist.

9. Prior to the military *coup*, January, 1971.

10. Modified, but not essentially, following the 1971 *coup* and counter-*coup*.

11. In Egypt the Communist Party was outlawed and Communists imprisoned despite the Soviet military build up. Only in 1972 were they released.

Chapter Twenty-seven

Ending
Imperialism

We shall find as we proceed that the eradication of imperialism involves a revolution in the political and economic structures of the world. The consequences are so great and the intermediary factors so incalculable that one hesitates to present anything in the nature of a blue print. Yet we must look forward ruthlessly if the transition is to be made and remorselessly face what is involved. It is with the hope that the proposals made here will contribute to the fundamental thinking required that we venture to suggest the basis of the new order towards which we must move, conscious that events may shatter its evolution.

Cultural

First, cultural domination. This must be ended from within, but the developed countries and the United Nations can assist.[1] UNESCO should be provided with funds to permit it to expand its service to the peoples of Africa and Asia by close co-operation with them not only in the widest production of textbooks which reflect their histories and their contributions to civilisation and thought and crafts but in the publication of work by new writers and artists, and in the encouragement of drama, sculpture, painting and the crafts. Another large area of development would be by the use of slides and radio for national education and, later, by television films.

In their resistance to cultural domination there is some danger that the new nations will dismiss the philosophies, literature and art of other civilisations, but this should not be more than a passing phase. The developed nations have also to realise that all enlightenment did not have its birth in Greece, Rome and Christianity and that the history and cultures of other peoples are necessary to get the whole picture. There is a welcome recognition of this in published works and at the Universities, but not yet sufficiently in our schools.

Military

As already mentioned, the present tendency is for both the West and the East to withhold troops from the Third World and to send arms, instructors, finance and armament-making technicians; but at the time of writing the American forces are still in Indo-China, the Portuguese in their African possessions, the French in their ex-colonies and the British in Oman,[2] Malaysia and Hong Kong. In addition, there are American or British bases and airstrips in the Caribbean islands and the Mediterranean and across the Indian Ocean; military outposts at many strategic points; defence alliances in western and south-east Asia; troops trained domestically for service under tropical conditions; and American, Russian, British and French fleets look uneasily at each other in the Mediterranean and Indian Oceans. These facts reflect the Cold War rather than deliberate imperialism, but they technically constitute imperialism in that they represent the domination of the great powers over the rest of the world.

Indo-China and the Middle East are the two most critical areas of military intervention. In both cases negotiations have proved fruitless over many years. The time has come when the United Nations should take far bolder and decisive action. It should summon Geneva Conferences with all the interested governments and parties present to thrash out settlements. In the case of the Middle East there would be the difficulty that the Arab nations will not agree to direct negotiations, but this should not apply in the presence of other delegations, or even if it did the representatives of the two sides could meet separately in the first instance. There are two other issues where the United Nations should take early action: the disputes over frontiers between the Soviet Union and China and between China and India. They should be soluble given authoritative initiative.

There are complications for which the great powers are not immediately responsible. Asian and African nations are asking both West and East to provide arms for their own quarrels, of which the Nigerian civil war and the war between West and East Pakistan are examples. There is a history of imperialist implication in these conflicts, but they also represent the continuance of deep-rooted racial animosities which show that political settlements are also necessary within Asia and Africa. This is a hard fact, however; foreign arms are responsible for the destructiveness of regional and local wars which could not be maintained long without them.

To end military and arms intervention and the financing of armament industries in the Third World would require comprehensive international action. It could be done, but it would need a settlement of the 'Free World *v*. Communist' confrontation and a transformation in the economies of the industrialised countries which are so largely geared to war preparations. For example, France (second only to the USA in this) in 1970 exported £530 million worth of arms, employing 300,000 people, and its leading customer was South Africa. These changes demand a basic revolution in social and international structures.

Nevertheless, if there were a serious desire and an acceptance of its consequences, there is already the beginning of the administration which could end military imperialism. Military presence and aid in arms are authorised by governments and can be stopped by governments. Arms can be exported by manufacturers only under licence, and governments could prohibit the traffic entirely, though they would also have to control a black market which cleverly evades detection. If any government declined to co-operate, there could be a mandatory decision by the United Nations with an international inspectorate to ensure compliance.

Similarly, many governments already control the export of capital, and all could prohibit its use for financing armed forces and armament industries abroad if this were their determination; if instructors and technicians went, their citizenship could be withdrawn. Again there could be a UN mandatory decision and sanctions in the background. With the present character of governments these prohibitions are admittedly immediately unrealisable. Some governments, including the British, even have salesmen to push the purchase of arms, and to all nations the orders are important to balance trade. The point we are making is that the machinery exists for applying a prohibiting policy if we had governments representing societies consistent with it in outlook and pattern.[3]

We should not have solved the problem even if all military and arms intervention by the great powers were stopped. Unless we move forward to a world of governments which repudiate physical conflict entirely, the new nations themselves would still arm and make arms, not so effectively without external assistance, yet enough to be a menace. The fact must also be faced that any difficulties put in their way in producing arms might be resented, just as the nuclear non-proliferation treaty was resented whilst the great powers retained their arms. This reaction could be met only by impressive disarmament on the part of the powers. The problem is additionally complicated by the ease with which energy for civilian purposes can be perverted to war purposes. The atomic plants of India and Israel could produce nuclear weapons tomorrow. One is driven once more to the conclusion that these issues can be solved only by the harmonisation of nations and disputes in a new international order.

Economic

The economic domination of the poorer nations by the rich is the most pervasive, penetrating and permanent form of imperialism. The developing nations require capital to remove the imbalance of economies left by the occupying powers; they need industrial expansion to partner their land production and technical assistance as well as aid to spread education and social services. At present, as shown earlier, these are provided at heavy cost to the recipient and large profit to the source, which amounts often to foreign ownership of a large part of the economy, and, even when aid is donated, it is often accompanied by economic and political obligations. Can this domination and exploitation be removed?

They are fundamentally a reflection of the very basis of society. In the industrial West the economy is geared to the motive of sectional profit making, which necessarily determines the character of financial and industrial participation overseas no less than at home. In addition, all governments, including communist, use the need for investment and aid to influence developing countries politically. These factors are inherent in domestic structures and international relationships and cannot be eradicated without removing the cause. We shall conclude this survey by arguing that a fundamental change in the economic system of the West and a political transformation, East and West, are required if imperialism is to be ended. Meanwhile, we look at the direction of the changes which are needed, some of which can be currently applied.

Aid Through the United Nations

Let us take aid first. To recap: so long as it is bilateral it is bound, given present power rivalries, to influence the recipient even when no strings are ostensibly attached; in many instances aid is deliberately directed to countries which are ideologically sympathetic to the donor, and often there is an understanding that when the aid involves the purchase of manufactured goods, these shall be bought from the donor country even though they may be cheaper elsewhere. To overcome the political bias of aid and its economic restrictions it would be necessary to channel it through an international body. The United Nations agencies are the best example of international aid, and the most desirable action would be to revive the Special Fund for Economic Development, to require all aid to be distributed through it, and to insist on contributions from member-states proportionate to their wealth. But we have to face the fact that this is not likely to happen whilst ideological pressures and power rivalries dominate the world.

Socialisation

The problem of private investment is still more complex. In 1969 *The Times* (August 19) contained a leading article entitled 'African Owners'. It discussed the difficulties of foreign companies controlling African industries when they confront claims that their enterprises shall be Africanised. The occasion for the article was Zambia's decision to take a fifty-one per cent controlling interest in its rich copper mines. The companies had been granted leases in perpetuity during the Rhodesian period, for which Zambia substituted twenty-five years, and an arrangement was made that the Government would pay compensation from the returns received from its half and more ownership. Whilst the management remained for a time British, *The Times* recognised the 'strong African motives extending throughout the continent' in favour of nationalisation. It stated two of these motives. The first was the feeling that African wealth should be owned 'by the black inhabitants, not by expatriates'; the second was 'the growing African ambition to manage commercial and mining enterprises, not just to work for white managements'. In November 1970 Zambia went much further in Africanising the economy. It announced that it would acquire a fifty-one per cent interest in foreign banks, including Barclay's DCO, and in the main foreign-controlled industrial companies, including tobacco and transport. The Government would take over entirely insurance and building, and gave notice that within fourteen months all expatriates engaged in wholesale trading must close their businesses or sell them to Zambians; by January 1972 all retail trade would be in Zambian hands. This was drastic socialisation and Africanisation, but it reflected a tendency over a large part of Asia and Africa. In greater or less degree it was happening in India under Mrs Indira Gandhi, in communist Siberia, Mongolia, China and Vietnam, in Burma, Iran, Iraq, Syria, the UAR (Egypt), Libya, Algeria, Sudan, Senegal, Mali, Guinea, Uganda, Tanzania, Somalia, Sierra Leone and the two Congos. The area of economic imperialism, although still vast, was becoming restricted. This tendency will grow, replacing half ownership by full ownership, communist in intention in northern and central Asia, in Africa mostly socialist, and sometimes only pragmatic.

Apprehension was felt that the indigenous peoples had not trained persons capable of take over management. This was argued when the UAR nationalised the Suez Canal, but in fact the new management proved remarkably efficient. Fear of collapse was expressed when other governments nationalised industries, again to be disproved. The fact was overlooked that many hundreds of Africans and Asians were training technically in Europe and America, as well as at institutions in their own countries, and that the old disproportion of legal over technical students was disappearing. Moreover, when native executives were not available it was possible to employ expatriates temporarily whilst Africans or Asians learned from experience. *The Times* in the article quoted remarked that it would be foolish to assume that African-owned enterprises could not work successfully and warned that with every successful African seizure of control the demand for nationalisation would grow in other African countries. This development is the first challenge to external financial and industrial domination, to economic imperialism.

International Conventions

If we frankly accept that in the course of time political freedom will logically be followed by economic emancipation, and if we plan to help this evolution and to make the transition orderly and successful, we must respond by adjustments outside the developing countries to supplement what is occurring within them. We have international conventions to prevent extreme forms of the exploitation of labour. Why not against exploitation of peoples by external finance? Certain conditions could be laid down for foreign investment which could remove considerably the ill effects which so frequently accompany its operations and which would give the promise of ultimate freedom from dependence upon it. Such a convention might include these proposals: (1) investments should be in the form of loans repayable within a period reflecting the resulting increased production, (2) a maximum rate of interest at a reasonable level should be fixed,[4] (3) majority ownership of industries would be with the national government, with provision for payment for shares within a limited period from revenue received, (4) an indigenous staff should be trained in skills and management, (5) beginning at a living level, wages and salaries should be increased with production and (6) trade unions should be encouraged, with increasing workers' participation in the administration of the industry as competence grew from experience. This assumes that industries so financed would succeed, but financiers would not be likely to risk their money unless they were confident. When failures occurred, national governments would be required to meet their obligations from revenues otherwise raised. Developments of social value not expected to give an economic return would be financed from aid rather than investment or from loans for which the government would be responsible. A convention as drastic as the one proposed here might not be acceptable to governments representing the USA and western Europe, but even a less forthright agreement would embody the valuable principle of some international responsibility for the effects of external financial penetration of developing countries and of their right to move towards economic liberation. As public opinion became aware of the problem the terms could be progressively extended.

Such a convention would not, however, remove bilateral bargains or the political rivalry of the two power *blocs*. Investing nations could still exert pressures in their own interests and reflect ideological purposes rather than need. The only effective control of these motives would be the channelling of all investment through an international body such as has been suggested for governmental aid, but one must acknowledge that this would be impracticable within the economic system of the West and whilst power pressures continue both from East and West. Some advance might be made through an agency such as the World Monetary Fund and the World Bank if they were under representative international supervision. The most appropriate body would be a commission of the United Nations.[5]

Stabilising Fair Prices

There is also the need to ensure that the standard of life of the
peoples of the developing countries shall not be prejudiced by low
prices for their products. There are now trade agreements fixing
world prices for many commodities, but the pressure from both
receiving governments and industry is to keep them low; governments have an interest in reducing the cost of imports and controlling the price of food, and industry seeks cheap raw materials. As
we have shown, however, low prices impoverish millions of people
in the developing countries, and this in turn reduces world purchasing power with disastrous consequences on employment in the
industrialised countries. At present the highly organised and co-
ordinated corporations which negotiate the trade agreements have
the whip-hand over those in the developing countries who produce
primary commodities. There is therefore a need for an international commission, associated with the expanded economic arm of
the United Nations, later proposed (on which the developing
countries would have representation), whose function should be
the supervision of the fixing of prices and stabilising them over a
period of years, so guaranteeing continuing security. This could
bring a revolution in the living conditions of the peoples of the
developing nations.

Poverty and Population

The nations of the Third World are the nations of poverty and
hunger. Whilst the richer nations have not yet reached their aid
target of one per cent of their gross national product, the Secretary-
General of NATO chides them for not contributing five per cent
for European defence. We may wake up too late to realise that
before the end of this century the growth of population may have
so outstripped food production and its equitable distribution that
starvation will be suffered by millions. The present activities of
international agencies and voluntary organisations, often splendid
in technique and service, are losing the race, despite modern
devices. Some breakthrough was made by the 'Green Revolution'
initiated by Dr Norman Borlang for which he was awarded the
Nobel Peace Prize. By cross-fertilisation he developed new strains
of both rice and wheat which transformed production in India,
Pakistan, Ceylon, the Philippines, Nigeria and Colombia, spread-

ing to other food-growing countries. Within a few years production in India and Pakistan increased by fifty per cent. It is claimed that Pakistan became self-sufficient in 1970 and that India expected to be so by 1972, though in both cases one wonders how far this reflected only the monetary demand leaving many thousands underfed.[6] The 'Green Revolution' gave us a breathing space, but not more. There was a rumour in Pakistan that the new wheat would make sterile all women who ate it. 'If only that were true,' remarked Dr Borlang, 'we would really merit the Nobel Peace Prize,' adding that the real problem is that too many people are coming on the scene too fast.[7]

That is the problem given present production and distribution, but it would not be if the potentialities of production and equitable distribution were fulfilled. Adequate production involves two necessities: all that modern techniques can contribute to the present areas of production and, secondly, a point still to be grasped, the vast possible extension of that area. The former could be met by the expansion of the Food and Agricultural Organisation in co-operation with the kind of laboratories which enabled Dr Borlang to make his researches and with the Rockefeller and Ford Foundations which financed his studies and their application. This would require a large increase in FAO allotted funds, a test of the sincerity of the UN member-states and, also, if we are not being over-critical, a more far-reaching conception of horizons. Brown, Orange and Red Revolutions (the reader can identify the crops) should follow the Green Revolution, and an immense expansion made in the regional work FAO has done in providing training, fertilisers and up-to-date agricultural equipment.

When we look at potential new areas of food production there are two which, compared with their possibilities, are now almost untapped: the deserts and the oceans. One-seventh of the earth's surface is sandy desert, a much wider area arid land. It has now been proved in Israel and elsewhere that sand can be converted into fertile soil in three years by water treatment. There are two sources from which the deserts could be flooded with water: the rivers and lakes which lie underneath them, and the seas by desalination. It is known that water exists beneath many of the deserts. In the Sahara French geologists have said 'we are walking on water'; in the days of the Roman empire deep wells were dug, still to be found unused. The deserts are dry because they are sand and rainfall is limited, but on many rain falls torrentially for a few days, seeping through to rocks beneath. There the rivers flow, the lakes lie; the water has only to be brought to the surface to fertilise the sand. If it were oil the pumping apparatus would quickly have been installed; indeed, when oil is found water is often near by and has to be cemented off to prevent dilution. We have now to appreciate that for the future of mankind water is as necessary as oil. Bring it to the surface for this purpose, applying nuclear power for life instead of death, and the deserts could be made to blossom into fertility.

The desalination of the oceans is held up at present by the cost. It is an irony that a pioneer in utilising the known apparatus is small Kuwait which can afford to do so from its revenue from oil; but there is little doubt – it may be before these words are printed – that less costly methods will be found, and then deserts all over the world could be channelled and fertilised. There will be a huge new area for food production.

The second insignificantly used sources of food are the oceans themselves. The time will come when they will be farmed as land is farmed. The food potential here is immense; fish and other edibles below the surface. Proposals are now being made that the sea-beds should be internationalised as the 'heritage of all mankind' to prevent their use for war and for private or uninational exploitation of minerals. It is equally important that the seas themselves should be internationalised and developed for food. Add the seas to the deserts, and we have areas of food production to catch up with the growth of world population for a century and more. By that time family planning should have populations disciplined to the available resources of the world.

Disease is almost as great a calamity as hunger in the Third World – the expectation of life is under forty years, the appalling number of infants still dying in their first year, the sicknesses which accompany malnutrition. In many countries there is only one doctor for forty thousand of the population and dispensaries and hospitals are few and far between. The World Health Organisation requires vast extension, with more money, more staff, more projects, including preventive activities. This would be among the priorities in an internationally-minded world.[8]

There is a problem unrelated to imperialism which we should have in mind when considering international action to prevent distress. Earthquakes, volcanic eruptions, hurricanes and tidal waves have caused disaster and loss of life comparable to the casualties of war. When they occur, governments and peoples rush aid but, as the calamity in East Pakistan in 1970 showed, there are delays and confusion because of the absence of preparation and consideration. There should be in association with the United Nations an International Rescue Organisation with stocks of food, medicines, mobile clinics and surgeries, personnel and planes immediately available. And there is another problem: the danger of pollution to which we awoke in the seventies. Many preventive steps can be taken within nations, but there is the defiling of sea and air and of territories by industry and war, which require international action. This should be a further function under United Nations auspices when it really becomes the positive organ of world betterment.[9]

Notes

1. The Universities of Asia and Africa will help to correct the exclusively Western higher education of the earlier leadership, though the standard of scholarship of the latter still attracts students who can afford it. One would like to see a greater exchange of staff and students.

2. Britain's Conservative Government in 1971 caused some surprise by confirming the decision of the preceding Labour Government to withdraw the main British forces from the area, but left the door open for the future.

3. Anti-imperialism involves one exception to the prohibition of arms and personnel. It could not be applied logically to forces engaged in conflict with colonialist occupation or with apartheid regimes. The principle might be accepted that by decision of the General Assembly help would be legitimate to those engaged in asserting the provisions of the Charter of the United Nations.

4. The communist countries, the Soviet Union and its associates and China, already provide finance at very low rates of interest, generally $2\frac{1}{2}$ per cent, sometimes interest free. The terms of the agreement for the construction of the railway from the copperbelt of Zambia to Dar-es-Salaam, the Tanzanian capital and port, illustrate the easy terms which the Chinese offer. Their loan of about £168 million will be shared equally by Zambia and Tanzania, with repayment over thirty years, beginning only in 1983. Local costs will be met by the African states through sales of Chinese goods, which will not have to be paid for until 1983 under a credit agreement which the Chinese have conceded. The facilities

offered by the communist governments are not, of course, entirely disinterested. They also seek political influence.

5. There was a disastrous conflict between rich and poor nations at the United Nations Conference on Trade and Development held at Santiago in May 1972. The developing nations asked for participation in the International Monetary Fund and an equitable share of the Special Drawing Rights which distribute currency. The industrialised countries resisted, promising only to consider later how a link could be made. Increased aid to the very poorest countries was pledged and the monopoly exploitation of the shipping companies carrying trade with developing countries was placed under some control. But the total effect of the conference was disillusioning to the nations of Asia, Africa and Latin America.

6. It was said in India that the 'Green Revolution' had actually increased the income gap between large farm owners and peasant farmers.

7. *The Times* (November 12, 1970).

8. On the other hand, the saving of lives is already having the effect of population growth. This emphasises the need for new sources of food production.

9. In June 1972 the United Nations held a conference on environment at Stockholm, attended by delegations from 113 nations, unhappily not including the Soviet Union and other communist countries because East Germany was not invited.

Chapter Twenty-eight

World
Transformation

(The United Nations,
Synthesis of Liberty
and Socialism)

The United Nations

The alternative to imperialism is internationalism and the instrument for its overall administration should be found in the United Nations, transformed, expanded and moving towards world government. The United Nations lost authority in the seventies. It had watched the Vietnam war unable to intervene. It had stood aside from the conflicts which led to two million deaths in Nigeria and the massacre of millions in Bangladesh. It had gained prestige from its termination of the British–French–Israeli attack on the Suez Canal, but was incapable over years to bring an end to the Middle East confrontation. It had carried strong resolutions on Rhodesia, South Africa, South West Africa and the Portuguese colonies but was reluctant to implement them. The most promising steps towards peace were made independently: the American–Russian talks on the limitation of strategic weapons, Willi Brandt's initiative for agreements with the Soviet Union and Poland, the Finnish mission to make practicable the communist proposal for a European conference on security and co-operation. Scepticism grew about the role of the United Nations.

But there it is, the one hope of association and communication by all nations in a world growing technically smaller and more interdependent. Its most serious representative limitation, the absence of communist China with a fifth of the earth's population, was put right in the first month of 1972.[1] The new nations from Asia and Africa continuously seize the opportunities of membership to press constantly their opposition to any continued racial supremacy and use the Committee on Colonialism to denounce challengingly Britain, Portugal and South Africa. It is probably true, however, that the unrealistic demands of the Afro-Asians and their over-representation in the Assembly measured by population contributed to doubts about the United Nations. Rightly, they condemned South Africa's annexation of South West Africa, but it weakened UN authority when the Assembly assumed administration without the means to take over.

Not unnaturally some of the larger nations with populations of fifty millions upwards resent the equal votes of nations with a few hundred thousand. This imbalance is protected by the right of veto of the big powers in the Security Council, but when this right is used resentment is felt. Increasingly it is seen that the United Nations cannot be an effective world body under this constitution or without an instrument to enforce its decisions. U Thant proposed that the smaller nations should be grouped, retaining the right to speak but with one vote only for each group. More changes than this, particularly in its ability to implement its decisions, will be required if the UN is to become authoritative.

Extended Functions

Consider its function in relation to the problems of colonialism and neo-colonialism we have discussed. We have suggested that it should have the overall protection of the scattered islands too small to become economically viable. If it is to fulfil these duties the Trusteeship Council would require to be strengthened in representation and greatly in staff. The UN, we have suggested, should also take a positive part in facilitating negotiations for the federation of groups of islands or for their association with mainland neighbours. Hong Kong is an example; its future, poised between Britain and China, is an international and not merely a bilateral issue. To prevent war and end world poverty, the UN would have to extend its authority and organisation still more; this we discuss later. For these services the UN should not have statesmen merely seconded by governments. The highest distinction for a statesman should be an appointment to its permanent staff.

International Police Force

If the United Nations is to become more than a forum of nation-states, if it is to extend its intervention, already made in the Korean war, the Suez attack, the Congo (Kinshasa), Cyprus and by sanctions in Rhodesia, it must act when its principles are repudiated by dissident member-states. The issue of the use of force has to be faced. If, for example, sanctions are to be applied effectively to southern Africa, they might require to be maintained, as already indicated, by a naval blockade. It is a little hypocritical to say that on principle force should not be used. It was used against communist North Korea in a full-scale war. Was the danger that all Korea would go communist a greater threat to freedom than the continuous suppression of the African population of southern Africa?

The great powers now assume the right to police peoples in other territories: America in Vietnam and South-East Asia (even if in the future vicariously by the supply of arms), the Soviet Union in Czechoslovakia, Britain in Borneo and Oman, China in Tibet. If there is need for a police force it should be a world force. The principle is not new. We had a UN peace-keeping force in the Middle East, unfortunately rejected on Israeli territory and liable to fatal recall by the UAR. We have it in Cyprus. If we were really internationally minded there would be only one armed force and only one armament reserve, and they would belong to the United Nations, which should have the authority to keep the peace whenever the threat of violent conflict arose.

The peace-keeping force should be in reserve, in the background. Positive intervention by the United Nations to settle issues before they reach the stage of physical conflict should be in the foreground. There should be an influentially representative UN Commission whose duty it would be to initiate negotiations whenever explosive differences became apparent, both between states and within states. The calamitous Nigerian and Pakistani wars might have been avoided if the supranational status of the United Nations had been recognised and the civil strife in Northern Ireland could be contained. National sovereignty should no longer be a barrier to intervention when warlike hostilities are threatened or occur.[2]

An Economic Arm

The proposals we have made for the limitation and final elimination of economic imperialism would require a large extension of the authority and organisation of the United Nations. Nothing less is necessary than an economic arm as important as the present political arm. It should have a Secretary-General and staff of status equal with the present Secretary-General and staff, co-ordinated but distinct. Consider the practical implications of our proposals; the distribution of all governmental aid through the UN, the enforcement of a code conditioning private investment (progressing to its international channelling), a Commission to supervise prices of primary commodities, a vast scheme of international development to end world poverty, including the fertilising of the deserts and farming of the seas. All this would involve immense planning by the best experts the world could provide in continuous session and administration, supported by a staff effective in size and quality. It would be the constructive function of the United Nations, turning the minds of governments and peoples from their obsession with war preparations, diverting their expenditure on defence to creation, building a world in which co-operation for human well-being and its accomplishment would sublimate the motives and conditions for war.

Impotence Under Imperialist Domination

We have assumed that the United Nations will continue as the instrument of world transformation, but there is the possibility that it will fail as the League of Nations failed. It may (Heaven forbid!) be destroyed by war as was the League, but the conflicting strains accompanying the transition to a new international order may also prove too great to be reconciled. Whilst capitalist and communist countries have so far co-existed within it, the major decisions in international affairs are made not by the concensus of opinion in the UN, but by the two super-powers. America determine's what happens in South-East Asia and America and Russia together determine what happens in the Middle East. There is also the power of the industrialised West in southern Africa; the United Nations may carry resolutions but no action is taken because of British and West European economic interests. The United Nations are intolerant when up against the reality of power.

We have to ask if it is conceivable that the proposals we have made for ending imperialism will be implemented whilst the profit-inspired economy of America, Britain and Western Europe persists and whilst their representatives have not only the power of veto in the United Nations, but behind it the real power to control action. Can we believe that economic imperialism will be eliminated by the United Nations whilst the governments which practise it have commanding authority within it? Can we believe that military imperialism will be ended whilst military might remains with governments in competition with each other for influence in the Third World?

We recognise that our proposals for United Nations action are unreal under the present circumstances of the world. The hard but inescapable fact is that the United Nations organisation is incapable of establishing an alternative to empires whilst power rests with imperialist governments. If imperialism is not ended at its sources, the UN will fail to meet the outstanding challenge of our time.

Racial Discrimination

We have referred earlier to the persistence of racial and tribal conflicts within the new nations, perhaps the most distressing sequence to their independence. These largely reflect the artificial frontiers left by colonialism and readjustments, such as happened in Bangladesh in 1972, may still be required. These could be facilitated by comprehensive organisations like the OAU, the Arab League and the conference of South-East Asian nations.

Racialism is also evident within imperialist nations and must be eliminated if their white populations are to become responsive to world action. Prejudice against Blacks is still strong in the US, an inheritance of slavery, and in Britain, an inheritance of white supremacy in the empire. The danger is that in both countries a large part of the coloured population will become a segregated labouring class, confined to the harshest forms of unskilled work and accommodated in ill-housed ghettoes. The British Government has made racial discrimination in public places, housing and employment illegal, and many American states have anti-discrimination laws. But social and economic discrimination persists, incited by housing shortages and unemployment as well as by colour prejudice. Only as fundamental changes in society take place, and as association and experience under equal conditions diminish racial feelings, will this poison in human relations, implicitly affecting the realisation of an inter-racial world, be lessened and removed.

The Triangle of Power

There is the incalculable effect on the world, and not least on the Third World, of the critical triangle of the great powers, China, America and Russia.[3] South-East Asia is the crucial area for China and America, but in fact China's behaviour towards Vietnam should be reassuring rather than frightening. Peking supplied arms but refrained from direct intervention, reflecting her theory of invincible people's war. It is almost certainly wrong to assume that in the foreseeable future China will engage in manned participation in revolutions outside its borders; in areas of conflict both America and China are likely to fight more by arms than by armies. Ultimately America must reconcile herself to the likelihood that, in the absence of effective political democracy to allow the ending of feudalism and external economic domination, a large part of the region of South-East Asia will adopt some form of Communism by its own volition. President Nixon's visit to China in February 1972 was a turning point. It meant the acceptance by China of co-existence, a modification of previous policy. The *communiqué* at the end of the visit reiterated differences on Indo-China, Korea and Taiwan and it conceded more to Peking than to Washington; notably Nixon agreed to the ultimate withdrawal of US troops from Taiwan, much to the dismay of Chiang Kai-shek and his government. It also had the important effect for the Far East of prompting Japan to say, in contradiction of earlier policy, that the island belonged to China. In bridging the gulf between the USA and Communist China and in its initiative for peace, President Nixon's visit was of historic importance.

China has joined the United Nations and hope for the future lies in an adjustment of her policy as she concentrates on safeguarding her own construction, in the same way that there was a readjustment of Russian policy. Already, however, China has made it clear that she will maintain her championship of the rights of the Third World, a powerful new influence. There is some reality in the fear of conflict between Russia and China, contesting the leadership of Communism, but there is the chance that in time co-operation may replace rivalry as both, despite many differences, have basically the same economic system and neither will wish to risk nuclear destruction. It may be that we shall have to await the arrival of new leadership before accord comes.

The visit of President Nixon to Moscow, in May 1972, was perhaps even more historic than his visit to China. It brought a surprising series of agreements regarding economic exchanges, co-operation in space, cultural contacts and lessening competition in nuclear arms. There was no open accord on Vietnam, though it is possible that some collaboration towards a settlement was privately accepted. All this was good for the peace of the world, but in this closer association of the greatest powers – America, Russia and China, perhaps extending to Japan – a new issue is implicit which may become of fundamental importance. Are they to determine the future of the world, with the remaining nations, more than one hundred, excluded from influence? This would be a further form of imperialism, which emphasises the importance of the establishment of the new democratic international order which we are advocating.

The Revolution Required

A basic change in attitudes and systems is required before the transformation we have patterned can fully take place. People must feel that they are world citizens if they are to accept what in effect is world government. Racial equality and co-operation must become as instinctive as racial supremacy and segregation. Nationalism must become internationalism.

The causes of the division in the world are complex. Perhaps they can be classified under six heads: (1) the remaining denial of nationhood, satisfaction of which must precede internationalism, (2) the extent to which racial inequality is still practised, (3) the cultural, economic and military domination of less developed peoples by great powers, (4) the division of rich and poor, both between nations and within nations, (5) the existence of conflicting economic systems, concentrated at the extremes by the USA and the USSR (China challenging) and (6) the contrast between democracy with personal freedoms and authoritarian regimes with suppressions of thought and action.

Many of the reasons for these divisions have been discussed in these pages, but except by implication we have not so far considered the form which new social structures in West and East must take if imperialist incentives are to be removed. Logical thinking must bring us to the conclusion that whilst these structures and conflict between them persist economic exploitation and political imposition cannot be ended. This is basic. Imperialism is not an excrescent fungus. It is an integral part of the trunk of our present social and political systems.

One thing our survey of the working of modern imperialism has shown: it has always been exercised for profit and supplemented by a desire for national prestige. That was the aim of the early traders and it became institutionalised in the chartered companies given governmental power by their nations. It was carried on by the slave trade, it was reflected in the cheating of chiefs for mines and land, and it became integrated, as the industrial revolution proceeded, in the economic relations of the developed countries to the peoples of the Third World. It is not enough to say that this was accompanied by civilising progress because over three hundred years, from Clive to Cecil Rhodes and later, far more has been extracted than has been expended on education, health, road-making and other amelioratives. Colonialist governments have found administration costly, but private interests have gained and it is these which have exploited and taken possession of the economies.

The economic system which evolved from the industrial revolution institutionalised the profit-making incentive which matured in modern economic imperialism. One cannot expect financiers and industrialists whose purpose at home is to make profits to exclude profit-making from overseas territories. Within the existing economic system investment in Africa, Asia and Latin America and possession of their industries is inevitably for profit. It is clear, therefore, that imperialism is inseparable from the capitalist structure of the West. Indeed, it is not distinct. It *is* capitalism, and its ill effects at home and abroad are similar. We have listed among the causes of division in the world the contrast of riches and poverty not only between nations but within nations. When one thinks this issue through, it is seen that the home economies of the West are a kind of domestic imperialism, a class possessing the major features of the economy with consequent good living for some and poverty for many. Substitute race for class, and we have a microcosm of imperialism overseas.

It may be argued that the motive of profit and riches preceded the capitalist system and is inherent in human nature. This is true; the early mercantile raiders, Clive and Warren Hastings in India, the slave traders, were concerned with what they could grab. Ever since the earliest tribal communities the motive of gain has dominated life; it will be a long time before it is sublimated to service and egalitarianism. But human nature is not limited to personal or group enrichment. It also includes compassion (reflected widely in the ending of the slave trade), a sense of justice and of the right to liberty, a sense of human brotherhood and a desire to serve. It is these attributes which we now assume are progressive and contributing to the advance of civilisation. Our task is to establish an international order and a social system which, because based on justice and freedom, will reflect these human characteristics.

Communism and Imperialism

There can be no doubt that the capitalist motive has been the main contributor to the modern exploitation of the dependent continents by the USA, Britain, France, the Netherlands, West Germany, Italy and now Japan. When we say this we have to meet the challenge that we ignore communist imperialism. Let us try to reach the truth about this. Communist ideology rejects imperialism. Lenin wrote his great book on the subject and the Second Congress of the Communist International issued a classic statement of opposition. But the communist definition of imperialism relates it only to the sphere of monopoly capitalism and our definition is wider. We think it is true to say – as we should expect it to be – that communist states have never repudiated in action their own conception of imperialism; they have never sought to control the life of other peoples in the interests of private profit. But they have repudiated the more comprehensive definition of imperialism which we have adopted. In Eastern Europe the Soviet Union has twice intervened in Czechoslovakia against administrations of which it did not approve, and has done so once in Hungary. China occupied Tibet and overthrew its pattern of society. Communist states have repeatedly had to balance the priorities between self-determination and the expansion of Communism. In Eastern Europe, force has been used to impose even particular conceptions of Communism, action which is imperialist by our definition.

When that has been said, the contribution which communist states and parties to the cause of anti-imperialism should be recognised. In Asia and Africa the provision of financial and military aid by both Russia and China has generally been in the interests of anti-imperialist and socialist purposes, even though the balance of power in the Cold War and rivalry between them have also been factors. Their delegations in United Nations Assemblies have consistently opposed white supremacy, and communist states have given training to freedom fighters in southern Africa. Despite this, it is important for us to realise when considering an alternative pattern for the world that the new nations have declined to become identified with the communist *bloc*. This attitude has reflected the self-reliance of peoples who are determined to be unaligned and even when committed to Socialism, wish to work out for themselves the nature of their future society.

Freedom is Indivisible

We have included in our list of the causes of a divided world the absence of liberty of thought within authoritarian states, near-fascist or communist. The denial of libertarian democracy is publicised as the basic reason for the confrontation of the 'free world' with the communist world, though there can be no doubt that the real reason is the challenge of the communist economic system to capitalism; the fact that the political democracies accept dictatorial Portugal and Greece as allies show that freedom is not the criterion. Nevertheless, the issue of personal liberty – freedom of thought, writing, speech, religion, movement and of participation in government – these democratic liberties are of profound importance in seeking a new international order which will be free from exploitation. It may be argued that this has little to do with imperialism; the accusing finger can be pointed to many newly independent nations which pay little regard to personal freedoms. But, fundamentally, when we endeavour to end cultural, military and economic domination, freedom is the essence of our purpose, and freedom is indivisible. One cannot philosophically or logically denounce the denial of national freedom and acquiesce in the denial of personal freedom.[4]

All liberals were shocked even as late as the seventies when we read of the imprisonment of writers in Soviet Russia for the expression of views unacceptable to the authorities, and those who had campaigned for African and Asian freedom were the most distressed when some of their independent governments arrested and detained political opponents without trial.[5] But we must look at these events in the perspective of time. The comparative liberty and tolerance within Britain and Western Europe in this sphere are due to long years of democratic growth during which freedom has had many martyrs. In the communist countries there were social and economic revolutions and in Africa a political revolution which required safeguards for the security of the new order. Many of us hold that these restrictions were overdone and continued too long, but it is not possible to believe that as education creates new self-respecting generations the prohibitions of freedom of thought and personal rights can persist. The right to liberty is so rooted in the human nature which we have decried in other respects that the demand for expression will be inevitable and, indeed, essential because criticism of the present is the dynamism for the future. But we must not get this issue of personal liberty out of proportion. The fulfilment of the potentialities of personality is prevented more by dehumanising poverty than by restrictions on thought. The starved and half-starved peoples of Asia, Africa and Latin America are little concerned about freedom of the mind. The opportunity to live comes first.

Synthesis of Socialisation and Liberty

So as we look forward to a new international order to replace imperialism we conclude there are two essentials. First, gain for individuals and groups must cease to be the incentive within the economies and, second, freedoms of personality must be recognised. Capitalist countries must accept social orders embodying service and co-operation, in which domination by sectional ownership of the economy and wealth is ended. Communist countries must establish personal liberty. This will be a synthesis of West and East, freedom of thought together with social ownership. Yet we must face the fact that to end imperialism it is the latter which is fundamental. As mentioned above, liberty of thought will evolve with education, but the change in the basis of capitalist societies involves a conscious effort of transformation which amounts to a social and international revolution. It will be resisted by the powerful vested interests which now profit from the three continents of the Third World, and which increasingly penetrate across all frontiers in great multi-national combines. This revolution is the formidable task which challenges us today. It will be seen more and more that the peoples of the capitalist countries and of the overseas ex-colonial countries have a common cause. The struggle against international capitalism must become international.

The new world order must be based on the libertarian socialist principles we have described, but their application may take different forms. In essence the object is to extend democracy, to allow peoples to *participate*, possessing in common not only the governmental apparatus but the economies which determine their lives, their work, their family well-being, and co-operatively controlling them. This is not the place to detail the possible forms of organisation, but clearly if there is to be a conscious and active participation social ownership must be applied not in distant centralised bureaucracies but in intimate self-government within industries and services and in devolution to local communities. Social ownership is not necessarily under governmental ownership. Particularly in agriculture, co-operatives could be the instrument.

We seem to have digressed from the subject of imperialism, but essentially the problem confronting the world is the right of peoples to control their own lives. That is the case against imperialism, and it cannot be satisfied unless the principle is accepted at the sources of imperialism. It is at the roots the issue of participating democracy. To construct societies and an international order which embody this principle is the responsibility of the generation now emerging. The author is aware that his proposals will appear Utopian and that they ignore the power of the new capitalist imperialism reflected in the vast multi-national associations of finance and industry which are becoming stronger even than governments; but throughout the world there is now new thinking which in the course of time may be expected to lead to co-ordinated action by means which events beyond our ken will determine. It is our hope that the ideas expressed here will help towards that realisation.

Notes

1. Divided Korea, Vietnam and Germany are still excluded. The two Germanies are likely to be accepted before the end of 1973.

2. In June 1972 a tribal war in Burundi led to the massacre of many Tutsis and 100,000 Hutis. It was regarded as an internal matter outside the scope of the United Nations.

3. To these three great powers should be added Japan, whose financial investments abroad have made it almost a world-wide instrument of economic imperialism.

4. We will not delay to argue what should be the limitation of personal action. Broadly, restriction is justifiable when such action becomes domination, exploitation of others or in self-interest at the expense of others.

5. This is the practice of all governments under stress. Britain applied internment without trial in Northern Ireland in 1971–2.

Chapter Twenty-nine

Conclusions

To sum up our proposals:

Colonialism and Racialism

1. The era of political empires is passing.

2. Most of the remaining colonies are in transition. The larger and more viable territories should proceed to independence. The small islands should pass to Trusteeship under a United Nations Commission with the right to decide between (*a*) confederation in groups enjoying independence, (*b*) association with a mainland state or (*c*) self-government under UN protection.

3. The Commonwealth should consist of Members who practise its Declaration of Principles. (See Appendix on page 566.)

4. Continued colonialism should be declared incompatible with membership of the Community of Nations. Portugal denies the principle of self-determination. The Portuguese Government and representatives of the African communities in its overseas possessions should be asked to enter discussions with the United Nations to implement self-determination. Should this be rejected, notice should be given that, unless within a limited period self-determination be accorded, Portugal would be excluded from the United Nations, and all international relations – political, economic, transport and communications – ended. This would involve exclusion from NATO.

5. The denial by a State of human rights to peoples of particular races should also be regarded as incompatible with the code of civilised nations. Representatives of the Republic of South Africa and of the Administration of Rhodesia, respectively, together with representatives of their non-white populations, should be invited to meet UN representatives to implement racial equality. In the event of refusal, they should be given notice as proposed above for Portugal. In the case of the Republic, the transference of South West Africa (Namibia) to UN administration preparatory to independence should be made a condition.

Imperialism

6. Empires do not consist only of political domination. Imperialism persists in cultural, military and economic domination.

7. Cultural domination will disappear with indigenous education, though integration of cultures will advantageously continue. UNESCO should co-operate in the publication of textbooks, literary works and works of art, and the presentation of films.

Military Domination

8. The military domination of the rest of the world by the USA and the USSR is in essence imperialism. Final power over all our lives is in their hands. Every step towards disarmament should be encouraged. The goal should be the abolition of national armed forces and the existence only of a UN peace-keeping force.

9. Within the Third World military domination largely reflects the Cold War and the protection of private interests. The transference to external territories of troops and weapons, as well as of finance and techniques for military and arms production purposes, should be prohibited unless authorised by the UN General Assembly for aims consistent with the Charter.

10. Whilst, so far as one can judge, the majority of peoples in Eastern Europe accept association with the Soviet Union, Russia exerted military domination particularly in Czechoslovakia and Hungary. The assertion of self-decision will grow, following the lead of Yugoslavia and later of Roumania and Albania. The projected Conference for European Security and Co-operation should encourage this.

11. World War is threatened from the antagonistic triangle of America–Russia–China. Major divisive causes are Indo-China and the Middle East. Geneva Conferences, with all the involved governments represented, should be held to resolve these conflicts. The UN should negotiate settlements of Soviet–Chinese and Chinese–Indian frontiers. China's membership of the UN should help.

Economic Domination

12. Economic domination is now the main instrument of imperialism. More is extracted annually from the developing nations in

interest and dividend payments than is contributed by the industrial powers in aid and investment.

13. Governmental aid is given not only to meet human needs but to exert political pressures and frequently is conditional upon purchases from the donor countries. All governmental aid should be channelled through UN agencies without requiring interest payments and member-states required to contribute proportionately to their *per capita* income.

14. Private investment should not be included in the calculation of aid since it is profit-making. It should be subject to an International Convention providing, among other things, for majority share-holding by the recipient states, repayment from the revenue of the industry, a maximum rate of interest, and the training of indigenous personnel in skills and management.

15. Ideally all private investment should be channelled through the UN Fund for Economic Development, but this is not realisable whilst profit-making remains the motive.

16. The standard of life of the peoples of developing countries depends upon world prices. Any lowering of their purchasing power causes unemployment in the industrialised countries. There should be an international commission associated with the UN to supervise trade agreements which fix prices and to plan stabilisation of demand over a period of years.

17. The population explosion threatens the starvation of millions by the end of the century. To meet the needs of the coming generations there should be international projects to fertilise the deserts and farm the oceans.

The United Nations

18. The United Nations must become an instrument of world action, the nucleus of world government. It should have an economic arm as important as its political arm to fulfil the proposals made here. This constructive work would reduce the obsession with armaments and war.

19. The finance, staff and activities of the UN agencies should be greatly extended. There should be agencies for relief from natural disasters and to prevent pollution of sea and air.

20. *The fact should be faced, however, that so long as the United Nations reflects the imperialist powers and the East–West confrontation, the UN cannot be the instrument of the necessary world*

transformation. The first need is to transform the dominant member states themselves. Unless imperialism is overthrown at its source the UN will be incapable of establishing the international order which is the alternative to empires.

Racial Discrimination

21. Racial and tribal conflicts have persisted within the new nations following independence. This largely reflects the artificial frontiers left by colonialism. Readjustments may be required, illustrated in Bangladesh in 1972. Comprehensive organisations like the OAU, the Arab League and the conference of South-East Asian nations could negotiate these. Racial tension within imperialist nations also prejudices the establishment of a multi-racial international order. Britain has made discrimination illegal in public places, housing and employment and many American states have similar laws, but large sections of the non-white populations are segregated to inferior employment and housing. This will be overcome only by fundamental social changes and the decrease of racialist feeling by association in conditions of equality.

Capitalism the Main Cause

22. Modern imperialism is inseparable from capitalism. Exploitation of the developing countries is an extension of the exploitation of domestic peoples by class ownership of the economies, basically the same as economic colonialism.

23. If exploitation of developing countries is to cease, the capitalism of the West extending to Japan must be transformed to a society where service replaces profit as the motive of the economy.

24. In growing numbers in Asia, Africa, the Caribbean and South America the nations are challenging economic imperialism by socialising their economies.

Freedom Indivisible

25. Confrontation between the capitalist and communist powers leads to intervention in the Third World by both. Whilst the root cause of the conflict is the communist challenge to capitalist interests, there is also the gulf between democratic liberties and authoritarianism.

26. The final condemnation of imperialism is the repression of freedom. Freedom is indivisible. One cannot logically ask that a people shall be free in national relationships without claiming that an individual should be free within a state. Our thinking of the new order of society must proceed to the double aim of freeing peoples from external domination and of freeing individuals from internal domination.

27. Revolutionary changes, such as the establishment of communist regimes and of independent states, have historically been accompanied by suppression of liberties to maintain the new status. Power corrupts and suppression has been over severe and over long, becoming dictatorship. This has happened in new nations freed from colonialism. Mass education can be expected to lead to insistence upon democratic freedoms and participation.

The New Order

28. The new order should end both capitalism and authoritarianism. It should be based on the principles of Libertarian Socialism, combining community ownership of economies and service rather than profit-making with fundamental personal liberties. Structures expressing this principle will vary but will express the antithesis of imperialism which is domination by a few over the many.

29. It involves the adoption of the same principle in an international order which, whilst recognising the liberty of peoples and of cultural and racial identity in democratic autonomy, will express the co-operation of all peoples in moving towards world government, with the aims of ending poverty, disease and war and providing the conditions of human fulfilment.

Select
Bibliography

This is very selective. The author has a list of over 2,000 books which are relevant, but only a fragment can be included. He apologises for omissions of subjects and books of which he is conscious; these include official reports. It is regretted, also, that the list is limited to works in the English language.

General
Cambridge Histories, Ancient, Medieval and Modern; *Outline of History*, H. G. Wells; *Glimpses of World History*, Jawaharlal Nehru.

Theory
The Levellers, H. N. Brailsford; *The British Empirical Philosophers*, A. J. Ayer and Raymond Winch; *Imperialism: A Study*, J. A. Hobson; *On Colonialism*, K. Marx and F. Engels; *Imperialism, the Highest Stage of Capitalism*, V. I. Lenin; *Marxism and the Colonial Question*, J. Stalin; *History of the International*, J. Braunthal; *Writings of Mao Tse Tung*; *The Imperial Idea and its Enemies*, A. P. Thornton; *Critics of Empire*, B. Porter.

British Empire
The Cambridge History of the British Empire; *The Evolution of the British Empire and Commonwealth from the American Revolution*, A. L. Burt; *The Origins of the British Colonial System*, G. L. Beer; *The Crisis of Britain and the British Empire*, R. P. Dutt; *Unscrambling an Empire, 1956–66*, W. P. Kirkman.

North America
Anglo-America, W. H. Parker; *The Reign of George III*, J. Steven Watson; *The American Commonwealth*, Lord Bryce; *The Indian Tribes of North America*, J. R. Swanton (ed.); *Colony to Nation* (Canada), A. R. M. Lower; *The French Canadians, 1760–1945*, M. Wade.

Ireland

The Making of Modern Ireland, 1603–1923, J. C. Beckett; *The Irish Question, 1840–1921*, N. Mansergh; *The Irish Republic*, D. Macardle; *The Resurrection of Hungary: a Parallel for Ireland*, Arthur Griffith; *Socialism and Nationalism*, James Connolly; *The Green Flag*, E. E. Robert; *Mutiny at the Curragh*, A. P. Ryan; *Ulster, 1972*, Sunday Times Insight Team; *The Irish Crisis*, Desmond Greaves.

India, Pakistan, Bangladesh

Oxford and Cambridge Histories of India; *The First Indian War of Independence, 1857–59*, K. Marx and F. Engels; *Lokmanya Tilak*, D. V. Tahmankar; *Mahatma Gandhi and the Nehrus*, B. R. Nanda; *Nehru: A Birthday Book*; *India Today*, R. P. Dutt; *The Foundations of New India*, K. M. Pannikar; *The Partition of India*, C. H. Philips and D. Wainwright; *Pakistan: Old Country, New Nation*, Ian Stephens; *Pakistan: A Political Study*, Keith Callard; *Bangladesh: Genocide and World Press*, F. Q. Quaderi (ed.).

South East Asia

South East Asia: Its Historical Development, J. F. Cady; *South East Asia*, H. G. Dobby; *The Colonial Period in South East Asia*, V. Purcell; *Ceylon: The Portuguese Era*, P. E. Pieris; *Dutch Power in Ceylon, 1658–87*, S. Arasaratnam; *Ceylon under the British Occupation, 1795–1833*, C. R. de Silva; *Europe and Burma* (to 1886), D. G. E. Hall; *British Rule in Burma, 1824–1942*, G. E. Harvey; *Burma from Kingdom to Republic*, F. N. Trager; *French Indo-China*, V. Thompson; *Focus on Indo-China*, Malcolm Salmon; *The Furtive War: The United States in Vietnam and Laos*, and *Vietnam North: A First Hand Report*, Wilfred G. Burchett; *Vietnam*, Mary McCarthy; *Vietnam: the Truth*, W. Warbey; *Ho Chi Minh*, C. Fenn; *Fire in the Lake*, Frances Fitzgerald; *Malaya and Its History*, Sir R. Winstedt; *Singapore and Malaysia*, M. E. Osborne; *Raffles of the Eastern Isles*, C. E. Wurtzburg; *A History of the East Indian Archipelago*, H. M. Vlekke; *Indonesia*, B. Grant; *The Republic of Indonesia*, Dorothy Woodman; *Nationalism and Revolution in Indonesia*, G. McT. Kahin; *The White Rajahs* (Sarawak), S. Runciman; *The Philippines: A Nation in the Making*, F. M. Keesing; *Philippine Nationalism*, A. Chapman; *The Forest*, W. J. Pomeroy; *A History of Hong Kong*, G. B. Endacott.

Middle East

The Arab–Israeli Dilemma, F. Khouri; *Both Sides of the Hill*, J. and D. Kimsche; *Communism and Nationalism in the Middle East*, W. E. Laquer; *The Emergence of Arab Nationalism*, Z. N. Zeine; *The Arab Cold War*, M. Kerr; *Crossroads to Israel*, C. Sykes; *Israel, Years of Challenge*, Ben Gurion; *Palestine: Loss of Heritage*, Sami Hadawi; *The Empire of Oil*, H. O'Connor.

Africa

An African Survey, Lord Hailey; *Africa*, W. Fitzgerald; *Inside Africa*, John Gunther; *Africa Handbook*, Colin Legum (ed.); *Africa: Its People and their Cultural History*, C. R. Murdock; *Political Africa*, R. Segal; *Africa; Britain's Third Empire*, G. Padmore; *Struggle for Mastery in Europe*, A. J. P. Taylor; *African Political Parties*, T. Hodgkin; *The British in Africa*, D. Taylor; *The Dual Mandate in British Tropical Africa*, F. J. D. Lugard; *British Policy in Changing Africa*, Sir Arthur Cohen; *Black Mother*, Basil Davidson; *Lugard: the Years of Adventure, 1858–98* and *Lugard: the Years of Authority, 1898–1945*, Margery Perham; *The Penguin Books on Africa*; *African Liberation Movements*, R. Gibson; *Organising African Unity*, J. Woronoff; *Pan-Africanism*, Colin Legum; *Pan-Africanism or Communism*, G. Padmore; *Africa Must Unite*, Kwame Nkrumah.

North Africa and Mediterranean

History of French Colonial Policy (also West and Equatorial Africa), S. H. Roberts; *Egypt and the Fertile Crescent, 1516–1922*, P. M. Holt; *Secret History of the British Occupation of Egypt*, Scawen Blunt; *Egypt's Ruin*, T. Rothstein; *British Imperialism in Egypt*, Elinor Burns; *Nasser's Egypt*, P. Mansfield; *The Philosophy of the Revolution*, C. A. Nasser; *Egypt Since the Revolution*, P. J. Vatikiotis; *No End of a Lesson: the Story of Suez*, H. A. Nutting; *Egypt in the Sudan, 1820–1881*, R. L. Hill; *British Policy in the Sudan, 1882–1902*, M. E. T. Shibeika; *A Modern History of the Sudan*, P. M. Holt; *The Southern Sudan; Background to Conflict*, M. O. Beshir; *The Economic and Social Development of Libya*, United Nations; *Tunisia: the Politics of Modernisation*, C. A. Micaud and others; *Tunisia Since Independence*, C. H. Moore; *The Passing of French Algeria*, D. C. Gordon; *Moroccan Drama*, R. Landau; *Ben Bella*, R. Merle; *History of Gibraltar*, J. Bell; *The Maltese Islands and Their History*, T. Zammit; *Cyprus in History*,

D. Alastos; *Cyprus: The Dispute and the Settlement*, Royal Institute of International Affairs; *Bitter Lemons*, L. Durrell.

East Africa

A History of East Africa, K. Ingham; *East Africa Through a Thousand Years*, G. S. Were and D. A. Wilson; *East Africa: The Search for Unity*, A. J. Hughes; *The Asians of East Africa*, L. Hollingsworth; *East Africa Rebels*, F. B. Welbourne; *Ethiopia: A New Political History*, R. Greenfield; *Ethiopia and Haile Selassie*, C. Stanford; *The Modern History of Somaliland*, J. M. Lewis; *Kenya*, Norma Leys; *Kenya: A Political History*, G. Bennett; *Facing Mount Kenya*, J. Kenyatta; *Historical Survey of the Origin and Growth of Mau Mau*, F. D. Carfield; *Who Killed Kenya?* Colin Wells; *Kenyatta*, J. Murray-Brown; *Mau Mau and the Kikuyu*, L. S. B. Leakey; *The Trial of Jomo Kenyatta*, Slater Montagu; *Mau Mau from Within*, D. L. Barnett; *Last Chance in Africa*, Negley Farson; *Must We Lose Africa?* (Uganda), Colin Legum; *The Rise and Fall of Germany's Colonial Empire* (also Togoland and S.W. Africa), M. E. Townsend; *The Making of Tanganyika*, J. Listowel; *The Political Development of Tanganyika*, J. C. Taylor; *Zanzibar: Background to Revolution*, M. E. Lofchie.

Central Africa

A History of Africa South of the Sahara, D. L. Wiedner; *Story of the Rhodesias and Nyasaland*, A. J. Hanna; *The Two Nations*, R. Gray; *Race and Nationalism*, T. M. Franck; *A New Deal in Central Africa*, C. Leys and C. Pratt (eds.); *Britain and Nyasaland*, Griff Jones; *Dawn in Nyasaland*, G. Clutton-Brock; *A History of Northern Rhodesia*, L. H. Gann; *North of the Zambesi*, L. F. G. Anthony; *Year of Decision: Rhodesia and Nyasaland in 1960*, P. Mason; *Handbook to the Federation of Rhodesia and Nyasaland*, W. V. Brelsford; *Unholy Wedlock*, H. Franklin; *Zambia*, R. S. Hall; *A Humanist in Africa*, Kenneth Kaunda; *Cecil Rhodes*, Basil Williams; *Rhodesia: A Human Geography*, G. Kay; *Crisis in Rhodesia*, N. M. Shamuyarvia; *The African Voice in Southern Rhodesia*, T. O. Ranger; *Rhodesia*, Judith Todd.

West Africa

Survey of North West Africa, N. Barbour; *An Introduction to the History of West Africa*, J. D. Fuge; *West Africa*, R. J. H. Church; *Land and People of West Africa*, C. R. Niven; *New Nations of West Africa*, R. Theobald; *West Africa and the Commonwealth*, D.

Austin; *The French Union*, H. Deschamps; *The Emerging States of French Equatorial Africa*, V. Thompson and R. Adloff; *Senegal: a Study in French Assimilation Policy*, M. Crowder; *Politics in Ghana, 1946–60*, Dennis Austin; *The Gold Coast Revolution*, G. Padmore; *Dark Days in Ghana*, Kwame Nkrumah; *A History of Sierra Leone*, C. Fyfe; *Political Change in a West African State*, M. Kilson; *History of Nigeria*, Alan Burn; *Land and People in Nigeria*, K. M. Buchanan and J. C. Pugh; *The Dual Mandate in British Tropical Africa*, F. J. D. Lugard; *Nigerian Background to Nationalism*, J. S. Coleman; *Nigerian Perspectives*, T. L. Hodgkin; *The Congo and the Founding of the Free State*, H. M. Stanley; *The Belgian Congo and the Berlin Act*, A. B. Keith; *Belgian Congo*, R. Slade; *Congo: Background of Conflict*, A. P. Merriam; *Political Awakening in the Belgian Congo*, R. Lemarch; *Congo My Country*, Patrice Lumumba; *Katanga*, R. J. Grant; *To Katanga and Back*, C. Cruise O'Brien; *The Congo Since Independence*, C. Hoskyns.

Portuguese Africa
The Portuguese Seaborne Empire 1615–1852, Brian Bunting; *Portuguese Africa*, R. H. Chilcote; *Portugal and Africa*, R. J. Hammond; *Portugal in Africa*, James Duffy; *Revolution in Guinea*, Amilcar Cabral; *The Liberation of Guiné*, Basil Davidson; *Angola in Ferment*, T. Okuma; *The Angolan Revolution*, J. A. Marcum; *The Struggle for Mozambique*, Eduardo Mondlane.

Southern Africa
Oxford History of South Africa, M. Wilson and L. Thompson; *Southern Africa*, B. Fagan; *The Story of an African Farm*, Olive Schreiner; *Southern Africa in Transition*, J. A. Davis and J. K. Baker; *Class and Colour in South Africa 1850–1950*, H. J. and R. E. Simons; *Violence in Southern Africa*, P. Mason; *Guilty Land*, P. van Rensberg; *The Discarded People: An Account of African Resettlement in South Africa*, Father C. Desmond; *The Dynamics of the African National Congress*, E. Feit; *Liberalism in South Africa*, Janet Robertson; *My Life and the I.C.U.*, C. Kadalie; *South West Africa: The Factual Background*, Sir Charles Dundas; *South West Africa*, Ruth First; *The Struggle for a Birthright*, Mary Benson; *Return to the Fairy Hill* (Botswana), Naomi Mitchison; *Seretse Khama and the Bamangwato*, J. Mockford; *The Swazi*, H. Kuper; *History of the Basuto: Ancient and Modern*, D. F. Ellenberger and J. C. Macgregor; *The Rise of the Basuto*, G. Tylden.

The Caribbean

From Columbus to Castro: The History of the Caribbean, Eric Williams; *A Short History of the West Indies*, J. H. Parry and P. M. Sterlock; *The West Indies, Past and Present*, A. Macmillan; *Democracy and Empire in the Caribbean*, P. Blanshard; *Jamaica, the Blessed Island*, Lord Olivier; *They Seek a Living* (Jamaicans), Joyce Egginton; *Netherlands West Indies*, W. Nvan Pall; *History of Indians in British Guiana*, D. Nath; *British Guiana*, R. T. Smith.

Latin America

The Fall of the Spanish American Empire, S. D. Madariaga; *Nationalists Without Nations and Alliance Without Allies*, V. Alba; *The Great Fear*, J. Gerassi; *Arms and Politics in Latin America* and *Generals versus Presidents*, E. Lieuwen; *Obstacles to Change in Latin America*, C. Veliz; *Latin America: New World, Third World*, S. Clissold; *Capitalism and Underdevelopment in Latin America*, A. G. Frank; *The Speeches and Writings of Che Guevara*; *Guerilla Movements in Latin America*, R. Gott; *Guerillas in South America: The Technique of the Counter-State* and *Roads to Power in Latin America*, L. M. Vega; *Revolution in the Revolution*, R. Debray; *The Cuban Revolution* and *Latin America*, B. Goldenberg; *Cuba*, H. Thomas; *Change in Latin America: the Cuban and Mexican Revolutions*, D. C. Villegas; *Land and Society in Colonial Mexico*, M. Chevalier; *Ideology and Program of the Peruvian Aprista Movement*, H. Kantor; *Land Reform and Social Revolution in Bolivia*, B. Heath, C. J. Erasmus, H. Bencher.

Neo-Colonialism

The Wretched of the Earth, Franz Fanon; *The Third World in World Economy*, Pierre Jalée; *Neo-Colonialism: the Last Stage of Imperialism*, Kwame Nkrumah; *Africa – the Roots of Revolt* and *Introduction to Neo-Colonialism*, Jack Woddis; *Aid as Imperialism*, Theresa Haines; *Aid and Liberation*, Judith Hart; *The African Bourgeoisie*, Leo Kerr; *National Unity and Regimentation in Eight African States*, M. Carter (ed.); *Socialist Ideas in Africa*, Idris Cox.

Index

n denotes significant reference in *Notes*

THE WORLD AFTER THE COLONIAL REVOLUT

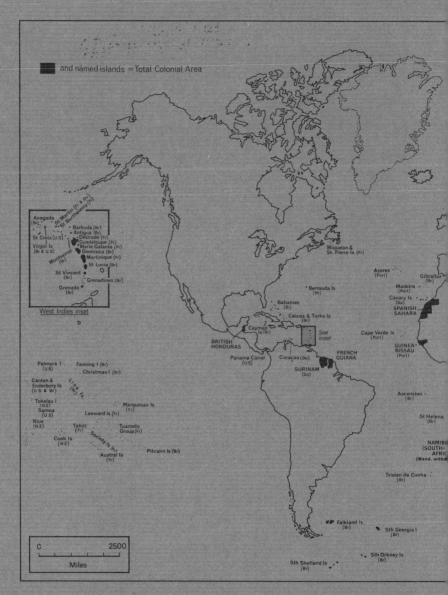

▨ and named islands = Total Colonial Area

West Indies inset

Anegada (Br)
St Martin (Fr & Du)
St Barthélemy (Fr)
Barbuda (Br)
Antigua (Br)
St Croix (U S)
Désirade (Fr)
Guadeloupe (Fr)
Virgin Is (Br & U S)
Marie Galante (Fr)
Dominica (Br)
Montserrat (Br)
Martinique (Fr)
St Lucia (Br)
St Vincent (Br)
Grenadines (Br)
Grenada (Br)

Miquelon & St. Pierre Is (Fr)

Azores (Port)
Gibraltar (Br)
Madeira (Port)
Bermuda Is (Br)
Canary Is (Sp)
SPANISH SAHARA
Bahamas (Br)
Caicos & Turks Is (Br)
Cayman Is (Br)
See inset
Cape Verde Is (Port)
GUINEA-BISSAU (Port)
BRITISH HONDURAS
Panama Canal (U S)
Curaçao (Du)
FRENCH GUIANA
SURINAM (Du)

Palmyra I (U S)
Fanning I (Br)
Christmas I (Br)
Canton & Enderbury Is (U S & Br)
Line Is (Br)
Ascension (Br)
Tokelau I (N Z)
Samoa (U S)
Marquesas Is (Fr)
Leeward Is (Fr)
St Helena (Br)
Niue (N Z)
Tahiti (Fr)
Tuamoto Group (Fr)
Cook Is (N Z)
Society Is (Fr)
Pitcairn Is (Br)
NAMIBI (SOUTH-AFRIC (Mand. witho
Austral Is (Fr)
Tristan da Cunha (Br)
Falkland Is (Br)
Sth Georgia I (Br)
Sth Orkney Is (Br)
Sth Shetland Is (Br)

C 2500
Miles

See endpaper at the front of the book for The World before the Colonial Revolution (1945